W9-AAQ-357

"THE GOOD WAR"

OTHER BOOKS BY STUDS TERKEL

STUDS TERKEL

AN ORAL HISTORY OF WORLD WAR TWO

"THE GOOD WAR"

THE NEW
PRESS

NEW
YORK

© 1984 by Studs Terkel.
All rights reserved. No part of this book may be reproduced, in any form,
without written permission from the publisher.

Grateful acknowledgment is made to the following for permission
to reprint previously published material:

CBS Songs, and Ched Music: A portion of the lyric "Don't Sit Under the Apple
Tree (with Anyone Else But Me)" by Lew Brown, Charles Tobias, and Sam
Stept. Copyright 1942, 1954 by Robbins Music Corporation. Copyright
renewed 1970 by Robbins Music Corporation, and Ched Music. Rights of Robbins Music assigned to CBS Catalogue Partnership. All rights controlled and
administered by CBS Robbins Catalog Inc. All rights reserved. International
copyright secured. Reprinted by permission of CBS Songs, and Ched Music.

Cherry Lane Music Publishing Co., Inc.: A portion of the lyric "That's What I
Learned in School Today" a.k.a. "What Did You Learn in School Today" by
Tom Paxton. Copyright © 1962 by Cherry Lane Music Publishing Co., Inc. All
rights reserved. Reprinted by permission.

Norman Corwin: Excerpt from a coast-to-coast radio program, "On a Note of
Triumph," V-E Day, May 8, 1945. Reprinted by permission of Norman Corwin.

MCA Music: A portion of the lyric "Boogie Woogie Bugle Boy," words and
music by Don Raye and Hughie Prince. Copyright 1940, 1941 by MCA Music,
A Division of MCA INC., New York, N.Y. Also the lyric "The Sinking of the
Reuben James," words and music by Woodie Guthrie. Copyright 1942 by MCA
Music, A Division of MCA INC., New York, N.Y. Copyright renewed.
Reprinted by permission. All rights reserved.

New Directions Publishing Corp.: For excerpt from "Insensibility" by Wilfred
Owen, from *Collected Poems of Wilfred Owen*. Copyright © 1963 by Chatto &
Windus Ltd. Reprinted by permission of New Directions Publishing Corp.

Simon and Schuster, Inc.: For excerpt from *Science and Human Values* by
Jacob Bronowski. Copyright © 1956, 1965 by Jacob Bronowski. Reprinted by
permission of Julian Messner, a Division of Simon & Schuster, Inc.

LIBARY OF CONGRESS CATALOGING-IN-PUBLICATION DATA
Terkel, Studs, 1912–
"The good war".
1. World War, 1939–1945—Personal narratives.
I. Title.
D811.A2T45   1984   940.54   82-4271
ISBN 1-56584-343-6

Published in the United States by The New Press, New York
Distributed by W.W. Norton & Company, Inc., New York

Established in 1990 as a major alternative to the large commercial publishing houses, The New Press is a nonprofit book publisher. The Press
is operated editorially in the public interest, rather than for private
gain; it is committed to publishing, in innovative ways, works of educational, cultural, and community value that, despite their intellectual
merits, might not normally be commercially viable. The New Press's
editorial offices are located at the City University of New York.

Some of the names in this book have been changed.

Production management by Kim Waymer, The New Press
Printed in the United States of America

9 8 7 6 5

FOR JAMES CAMERON,
master of his trade

NOTE

The title of this book was
suggested by Herbert Mitgang,
who experienced World War Two
as an army correspondent. It is a phrase
that has been frequently voiced by
men of his and my generation,
to distinguish that war from other
wars, declared and undeclared.
Quotation marks have been added,
not as a matter of caprice or
editorial comment, but simply
because the adjective "good" mated
to the noun "war" is so
incongruous.

In memory, we find the most complete release from the narrowness of presented time and place. . . . The picture is one of human beings confronted by a world in which they can be masters only as they . . . discover ways of escape from the complete sway of immediate circumstances.

—F. C. Bartlett, *Remembering*

What did you learn in school today, dear
little boy of mine?
What did you learn in school today, dear
little boy of mine?
I learned that war is not so bad
I learned about the great ones we have had
We fought in Germany and in France
And I am someday to get my chance
That's what I learned in school today
That's what I learned in school.

—A song by Tom Paxton

ACKNOWLEDGMENTS

A suggestion, softly offered at lunch by my editor, André Schiffrin, sprang forth the idea for this book. It was the sixth such occasion. Further suggestions by Ursula Bender and Tom Engelhardt helped considerably. Others at Pantheon Books—Jeanne Morton, Carolyn Marsh, and Iris Bromberg—came through in the practice of their respective crafts.

I might have been somewhat hesitant to undertake this project had I not been certain that Cathy Zmuda, an empress among transcribers, would be deftly working words from cassette to typed page. Dorothy Constance and Grace Zmuda assisted during an emergency—i.e., a deadline.

During my travels across the country, I was in the good hands of knowing companions, who were cicerones as well as chauffeurs. Tony Judge volunteered on several occasions in several states: Massachusetts, New Jersey, Tennessee, and parts of Kentucky, as well as California, northern and southern. Tony Lucki covered a good piece of Massachusetts real estate with me. Dave Nichols not only came through with hot leads; he knew Indiana roads forwards, backwards, and sideways. Mike Edgerly took me along the bluegrass country of Kentucky, as well as the Cumberlands.

I owe a special debt to the members of the UCLA Home Front Film Project, especially Stephen Schechter, for leading me to at least a dozen rememberers who appear in this book.

A toast to the scouts who tipped me off to a regiment of others: Ruth Adams, Robert L. Allen, Les Bridges, Mike Briggs, Cooper Brown, Cathy Cowan, John Dower, Sonja Ellingson, Carmelina Esposito, Jules Feiffer, Hamilton Fish III, Ron Freund, Rebecca Goalby, Bill Hohri, Diane Hutchinson, Kim Lady, Pat Lofthouse, the late Hans Mattick, Alice McGrath, Marylouise Oates, Irving Paley, Rudy Rasin, John Rasmus, Frank Rowe, Bob Rudner, Harrison Salisbury, Isabel Stein, Ida Terkel, Steve Veenker, John Wickes, Joan Wood, and Jerry Zbiral. (I suspect a number of these named are unaware of inestimable help they gave me; it may have come in the form of a casual comment, or as a letter or an address or phone number scrawled on a scrap of paper.)

For the sixth time around, I thank my colleagues at WFMT, Chicago, not only for allowing me frequent leaves of absence but for assuming burdens over and beyond the call of duty: Ray Nordstrand, Norm Pellegrini, Lois Baum, Jim Unrath, Andrea D'Alessio, Carol Martinez, Wanda Rohm, Nancy Joyce; and especially Sydney Lewis, George Drury, and Matt McDonnell.

To all of this battalion, a salute.

CONTENTS

BOOK TWO

BOOK THREE

BOOK FOUR

"THE GOOD WAR"

INTRODUCTION

"I was in combat for six weeks, forty-two days. I remember every hour, every minute, every incident of the whole forty-two days. What was it—forty years ago?" As he remembers aloud, the graying businessman is transformed into a nineteen-year-old rifleman. Much too tall for a rifleman, his mother cried.

This is a memory book, rather than one of hard fact and precise statistic. In recalling an epoch, some forty years ago, my colleagues experienced pain, in some instances; exhilaration, in others. Often it was a fusing of both. A hesitancy, at first, was followed by a flow of memories: long-ago hurts and small triumphs. Honors and humiliations. There was laughter, too. *

In 1982, a woman of thirty, doing just fine in Washington, D.C., let me know how things are in her precincts: "I can't relate to World War Two. It's in schoolbook texts, that's all. Battles that were won, battles that were lost. Or costume dramas you see on TV. It's just a story in the past. It's so distant, so abstract. I don't get myself up in a bunch about it."

It appears that the disremembrance of World War Two is as disturbingly profound as the forgettery of the Great Depression: World War Two, an event that changed the psyche as well as the face of the United States and of the world.

The memory of the rifleman is what this book is about; and of his sudden comrades, thrown, hugger-mugger, together; and of those men, women, and children on the home front who knew or did not know what the shouting was all about; and of occasional actors from other worlds, accidentally encountered; and of lives lost and bucks found. And of a moment in history, as recalled by an ex-corporal, "when buddies felt they were more important, were better men who amounted to more than they do now. It's a precious memory."

Hard Times: An Oral History of the Great Depression (New York: Pantheon Books, 1970), p. 3.

On a September day in 1982, Hans Göbeler and James Sanders are toasting one another in Chicago. Mr. Göbeler had been the mate on a German submarine, U-505. Mr. Sanders had been the junior flight officer on the U.S.S. *Guadalcanal*. Thirty-eight years before, one tried his damndest, as a loyal member of his crew, to sink the other's craft about two hundred miles off the coast of West Africa. Now they reminisce, wistfully.

"Every man, especially the youth, can be manipulated," says Mr. Göbeler. "The more you say to him that's the American way of life, the German way of life, they believe it. Without being more bad than the other is. There's a great danger all the time." Mr. Sanders nods. "It could happen. People could be fooled. Memory is short."

For me, it was forty-odd years ago. I was in the air force, 1942–1943. I never saw a plane; if I did, I wouldn't have had the foggiest idea what to do with it. Mine was limited service. Perforated eardrum. It was stateside all the way, safe and uneventful. Yet I remember, in surprising detail, the uneventful events; and all those boy-faces, pimply, acned, baby-smooth. And bewildered.

From Jefferson Barracks, Missouri, to Fort Logan, Colorado, to Basic Training Center 10, North Carolina, my peregrinations were noncombative in nature. How I became a sergeant may have had something to do with my age. I was ten years older than the normal GI and, willy-nilly, became the avuncular one to the manchildren. Special Services, they called it.

The other barracks elder was a crooked ex-bailiff from New Orleans. He was forty. Propinquity, the uniform, and the adventure made us buddies. Even now, I remember those wide-eyed wonders, our nightly audience, as Mike and I held forth. Who knows? Perhaps we were doing the state some service in giving these homesick kids a laugh or two. In any event, they were learning something about civics hardly taught in school, especially from Mike.

When he and I, on occasion, goofed off and, puffing five-cent Red Dot cigars, observed from the warm quarters of the PX toilet our young comrades doing morning calisthenics in the biting Rocky Mountain air, it was without any sense of shame. On the contrary. Mike, blowing smoke rings, indicated the scene outside and, in the manner of General Mac-Arthur, proclaimed, "Aintchu proud of our boys?" I solemnly nodded. The fact is we were proud of them; and they, perversely, of us. Memento mores.

Seated across the celebratory table from Hans Göbeler and Jim Sanders, I think of the nineteen-year-old rifleman. "It was sunshine and quiet. We were passing the Germans we killed. Looking at the individual German dead, each took on a personality. These were no longer an abstraction. They were no longer the Germans of the brutish faces and the helmets we saw in the newsreels. They were exactly our age. These were boys like us."

"Boys" was the word invariably used by the combat-protagonists of this book. The references were to enemy soldiers as well as our own. The SS were, of course, another matter. Even the most gentle and forgiving of our GIs found few redeeming attributes there. So, too, with the professional warrior of Imperial Japan. As for the Japanese citizen-soldier, let a near-sighted, bespectacled American corporal (now a distinguished near-sighted, bespectacled economist) tell it: "In Guam, I saw my first dead Japanese. He looked pitiful, with his thick glasses. He had a sheaf of letters in his pocket. He looked like an awkward kid who'd been taken right out of his home to this miserable place."

Paul Douglas, the liberal Illinoisan, volunteered for the marines at fifty "to get myself a Jap." True, it did no harm to his subsequent campaign for the United States Senate. There was nothing unusual in Mr. Douglas's pronouncement. "Jap" was a common word in our daily vocabulary. He was a decent, highly enlightened man caught up in war fever as much as fervor. It was the doyen of American journalists, Walter Lippmann, who strongly urged internment for Niseis and their fathers and mothers.

For the typical American soldier, despite the perverted film sermons, it wasn't "getting another Jap" or "getting another Nazi" that impelled him up front. "The reason you storm the beaches is not patriotism or bravery," reflects the tall rifleman. "It's that sense of not wanting to fail your buddies. There's sort of a special sense of kinship."

An explanation is offered by an old-time folk singer who'd been with an anti-aircraft battery of the Sixty-second Artillery: "You had fifteen guys who for the first time in their lives were not living in a competitive society. We were in a tribal sort of situation, where we could help each other without fear. I realized it was the absence of phony standards that created the thing I loved about the army."

There was another first in the lives of the GIs. Young kids, who had never wandered beyond the precinct of their native city or their small hometown or their father's farm, ran into exotic places and exotic people, as well as into one another, whom they found equally exotic.

"The first time I ever heard a New England accent," recalls the midwesterner, "was at Fort Benning. The southerner was an exotic creature to me. People from the farms. The New York street-smarts." (Author's note: The native New Yorker was probably the most parochial, most set in his ways, and most gullible.)

One of the most satisfying moments during my brief turn as a "military man" came at a crap game. It was in Jefferson Barracks. A couple of hotshots from New York and Philadelphia had things seemingly going their way. I and several others lost our pokes in short order. Along came this freckled, skinny kid off an Arkansas farm, his Adam's apple bobbing wildly. It appeared that the easterners had another pigeon. An hour or so later, the street-smart boys were thoroughly cleaned out by the rube. It was lovely. City boys and country boys were, for the first time in their lives, getting acquainted.

"When I woke up the first morning on the troop train in Fulton, Kentucky, I thought I was in Timbuktu. Of course, I was absolutely bowled over by Europe, the castles, the cathedrals, the Alps. It was wonderment for a nineteen-year-old."

Of course, there were songs learned that their mothers never taught them. And swearing. And smoking. "We were told that the next morning we would be on the attack. By this time, I had taken up cigarette smoking, wondering what my mother would think when I came back. I felt sickish, I was cold, I was scared. And I couldn't even get one last cigarette."

In tough circumstances, as a war prisoner or under siege or waiting for Godot, what was most on the soldier's mind was not women nor politics nor family nor, for that matter, God. It was food. "In camp," a prisoner of the Japanese recalls, "first thing you talked about is what you wanted in your stomach. Guys would tell about how their mother made this. Men would sit and listen very attentively. This was the big topic all the time. I remember vividly this old Polack. One guy always wanted him to talk about how his mother made the cabbage rolls, the *golabki*. He had a knack of telling so you could almost smell 'em. You'd see some of the fellas just lickin' their lips. Tasting it. You know?"

Food. Fear. Comradeship. And confusion. In battle, the order of the day was often disorder. Again and again survivors, gray, bald, potbellied, or cadaverous, remember chaos.

The big redhead of the 106th Infantry Division can't forget his trauma. "So there I am wandering around with the whole German army shooting at me, and all I've got is a .45 automatic. There were ample opportunities, however, because every place you went there were bodies and soldiers laying around. Mostly Americans. At one time or another, I think I had in my hands every weapon the United States Army manufactured. You'd run out of ammunition with that one, you'd throw it away and try to find something else."

The lieutenant had an identical experience some five days after D-Day. "We were in dug-in foxholes, in a very checkered position. There were Germans ahead of us and Germans in the back of us. Americans over there ahead of these Germans. There was no straight front line. It was a mess."

A mess among the living, perhaps. There was order, of a sort, among the dead. At least for the Germans. A Stalingrad veteran is haunted by the memory of the moment. "I was sleeping on the bodies of killed German soldiers. The Germans were very orderly people. When they found they didn't have time to bury these bodies, they laid them next to each other in a very neat and orderly way. I saw straight rows, like pieces of cordwood. Exact."

A woman, born in 1943, cannot forget the camp photographs in *Life*. She had been casually leafing through some old issues in a Pennsylvania school library. She was twelve at the time. "In those grainy photos, you first think it's cords of wood piled up. You look again, it shows you human beings. You never get the picture out of your eye: the interchangeability of the stacks of human bodies and the stacks of cords of wood. There is something curious about the fascination with horror that isn't exhausted anywhere. Prior to finding these pictures, there were merely hints of something to a sheltered girl, nothing she could put together."

Between the winter of 1941 and the summer of 1945, Willie and Joe, dogfaces, and their assorted buddies grew up in a hurry. It wasn't only the bullet they bit. It was the apple. Some lost innocence, abroad. "I went there a skinny, gaunt mama's boy, full of wonderment," says the rifleman. "I came back much more circumspect in my judgment of people. And of governments."

Others were not quite so touched. "I got one eye. My feet hangs down. I got a joint mashed in my back. I got a shoulder been broke. Feel that knot right there." The Kentucky guardsman offers a litany of war wounds, but is undaunted. "I'd go fight for my country right today. You're darn right. I'd go right now, boy."

They all came back home. All but 400,000.

At home, the fourteen-year-old Victory girl grew up in a hurry, too. "What I feel most about the war, it disrupted my family. That really chokes me up, makes me feel very sad that I lost that. On December 6, 1941, I was playing with paper dolls: Deanna Durbin, Sonja Henie. I had a Shirley Temple doll that I cherished. After Pearl Harbor, I never played with dolls again."

After the epochal victory over fascism, the boys came back to resume their normal lives. Yet it was a different country from the one they had left.

In 1945, the United States inherited the earth. . . . at the end of World War II, what was left of Western civilization passed into the American account. The war had also prompted the country to invent a miraculous economic machine that seemed to grant as many wishes as were asked of it. The continental United States had escaped the plague of war, and so it was easy enough for the heirs to believe that they had been anointed by God.*

We had hardly considered ourselves God's anointed in the thirties. The Great Depression was our most devastating experience since the Civil War. Somewhere along the line, our money machine had stripped its gears.

A Wall Street wise man, adviser to four presidents, non-explained: "The Crash was like a thunderclap. Everybody was stunned. Nobody knew what it was about. The Street was general confusion. They didn't understand any more than anybody else. They thought something would be announced." He neglected to tell me by whom.

The sixteen million Americans out in the cold reached for abandoned newspapers on park benches and—would you believe?—skipped over the sports section and flipped feverishly to Help Wanted. A hard-traveling survivor recalls an ad being answered at

*Lewis H. Lapham, "America's Foreign Policy: A Rake's Progress," *Harper's*, March 1979.

the Spreckels sugar refinery in San Francisco: "A thousand men would fight like a pack of Alaskan dogs to get through. You know dang well, there's only three or four jobs."

With the German invasion of Poland in 1939, it all changed. The farewell to a dismal decade was more than ceremonial: 1939 was the end and the beginning. Hard Times, as though by some twentieth-century alchemy, were transmuted into Good Times. War was our Paracelsus.

True, the New Deal had created jobs and restored self-esteem for millions of Americans. Still, there were ten, eleven million walking the streets, riding the rods, up against it, despairing. All this changed under the lowering sky of World War Two. What had been a country psychically as well as geographically isolated had become, with the suddenness of a blitzkrieg, engaged with distant troubles. And close-at-hand triumphs.

Our huge industrial machine shifted gears. In a case of Scripture turned upside down, plowshares were beaten into swords (or their twentieth-century equivalents: tanks, mortars, planes, bombs). In the words of President Franklin D. Roosevelt, Dr. New Deal was replaced by Dr. Win The War.

Thomas (Tommy the Cork) Corcoran, one of FDR's wonder boys, remembers being called into the Oval Office: " 'Tommy, cut out this New Deal stuff. It's tough to win a war.' He'd heard from the people who could produce the tanks and other war stuff. As a payoff, they required an end to what they called New Deal nonsense."

James Rowe, who had been a young White House adviser, recalls: "It upset the New Dealers. We had a big PWA building program. Roosevelt took a big chunk of that money and gave it to the navy to build ships. I was shocked. A large number of businessmen came down as dollar-a-year men. Roosevelt was taking help anyplace he could get it. There was a quick change into a war economy."

And prosperity came. Boom had a double meaning.

For the old Iowa farmer, it was something else. Oh yes, he remembered the Depression and what it did to the farmers: foreclosures the norm; grain burned; corn at *minus* three cents a bushel; rural despair. Oh yes, it changed with the war. "That's when the real boost came. The war—" There is a catch in his voice. He slumps in his rocker. His wife stares at the wallpaper. It is a long silence, save for the *tick-tock* of the grandfather's clock. "—it does something to your country. It does something to the individual. I had a neighbor just

9

⬝

as the war was beginning. We had a boy ready to go to service. This neighbor told me what we needed was a damn good war, and we'd solve our agricultural problems. And I said, 'Yes, but I'd hate to pay with the price of my son.' Which we did." He weeps. "It's too much of a price to pay."

The retired Red Cross worker wastes no words: "The war was fun for America. I'm not talking about the poor souls who lost sons and daughters. But for the rest of us, the war was a hell of a good time. Farmers in South Dakota that I administered relief to and gave 'em bully beef and four dollars a week to feed their families, when I came home were worth a quarter-million dollars, right? It's forgotten now."

It had, indeed, become another country. "World War Two changed everything," says the retired admiral. "Our military runs our foreign policy. The State Department has become the lackey of the Pentagon. Before World War Two, this never happened. Only if there was a war did they step up front. The ultimate control was civilian. World War Two changed all this."

It is exquisite irony that military work liberated women from the private world of *Küche, Kinde, Kirche*. "I remember going to Sunday dinner one of the older women invited me to," the ex-schoolteacher remembers. "She and her sister at the dinner table were talking about the best way to keep their drill sharp in the factory. I never heard anything like this in my life. It was just marvelous. But even here we were sold a bill of goods. They were hammering away that the woman who went to work did it to help her man, and when he came back, she cheerfully leaped back to the home."

Though at war's end these newborn working women were urged, as their patriotic duty Over Here, to go back home where they "naturally belonged" and give their jobs back to the boys who did their patriotic duty Over There, the taste for independence was never really lost. Like that of Wrigley's chewing gum, found in the pack of every GI, its flavor was longer-lasting. No matter what the official edict, for millions of American women home would never again be a Doll's House.

War's harsh necessity affected another people as well: the blacks. Not much had happened to change things in the years between the two world wars. Big Bill Broonzy, the blues singer, commemorated his doughboy life in World War One:

When Uncle Sam called me, I knew I would be called the real McCoy.
But when I got in the army, they called me soldier boy.
I wonder when will I be called a man?

As in 1917, black servicemen were almost exclusively in labor battalions: loading ships, cleaning up, kitchen work, digging one thing or another. They were domestics abroad as well as at home. Mythology had long been standard operating procedure: blacks were not to be trusted in combat. To this, Coleman Young offered a wry touch of history: "The black Tenth Cavalry was with Teddy Roosevelt at San Juan Hill. They saved his ass." As the war dragged on, and casualties mounted alarmingly, black soldiers were sent up front. Grudgingly, they were allowed to risk their lives in combat. Lieutenant Charles A. Gates tells of the 761st Tank Battalion. All black. "We were very well disciplined and trained. The German army was confused. They couldn't see how we could be in so many places at the same time." There was astonishment on the part of our generals as well as theirs. It took thirty-five years for the 761st to get a Presidential Unit Citation.

These were rare adventures for black GIs in World War Two. A schoolteacher recalls his days as a sergeant with the Quartermaster Corps: "That's where most of us were put. We serviced the service. We handled food, clothing, equipage. We loaded ammunition, too. We were really stevedores and servants."

At home, things were somewhat different. Like women, blacks were called upon. Their muscles and skills, usually bypassed, were needed in defense plants. The perverse imperatives of war brought about relatively well-paying jobs for black men and women who would otherwise have been regarded with less than benign neglect. Even this might not have come about had it not been for the constant pressure from the black community.

"I got a call from my boss. 'Get your ass over here, we got a problem.'" Joseph Rauh, working in Washington, remembers June of 1941. "'Some guy named Randolph is going to march on Washington unless we put out a fair employment practices order.* The President says you gotta stop Randolph from marching. We got

*A. Philip Randolph, president of the Brotherhood of Sleeping Car Porters. He and other black leaders were planning a march urging the administration to pass a fair employment practices act.

defense plants goin' all over this goddamn country, but no blacks are bein' hired. Go down to the Budget Bureau and work something out.' "

It was not noblesse oblige that brought forth Executive Order 8802, establishing the Fair Employment Practice Committee.

Wartime prosperity had extended into an exhilarating period of postwar prosperity. The United States had become the most powerful industrial as well as military power in the world. Its exports were now as truly worldwide as its politics. For the returning GI, it was a wholly new society. And a new beginning.

"I had matured in those three years away," says the middle manager of a large corporation. He had come from a family of blue-collar workers in a blue-collar town. "I wanted to better myself more than, say, hitting the local factory. Fortunately, I was educated on the GI Bill. It was a blessing. The war changed our whole idea of how we wanted to live when we came back. We set our sights pretty high. All of us wanted better levels of living. I am now what you'd call middle class."

The suburb, until now, had been the exclusive domain of the "upper class." It was where the rich lived. The rest of us were neighborhood folk. At war's end, a new kind of suburb came into being. GI Joe, with his persevering wife/sweetheart and baby, moved into the little home so often celebrated in popular song. Molly and me and baby makes three. It was not My Blue Heaven, perhaps, but it was something only dreamed of before. Thanks to the GI Bill, two new names were added to American folksay: Levittown and Park Forest.

A new middle class had emerged. Until now, the great many, even before the Depression, had had to scuffle from one payday to the next. "When you went to the doctor's," remembers the California woman, "it may have been ten dollars, but that was maybe a third of my father's salary as a milkman."

"The American myth was alive," reminisces a Sioux Falls native. "Remember the '49 cars in the *National Geographic?* Postwar cars. New design, new body style. In the colored Sunday funnies there'd be ads for the new cars. We'd been driving Grandpa Herman's old prewar Chrysler. It was the only car on the block. Now everybody was getting a car. Oh, it was exciting."

It was, indeed, a different world to which Telford Taylor returned from Germany. He had been the chief American prosecutor during twelve of the thirteen Nuremberg trials. "When I came back home in 1949, I was already in my early forties. I'd been away from home seven years and was out of touch with things politically. I thought that Washington was still the way I'd left it in 1942. By 1949, it was a very different place. I had left Washington at a time when it was still Roosevelt, liberalism, social action, all these things. When I came back in the late forties, the Dies Committee . . . the cold war. I was a babe in the woods. I didn't know what hit me."

The cold war. Another legacy of World War Two.

The year Telford Taylor returned to the States, Archibald Mac-Leish wrote a singularly prescient essay:

> Never in the history of the world was one people as completely dominated, intellectually and morally, by another as the people of the United States by the people of Russia in the four years from 1946 through 1949. American foreign policy was a mirror image of Russian foreign policy: whatever the Russians did, we did in reverse. American domestic politics were conducted under a kind of upside-down Russian veto: no man could be elected to public office unless he was on record as detesting the Russians, and no proposal could be enacted, from a peace plan at one end to a military budget at the other, unless it could be demonstrated that the Russians wouldn't like it. American political controversy was controversy sung to the Russian tune; left-wing movements attacked right-wing movements not on American issues but on Russian issues, and right-wing movements replied with the same arguments turned round about. . . .
>
> All this . . . took place not in a time of national weakness or decay but precisely at the moment when the United States, having engineered a tremendous triumph and fought its way to a brilliant victory in the greatest of all wars, had reached the highest point of world power ever achieved by a single state.*

The ex-admiral says it his way: "World War Two has warped our view of how we look at things today. We see things in terms of that war, which in a sense was a good war. But the twisted memory of it encourages the men of my generation to be willing, almost eager, to use military force anywhere in the world."

*MacLeish's piece of 1949, "The Conquest of America," was reprinted in the *Atlantic Monthly*, March 1980.

In a small midwestern rural town, a grandmother, soft and gentle, is certain she speaks for most of the townsfolk. "People here feel that we should have gone into Vietnam and finished it instead of backing off as we did. I suppose it's a feeling that carried over from World War Two when we finished Hitler. I know the older men who fought in that war feel that way."

Big Bill Broonzy put it another way. It happened quite inadvertently one night in a Chicago nightclub. He had been singing a country blues about a sharecropper whose mule had died. It was his own story. During the performance, four young hipsters made a scene of walking out on him. I, working as MC that night, was furious. Big Bill laughed. He always laughed at such moments. Laughin' to keep from cryin', perhaps. "What do these kids know 'bout a mule? They never seen a mule. How do you expect somebody to feel 'bout somethin' he don't know? When I was in Europe, all those places, Milano, Hamburg, London, I seen cities bombed out. People tellin' me 'bout bombin's. What do I know 'bout a bomb? The only bomb I ever did see was in the pictures. People scared, cryin'. Losin' their homes. What do I know 'bout that? I never had no bomb fall on me. Same thing with these kids. They never had no mule die on 'em. They don't even know what the hell I'm talkin' 'bout."

Big Bill, at that moment, set off the most pertinent and impertinent of challenges: Must a society experience horror in order to understand horror? Ours was the only country among the combatants in World War Two that was neither invaded nor bombed. Ours were the only cities not blasted into rubble. Our Willie and Joe were up front; the rest of us were safe, surrounded by two big oceans. As for our allies and enemies, civilian as well as military were, at one time or another, up front: the British, the French, the Russians (twenty million dead; perhaps thirty million, says Harrison Salisbury), as well as the Germans, the Italians, the Japanese. Let alone the Slavs of smaller spheres. And, of course, the European Jews. And the Gypsies. And all kinds of *Untermenschen.*

True, an inconsolable grief possessed the families of those Americans lost and maimed in the Allied triumph. Parks, squares, streets, and bridges have been named after these young heroes, sung and unsung. Yet it is the casual walkout of the four young hipsters in that Chicago nightclub that may be the rude, fearsome metaphor we must decipher.

The elderly Japanese *hibakisha* (survivor of the atom bomb), contemplates the day it fell on Hiroshima. He had been a nineteen-year-old soldier passing through town. "The children were screaming, 'Please take these maggots off our bodies.' It was impossible for me, one soldier, to try to help so many people. The doctor said, 'We can't do anything. Sterilize their wounds with salt water.' We took a broom, dipped it into the salt water, and painted over the bodies. The children leaped up: 'I'm gonna run, I must run.'" The interpreter corrects him: "In the local dialect, it means 'thank you.'"

The tall young rifleman understands the horror. He was being retrained, after his European near-misses, for the invasion of Japan when the first atom bomb was dropped. "We ended halfway across the Pacific. How many of us would have been killed on the mainland if there were no bomb? Someone like me has this specter." So does his quondam buddy: "We're sitting on the pier in Seattle, sharpening our bayonets, when Harry dropped that beautiful bomb. The greatest thing ever happened. Anybody sitting at the pier at that time would have to agree." The black combat correspondent sees it somewhat differently: "Do you realize that most blacks don't believe the atom bomb would have been dropped on Hiroshima had it been a white city?" Witnesses to the fire bombings of Dresden may dispute the point.

The crowning irony lay in World War Two itself. It had been a different kind of war. "It was not like your other wars," a radio disk jockey reflected aloud. In his banality lay a wild kind of crazy truth. It was not fratricidal. It was not, most of us profoundly believed, "imperialistic." Our enemy was, patently, obscene: the Holocaust maker. It was one war that many who would have resisted "your other wars" supported enthusiastically. It was a "just war," if there is any such animal. In a time of nuclear weaponry, it is the language of a lunatic. But World War Two . . .

It ended on a note of hope without historic precedent. *On a Note of Triumph* is what Norman Corwin called his eloquent radio program heard coast-to-coast on V-E Day, May 8, 1945.

> *Lord God of test-tube and blueprint*
> *Who jointed molecules of dust and shook them till*
>   *their name was Adam,*
> *Who taught worms and stars how they could live together,*
> *Appear now among the parliaments of conquerors and*
>   *give instruction to their schemes:*

Measure out new liberties so none shall suffer for his
father's color or the credo of his choice. . . .

The day of that broadcast is remembered for a number of reasons by a West Coast woman. "V-E Day. Oh, such a joyous thing! And San Francisco was chosen for the first session of the UN. I was ecstatic. Stalin, Churchill, and Roosevelt met, and somehow war never again would happen." She was an usher at the War Memorial Opera House, where the UN first met in June of '45. "I was still in my little Miss Burke School uniform. Little middy and skirt. I was part of it. And so deeply proud. When the Holocaust survivors came out, I felt we were liberating them. When the GIs and Russian soldiers met, they were all knights in shining armor, saving humanity." She laughs softly. "It's not that simple. World War Two was just an innocent time in America. I was innocent. My parents were innocent. The country was innocent. Since World War Two, I think I have a more objective view of what this country really is."

The Red Cross worker thinks of then and now. "To many people, it brought about a realization that there ain't no hidin' place down here. That the world is unified in pain as well as opportunity. We had twenty, twenty-five years of greatness in our country, when we reached out to the rest of the world with help. Some of it was foolish, some of it was misspent, some was in error. Many follies. But we had a great reaching out. It was an act of such faith." He tries to stifle an angry sob. "Now, we're being pinched back into the meanness of the soul. World War Two? It's a war I still would go to."

The ex-captain, watching a Dow-Jones ticker, shakes his head. "I don't have as much trust in my fellow man as I once did. I have no trust in my peers. They're burnt-out cases. In the war, I was trying to do something useful with my life . . ."

A thousand miles away, the once and forever tall young rifleman, though gray and patriarchal, stares out the window at the Chicago skyline, the Lake, and beyond. "World War Two has affected me in many ways ever since. In a short period of time, I had the most tremendous experiences of all of life: of fear, of jubilance, of misery, of hope, of comradeship, and of endless excitement. I honestly feel grateful for having been a witness to an event as monumental as anything in history and, in a very small way, a participant."

A SUNDAY MORNING

JOHN GARCIA

A huge man, built along the lines of a sumo wrestler. He manages a
complex of apartment buildings in Los Angeles. He could quite easily
be the bouncer, too. He is resigned to the assortment of illnesses that
plague him; his manner is easygoing. "With my age, my love for food,
that's caused diabetes, the whole bit." He is a Hawaiian.

I was sixteen years old, employed as a pipe fitter apprentice at Pearl
Harbor Navy Yard. On December 7, 1941, oh, around 8:00 A.M., my
grandmother woke me. She informed me that the Japanese were
bombing Pearl Harbor. I said, "They're just practicing." She said,
no, it was real and the announcer is requesting that all Pearl Harbor
workers report to work. I went out on the porch and I could see the
anti-aircraft fire up in the sky. I just said, "Oh boy."

I was four miles away. I got out on my motorcycle and it took me
five, ten minutes to get there. It was a mess.

I was working on the U.S.S. *Shaw.* It was on a floating dry dock.
It was in flames. I started to go down into the pipe fitter's shop to
get my toolbox when another wave of Japanese came in. I got under
a set of concrete steps at the dry dock where the battleship *Pennsyl-*
vania was. An officer came by and asked me to go into the *Pennsyl-*
vania and try to get the fires out. A bomb had penetrated the marine
deck, and that was three decks below. Under that was the magazines:
ammunition, powder, shells. I said, "There ain't no way I'm gonna
go down there." It could blow up any minute. I was young and
sixteen, not stupid, not at sixty-two cents an hour. (Laughs.)

A week later, they brought me before a navy court. It was determined that I was not service personnel and could not be ordered.
There was no martial law at the time. Because I was sixteen and had
gone into the water, the whole thing was dropped.

I was asked by some other officer to go into the water and get
sailors out that had been blown off the ships. Some were unconscious,

some were dead. So I spent the rest of the day swimming inside the harbor, along with some other Hawaiians. I brought out I don't know how many bodies and how many were alive and how many dead. Another man would put them into ambulances and they'd be gone. We worked all day at that.

That evening, I drove a truckload of marines into Palolo Valley because someone reported that the Japanese had parachuted down there. Because of the total blackout, none of the marine drivers knew how to get there. It was two miles away. There were no parachuters. Someone in the valley had turned their lights on and the marines started shootin' at that house. The lights went out. (Laughs.)

I went back to my concrete steps to spend the night there. Someone on the *Pennsylvania* was walking along the edge of armored plate. He lit a cigarette. All of a sudden, a lot of guns opened up on him. I don't know if he was hit.

The following morning, I went with my tools to the *West Virginia*. It had turned turtle, totally upside down. We found a number of men inside. The *Arizona* was a total washout. Also the *Utah*. There were men in there, too. We spent about a month cutting the superstructure of the *West Virginia*, tilting it back on its hull. About three hundred men we cut out of there were still alive by the eighteenth day.

How did they survive?

I don't know. We were too busy to ask. (Laughs.) It took two weeks to get all the fires out. We worked around the clock for three days. There was so much excitement and confusion. Some of our sailors were shooting five-inch guns at the Japanese planes. You just cannot down a plane with a five-inch shell. They were landing in Honolulu, the unexploding naval shells. They have a ten-mile range. They hurt and killed a lot of people in the city.

When I came back after the third day, they told me that a shell had hit the house of my girl. We had been going together for, oh, about three years. Her house was a few blocks from my place. At the time, they said it was a Japanese bomb. Later we learned it was an American shell. She was killed. She was preparing for church at the time.

My neighbors met me. They were mostly Japanese. We all started to cry. We had no idea what was happening, what was going to happen.

▾

Martial law had been set in. Everyone had to work twelve hours, six to six. No one on the streets after 6:00 P.M. No one on the streets before 6:00 A.M. The military took over the islands completely. If you failed to go to work, the police would be at your door and you were arrested. You had to do something, filling sandbags, anything. No one was excused. If you called in sick, a nurse would come to your house to check on you. If you failed to be there or were goofing off, you went to jail. All civil liberties were suspended.

There was no act of treason by anyone that I know of. There were spies, but they were all employed by the Japanese embassy. If they had arrested the ordinary Japanese, there would be no work force at Pearl Harbor. There were 130,000 Japanese on the islands. There'd be no stores, no hotels, nothing. You'd have to shut the city down. They suffered a lot of insults, especially by the servicemen. They took it without coming back.

I tried to get in the military, but they refused. They considered my work essential for the war effort. I was promoted to shop fitter and went from $32 a week to $125. But I kept trying for a year to get in the fight. Finally, I wrote a letter to President Roosevelt. I told him I was angry at the Japanese bombing and had lost some friends. He okayed that I be accepted. I went into the service and went down to $21 a month. (Laughs.)

My grandmother signed for me because I was only seventeen. She said she would never see me alive again. It turned out prophetic because she died one day before I got home. January 1946.

They wanted to send me to Texas for training. I got on the stick and wrote to the President again. I wasn't interested in Texas, I wanted to go into combat. I got an answer from the White House requesting that I be put into a combat outfit. I got thirty days washing dishes for not following the chain of command. (Laughs.)

"When I went into the military, they asked, 'What race are you?' I had no idea what they were talking about because in Hawaii we don't question a man's race. They said, 'Where are your parents from?' I said they were born in Hawaii. 'Your grandparents?' They were born in Hawaii. 'How about your great-grandparents?' I said they're from Europe, some from Spain, some from Wales. They said, 'You're Caucasian.' I said, 'What's that?' They said, 'You're white.' I looked at my skin. I was pretty dark, tanned by the sun. I said, 'You're kidding.'

(Laughs.) They put me down as Caucasian and separated me from the rest of the Hawaiians.

"Some of my new buddies asked me not to talk to three of the men. I asked why. They said, 'They're Jews.' I said, 'What's a Jew?' They said, 'Don't you know? They killed Jesus Christ.' I says, 'You mean them guys? They don't look old enough.' They said, 'You're tryin' to get smart?' I said, 'No. It's my understanding he was killed about nineteen hundred years ago.'"

I joined the Seventh Infantry Division in time for the run to Kwajalein in the Marshall Islands. It took six days to take it. We went back to Hawaii. I don't know what we were preparing for, but we practiced and practiced and practiced swimming, some other Hawaiians and me. I said, "Eleanor must be coming here." I was taken to the FBI in Honolulu and asked how did I know the President was coming. I said I don't know. They said, "You said Eleanor was coming." I said, "Yeah, I just figured somebody important was coming because we've been practicing this show for two months." They said, "Okay, keep your mouth shut."

All of a sudden one day they told us there'd be a swimming show. We threw oil in the water, set the water on fire, and dove into it. Then they told us to get dressed and get ready for the parade. We were all searched for ammunition. No one could have ammunition in his rifle, no pocket knives. But we had bayonets. (Laughs.) As we went past the parade stand, we saw General MacArthur and President Roosevelt.

We knew something was up but we didn't know where we were gonna go. A rumor came down that we were going into Africa after Rommel. The main body of the Seventh had trained in the Mojave Desert, but was sent to the Aleutians. They had figured on Africa. So we thought for sure it was Africa for us. We got orders for the Pacific. They said Yap.

"I had been made a sergeant by this time because we were given jungle training and I knew the tropics. So they sent me to Alaska. (Laughs.) After three weeks, they had to send me back because I was shaking. It was too damn cold. (Laughs.)"

Several nights later, a broadcast came from Tokyo Rose: "Good evening, men of the Seventh Infantry. I know you're on your way to the Philippines." She was right. (Laughs.) We were there from October of '44 until March of '45. Totally combat.

I fought very carefully, I fought low. There were a couple of Japanese boys, our interpreters, who were a little bit heroic. They would climb on board a Japanese tank going by, knock on the things, converse in Japanese, and as soon as the door popped open, they'd drop a hand grenade—boom!

Our next stop was Okinawa. We landed there on April 1, '45. No opposition. Several days later, we got word that President Roosevelt had died. We were all sort of down—boom! They said a man called Truman replaced him. I said, "Who is Truman?" We were there eighty-two days. I did what I had to do. When I saw a Japanese, I shot at him and ducked. Shot and ducked, that's all I did. I was always scared until we took Hill 87.

We buried General Ushijima and his men inside a cave. This was the worst part of the war, which I didn't like about Okinawa. They were hiding in caves all the time, women, children, soldiers. We'd get up on the cliff and lower down barrels of gasoline and then shoot at it. It would explode and just bury them to death.

I personally shot one Japanese woman because she was coming across a field at night. We kept dropping leaflets not to cross the field at night because we couldn't tell if they were soldiers. We set up a perimeter. Anything in front, we'd shoot at. This one night I shot and when it came daylight, it was a woman there and a baby tied to her back. The bullet had all gone through her and out the baby's back.

That still bothers me, that hounds me. I still feel I committed murder. You see a figure in the dark, it's stooped over. You don't know if it's a soldier or a civilian.

I was drinking about a fifth and a half of whiskey every day. Sometimes homemade, sometimes what I could buy. It was the only way I could kill. I had friends who were Japanese and I kept thinking every time I pulled a trigger on a man or pushed a flamethrower down into a hole: What is this person's family gonna say when he doesn't come back? He's got a wife, he's got children, somebody.

They would show us movies. Japanese women didn't cry. They would accept the ashes stoically. I knew different. They went home and cried.

I'd get up each day and start drinking. How else could I fight the war? Sometimes we made the booze, sometimes we bought it from the navy. The sailors stole it from their officers. (Laughs.) Sometimes it cost us seventy-five dollars a bottle, sometimes it cost us a Japanese flag. You'd take a piece of parachute silk, make a circle on it, put a few bullet holes in it, give it to the navy, and they'd give you a bottle of whiskey.

I drank my last drink on the night of August 14, 1945, I think it was. When we heard from Swedish radio that the Japanese wanted to contact the Americans in order to end the war, we just went wild. Every soldier just took a gun and started shooting. I got into my trench and stayed there because the bullets were all over. Thirty-two men out of our outfit were killed that night by stray celebrating bullets.

I haven't touched a drop since. I wasn't a drinking man before. I started in the Philippines when I saw the bodies of men, women, and children, especially babies, that were hit by bombs. They were by the side of the road, and we would run over them with our tanks.

Oh, I still lose nights of sleep because of that woman I shot. I still lose a lot of sleep. I still dream about her. I dreamed about it perhaps two weeks ago . . . (He lets out a deep breath; it's something more turbulent than a sigh.)

Aaaahh, I feel that if countries are gonna fight a war, find yourself an island with nobody and then just put all your men in there and let them kill each other. Or better, send the politicians, let them fight it out. Yeah, like this stupid race that we're having of atomic wars. So much money is being devoted to killing people and so little to saving. It's a crazy world.

I was a policeman for fifteen years in Washington, D.C. When I was involved in a hostage situation, I just waited. Eventually, the person gave up. There's no need to be playing gung ho and going in there with guns blazing. I worked always in black neighborhoods. I would not shoot. I would talk and talk and talk. In one instance, there were three men holed up. I took off my gun and I went in. I said, "You guys can kill me, but you're not gonna walk out of here because there's a lot of men waiting for you. You can give me your gun and walk out and do some time, but you're not gonna do it inside of a box." They said, "Man, you're crazy." I said, "I don't think you are." All three of them gave me the gun, and we walked out. It's just that I'm not a killer.

Santa Rosa, California. He came in during the conversation with his younger brother, Frank. He is a lawyer, successful, solid, and though easy with talk, is matter-of-fact in style.

I'd been to mass at Saint Rose and was on the floor reading the funny paper when we got the news of Pearl Harbor. We had the radio on, probably listening to Glenn Miller or Benny Goodman. It didn't really mean a thing for a while. Of course, we already had a brother, Bill, who was already in Canada, training to fly Spitfires. But these places were so far away from us. It just didn't seem possible that we were at war.

A friend and I were in San Francisco that Sunday night. We were stopped on the Golden Gate Bridge by a national guardsman. He looked in the car. It was a battered Chevvy. We heard later that a woman was killed on the bridge that night because she didn't respond to a guardsman's order to halt.

We decided to drive downtown. That was an eye-opener. Market Street was bedlam. The United Artists Theatre had a huge marquee with those dancing lights, going on and off. People were throwing everything they could to put those lights out, screaming Blackout! Blackout! The theater people had not been told to turn them off. Once in a while, they'd hit a light.

No cars could move. The streets were full of people, blocking the tracks, the trolley line. People were throwing rocks, anything they could find. A streetcar came along, one of those old-fashioned, funny San Francisco streetcars. It had a big round light. A man ran up with a baseball bat and smashed the light. But the city was lustrous, all the office building lights were on. I said to my friend, "Let's get the hell out of here before they smash our headlights."

I was a senior at the University of San Francisco. I had room and board with a lady and her daughter. I flipped on the lights because it was pitch dark. Mrs. Kelleher screamed, "Dennis, turn the lights out! The Japs are comin'! The Japs are comin'!" She and her daughter were sitting on the couch, clutching one another in absolute abject terror. "The Golden Gate Bridge has been bombed!" I said, "Mrs. Kelleher, I just drove over there a few minutes ago. There's nothing wrong with the bridge." But they were so terror-stricken, I turned out the lights.

Their son Frank was in the ROTC at USF. He got a call: For God's sake, get over here. We're gonna make a stand at the university! They'd been listening to the radio all day and were convinced the Japanese were here. They had landed all over the coast and had taken the Presidio. They would repeat it on the radio, again and again. Total hysteria.

The next morning, when we discovered that there weren't any Japs on the corner of Twelfth and Balboa, the fear subsided. We made it through the black night and we weren't bombed. We had our breakfast and everything was pretty routine. We were simmering but we weren't boiling.

Bill, who was in Canada, called our mother to find out if we were okay. He'd heard in Canada that San Francisco had been bombed and most of the West Coast. Mrs. Thurston, our doctor's wife, packed up and left. Back to Alabama, where she came from. The doctor said, "You go, I'm not leavin'." She took the jewelry, all the money, everything, and left him alone in the big beautiful house.

Within a week we had a company of Texas National Guard boys. Six or seven hundred of them, camped in the old Fairgrounds building. They had been sent here to protect us. Everybody came out here to protect us from the anticipated invasion. The papers didn't help any. The *Examiner* had a headline: Japanese Invade West Coast. All we had out here were Hearst papers. We reacted like a bunch of nuts.

I went down to San Francisco to enlist. I couldn't pass the eye test for the navy. I thought, The army will get me if I don't get my butt out of here. So I hopped down and got my seaman's papers and climbed aboard a Standard Oil tanker and got the hell out of there as fast as I could.

MAYOR TOM BRADLEY

He is mayor of Los Angeles. He was a young policeman in 1941: "I had been on the job for about a year."

Immediately after Pearl Harbor, there was bedlam. Sirens going off, aircraft guns firing. It was panic. Here we are in the middle of the night, there was no enemy in sight, but somebody thought they saw the enemy. (Laughs.) They were shooting at random.

All policemen were ordered to their respective stations, to be on the ready for whatever. We were all herded into the station, awaiting orders. None came, because there was nothing. (Laughs.) It was panic that simply overwhelmed us.

RON VEENKER

He is a teacher at a small college in Kentucky. He is forty-four.

He was raised in a Frisian community in Sioux Falls, South Dakota. "Frisian is a kind of Middle German language. They who knew High German in this community kept a very low profile. Every once in a while they'd break out in German, someone would say shoo, shoo, shoo, shoo, shoo. There was one fellow who would not shut up with the German. Everybody was afraid the whole community would suffer because of him. Anybody who had a German background was almost a pariah.

"But if we wanted to be in big trouble, we'd get angry and call the other kid a dirty Jap rat. That was the filthiest thing you could say."

I was four years old when the silence on December 7 terrified me. There had always been a lot of hilarity on Sundays. Not this time.

I was five when I visited California to stay with my other grandmother. We were standing at a trolley stop. A Japanese man about fifty-five, all bent over, smiling, came up. He had a pack of gum with a stick extended, which he handed to me. He had nothing but kindness on his face. I intuited it. Kids and dogs, you know. (Laughs.) My grandmother picked me up and ran two blocks, lickety-kite. And waited for the trolley at another stop.

Very soon after that, I noticed that all our neighbors were not there any more. Nobody talked about it. These were Japanese truck-garden people, who had been there a long time. Their homes had pagoda architecture. I walked down this lane past all their homes on my way to school in the morning. It was so quiet, it was eerie. I had been used to hearing people. They'd been taken away.

I'd been told the Japanese were something to fear. Even their empty homes I feared. I would start to whistle. I'll never forget the song "Pistol-Packin' Mama." I'd start to sing at the top of my lungs and I'd run. Every morning I'd come to school so tired. I would have been about seven then.

My great-grandmother was still alive. She was an alcoholic. My grandmother would give the old woman a jug of wine and go off to work. Great-Grandma would sit there, get bombed all day. I awakened one night, hearing a great commotion. Like airplanes going over. I swear I could hear flak from the anti-aircraft. I looked out the window and saw searchlights. There were explosions in the sky. Down below, I saw my great-grandmother wandering around the back yard in a nightgown, dazed. I've always associated that with the rumor that the Japanese once attacked Los Angeles.

PETER OTA

I think back to what happened—and sometimes I wonder: Where do I come from?

He is a fifty-seven-year-old Nisei. His father had come from Okinawa in 1904, his mother from Japan. He's an accountant. His father had worked on farms and in the coal mines of Mexico. After thirty-seven years building a fruit and vegetable business, he had become a successful and respected merchant in the community. He was a leader in the Japanese Chamber of Commerce of Los Angeles.

On the evening of December 7, 1941, my father was at a wedding. He was dressed in a tuxedo. When the reception was over, the FBI agents were waiting. They rounded up at least a dozen wedding guests and took 'em to county jail.

For a few days we didn't know what happened. We heard nothing. When we found out, my mother, my sister, and myself went to jail. I can still remember waiting in the lobby. When my father walked through the door, my mother was so humiliated. She didn't say anything. She cried. He was in prisoner's clothing, with a denim jacket and a number on the back.

The shame and humiliation just broke her down. She was into Japanese culture. She was a flower arranger and used to play the *biwa*, a Japanese stringed instrument. Shame in her culture is worse than death. Right after that day she got very ill and contracted tuberculosis. She had to be sent to a sanitarium. She stayed behind when we were evacuated. She was too ill to be moved. She was there till she passed away.

My father was transferred to Missoula, Montana. We got letters from him—censored, of course—telling us he was all right. It was just my sister and myself. I was fifteen, she was twelve. In April 1942, we were evacuated to Santa Anita. At the time we didn't know where we were going, how long we'd be gone. We didn't know what to take. A toothbrush, toilet supplies, some clothes. Only what you could carry. We left with a caravan.

Santa Anita is a race track. The horse stables were converted into living quarters. My sister and I were fortunate enough to stay in a barracks. The people in the stables had to live with the stench. Everything was communal. We had absolutely no privacy. When you went to the toilet, it was communal. It was very embarrassing for women especially. The parent actually lost control of the child. I had no parents, so I did as I pleased. When I think back what happened to the Japanese family . . .

We had orders to leave Santa Anita in September of 1942. We had no idea where we were going. Just before we left, my father joined us. He was brought into camp on the back of an army state truck, he and several others who were released from Missoula. I can still picture it to this day: to come in like cattle or sheep being herded in the back of a pickup truck bed. We were near the gate and saw him come in. He saw us. It was a sad, happy moment, because we'd been separated for a year.

He never really expressed what his true inner feelings were. It just amazes me. He was never vindictive about it, never showed any anger. I can't understand that. A man who had worked so hard for what he had and lost it overnight. There is a very strong word in Japanese, *gaman.* It means to persevere. Old people instilled this into the second generation: You persevere. Take what's coming, don't react.

He had been a very outgoing person. Enthusiastic. I was very, very impressed with how he ran things and worked with people. When I saw him at Santa Anita, he was a different person.

We were put on a train, three of us and many trains of others. It was crowded. The shades were drawn. During the ride we were wondering, what are they going to do to us? We Niseis had enough confidence in our government that it wouldn't do anything drastic. My father had put all his faith in this country. This was his land.

Oh, it took days. We arrived in Amache, Colorado. That was an experience in itself. We were right near the Kansas border. It's a desolate, flat, barren area. The barracks was all there was. There were no trees, no kind of landscaping. It was like a prison camp. Coming from our environment, it was just devastating.

School in camp was a joke. Let's say it was loose. If you wanted to study, fine. If you didn't, who cared? There were some teachers who were conscientious and a lot who were not. One of our basic subjects was American history. They talked about freedom all the time. (Laughs.)

After a year, I was sent out to Utah on jobs. I worked on sugar beet farms. You had to have a contract or a job in order to leave camp. The pay was nominal. We would have a labor boss, the farmer would pay us through him. It was piecework. Maybe fifteen of us would work during the harvest season. When it was over, we went back to camp.

If you had a job waiting, you could relocate to a city that was not in the Western Defense Command. I had one in Chicago, as a stock boy in a candy factory. It paid seventy-five cents an hour. I was only in camp for a year. My sister was in until they were dismantled, about three and a half years. My father was in various camps for four years.

I went from job to job for a year. I had turned draft age, so I had to register. It's ironic. Here I am being drafted into the army, and my father and sister are in a concentration camp waiting for the war to end.

I was in the reserve, not yet inducted, in the middle of 1944, when I received a wire from my father saying that my mother was very ill. I immediately left Chicago for Amache, Colorado, to get my clearance from the Western Defense Command. It took several days. While I was waiting, my mother passed away.

Since we wanted her funeral to be at the camp where my father and sister were, I decided to go on to California and pick up her remains. At Needles, California, I was met at the train by an FBI agent. He was assigned to me. He was with me at all times during my stay there. Whether I went to sleep at night or whether I went to the bathroom, he was by my side.

As soon as we stepped off the train at the Union Station in Los Angeles, there was a shore patrol and a military police who met me. They escorted me through the station. It was one of the most . . . (He finds it difficult to talk.) I don't even know how to describe it. Any day now, I'd be serving in the same uniform as these people who were guarding me. The train stations at that time were always filled. When they marched me through, the people recognized me as being Oriental. They knew I was either an escaped prisoner or a spy. Oh, they called out names. I heard "dirty Jap" very distinctly.

After we got to the hotel, the FBI agent convinced the military that it wasn't necessary for them to stay with me. But he had to. He was disgusted with the whole situation. He knew I was in the reserve, that I was an American citizen. He could see no reason for him to be with me. But he was on assignment. We spoke personal things. His wife was having a baby, he couldn't be with her. He thought it was ridiculous.

I was in the armored division at Fort Knox. We were sent to Fort Mead for embarkation when the European war ended. They didn't know what to do with us Japanese Americans. We were in our own units. Should they send us to the Pacific side? They might not be able to tell who was the enemy and who was not. (Laughs.)

The war ended while I was at Fort McDowell on San Francisco Bay. That was the receiving point for Japanese prisoners captured in the war. I went back with a boatload of them. I didn't know how they'd react to me. I was very surprised. The professional soldiers who were captured during the early days of the war in Guadalcanal, Saipan, never believed the war ended. They would always say, when the subject came up, it was propaganda. The civilian soldiers were very different. We could get along with them. They were very young —*boheitai*, boy soldiers. We could relate to them as to children. They were scared. They had nothing to go back to. Okinawa was devastated. A lot of them lost their families.

My furloughs were spent in camp, visiting my father and sister. Going to camp was like going home for me, to see my family. We made the best of what we had. We celebrated Christmas in the American fashion. We tried to make our lives go easy.

We came back to Los Angeles at the end of the war, believing that there was no other way but to be American. We were discouraged with our Japanese culture. My feeling at the time was, I had to prove myself. I don't know why I had to prove myself. Here I am, an ex-GI, born and raised here. Why do I have to prove myself? We all had this feeling. We had to prove that we were Americans, okay?

My mother and father sent me to a Japanese school teaching the culture. My wife and I did nothing with our children in that respect. We moved to a white community near Los Angeles. It was typical American suburb living. We became more American than Americans, very conservative. My wife and I, we talk about this. We thought this was the thing we had to do: to blend into the community and become part of white America.

My children were denied a lot of the history of what happened. If you think of all those forty years of silence, I think this stems from another Japanese characteristic: when shame is put on you, you try to hide it. We were put into camp, we became victims, it was our fault. We hide it.

My oldest daughter, Cathy, in her senior year at college, wanted to write a thesis about the camp experience. She asked if we knew people she might interview. Strange thing is, many people, even now, didn't want to talk about it. Some of the people she did talk to broke down. Because this was the first time they had told this story. This is the same thing I did. When I first went into detail, it just broke me up. When it came out, I personally felt good about it. It was somethin' that was inside of me that I've wanted to say for a long time.

How do the Sansei feel about it—your daughter's generation?

Very angry. They keep saying, "Why did you go? Why didn't you fight back?" They couldn't understand it. They weren't raised in our culture. Today, I would definitely resist. It was a different situation at that time. This is what we tried to explain to our daughter. Today if this happened, I think a majority of the Japanese would resist.*

When I think back to my mother and my father, what they went through quietly, it's hard to explain. (Cries.) I think of my father without ever coming up with an angry word. After all those years, having worked his whole life to build a dream—an American dream, mind you—having it all taken away, and not one vindictive word. His business was worth more than a hundred thousand. He sold it for five. When he came out of camp, with what little money he had he put

*Jun Kurose, a Nisei internee from Seattle: "When we were told to evacuate, the American Friends Service Committee said: 'Don't go, we will help you.' . . . Some of the Japanese were saying: 'Stay out of this, you're making it rougher for us.' If we'd listened to the Friends, we might have been able to avert much suffering. We went willingly, we really did." (From *American Dreams: Lost and Found* [New York: Pantheon Books, 1980], p. 168).

a down payment on an apartment building. It was right in the middle of skid row, an old rooming house. He felt he could survive by taking in a little rent and living there. My sister worked for a family as a domestic. He was afraid for her in this area. He died a very broken man.

My wife and I, we're up on cloud nine right now. Our daughter just passed the California bar. Guess what she's doing? She works for the redress and reparations group in San Diego.* How's that?

YURIKO HOHRI

She lives with her husband in Chicago. He is national chair of the Council for Japanese American Redress. She is active, too.

The war became real for me when the two FBI agents came to our home in Long Beach. It was a few months after December 7. It was a rainy Saturday morning. My three sisters, my mother, and myself were at home doing the chores. I was twelve.

A black car came right into the driveway. One man went into the kitchen. As I watched, he looked under the sink and he looked into the oven. Then he went into the parlor and opened the glass cases where our most treasured things were. There were several stacks of *shakuhachi* sheet music. It's a bamboo flute. My father played the *shakuhachi* and my mother played the *koto*. At least once a month on a Sunday afternoon, their friends would come over and just enjoy themselves playing music. The man took the music.

I followed the man into my mother and father's bedroom. Strangers do not usually go into our bedrooms when they first come. As I watched, he went into the closet and brought out my father's golf clubs. He turned the bag upside down. I was only concerned about the golf balls, because I played jacks with them. He opened the *tansu*, a chest of drawers. My mother and sisters were weeping.

My father was at work. He took care of the vegetable and fruit sections for two grocery stores. He was brought home by the agents. He was taken to a camp in Tujunga Canyon. My grandmother and I went to visit him. It was a different kind of visit. There was a tall

---

*A movement for redress of grievances has come into being on behalf of Japanese Americans who were interned during the war years.

barbed-wire fence, so we were unable to touch each other. The only thing we could do was see each other. My father was weeping.

Our family moved to my grandmother's house—my mother's mother. At least six of my uncles were at home, so it was very crowded. My next recollection is that my mother, my three little sisters, and I were on this streetcar. My mother had made a little knapsack for each of us, with our names embroidered. We had a washcloth, a towel, soap, a comb. Just enough for us to carry. It was the first time we took a streetcar. Because we always went by my father's car.

We went to Santa Anita. We lived in a horse stable. We filled a cheesecloth bag with straw—our mattress. The sides of the room did not go up to the ceiling, so there was no privacy at all. They were horse stalls. We'd have fun climbing up. The floors were asphalt. I do remember what we called stinky bugs. They were crunchy, like cockroaches, large, black. Oh, it's really—(Laughs, as she shakes her head.) We had apple butter. To this day, I cannot taste apple butter.

She shows her internee's record, which she had saved all these years: her name, birthdate, internment date, places of internment. At the bottom of the sheet, in large print: KEEP FREEDOM IN YOUR FUTURE WITH U.S. SAVINGS BONDS.

Our teachers were young Nisei internees. There was a lot of rotation among them. The schooling was informal. Oh, I learned how to play cards there.

In the mornings, a man would knock on the door. There was a sort of bed check at night. There were searchlights always going.

All during this time, I was writing letters to Attorney General Biddle. I was asking him to release my father. I said we are four growing girls. We need our father here. Period.

We left Santa Anita in October 1942. It was a very long train with many, many cars. The stops were made at night with all the shades drawn. We wound up in Jerome, Arkansas. It was in the swamps. The toilet facilities had not yet been finished. The minute we got off, we had to go to the bathroom. I was standing in line, next thing I know people were looking down at me. I had fainted.

We could hardly walk because the clay would grab hold of your shoe or boot. It was very cold. They issued us all navy peacoats. You could see the soldier with his gun in the tower. It was trained in our direction.

My father was released shortly before we left Jerome. He appeared one day in April 1944. He said this was no place for a family to be reared. We left before other families because my father had a sponsor. This is where the American Friends Service Committee came into our lives. Our sponsor was a Quaker who lived in Des Moines, Iowa.

All I remember of Des Moines is that I was much ahead of my class in algebra. I think it had something to do with my Nisei algebra teacher in camp. His name is Paul Shimokobo. He later became my neighbor in Chicago. He died a few years ago. He must have been a very good teacher.

My classmates were sort of standoffish. But there was a black girl, Marguerite Desleigh. She treated me like an ordinary person. She invited me to her home. It was very beautiful. We became friends.

What else can I say? I'm just pleased to be alive.

FRANK KEEGAN

He is Dennis Keegan's younger brother. Though he's touching sixty, his manner is that of a young man, an enthusiastic one. If there is ever a desperate moment, it is genially concealed. His easy-talking repertoire includes funny stories, of course.

He is an educator and a lecturer.

We heard that the Japanese had destroyed our fleet and would come here by sea. There was considerable talk of a Japanese midget submarine fleet.

I was sixteen, a yell leader and C student at high school and very small. Because the Japanese were small, I thought I was their match. On Monday, December 8, about six of us were in a '36 Model A Ford, three in front, three in the rumble seat, heading for Bodega Bay with our armament. Paul Henderson, a senior, had a .22. I had a 410. Scotty Webb had a little shotgun. Somebody else had a BB gun. We loaded our guns, hid behind the dunes, and waited for the Japanese assault. (Laughs.)

We knew these dunes better than the Japanese, 'cause we went on picnics and we hugged girls and we drank beer and things like that.

We peered, we saw nothing. But we knew the Japanese were subtle, deceitful. We waited and waited, until it got dark. There were no jokes. We were deadly serious.

We told our parents we were going back early the next day. There was a general feeling of approval. We're country boys out here. It was very ordinary to shoot rabbits. They said, "Would you want us to pack a lunch?" (Laughs.)

We were dreadfully frightened of the Japanese. For years we were told of the yellow hordes. We had the Oriental Exclusion Act. Even before Pearl Harbor we were scared of them.

We were terribly disappointed the next day because we never saw a Japanese submarine. And the next day. By that time, the lunacy of the moment had sort of dissipated. But we went out there to do the only thing we knew how: take a gun and defend our land.

My big brother, Dennis, joined the merchant marines. He had eye problems. My middle brother, Bill, at eighteen, joined the Royal Canadian Air Force, before Pearl Harbor. He was killed in a Spitfire over Scotland when he was twenty. I always wanted to go to sea, so I joined the merchant marine at eighteen.

I was in Pearl Harbor six or eight times. We hit the Marianas, Guam, Saipan, shortly after the invasion. I was in for almost three years. I worked my way up to be a bo'sun at nineteen.

These were Liberty ships, nine, ten knots an hour, very slow. They had huge holds. They were the workhorses. Rosie the Riveter at the Kaiser shipyards in Sausalito put them together in thirty days. Every once in a while, they'd break up because Rosie missed a rivet. (Laughs.)

The longest trip I ever took was to India, by way of Tasmania. We were forty days at sea. The Indian Ocean was a very dangerous part of the world at that time. I was still an altar boy when the order came for short-arm inspection. I didn't understand and said to my bunkmate, "I think my left arm is shorter than my right." He said, "You asshole, they're talking about your prick." I was that innocent.

At Hobart, Tasmania, we were heroes—"Oh Yank, oh Yank." The two fingers, the Churchill thing. They wanted our autographs, free drinks. Fathers and mothers would be delighted to bring a sailor to spend a weekend with the daughter and mom's home cooking. We were gonna stop the Japanese from coming down. They had parts of Borneo at the time, and Australia, New Zealand, Tasmania were scared to death. When you first come in you're a hero, but enough sailors come through these ports, and social disease, alcoholism, rape, mayhem, and they're not popular any more. I learned a lot on that merchant ship. (Laughs.)

We were in the Hebrides when we heard about the huge bomb that decimated Hiroshima. We said, Thank God that's over. A hundred thousand, two hundred thousand Japanese? Too bad. It's over, that's what it meant. Nice goin', Harry. You did it to 'em, kid. That's how guiltless I was. He saved our lives, he terminated the goddamn thing.

When the war was over, we were disoriented. We didn't know quite what to do. I was getting paid off on the last ship when Franklin Roosevelt died. I remember being paid twenty-five fresh, clean one-hundred-dollar bills. I'd saved about three thousand dollars, and got through college.

If it weren't for the war, I would be selling you insurance right now.

A CHANCE ENCOUNTER

ROBERT RASMUS

I've lived about thirty-eight years after the war and about twenty years before. For me it's B.W. and A.W.—before the war and after the war. I suspect there are a lot of people like me. In business, there'll be times when I say, This really worries the heck out of me, but it's really minor compared to having to do a river crossing under fire. (Laughs.)

He is six feet four or five, graying. He is a business executive, working out of Chicago. Obviously he's kept himself in pretty good shape. His manner is gentle, easy, unruffled.

I get this strange feeling of living through a world drama. In September of '39 when the Germans invaded Poland, I was fourteen years old. I remember my mother saying, "Bob, you'll be in it." I was hoping she'd be right. At that age, you look forward to the glamour and have no idea of the horrors.

Sure enough, I was not only in the army but in the infantry. Step by logistic step, our division was in combat. You're finally down to one squad, out ahead of the whole thing. You're the point man. What am I doing out here—in this world-cataclysmic drama—out in front of the whole thing? (Laughs.)

You saw those things in the movies, you saw the newsreels. But you were of an age when your country wasn't even in the war. It seemed unreal. All of a sudden, there you were right in the thick of it and people were dying and you were scared out of your wits that you'd have your head blown off. (Laughs.)

I was acutely aware, being a rifleman, the odds were high that I would be killed. At one level, animal fear. I didn't like that at all. On the other hand, I had this great sense of adventure. My gosh, going across the ocean, seeing the armies, the excitement of it. I was there.

This wouldn't have been true of most, but I was a skinny, gaunt kind of mama's boy. I was going to gain my manhood then. I would forever be liberated from the sense of inferiority that I wasn't rugged. I would prove that I had the guts and the manhood to stand up to these things. There were all these things, from being a member of the Western world to Bobby Rasmus, the skinny nineteen-year-old who's gonna prove that he can measure up. (Laughs.)

I remember my mother during my thirty-day furlough. Continuous weeping. She said, "Bob, you've got to tell your captain you're too tall to be a rifleman." (Laughs.) The only way I could get her off that was to say, "I'll tell him, Ma." Of course, I didn't.

I was in training at Fort Benning, Georgia. If you got sick and fell back more than a week, you were removed from your battalion. I got the flu and was laid back for eight days. I was removed from my outfit where all my buddies were. I was heartbroken.

My original group went to the 106th Division and ended up being overwhelmed in the Battle of the Bulge. I remember letters I sent my buddies that came back: Missing in action. Killed in action. These were the eighteen-year-olds. It was only because I got the flu that I wasn't among them.

When I went in the army, I'd never been outside the states of Wisconsin, Indiana, and Michigan. So when I woke up the first morning on the troop train in Fulton, Kentucky, I thought I was in Timbuktu. Of course, I was absolutely bowled over by Europe, the castles, the cathedrals, the Alps. It was wonderment. I was preoccupied with staying alive and doing my job, but it seemed, out of the corner of my eye, I was constantly fascinated with the beauty of the German forests and medieval bell towers. At nineteen, you're seeing life with fresh eyes.

The first time I ever heard a New England accent was at Fort Benning. The southerner was an exotic creature to me. People from the farms. The New York street-smarts. You had an incredible mixture of every stratum of society. And you're of that age when your need for friendship is greatest. I still see a number of these people. There's sort of a special sense of kinship.

The reason you storm the beaches is not patriotism or bravery. It's that sense of not wanting to fail your buddies. Having to leave that group when I had the flu may have saved my life. Yet to me, that kid, it was a disaster.

Kurt Vonnegut, in *Slaughterhouse Five,* writes of the fire bombing of Dresden and the prisoner-of-war train in Germany. A lot of my buddies who were captured were on that train. I didn't know that until three days ago when a middle-aged guy with white hair like mine stopped me on the street and said, "Hey, aren't you Bob Rasmus?" I said, "Aren't you Red Prendergast?" He'd been in the original training group, gone to the 106th Division, taken to Germany, was on the troop train that got strafed. I knew him for about five months, thirty-nine years ago, and had never set eyes on him since. I was only in combat for six weeks, but I could remember every hour, every minute of the whole forty-two days.

In Boston Harbor, we actually saw the first visible sign of the war: an Australian cruiser tied up next to the troop ship. There was a huge, jagged hole in the bow. The shape of things to come. There was a lot of bravado, kidding.

Our impression of France, those of us who grew up in the thirties, was French maids, French poodles, a frivolous type of people. So it was striking to see these stolid peasants walking behind horse-drawn plows. The area we were in had not yet been hit by the war. I was struck by the sheer beauty of the countryside, the little villages, the churches. This sort of thing the impressionists did.

Going to the front, I can remember the cities in Belgium: Liège, Namur. We were going through towns and villages. We were hanging out of the cars of the trains and on the roofs. We had all this extra candy from our K rations and would just throw them out to the kids. There was a sense of victory in the air. They had already been liberated. They were elated.

All of a sudden, the tone changes. You get off the train on the border in that little corner of Holland and Germany. We're near Aachen, which had been absolutely leveled by Allied bombings. Rubble, nothing but rubble. Here was the ancient city of Aix-la-Chapelle, just a sea of rubble. We've had forty-eight hours enjoying being part of the victorious army. Now the party's over. You're within a few miles of the front. You're off the train into trucks. You hear gunfire in the distance.

Everybody sobered up very rapidly. We drove on for a few miles and there was a second city, Düren, totally wiped out. It was one of the most bombed-out cities in Germany. Now we're moving forward on foot.

They moved us into what they called a quiet front. Our division occupied a frontage on the Rhine, south of Cologne. We simply relieved another division that had been there, the Eighth. We moved into the same foxholes. You know it's getting close. It's still sort of exciting. Nobody's gotten killed yet. To me, it was interesting because of the architecture. From the distance I could see the Cologne cathedral, with the twin towers.

We stayed in bombed-out buildings. It was almost surreal. Here's a cross-section of a four-story, where every room is open to the atmosphere on one side and there's another room that is still intact. This was true all the way through Europe.

The very first night, our squad was in comfortable quarters. Our one side was completely open, but on the other side were beds and kitchens and what-not. It was almost theatrical. Since the Germans were the enemy and evil, we never had any sense of guilt that we were in somebody's apartment. Any abuse of the apartment, like throwing dishes out the window, was what they deserved. Whatever was there in the way of food and drink, we would make use of.

One of the things we had was this old music box. It could play whole melodies. We had two disks. One was "Silent Night" and the other was "We Gather Together to Ask the Lord's Blessing." I had a typical Lutheran churchgoing background. Here am I hearing a Christmas carol and a hymn that I'd sung many times in church.

I was sort of schizophrenic all through this period. I was a participant, scared out of my wits. But I was also acutely aware of how really theatrical and surreal it was.

Three days later we pulled out, crossed the Rhine, and cut off a German pocket. As we were moving out of this area of sheared-off buildings, there were courtyards with fruit trees in blossom. And there were our heavy mortars blasting away across the river. I had been seeing shadowy figures moving around. Were they infiltrators or just a bush that I was imagining? And there in sight was the Cologne cathedral amidst all this wreckage.

We've seen a little of the war now. We've seen planes dropping bombs over on the other side. We've sent out patrols, have captured prisoners. But we really hadn't been in it ourselves. It was still fun and dramatics. When the truck took us from Cologne south through Bonn, for me it was, Hey, Beethoven's birthplace! But when we crossed a pontoon bridge and I saw a balloon of fire, I knew the real combat was going to begin. I had the feeling now that we were gonna be under direct fire, some of us were gonna be killed. But I was also enormously affected by the beauty of the countryside. We were in rolling hills and great forests. It stretched out for mile after mile. I could almost hear this Wagnerian music. I was pulled in two directions: Gee, I don't wanna get killed. And, Boy, this is gorgeous country.

Our uniforms were still clean. We were still young kids who hadn't seen anything. You could see these veteran troops. Their uniforms were dirty, they were bearded, there was a look in their eyes that said they'd been through a lot. A sort of expression on their faces—You're gonna find out now. A mixture of pity and contempt for the greenhorns.

We started seeing our first dead, Germans. You drew the obvious inference: if Germans were dead, the Americans were getting killed farther up the line. Night fell, we were up within a couple of miles of where the action would begin. We were passing through our artillery emplacements. Incessant firing. It was reassuring to see how much artillery we had, but disturbing to see all these German dead. I had never seen a dead body before, except in a funeral home.

We were told that the next morning we would be on the attack. I remember the miserable cold. By this time, I had taken up cigarette smoking, wondering what my mother would think when I came back. (Laughs.) I felt sickish, I was cold, I was scared. And I couldn't even get one last cigarette.

We were awakened before dawn. I honestly don't know whether I dreamed it or whether it really happened. I've asked buddies I've seen since the war: Can you remember these ambulances and army surgeons getting their gear out? I have such an absolute recollection of it, but nobody else remembers it. It had a dreamlike quality: just seeing surgeons ready to work. Here we were still healthy, still an hour or two away from actual combat. It added to the inevitability that really bad, bad things were going to happen.

Our platoon of thirty men was to take a small town. At the time, I was a bazooka man. I'll never forget that sense of unreality as we were moving through the woods to this village, which we could just see a few hundred yards away. There were sheep grazing in the fields. By now there's gunfire: machine guns, rifle fire, mortar shells.

You'd lost your sense of direction. This was not a continuous front. These were piercing, probing actions. You'd take a town, then to the next river, then across the river and then the next one. This was the first. Now I can see actual mortar shells landing in this meadow. German 88s. They were hitting the tile roofs of these houses and barns. My initial reaction: they're not hurting anything. Oh, a few tiles being knocked loose, but it's still a beautiful sunny day. The meadow is lovely. Here we are in a medieval village. This reaction lasted three seconds. These sheep started getting hit. You were seeing blood. Immediately you say, Soon it's gonna be us torn up like these animals. You sense all these stages you've gone through. And now (laughs), the curtain has gone up and you're really in it.

We captured that town without any casualties. I think the German troops had moved out. My confidence is coming back a little. Gee, we captured a town and didn't even see a German. Later that afternoon, we were moving up to take another town. We have a sense that things aren't going too well. We seem out of radio contact with the other rifle companies. I sense an apprehension by our officers.

All of a sudden, we spotted a group of German soldiers down by the slope of this hill, perhaps fifty. We were strung out, a couple of platoons. We would be on the ground, get up on command, and start firing right into this group of Germans. We did catch them by surprise. They responded quickly, firing back, machine guns and rifles. We had them well outnumbered, our company, about 240. We did the march-and-fire. It was a new maneuver we'd never done in training. We learned. I noticed that some of our guys were getting hit. It was all in a few minutes. We killed most of the Germans. A few might have gotten away, but we wiped them out. Our guys were getting killed, too. Irony again, the first one killed was our platoon sergeant.

You have to understand the culture of our company. Most of our privates were college types. They had been dumped en masse into these infantry divisions. The cadre of noncommissioned officers were old-timers. They were mostly uneducated country types, many of them from the South. There was a rather healthy mutual contempt between the noncoms and the privates. This sergeant was the most hated man. One of the nineteen-year-olds, during maneuvers, was at the point of tears in his hatred of this man who was so unreasonable and so miserable. He'd say, "If we ever get into combat, I'm gonna kill 'im. First thing I'll do." Who's the first one killed? This sergeant. I'm sure it was enemy fire. I would bet my life on it. I'm sure the guys who said they would kill him were horrified that their wish came true.

My best friend was leaning against a tree. We were waiting for further instructions. He had this sly grin on his face. I was so aghast. It didn't occur to me that one of our people had done it. I'm really sure we didn't. "I'm gonna kill 'im" is said a million times. Added to the horror of our first dead is that he's the one all of us hated so much.

I'm sure our company was typical. We had x percent of self-inflicted wounds. There's no question that a guy would blow his toe off to get out of combat. People would get lost. These combat situations are so confused that it's very easy to go in the other direction. Say you get lost, get sick, get hurt. By the time you get back to your outfit, a couple of days have gone by.

We remember examples of Caspar Milquetoast: ordinary people showing incredible heroism. But you have to accept the fact that in a cross section of people—in civilian life, too—you've got cowards and quitters. Our radio man shot up his radio: he thought we were going to be captured. Panic. I became a bazooka man because our bazooka man threw his weapon away and I picked it up. He ran off.

Our captain said, "Pick up the bodies. We don't leave our dead to the enemy." We're now cut off and have to join the rest of our battalion. We had to improvise stretchers. I took off my field jacket and turned the arms inside out. We poked rifles through the arms and fashioned a stretcher. We got the sergeant on ours and, jeez, half his head was blown off and the brains were coming out on my hands and on my uniform. Here's the mama's boy, Sunday school, and now I'm really in it.

I remember lying in that slit trench that night. It was a nightmare. I'd now seen what dead people look like, the color out of their face. I think each person in my squad went through this dream of mine. Daylight came and we moved out into another town. This is twenty-four hours of experience.

Those who really went through combat, the Normandy landings, the heavy stuff, might laugh at this little action we'd been in, but for me . . . We were passing people who were taking over from us, another company. We had one day of this. Our uniforms were now dirty and bloody and our faces looked like we'd been in there for weeks. Now *we* had the feeling: You poor innocents.

We weren't able to bring those bodies back with us. The mortar fire became too much. The next morning, our squad was assigned to go back and recover the bodies. It was sunshine and quiet. We were passing the Germans we killed. Looking at the individual German dead, each took on a personality. These were no longer an abstraction. These were no longer the Germans of the brutish faces and the helmets we saw in the newsreels. They were exactly our age. These were boys like us.

I remember one, particularly. A redhead. To this day, I see the image of this young German soldier sitting against a tree. This group was probably resting, trying to make their escape. The whole thing might have been avoided had we been more experienced and called down in German for them to surrender. They probably would have been only too glad. Instead, out of fear, there was this needless slaughter. It has the flavor of murder, doesn't it?

What I remember of that day is not so much the sense of loss at our two dead but a realization of how you've been conditioned. At that stage, we didn't hate the Germans just for evil the country represented, their militarism, but right down to each individual German. Once the helmet is off, you're looking at a teen-ager, another kid. Obviously you have to go on. There are many, many more engagements.

A few days, later, we're in Lüdenscheid. It's near the Ruhr pocket. Two Allied armies had crossed the Rhine fifteen miles apart. It's a pincer movement, closing in a pocket of 350,000 Germans. Under Field Marshal Model, I believe. They just don't surrender overnight. They're gonna fight it out. Our job, all the way through Germany, was to move as fast as you could on trucks, on tanks, until you came up against resistance. Some towns fell without a battle. Others, quite a bit of resistance. You'd assume the worst.

You were constantly behind the lines and then moved up. You'd pass through your artillery and you knew you were getting closer. Pretty soon things would thin out. Just an hour earlier there were an awful lot of GIs around. As you got closer to action, it was only your platoon, and then it was your squad ahead of the other two. You were the point man for the squad.

I thought, This is incredible. We've got these great masses of troops, of quartermasters and truckers and tanks and support troops, and then all of a sudden it's so lonely. (Laughs.) You're out ahead of the whole thing.

In Lüdenscheid, we were in the hills looking down. It was dead silence in the town, except that you became aware of German ambulances with the big red crosses on the roofs. We didn't know whether it was a trick. There was something mysterious about that sight. The bells started tolling in the city. You didn't know what to make of it. Was this the opening of a major battle? Were they going away? There was very little resistance and we took the town.

Now I began to get an inkling of some other evil abroad. We were very much aware that the Germans had mobilized the Poles, the French, the captive countries, into workers on farms and in factories. As each town was captured, you were liberating Slavs, Poles, French, whatever. It was often highly emotional. The idea of those death camps still hadn't reached us at all. I marvel as I think back on it. When we took Lüdenscheid, our platoon stayed overnight in what was a combination beer hall, theater, festival-type thing, with a stage and a big dance floor. There in the middle of the floor was this mountain of clothing. I realize now that was probably the clothing they'd taken from the people that went to Dachau or another camp. It really didn't register with us what that might have been. You knew this wasn't just a Salvation Army collecting clothes. I remember it because that was the day Roosevelt died.

Every town had a certain number of slave laborers. It might range from handfuls to hundreds, depending on whether there was industry in that town. The final one we captured in the Ruhr was Letmathe. There was a large number of Italian laborers who worked in a factory. There were quite a few Russians. The military government hadn't yet moved in. I remember the Russians taking the horses and running them up and down the street to get their circulation up and then kill them for food. A Russian was going to kill the horse with a hatchet. I wasn't up to shooting the horse myself, but I let him use my pistol. We were aware of the starvation and the desperate measures they would take.

You had these spontaneous uprisings where the slave laborers and war prisoners the Germans had in these towns would just take over. It was very chaotic.

I remember where a Russian was in the process of strangling a German in the cellar of our building. This was a moment of truth for me. I was still nurturing the notion that every individual German was evil and the Russians were our allies. Somehow I got the picture that the Russian was carrying out vengeance. He claimed this German had killed his buddy. In that confused situation you couldn't tell whether it was true or whether it was a grudge carried out or what. It didn't take much deliberation to stop it. The Russian broke out in tears when I wouldn't let him kill the German. He just sobbed. Reflecting on it later, I had reason to believe his story was true. But I wasn't up to letting it happen.

We were aware that the Russians had taken enormous losses on the eastern front, that they really had broken the back of the German army. We would have been in for infinitely worse casualties and misery had it not been for them. We were well disposed toward them. I remember saying if we happen to link up with 'em, I wouldn't hesitate to kiss 'em.

I didn't hear any anti-Russian talk. I think we were realistic enough to know that if we were going to fight them, we would come out second best. We hadn't even heard of the atomic bomb yet. We'd just have to assume that it would be masses of armies, and their willingness to sacrifice millions of troops. We were aware that our leaders were sparing our lives. Even though somebody would have to do the dirty work in the infantry, our leaders would try to pummel the enemy with artillery and tanks and overpower them before sending the infantry in. If that was possible.

I've reflected on why people my age and with my experience don't have that spontaneous willingness to be part of the nuclear freeze. It's the sense that the Germans were willing to lose millions of men. And they did. Every German house we went to, there would be black-bordered pictures of sons and relatives. You could tell that most of them died on the eastern front. And the Russians lost twenty million.

Later, we were back in the States being retrained for the Japanese invasion. The first atom bomb was dropped. We ended halfway across the Pacific. How many of us would have been killed on the mainland if there were no bomb? Someone like me has this specter.

In the final campaign down through Bavaria, we were in Patton's army. Patton said we ought to keep going. To me, that was an unthinkable idea. The Russians would have slaughtered us, because of their willingness to give up so many lives. I don't think the rank of the GIs had any stomach for fighting the Russians. We were informed enough through press and newsreels to know about Stalingrad. I saw the actual evidence in those black-bordered pictures in every German household I visited. Black border, eastern front, nine out of ten.

I have more disapproval of communism today than ever. I think our government did try to stimulate a feeling about good Uncle Joe. The convoys to Murmansk. We had this mixed feeling: Gee, we're glad they did the lion's share, the overwhelming bulk of the dying, the breaking the back of the German armies. And individually, they can't be all that bad. In any case, we don't want to fight 'em. (Laughs.)

The thing that turned me against the Vietnam War was an issue of *Life* magazine in '68. It had a cover picture of the hundred men that died in Vietnam that week. I said, Enough. I don't want to stand here as a veteran of World War Two saying that we somehow took a stand that was admirable. We are bad as the rest if we don't think independently and make up our own minds. We were willing to go along as long as it seemed an easy victory. When it really got tough, we started re-examining.

World War Two was utterly different. It has affected me in many ways ever since. I think my judgment of people is more circumspect. I know it's made me less ready to fall into the trap of judging people by their style or appearance. In a short period of time, I had the most tremendous experiences of all of life: of fear, of jubilance, of misery, of hope, of comradeship, and of the endless excitement, the theatrics of it. I honestly feel grateful for having been a witness to an event as monumental as anything in history and, in a very small way, a participant.

RICHARD M. (RED) PRENDERGAST

I was walking down the street and I saw this fellow, about six foot four or five. He looked vaguely familiar. I tapped him on the shoulder and I said, "Pardon me, weren't you at Fort Benning in 1943?" And he says, "Yes, and you're Red Prendergast." Thirty-nine years later and I still recognized him instantly. He hasn't changed a bit. He's still tall and slim.

We were practically bunkmates all through basic training. As fate would have it, Bob got ill a week before we shipped out. He was heartbroken. But as it turned out, it was the luckiest thing ever happened to him. (Laughs.) My whole group went into the 106th Infantry Division, which was completely destroyed in the Battle of the Bulge.

He is a large, big-boned man, heavy-set, graying. He brings to mind a retired football lineman. He is vice-president and sales manager of a Chicago trade magazine.

I was on heavy weapons. Heavy weapons is about five hundred yards behind the rifles. I was on 81-millimeter mortar. They tried to get larger guys on that because it's heavy stuff. You carry forty-two pounds of metal on your shoulder all the time. Plus your normal gear.

We replaced the Indianhead Second Division. They'd been through everything, had something like three hundred percent casualties. As they dropped, new men replaced 'em. The new men didn't last very long. We were in pillboxes that were all facing the wrong way. They were at the Siegfried Line, German-built pillboxes, all pointing toward France. (Laughs.) So they were no good to us.

We had two regiments spread out over twenty-three miles of front, which is much too thin. They said don't worry about it. (Laughs.) We didn't worry about it. Every morning we'd fire three rounds, and late in the afternoon we'd go out and fire three more. We were sending out night patrols. I participated in a few, largely uneventful. Occasionally, we'd pick up prisoners. A great many of these were Polish and Hungarians who has been pressed into the German army. They weren't terribly enthusiastic. They were telling us there's a big buildup back there, tanks all over the place. We would send the information back, and nobody seemed to pay any attention.

On the morning of December 16, we were suddenly under a fantastic barrage. Every tank in Europe came over the hill, all the panzers in the world. We had no tanks at all. The weather was such that we had no air support. They went over our rifles like they weren't even there. We were completely cut off and surrounded. We ran through the hills, firing at anything.

We had, say, two platoons, maybe sixty men. We were in this huge forest. This was the Ardennes—the Schnee Eifel, snowy mountains. We were fighting on the run. We had no food, no vehicles, no ammunition. We had no place to run because they were behind us, too. As we were crossing a little stream, I said, "Why don't we throw these mortars in the stream? They're no good to anybody." An officer with us said, "No, you can't destroy government property." (Laughs.) So the next stream we went to, I dumped mine. The military mind, I guess.

So there I am wandering around with the whole German army shooting at me, and all I've got is a .45 automatic. There were ample opportunities, however, because every place you went there were bodies and soldiers laying around. Mostly Americans. At one time or another, I think I had in my hands every weapon the United States

Army manufactured. You'd run out of ammunition with that one, you'd throw it away and try to find something else. One time I had a submachine gun, first experience I ever had with one.

Snipers were a big problem. When we'd get into an area that had been occupied by the Germans, they usually left a couple of guys up in the trees. (Laughs.) They shot a major right out from under me. This was another case of the military mind. It was always protocol for the lower rank to walk on the left of an officer. So he insisted I walk on his left. (Laughs.) He said, "You're gonna be my body-guard." Of course, everybody in the German army knew that the lesser rank walked on the left. (Laughs.) The major got one right through the neck.

Somehow we fell in with a larger group. There was a small village ahead. Whoever was in charge said we're gonna attack the village. We lined up as in skirmishes. There was no cover, no concealment, no nothing. There was a wide-open space, and we attacked. We got heavy fire comin' back and we hit the ground. Suddenly somebody started waving flags, and the town was occupied by us. We were shooting at each other. The whole thing was total confusion. There were very few casualties in that one, I'm happy to say.

We're carrying our wounded with us, quite a few. We're out of food, we haven't eaten in a couple of days, I'd say about 150 of us. Suddenly we're encircled on top of this snow-covered hill. There we lay in the snow and the Germans, all around us, are shooting anything that moves. They fire a small cannon, a 20- or 40-millimeter. We're not shootin' back because nobody's got ammunition. We had assembled a mortar with nothin' to shoot out of it. So we took that apart, and I stood the faceplate up. It's like a waffle iron, and I lay behind it. One of our second gunners, a kid from Pennsylvania, said, "Can I come over and hide with you?" I said sure. He wasn't there five minutes and he got his leg blown off. I think he bled to death. That was the way things went.

This is the nineteenth. We've been running around these hills for some time, accomplishing nothing. (Laughs.) The sun was going down, about three-thirty, the flag of truce came, and a German officer came up. They were wearing white suits. These were the elite, the crack troops of the German army. He said to us in perfect English, to our colonel, "You've been up here for quite a while and you haven't fired a shot since noon. We strongly suspect you don't have ammunition. If you don't come down in twenty minutes, none of you are coming down." Our officer in charge gave that a thought for about three minutes (laughs) and he said, "All right, everybody, destroy your weapons." All I had was this beautiful .45 that I'd been treasuring. I took it all apart and threw it in the snow.

All of 'em came up. They took our wristwatches, our fountain pens, and any cigarettes they could find.

"When we were in the pillbox, before the Battle of the Bulge started, they used to send us a carton of cigarettes per man every day. When it was obvious we'd have to get out of there, we all filled our pockets with cigarettes. We were wearing combat boots with the blouse. I put four packs of cigarettes inside my trouser blouse on both sides. Down the cuff, as it were. Boy, did they want those cigarettes. They say, at the stalag we went to, if you had a hundred cartons, a guard would take you to the Dutch border. I don't know if it's true, because nobody ever had a hundred cartons. (Laughs.) They didn't get the ones in my trousers. When we got to the stalag, we were semimillionaires, my buddies and I."

They were furious that we'd destroyed our weapons. Actually their P-38s and Lugers were superior pistols, but they liked .45s for souvenirs. They took my overshoes, which is the worst thing that happened to me. They passed 'em around: they were too big. There was nobody that they'd fit—I have a size 14. So they took a knife and cut 'em up, so nobody could use 'em. From there we marched a long, long way under guard. My feet are frostbitten today. From October to May, I don't feel like I have any toes at all. Once you've got it, you've got it.

This fella that I graduated from Mount Carmel with, he had no business in the infantry anyway. He had big, thick glasses, he had fallen arches. I ran into him on the road after we were captured. I said, "Stick with me, I don't know how this is gonna work out. But if anybody survives, I will. So hang in and we'll be all right."

They'd have us pull off the road and sleep in the ditches. I'd put my raincoat on the ground and my overcoat over that, and he and I would sleep on top of that. Then we'd put his raincoat and his overcoat on top of us. That kept us warm. One night I woke up shivering. He was gone and the coats were gone. I never saw him again. First thing I found out when I got home is he starved to death.

The march in the snow took two or three days. It seemed like a hundred miles. They put us on these trains—cars that were built for forty men and eight horses. They put sixty of us in there. They can only travel at night, because the American and British bombers'd knock out anything that moved during the day. They gave us a bag of crackers and a hunk of cheese before we got on. That was all the rations we were allowed. The train ride was supposed to be a very short one, but it wasn't. The Allies were always bombing the railroad tracks. They had repair crews out there constantly. (Laughs.)

They had no POW markings on the cars. It looked like a troop train. Along comes the RAF on one of their famous night raids. They drop flares and they see this big beautiful train, a very lovely target. They just pasted us somethin' terrible. We couldn't get out of the cars. They had barbed wire across the window and there was only one window. Finally someone, with just sheer brute strength and cutting his arms severely, knocked the barbed wire out. Some of our guys got out. They were running up this hill, right into the attacking bombers and fighter planes. About five hundred people died that night. Allied bombers killed Allied prisoners. Just one of those goof-ups that happened so often in war. One of the reasons I didn't go out the window, I couldn't find my shoes. I was rubbing my frostbitten feet.

We got on that train about the twenty-third. We got off the day before New Year's Eve. Seven days. Thirst was the big thing. And cold. Cold I remember very well. There were two benches and a potbellied stove at one end of the car. Of course, there was nothin' to burn. When they finally let us out, they were absolutely furious that we'd burned up their benches. What the hell do you expect us to do? (Laughs.)

When we arrived at Stalag 4-B, the first thing they do is delouse us. I had heard all these horror tales about the extermination camps, where they get the Jews or political prisoners and they say, Okay, you go in for a nice shower. They'd go in and get gassed instead from a shower nozzle. They'd tell us the same thing. (Laughs.) We go into this huge tile room, maybe fifty or sixty shower nozzles. I thought, Oh-oh, this is it. (Laughs.) It turned out to be a nice hot shower. That was bad news, too. We hadn't washed in weeks. The hot shower opened all the pores and we went out and marched twenty minutes to the barracks. I caught the flu.

We go into these barracks. The British need us like a kick in the nose. They had everything nice. They had little curtains, and most of 'em were wearing civilian clothes. They had regular mail service to England. And they had laundry service. They used to send their dirty clothes back to England. It was really a nutty setup. They'd been there since Dunkirk and were pretty well established. They had their own escape committees and a grievance committee. The English were always working out escapes. They ran the place.

In come this wave of prisoners from the Battle of the Bulge. They didn't know what to do with us. They were very hospitable, though. We all had to double up in bunks. There weren't enough to go around.

We'd have this early-morning roll call. That was hilarious. They had a terrible time keeping track of how many people they had in those barracks.

The Russian soldier—once a Russian soldier is captured, they consider him dead. It was quite common after the war that these prisoners did not want to go back to Russia, because they'd go right on to another camp in Siberia. For the disgrace of being captured.

They were treated terrible. They weren't getting anything. We weren't getting much, but we were taken care of by the Geneva Convention and the Red Cross. They had nobody on their side, because the Russians did not recognize the Red Cross. The Germans gave them absolutely nothing. If one or two of their members died during the night, they would bring the bodies out in the morning for the head count. They'd stand 'em up and count heads. That's how many rations you'd get. Instead of three hundred bowls of soup, they'd get three hundred and two bowls of soup, two for the dead guys. They'd throw the bodies out after the food had been distributed.

Twenty-three of us were taken out of Stalag 4-B and were sent to a chemical factory, Bykguldenwerk, about ten miles outside of Dresden. Which was no place to be, as it turned out. Our principal job there was shoveling coal, which we did ten, twelve hours a day. They had big furnaces to keep the chemicals goin'. We did all that on one bowl of turnip soup and a seventh of a loaf of bread a day. Ersatz bread. I've never been able to look a turnip in the eye since. I was never too nuts about turnips before the war. And I'm doubly not nuts about 'em now.

We could always escape, that was no problem. But where are you gonna go, not speaking the language? You're hundreds and hundreds of miles from any familiar face. And everybody's carryin' a gun— mailmen, streetcar conductors. One night in February, oh, it was bitter cold, about twenty below zero, and two guys escaped. They were captured by a troop of German boy scouts, who beat the living hell out of them. Brought 'em back on stretchers. That also discouraged us from further thoughts of escape. (Laughs.)

The night they escaped, it was too cold for the guards to go out, so they put a guard dog out. Big, vicious German shepherd. We killed the dog and ate it. (Laughs.) We had a little stove in there and cooked the damn dog. (Laughs.) We drew cards for the bones. I got the jaw —with a few teeth.

How'd it taste?

Terrific. Just like a T-bone. But we had a problem. We hadda get rid of the claws and teeth and the fur. We had a helluva time doing it, but we managed. They never figured out what happened to the dog. 'Cause the fence was forty feet high and there's no way in the world the dog was gonna get over that fence. With barbed wire at the top.

There was an old German woman, Anna, worked in the factory, a cleaning woman. She used to take pity on me and smuggle me an apple. On the other hand, we had a ferocious beast of a foreman. His son was a prisoner of war in America, and he was convinced by German propaganda that we were torturing his son. He in turn made life a hell on earth for these guys. He picked on one kid, Murphy, who finally cracked.

There was a little old man, Alf, Alfred Winkler, a jack-of-all-trades. Alf was the biggest goldbrick in the history of the world. This guy had hiding places all over the factory. They were always screaming, Alf Vinkler, vere are you? After an hour or so, he'd come toddling out: Anybody looking for me? They decided Alf could use an assistant. He needed a six-foot-three redhead for an assistant like he needed another nose (laughs), 'cause I couldn't fit in his hiding places. He was absolutely frustrated, the poor guy. They could always find him 'cause they could always find me.

They needed all the able-bodied men at the fronts, in either Russia or the western front, so the guards we got were crippled or ancient. We had one old guy who was a schoolteacher who had been drafted. He musta been sixty-five, and he could no more have got that gun off his shoulder than he could jump off the roof. We had one guy with a wooden leg. And another one who spoke English pretty well and his whole head was plastic surgery. He used to come in and tell us we were really crazy to be fightin' the Germans. We should all be joinin' the Germans in fightin' the Russians.

In the stalag, they were raising what they called the Legion of Saint George among Allied prisoners. They were supposed to join this legion and go off to the eastern front and fight the Russians. They were trying to recruit Americans and English. I never really knew anybody that signed up for it. The English said it was some kook, somebody off his rocker.

It was Easter Sunday, I think. Our shirts were worn out. We were issued German army shirts. We're laying around the yard and out of nowhere come six P-38s, American. They made a low pass and they see all of us in our German army shirts. (Laughs.) They came back and they strafed. They bombed our factory.

A couple of nights later, a guard came in around midnight. He said, "The civilians are very upset. They want to lynch you guys because you're Americans." He says, "The Russians are not far away. We propose to pack up and take off toward the American lines." He says, "Now you need us to save you from the people. We need you for when we get to the Americans, you can tell 'em that we didn't treat you so bad." If the Russians ever found 'em, goodbye, Charlie.

So we took off in the middle of the night, headin' for the American lines. We ran into a group of fifty English soldiers also under guard. Next day, thirty or forty Frenchmen. A bunch of Bulgarians. A bunch of Polish. Pretty soon our column of twenty-three had grown into a long one. Hitler's last order was to kill all the prisoners, which was patently out of the question. Forget it. After Hitler killed himself in the bunker, Admiral Doenitz took over. His first order was to keep the prisoners out of everybody's hands because that's their only bargaining point. So one day we march like crazy to the American lines. The Americans make a push, and we march back to the Russians. The Russians make a push, back to the Americans. I walked through the town of Meissen six times. I got to feel like I knew the town. (Laughs.)

We hear guns behind us, the Russians are very, very close. So they herd us all into a great big field. They said, "Now, don't go anyplace." We said, "Oh, we wouldn't dream of it." (Laughs.) They took off their uniforms, put on civilian clothes, jumped on bicycles, and took off like birds for the Americans.

There we are in the middle of Germany. Oh Christ, there musta been two, three hundred of us by this time. I really felt sorry for the

German farmers. We were like army ants. As this horde of prisoners came over the hill, farmers would just shake their heads, 'cause we ate everything in sight. Any form of livestock went. All their barns and fences were torn down to make fires. They'd have mountains of seed potatoes, that they were saving to plant for the following year. So long! We ate those like popcorn. (Laughs.) We must have wiped out the potato plant crop for 1946.

There we were, free again. By now I've got this big, huge, shaggy red beard. Filthy, of course. We look like pirates. We didn't know what to do or where to turn. Most of the guys disappeared, just took off in little groups.

My two buddies and I are still standing there when the Russians arrived. They come roarin' into town, on horseback, on motorcycles. And all drunk. (Laughs.) None of 'em in uniform. A lot of 'em Mongolians that couldn't even talk to each other. They took that town apart, absolutely destroyed it.

How'd they treat you guys?

Great. They came up to us, gave us guns. They said, "Let's go. We think we can catch those guards." I think they probably did catch some of 'em, the slower ones. I said, "Well, I don't think I'm in hot pursuit of the fellas." I said "The big thing is to eat." So three of us took off.

Most of 'em headed for the American lines, tryin' to get back. We did too, eventually. But we took our own sweet time about it. We would go down the road and if some German would come down, say, driving a Volkswagen, we'd flag 'im down. With our guns going, we take his car and we drive until we run out of gas. Then we'd set fire to it. (Laughs.)

We would go until we found a house. We'd knock on the door. Whoever came, we would usher them outside and go in and eat everything in sight. If they were nice, we'd leave them alone. If they weren't, we'd set fire to their house. We were really nasty fellows.

May 7 we were in this barn and a pretty little girl with flaxen braids came in and said, "Der Krieg ist über." The war is over. I said, "You crazy little girl, go home." I didn't believe her. Of course, it was over.

We're in this town waiting to be flown out. My two buddies and I found an abandoned apartment building still in fairly good shape.

We had sleeping bags and threw them on the floor. I'm still carryin' this .32 automatic. We're laying there and all of a sudden I hear the door creaking open. I thought, oh-oh. I pull out the .32. I'm just about to squeeze one off and there's a flashlight, very low to the ground. I said, "Who's there?" It was a little boy about six years old. I said, "Vas vants you?" or whatever—I could speak a little German. He said, "Mein teddy bear." He used to live there. And I almost blew him away.

They flew us to Camp Lucky Strike in France. They had these huge camps for repatriated ex-prisoners. The lines were interminable, thousands of released prisoners. They said, Anybody that wants to take some of his back pay and a two-week furlough in London is free to do so. My two buddies and I signed up for that. We managed to get on a hospital ship back to the States as KPs, because everybody else on the boat was immobilized.

They took us down to Camp Shanks. The KPs were German prisoners. We're goin' through the chow line and this big guy in front of me, a paratrooper, asks for two cartons of milk. You know the German military mind, someone told these guys one carton per man. So the German says no. (Laughs.) Well, everybody jumped over and beat the bejesus out of these Germans. The next day, there was a regiment of Nisei troops, the Japs, who had fought very hard in Italy. They were there for a rest. They were made KPs.

We each got a sixty-day furlough back home. I had all kinds of back pay and reparations money. I got somethin' like $350 from the German government for my wristwatch and various things stolen from me. My sixty days are up and I get orders to report to Hot Springs, rest and rehabilitation. Massage, baths, everything. The town was dull, but I could stand a little dullness by this time.

So I get my orders: Fort Lawton, Seattle, Washington. Going off on the invasion of Japan. We're sitting on the pier, sharpening our bayonets, when Harry dropped that beautiful bomb. The greatest thing ever happened. Anybody sitting at the pier at that time would have to agree.

I was tempted to re-enlist. They offered me a job as sergeant major, which is the highest-paying noncom officer job in the army. What was I—twenty years old? I could retire at thirty-seven. I was really thinking about it. I told my mother. She said, "Forget it. I've got you signed up at Notre Dame."

The GI Bill made all the difference in the world to me. I could never have afforded college. I don't know if I'd have been a blue-collar worker. Certainly not what I'm doing now.

Looking back on the war, in spite of the really bad times, it was certainly the most exciting experience of my life. As a character in *Terry and the Pirates* once put it so eloquently, "We shot the last act in the first reel." As I see it, at that young age, we hit the climax. Everything after that is anticlimactic.

TALES OF THE PACIFIC

E. B. (SLEDGEHAMMER) SLEDGE

*Half-hidden in the hilly greenery, toward the end of a winding country
road, is the house he himself helped build. It is on the campus of the
University of Montevallo, a forty-five-minute drive from Birmingham,
Alabama.*

*On the wall near the fireplace—comforting on this unseasonably cool
day—is a plaque with the familiar Guadalcanal patch: "Presented to
Eugene B. Sledge. We, the men of K Co., 3rd Bn., 5th Reg., 1st Marine
Div., do hereby proudly bestow this testimonial in expression of our great
admiration and heartfelt appreciation to one extraordinary marine, who
had honored his comrades in arms by unveiling to the world its exploits
and heroism in his authorship of* WITH THE OLD BREED AT PELELIU AND
OKINAWA. *God love you, Sledgehammer. 1982." It is his remarkable
memoir that led me to him. **

*Small-boned, slim, gentle in demeanor, he is a professor of biology at
the university. "My main interest is ornithology. I've been a bird-watcher
since I was a kid in Mobile. Do you see irony in that? Interested in birds,
nature, a combat marine in the front lines? People think of bird-watchers
as not macho."*

There was nothing macho about the war at all. We were a bunch of
scared kids who had to do a job. People tell me I don't act like an
ex-marine. How is an ex-marine supposed to act? They have some
Hollywood stereoptype in mind. No, I don't look like John Wayne.
We were in it to get it over with, so we could go back home and do
what we wanted to do with our lives.

I was nineteen, a replacement in June of 1944. Eighty percent of
the division in the Guadalcanal campaign was less than twenty-one
years of age. We were much younger than the general army units.

To me, there were two different wars. There was the war of the guy

*Novato, Calif.: Presidio Press, 1981.

on the front lines. You don't come off until you are wounded or killed. Or, if lucky, relieved. Then there was the support personnel. In the Pacific, for every rifleman on the front lines there were nineteen people in the back. Their view of the war was different than mine. The man up front puts his life on the line day after day after day to the point of utter hopelessness.

The only thing that kept you going was your faith in your buddies. It wasn't just a case of friendship. I never heard of self-inflicted wounds out there. Fellows from other services said they saw this in Europe. Oh, there were plenty of times when I wished I had a million-dollar wound. (Laughs softly.) Like maybe shootin' a toe off. What was worse than death was the indignation of your buddies. You couldn't let 'em down. It was stronger than flag and country.

With the Japanese, the battle was all night long. Infiltratin' the lines, slippin' up and throwin' in grenades. Or runnin' in with a bayonet or saber. They were active all night. Your buddy would try to get a little catnap and you'd stay on watch. Then you'd switch off. It went on, day in and day out. A matter of simple survival. The only way you could get it over with was to kill them off before they killed you. The war I knew was totally savage.

The Japanese fought by a code they thought was right: *bushido*. The code of the warrior: no surrender. You don't really comprehend it until you get out there and fight people who are faced with an absolutely hopeless situation and will not give up. If you tried to help one of the Japanese, he'd usually detonate a grenade and kill himself as well as you. To be captured was a disgrace. To us, it was impossible, too, because we knew what happened in Bataan.

Toward the end of the Okinawa campaign, we found this emaciated Japanese in the bunk of what may have been a field hospital. We were on a patrol. There had been torrential rains for two weeks. The foxholes were filled with water. This Jap didn't have but a G-string on him. About ninety pounds. Pitiful. This buddy of mine picked him up and carried him out. Laid him out in the mud. There was no other place to put him.

We were sittin' on our helmets waitin' for the medical corpsman to check him out. He was very docile. We figured he couldn't get up. Suddenly he pulled a Japanese grenade out of his G-string. He jerked the pin out and hit it on his fist to pop open the cap. He was gonna make hamburger of me and my buddy and himself. I yelled, "Look out!" So my buddy said, "You son of a bitch, if that's how you feel about it—" He pulled out his .45 and shot him right between the eyes.

This is what we were up against. I don't like violence, but there are times when you can't help it. I don't like to watch television shows with violence in them. I hate to see anything afraid. But I was afraid so much, day after day, that I got tired of being scared. I've seen guys go through three campaigns and get killed on Okinawa on the last day. You knew all you had was that particular moment you were living.

I got so tired of seein' guys get hit and banged up, the more I felt like takin' it out on the Japanese. The feeling grew and grew, and you became more callous. Have you ever read the poem by Wilfred Owen? The World War One poet? "Insensibility." (He shuts his eyes as he recalls snatches of the poem and interpolates) "Happy are the men who yet before they are killed/Can let their veins run cold. . . . And some cease feeling/Even themselves or for themselves. Dullness best solves/The tease and doubt of shelling." You see, the man who can go through combat and not be bothered by the deaths of others and escape what Owen calls Chance's strange arithmetic— he's the fortunate one. He doesn't suffer as much as the one who is sensitive to the deaths of his comrades. Owen says you can't compare this man to the old man at home, who is just callous and hardened to everything and has no compassion. The young man on the front line develops this insensitivity because it is the only way he can cope.

You developed an attitude of no mercy because they had no mercy on us. It was a no-quarter, savage kind of thing. At Peleliu, it was the first time I was close enough to see one of their faces. This Jap had been hit. One of my buddies was field-stripping him for souvenirs. I must admit it really bothered me, the guys dragging him around like a carcass. I was just horrified. This guy had been a human being. It didn't take me long to overcome that feeling. A lot of my buddies hit, the fatigue, the stress. After a while, the veneer of civilization wore pretty thin.

This hatred toward the Japanese was just a natural feeling that developed elementally. Our attitude toward the Japanese was different than the one we had toward the Germans. My brother who was with the Second Infantry Division in the Battle of the Bulge, wounded three times, said when things were hopeless for the Germans, they surrendered. I have heard many guys who fought in Europe who said the Germans were damn good soldiers. We hated the hell of having to fight 'em. When they surrendered, they were guys just like us. With the Japanese, it was not that way. At Peleliu, my company took two prisoners. At Okinawa, we took about five. We had orders not to kill the wounded, to try to take prisoners. If they surrendered, they'd give you information. But the feeling was strong . . . Some guys you meet say they didn't kill any wounded. They weren't up there living like animals, savages.

Our drill instructor at boot camp would tell us, "You're not going to Europe, you're going to the Pacific. Don't hesitate to fight the Japs dirty. Most Americans, from the time they're kids, are taught not to hit below the belt. It's not sportsmanlike. Well, nobody has taught the Japs that, and war ain't sport. Kick him in the balls before he kicks you in yours."

I've seen guys shoot Japanese wounded when it really was not necessary and knock gold teeth out of their mouths. Most of them had gold teeth. I remember one time at Peleliu, I thought I'd collect gold teeth. One of my buddies carried a bunch of 'em in a sock. What you did is you took your K-bar (he displays a seven-inch knife), a fighting knife. We all had one because they'd creep into your foxhole at night. We were on Half Moon Hill in Okinawa about ten days. It happened every night.

The way you extracted gold teeth was by putting the tip of the blade on the tooth of the dead Japanese—I've seen guys do it to wounded ones—and hit the hilt of the knife to knock the tooth loose. How could American boys do this? If you're reduced to savagery by a situation, anything's possible. When Lindbergh made a trip to the Philippines, he was horrified at the way American GIs talked about the Japanese. It was so savage. We *were* savages.

When I leaned to make the extraction, as the troops used to say, this navy medic, Doc Castle, God bless his soul, said, "Sledgehammer, what are you doing?" I says, "Doc, I'm gonna get me some gold teeth." He said, (very softly) "You don't want to do that." I said, "All the other guys are doin' it." He says, "What would your folks think?" I said, "Gosh, my dad is a medical doctor back in Mobile, he might think it's interesting." He said, "Well, you might get germs." I said, "I hadn't thought of that, doc." In retrospect, I realized Ken Castle wasn't worried about germs. He just didn't want me to take another step toward abandoning all concepts of decency.

I saw this Jap machine-gunner squattin' on the ground. One of our Browning automatic riflemen had killed him. Took the top of his skull off. It rained all that night. This Jap gunner didn't fall over for some reason. He was just sitting upright in front of the machine gun. His arms were down at his sides. His eyes were wide open. It had rained all night and the rain had collected inside of his skull. We were just sittin' around on our helmets, waiting to be relieved. I noticed this buddy of mine just flippin' chunks of coral into the skull about three feet away. Every time he'd get one in there, it'd splash. It reminded me of a child throwin' pebbles into a puddle. It was just so unreal. There was nothing malicious in his action. This was just a mild-mannered kid who was now a twentieth-century savage.

Once on another patrol, on Okinawa, I saw Mac take great pains to position himself and his carbine near a Japanese corpse. After getting just the right angle, Mac took careful aim and squeezed off a couple of rounds. The dead Japanese lay on his back with his trousers pulled down to his knees. Mac was trying very carefully to blast off the head of the corpse's penis. He succeeded. As he exulted over his aim, I turned away in disgust. Mac was a decent, clean-cut man.

We had broken through the Japanese lines at Okinawa. I had a Thompson submachine gun and went in to check this little grass-thatched hut. An old woman was sitting just inside the door. She held out her hands. There was an hourglass figure tattooed on it to show she was Okinawan. She said, "No Nipponese." She opened her kimono and pointed to this terrible wound in her lower abdomen. You could see gangrene had set in. She didn't have a chance to survive and was obviously in great pain. She probably had caught it in an exchange of artillery fire or an air strike.

She very gently reached around, got the muzzle of my tommy gun, and moved it around to her forehead. She motioned with her other hand for me to pull the trigger. I jerked it away and called the medical corpsman: "There's an old gook woman, got a bad wound." This is what we called the natives in the Pacific. "Hey, doc, can you do anything?"

He put a dressing on it and called someone in the rear to evacuate the old woman. We started moving out when we heard a rifle shot ring out. The corpsman and I went into a crouch. That was an M-1, wasn't it? We knew it was an American rifle. We looked back toward the hut and thought maybe there was a sniper in there and the old woman was acting as a front for him. Well, here comes one of the guys in the company, walking out, checking the safety on his rifle.

I said, "Was there a Nip in that hut?" He said, "Naw, it was just an old gook woman. She wanted to be put out of her misery and join her ancestors, I guess. So I obliged her."

I just blew my top: "You son of bitch. They didn't send us out here to kill old women." He started all these excuses. By that time, a sergeant came over and we told him. We moved on. I don't know what was ever done about it. He was a nice guy, like the boy next door. He wasn't just a hot-headed crazy kid. He wanted to join the best. Why one individual would act differently from another, I'll never know.

We had all become hardened. We were out there, human beings, the most highly developed form of life on earth, fighting each other like wild animals. We were under constant mortar fire. Our wounded had to be carried two miles through the mud. The dead couldn't be removed. Dead Japs all around. We'd throw mud over 'em and shells would come, blow it off, and blow them apart. The maggots were in the mud like in some corruption or compost pile.

Did you ever get to know a Japanese soldier?

One of the few we captured at Okinawa was a Yale graduate. He spoke perfect English, but we never said anything to him. I must be perfectly honest with you, I still have a great deal of feeling about them. The way they fought. The Germans are constantly getting thrown in their face the horrors of nazism. But who reminds the Japanese of what they did to China or what they did to the Filipinos? Periodically, we remember Bataan.

It always struck me as ironic, the Japanese code of behavior. Flower arranging, music, striving for perfection. And the art of the warrior. Very often, we'd get a photograph off a dead Japanese. Here would be this soldier, sitting in a studio, with a screen behind and a table with a little flower on it. Often he'd be holding a rifle, yet there was always that little vase of flowers.

We all had different kinds of mania. To me, the most horrible thing was to be under shellfire. You're absolutely helpless. The damn thing comes in like a freight train and there's a terrific crash. The ground shakes and all this shrapnel rippin' through the air.

I remember one afternoon on Half Moon Hill. The foxhole next to me had two boys in it. The next one to that had three. It was fairly quiet. We heard the shell come screeching over. They were firing it at us like a rifle. The shell passed no more than a foot over my head. Two foxholes down, a guy was sitting on his helmet drinking C-ration hot chocolate. It exploded in his foxhole. I saw this guy, Bill Leyden, go straight up in the air. The other two kids fell over backwards. Dead, of course. The two in the hole next to me were killed instantly.

Leyden was the only one who survived. Would you believe he gets only partial disability for shrapnel wounds? His record says nothing about concussion. He has seizures regularly. He was blown up in the air! If you don't call that concussion . . . The medics were too busy saving lives to fill out records.

Another kid got his leg blown off. He had been a lumberjack, about twenty-one. He was always telling me how good spruce Christmas trees smelled. He said, "Sledgehammer, you think I'm gonna lose my leg?" If you don't think that just tore my guts out . . . My God, there was his field shoe on the stretcher with this stump of his ankle stickin' out. The stretcher bearers just looked at each other and covered him with his poncho. He was dead.

It was raining like hell. We were knee-deep in mud. And I thought, What in the hell are we doin' on this nasty, stinkin' muddy ridge? What is this all about? You know what I mean? Wasted lives on a muddy slope.

People talk about Iwo Jima as the most glorious amphibious operation in history. I've had Iwo veterans tell me it was more similar to Peleliu than any other battle they read about. What in the hell was glorious about it?

POSTSCRIPT: *During the next day's drive to the airport, he reflected further: "My parents taught me the value of history. Both my grandfathers were in the Confederate Army. They didn't talk about the glory of war. They talked about how terrible it was.*

"During my third day overseas, I thought I should write all this down for my family. In all my reading about the Civil War, I never read about how the troops felt and what it was like from day to day. We knew how the generals felt and what they ate.

"We were told diaries were forbidden, because if we were killed or captured, any diary might give the Japanese information. So I kept little notes, which I slipped into the pages of my Gideon's New Testament. I kept it in a rubber bag I got off a dead Jap. I committed the casualties to memory. We had more than a hundred percent in Okinawa and almost that many at Peleliu.

"Any time we made an attack, I recited the Twenty-third Psalm. Snafu Shelton says, 'I don't know what it is that got us through. I was doin' a hell of a lot of cussin' and Sledgehammer was doin' a hell of a lot of prayin'. One of those might have done it.' Some of the survivors never knew I was keepin' notes: 'We just thought you were awfully pious.' Some of the guys were very religious. But some of 'em, after a while, got so fatalistic they figured it was nothing but dumb chance anyway."

ROBERT LEKACHMAN

He is a professor of economics at the City University of New York. "I was drafted right after Pearl Harbor. The army provided me with my first steady job."

I was a helplessly awkward intellectual sort of kid, with no mechanical skill. I tried to enlist in the navy, but the navy was snotty in those days. People with less than twenty-twenty vision and a bad bite were out. I was utterly useless, so they put me in the infantry.

I was sent down to Fort Jackson, South Carolina. The Statue of Liberty Division, the Seventy-seventh. My unit was a mixture of New Yorkers and southern boys. The officers and noncoms were southern. The first week, my platoon sergeant said, "You're a college kid. There's no reason why you shouldn't go to OCS." After he watched my performance as a soldier, he never mentioned it again. (Laughs.)

My ineptitude was my salvation. The people who went to OCS turned into second lieutenants and got slaughtered in heaps in Japan and in the Pacific, where my unit ultimately went. Though I was unable to shoot accurately and couldn't put one foot after the other in the right sequence, I could type. I was installed in regimental headquarters. I would write letters for people and hold their money and lose money in card games because I was a terrible player. (Laughs.) The experience had a personal meaning to me. It made me a bit less timid. I found that I could cheerfully get along with various kinds of people. Of course, as a militarist I was a dismal failure.

Our first operation was in Guam. That was the first time I saw a dead Japanese. He looked pitiful, with his thick glasses. He had a sheaf of letters in his pocket. He looked like an awkward kid who'd been taken right out of his home to this miserable place.

It was perfectly safe for people like me. The casualty rate among clerks was close to zero. Next came Leyte in the Philippines. Here's where MacArthur waded onto the beach and said, "I have returned." It took several months to pacify the Japanese, who hadn't heard the news apparently. Then came the Okinawa bloodbath. A dreadful affair. At the end of the three campaigns, I computed my regiment's casualty list. It was 140 percent.

I found myself ghost-writing. The company commander was supposed to write a personal letter of condolence to the parents or wife or next of kin. He'd give me a name of a young kid, particularly in Okinawa, who came up to the line and got killed the next day. What was there personal that could be said? What could I say that would console the family? So it was a case of creative fiction. I also became something of an expert in writing citations for medals. This was really creative fiction. There was an awful lot of hustling for awards. Each one was worth five points. People were shipped back home in the order of points accumulated. But there were so many genuine acts of bravery, too.

In the Pacific, there were none of the European diversions. What you tended to see were miserable natives and piles of dead Japanese and dead Americans. I was not a virulent hater of the Japanese. I didn't collect ears, as I knew some others did. We had been fed tales of these yellow thugs, subhumans, with teeth that resembled fangs. If a hundred thousand Japs were killed, so much the better. Two hundred thousand, even better. I wasn't innocent, either. You couldn't escape it. When I heard about Hiroshima, I felt great: we won't have to invade Japan.

Towards the end of Okinawa, people who had been in all three campaigns were really zonked out. There was a rash of guys shooting themselves in the foot, anything to get hospitalized. One guy deliberately scratched a jungle-rot infection until it got so bad he had to be sent back to Hawaii. But I heard of no fragging of unpopular officers, as in Vietnam.

Unlike Vietnam, it wasn't just working-class kids doing the fighting. You go to college faculty clubs today and on the walls are long lists of graduates who died in the Second World War. It was the last time that most Americans thought they were innocent and good, without qualifications.

There were black marketeers on the home front, people who were, as usual, hustling for themselves. But most Americans at home did observe price controls and rationing. Soldiers who came home on leave were treated with respect by the folks, unlike the Vietnam veterans. They bought war bonds: Buy yourself a tank. It was an idealistic war. People still believed.

The boys came home, eager to make up for lost time. Newly married, and Levittown selling homes for six or seven thousand dollars, four percent mortgages, no down payment. A postwar boom that lasted until 1969. Eisenhower was the perfect symbol of the period. It was as though a massive dose of Sominex were administered to the whole population. There was now less concern for those beyond your immediate family. Making it yourself was what it was all about in the fifties.

The GI Bill produced an educational explosion. If you wanted to educate yourself, you got a good deal. Like millions of others, I went back to school. I got full tuition at Columbia.

It was a decade in which most people were doing well. There were the usual losers, who weren't doing so great. The rural workers, pushed out by agricultural machinery and shoved into the big cities. But if you were a nice white middle-class family, life was pretty good.

I think everybody still felt good about the war in '47, '48, '49. One wonders: could Truman have unilaterally committed American troops to Korea unless there had been the lingering romance of the Second World War? I rather doubt it. I think things began to sour and innocence end in, say, 1952 and 1953, as the Korean War dragged on.

In the war we remember best, there were lots and lots of people who suddenly realized what they were capable of. They were real heroes, not just those who got fake citations. Sometimes, unexpected people. The only person I knew who won a Congressional Medal of Honor was a conscientious objector who was in the medical corps. He ran up a hill under fire, dragging God knows how many people back to safety.

When they meet some old buddy, they lift a glass together and talk about the old days. They felt they were more important, were better men who amounted to more than they do now. It's a precious memory.

Along U.S. 127, on the outskirts of Harrodsburg, Kentucky, reposes an old army tank. A white star imprinted, U.S. Army. W35. It is a replica of the tank of Company D, 192nd Tank Battalion. It is the town's hallmark: a monument to the sixty-six young men of the company, all from Harrodsburg. Twenty-nine died in the defense of Bataan and Corregidor. Thirty-seven survived. Of the survivors, twelve had died at the time of my visit. One had been killed by his wife.

While Wilson's wife quietly crochets in the living room, we are seated in his "war room." There is a whole shelf of books on one subject: Bataan. On the walls, as well as on the desk, are medals, ribbons, certificates; photographs of a prison camp, of a Kentucky colonel; a knife; notices of American Legion and Disabled Veterans conventions— "I'm a member of 'em all, a life member. I built this house in 1966 as a wheelchair house. See, it's made for a wheelchair all the way round."

The photograph on the desk of young Maurice E. (Jack) Wilson, as a tech sergeant, bears a remarkable resemblance to that of a more heavy-set Robert Mitchum in one of those World War Two films.

As he urges newspaper clippings, xeroxed letters, old postcards, news releases into my hand, his words tumble out, one on top of the other. He is a man possessed.

He is the acknowledged, though informal, historian of Company D, 192nd Tank Battalion.

I joined the Kentucky National Guard with the Thirty-eighth Tank Company in 19 and 33. We went through Harlan County coal-minin' strikes, went through Kentucky floods, guarded convicts down to Frankfort. We drilled every Monday night. I got a dollar a drill. Fifteen days out of every year we went to Fort Knox on training.

In 19 and 41, we went on Louisiana maneuvers. Lieutenant General George Patton, Jr. said the 192nd Tank Battalion had showed up so good, they had selected them to go overseas.

Those was over twenty-eight years old had a chance to get out, and those that had dependents. I was around close to that. And with this eye I got hurt on the firin' range, I said, "I'll accept a discharge if you tell me are ya gonna give me a disability on it. I'm a poor boy, just an old farmer, and I don't want to pay a doctor bill all my life." So they say, "It hasn't happened long enough." I done been in the hospital eighty-nine days with it. And I said, "I won't sign a discharge that I'm well and okay." I didn't know the war was gonna start and I'd be a prisoner of war, or I'da went and signed two or three discharges. (Laughs.)

We hit Frisco and went on Angel Island. Then they loaded us, sixty-six boys from Harrodsburg, onto ships and we went over to the Hawaiian Islands. And there was a cruiser and we landed in Luzon at Manila. It was under sealed orders. It was November 20, 19 and 41. We went on to Fort Stotsenburg. It just wasn't a mile and a quarter over to Clark Field. As soon as we got there, we suspicioned somethin', but we didn't know what was goin' on. They never told us nothin' about it.

That one day, December 8, about twelve o'clock, we all went up to the chow truck and we looked up at the sky. There was fifty-four planes. I said, "Look what pretty planes we got." They was all silver-lookin'. About that time, they commenced droppin' those bombs out on the hangars. The bombers went by and here come the fighters down, shootin' them shells off toward us. It's fallin' around like hail. Of course, I run underneath the command tank.

We found one of our boys that had shrapnel from one of the bombs had cut half his head off. His name was Robert Brooks and he's from Sadieville, Kentucky. He lied about his race. We was all white, see? And he lied to get in a white outfit. He was yellow-complected, had kinda kinky hair. I called him Nig all the time and I didn't know he was a nigger, see? We found out that he was the first boy killed in the armed forces in the Philippines in World War Two. They named the parade ground at Fort Knox after Robert Brooks. They found out his mother and father in Sadieville, they was niggers and sharecroppers. So this general out there in Fort Knox said tell them people, regardless of race, creed, or color, that he was still one of the heroes of Kentucky and wanted them to be invited to the celebration.* But his mother and father wouldn't come. They didn't like it much because the boy had lied about his race to get in the white outfit.

We didn't know he was colored, because he came to Harrodsburg, spent the weekend sometimes with a lotta white boys. That would be

*Major General Jacob L. Devers, Chief of Armored Force, ordered that the field be named in Brooks's honor: "For the preservation of America, the soldiers and sailors guarding our outposts are giving their lives. In death, there is no grade or rank. And in this, the greatest Democracy the world has known, neither riches nor poverty, neither creed nor race draws a line of demarcation in this hour of national crisis."

somethin' unusual for a nigger. Nowadays it would be a different thing. But back in '41 . . .

Kenneth Hourigan, another of the Harrodsburg 66, whose tales are not as oft-told as Wilson's though he shares the same experiences (in fact, some of their anecdotes are identical), remembers Brooks: "We didn't know he was colored, but we always thought he was cuttin' up and laughin' kinda like a colored guy. But you couldn't really tell by the looks of him. I mean, he was just one of the boys."

All the airplane hangars had been destroyed. About dinnertime, that's when the Japanese came over an' caught all our airplanes down on the ground. The Japanese got to landin' just ship after ship of soldiers. Oh, they come in there by the thousands. We just couldn't fight that many, but we did the best we could.

We went an' left there and come through Manila. I said to the boys, "Listen, I had a brother in World War One. He told me if I ever come to Manila to go into the Silver Dollar Bar." So we pulled up there. All the counter was inlaid with silver pesos, one almost touchin' the other. We was in there pryin' them things out because we knew the Japanese was landin'.

So this captain found a buddy of his from his hometown and he said, "Wilson, you cain't see how to command a tank, so I'll put you here in the kitchen to be a mess sergeant." We didn't have anything to eat. Killed all the horses and mules and cut all the legs off an' skinned 'em and tried to eat the meat. Too tough to cook. We tried to grind that meat and season it up. I said, "What kinda leg is that?" Someone said it's off a Indian cow. I said, "Indian cow nothin'. I rode behind that thing the other night in Manila passin' one of them low buggies." (Laughs.) I knew it was a horse's leg 'cause the bones was too big. They finally give us three cans of salmon and two round loaves of bread to feed eighty men with.

I found this private behind the bushes and he had a whole can of salmon and bread. I said, "All these boys gotta have somethin' to eat. You wanna starve 'em?" And he jumped up an' give me the prettiest black eye I ever did see. He was too big. He could whip the devil outa me. So I hadda go ahead and let 'im eat the salmon and bread.

So the captain said, "Wilson, I'm gonna take your stripes away from you and reduce you down and give it to the man who can find us some food." I said, "I'm a three-grade sergeant. I've gotta be court-martialed. I've done nothin' to be court-martialed for." He said he could do any damn thing he wanted. I was reduced down to private.

He said I got dust in my eye and I couldn't see how to command a tank, and he put me in the rear echelon, and there wasn't no rear 'cause the Japanese shootin' us with shells right over our head all the time. So when I surrendered, I surrendered as a private.

We kept on afightin' in Bataan and the Japanese kept on comin' on us an' hittin' us down. Bataan Bay goes up to Manila. The boys reports they're ready to surrender. So me and about twenty-five other boys decided we wasn't gonna surrender. We was goin' down and get over to Corregidor, which was right across the water about four miles.

We see this cave an' an old man, looked like maybe seventy-eight. He was half Chinese and half Spanish an' he had a boat. But the motor won't run. We had tank mechanics an' they got it to runnin'. We went by and seen several drums of gasoline, so we loaded up and we was gonna go to Australia. Lay over in the daytime and travel at night. I had a can of sardines. Somebody else had a can of pork and beans in his shirt. We put it in one large can and said one guy eats, we all eat.

Two of the guys robbed a bank in Bataan. Pesos—they had their shirts all full. They just went in an' told the man, "Hand over the money. The Japanese are gonna get it anyhow." They put all their money in the pot an' if we need anything to buy, we'll buy.

We got ready to pull away and there's a man on another barge over there and he pulled out that sub-Thompson machine gun an' hollered over, "If you don't come by here and pick me and my men up and take us to Corregidor, I'm gonna start shootin'." So we went on to Corregidor.

We went up the bank there to a small tunnel. They had the barracks back in there. Outa concrete, real nice, but you didn't have room to squat down, you didn't have room to stand up. And we didn't have no cigarettes. Last package I bought in Bataan, I had to give twenty pesos for it. That was ten dollars.

The Japanese come and we had to surrender. We took our pistols and throwed them over in the ocean. I've seen boys light cigarettes with fifty-dollar bills and hundred-dollar bills. Some of 'em cut the threads of their clothes an' tuck bills in there.

My brother was in the navy over in Hong Kong. He had a twelve-dollar gold piece and he made me a ring out of it. It had my initial on it. The Japanese seen that ring, he pulled it and he took skin and all off. Another ol' boy I couldn't keep from laughin' at. He had a pair of Florsheim shoes, prettiest shiny things I ever did see. I had told him at Fort Drum, "You better not take 'em, that's too nice-lookin'." As soon's he got on that boat, the Japanese looked down an' said changee, changee. This boy's foot was bigger than this Japanese shoe. The Japanese said, "I fix it, I fix it." He cut the toe cap off and this boy's toes stuck out about that far over the end of the soles. (Laughs.) An' I got to laughin' at 'im.

Some of these boys said, "Wilson, we're gonna make an escape." I said, "You haven't got a chance. Any white man out there is enemy. And these Filipinos are getting hungry, an' if they offer 'em ten or fifteen pesos reward, they gonna squeal on you." I said, "Of course, we're over here fightin' for 'em, but they're hungry, they'll do anything for food." They said they're goin' underneath the fence that night. I said, "Don't do it, boys." They said, "Come and go with us." No, I've got dinky fever. It wasn't quite as bad as malaria, but if you don't have the quinine, it was malaria.

They was gone three or four days and the Japanese caught 'em. They tied 'em up to the fence post and made 'em squat down on their knees. Took the hat off 'em, an' blisters on their face big as goose eggs in that hot sun. They kept 'em out there for three days. Finally, the Japanese went and dug a hole up on the ridge. They took them boys up there an' they took their blindfolds off of 'em. They offered one of 'em a cigarette. That boy took a draw off it an' flipped it right in the Japanese' face. They offered another one a drink of water. He took a little taste of it and throwed it right in the Japanese' face. Then they put the blindfolds back on 'em, got back, an' commenced shootin'. All these boys went back in that hole. I coulda been one of 'em.

We went up to a sugar plantation. The Japanese lined us up to a big pile of rock. We had to pick up rock an' pass it over to the next guy. They done got mad an' took our caps off. In that ship we got real white, no sunshine on our faces. And we had them blisters come on our face, looked like eggs. They wouldn't give us no water to drink. We went for four days. Somebody said all you gotta do is pull your buttons off your shirt and suck on 'em and that would cause saliva in your mouth an' put moisture in it. I think I had done pulled every button off the shirt.

This officer, he went up to the Japanese and told 'em, "My men's gotta have water." So they said, "We'll give you a barrel, get water in the creek." On the banks of the creek were these Filipino huts. Back behind it, they had a little ol' toilet. When their droppin' fell down it went right in the creek. We had to dip water outa that. We knocked the stuff away an' dip up a bucket of water. The only way we could drink it, we had to put chlorine in it. In order to keep from takin' diphtheria an' everything else. We had it so strong, it would almost draw your mouth.

Kenneth Hourigan, sergeant, recalls a thirst and something unexpected: "After we were captured, we hadn't had any water for two or three days. We was in line and I was lucky enough to get pretty close to the head of that line to the spigot. The line was a good half-mile long. The guys were just thirsty, boy. Somebody bucked me like that and shoved in front of me. I looked up. That colonel, I remembered him from giving us such a hard time. I kinda bucked him back and he come back at me again. I kicked him in the rear and here come a Jap. He wanted to know what was goin' on. I said to myself I'm in trouble, him a colonel and me just a sergeant. I told him, 'Because he's got those chickens on his shoulder, he broke the line.' That Jap, he knocked him down with a rifle and was takin' him to the rear of the line. The last I seen him, he was kickin' his butt. The Jap took up for me."

Meantime, I had a carbuncle on my back. It had eight heads. It hurt. I tried to get an American to lance it. He said, "I don't have no tools, the Japanese take 'em all away." I had to lay on the concrete floor in a big wire house. If you turned over at night, you'd turn over on the guy next to you. That much room. Go to sleep on my side and I'd turn over an' hit that place an', boy—up I'd come. All night, same thing.

In about twelve days, they come an' picked out eighteen big broad-shouldered guys, looked like football players. We never seen no more of 'em. Somebody tol' me last year, at Louisville when they had the defenders of Bataan an' Corregidor, what they did. They got out to drinkin' one night an' they got their guns and just shot 'em all down.

We got these Japanese landin' barges an' we went down to Dewey Boulevard in Manila. That's all the big fine millionaires' homes. They made us jump out in the water way up to our neck and wade through. We got up to the main street, front of all these homes. We marched down through there. The Filipinos had put tubs of water and they hung cups all the way around it. We'd reach down an' get a drink of water. Sometimes a Filipino would throw cigarettes out on the ground, so's we'd walk over an' pick one up. But if a Japanese caught 'em, boy, they'd slap 'em, beat 'em up.

Then I went to Bilibid prison an' I took to diarrhea, so I messed up my shorts. They loaded us up on boxcars, eighty and ninety men to a boxcar. They didn't have room to squat down. It was hot in those metal things, an' boy, when that sun was comin' down on us. They stopped to take on water. When they did, these Filipinos come by the door an' tryin' to sell rice cakes. I motioned to the guard that I had to take my pants down, that I had diarrhea. He was out with a gun. So I stood right there beside the women, squattin' down there with my pants down. I wanted to show a little respect, see? But they thought I was fixin' to make a getaway. Oh, it was pitiful.

They made us march. We went for about a fifteen- or twenty-mile walk. From there out to Cabanatuan. Me an' another boy, we went out on a detail. He got whatever he could get and divided it up with me. Whatever I got, I divided up with him. He caught diarrhea, and my god, he died in five days' time. And he was from Mississippi. He was eatin' pony sugar. It's a mound of sugar about the size of a pound of round soap. It's got straw an' stuff in it and ol' cleanin's. We's eatin' that ol' dirty stuff.

Now they wanted twenty-five acres to put corn in. They didn't have a mule, horse, tractor and plow, or nothin'. They put a hundred of us out there with grubbin' hoes and shovels, bent over, diggin'. We come to a big anthill and down there a snake. Japanese get mad if you kill a snake. They wanted you to tell 'em. They'd put a fork over it an' caught it. He told me, "You hold it tight back here." So I held that poison snake. He said, "I'll show you how to work it." He cut that thing down through the skin, clear on down, and he brought them entrails up, level with his head, then he whacked the thing off. See, he could speak a little English. Said all the poison's right up here. None got in that meat. He took the rest of that skin off and built him a fire an' put a shovel over it like a oven and they put it on a wire and roasted that snake. They gimme a little piece of it. He said, "Good, ain't it?" I said, "Sure is good." He said, "Better than pig, ain't it?"

Several nights, an old cat kept arubbin' up against my leg when I would be eatin'. At that time we was havin' fish heads. Japanese eat the fish an' give us the heads, boiled in water. Sometimes an eye'd pop around your mouth like a grain of corn. Anyhow, I missed the cat one night. I said, "Boys, anybody seen my cat?" They says a couple of sailors killed the cat: "They over there cookin' it." See, we got a Red Cross about once ever' six months an' it weighed about twelve pounds. Two or three little cans of butter in it. These boys saved about a spoonful of it and they was fryin' that cat in butter. The limey doctor went out there to stop 'em, but got a piece of it himself. This little bitty ol' boy that lied about his age to get in the service, he says, "Boys, gimme piece o' that cat so I can go back home an' tell the folks I've eaten cat." These boys said, "Listen, you just go back home an' tell the folks you seen some guys eatin' cat. You don't get none of this damn cat." (Laughs.)

Ken Hourigan, across the town, has his own recollections. "We caught a cat in camp. We fried it up in coconut oil. This American officer come along and he said, 'Now listen, boys, we're starvin' to death in here now. If the Japs find out you doin' that thing, we don't get nothin'.' We went and fried it up and had it on a big piece of tin layin' there. And by golly, this guy looked up and he's grinnin'. 'That does look pretty good,' he says. And damn if I thought he wasn't gonna eat it all. One little boy said, 'Gimme a piece of that cat so I can go home and tell 'em I ate a piece of cat.' I said, 'You go home, tell 'em you saw me eat a piece of cat.' (Laughs.)
"We had a pup there at camp, a little collie. We fed him rice. He got run over by a truck. This big old boy, he reached down, got that dog by the tail, and took him out on the job. We worked in a steel mill, un-loadin' ships and steel. He took that dog up and when we cooked that rice and things, he told me as I was goin' by, 'You want a good sand-wich?' Yeah, boy, I'm starvin' to death. He took the bottom out of that rice cake and a slab of that dog between it. It taste pretty good, you know."

They had these cows with a big hump on 'em. They confiscated 'em offa some Filipino and brought 'em into camp. The only time they gave us one is when one of 'em died. We'd cut it up, had a big kettle there, you boiled your soup in. Sometimes they give us boiled bean leaves. Boy, they's as bitter as quinine. They'd dig the sweet potatoes an' give us the vines. We called 'em whistle weeds. (He indicates a photograph on the wall) There's my picture in the Japanese prison camp. I lost ninety-five pounds when that was taken. I weighed two hundred when they caught me, an' when they turned me loose I weighed one hundred and five.

In September 19 and 43, they run us into Formosa. They thought the Americans was after 'em. We had one boy with appendicitis. He was a Spanish boy from Albuquerque. They didn't even have no operatin' things or nothin'. They took two teaspoons, bent the handles, and put it down in there to hold it open. An' they reached out and got that boy's appendix an' cut it off with a razor blade. They just had enough ether to put him to sleep. When he'd come out, they run out of ether. When they got ready to sew him up, they hadda hold to him. The Japanese took a likin' to that boy. He stayed around the medics an' never had to do too much.

Finally we went on to Moji city in Japan, caught a passenger train, had all the shades pulled down, an' we rode up to Niigata. I worked there as a stevedore, unloadin' coal off the ships. We put it on this trestle. We had to put a pole on our shoulder with a basket of coal swingin' in front an' a basket swingin' in back to walk this plank an' fill up the railroad car.

In January 1944, I fell from the trestle about thirty-five feet. I broke a joint in my back an' am paralyzed. The Japanese come every day an' kicked me an' want me to go to work. They tried these guards at the war crimes. They wanted me to stay over there, but I never did learn the Japanese' names. We just nicknamed 'em, Green Eyes, White Angel, and such. I never did try to catch none of 'em.

I tell you what got me to fall off. About four o'clock in the afternoon, I had to urinate. I stepped over the edge of these ties. This boy back behind me didn't see me, you couldn't see over this coal, and he knocked me down. It wasn't two weeks before that I had seen a Japanese officer with his uniform an' a big saber in front of me. I saw an' I just kept pushin' an' I knocked him off. I believe that was the results I got, gettin' knocked off, because I pushed him.

It got down to zero weather and we didn't have no heat. We had to steal coal and bring it in the pocket of our coat. If the Japanese caught us with that coal in our pocket, why, they'd beat the devil out of us. If a boy died in Japan, the Japanese wouldn't furnish the wood to burn him up with, to cremate him. We hadda go out in the woods to cut down wood to cremate him. We took the boy's ashes back to the Japanese office.

Hourigan's remembrance: "We had to bury our own dead. There'd be a Jap undertaker ride in on a bicycle when one died, and he'd break his body up. I don't know how he done it. Had a pickle barrel about that high, he'd set 'em in that and wrap tissue paper, different colored, all around and put him on a little stand there. We never had a preacher. There was never a word said outa the Bible. They did have an old bugle there and he'd blow taps and that'd be it. There'd be a big pile of wood, and we'd set it on fire with gasoline and burn him.

"We'd pick up a tooth or anything we could find and put it in what looked like a shoe box and sew a white piece of silk around it and put his rank, serial number, and name and all that. When we left there, we carried every one of 'em out to the ship. Whatever remained, some ashes, we turned it over to the government and they'd put it in these urns and send 'em to the families."

The Japanese gave us numbers, not names. I was 431. Whenever they got to my number, I didn't know what to say and they come back to where I was and they started beatin' up on me. So I said, "Boys, I gotta learn how to count in Japanese." (Laughs.) (He indicates his number on the wall) Yon Hyaku-Sanju-Ichi. 'At's me, 431.

When the Japanese left our camp, we knew it was all over. They told us the Americans were unfair, that they dropped a bomb of some kind that killed two-hundred-and-forty-some-odd-thousand people. The war was *nai*. That means finished.

The night we dropped the atomic bomb, they lined up every one of us and had us put a rope around what clothes we had. We saw our planes were flyin' around and we went on top of the roof, we found some ol' yellow paint, and we put POW K5B. They dropped two packs of cigarettes apiece, candy bars, razor blades, clothes. The Japs done left camp. *Nai.*

We found out Americans were in Tokyo, so three hundred of us went down one night and got on a Japanese train an' we didn't have no tickets or nothin'. We got there, them girls was passin' around candy bars and all. They was WACs so-and-so. I said, "WACs? What's that?" All that happened since I been in. I flew to Yokohama, stayed there ten days, and we had a chance to buy a watch and a billfold. I got on another airplane and landed on the same airstrip that I helped build when I was a prisoner. I rode a ship out to San Francisco and they put us in Letterman Hospital. Stayed there eight or ten days. They didn't give us much of a checkup.

They called out my name one day: "Here's a check for Maurice E. Wilson. It's twelve hundred dollars." I said, "What do you mean, twelve hundred dollars? For three years and five months? I'm not gonna take that check." They said, "You got to." I said, "I don't have to do nothin'!" If I hadn't got to kickin', raisin' hell—I got about five thousand dollars, the way it was.

I got one eye. My feet hangs down. I got a joint mashed in my back. I got a shoulder been broke. Feel that knot right there. But I'd go fight for my country right today.

I knew why the boys were fightin' there in Vietnam. To keep them communists from gettin' on closer to us. Why, we don't wanna let 'em get too close to us. Just like these Cubans down here, I'da never let them Cubans come in here. Now we got to feed 'em. I might be hard-hearted, but let all them Cubans come out here, I'da got me a machine gun and made 'em turn around and go back.

If it was ever to come up again and they'd need me, I'd be ready to go. I'm not a draft dodger. You're darn right. I'd go right now, boy.

PETER BEZICH

"I'm sixty-two plus. You don't go any further than that. I was a carpenter by trade, construction. When I got outa the service, that was the handle I picked up. I carried it for thirty-five years. I get a pension from the carpenters and a pension from Uncle Sam. So that doesn't hurt too bad."

He points toward a Chicago skyscraper: "When they put this building up, I used to walk that outside beam, all the way to the roof."

He is six feet plus, large-boned. He is nobody you'd care to tackle, no matter what his age. "I could throw you over my shoulder," he says. It is not a boast; it is, I suspect, a simple matter of fact.

"I heard the Great White Father say that we've been attacked. So it was just a matter of time: the whole neighborhood was in the service. We're a closely knit three, four square blocks, near White Sox ball park. Irish, Croatian, Polish, Italian, Slav. They were all hard-workin' people.

"I was drafted in '42. When I came home, I found we lost a lotta buddies in my neighborhood."

I was infantry. Dogface. I never had a gun in my hand. Nothin'. Then we had our basic in Schofield Barracks. Oahu. Next stop for the Twenty-fourth Division: Sydney, Australia. I was with the Medical, as an aide man to the task force. We had our first casualty: the guy got hit by a streetcar. (Laughs.) That was our first war hero. The streetcars go on the wrong side of the street, and he stepped off the curb. There was Brisbane and Rockhampton. We were goin' towards the northern part. They had expected the Japanese to come from New Guinea. It never materialized because they were held at Bougainville by the Aussies. We went up to what they call Goodenough Island or somethin'. The beginning of '43. We had our escapades through New Guinea. It was my fortune or unfortune to run across a Japanese outpost involving cannibalism. We saw where their rumps were bein' eaten by their own.

What's there to say about combat? It's an ugly word. I'm a kook. My mind's always workin'. I even invented a bomb. There was a buddy of mine, Tut Grode from Neenah, Wisconsin. We sent it to Dr. Vannevar Bush in Washington, D.C. We got a big diploma and all that bull. It was an antipersonnel bomb. Much like what they use today. We called it a G-B bomb—Grode and Bezich. I like to kid around.

We had some bad eggs that were commanding officers. I was close to being court-martialed over that bomb. When I gave my coordinates of where I was, I gave it to my commanding officer to censor. In them days they used to censor your mail. He wanted to court-martial me for disclosing my position. There was a colonel in the outfit was a construction man. He says, "You fool around with Pete, you answer to me." Because it was man-to-man over there. You don't take this. Anyhow, it passed.

We went to this island, Panaon, where President Kennedy got shot up with the PT boats? I got a few little pins. The real hero in our family was my brother, Bill, who's retired down in Florida. He got about twenty-one awards. I got a Silver Star. Hand-to-hand.

He hesitantly hands me an old newspaper clipping—1943. It reads:

The Silver Star for gallantry recently was awarded Private Peter N. Bezich, son of Mrs. Philomena Bezich at 221 West 35th Street, for repeatedly crawling into no man's land to rescue and render first aid to wounded buddies. He's a medical aide man in the Philippines.

I was in every island in the Philippines. I was on the beach in Leyte when General MacArthur landed. They were taking movies of our great hero, of him comin' in with his hat. We're watchin'. All of a sudden we see 'im takin' off and comin' in again. This was the second take, so to speak. (Laughs.) I have returned, right? I didn't have my helmet on. He told me, "Where's your helmet?" I said, "Is it necessary?" He didn't have one on, just the crushed hat.

Oh, MacArthur, he was building his little palace there. While we were there, they put us on one-third rations. In the meantime, they're flyin' in furniture for his retreat, so to speak. Anybody that wrote back about it wrote, "Cancel the bonds." Remember, we were buying war bonds, even though we were in the service, or the folks were buyin' it. They says, "Forget it, we're not payin' for this guy's palace on the hill."

We were on the front lines for thirty-one days, waitin' for our relief. I almost lost my life in Davao. The commanding officer wanted us to give up our foxholes for another officer, who came to this hill where we were. He told me an' Charlie Browd, some Indian, he said, "Will you give up your foxholes to the colonel and his captain?" I said no way. (Laughs.) When you're out in the jungle, everybody digs their own hole. You don't play God to these guys. I got away with it. That's like me takin' your gun. You're at the front and I don't have a gun, so I take your gun?

We went down over the hill when the attack came. The two guys jumped into our holes. A mortar fell right in that hole and blew 'em to hell. If we'da stayed in those holes, that woulda been the end of us. The mortars were poppin' everywhere. They were hittin' us on the ridge. When you put yourself up on a ridge, they see you easy. We were up there for some thirty-one days before they come with another outfit to relieve us.

One guy got shot and I hadda carry him back to the clearing company. I carried him over my shoulder. I'm a strong guy, even now. I could throw you over like a sack of potatoes. Anyway, the guy got shot in the rump and he lived in Elgin. (Laughs.) After I took him to the clearing company, I hadda rejoin my outfit. On the way back, I got pinned down by the Japanese. Every time I'd move, you hear a shot. I found a little depression and I fell in. They were hittin' all around me. So I took my helmet on a stick and I stuck it on the other end of the ravine and I took off.

I came to the outfit. There's a monument in Davao—someday I hope to go down there and see it, because that's the closest I came to death. The guy that was layin' there said, "Don't stay there. The guy that was there just got hit." I said, "They can't shoot in the same place twice." Just for the hell of it, I rolled over and, sure enough, bullets were breakin' off the marble there. I'd like to go back and see those spots now. That's a monument in honor of some big Japanese industrialist.

There's this Pinamalayan. That's where I got a boat from the Japanese, an outboard. I was one of the first Americans to own property in the war. I beached it because we used to go out with it and we'd get strafed by our own men. So the captain said, "You either paint a flag on it or leave it." So it was beached and I left it there to the mayor. His name is Reyes.

I even kept correspondence with these people. They felt I saved this girl's life. This one woman was raped and shot in the groin by a Jap, so I went under her house and dragged her out. There was another Philippine woman, she didn't have the nutrition for somebody that had a baby. I helped her have a baby. Another one, she was sick. Philippine guerrillas came after me, they called me Doctor York. I don't know why. They gave me guns, eggs, chickens, everything.

They had a dinner in my honor when I came back with the task force. They carried me half a kilometer on their shoulders, to honor Doctor York. These Filipinos would adopt ya into the family. They opened up their local pub and drank this *tuba*. It was like a beer or booze. This guy Reyes chased everybody out and said, "My son is home!" And all these soldiers sayin', "Who the hell's his son?" "It's Pete, you know." And then they had that dinner for me. If you didn't taste everything that they put in front of ya, you hurt their feelings. They'd have a ten-course. (Laughs. Without pause, his tears flow, and he continues with some difficulty.)

There was an adjustment period back home, because there wasn't any work at that time. I joined the 52–20 club. I coulda been deferred —I was a precision-tool grinder when I left.

Oh yeah, we were fightin' fascism. Kids today don't even know what fascism is. We won the war but we lost the peace. Japan and Germany today, their technology and economy surpasses us. Even to this day, I'm bitter about Japanese and German goods.

We were friends of Russia, right? My dad even went to their rallies, the Soviet-American friendship rallies. This was during the war, and don't forget, we're a Slavic family. And they paid a price, twenty million dead people, right? You'd have to light a candle for that amount of humanity.

People in America do not know what war is. I do, and anybody that was in the service. The Russians know. The Polish know. The Jewish know. But the American people have no idea what all-out war is. We never tasted it. I hope we never do.

My brother, he was the all-American kid, Jack Armstrong. He's being elevated in the military. He's a career man. They're checking out his background and all that bull, the FBI. They came to my dad, to his job, and they said somethin' about Russia and all that. This is just after the war, right? And they said, "What're you? Communists or somethin'? You know Russia's our enemy." The curtain and all that stuff. My dad says, "Hey, weren't they fightin' with us?" The government was sayin' they're our allies, and all of a sudden they turn it around and the Russians are no good.

They wanted to know about my brother. Did he have any leanings to the left? Did he do this? Did he do that? I said, "You couldn't find a more all-American kid than my brother." He was in the Battle of the Bulge, yeah.

Now we come to my two sons and Vietnam. I get mad about that patriotism. If your house is on fire, I'll help you put out the fire. If you argue with your wife, I'm not gonna get in between. It's like we had our revolution here. When they talk about reds and redniks, we did our fighting here. The American Revolution. Look what the French did there. We got sucked in by the French.

My war's over, right? Then they come up with Vietnam. My one son was gettin' outa school and he went to Vietnam for a year and a half. The other son refused to be drafted. It wasn't on religious principles, because we're not church people. He said killing was against his principles. Steve didn't burn no draft cards. He said, "I'll go to Vietnam and build hospitals." He was in construction, with me. They even interviewed the guys at work. Steve was the nicest kid you could know. He's a do-gooder. He donates one day a week to Shedd Aquarium for no pay. He's an all-American kid. It's a shame. It has ruined his life.

What he did took more guts than what I did. These big heroes grab him, put 'im in handcuffs right away, like a criminal. It really hurts. They put him in county jail. The kid never had a ticket in his life. It's like takin' a flower and cuttin' it and just throwin' it in a corner.

Governor Thompson, he was the U.S. attorney, he kept sayin': "He's a nice kid, I got nothin' against him, but I gotta do my thing." He wanted to make a deal where they're gonna put him someplace where it won't be too bad. But Judge Hoffman,* he wouldn't even let the kid give his statement as to his feelings. When he started to talk, Hoffman ruled it out. He wouldn't let him talk to the jury, right? Lloyd Wendt† said he would come as a character witness. Hoffman says we don't need character witnesses.

My brother came here from Washington. He's got forty years in the service. He went in as a buck private. He was commissioned out in the field for his outstanding bravery. At this time, he was a colonel. Hoffman says, "You will not wear that uniform on the stand." They made him take off his army jacket with all the awards. I'm surprised that the U.S. Army let somethin' go like that. To me, that's disrespect to the uniform.

Steve got three years. He did full time. He wouldn't even take probation. He said, "I didn't commit any crime against society. I'm not here to"—how would you say?—"perpetuate this prison system." He says, "That's your thing, you put me here." He wouldn't work. Oh, they wanted to put him to work at a dollar-fifty an hour as a mechanic. For overhauling Volkswagen engines or somethin'. He says, "I didn't come here to work for somebody." (Laughs.)

They give 'im a hard time and I had to go up there. Warden gimme that pitch: "Pete, you're Catholic, I'm Catholic, and I'll see that the kid goes straight." I says, "You can lead a horse to water, but can't make him drink. You will not make him do nothin'. If you'll try, I'll have a dead son. But maybe somebody else will be dead, too."

When Steve was in jail, they beat 'im up. When I'd ask him for his feeling, he was never bitter. I'd say, "Aren't you bitter against Hoffman?" He'd say, "I don't hold nothin' against him. He's playin' his role in society the way he's programmed to." He was the kid who tried to tell Hoffman that he'd pick up a crippled bird or somethin'. He likes animals, birds, fish. He was a nature kid. His hope was to be in the woods somewhere.

The whole neighborhood, policemen, whatever, would come over and say, "We're a hundred percent with your kid. If we can help you in any way . . ." They said it took a lotta moxie. It's a neighborhood that were mostly World War Two veterans.

To me, World War Two was an experience that I wouldn't wanna repeat, but I'm glad I did my share. I think it would've been a

*The late Judge Julius Hoffman, who presided at the trial of the Chicago Seven.
†Chicago author and former newspaper editor.

catastrophe if Hitler would've won. We can be thankful for all the boys who lost their lives.

Let's face it, it's forty-some years ago and we forget. People are getting so mechanical in thinking, they forget.

ANTON BILEK

He's still wiry, with just a slight touch of middle-aged flab. His appearance is that of an old-time welterweight fighter. Or an Eddie Stanky–type infielder.

He runs a greenhouse and flower shop in Rantoul, Illinois, near the Chanute air base. "Nothin' but you and the flowers, and they don't talk back to you.

"Prior to the war, I was a go-getter. Now, I live on the only hill in town. I very seldom leave the place. I get up in the morning, tend my flowers, and I go back to sleep at night. I have my shot of bourbon and beer at night and stay away from people.

"I'd like to go back to the Philippines again. I got a lotta memories there. They've got the most beautiful cemetery in the world for our boys."

A lotta friends I lost. We had 185 men in our squadron when the war started. Three and a half years later, when we were liberated from a prison camp in Japan, we were 39 left. It's them I think about. Men I played ball with, men I worked with, men I associated with. I miss 'em.

I got in the Philippines in 1940 for a two-year term. I enlisted in 1939. I was nineteen. Jobs were hard to get. I was always interested in building things, especially aircraft. I wanted to pursue that, but I didn't have money for school. I found a little brochure: Join the air corps and learn a trade. So I joined, went down to Chanute, went through sheet-metal school. After I graduated, they shipped me to the Philippine Islands. I went right to Clark Field, about sixty miles due north of Manila.

He shows me a photograph of Clark Field in 1939. It is startlingly plain and bare.

There were only about 250 men there at the time. We had only one bomb squadron, the Twenty-eighth. I worked repairing the old B-10s.

Things were real slow then. In mid-1941, they started bringin' in the troops.

We could never believe that the Japanese would attack the United States of America. That was out of the question. So we didn't pay too much attention. We were going through alerts, starting in November. I was assistant machine gunner to old Sergeant Amos. It was an old Lewis machine gun from World War One, an air-cooled job.

On December 8—that's December 7 here—an alert sounded around nine o'clock. All the fighters and all the B-17s took off. We thought, Gosh, General MacArthur's payin' us a visit and we're showin' him. Soon all the airplanes came back. It was about eleven-thirty or so. I got through eating and went into the dayroom. I was thumbin' through a sports magazine and the radio was playin'. All of a sudden, the newscaster from Manila stops the music: "Clark Field's been bombed." He starts shouting: "The Japanese have attacked Clark Field."

I got up, looked out the window, and I didn't see any bombers. Everything's real calm. I sat down and told the guy next to me, "D'ya hear that?" He said, "Oh, Jesus, some of that crap." There's all kinda rumors floatin' around. I thought this is a good time for me to start writing down all these rumors and the date I heard 'em on. In a coupla months, it would be a good laugh. I went back to my bunk, had a little black address book, and I started writing the rumor of Pearl Harbor being bombed in the morning. We couldn't believe that. And now we're hearin' that Clark Field's been bombed. I'm sittin' here and there's nothing dropped. (Laughs.)

Just then the first sergeant ran in, shouting, "It's the real thing. Here they come!" I grabbed all my gear, a Springfield rifle, a World War One model, and threw my helmet on, my gas mask, and I ran out of the barracks.

As soon as I hit our little machine-gun pit, the bombs started droppin'. I stood up and says, "So that's what it sounds like." Amos grabbed me by the back of the pants and pulled me back. 'Cause I'd been seein' a lot of that stuff on newsreels, about what's goin' on in Poland, what's goin' on in Europe. The real thing is kinda surprising.

They leveled the whole field. Tremendous bombing. They didn't miss anything. All our airplanes had just come in and were being refueled.

When our airplanes first took off that morning, the Japs did come in. They hit the city of Baguio in the northern part of Luzon, and then went back to Formosa. Our planes couldn't find 'em, so they come back and were outa fuel. They didn't see the bombing, they were twenty thousand feet up. So they went to chow and got some lunch. And that's when the Japs come in to Clark Field. As they left, after leveling us, Amos and I got out of the pit. We were flabbergasted.

We look around and see all this devastation, airplanes burning, hangars burning, gas trucks burning. Men yelling and screaming. Wounded and dead all over the place. Jap fighters followed 'em in, about eighty of 'em. Just strafed everything that stood. Amos started shootin' at 'em with our little old putt-putt. (Laughs.) I stood by with the ammunition box. After it was over, we were kinda in shock.

This shouldn't have happened to us. We were Americans, they were Japanese. They weren't supposed to bomb us. This is the way we were talkin' about it. (Laughs.) We were always told that they all wore glasses and they didn't have a decent bombsight. And they didn't have any navy to amount to anything. They were usin' all our scrap metal, all our oil. You always thought that way. Jesus Christ, how the hell'd this happen?

For the next month, there wasn't much to do. We did help some of the squadrons repair their aircraft and make one good one out of maybe three or four bombed ones. Then they started shippin' the men out. We had nothing left any more, see? We lost a lotta men.

We flew the bombers down to the Del Monte pineapple plantation on Mindanao, oh, seven hundred, eight hundred miles south. It was the only other air base in the Philippines that could hold a B-17. We had about sixteen B-17s left out of thirty-five. And our P-40s, we had about fifty percent of those left. We had nothin' left to fight 'em with. We tried to use our planes strategically, but the Jap Zero was a better maneuverable aircraft than our P-40.

One thing that hurt us, we knew of Pearl Harbor, we had eight hours to do something and we didn't. We had airfields where we could have dispersed our craft. I've loaded fifty-five-gallon drums at different air bases throughout the Philippines. Consequently, we lost 'em. The Japanese had the run of the land.

We stayed there till Christmas Eve, 1941. We were thinking, Hell, we're gonna get the troops in here. They're gonna fly in supplies, stuff. We heard of a convoy that was coming in with fifty-four A-24 dive bombers. We didn't have a single dive bomber. We heard artillery was comin' over. That was the war plan, see? Battleships and everything. The navy would protect a convoy to come to the Philippines. But here was our navy resting on the mud flats of Pearl Harbor. We didn't know the damage inflicted on Pearl Harbor, how bad it was.

Christmas Eve, we get orders: retreat to the Bataan peninsula. About a hundred miles. The first sergeant said, "I need five volunteers. You, you, you—" the five of us he pointed at were the volunteers. (Laughs.) "You're gonna stay here at Clark Field while the rest of the men move out."

On December 22, General Homma's forces landed at Lingayen Gulf on the northern part of Luzon. Another force landed on Lamon Bay. They formed a pincer movement on Manila. MacArthur had about seventy thousand Filipino troops but no equipment. General Wainwright was at Lingayen, but he had just one little regiment of American infantry and some Filipinos. He didn't have any aircraft, no dive bombers. So they landed without opposition.

We five guys are still at Clark Field. Our shavetail, a second lieutenant, just came into the army out of college. A slim Jim. He didn't know what he was there for, either. Next morning, Christmas Day, Major Johnson pulls up in a staff car: "Lieutenant, this is your air base. This is your staff, these five privates. You have a gas truck and an oil truck." The gas truck is full of three thousand gallons of high-octane gasoline. "You will service any of our P-40s that makes a forced landing here. When you think it's fit to leave Clark Field, that's entirely up to you." And the major took off for Bataan.

We were there for four days. We could hear the fighting at Tarlac, about twenty miles north. We slept on mattresses on the airfield, in case aircraft did come in. We could see the flashes from the artillery and hear the boomin'. I nudged the lieutenant: "Don't you think it's time to leave?" (Laughs.) The shootin's gettin' pretty close, with three thousand gallons of gasoline. That's a big bomb in itself. All it takes is one tracer bullet into that thing. We gotta get that down to Bataan.

He says, "Tomorrow morning." We had our last meal—cleaned everything up. We had our last bacon and eggs for the next three and a half years.

He says, "Bilek, you ride shotgun on the gas truck." Two other fellas went with the oil truck. He followed us in a command car. We keep at maybe a mile or two intervals. In case a Jap fighter comes in, he won't get both of 'em. (Laughs.) It's a lot of BTUs in there for an explosion—British thermal units—boom!

The cab and the trailer were ill-mated. Here we gotta take this about a hundred miles through all kindsa traffic. A little bit of braking and you're gonna jackknife, 'cause there's a lotta weight in three thousand gallons of gas. If it turns up, we're gone. We do have a few hairy adventures but nothing drastic. We finally got to Bataan.

The first sergeant tells me I'm now with the Twenty-eighth Matériel Squadron: clerks, truck drivers, machinists, sheet-metal men. We all had Springfield rifles and were sent to the front as infantrymen. Some of the guys never fired a rifle in their life. The machine guns we had were all homemade, we took off the old P-40s that were destroyed. Our job was to keep in shape the last four P-40s we had left.

American troops were still at Corregidor, at the mouth of Manila Bay. They had big heavy guns there to stop any entrance into the bay. In March of '42, the Japanese were bringing in shiploads of more men, because they couldn't break our front line. We'd just blow the hell out of 'em. We had tremendous artillery, and the Filipino scouts were terrific. We held 'em back for about three months.

That last month, from March 3 to April 9, we had one P-40 left. We patched it up. We had this one fighter that looked like an airplane with the measles. We're still waiting for the convoy. MacArthur's tellin' us it's on the way. President Quezon of the Philippines was told personally by President Roosevelt that the United States will do everything to assist. All the time, they knew that nothing was coming. We always looked to see if the ships were in yet. But nothin' ever showed up.

One guy comes in with a letter he drafted to the President of the United States: "Dear Mr. President: Please send us another P-40. The one we have is full of holes." (Laughs.) So we got a laugh out of that.

They broke our line finally, and we started to retreat down to the tip of Bataan. The orders were to burn, destroy everything. We threw all our tools away, stuff was burnin', it was chaos— (A long pause, he is softly sobbing.) Son of a bitch. You see all these guys comin' back from the front, dirty and wounded and tryin' to find their outfit —(Very softly) God damn. Big ammunition dumps blowin' up all over the place. It was like another world.

While we're retreating, Bataan is hit with an earthquake. We're marchin' down the road and the earth is shakin' You don't know what the hell to do. Is the earth comin' to an end? Is that it? Is this hallelujah? Did we buy the farm?

The next morning, we got orders to get rid of all our arms and wait for the Japanese to come. General King had surrendered Bataan. They came in. First thing they did, they lined us up and started searchin' us. Anybody that had a ring or a wristwatch or a pair of gold-rimmed spectacles, they took 'em. Glasses they'd throw on the floor and break 'em and put the gold rims in their pockets. If you had a ring, you handed it over. If you couldn't get it off, the guy'd put the bayonet right up against your neck. Fortunately I never wore a ring. I couldn't afford one.

They moved us about on the road. Here was a big stream of Americans and Filipinos marchin' by. They told us to get in the back of this column. This was the start of the Death March. (A long, deep sigh.) That was a sixty-mile walk. Here we were, three, four months on half-rations, less. The men were already thin, in shock. Undernourished, full of malaria. Dysentery is beginning to spread. This is even before the surrender. We had two hospitals chuck-full of men. Bataan peninsula was the worst malaria-infected province of the Philippines.

The Japanese emptied out the hospitals. Anybody that could walk, they forced 'em into line. You found all kinda bodies along the road. Some of 'em bloated, some had just been killed. If you fell out to the side, you were either shot by the guards or you were bayoneted and left there. We lost somewhere between six hundred and seven hundred Americans in the four days of the march. The Filipinos lost close to ten thousand. At San Fernando, we were stuffed into boxcars and taken about thirty-five miles further north. The cars were closed, you couldn't get air. In the hot sun, the temperature got up there. You couldn't fall down because you were held up by the guys stacked around you. You had a lot of guys blow their top, start screamin'. From there, they marched us another seven, eight miles to Camp O'Donnell, which was built hurriedly for the Philippine army. It was built like the huts were built, of native bamboo and *nipa* and grass. There must've been about nine thousand of us and about fifty thousand Filipinos. Americans in one camp, Filipinos in the other. We had to leave after a month and a half. The monsoon season was starting. A hurricane blew down two of the barracks. Eighty men were killed. Just crushed.

I went blind, momentarily. It scared the hell out of me. I was at the hospital for about two weeks, and the doctor, an American, said, "There's nothing I can do with you. Rest is the only thing. Eat all the rice you can get. That's your only medicine." That's the one thing that pulled me through. He said, "You won't have to go on details." The Japanese were comin' in and they'd take two, three hundred and start 'em repairing a bridge that was blown up. We were losin' a lot of men there. They couldn't work any more. They were dyin'.

Every room at the hospital was full. They were built on stilts. It was cool underneath, where I was put. I started to swell. I got beriberi. Lack of vitamin B-1. Your kidneys stops functioning. The fluids just stay in your body. You blow up like a balloon. I was seein' guys die all around me. Americans, at 50 a day. Filipinos, around 350. We buried close to 2,000 Americans at Camp O'Donnell. They buried between 28,000 and 30,000 Filipinos.

They moved us to another camp at Cabanatuan, about fifty miles away. I rode on the back of a truck. My testicles were the size of a sixteen-inch softball. I couldn't wear pants. I was naked from the waist down. It was some ride.

I got rid of beriberi and started off with amoebic dysentery. You couldn't eat anything. You couldn't pass anything but mucus and blood. The biggest thing, you had to have a buddy-buddy system, somebody that'd get on your butt and make you eat the damn rice. I always remembered what the doctor told me and I ate it. Today, I love it.

The Japanese stayed away from the hospital. They were afraid they'd catch it. There was one ward in the hospital at Cabanatuan which we called Saint Peter's Ward. In this room were the guys who were on their last legs. They were down to seventy, eighty pounds, and unable to control themselves. They were stripped down, laid on the floor, and medics would come swab 'em off, move 'em over, and swab down the area they soiled. From June 11 to November we lost another fifteen hundred men.

This is still '42. In the first six months of captivity, we lost about four thousand men, almost one-third of the force we had on Bataan. Besides those, they brought in the men from Corregidor, when Wainwright surrendered.

Now they started shippin' men to Japan. They needed laborers there. So they got sixteen hundred men in an old freighter. They'd tell our commander to pick out the most healthful.

Around June 1943 I went to the well side. I worked on a large

farm. We grew sweet potatoes, cucumbers, squash, and tropical vegetables. We got some and I started to put on weight. We did get some
meat. Every once in a while, they'd butcher a carabao and we had
some beef soup.

In June of '44, they asked for another detail to go to Japan. I
volunteered for it. I talked to a buddy, Bob, who I knew from
Chicago. I said, "Let's get the hell out of here." We'd been hearing
some rumors where our troops are movin' up, gettin' some foothold
into the islands here. Down south, Guadalcanal and this stuff. When
they come in, they're not gonna come in like a ballet dancer. They're
gonna come in with both guns firin' from the hip. They can't afford
to be very fussy. We could be bombed by 'em or shot by 'em.

We went to Japan and were fortunate we chose that detail. The ship
that left right after us with another sixteen hundred men aboard was
torpedoed by one of our submarines. All sixteen hundred drowned.
We lost close to five thousand men killed by our U.S. Navy, on
freighters being transported to Japan. None of the ships were
marked, so our navy people didn't know this.

It was a mean old freighter, rusty goddamn thing, full of bedbugs.
It stunk to high heaven. It took us sixty days from Manila to Moji,
Japan. We stopped at Formosa for two weeks, loadin' up with salt.
It's the only ballast we had.

We worked in a coal mine in Omuta, about twenty-five miles east
of Nagasaki, across the bay. We were surprised at the nice quarters
we had. The food was tremendous. In other words, we got some
vegetables in our soup. One time we got a bun. For sixty days on the
boat, we had nothin' but wormy rice. You swallowed all the worms.
We called that our protein. They quarantined us, because we were
in such poor shape after sixty days of two dabs of rice a day. They
decided we needed some rest and a little bit more food, so we could
do some work in the mines.

The mines were the property of Count Mitsui, the industrialist. We
were really workin' for him. Plus they had Korean prisoners. The
Japanese who supervised us were, you might say, 4-Fs, either too old
for the army or somethin' wrong with 'em. We'd work, maybe six or
eight of us, with one Jap supervisor.

You did find some good Japs there. Some of the old men were nice
to us. But the majority could not see looking up at an American who
was much taller than him. This they hated with a passion. I got the
devil whaled out of me quite a few times because I couldn't under-

stand. The school they took us to, the Jap would hold up a shovel or a pick and say the Japanese word. You gotta remember all this. My first day in the mine, he talks to me and I couldn't understand. So he decked me. It made him feel good, I guess.

Once in a while you'd find a good Jap. Right away you learned his name. If you could get Fiji-san or Okamoto-san, he's a good one. Some of them guys would take you on the side and you'd sit down and rest. One time, at the end of the day, while I was waitin' for the little train to take our shift out, I laid back against the rock wall, put my cap over my eyes, and tried to get some rest. The guy next to me says, "God damn, I wish I was back in Seattle." I paid no attention. Guys were always talking about being back home. He said, "I had a nice restaurant there and I lost it all." I turned around and looked and it's a Japanese. He was one of the overseers. I was flabbergasted.

He said, "Now just don't talk to me. I'll do all the talkin'." He's talkin' out of the side of his mouth. He says, "I was born and raised in Seattle, had a nice restaurant there. I brought my mother back to Japan. She's real old and knew she was gonna die and she wanted to come home. The war broke out and I couldn't get back to the States. They made me come down here and work in the coal mines." I didn't know what the hell to say to the guy. Finally the car come down and I says, "Well, see you in Seattle someday." And I left. I never saw him after that.

One of the Japanese officers in our camp was born and raised in Riverside, California. He pitched for his college team. He was the chief interpreter. He was no good. He'd sneak around and listen to us in the dark, and if he didn't like what we were sayin', he'd turn us in.

Our camp was one of the worst. Both camp commanders were executed by war-crimes trial, and two of the guards, because of the treatment to war prisoners.

I lost about fifty pounds in the war. Once I came down with double pneumonia. This was the big killer, and I beat it. The doctor was elated. They'd given me up. No sooner do I get rid of it than I come down with beriberi again. I swelled up. This was the worst I had. I was so big I was like a walrus. I couldn't move. If I had to defecate, they'd roll me over on the side and put the bedpan up against my butt and then they'd wash me. Your hand is so big around, you could stick your finger in it and make a big hole. They had to make a special bed for me.

The work we were doin' was against the Geneva Convention. No prisoners were supposed to be used in any type of work that aided in the manufacture of war stuff for the enemy.

Now we were seeing the B-29s flying over on their way to Tokyo, and bombin' towns. They bombed our town. They burned it down. I was in the hospital with beriberi. I was one of the very few that couldn't go down into the bomb shelter, because I was immovable. Out of the window, I watched B-29s come over, one by one, layin' down their incendiaries.

When the Japs got rough, we knew they were catchin' hell. Our troops were givin' it to 'em. We knew what was happenin' from some of the good guards who told us: Tokyo was *nai*. No more Tokyo.

One day I knew they were really near. We were ready to go on our shift. It was a sunny day. You seldom saw the sun. I just sat there, took off my cap, held my face to the sun, and absorbed the rays. It felt so good. All of a sudden, here come two aircraft. They dropped bombs right outside the compound and zoomed off. I heard some of the guys yell, "They're ours!" So I go run out. By Christ, I saw 'em turn around and come back and they started machine-gunning. They shot up one corner of the hospital. They didn't know it was a hospital. They were after a gun emplacement.

The big thing about it is, they were fighter aircraft. Jesus, they're close. They had to be within three hundred miles to send fighters. This was like sittin', bein' given anything we wanted to eat. It was heaven. Here they are!

I guess it was August 9 when they dropped the A-bomb on Nagasaki. We were about twenty-five, thirty miles away. They dropped it around ten o'clock. There was nothin' between us and them but the bay. I felt the windows vibrate. The whole barracks shook. But it always shook when there was heavy demolition on Nagasaki. But this time, we turned around and there's the big mushroom, way up in the air.

We didn't know about Hiroshima. The guys said they must've hit an oil refinery for so much smoke to go up. We were due west of Nagasaki and prevailing winds usually come from the west. If there was any fallout, whether it hurt anybody in camp, I don't know.

A day or two after that, the end of the war. (Sighs deeply.) We were talkin' about it: What're you gonna do when the war's over? Well, I'm gonna get that son of a bitch, Fuji-san, that bastard beat me so many times. I'm gonna tear his toenails out or I'm gonna do this to 'im. Everybody had somethin' they were gonna do. (A half-laugh, half-cry.)

They got us all out on the parade ground. There were about nineteen hundred of us. About a thousand Americans, some Dutchmen, some Australians, some English. They lined us up and the Jap commander got up on his pedestal. And the interpreter (cries silently, sighs) he says, "Take care of yourself" (almost a whisper). He told us the war was over, and he turned around and left. The nineteen hundred men, you could hear a pin drop. Nobody said anything. Finally, some of the boys turned around and (cries; a long pause) they all walked back to the barracks. Nobody said a damn word. It was quiet, quiet. Just the shufflin' of feet. I went behind the first barracks there and I bawled like a baby.

It took a couple hours, and then the guys started yellin' and beatin' one another on the back. The day before that, they gave us a Red Cross parcel, with American food. They had these in camp for the past two years and they never gave us one of 'em. They had tons of food there brought in by the Red Cross ship. They also had medical supplies. And our doctors had been amputating legs without anesthetic.

The Japs left. They all took off. We were the only ones in camp. We didn't know where to go or what to do. We got the radio and we kept it turned on. Finally, American broadcasts start comin' over. It says: "All American prisoners, all prisoners of war, stay where you are. We're sending airplanes to look for you. Put a big POW on the barracks or on a parade ground, with sheets or paint or anything."

The B-29s found us and started droppin' us food. They told us there was an air base on the southern part of the island and told us they were flyin' in supplies from Okinawa. And they were flyin' back empty. We commandeered the first train we could, about a thousand of us. We found this air base. And they started flyin' us back to Okinawa, and from there to the Philippines.

The only thing you talked about is, What're ya gonna do? Where you gonna eat as soon as you get back? Everybody was goin' to Frisco. They wanted to go to Fisherman's Wharf. Everybody wanted to get some fried oysters or a big steak.

In camp, from the beginning to the end, you never talked of women. You never talked of sex. You never told stories. First thing you talked about is what you wanted in your stomach. Guys would tell stories about how their mother made this. Men would sit and listen very attentively. This was the big topic all the time.

I remember vividly this old Polack. One guy always wanted him to talk about how his mother made the cabbage rolls, the *golabki*. He had a knack of telling so you could almost smell 'em. He would say when he would be comin' home from school, he knew what he was gonna have to eat. When his mother made these *golabki*, he could smell 'em a block away. Oh, they'd get all excited. You'd see some of the fellas just lickin' their lips. Tasting it. You know?

I'm back home. It's all over with. I'd like to forget it. I had nothin' against the Japanese. But I don't drive a Toyota or own a Sony.

In 1967, I was working at Chanute air base as a civilian instructor. They sent me to the Pacific to teach men. This was during the Vietnam War. I went back to the Philippines. I went to Ben Hua in Vietnam, to Thailand, and I ended up in Japan.

I walked into the bachelor officer quarters. I threw down my orders on the desk and I says, "I need a room." There were about four or five Japanese working there. They were all standing around and talking, tellin' some kinda story and laughin'. That jabber just got me. I got hot all over and I banged on the desk: "Damn it, son of a bitch, come over here and give me the goddamn key to this room. Right now!" One guy ran over and gave me a key. He said, "You'll have to fill this form." I said, "Fill out shit." I took the form and said, "You want the goddamn thing? It'll be under my door." And I left. This—just the talk set me off. The staccato jabber I heard so much in the mines.

We should have dropped the A-bomb, yes. If we'd landed there with a force, we'd have killed off more people than were killed by the bomb. All the prisoners of war would have been killed, of course. I doubt if dropping it on an uninhabited place woulda done any good. Not to Japanese people. Maybe another people. They were a hard nut.

That war was different from Vietnam. Definitely. We were too easy in Vietnam, I believe. We had too many restrictions. Too many strings holdin' us back from things we shoulda done. Once you go to war, that's it. You can't say we can only do this and we can't do that. We needed more men like MacArthur and Patton.

I think we should be in any place that communism is threatening to take over. If we go in there, for God's sake, let's go in. Play the game like it should be or get the hell out. You can't go in halfway and the other guys all the way. That's not a good ball game.

He gently holds forth an old photo: men in baseball uniforms at Clark Field. He points to each man as he tells of him.

We had a ball club there. We played in Manila every weekend. Filipino teams, American teams, one Jap team. I pitched ball—I had a pretty good arm. At first base we had Max and O'Connell, they used to alternate. Both those men died at Cabanatuan. At second base was Andy Olds from Milwaukee. He was a Polack, a lovable guy. Andy made it back and he died of a heart attack shortly after he returned. At shortstop we had Armando Viselli. He was from Connecticut. Armando died in a reconnaissance flight over Lamon Bay on the twenty-second of December, 1941. At third base was Cabbage Clan, a Pennsylvania Dutchman—we called him Cabbage. He died when his ship was torpedoed off Mindanao. Torpedoed by a U.S. Navy submarine. We had two catchers. We had Beck. He was hit on the first day the Japanese bombed at Clark Field and his leg was badly mangled. He was shipped out on a hospital ship, and I don't know what happened to him. The other catcher was Dumas. He was from Massachusetts. Dumas was killed on the first day at Iba.

I'm the only one left out of the whole infield, the only one that came back. That's why I treasure that picture.

THE GOOD *REUBEN JAMES*

Have you heard of a ship
Called the good Reuben James
Manned by hard-fighting men
Of both honor and fame?

She flew the Stars and Stripes
Of this land of the free;
But tonight she's in her grave
On the bottom of the sea.

Tell me, what were their names?
Tell me, what were their names?
Did you have a friend
On that good Reuben James?

—Woody Guthrie

BILL BAILEY

Craggy-faced, bespectacled, six feet three, he's right out of a Rockwell Kent woodcut, crossed with American Gothic.

"My family came from Ireland and I was born in the slums of Jersey. Went to school up to fourth grade. When I was makin' my communion, the nuns sent my mother a letter: 'This boy is not going to make it unless he has a pair of shoes and a little suit of clothes.' My mother said, 'If you want him to wear shoes and a little suit of clothes, buy it for him. We haven't enough food to feed him, let alone shoes. He's going to make his communion if I have to bring him up to the altar naked. The Good Lord ran around with a potato sack wrapped around his ass, and if it's *good enough for him, it's good enough for anyone else.' Two days before communion, they bought the shoes and suit.*

"I'd go for days and days eating bread with salt on it or lard. The greatest thing I remember about wintertime, you'd reach out on the fire escape and pull in some snow, put condensed milk on it, and you had great ice cream. (Laughs.) When you come from that type of setup, you start questioning every goddamn thing."

He went to sea at fifteen. "I've been to just about all the countries of the world, seein' poverty I can't describe. It shook the hell out of me to see the marketplace—was it Ethiopia?—you go buy a piece of meat, you can't see the color, it's all covered with flies. Not just there. I could name a dozen places I been to, just as terrible. How the Christ can they take this? That's why I went to Spain in '36."

I'd been in Hamburg durin' the May Day demonstrations, just before the Nazis took over. Thirty-three, Hitler took over? This was '32. The storm troopers stood on the sidelines, jeered, and threw rocks. You could see the violence comin'. We're safe here in America. Nobody's payin' him any attention. Maybe we'll wake up in the mornin', just a bad dream. Or he may have a heart attack. Like a passing fad. Hell, I could see this son of a bitch was gonna eat up all Europe and eat us up.

One day, this was '35, I hear a guy named Simpson is dragged off the *Manhattan.* The ship's docked in Hamburg. Up comes a couple of storm troopers, bust in his locker, and find these stickers you put on subways: Fight Fascism. They work 'im over good, take him to court. There's a piece in the *New York Times:* American Seaman Accused of Being a Communist Working for the Underground. Arrested. Faces 20 Years.

You gotta have some friends someplace, so we decided we're gonna demonstrate at the pier of the *Bremen.* She was the flagship of the whole German merchant marine. Up on the bow of the *Bremen* was the swastika. Typical Hollywood style, they had big klieg lights shining down on that flag, when everything else was darkened. You could look outa your big hotel on Times Square, toward the waterfront, and whattaya see? This tremendous bright light and that red-and-black swastika. It was so brazen.

We said, We'll picket at the pier with placards askin' for the release of Simpson. Then somebody got the idea: Why don't we go aboard and take the goddamn flag off the bow of the ship? It sounded good. But to get to that flag was almost impossible. All the crew lives up in the bow. They see us movin' up, they're gonna beat the Christ out of us. We have to think of somethin'. We had a couple of Irishmen, real tough characters. We're gonna stand on the port side an' send a decoy down the starboard side an' create a little hollerin'. While they're doin' that, we're gonna dash up and get the flag.

All of a sudden, the *beep-beep*, the twenty-minute whistle: Everybody off, all ashore. The sailors got the bow blocked off. Meanwhile there's about ten thousand people on the dock demonstratin' and hollerin'. We decided it's now or never.

We sent up a guy by the name of Lowlife McCormick. The German mate says, "Get back." All I heard was a fist hit the guy's jaw. He toppled over, fell on his ass. McCormick took off. I was the third one pushin' my way up there. They got McCormick an' they're punchin' 'im. That left Blair, myself, and another Irishman.

As I worked my way up, Blair had some German, just beatin' the Christ outa him. He's jabbin' the German with a fountain pen. Blood comin' outa both faces. He hollers at me, "Keep goin'! Go!" The Irishman's gettin' it, too. Next thing I remember was over the hurdles. Bein' young then, all of nineteen years old, ya do all these goddamn things. Nowadays, I'd have a doctor alongside me.

With all the adrenaline pumpin', I found myself climbin' the last six little rungs. And there I had the swastika. When I did that, the scream from the dock was just deafening. I gave it one yank an' ripped the top part off. I kept yankin' to get the rest off an' the son of a bitch wouldn't come. Talk about panic. I looked down an' there's all kindsa fightin'. Some detective came aboard. A guy got shot. Passengers screamin', women goin' hysterical. A couple of our guys already laid out, unconscious, kicked in the head. I'm about ready to give up.

I notice a hand where my foot is. I want to stomp it, 'cause I think it's a Nazi comin' up to get me. It was Adrian Duffy. He said, "Hold the goddamn flag, Bill, and I'll snap, snap." I heard a switchblade come out and rip. The flag is free. I gave it one big jerk and it just floated down into the dirty Hudson.

Now, to get outa here. (Laughs.) People screamin', cops sendin' out alarm after alarm. People on the dock are happy. They've seen the Nazi flag for the first time get torn up. The skipper is hollerin' like a film director in Hollywood: "Go to the klieg, get that guy, lower a lifeboat, get another flag." Meantime, cops are comin' aboard. Two, three hundred. Okay, I jumped. They let go one, two, three, and laid me out flat as a goddamn doornail. I maybe got one guy, in the process, to belt.

There's blood all over me. They drag me to a little room. There's a guy layin' there. I seen two little eyes peerin' through this mess of blood. The cops says, "Is this him?" The guy says no. They took me out and walked me in again: "Okay, this is him." The guy says again, no. So they did it again. He looked at me again: no. He was a dumb son of a bitch, because the law of the cops is to pick anybody up and say that's him an' stick with it. If you can't get the guy who done it, get somebody.

It turns out this guy was Solomon, a Jewish detective, assigned to the *Bremen* to follow us guys around. He heard there was gonna be a fracas. He even tried to tell the steamship company. They said, "We don't need you cops, we'll take care of our own." When Solomon came chargin' up with a gun, the crew thought he was another demonstrator and they punched him out and stomped on 'im. By the time he reached for his badge an' kept sayin' "I'm a policeman," they stomped on 'im some more. That's the funny thing, a Jewish detective. Talk about just deserts, defendin' nazism.

The harbor patrol came up and they were nasty bad. Bang! Smash you right in the mouth. "Why, that son of a bitch beat up Solomon." "He beat up Solomon?" Bang! They really let ya have it.

We had six guys arrested. We didn't say who tore the flag down. We became known as the Bremen Six. The headlines in every newspaper throughout the country helped to make people see what the hell was goin' on. Goebbels issued an angry statement, so LaGuardia assigned ten detectives to go out to the German consulate. These were all Jewish detectives with names like Goldfarb, Ginsburg. Goebbels thought this was the biggest insult. He said, "We don't want these inferior bastards to guard any of our people." This could only happen in a city where you got a mayor that's a half Jew and half dago, somethin' like that. That's all LaGuardia needed. Man, he took off. He started layin' it on Goebbels. All this, you gotta remember, was 1935. The rest you know.

A few years later, there's a war and we're in it. I'm at the NMU* office, puttin' young kids aboard these ships by the dozens. Kids

*National Maritime Union.

who'd never seen a ship. I'd see these ships go out an' get torpedoed, some kids come back, a lot don't. Guys with frozen feet, toes off. These same kids goin' out again.

So I begin to say, How dare I sit behind a desk and ask these kids to go out? Out there is where I belong. I could never survive hereafter if the war ended and I didn't do some part. So I resign, go to engineering school, get my certificate. From then on, I sailed through the whole war as an engineer. My field was mostly the whole Pacific. Okinawa, the Solomons, Leyte, the whole Philippines. I didn't screw around. I took a rifle from the armory. (Laughs.) Me and another mate, we got right out there. The skipper says, "You can't do that. Suppose you guys get hurt?" (Laughs.)

We were the first ship in Subic Bay. Bullets were hittin' us all over the place. We went ashore and they brought us a couple of infantry. We still had our rifles, me and the mate. The only reason we got by is we had our uniforms on. The GIs didn't question us. They see these officers, gold braid, rifles in their hands.

We were never torpedoed. We seen submarines there where we were panicky. All we talked about on board was the war. You'd go completely bananas. What's gonna happen when it's finally over? What's the world gonna be like?

We were at sea when the chief engineer said, "I just heard over the radio that Roosevelt died." I said, "Jesus Christ! We grew up with that man practically." We called a ship's meeting and signed a document: We're behind the new President. Carry on till victory.

We're on our way to Okinawa, when we got word that the atom bomb dropped. I thought it was Adam, A-D-A-M. Somebody dropped an Adam bomb. What kinda bomb is that? They said it wiped out a city. I said, "This son of a bitch of an Adam, who the hell is he?" At that particular moment I said, "Gee, that's great." But secretly you had these feelings that somethin' was wrong. You couldn't place your hand on it, but you had a feeling.

And then bad things happened. That great camaraderie of savin' tinfoil, toothpaste tubes, or tin cans, all that stuff that made people part of somethin', that disappeared. Everybody was out for what they could get from then on. Everything changed.

I still think we're all part of somethin', call it the history of the human race, if you want to. I feel that if some guy ten years from now has got some halfway decent conditions, I wanna feel that I helped in some small way to make it possible for him to enjoy them conditions. I mean, that's the name of the game. I just want somebody to say, Them poor son-of-a-bitches, they musta taken a beating back in the old days. We don't know all the names, but glory to them, or somethin' like that. (Laughs.)

DAVID MILTON

A journalist.

In the first year of the war, merchant seamen had more casualties than anyone else. They were on the front line. I was an innocent eighteen-year-old in '42, shipping out of Boston on a Liberty ship. It took three, four weeks to load it. You'd see all these huge crates coming on board, labeled USSR: tanks, TNT, shells. Loaded to the gunnels. On the top decks, they put locomotives.

They started building these ships as rapidly as they could. They were very slow, plodding along at ten knots, totally helpless. In the beginning, all we had protecting us were little corvettes and destroyers. It was just a massacre. They stopped the convoys during the summer of '42. They resumed in the fall. That's when the Germans coordinated an attack of thousands of torpedo bombers and submarines. You took your life in your hands on those trips. This was before most of the American troops were involved. Merchant seamen were really in front of the front.

They recruited captains and seamen wherever they could find them. Ours had been a tanker captain, sailing for twenty-five years from Galveston to New York. He could do it in his sleep, but it's all he'd ever done. He didn't understand convoys: a hundred ships moving together. He had attended a navy conference where they explained signal hoists, whistle blasts, zigzags in order to avoid submarines. He didn't understand a word. He locked all these plans in his safe.

When we were three hundred miles off Boston, the whole convoy, a hundred ships, zigzags. He just keeps going straight. We're hit in the middle of the night by a 16,000-ton tanker. All our lifeboats were swept off the ship. We were wallowing in the sea. A ship on our convoy had been torpedoed a couple of hours before. You could still see the flames. The captain turned all the lights on and we saw this gaping hole in our side. These crates of TNT, explosives, were just floating out through the hole into the sea.

The captain hollered down to the first mate, "Is she taking water, Mr. Shurig?" The mate hollered back, "Taking water, hell, she's sinking." We got the ship back to Boston at a tilt, half under water. It went into dry dock for three months. I didn't want to stick around. I went off to New York to get on another ship. The ships were being sunk so rapidly by German submarines, I knew one seaman who was torpedoed twice in two weeks.

A number of my friends stayed on the ship I left. In the summer of '42, it made the really first North Atlantic convoy to Murmansk. It was hit right in the engine room. That's where I'd have been. Had I stayed on, I'd have undoubtedly been killed.

Murmansk, up in the Arctic Circle, was the only port open at the time. You leave Scotland, go all the way around the coast of Norway, up around the North Cape, and then down into Russia. The Germans had airfields all along Norway. Three days out of Scotland, you're under constant attack by bombers and submarines. That convoy lost something like seventy out of eighty ships.

It was kind of suicidal, but to an eighteen-year-old it was very exciting. I was so gung ho on the war. The National Maritime Union had been through tough fights with gangsters and thugs. It was a radical outfit. Many of them had fought in Spain. They saw this war as a continuation. The dangers of the Murmansk run didn't stop 'em. A lot of others, who found out where we were headed, got off.

If you were torpedoed, you would last maybe ten minutes in the freezing water. They gave you rubber suits to put on. It would take at least a half-hour to get into 'em. Even so, the chances are you'd freeze to death.

The time I went there, we had a number of screw-ups. We were carrying tanks and locomotives. In the middle of the Atlantic, these tanks broke loose in a big storm. They were Sherman tanks, twenty, thirty tons. As the ship would roll, these tanks would just slide through the hole and bang up against the bulkhead. Then they'd roll the other way, just shaking the ship apart. So we pulled out of the convoy. We headed into the sea, while the deck seamen went down below to secure those tanks. They were riding them like cowboys, trying to hook cables through. Finally, they got the tanks lashed down. The convoy just steamed off and left us. They didn't even leave a destroyer with us. One ship wasn't worth it. They were trying to protect a hundred ships.

There we were in the middle of the Atlantic all by ourselves. About five or six days later, we ended up on the coast of Ireland, because the captain got lost. We could have been interned for the war, because Ireland was neutral. We steamed back through some minefield and got to Scotland, where all the ships of our convoy were anchored. They thought we were lost, and here we showed up. (Laughs.) We finally took off for the northern run.

On a beautiful sunny day, we're filing singly through the Scottish islands. One ship runs on the rocks. A second one runs on the rocks. A third one runs on the rocks. Our bo'sun, on the bridge, says, "Captain, the ships are running aground." He just said, "Straight ahead." So we ended up on the rocks. Twenty million dollars worth of cargo. We pulled back into Edinburgh and the ship was unloaded.

This was '44. It was the time when we were getting ready for the invasion of France. Churchill wanted to locate old ships which would still run, or damaged ships like ours. They could be used as block ships in the Normandy invasion. That's where we ended up. We unloaded everything. They placed TNT charges throughout the ship, sawed holes in the bulkhead, so it was sunk to deck level, right off the beachhead. Sixteen ships did the job. All kinds of pontoons were attached to these ships. It made an artificial port in Normandy. It was Churchill's idea and a very good one.

They must have unloaded a million men or more and all their supplies. The Germans never believed it was possible. In two weeks, a huge storm came up and blew the whole harbor away. We came back to England with wounded soldiers right off the beach. The ship was up to deck level.

The third time I tried for Murmansk, I made it. It was early in '45. Convoys were safer now. They began to send aircraft carriers and cruisers and huge ships. Even so, we lost five or six ships. German pilots toward the end of the war were not as good. But it was still a deadly run. The Germans would fly very low and all our ships were firing at them. Shrapnel from these ships were coming onto ours.

The Russians used icebreakers in getting us through into Murmansk. Once you've passed, the ice closes in behind you. I'll never forget—I was twenty-one at the time—this Russian pilot came aboard. He had on a fur hat, a gold-buttoned black uniform, and polished black boots. The first mate hollers, "We're in the hands of the commies now!" (Laughs.) It's about twenty below. This fierce wind is blowing in this Russian's face, icicles on his eyebrows, his chin, his nose. Everyone else is huddled in the cabin. It was so co-o-o-old! He would open the door and say, "Two degrees port, three degrees starboard." And the wind would blow in and he'd close the door and stand out there in the wind, like a statue.

The convoy stopped. What's the matter? The Russians were hunting seals on the ice. That's what they ate. Our mate, who hated them, was cursing: "My God, we're fighting a war and these commies are getting seals." We ourselves got off and got some baby seals to bring back to the New York zoo as a contribution from the seamen.

We finally got to Murmansk with these huge locomotives on the very top of the deck. The Russians unloaded them right onto the tracks. They brought up freight cars and attached them to the locomotives. We unloaded the tanks right onto these flatcars. They'd right away fire up the locomotives and shoot right out to the front. I mean, they weren't playing around.

There was a very large Russian woman who was head of the whole dock. She was something. When I was having vodka at the bar ashore, a British captain told me this story. When his ship was unloaded, the iron beams were stacked on the dock. When they finished he told this woman, "You can put the beams back now, on ship." She said, "What beams? I thought they were cargo. They're already parts of tanks." He laughed: "You know better than that." She winked and slapped him on the back: "You rig up some wood. We need all the steel we can get." They'd use everything.

I remember hitchhiking through this deep snow, tryin' to catch up with this Russian truck. They couldn't stop because they'd get stuck in the snow. I'm running behind and some of these Russian women reached down, grabbed me, and pulled me up like a sack of potatoes. And slapped me on the back. (Laughs.) They were a formidable bunch.

For the first two years, half the ships going to Russia were being sunk. They weren't getting that many supplies. It was only toward the end of the war that they began to ship through the Persian Gulf. They built a railroad from Teheran to southern Russia, and ships went through the gulf. That's where the majority of the supplies came from. But this was after Stalingrad, when things were turning around.

All this time, certain columnists like Westbrook Pegler were clobbering the seamen: we're making all this money while the navy boys are sailing for twenty-seven dollars a month. Our answer was: The shipowners are makin' millions of dollars during the war. If they give up their profits during the war, we'll sail for the same wages as the navy. Otherwise, we're gonna fight for our union conditions. When these navy guys are released, they'll need some union conditions after the war.

On our ships, we had a big world map where the American enemies were, where the Russians were. Seamen were very international. There were Norwegians, Finns, Latvians, Egyptians, blacks, whites. It was a microcosm of the world. Talk about a polyglot bunch. I'd say my world view came from sailing the sea during World War Two.

ROSIE

PEGGY TERRY

She is a mountain woman who has lived in Chicago for the past twenty years. Paducah, Kentucky is her hometown. She visits it as often as her meager purse allows.

The first work I had after the Depression was at a shell-loading plant in Viola, Kentucky. It is between Paducah and Mayfield. They were large shells: anti-aircraft, incendiaries, and tracers. We painted red on the tips of the tracers. My mother, my sister, and myself worked there. Each of us worked a different shift because we had little ones at home. We made the fabulous sum of thirty-two dollars a week. (Laughs.) To us it was just an absolute miracle. Before that, we made nothing.

You won't believe how incredibly ignorant I was. I knew vaguely that a war had started, but I had no idea what it meant.

Didn't you have a radio?

Gosh, no. That was an absolute luxury. We were just moving around, working wherever we could find work. I was eighteen. My husband was nineteen. We were living day to day. When you are involved in stayin' alive, you don't think about big things like a war. It didn't occur to us that we were making these shells to kill people. It never entered my head.

There were no women foremen where we worked. We were just a bunch of hillbilly women laughin' and talkin'. It was like a social. Now we'd have money to buy shoes and a dress and pay rent and get some food on the table. We were just happy to have work.

I worked in building number 11. I pulled a lot of gadgets on a machine. The shell slid under and powder went into it. Another lever you pulled tamped it down. Then it moved on a conveyer belt to another building where the detonator was dropped in. You did this over and over.

Tetryl was one of the ingredients and it turned us orange. Just as orange as an orange. Our hair was streaked orange. Our hands, our face, our neck just turned orange, even our eyeballs. We never questioned. None of us ever asked, What is this? Is this harmful? We simply didn't think about it. That was just one of the conditions of the job. The only thing we worried about was other women thinking we had dyed our hair. Back then it was a disgrace if you dyed your hair. We worried what people would say.

We used to laugh about it on the bus. It eventually wore off. But I seem to remember some of the women had breathing problems. The shells were painted a dark gray. When the paint didn't come out smooth, we had to take rags wet with some kind of remover and wash that paint off. The fumes from these rags—it was like breathing cleaning fluid. It burned the nose and throat. Oh, it was difficult to breathe. I remember that.

Nothing ever blew up, but I remember the building where they dropped in the detonator. These detonators are little black things about the size of a thumb. This terrible thunderstorm came and all the lights went out. Somebody knocked a box of detonators off on the floor. Here we were in the pitch dark. Somebody was screaming, "Don't move, anybody!" They were afraid you'd step on the detonator. We were down on our hands and knees crawling out of that building in the storm. (Laughs.) We were in slow motion. If we'd stepped on one . . .

Mamma was what they call terminated—fired. Mamma's mother took sick and died and Mamma asked for time off and they told her no. Mamma said, "Well, I'm gonna be with my mamma. If I have to give up my job, I will just have to." So they terminated Mamma. That's when I started gettin' nasty. I didn't take as much baloney and pushing around as I had taken. I told 'em I was gonna quit, and they told me if I quit they would blacklist me wherever I would go. They had my fingerprints and all that. I guess it was just bluff, because I did get other work.

I think of how little we knew of human rights, union rights. We knew Daddy had been a hell-raiser in the mine workers' union, but at that point it hadn't rubbed off on any of us women. Coca-Cola and Dr. Pepper were allowed in every building, but not a drop of water.

You could only get a drink of water if you went to the cafeteria, which was about two city blocks away. Of course you couldn't leave your machine long enough to go get a drink. I drank Coke and Dr. Pepper and I hated 'em. I hate 'em today. We had to buy it, of course. We couldn't leave to go to the bathroom, 'cause it was way the heck over there.

We were awarded the navy E for excellence. We were just so proud of that E. It was like we were a big family, and we hugged and kissed each other. They had the navy band out there celebrating us. We were so proud of ourselves.

First time my mother ever worked at anything except in the fields —first real job Mamma ever had. It was a big break in everybody's life. Once, Mamma woke up in the middle of the night to go to the bathroom and she saw the bus going down. She said, "Oh my goodness, I've overslept." She jerked her clothes on, throwed her lunch in the bag, and was out on the corner, ready to go, when Boy Blue, our driver, said, "Honey, this is the wrong shift." Mamma wasn't supposed to be there until six in the morning. She never lived that down. She would have enjoyed telling you that.

My world was really very small. When we came from Oklahoma to Paducah, that was like a journey to the center of the earth. It was during the Depression and you did good having bus fare to get across town. The war just widened my world. Especially after I came up to Michigan.

My grandfather went up to Jackson, Michigan, after he retired from the railroad. He wrote back and told us we could make twice as much in the war plants in Jackson. We did. We made ninety dollars a week. We did some kind of testing for airplane radios.

Ohh, I met all those wonderful Polacks. They were the first people I'd ever known that were any different from me. A whole new world just opened up. I learned to drink beer like crazy with 'em. They were all very union-conscious. I learned a lot of things that I didn't even know existed.

We were very patriotic and we understood that the Nazis were someone who would have to be stopped. We didn't know about concentration camps. I don't think anybody I knew did. With the Japanese, that was a whole different thing. We were just ready to wipe them out. They sure as heck didn't look like us. They were yellow little creatures that smiled when they bombed our boys. I remember someone in Paducah got up this idea of burning everything they had that was Japanese. I had this little ceramic cat and I said, "I don't care, I am not burning it." They had this big bonfire and people came and brought what they had that was made in Japan. Threw it on the bonfire. I hid my cat. It's on the shelf in my bathroom right now. (Laughs.)

In all the movies we saw, the Germans were always tall and handsome. There'd be one meanie, a little short dumpy bad Nazi. But the main characters were good-lookin' and they looked like us. The Japanese were all evil. If you can go half your life and not recognize how you're being manipulated, that is sad and kinda scary.

I do remember a nice movie, *The White Cliffs of Dover*. We all sat there with tears pouring down our face. All my life, I hated England, 'cause all my family all my life had wanted England out of Ireland. During the war, all those ill feelings just seemed to go away. It took a war.

I believe the war was the beginning of my seeing things. You just can't stay uninvolved and not knowing when such a momentous thing is happening. It's just little things that start happening and you put one piece with another. Suddenly, a puzzle begins to take shape.

My husband was a paratrooper in the war, in the 101st Airborne Division. He made twenty-six drops in France, North Africa, and Germany. I look back at the war with sadness. I wasn't smart enough to think too deeply then. We had a lotta good times and we had money and we had food on the table and the rent was paid. Which had never happened to us before. But when I look back and think of him . . .

Until the war he never drank. He never even smoked. When he came back he was an absolute drunkard. And he used to have the most awful nightmares. He'd get up in the middle of the night and start screaming. I'd just sit for hours and hold him while he just shook. We'd go to the movies, and if they'd have films with a lot of shooting in it, he'd just start to shake and have to get up and leave. He started slapping me around and slapped the kids around. He became a brute.

Some fifteen years before, Peggy had recalled her experiences during the Great Depression. She and her young husband were on the road. "We were just kids. I was fifteen and he was sixteen. . . . It was a very nice *time, because when you're poor and you stay in one spot, trouble just seems to catch up with you. But when you're moving from town to town, you don't stay there long enough for trouble to catch up with you."**

One of the things that bothered him most was his memory of this town he was in. He saw something move by a building and he shot. It was a woman. He never got over that. It seems so obvious to say —wars brutalize people. It brutalized him.

The war gave a lot of people jobs. It led them to expect more than they had before. People's expectations, financially, spiritually, were raised. There was such a beautiful dream. We were gonna reach the end of the rainbow. When the war ended, the rainbow vanished. Almost immediately we went into Korea. There was no peace, which we were promised.

I remember a woman saying on the bus that she hoped the war didn't end until she got her refrigerator paid for. An old man hit her over the head with an umbrella. He said, "How dare you!" (Laughs.)

Ohh, the beautiful celebrations when the war ended. They were selling cigarettes in Paducah. Up until that hour, you couldn'ta bought a pack of cigarettes for love or money. Kirchoff's Bakery was giving away free loaves of bread. Everybody was downtown in the pouring rain and we were dancing. We took off our shoes and put 'em in our purse. We were so happy.

The night my husband came home, we went out with a gang of friends and got drunk. All of us had a tattoo put on. I had a tattoo put up my leg where it wouldn't show. A heart with an arrow through it: Bill and Peggy. When I went to the hospital to have my baby— I got pregnant almost as soon as he came home—I was ashamed of the tattoo. So I put two Band-Aids across it. So the nurse just pulls 'em off, looks at the tattoo, and she says, "Oh, that's exactly in the same spot I got mine." She pulled her uniform up and showed me her tattoo. (Laughs.)

I knew the bomb dropped on Hiroshima was a big terrible thing, but I didn't know it was the horror it was. It was on working people. It wasn't anywhere near the big shots of Japan who started the war in the first place. We didn't drop it on them. Hirohito and his white horse, it never touched him. It was dropped on women and children

Hard Times: An Oral History of the Great Depression (New York: Pantheon Books, 1970), p. 48.

who had nothing to say about whether their country went to war or not.

I was happy my husband would get to come home and wouldn't be sent there from Germany. Every day when the paper came out, there'd be somebody I knew with their picture. An awful lot of kids I knew, went to school and church with, were killed.

No bombs were ever dropped on us. I can't help but believe the cold war started because we were untouched. Except for our boys that went out of the country and were killed, we came out of that war in good shape. People with more money than they'd had in years.

No, I don't think we'd have been satisfied to go back to what we had during the Depression. To be deprived of things we got used to. Materially, we're a thousand times better off. But the war turned me against religion. I was raised in the fundamentalist faith. I was taught that I was nothing. My feeling is if God created me, if God sent his only begotten son to give his life for me, then I am something. My mother died thinking she was nothing. I don't know how chaplains can call themselves men of God and prepare boys to go into battle. If the Bible says, Thou shalt not kill, it doesn't say, Except in time of war. They'll send a man to the electric chair who in a temper killed somebody. But they pin medals on our men. The more people they kill, the more medals they pin on 'em.

I was just so glad when it was over, because I wanted my husband home. I didn't understand any of the implications except that the killing was over and that's a pretty good thing to think about whether you're political or not. (Laughs.) The killing be over forever.

SARAH KILLINGSWORTH

She manages a complex of apartment buildings in Los Angeles: the portrait of a stately dowager.

"I come from Clarksville, Tennessee, in 1935, as a personal maid for a beauty-contest winner. She played small bits in the movies and lost her contract. So I got a job with the E. F. Hutton family as a live-in maid, cook, housekeeper. I was always jobbin' around and managin'."

The war started and jobs kinda opened up for women that the men had. I took a job at a shoe-repair place on Wilshire Boulevard.

Cleanin' shoes and dyin' shoes, the same thing that men did. They started takin' applications at Douglas, to work in a defense plant. I was hired.

I didn't want a job on the production line. I heard so many things about accidents, that some girls got their fingers cut off or their hair caught in the machines. I was frightened. All I wanted to do was get in the factory, because they were payin' more than what I'd been makin'. Which was forty dollars a week, which was pretty good considering I'd been makin' about twenty dollars a week. When I left Tennessee I was only makin' two-fifty a week, so that was quite a jump.

I got the job workin' nights in the ladies' rest room, which wasn't hard. We had about six rest rooms to do. They would stay up all night and they would be sleeping. I had bought some of those No-Doz tablets, and I would give them a No-Doz so they could stay awake all night. This was the graveyard shift. Some of 'em had been out drinkin', and we would let them take a nap for about fifteen minutes. We would watch out for them, so their supervisor wouldn't miss 'em. We'd put the sign out: Closed. We'd wake 'em up, and sometimes they'd give us tips. They would give me fifty cents for a tablet or a cup of coffee, so they could stay awake. Especially on weekends.

They weren't interested in the war. Most of them were only interested in the money. Most of us was young and we really didn't know. All we were after was that buck. I didn't care about the money. That was a big salary for me, I was satisfied with that.

My husband was in the service. He had been drafted. While he was there, he got promoted to chaplain. He wasn't a minister, just always a religious man. He tried everything to keep from goin' out on that battlefield. He didn't see much action. He just devoted most of his time around the kitchen. Right after he got out, I divorced him. You weren't in love in the first place, I call your first marriage a trial marriage. Most of the girls married soldiers at that time because that was a sure income. You knew you were gonna get a check. They had a song about fifty dollars a month once a day. Fifty dollars a month was a lot of money, you could live offa that. I was payin' twenty-five dollars a month rent, so I could live off the other twenty-five dollars. And then I did a little sewin'. I've always been the type of person could always find work to do, so I never suffered too much. I didn't marry my husband because he was a soldier. We were married before the war. I stayed single for about five years and then I married again.

I do know one thing, this place was very segregated when I first come here. Oh, Los Angeles, you just couldn't go and sit down like you do now. You had certain places you went. You had to more or less stick to the restaurants and hotels where black people were. It wasn't until the war that it really opened up. 'Cause when I come out here it was awful, just like bein' in the South.

I was relating this to my daughter last night. What am I gonna relate to my children? "You young people are makin' money and you're doin' well," I says. "You would never struggle and go through the hardships that I went through to get where I am today." So she said, "In other words, from rags to riches." I said, "That's just the way you would probably explain my life: from rags to riches."

For a person that grew up and knew nothin' but hard times to get out on my own at eighteen years old and make a decent livin' and still make a decent person outa myself, I really am proud of me.

I had so many opportunities to go wrong. I was waitin' on the bus on Wilshire, girls were there. Prostitutes would come up and tell you, "What kind of work do you do?" I'd tell 'em I'm doin' domestic work. They'd say, "We got good jobs. You could make as much money in one day as you do in a month." They'd go out and date these white fellas and spend the night with 'em. I was never interested in that kind of life, because I wasn't raised that way.

Some of the people I worked with saved money. Some of 'em, they were just out havin' a good time. They were just makin' this big money and they were spendin' it as fast as they were makin' it.

I also had a restaurant, which we opened when my husband got out of the army. The prostitutes used to come in. I had good, good business. They had a red-light district in San Bernardino, where the soldiers would all go. Some of the girls were married, very attractive women. Their husbands would take them down there and they would pick 'em up on weekends. They called 'em pimps in those days. The girls were high-class, they didn't work on the streets. But I was always a strong person. I could never be tempted. I was never interested in selling my body for a few dollars.

I really didn't know what the war was about. I was in the house one day and all of a sudden they started yellin' about the war, war, war. Roosevelt had declared war. Well, they know that when there's a war, somebody's gonna get a job. This was during the Depression, so I think people were kinda glad the war had started. So right away they started hirin'. I think the war had kind of a pleasure. People didn't realize the seriousness of the war. All they were thinkin' about is they had lived in these Depression days. It was so hard to come by a dollar.

Those who had to go, that was the sad part. I had a brother that went to war, my youngest. He come back. The war helped some people because they come back, they took trades, learned to do things. My brother come back and now he is very successful. I think the army really made a man out of him. He works at Rockwell in the missile department and he's a supervisor. He wouldn't have known what to do if he hadn't gone in the army.

I have a friend tells us different things he experienced in the war. We sit up and listen to him. He was really in the battle zone. He was injured. Right now he's losing his hearing, he's losing his eyesight. He was so proud he really didn't tell them how he had got the hand grenade. He couldn't even get a pension and he didn't get a medical discharge. Yet he was in the hospital there for a long time, you know. He injured his spine 'cause he had to grab a rope and swing over a branch. Well, he missed the rope and fell and struck his back. He had to have surgery on his spine. They told him it was a fifty-fifty chance whether he'd ever walk again. He's walkin', but he's been affected a lot, uh-huh.

They didn't mix the white and black in the war. But now it gives you a kind of independence because they felt that we gone off and fought, we should be equal. Everything started openin' up for us. We got a chance to go places we had never been able to go before.

In ways it was too bad that so many lives were lost. But I think it was for a worthy cause, because it did make a way for us. And we were able to really get out.

DELLIE HAHNE

Toluca Lake, North Hollywood: all strata of society live within these precincts. Posh estates; a depressed community where "all the billboards are in Spanish"; an area in transition, of "average homes," where she lives.

She had retired a year ago, after thirty-three years as a music teacher

in Los Angeles schools. She still puts in two days a week with handi-
capped children. "I do a little writing."

Her trim figure and her quick movements give the lie to her years.

While my conscience told me the war was a terrible thing, bloodshed
and misery, there was excitement in the air. I had just left college
and was working as a substitute teacher. Life was fairly dull. Suddenly, single women were of tremendous importance. It was hammered at us through the newspapers and magazines and on the radio.
We were needed at USO, to dance with the soldiers.

A young woman had a chance to meet hundreds of men in the
course of one or two weeks, more than she would in her entire
lifetime, because of the war. Life became a series of weekend dates.

I became a nurse's aide, working in the hospital. Six or eight weeks
of Red Cross training. The uniform made us special people.

I had a brother three years younger than I. He was a cadet at the
Santa Ana Air Base. Your cadet got to wear these great hats, with
the grommets taken out. Marvelous uniform.

I met my future husband. I really didn't care that much for him,
but the pressure was so great. My brother said, "What do you mean
you don't like Glenn? You're going to marry him, aren't you?" The
first time it would occur to me that I would marry anybody. The
pressure to marry a soldier was so great that after a while I didn't
question it. I have to marry sometime and I might as well marry him.

That women married soldiers and sent them overseas happy was
hammered at us. We had plays on the radio, short stories in magazines, and the movies, which were a tremendous influence in our
lives. The central theme was the girl meets the soldier, and after a
weekend of acquaintanceship they get married and overcome all
difficulties. Then off to war he went. Remember Judy Garland and
Robert Walker in *The Clock*?

I knew Glenn six weekends, not weeks. They began on Saturday
afternoon. We'd go out in herds and stay up all night. There was very
little sleeping around. We were still at the tail-end of a moral generation. Openly living together was not condoned. An illegitimate child
was a horrendous handicap. It was almost the ruination of your life.
I'm amazed and delighted the way it's accepted now, that a girl isn't
a social outcast any more.

The OWI, Office of War Information, did a thorough job of con-
vincing us our cause was unquestionably right. We were stopping

Hitler, and you look back at it and you had to stop him. We were saving the world. We were allied with Russia, which was great at that time. Germany had started World War One and now it had started World War Two, and Germany would be wiped off the face of the map. A few years later, when we started to arm Germany, I was so shocked. I'd been sold a bill of goods—I couldn't believe it. I remember sitting on the back porch here, I picked up the paper, and I read that our sworn enemy was now our ally. The disillusionment was so great, that was the beginning of distrusting my own government.

Russia was the enemy from the time I was born right up to '40. Then Russia became our ally. It's funny nobody stopped to think that this was a complete turnabout. As soon as the war was over, we dropped Russia. During the war, I never heard any anti-Russian talk.

There was a movie and there were two Russian artillery women. This woman could not speak English. She had been obviously, painfully coached. The announcer said, "If you were to meet a German now, what would you do?" And she says, (very slowly) "My hand would not falter." And everybody cheers and claps. There were some who said, What bullshit is this? Even so, we knew the importance of loving the Russians and being told that what they were doing was great.

I had one of those movie weddings, because he couldn't get off the base. My parents approved. My mother had a talk with the head of the army base. She wanted to know why the guy I was to marry was restricted to quarters. He said they were having nothing but trouble with this guy. The major advised her to think twice before permitting her daughter to marry a man like this: he was totally irresponsible. My mother told me this, and we both laughed about it. He was a soldier. He could not be anything but a marvelous, magnificent human being. I couldn't believe for one minute what this major had said. He was given a weekend pass and we were married.

Shortly after that he was thrown out of the air force. This was my first doubt that he was magnificent. So he became a sergeant, dusting off airplanes. He was sent to various parts of the country: Panama City, Florida; Ypsilanti, Michigan; Amarillo, Texas. I followed him.

That's how I got to see the misery of the war, not the excitement. Pregnant women who could barely balance in a rocking train, going to see their husbands for the last time before the guys were sent overseas. Women coming back from seeing their husbands, traveling with small children. Trying to feed their kids, diaper their kids. I felt sorriest for them. It suddenly occurred to me that this wasn't half as much fun as I'd been told it was going to be. I just thanked God I had no kids.

We didn't fly. It was always a train. A lot of times you stood in the vestibule and you hoped to Christ you could find someplace to put your suitcase and sit down. No place to sleep, sit up maybe three, four nights. The trains were filthy, crowded.

You'd go live with your husband, far from home. In the town, provision was made for the service wife. They needed all the woman-power they could get. You'd work in a factory or a restaurant. In some towns, your husband had a regular day off. They would allow you to have that day off. The townspeople were accommodating because they needed us. But you never got the feeling that you were welcome. It was an armed truce.

In Amarillo, I went to the store to buy a loaf of bread. I am next. The woman deliberately waits on two or three women who are after me. She knows these women and I'm an outsider. I opened a checking account and they threw my check out without a word of explanation. Account closed. The landlady returned the check to me furious. It was the first check I had written my whole life. The bank manager told me, curt and cold, I had signed my signature card Dellie Hahne and I had signed my check Mrs. Dellie Hahne. In any other person, they'd say, "Look, you made a mistake. This is how you write a check." It was the immediate cold, contemptuous dismissal. I was an outsider.

I felt one step above a camp follower. In some cases, I was asked to produce my marriage license. Most cases, you paid your rent in advance. Lot of times you were told, leave your door open if, say, one of your husband's friends came over. We were looked down upon. Yet they got very rich on the soldiers.

On V-J Day, I went out in the street and all the people were milling around. I talked to a man who was so dazed I thought he was a psychiatric case. He said he lived on a farm and came to Panama City to work in the shipyards. The war ended, half an hour later he was dismissed. He said, "I don't have a dime saved up. I got a kid. I don't know where the hell to go."

I ran across a lot of women with husbands overseas. They were living on allotment. Fifty bucks a month wouldn't support you. Things were relatively cheap, but then we had very little money, too. It wasn't so much the cost of food as points. I suspected the ration system was a patriotic ploy to keep our enthusiasm at a fever pitch.

If you wanted something you didn't have points for, it was the easiest thing in the world . . . Almost everybody had a cynical feeling about what we were told was a food shortage.

When it started out, this was the greatest thing since the Crusades. The patriotic fervor was such at the beginning that if "The Star-Spangled Banner" came on the radio, everybody in the room would stand up at attention. As the war dragged on and on and on, we read of the selfish actions of guys in power. We read stories of the generals, like MacArthur taking food right out of the guys' mouths when he was in the Philippines, to feed his own family. Our enthusiasm waned and we became cynical and very tired and sick of the bloodshed and killing. It was a completely different thing than the way it started. At least, this is the way I felt.

We had a catchphrase: The War Against Fascism. I remember a Bing Crosby movie. I think he's a cabdriver and some guy is dictating a letter in the cab to a secretary. Crosby's singing a song. The businessman says, "Will you cut it out?" And Crosby says, "The world would be a better place if we didn't have so many dictators." The catchwords and catchphrases again. This was the war to stop Hitler, stop Mussolini, stop the Axis.

There were some movies we knew were sheer bullshit. There was a George Murphy movie where he gets his draft induction notice. He opens the telegram, and he's in his pajamas and bare feet, and he runs around the house and jumps over the couch and jumps over the chair, screaming and yelling. His landlady says, "What's going on?" "I've been drafted! I've been drafted." Well, the whole audience howled. 'Cause they know you can feed 'em only so much bullshit.

If a guy in a movie was a civilian, he always had to say—what was it? Gene Kelly in *Cover Girl?* I remember this line: "Well, Danny, why aren't you in the army?" "Hell, I was wounded in North Africa, and now all I can do is keep people happy by putting on these shows." They had to explain why the guy wasn't in uniform. Always. There was always a line in the movie: "Well, I was turned down." "Oh, tough luck." There were always soldiers in the audience, and they would scream. So we recognized a lot of the crap.

There were some good books, *Mrs. Miniver* by Jan Struther. She asked herself why did it take a war to get government to paint its curbstones white so that people wouldn't trip at night? Why did it take a war to bring out the poverty and injustice? There were a lot of people who didn't want to fight. Why the hell fight for this country?

What did this country do for me? There was a book called *This Above All*. The theme was first we win the war, *then* we settle your poverty and your wretched childhood and your neglect and your want. You go overseas, you come back, you'll get . . . All they did get is the GI Bill of Rights, going to school. As for the rest of it . . .

Most soldiers were resentful of guys who were not in uniform. There was a term, 4-F bastards. If two guys in cars were fighting it out, the uniformed guy stuck his head out the window: "Oh, you 4-F bastard!" They didn't want to be handed a bill of goods that the men not in uniform were sorry, or the man in uniform was happy as a lark. He wasn't. He was sick of the whole damn thing.

The good war? That infuriates me. Yeah, the idea of World War Two being called a good war is a horrible thing. I think of all the atrocities. I think of a madman who had all this power. I think of the destruction of the Jews, the misery, the horrendous suffering in the concentration camps. In 1971, I visited Dachau. I could not believe what I saw. There's one barracks left, a model barracks. You can reconstruct the rest and see what the hell was going on. It doesn't take a visit to make you realize the extent of human misery.

I know it had to be stopped and we stopped it. But I don't feel proud, because the way we did it was so devious. How many years has it been? Forty years later? I feel I'm standing here with egg on my face. I was lied to. I was cheated. I was made a fool of. If they had said to me, Look, this has to be done and we'll go out and do the job . . . we'll all get our arms and legs blown off but it has to be done, I'd understand. If they didn't hand me all this shit with the uniforms and the girls in their pompadours dancing at the USO and all those songs—"There'll Be Bluebirds over the White Cliffs of Dover"—bullshit!

If only we had a different approach, that's all I'm asking for. If you have to live through a war, be truthful. Maybe you have to get people to fight a war, maybe you have to lie to them. If only they'd said that this isn't the greatest of all worlds, and there's graft and corruption in Washington, and kids are going without milk so some asshole can take a vacation in Florida. If they'd done that, I wouldn't feel so bad.

My brother was killed. Not even overseas. He was killed in North Carolina on a flight exercise. It ruined my mother, because she just worshipped my brother. He was the only boy. I don't think she ever recovered from it.

There was *one* good thing came out of it. I had friends whose mothers went to work in factories. For the first time in their lives, they worked outside the home. They realized that they were capable of doing something more than cook a meal. I remember going to Sunday dinner one of the older women invited me to. She and her sister at the dinner table were talking about the best way to keep their drill sharp in the factory. I had never heard anything like this in my life. It was just marvelous. I was tickled.

But even here we were sold a bill of goods. They were hammering away that the woman who went to work did it temporarily to help her man, and when he came back, he took her job and she cheerfully leaped back to the home.

There was a letter column in which some woman wrote to her husband overseas: "This is an exact picture of our dashboard. Do we need a quart of oil?" Showing how dependent we were upon our men. Those of us who read it said, This is pure and simple bullshit. 'Cause if you don't know if you need a quart of oil, drive the damn thing to the station and have the man show you and you'll learn if you need a quart of oil. But they still wanted women to be dependent, helpless.

I think a lot of women said, Screw that noise. 'Cause they had a taste of freedom, they had a taste of making their own money, a taste of spending their own money, making their own decisions. I think the beginning of the women's movement had its seeds right there in World War Two.

POSTSCRIPT: *"I had two children, and in seven years, a long time, I realized I was married to a totally irresponsible man. The major knew exactly what he was talking about when he warned my mother. He was a gambler and a drunk and a woman-chaser. So I divorced him and was left without a dime. It was a grim struggle. I was taking home around $273 in those days and child care took $100. So all I had was money for food and a couple of medical bills. The rest of the bills were put aside until the next month. I went in a hole twenty, twenty-five dollars a month. Plus no work in the summertime. I had to find a job to keep the three of us alive.*

"I don't think I'd have married so foolishly, if it weren't for the war. If I hadn't married a uniform. I wouldn't marry a civilian that fast. The man was a soldier. Somebody had to marry him, and I married him. The war directly influenced the rest of my life."

Film critic, The New Yorker.

During the war years, the whole spirit of the country seemed embodied in *Life* magazine. Its covers featured GI Joes, girls, and generals. The GIs were always clean-cut, wonderful kids. And so were the girls they dated. This was carried through in the movies. Everybody was patriotic and shiny-faced. Wiped clean of any personality. Even after the war, when William Wyler made *The Best Years of Our Lives,* a sensitive movie, by no means cheerful—even that had the look of a *Life* magazine cover.

A lot of the movies were very condescending to Europeans and Asiatics. There were films like *Bataan,* with Robert Taylor screaming epithets about the Japs. I was in my early twenties and was seeing them all. Oh, I hated the war movies, because they robbed the enemy of any humanity or individuality. In all these films you were supposed to learn a lesson: even the German or the Japanese who happened to be your friend, even the one who was sympathetic, had to be killed because he was just as dirty as the others. Even those who were trapped trying to save American lives were weaklings and untrustworthy. We had stereotypes of a shocking nature. They could never be people, who were just caught in the army the same way Americans were and told what to do. They always had to be decadent, immoral, rotten people, sneaks.

In contrast, there was *The Grand Illusion,* one of the great war films of all time. It would not have gone over during World War Two. It was sympathetic to the Germans in World War One. It showed that not all Germans were behind the war. It had a poetic understanding.

Compare that with the shameful movie Alfred Hitchcock made, *Life Boat.* Once again you had to learn what the master race was all about. Walter Slezak was the Nazi. It took a tough American working-man, John Hodiak, to deal with him. The other Americans were too weak, too liberal, too pacifistic. That was the message. The German represented everything terrible. He mouthed all the clichés.

Even more grotesque was *Tomorrow the World,* in which a little Nazi boy was the enemy. In *The White Cliffs of Dover* the people know that the war is coming home because two little German children are already warlike. *Mrs. Miniver*—oh God, that was a disgusting picture.

It was about the wonders of the British class system when you really got to it. The church had its roof blown off at the end, but the people gathered inside the roofless church and sang "Onward, Christian Soldiers."

The Clock was a popular movie. But it had none of the nasty quality you got in so many others. It was Judy Garland and Robert Walker as two kids who meet in New York. He's a soldier who has to leave in a couple of days. They meet, they fall in love and are separated. It was a soft, sentimental romance, charmingly done. That was the kind of thing people could love. I don't think that the big action films were ever popular with women.

Of course, we had an incredible switch after the war. We had those wonderful Russians, being tortured by Nazis, and suddenly, we had the Russians as bums. (Laughs.) That period was one of the last moments in modern history when Americans were viewed as liberators. It's so interesting to see Italian films of that time, where the people are longing for the Americans to arrive. So there's something a little warming about that period. It was a good time for the country. It believed in itself, despite people who really knew better.

The Americans were stereotyped, too. They were always clean-cut, wonderful kids from the Midwest, who had funny ethnics, Italians or Jews, as buddies, who were from Brooklyn. The films were condescending to everybody. The Americans from the Midwest were always so innocent they didn't know a thing. They were virginal boys. There was a sickly undercurrent.

By the time we got to later wars, there was more of a sense that people knew a little something about what they were about. In the Vietnam stories reported, you didn't assume that all the boys were twelve-year-olds at heart. In World War Two, there was still this image of the American GI giving candy bars to the European kids he liberated. Of course, American boys did that. (Laughs.) Chocolate and gum became synonymous with GIs.

Soldiers actually used the techniques they saw in the movies. If you were walking down the street and a guy in uniform tried to stop you and you weren't interested, he would say, That's what we're fighting for, that's what we're giving our lives for. They tried to make you feel guilty for not wanting to go to bed with them. They were going out and dying to protect you. Soldiers and sailors used the same techniques they saw the smart-guy characters play on the screen. These innocent boys.

There *was* still hope. It wasn't until the world became divided pretty much by the Russians and the Americans and Europeans that the hope had gone out. Now, almost every place on earth is a trouble spot. All the fights that seemed to be settled have started up again. So there's a general sense of hopelessness and powerlessness. You remember the pictures of Winston Churchill? On the cover of *Life?* That bulldog face and that big fat cigar. The idea was there were men in charge who knew something. You couldn't pose leaders in that style any more. People would laugh at it.

Hope didn't really seep out until the counterculture period in the sixties. Even if you went to see a western, the Indians often looked like Vietnamese and the Americans were brutal racists. So you started to hate yourself when you went to the movies. It satisfied an almost masochistic feeling among the younger moviegoers. I think that's when older people stopped going to the movies.

I've always been a movie person, but the war years really put a strain on my patience. I got so angry. It was so difficult to deal with, because in some intangible way they did represent the essence of war propaganda.

EVELYN FRASER

Her gray hair is bobbed, Dorothy Parker fashion: "I'd probably have had an Afro if I had enough hair." She has, this week, retired after twenty-three years as a proofreader for the Chicago Tribune.

I was a WAC, yes. A captain in Public Information. I had two tours of duty in Germany. The shocking thing was to walk among Germans and see them as human beings, and then see Dachau. It was so difficult to put together. My translator, a survivor of the Holocaust, had such a sense of guilt because he survived.

I'd been a reporter in Evansville, Indiana. I did a story on the WACs in training at Fort Oglethorpe. I thought it would be an even better story if I volunteered. I never thought they'd accept me because I'm so neurotic. I'd be a woman 4-F and that would be another story.

So I'm having these examinations with about sixteen others, big, healthy girls. This psychiatrist is mad as the very devil. I couldn't understand it. Finally it's my turn: "Are you pregnant?" I said, "I wasn't when I came in." It turns out I was the only one that passed. The other sixteen weren't accepted because they got mad at him for asking such questions. It just amused me. I was in the army. Jeez, now I have to go all the way through with this.

At camp in Georgia, where I had done this story, I'd been treated as an important reporter by the colonel. Now I was in fatigues, doing KP. The colonel didn't recognize me. When I reminded him, he was really flustered. (Laughs.)

You wake up one morning in this barracks, with all these people. You've never been able to sleep without the shades down. And here I am. What have I done?

I'm heading for my duty station in Camp Breckenridge, Kentucky. I have this bundle of orders. I'm the only woman on the train. This sailor sits down by me: "Hey, honey, where you going?" I said, "I can't tell you. Classified orders." (Laughs.) Naturally he laughed, he and the others. They didn't take us very seriously.

It was awkward for the men. I'd been brought into Camp Atterbury for administrative work. This lieutenant wouldn't tell me a thing about the job. He was afraid I was going to replace him and he'd have to go overseas. I beat him to it: "Look, you can put everything on the desk now. I'm going overseas and you can stay here." (Laughs.) When we came along, the men in clerical jobs were none too happy. We replaced them for combat overseas. That was the whole idea. Nobody wants to go overseas to fight.

I went in in September of '43 and was commissioned in May of '44. In basic training we were around all these women. You seldom encountered a male. When I got on the bus with a weekend pass, I heard male voices and little children's. You didn't realize how much you missed those voices.

I was a recruiting officer in Cleveland. I had to find out what the resistance to the WACs was about. There were stories that our women were promiscuous and it wouldn't be a nice place for a nice girl. We took only high school graduates, so few of the women passed. You'd be surprised the number of women we had to reject for physical reasons. There were lots of high school graduates with syphilis who didn't know they had it. Black and white. It was incredible to me. I had thought everybody was fairly healthy.

When I was in Paris I met this black WAC captain. They had a segregated detachment over there. They were beautiful girls, well qualified. I said, "I guess you girls are having an awful lot of fun over here." Because there were so many black soldiers in Paris. She says, "No, they're having a terrible time. All the black soldiers are taking out the white French girls."

At that time VD was rampant among our soldiers. It was an epidemic. The officers couldn't understand why the men didn't stop at the stations for treatment, after they had contact with the women. This was in Germany. It seemed obvious to me. I took my bars off and went to an enlisted club. I found out. These fellas, if they were out after bed check, would not stop at the pro station. So I suggested to the general, why not put a pro station in the barracks? They wouldn't have to worry about being late for bed check. He told his male officers it's funny that they had to have a WAC suggest such a practical thing. (Laughs.)

In late '45, I was in Vienna. The four powers were there. I wanted to see the Danube. We get in our jeep and we're crossing the bridge and this Russian soldier holds a rifle at us. Then I saw some husky-looking Russian gals with real thick stockings walking across the street. They glared at us. I couldn't understand where this had broken down, see? Maybe if we had handled it better in some way and tried to be more cordial, it might have helped. But we were so busy selling them watches. All the Russians wanted watches, and our people were so busy getting all the black-market Mickey Mouse watches from the United States.

I was there, near the Saar, the French zone, when we had taken over the occupation. Of course, the French had taken all the latrines and everything back to France. They took all this old junk, and the Russians took all this old junk. We had to completely rebuild it. That's why Germany has got such nice new facilities. (Laughs.) Our money. The French and Russians took all the obsolete stuff.

I had to give every officer a Why We Fight orientation. I used to give them one where I'd say how the Russians were our friends and how we were fighting together. Next minute, they expected us to give a lecture about the communists. A complete reversal, a change of gears. This really was disillusioning.

I saw all those cemeteries in Europe of eighteen-year-old boys, with all the little crosses. I talked to mothers who came over to see those crosses. I tried to persuade them not to bring the body home. Truthfully, I don't think they know, in many cases, what remains are in that grave. You'd get an arm here, a leg there.

If it weren't for the war, I'd have probably stayed in Evansville as a newspaperwoman. Maybe got a job in Indianapolis or Chicago. (Laughs.) I wouldn't have traveled as extensively as I did. It really changed my life. A young woman my age never had an apartment away from her parents. My mother would have thought I was a fallen woman. This way, I could gloriously go off on my own and be on my own.

I used part of the GI Bill to go to Northwestern and then full time to Roosevelt U. I'd never had accounting and all those dull subjects. I thought it would be a good exercise. It helped. I can balance my checkbook now. (Laughs.)

Dachau? I saw the lampshades made out of skin. I saw a lot of the children who had been in the camps. We had Christmas parties for them. They didn't even know how to open a package. It was incredible. Then you looked at these Germans, and they were people like —(laughs)—everybody.

What we've learned, I think, is that we should examine everything very carefully before we get into any kind of conflict. They design a weapon. We design a weapon. Where's it going? I don't know what the answer is. Unfortunately, the dead can't speak. I wonder what they'd say.

BETTY BASYE HUTCHINSON

On first meeting her, you sense that she had once upon a time been a beauty queen. She is sixty.

I was in the class of '41, the last high school class. You see? By that winter Leslie Bidwell would be dead at Pearl Harbor. My class would be dying.

Oroville was a little mining town eighty miles above Sacramento. My stepfather was a tenant farmer and owned just a little bit of land. He had just got electricity three years before. We lived in the kitchen because that's where it was warm. My stepfather kept things to himself. He would read the papers, but he never shared. My mother was busy feeding all her kids. I was the first one of nine children to graduate from high school.

I was dancing at Fresno State, at a big ball, when I first realized

Pearl Harbor had happened. It was a whole week later. I was a hayseed Basye.

Immediately, I was going to become a nurse. That was the fastest thing I could do to help our boys. Here I was only one semester at Fresno State, and by February 5, I was out at the hospital as a registered nurse.

It was expensive for me. You had to pay something like twenty dollars a month to live at the nurses' home. I didn't have any money. Fortunately, the Cadet Nurse Corps came into existence. The government paid for us to become nurses. That really saved me.

I remember February 5, '42. Our superintendent called us all together. Two little Japanese girls, sitting in front, who had come into class like me—why in the world are we saying goodbye to them? I couldn't understand what had happened. They were gone and I never, never saw them again. It must have been okay if President Roosevelt said it was okay. But I knew those girls should have been nurses.

I wanted to really have something to do with the war. It meant my kid brother on a tanker in the Mediterranean, delivering oil to Africa, to Italy. It meant losing several more Oroville schoolmates. It meant my boyfriend, whom I'd been engaged to ever since we left high school. He'd joined the marines and was gone. It meant just an end to all that life I had known just a few months before.

"He was president of the student body. I was an athlete, a drum majorette, everything. In February of '42, I was all-American drum majorette. I was offered a movie contract. I was going to be a star in this thing, this movie called Twirl Girl. *(Laughs.) I was in nurse's training when the call came in. I just said, 'Thank you, but I have to go back to duty.'*

"It was that picture in all the national papers. Cheesecake. I don't think the word 'cheesecake' had been invented yet. I had a baton under my arm and I was standing on a pedestal. Posed, with one leg up. Really short skirt and little velvet boots on. (Laughs.) My hair was full and long and red.

"It was one of the first available pinup pictures. Suddenly the fan mail started coming in. I still have clippings, letters from all over the world. 'Cause I was busy at the hospital, they would come to my aunt. The poor postman would carry boxes of this mail. The college began to send these pictures out to the boys who would write from different places and ask for a picture. Servicemen.

"I have one in French I've never translated. One from Argentina. One

of them said, 'As soon as the war is over, we'll get together and we'll have a wonderful time. Would you please wait? You are the most beautiful person I've ever seen, but you look wholesome.' It was just that kind of time."

All the regular nurses began to drop out and join the army. Many of my instructors left. We were down to just a skeleton crew at the county hospital. In Fresno. The student nurses were running the whole hospital.

You were supposed to stay in for three years as a student nurse, but the army took us out six months early. We went down to our first military assignment at Hoff General Hospital in Santa Barbara. We were given uniforms with a nice little cocky beret. It was basic training really, because most of us were gonna go into the service. About six months later, we went back to Fresno to graduate, get our pins, and say goodbye. The day President Roosevelt died, I was an official army nurse. I felt even more committed to go ahead.

I was on an orthopedic ward. Quite a few wounded paratroopers. I remember rubbing the backs of these people who had casts from head to foot. You could hardly find their backs through all these bandages and pulleys. It's not like plastic surgery where the really deformed people are. I was struck by the horror of it, but it wasn't as bad as what was to come.

Now I go to Dibble General Hospital in Menlo Park. In six weeks, we became so skilled in plastic surgery that they wouldn't let us go. Six-week wonders. It was coming to the end of the war and now they needed plastic surgery. Blind young men. Eyes gone, legs gone. Parts of the face. Burns—you'd land with a fire bomb and be up in flames. It was a burn-and-blind center.

I spent a year and a half in the plastic-surgery dressing room. All day long you would change these dressings. When you were through with those who were mobile, who would come by wheelchair or crutches, you would take this little cart loaded with canisters of wet saline bandages. Go up and down the wards to those fellas who couldn't get out of bed. It was almost like a surgical procedure. They didn't anesthetize the boys and it was terribly painful. We had to keep the skin wet with these moist saline packs. We would wind yards and yards of this wet pack around these people. That's what war really is.

I'll never forget my first day on duty. First Lieutenant Molly Birch introduced me to the whole floor of patients: "This is Lieutenant Basye." They'd say, What? Hayseed? Oh, Basie. Oh, Countess. So I got the name Countess.

I was so overwhelmed by the time I got to the third bed: this whole side of a face being gone. I wouldn't know how to focus on the eye that peeked through these bandages. Should I pretend I didn't notice it? Shall we talk about it? Molly led me down to the next bed: The Nose, she called him. He had lost his nose. Later on, I got used to it, all this kidding about their condition. He would pretend to laugh. He would say, "Ah yes, I'm getting my nose." He didn't have any eyebrows, a complete white mass of scars. The pedicle was hanging off his neck. He had no ears—they had been burned off. They were going to be reconstructed. But the nose was the important thing. Everyone nicknamed him The Nose. He didn't mind—well, I don't know that. Molly was right. She was giving them a chance to talk about what happened. At the time, I couldn't stand it.

As soon as we got back to the nurse's station behind glass, I went to the bathroom and threw up. Then she knew. She didn't introduce me to the patients who were in the private room that day, 'cause they were far the worst. They couldn't get up and couldn't joke so much. The next day she took me to them, one at a time. I was beginning to anesthetize myself.

I remember this one lieutenant. Just a mass of white bandages, with a little slit where I knew his eyes were. This one hand reaching out and saying, "Hi, Red." There were many, many, many more with stumps, you couldn't tell if there was a foot there or not, an eye, an arm, the multiple wounds. It wasn't just the one little thing I was used to in nurse's training. This is what got to me.

Oh, there were breakups. The wife of The Nose was going to divorce him. What can we do to make her understand? That was the talk all over. The doctor wanted her to understand it'll take time, he'll get his face back. But they broke up. She couldn't stand it. That was pretty common.

Sitting at the bedside of this young flyer who went down over Leyte. He got his own fire bomb. Next to his bed is a picture of this handsome pilot beside his P-38. He wants to be sure I see it: "Hi, Red, look. This is me." He was never gonna leave that bed until he got his face back. That handsome photograph he insisted be there, so that's the person you'll see.

He was very hard to manage because he would scream when they changed his dressing. He was insistent that he never was gonna leave that room until they brought him back to where he was before. The staff couldn't quite figure this out. Why isn't he quiet? Why can't he be brave when they're changing his dressing? What does he think we are, miracle makers? This mystique builds up that Bill can't handle it as well as the others. Be brave, be brave.

I can't say I ever really became used to it. But I became more effective as a nurse and adopted a kind of jocularity. I began to be able to tell jokes, banter back and forth. When I'd come in pushing the cart, there'd always be hooting and yelling: Hey, Red, Hayseed, Countess, come in, I got a cookie for you. There was a lot of alluding to sexuality. One said to me, "Why do you always walk that way?" I didn't know how I walked, but I had a walk. I said, "I don't know." And they all howled.

Having pretty young nurses around was very important to them. You were not supposed to date enlisted men, but you could date officers. I escorted Bill, the pilot, for the first outing out of his room. I talked him into escorting me to the officers' club. He still had a bandage on his one eye, terrible scars, one side of his face gone, and these pedicles of flesh. You look absolutely grotesque and you know. We had a drink at the club. He looked around and saw other cases there. So he began to get used to it.

One of the nurses in charge fell in love with an enlisted man. She carried on a very quiet love affair with him. We never alluded to it. After about a year, they were married. It was always a secret in those days. It was discouraged. I've always had the theory that they made us officers to keep the army nurses for the officers. We were just technicians. I was just a twenty-two-year-old kid who knew how to do bedpans. Why was I an officer? I feel it was a way to keep us away from the hordes and keep us for the officers. Oh, there was a terrible class feeling.

The doctors were the givers of gifts to these men. They were gods on a pedestal. The elusive, mobile god, who moves in and out and doesn't stay there very long, under a terrible amount of pressure. The nurses were counsel when marriages broke up. The doctors were busy someplace else.

V-J Day occurred while I was still at the hospital. Oh, wow! Just total chaos. Our superintendent of nurses led a conga line up and down the hospital, serpentine, up past every bed. This took hours, because it was ward after ward. (Laughs.) Everybody joined in. Absolute bedlam.

The hospital closed and they sent the patients out to other places. Plastic surgery was going to go on for years on these people. I went down to Pasadena. This is '46. We took over the whole hotel, one of the big, nice old hotels right there on the gorge. All my friends were still there, undergoing surgery. Especially Bill. I would walk him in downtown Pasadena—I'll never forget this. Half his face completely gone, right?

Downtown Pasadena after the war was a very elite community. Nicely dressed women, absolutely staring, just standing there staring. He was aware of this terrible stare. People just looking right at you and wondering: What is this? I was going to cuss her out, but I moved him away. It's like the war hadn't come to Pasadena until we came there.

Oh, it had a big impact on the community. In the Pasadena paper came some letters to the editor: Why can't they be kept on their own grounds and off the streets? The furor, the awful indignation: the end of the war and we're still here. The patients themselves showed me these letters: Isn't it better for them if they're kept off the streets? What awful things for us to have to look at. The patients kidded about that. Wow, we're in Pasadena.

This was my slow introduction to peacetime, through the eyes of that woman when she looked at my friend Bill. It's only the glamour of war that appeals to people. They don't know real war. Well, those wars are gone forever. We've got a nuclear bomb and we'll destroy ourselves and everybody else.

I swallowed all this for years and never talked about it. 'Cause I got busy after the war, getting married and having my four children. That's what you were supposed to do. And getting your house in suburbia. You couldn't get anybody to really talk about the war. Oh, the men would say, When I was in Leyte—buddy-buddy talk. Well, their buddies got killed, too. They never talked of the horrors.

My husband had been in the South Pacific. You could never get the father of my four children to talk about the war. It was like we put blinders on the past. When we won, we believed it. It was the end. That's the way we lived in suburbia, raising our children, not telling them about war. I don't think it was just me. It was everybody. You wouldn't fill your children full of these horror stories, would you?

When I think of the kind of person I was, a little hayseed from Oroville, with all this altruism in me and all this patriotism that sent me into the war! Oh, the war marked me, but I put it behind me. I didn't do much except march against Vietnam. And my oldest son, I'm happy to say, was a conscientious objector.

It's just this terrible anger I have. What is this story I want to tell? I even wrote short stories for myself. I started an autobiography, and always the war came up. This disappointment. We did it for what? Korea? Vietnam? We're still at war. Looking back, it didn't work.

In 1946, my house burned with all my mementoes. The only thing that was saved, inside a hope chest, was this scrapbook of burned-edged pictures. Of me, when I was in the service.

Today, we're going through the *romance* of war. Did you see *The Winds of War?* It was nothing, worse than nothing. It didn't tell us what's wrong with war or the reality of war. They showed that picture of Pearl Harbor, that pretty place, all bombed up. Wasn't he on the hill, looking down, the hero? I was trying to find some saving grace. But it wasn't like you were there. Somebody should have said, See, underneath this water is Leslie Bidwell. He died, you see?

NEIGHBORHOOD BOYS

MIKE ROYKO

A columnist for the Chicago Tribune, *he is the city's most widely read journalist.*

I was nine years old when the war started. It was a typical Chicago working-class neighborhood. It was predominantly Slavic, Polish. There were some Irish, some Germans. When you're a kid, the borders of the world are the few blocks of two-flats, bungalows, cottages, with a lot of little stores in between. My father had a tavern. In those days they put out extras. I remember the night the newsboys came through the neighborhood. Skid-row kind of guys, hawking the papers. Germany had invaded Poland: '39. It was the middle of the night, my mother and father waking. People were going out in the streets in their bathrobes to buy the papers. In our neighborhood with a lot of Poles, it was a tremendous story.

Suddenly you had a flagpole. And a marker. Names went on the marker, guys from the neighborhood who were killed. Our neighborhood was decimated. There were only kids, older guys, and women.

Suddenly I saw something I hadn't seen before. My sister became Rosie the Riveter. She put a bandanna on her head every day and went down to this organ company that had been converted to war work. There was my sister in slacks. It became more than work. There was a sense of mission about it. Her husband was Over There. She went bowling once a week. They had a league. I used to have to go with her, because the presence of her little brother would discourage guys from making passes at her.

There was one sad case in the neighborhood. This woman's husband was overseas. I remember her as very attractive. She became pregnant: the neighborhood pariah. If they could have shaved her head and walked her through the streets, they'd have done it. She was an outcast and the talk—talk, talk, talk—of the neighborhood. She was very lonely.

If a guy came into the tavern with the wife or girlfriend of a guy who was overseas, somebody might have gone after him.

There was talk in the neighborhood about one guy who got a Dear John letter. The girl wasn't from our neighborhood, but it made for a lot of talk. He was one of ours. It was an "I am pregnant" letter. The pill sure would have saved a lot of unnecessary heartbreak during the war. (Laughs.)

There was the constant idea that you had to be doing something to help. It did filter down to the neighborhood: home-front mobilization. We had a block captain. It was always some goof who wanted somethin' like that, who could become a little official fellow. A sort of neighborhood guy who nobody would have ever noticed under normal circumstances. But he had his white helmet. He was the air-raid warden.

The siren would go off and everybody would turn off the lights. He would go around the neighborhood banging on doors and yelling, "Your lights are on." He'd write down people's names if they had a little light on in their apartments. I didn't like this. My parents were downstairs running the tavern, so I'd have to turn out these damn lights. My younger brother and I would sit there in this absolutely pitch-black apartment. We were afraid that if we didn't, the air-raid warden would come by and the FBI would come and terrible things would happen. I remember the guy because he was later arrested on some child-molesting charge. (Laughs.) He was the neighborhood creep.

We were all supposed to save fat—bacon grease and chicken fat. We believed that it would be used to make nitroglycerine. I don't think anybody ever turned it in. In our back yard, we had big coffee cans of fat and grease. The rats in the neighborhood must've had a hell of a good time.

We'd listen to the radio every night. My father would turn it on to find out what was happening. The way a kid's mind could be shaped by those dulcet voices. The world was very simple. I saw Hitler and Mussolini and Tojo: those were the villains. We were the good guys. And the Russians were the good guys too. The war was always being talked about in the bar. Everybody was a military strategist.

The big event was my brother-in-law coming home, my sister's husband. He had been a combat soldier all the way through. He had all his ribbons and medals on. He was the family hero. It was a constant thing in the neighborhood, guys comin' home from the war.

Everybody was tacking GI on to everything. Do you know how many GI Lounges sprang up? Immediately after the big bomb was dropped on Japan, somebody opened the Atom Bomb Lounge on Milwaukee Avenue. Nobody really understood what happened. People couldn't grasp it. I don't remember any horror or regret. It was *our* weapon.

There were so many ex-GIs in the tavern. There wasn't a lot of sitting around talking about I did this, I did that. They just went about their business. The majority of guys from my neighborhood did not use the GI Bill for school. They used it for a loan for a home.

That's when the younger couples started moving out. Guys got married and went lookin' to live somewhere else. The neighborhood got older and never really recovered. The guys went out to Park Forest, Rolling Meadows. They were the new suburban pioneers. Now that they fought, they came back and believed they were entitled to this type of life.

Before the war, most of these people traveled by public transportation. Few people had cars. My father was considered a big heap because he had a La Salle. It was a distinctive thing to own a car. Now, everybody had a car.

After the war my father put in a two-piece band that'd play on Friday night, a drummer and an accordion player. Pop songs, polkas, weddings. Every weekend there were weddings. These soldiers coming back were getting married. That's when the baby boom started. They were working, they had money. They were going out on Friday and Saturday nights. The vitality of the neighborhood was tremendous—until the move to the suburbs.

Then came our first embarrassing war. Guys my age really got shafted when the Korean War came along. I was seventeen when it started—'49? I went in at the end of '51. I wondered, What is this? I didn't know anyone who was in Korea who understood what the hell we were doing there. We're here to stop the commies? Hell, when you looked at the way South Korea was run—I saw Koreans beaten to death by Korean police.

We were over there fighting the Chinese, you know? Christ, I'd been raised to think the Chinese were among the world's most heroic people and our great friends. Remember the little baby in the rubble? The incredible photograph that was used for propaganda against the

Japanese? And Chiang Kai-shek was a great man, we were told. Our guy. And Pearl Buck. (Laughs.)

I was still mad at the Japs. The Japanese are now our friends, our pals. I'm going from Japan to Korea, where I'm supposed to fight the Chinese, who are now our enemies. A few years earlier, I was mad at the Japanese and I was supposed to love the Chinese. Now I gotta love the Japanese and hate the Chinese. (Laughs.) That's when I decided something's wrong.

I remember coming back from Korea, the hostility, the indifference. I was almost embarrassed being in Korea because we didn't win. We cut a deal. We got a draw. We had failed where our older brothers had won.

Bataan, Wake Island, Anzio, Normandy. And all those movies. I took a vacation in Florida recently and every time I looked up at a palm tree, I expected a Jap sniper up there. In these movies, every tree had a little Nip sittin' up there, a rotten little Nip tryin' to kill William Bendix. (Laughs.) If I lived in Florida, do you know what I'd do? I'd stuff a dummy and put a Japanese face on him and hide him up in a palm tree with a rifle stickin' out.

Our guys were good guys and the other side was all evil. That was years before anybody made a movie in which they showed any compassion, any understanding at all for the others—that they were human beings.

PAUL PISICANO

He is an architect, living in Manhattan. He is fifty-two and "one hundred percent Sicilian."

It was an Italian-speaking neighborhood in New York. We were a whole bunch of people who were just breaking into the system. We all talked Italian at home. We talked a dialect we thought was Italian, but was New York Italian.

Mussolini was a hero, a superhero. He made us feel special, especially the southerners, Sicilian, Calabrian. I remember the Abyssinian War, about 1935. I was five. It was talked about as a very positive thing. We had the equivalent of your pep rallies for football teams. To us it was a great victory. We never really got down on

Mussolini. He was applauded. Then he went into Greece. He wasn't doing too well (laughs) and had to be bailed out by the Germans, remember? We were awfully disappointed by that.

It was us against the outside. One block against another block. We had less of a sense of nation than, say, the Israelis did. We were never comfortable with the northern Italians. We were Palestinians. (Laughs.)

It was very painful to live in America. You sorta wanted not to talk about it. Prior to Pearl Harbor, you tried not to talk about the Italian thing. We were very disappointed with their performance in the war. They weren't really heroes. They were brought up on this great macho crap. Our heroes were Joe DiMaggio and Phil Rizzuto. When the Yankees won the pennant in '41, they were our biggies. Crosetti was replaced by Rizzuto—I mean, it was an honorary Italian position, shortstop. The Yankee Italians were our heroes. The Cubs ultimately got Cavarretta and Dallessandro, but they didn't count.

You go to movies once a week, right? All you see are Italian guys surrendering to the British. Remember Africa? (Laughs.) That was terrible. You grow up, you're gonna be King Kong. All of a sudden all the guys that look like you are running with their arms in the air. I was ten, eleven, and very impressionable. See, the Italians were chumps.

The surrendering happened early. Now the whole neighborhood was not for Mussolini and not really against him. But if he went away, it would be good. We were against Hitler and it was easy to be against the Japanese, but it was still hard to be against Italians.

There were very few Italian-American confrontations. We pulled a deal with the Mafia in Sicily. Charlie Poletti, our lieutenant governor, became American military governor of Sicily. Suddenly all the Italian troops disappeared and went home. That's the first time I saw my father's town on the map. They had one of these big blowups of where the Americans were. I was proud as hell. Serradifalco was in the *Daily News* for the first time. 'Cause up to then, what did I know? I cut it out of the paper and showed it to my father. He grunted.

There were the American invasions, Anzio beachhead. And there was the great game of when Italy would become cobelligerent. Remember the Badoglio government? Our neighborhood followed this very closely.

At a certain point, Mussolini went in for a vote of confidence from his guys. They didn't give it to him, his own Fascist cabinet. He went to the king and this little guy, Victor Emmanuel, surprisingly said, Okay, you lose. (Laughs.) Someone said to him, Hey, you better get out of here, they're gonna kill you. So Mussolini gets hustled out of Piazza Venezia, goes to a ski resort where the Germans rescued him. They made him hide. They had the three fattest guys in the world take off in his glider. It was weird. Now the Italians are on our side, they're not our side.

Mussolini got the same fate as Lyndon Johnson. If Johnson had delivered a victory, he would have run for re-election and won. (Laughs.) The world hates losers. Mussolini was a loser, that's all. If Mussolini had won, he'd have been treated like Franco. Losers get hung. At least he had a great operatic finish: hanging by the heels.

Badoglio and the king made peace with us, and the Germans occupied all of Italy. There was a great sense of relief in the neighborhood. It was like getting the side out in a ball game. Finally, somebody comes in and puts out the fire. You're not gonna win the game, but at least you're not puttin' up runs. We won the war when the Italians gave up. (Laughs.) That's a fact. We had a V-J Day celebration.

What about the young Italian American soldiers?

They had to prove something, something macho. We have a system that neuters people in terms of background. We were heavy on the Italian feeling in America. We were more Italian than Italians. We always had a transient sense of our stay here. My uncle never became a citizen until he was in the army. Ninety days after you go in the army, you automatically became a citizen. It was still a ninety-day free home trial. (Laughs.)

Staying in America was something that you did to make money. You didn't stay in America to lead a good life. Nobody ever confused America with leading the good life. That happened after the war. Before the war, you always alluded to the return some way or other. It never happened, damn it.

I was born here, but I spoke Italian. We kept the tradition. There was always a sense of returning. I go back there, I feel very Sicilian. I feel at home there. Home is where the smells are good. You walk into any kitchen and it all smells like you want to be there. You don't get that here. This may explain the pro-Mussolini feeling. You can't call it an umbilical cord, but the connection was formidable. They never really cut it.

During the war, there was an implied sense of guilt. It was on all of us. So the sense of relief was tremendous. Remember when Sergeant John Basilone came home? He was the Italian American Medal of Honor winner. They have a bridge on the Jersey Turnpike named after him. He was our hero. He did the right things, but he did them in the Pacific. He was shooting gooks, so that's okay.

It would be very painful to see that same act of courage demonstrated against Italians. Even if he did it, he would have been forgotten about. With the Germans it would be different. Italians have always hated Germans. The Germans through their Austrian clients have always done maximum mayhem to the Italians.

As for blacks, there was a difference before the war and after the war. We thought Joe Louis was wonderful. He was such a champion, he was indisputable. Nobody was gonna ruffle Louis. We knew all the fighters. Prewar, Louis dominated the fight game. He was so imposing. It was a question of *when* he knocked you down. Everybody listened to the fights. If you walked down the neighborhood, everybody had the fight on. Louis knocked out Mauriello in the first round. He was a bartender from my neighborhood. It was equivalent to losing the South Bronx.

You enlisted to go into the marines or go into the navy. You never enlisted to defend America. No, America was like your boss. (Laughs.) You don't want to see anybody slash your boss's tires. It was a false patriotism. You had to be. You were Italian. There was no connection. It was a drifting thing.

Since the war, Italo-Americans have undergone this amazing transformation. They're now the most right-wing. There was a general black dislike before the war, like you disliked Jews. We had Jews lived in our apartment building, but that's different. That's my Jew. Keep your hands off him or you get killed. (Laughs.) But blacks didn't exist. We had two black guys in school and they were nice. There was never a threat. They didn't threaten us on the employment level. But after the war . . .

There were riots in Harlem in '45. I remember standing on a corner, a guy would throw the door open and say, "Come on down." They were goin' to Harlem to get in the riot. They'd say, "Let's beat up some niggers." It was wonderful. It was new. The Italo-Americans stopped being Italo and started becoming Americans. We joined the group. Now we're like you guys, right?

We went to college. Our whole neighborhood became professionals. All the guys whose mothers spoke Italian, every one of 'em is an engineer or a pharmacist. If you were an asshole, you became a pharmacist. My brother's a metallurgist. We were better than pushy Jews. We were pushy Italians. Now we're solid citizens.

Everybody started to get a piece of the rock. Everybody wanted to have a house away from the niggers. Now guys were talking about niggers: I gotta move out or my kids . . . The whole sense was to make money. We became respectable. We lost class.

We had all lived in one big apartment house my father built. He built a wine cellar. The guys, after they'd worked hard all day—not in offices, in factories—they'd have their dinner, there was no TV, they'd go downstairs, during the grape season, and they would crush. It was a communal effort. Everybody in the apartment house worked on the harvest. It was *The Most Happy Fella* in the Bronx. (Laughs.) My father would provide the machinery. Big vats of wine. Everybody would have his own grapes. The whole cellar was a vineyard. After the war, nobody used the wine cellars. The whole sense of community disappeared.

You lost your Italianness. There used to be four, five Italian bakeries in the neighborhood. You'd speak Italian. When I was a little kid, I was ashamed to speak Italian, but I did. On hot days in New York, they sat in front of the apartment houses and spoke Italian. At a certain point, somethin' happened. With the Bond bread, with the white bread, they started to speak English to each other. At the end of the war, the supermarket came. We made some money. We could see what the society wanted and we delivered. We became right-wing. Respect, respect, respectable.

Suddenly we looked up, we owned property. Italians could buy. The GI Bill, the American Dream. Guys my age had really become Americanized. They moved to the suburbs. I think American suburbs are bound by their antiblack sentiments. That's the common denominator. They're into it very easily, it seems. They feel they've achieved.

But they're worse off than they were before. That's the part they don't understand. They really haven't been assimilated. They're just the entrepreneurial rough-riders. They'll still take a tougher tack than most guys, getting what they want. Not one of my friends has taken an intellectual direction. The war bred the culture out of us. The opera, all the good things. My father could whistle every damn opera I ever heard. Of course every house had Caruso records. There wasn't a family that didn't have a lift-up phonograph. Opera was like cars for us. What the automobile is to Americans, opera was for us. My friends in the suburbs know nothing about opera, nothing about jazz. Just making money.

But they're still losers. When one of these guys walks into a room and he's got money, everybody presumes his money is ill-gotten, because he's Italian. The presumption is, unless his stuff is chronicled properly, it's illegal. He is still not respected. In fact, there's less respect now than we used to get when we were janitors. These dumb bastards, now that they're doctors and lawyers, don't believe it.

We came over here as the most independent, labor-oriented group, even more than the Jews from Eastern Europe. Sacco and Vanzetti were not weird wops. Their sense of struggle—*la lotta*—was very Italian. *La lotta continua*—the struggle continues. The struggle has been part of the Italian culture.

I remember when my grandmother went on strike. Her union was her life. She was an Italian dressmaker. We were in building trades, too. They were once strong unions. Now they've become corrupt. They're doing their best to subvert unions. Oh, God, I see the war as that transition piece that pulled us out of the wine cellar. It obliterated our culture and made us Americans. That's no fun.

JACK SHORT

If you searched for the archetypal middle-class Middle American, he would be a likely candidate. Bespectacled, medium height, a bit on the portly side, he could pass without undue notice in any middle-management society. He is fifty-seven years old and has lived all his life in a northeastern town within two hours commuting distance from New York. He has worked for IBM for thirty-two years. "I joined the corporation after I came out of the service and after I finished college on a GI Bill." He is in the finance department, and "it's been a very enjoyable type of career."

Right after D-Day, early June, '44, I landed in Liverpool. It seems that a few days later we landed at Omaha Beach. As you looked up on the beach, you could actually see the making of GI cemeteries. That was your first shock, regardless of all the combat training you had.

It just seemed like there was no set front. You'd go into areas where there were Germans and you'd just keep going and going. It just seemed like the war was almost over. We just raced across Germany and ended just outside Leipzig. The war ended. The Germans had surrendered.

Just before the surrender, we came across a concentration camp in Nordhausen. The Germans took off. It was unbelievable. The dying and the many dead stacked up like cordwood. I was just turning twenty then. Our company commander chased us all out of the camp, because of the disease. I guess you could get typhoid. He went back and he took a whole series of pictures. He gave each of us a set. I have them home yet. Every once in a while if you want to refresh your memory, you take those out and look at 'em. People living like animals.

We didn't get to talk to any of them. The army moved in medical supplies and food and had to bury the dead. You read these things, you heard these things, but you never believed 'em. It's typical of American people, I guess. You don't believe it until you see it. You look at the war and say, Gee, was that something I really experienced? Many people are forgetting that there was a World War Two.

In a way, World War Two had a positive impact on me as an individual. I can say I matured in those three years. I certainly did want to obtain an education. I wanted to better myself rather than, say, hitting a local factory. I didn't want to be a blue-collar worker. This was basically all we had in our area. Fortunately, I was educated on the GI Bill. I obtained a nice position in the company, have a nice family. Everything in my lifetime since the war has been positive. I don't mean that war is positive. They're all negative as far as I'm concerned.

The war changed our whole idea of how we wanted to live when we came back. We set our sights pretty high. If we didn't have the war, in Poughkeepsie, the furthest you'd travel would be maybe New York or Albany. But once people started to travel—People wanted better levels of living, all people.

I come from a working-class family. All my relatives worked in factories. They didn't own any business. They worked with their hands. High school was about as far as they went. I went to college, studied accounting, and that's all I've been doing for thirty-two years.

In the service, I was with people, some of 'em came from the farm country, some of 'em worked in the auto factories out in Detroit, some came from the South who worked on somebody else's farm. I said, Hey, you don't want to do the things these people are doin'. I thought to myself, this isn't what I want out of life. I want to have a good job, a respectable life.

Fellas I had gone in the service with, five or six, we all had the same feeling. We all went back to school. One's an engineer today, another one's a pharmacist. We just didn't want to go back and work in a factory in the hometown. The GI Bill was a blessing. It paid for 99 percent of your college expenses and gave you money each month to live on. That's the best thing the government came out with after the war. Yet it was bad in a way. Twenty dollars a week for fifty-two weeks. A lotta people just sat, they didn't even look for jobs. Just like welfare. I think in the long run it might have been detrimental.

It was funny when we first came back to go to college. We had a sprinkling of younger people coming right out of high school. I can tell you they were so used to studying that they certainly made us look not too good for the first year or so, until we got our skills back to rights. But they did help us. It was amazing that the young kids helped the GI to get back to studying. I got out in three and a half years, 'cause I figured I was gettin' too old to stay in school, I better get out and start earnin' a living. I was twenty-five. In 1950, I got a job with the corporation and have been there ever since.

I sort of listen to young people now. The first feeling you had during Vietnam, you were against 'em. Get in line, do your thing, stop this protesting. I did it, you have to do it too. We found out after that it was wrong. You wonder now: were they right? The whole thing was just one big mess. Then you start to wonder the same thing about World War Two. Did we get pulled in by the same kind of thing that pulled us into Vietnam?

You try not to talk about the sad points as much as about the funnier points. Those seem to be the stories you remember. Today, a lot of people talk about World War Two like they're glory points —I did this, I did that. I never discuss what I did in the service with my children. I told them some of the funnier stories. They do not know all the things that happened during the World War. I prefer that they don't.

DON McFADDEN

A retired deputy sheriff, Los Angeles County.

I was sixteen, too young to sign up, when the war broke out. The next year, I went to work in a foundry, filing castings for airplanes. Hey, I felt, I'm makin' a contribution to the war effort. I was told to collect some of this magnesium dust for chemical analysis. They tried to catch it in a paper bag, if you can imagine it. This bag was tied to a grinding stone. I had this magnesium powder on me, a spark hit it, and I started on fire. I panicked. A couple of workers knocked me down. I was burned from the waist up. My hands really bad, third-degree burns. My face was okay, but the rest of me was raw meat.

I spent the summer of '42 in the hospital. That brought the war home to me. I thought, I'm really a civilian casualty of the war. I took 'em to court and tried to prove negligence, because they didn't have the proper safety facilities. They threw it out, of course. But being young, I recovered and bounced back.

Los Angeles was just a beehive, twenty-four hours a day. In those days, it was fairly easy to get around. Streetcars. The defense plants were moving full time, shipyards and all the rest. Downtown movies were staying open twenty-four hours a day. And restaurants. You could go downtown at two in the morning, it'd be like Saturday. Any time would be Saturday night. Streets were full of people.

So many people came out here to work in the defense industry. There'd been a big influx before that because of the Depression, people coming up from the Dust Bowl. When they got into aircraft production and the shipyards, they did pretty well. They own a lot of property in San Fernando Valley. (Laughs.) Oh, Los Angeles boomed.

In the summer of '43, they had these zoot-suit riots. Zoot suit was a style of dress, mostly Mexican American kids went into it at that time. It actually started in East L.A., and they would spread out to

Hollywood and down around the beach. Once in a while they'd have a ruckus, okay? They were called rat packs.

There were some sailors down at the beach. Apparently, they got into some kind of confrontation with these zoot-suits. A sailor had been stabbed, that was the word. When the word got back to San Diego, where all the servicemen were—well, you know the navy and the marines. (Laughs.) This was in June of '43. Thousands of servicemen came up en masse. They started out in East L.A. They started grabbing anybody that had a zoot suit on. Anybody wearing that was fair game. They just really did a number on 'em—ripped their clothes up, beat 'em up. Then it spread downtown, and the police really had a problem.

I heard about it on the radio and was reading about it. This had been going on maybe a week. One night myself, my brother, and two friends decided to go down and see what was going on, right? We figured: Hey, we're big men. We're gonna get involved in this. We really just wanted to see firsthand what was happening.

They had the streets blocked off for about six blocks. No traffic at all on Main Street. Pretty soon, we see these servicemen confronting the zoot-suiters. Sometimes they didn't even have zoot suits on. If they happened to be Mexican, that was enough.

We walked into a little restaurant on Main Street, just standing there, nothing going on. All of a sudden, I see a guy in civilian clothes, he's really giving my brother a hard time. I'm wondering what's goin' on, we weren't doing anything. He just grabs him and hauls him outside. My brother was fourteen at the time. One of my buddies went out to talk to him, and he starts doing the same thing to him—grabbed 'im and shakin' him.

It turned out he was a detective. He is in plain clothes and didn't identify himself. So I went out and said, "What's going on?" He kinda came on strong, so I took a swing at him. (Laughs.) That was my mistake. I was seventeen and in good shape. I don't know what ever made me do it. Down the street, there were a couple of six-foot-six motorcycle cops. They had their clubs out. They ran down and really started takin' care of me. They did a number on my head with their clubs. I covered up and it was all over. I did get cut up, but at that time I had a little more hair than I got now, so it gave me some padding.

We were all under curfew age, so they took us to jail for violation. We ended up in about half a dozen jails. We went to the old Plaza jail that was really old. It was still made out of adobe. (Laughs.) They took us to the Georgia Street jail. They put three of us in one cell. We were the only non-zoot-suiters there, the only non-Mexicans.

The rest of the jail was packed with all these zoot-suiters. They'd been picking 'em up all over town, not because they'd done anything wrong, but because they were victims and they were tryin' to keep 'em from gettin' hurt. Most of 'em had their clothes in shreds. Their tailor-made suits were just hangin' on 'em. They'd been really worked over.

All these taunts were going back and forth between the three of us and all these zoot-suiters. You no-good zoot-suiters and this and that. (Laughs.) We were tryin' to rile 'em. How's it feel to be in jail? Of course, they didn't put us in with them or we'da probably been beaten up. We really didn't have anything against 'em. We were just out for a lark. Anyway, we ended up bein' transferred to another jail. We spent the night there. My parents couldn't find out what happened to us. They hadn't been notified. The next afternoon, they came and got me out.

A lotta people got hurt, a lot of innocent people, a lot of these young Mexican kids. I saw a group of servicemen stop a streetcar. They spotted one zoot-suiter on it. They got on, he couldn't get off. They carried him off unconscious. Here's a guy riding a streetcar and he gets beat up 'cause he happens to be a Mexican. I actually saw that happen.

Servicemen would go into theaters in downtown L.A. They'd go up and make the projectionist shut off the movie, right? Turn the lights on. They'd go down both aisles. Any zoot-suiters they saw (laughs), they'd drag him right out by his seat and—(clap hands)—beat him, tear his clothes up, what have you. They were mostly sailors and marines. They came from San Diego.

I went in the service, the navy, in August of '43. I got out in April of '46. I think the war pulled us out of isolation and pulled us out of the Depression. And L.A. became a big metropolis—too big, actually. (Laughs.)

It was just an interesting time to be alive, and history was being made. There was a feeling of optimism. It will be a better world—afterwards, you know. I'm not really too optimistic about what's happening today.

The war made me grow up a lot faster. It was good for me because of the discipline I received. It probably kept me out of serious trouble. I was a wild kid and had friends that did some crazy things. (Laughs.) By the grace of God, we survived without endin' up in jail.

MAYOR TOM BRADLEY

We were called out at the time of the so-called zoot-suit riots. It spread from Watts to downtown Los Angeles. Waves of servicemen came to town, and they were indiscriminatingly jumping and fighting both Hispanic and black youth on the streets of downtown Los Angeles.

Those riots affected my life. I was to receive my induction papers to report the following week for training, and then my unit would be off to England in a matter of weeks. I had been all set to go. My wife was about to deliver, and I went to my draft board to see if there was any chance of getting an extension. This was three days after the riots erupted in Watts. The chairman of my draft board said, "Aren't you handling these little thugs who broke out my windows?" They were smashing windows in the fighting that went on. "Yes, I'm handling those cases." "Well, we need you here right now. You tear up your induction papers and we'll send you some new ones in a month or so."

I waited a month, two months, three months. No papers came. I was caught up in what I was doing. Four or five months later, I received a reclassification. Essential service, law enforcement, exempted me from induction. I knew some of the fellows who were scheduled for induction at the same time. With very little training, they were shipped off to England and scattered all over Europe. I would have been right in the middle of the battle. I might be in a grave somewhere.

MICKEY RUIZ

He is an upholsterer in Los Angeles.

He was one of the twenty-two Mexican American defendants in the Sleepy Lagoon case. It was a celebrated trial in Los Angeles in 1942.

The defendants ranged in age from seventeen to twenty-two. They were known as pachucos or zoot-suiters. They had crashed a party of other Chicano young people. There was a killing.

Alice McGrath, who was active in their defense, recalls the anti-Mexican feelings in the community: "The so-called zoot-suit riots took place smack in the middle of our case. They ought more properly to have been called the servicemen's riots, newspaper-inflamed. The newspapers ran pictures of the crowds cheering on the servicemen against the zoot-suiters."

Ruiz was one of the three sentenced to five years to life. The California Appellate Court unanimously reversed the decision. He was set free after eighteen months at San Quentin.

My dad, he worked in the copper mines in Arizona. He was disabled. We were poor, but I didn't feel poor. I didn't know what poor was. My mamma loved me, my daddy loved me. The neighborhood was nice. I wasn't aware of any anti-Mexican feeling. I never thought of it. Although later, when we tried to go to a dance, like at the Palomar, we couldn't get in 'cause they said no Mexicans allowed.

The war came and Walter Villa, a friend of mine, went off to fight. This guy was probably the best athlete I've ever known. He went off into the medics. In the Pacific. He was killed in a hurry.

I was drafted early in 1945. I went, but I wasn't anxious to go. I go up to the draft board and they had me playin' with blocks. They classified me as illiterate—I couldn't read or write. So they gave me a deferment. I go back in six months and I thought I'm gonna get another deferment. But me and my big mouth, I turn around and I tell this sergeant, "Say, sergeant, didn't I see you here six months ago?" The guy says, "Wait a minute." I guess he figured if my memory was that good . . . (Laughs.) Next thing I knew, I was in the army. (Laughs.)

I was shammin' a little bit, but I guess I wasn't too bright. They sent me to Dumb School. There was a camp up north, called Camp McQuade. This is where illiterates were sent. While you're being processed, they ask you what you wish to do. I figure as long as I'm in the army, I'll shoot for the next best thing. I figure I'll go in the paratroopers. This corporal looks at my record and says, "Uh-uh, mister, not you. You're goin' to Dumb School."

They sent us to Korea, because it was under Japanese domination at that time, until we took over. I didn't get to see any action.

After I came home on leave, I didn't want to go back, so they came and got me. (Laughs.) I was still in a fog. I was just goin' through the motions, ever since the trial and the time in the joint. I may have come out to take a peek and didn't like what I saw, went right back into my fog.

I didn't like the army. My prison record—it follows you regardless. I remember one night at Fort MacArthur, I go into the barracks and I just happened to look at the bunk next to me. I saw a wallet there. I looked around and happened to see a guy over in the corner. I'll be damned, they wanna find out who's doing what. I go to the officer of the day and I tell him, "Hey, there's a wallet in one of the bunks over there." They weren't surprised. They just wanted to turn around and catch somebody.

Maybe it's me. I was a little bit more aggressive than I should have been in a lot of ways. I'm happy-go-lucky. Maybe I was just too loud. It seemed like I was always gettin' in trouble. Always diggin' these 6 by 6 by 6 holes, and coverin' 'em up myself.

I came back out of the army and I did a lot of goof-up. I still wasn't ready to face life. The army didn't help. I turned around and went back to prison again. Everything changed about twenty-five years ago, when I gave my wife my earnings from my paycheck. I wouldn't give her nothin' before. This last time I said, "Okay, Mamma, you take care of business from now on." Since then, everything has been nice.

DEMPSEY TRAVIS

A real estate broker and writer on Chicago's South Side.

The army was an experience unlike anything I've had in my life. I think of two armies, one black, one white. I saw German prisoners free to move around the camp, unlike black soldiers, who were restricted. The Germans walked right into the doggone places like any white American. We were wearin' the same uniform, but we were excluded.

This was Camp Shenango, Pennsylvania, about thirty-five miles east of Youngstown, Ohio. When I arrived, I stepped into mud up to my knees. The troop train was Jim Crow. They had a car for black soldiers and a car for whites. They went to their part and sent us to the ghetto. It seems the army always arranged to have black soldiers back up against the woods someplace. Isolated. We were never near the main gate. If you went through camp as a visitor, you'd never know black soldiers were there, unless they happened to be working on some menial detail.

They didn't have a PX that black soldiers could use. There was a white PX, but we could not use it. They set up a temporary situation in the barracks where a guy had some candy bars and a Coke. At the white PX, you could buy almost anything. We had nothin'. There was no black servicemen's club. No place for recreation. The only thing guys could do is shoot craps and play cards. If lucky, they might get a pass to Sharon, about fifteen miles away.

Although there were five theaters on the post, there were none that black soldiers could use. After we'd been there a couple of weeks, they decided to put a makeshift theater right in the center of the black area. You could get maybe a couple of hundred guys in, so they had to run it in shifts. A friend named Kansas and I had decided we'd go to the theater that night. When we looked out, the line was so damn long, we knew we'd never get in. So we made the second shift. *Wuthering Heights* was the picture.

As we walked out of the theater, there was a group of black soldiers standing around in a big discussion. Some black soldier's eye had been kicked out for going into the PX to get a beer. The guys were talking: We've got to do something about it. Kansas and I just walked into this.

Within minutes, a caravan of six trucks loaded with white soldiers in battle-color fatigues, like they had in jungle warfare, looked like green leaves, camouflage, they drove up and surrounded the area. Cut the street off. The lights went out and they start firing. Firing, firing, firing, just shooting into the goddamn crowd. Everybody started scrambling like hell. I must have run maybe five feet and fell, my friend Kansas beside me. I put my hand on my leg and I could feel something warm running down my pants.

Funny thing is I thought I'd be very religious at that point. Whereas, I was just filled with hate. I'd say, The rotten son-of-a-bitches. I just cursed. Meantime, shooting is still going on and men are screaming. Then the shooting subsides. Then comes the Red Cross. The guys start walking through the crowd with flashlights.

"This one is dead." "This one is bad." I don't know how many died and how many were wounded.

When they got to me, they said, "He'll live. He just seems to be shot in several places." I was shot three times. Then they looked at my friend. They threw a flashlight on him. They said, "He'll make it. Niggers don't die when you shoot 'em in the head." This was a Red Cross worker.

They took us both to the ambulance. Two guys were sitting in front. The one says to the driver, "Why we be doin' this to our own soldiers?" Driver says, "Who ever told you niggers were our soldiers? Where I come from"—I detected a southern accent—"we shoot niggers like we shoot rabbits." This stayed with me. This sound of these two men talking about two disabled black soldiers. Shot not by the enemy but by Americans.

We finally arrived at the base hospital and they rolled me into the corridor. They rolled Kansas into a little room that was probably four, five feet from where I was. I could see him on his bed. The doctor looked at him, went through this raising-your-eyelid thing. Then he started pumping his legs up about six or seven times. He pulled the light out and closed the door. No one had to tell me. Kansas was dead.

That night I was rolled into a ward with other soldiers. I recognized some of the guys who had been shot. Within forty feet of me were about twelve or fourteen of these guys.

There was a belief that I would never walk again. Doctors said, "You seem to be paralyzed." Well, that certainly disturbed the hell out of me. There's a guy next to me screamin' and hollerin'. Somehow, this information never reached the newspapers.

The Red Cross evidently contacted my parents. I hadn't been in the hospital forty-eight hours when I looked up and here comes my father. My father with a big cigar in his mouth, lookin' proud. He's a stockyard worker, but never been outside Chicago since comin' from Georgia. He had a walk and a proudness and an importance that you just couldn't believe. My mother, just the opposite. A very mild woman, but a smile that is so infectious it just brightens up the room. She saw me and her eyes just started blazing with tears and smiling ... (Cries.) Shit, when you go back and try to remember, that's hard. I mean, that's hard.

(Laughing and crying at the same time) Oh, God, I was so glad to see my parents. Overwhelming to be twenty-one years old and just totally out of it, thinking that I would never walk again. They told my parents that they would have to ship me out to the general hospital in Butler, Pennsylvania. Whatever operation was needed was not gonna take place here.

Before I was shipped out, an unusual thing happened. The FBI or the CIA or G-2, I don't know which, took a special interest in my case. They kept probing me at my bedside: Who did the shooting? As if I would know. How did it happen? Where were you? What were you doing prior to this happening? I told them I was in the theater and just walked out. The general hospital is about fifty or sixty miles from Shenango. Never will forget the rolling hills of Pennsylvania. Seemed like these doggone ambulances had no springs. Every damn bump all the way. Arriving there, they put me in private quarters. The army at that time was still very Jim Crow, even with sick people. I was isolated.

The same man showed up again, civilian clothes, black pants, the whispering, the same series of questions. He assured me I'd be taken care of here.

I found out later that my IQ was higher than anybody else's in the group that had been shot. They probably thought I was the ringleader. I had no idea I had a high IQ. (Laughs.) They didn't send anybody else out here except me. They put a screen in front of my bed. Red Cross is passing out candy and when this person reached my door, I heard another person say, "Oh, don't go in there. They got a coon in that room." (Laughs.)

A doctor showed up, examines me, and says, "I think I can relieve you of this problem. It's gonna take a series of operations. You may be able to walk, but never as you walked before. Probably a serious limp."

That set off a set of circumstances that I'd never dealt with before. Mary, the woman who had been advised not to come into my room, a little white woman about four feet six, came in. She said, "What would you like, candy, a magazine, a book?" I said, "I'll take 'em all." (Laughs.) We struck up a friendship. She said, "I notice nobody's been in to see you. As soon as the doctor gives me permission, I'm gonna take you for a ride."

My fever was running high as hell. Once it subsided, I went through X-rays and they determined how they're gonna take out these bullets with the least amount of permanent injury. I had shrapnel across the back, right here through the thick—buttocks. It caught me as I was falling. This one, half an inch deep, wide as my small finger. If I weren't falling, that one would've signed me off.

When they finally decided to operate, the two doctors couldn't agree on the diagnosis. One was a Wasp and one was a Jewish fella. They argued in front of me. I was a nonperson. Finally, the Jewish guy won and the other resigned from the case. He took one bullet out, left one in. He said, "If we remove it, it'll cause a new kind of problem." Through some miracle, the operation was partially successful. I had to drag my leg a bit, but I could feel the strength coming back.

On a thirty-day furlough, I returned to Chicago the fall of '43. I visited some of the clubs, Rum Boogie, Club de Luxe, Club de Lisa. Oh God, it was wonderful. I was still limping, but I saw improvement.

My mother didn't want me to go back. She started writing letters to congressmen, senators, even to President Roosevelt. She told them of my experience. But I went back.

I didn't walk as well as I thought I should. But this new doctor said, "Goddamn it, boy, walk down that hill. We're gonna send you back to Shenango." I didn't have any money, so Mary let me have five dollars.

When I got back to Shenango, I discovered something. They had built a major service center for the black servicemen. They had opened up the main theater and blacks were permitted to go. (Laughs.) It appears that you had to kill some guys. There was never an inquiry, to my knowledge.

A fellow I met a couple of years later told me he was at Shenango the night of the shooting. He spent the night under the bed. Later that night, the black guys broke into the ammunition place and got armed. This thing was not really quelled for forty-eight to seventy-two hours. It didn't die right that night. He said, "All I could hear is gunshot fire throughout the night." The next day, he said, his whole outfit was shipped out overseas.

They decided that what I needed improvement on was not my legs so much as my attitude. I should see a psychiatrist. Then they decided to talk about my career. Isn't that a bitch? This guy said, "You can be any damn thing you wanna be. You got an IQ over 137." I said, "What does that mean?" He said, "It means you're a candidate for OCS." You can do this, you can do that, you can do the other. I wasn't impressed. I was a musician.

They decided they were gonna make me a leader. (Laughs.) They put me in charge of a troop movement going to Camp Lee, Virginia.

I thought I'd seen everything. We changed trains at Washington, D.C. I thought this being the capital of the country, I could go and get me a Coke. Ha ha. (Laughs.) The woman said, "Boy, you don't drink no Cokes here. Go downstairs." I said, "God, this is Washington, D.C." (Laughs.) She looked at me like I was crazy. I guess I was. On the train to camp, we looked out of the back of the car and saw the dome of the Capitol. I said, What the hell does that mean? It didn't mean what I read in my civics books at DuSable High.

In Richmond—Camp Lee is nearby—we see German PWs riding streetcars in front, the blacks in the back. It was the first time that I saw black and white water fountains. In the theater at Camp Lee, I saw black officers and black enlisted men sitting in the back, behind a rope. In front were white officers and white enlisted men. The black officers seemed to show such pride. The thought went through my mind: How can you be proud sitting behind a rope? They're telling you, Boy, you are nothing. We're gonna rope you off.

Although there were many empty white barracks, we lived in tents. We used to sit in these damn tents in the hot sun waiting for some available space in the camp's black belt. It lasted some six or eight months.

The lying and dreaming that soldiers would do among themselves is unbelievable. I'd only finished high school, but these sophisticates from Philadelphia, from Baltimore, were talking about what colleges they'd been to. Black colleges. They were gonna do this, they were gonna do that. This is a training camp for quartermasters. These guys with college training were sent to cooking schools, digging schools, motor vehicle.

I was sent to the administrative school. This puts you in a position to become a master sergeant. I was there three days and yanked: "We have orders to ship you out in charge of another cadre to Aberdeen Proving Ground, Maryland." I said, "Why?" I liked this school. I was learning how to type. I'm trying to become an elitist, you see. (Laughs.) I had decided I was gonna make something of myself as a good soldier.

At Aberdeen I'm assigned to all these guys doing KP duty, kitchen police, trash detail, truck detail, pickin' up garbage. For three weeks, I'm layin' around. I don't really have an assignment. One day an officer sends for me: "Travis, I see you have a good record. What would you like to do?" What can I do? I'm a musician. He said, "We don't have a band here. But your IQ indicates you can do much more than that."

The next day I see a Major Sloan, a tall, red-faced, freckled, moon-shaped-faced, big-blue-eyed ex-Texas Ranger. He said, "Can you type?" I said, "No, sir." "Have you ever worked in an office?" "No, sir." He reaches into the drawer and pulls out a typing book. He calls in a corporal and says, "You give Private Travis that desk behind you. He's gonna learn how to type." I'll never forget Major Sloan. He recognized that as a piano player I used my fingers, and it wouldn't take much for me to become a typist.

He kept at me for about a month. I got up to fifty-five words a minute. He called me back: "Have you ever worked in a store?" "No, sir." He said, "I want you to work in the post exchange as a clerk." In about three months, he said, "We're gonna make you assistant manager." Within two months, I was the manager. This was a black PX. But that was not enough for him. He decided he wants me to manage the white PX as well. This was early '45, just before Roosevelt died. They were beginning to integrate the facilities. So I was the first guy to become manager of an integrated PX in the state of Maryland. I won first prize for the best-managed store in the Aberdeen Proving Grounds.

Sloan brought the post commander down to me, a general: "We're gonna have the newspapers take pictures of you, 'cause we're very proud of what you're doin'." A couple of days later, he came back: "Travis, that picture will never appear in the paper. Those fellas can't stand the idea of a black man being able to operate a post exchange in this manner." The picture never appeared.

I found the most sympathetic white men in the army were actually southerners. I found this to be true in civilian life as well. The best breaks I've got as a businessman have come from guys out of Alabama and Georgia. If they decide they're gonna go with you, they go all the damn way. And no forked tongue. (Laughs.)

What about your limp? I don't notice any.

Bit by bit, it disappeared as my leg got stronger. I still have the bullet in my hip. No compensation. Of course not.

I was in from September 9, 1942, to February 2, 1946. When I was about to get discharged, Major Sloan said, "Why don't you stay?

I want to send you to officer candidate school. You'd make a damn fine officer." But I'd had enough. I said, "Let me out as early as you can, so I can at least go to school under the GI Bill."

"I took entrance exams at Roosevelt, at DePaul, at Northwestern. I got three letters back saying pretty much the same thing: Look, you dumb son of a bitch, don't ever try to get into college, 'cause you just ain't got what it takes. Try usin' your arms, try usin' your back. They never said, Try usin' your head.

"I was so goddamn depressed, I did what my father did. I went to work at the stockyards. As a laborer, a Georgia mule. At noontime, all the guys would gather around me as I told stories. The foreman, a big Irishman, came up to me: 'I'm gonna fire you. Know why? You're too smart to be out here. You can do better than this. You should be doin' income tax or somethin'.'

"So I started working out income tax problems for relatives and friends. I didn't know anything about income tax, but if you can count, you can figure out a form. In the meantime, an old teacher met me on the street and said, 'Why don't you try Englewood Evening Junior College? You don't have to take an entrance exam.' I enrolled in Accounting 101 and Sociology 101. It restored my confidence. I enrolled at Wilson Junior College and I ended up in remedial everything: reading, writing. I was stupid enough to enroll in American Literature 117. I remember turning in my first paper on Silas Marner. *The teacher was furious. He thought it was a joke. It was that bad. It was my crazy stubbornness that persuaded him not to kick me out. One day, it just came to me, the whole meaning, the whole concept.*

"No person who learned to read normally at the regular age can understand this experience. To learn to read as a man twenty-seven years old! It's just like somebody lifted a veil off your eyes. (Laughs and cries.) I went to Roosevelt and finished two years in one. That's the story of me and the GI Bill. It paid my tuition and that made the difference. If anything positive came out of the war, that was it."

My mother was glad I was alive. My father was always kind of laid-back and important. He was not an emotional man. All the emotion was on my mother's side. And on my side. (Laughs.) He didn't appreciate how much I loved him until I started getting these promotions in the army. I would send him a box of cigars and he would talk of "my boy, the sergeant." While I was still in the army, he died. On my emergency furlough, I saw him that last day at County Hospital. His last words were, "Boy, you're the man of the house now. You gotta take care of your mother." My mother's eighty-six now and I'm still takin' care of her.

Those four years in the army are the turning point in my life. I learned something about men. I learned something about racism. I learned something about values. I learned something about myself. I don't think I'd have that experience any other place or time. Under no other circumstance would I have seen so many men in one setting, where I could evaluate them and myself. Imagine Major Sloan! Would you believe that he insisted I study the Bretton Woods Reports and explain it to the troops? I, who could hardly read. See the boy run. The cat jumped the fence. How can I ever forget this experience and this man?

I see World War Two as having been a step on the first rung of the ladder. But I wouldn't want to wish it on anybody else.

WIN STRACKE

A Chicago balladeer, founder of the Old Town School of Folk Music.

I was in the Sixty-second Coast Artillery. I got a little tired of being with the command post. When we were in the uplands of Algeria, I asked to be transferred to one of the guns. These were 40-millimeter Bofors. There were fifteen men to a gun.

You had fifteen guys who for the first time in their lives were not living in a competitive society. We had no hopes of becoming officers. I liked that feeling very much. There's a job to be done and everyone pitches in, some more than others. For the first time in their lives, they could help each other without fear of losing a commercial advantage. Without cutting each other's throat or trying to put down somebody else through a boss or whatever.

The army was a totally different experience from any I had in civilian life, where you competed for jobs. There was nothing of that here. I enjoyed that. It stayed with me during the entire war. I was in for three years and four months, June of '42 to September of '45.

It was forty years ago, but all these guys still remember it. We have battery reunions, although there's a gradual dying off. This was the most important experience these guys would ever have. Mine, too. I think it must have altered the character of these guys and their relations with their neighbors. Maybe I've romanticized it. I don't know.

I don't think very many were ideologically motivated. Some couldn't tell the difference between the Nazis and our allies. They did things that infuriated the French. When we landed in southern France, I remember seeing our guys picking up melons around the vine, breaking them, and throwing them away. They acted like boors. They were very complimentary to the Germans when we finally got to Germany and saw the autobahns. And how clean they were. The Germans kept their manure piles in the back yards and the French kept them in their front yards. Because they were proud of them, I guess.

I can remember heated discussions when John L. Lewis pulled out the miners. Oh, the terrible bitterness. "Those sons-o'-bitchin' miners are makin' a hundred and fifty or two hundred bucks a week and we're bustin' our asses for a hundred dollars a month. They oughta string 'em up." I don't think too many of the guys had worked at decent jobs. When I was filling out my questionnaire—I'd been making close to two hundred a week—I modified it to, say, a hundred and twenty-five. The guys thought I was lying. (Laughs.) But with the gun, these things were gradually solved.

I remember a Christmas morning on the outskirts of Palermo. Good-conduct medals were being handed out. You'd get one if you didn't get the clap during the preceding year. (Laughs.) We were standing in the middle of the gun positions and sang familiar Christmas carols. Someone was playing a mouth harp. Right in the middle of a carol, a boy about twelve in an Arab dress—a Mediterranean dress which probably hadn't changed in two thousand years—came through the gun position, driving his sheep. I immediately had the fantasy of seeing a boy like the young Jesus going about his work. It was a memorable experience.

When I was at Aix-en-Provence the following Christmas, I was asked to sing for the children of French prisoners of war. Monsieur Puel, the town's leading barrister, requested "Mon Bon Sapin." (Sings) "Mon bon sapin . . ." I said, "That's 'O Tannenbaum,' isn't it?" He said, "Oh, no, that's an old French folk song." Then he asked me to sing "O Douce Nuit"—O Sweet Night. (Sings a few bars in French.) It was "Stille Nacht, heilige Nacht." He insisted it was an

Alsatian song which was originally sung in French.

We were in Mannheim, Germany, when the war in Europe ended. We were sent to various batteries in preparation for coming home. I was in Fulda, where my namesake, Saint Winfrid, converted the tree-worshipping Germans to Christianity. My family came from this area.

On the very day we dropped the bomb on Hiroshima, August 6, 1945, I was walking down a lovely German road. It was a beautiful time of the year. Everything was lush and green. I had decided to visit my brother-in-law, who was stationed in Bad Bischofsheim.

I see a farm wagon approaching from a distance. There was a young German sitting on the crosstrees. He was virile and full of ginger. He was singing. I could barely hear him. I continued to walk as he approached. It was apparent that he was not going to give me any attention. As we came closer, I recognized the song. It was an aria from a German light opera, *Der Waffenschmied*—The Armorer. I had sung the title role at the University of Chicago just a few months before I was drafted. I sensed an arrogance about him. I assumed he thought he was going to give this American GI a lesson in German culture. He was getting his kicks, there was no doubt about it.

As he started the verse "Auch ich war ein Jünglein mit lockigem Haar"—I was a young man with curly hair, but look at me now— I was almost as bald then as I am now. (Laughs.) As he finished the verse, as we were exactly opposite each other, I sang out and took the chorus away from him: "Ja, das war eine glückliche Zeit"—Yes, that was a wonderful time.

I resisted the impulse to look at him. I kept my eyes straight ahead. I just wanted him to get the shock. I kept walking without giving him a glance. Finally, after about a quarter of a mile, I couldn't resist any more. I looked back. There he was staring at me. If he had been at Stalingrad, I don't think he'd have been shocked as much as he was at that moment. I felt he had been looking back at me all the time. Bewildered, I'm sure. He must have had a very rude awakening. It was a grand moment for me. I was showing him it was not only his culture, it was mine. It was the culture of anyone in the world who loved music.

I came back from the war primarily concerned with making a living to support my new family. I studied voice, paid for by the GI Bill. I don't think I had any illusion about a change in the world. For the first time in our lives, we were in a tribal sort of situation, where we could help each other without fear. I had realized it was the absence of competition and boundaries and all those phony standards that created the thing I loved about the army.

JOHNNY DeGRAZIO

He has the appearance of a jockey who has put on a pound or two. Two subjects possessed him: World War Two and gambling. It was as a matter of course that we wound up at a greasy spoon in Chicago: OPEN ALL NITE. He has been a cabdriver for fifteen years. I was his fare. Of course, I did not reach my destination on schedule.

I got drafted in World War Two, naturally, like everybody else. I was real patriotic. I wanted to be up front and everything else.

I come from a neighborhood where you done anything a little bit awkward, you were a sissy. Or you didn't have this pride or things like that. When I got drafted and found out it was for noncombatant, I resented that. Then I got the inkling: I volunteered for the paratroopers. And the guy says, "You're better off here." He said, "We need you over here" and shit like that. He wanted more or less to make a dog robber outa me. A dog robber is a guy that cleans the officer's quarters, shines his shoes, takes this, drives a jeep, and everything. I says, "Mister, I come here to fight. I don't wanna be no dog robber." I says, "I ain't goin' back to no neighborhood to tell 'em I come here to shine shoes." So he says, "Get outa here."

I come from a neighborhood where pride was pride. Lotta people say, "You might not have anything, but you still got your pride." To me, pride is somethin'. In other words, joinin' the army, you were supposed to fight for your country, not this bullshit. You know, of medic roller. Of course, everybody's got their part. To me, it was somethin' else. When we got overseas, to England, the job was actually to uncrate the equipment, take it to their destination, and bullshit like that. What the heck was it?

This was in England during wartime. English people are hurtin', right? Blackout, rationin', everything, okay? Mess sergeant, he's gettin' all the food, right? Now he's takin' this food to the officers and exchangin' it for booze and soap and whatchacallit. An' they're gettin' all the broads, the English broads. They finally did nail 'im and he got busted. He was sellin' some of the booze to us at double the price. They had it made over there, the officers and the mess sergeant. You know, like anything else, hand-in-hand.

In basic trainin', too. This hand-in-hand. You're first processed, they hand you the clothing, and ten minutes later they says everything's gotta be on hangers, buttoned up an' everything else. Ten minutes later comes a guy sellin' hangers a nickel apiece. After the soldiers left, this guy says, "Leave the hangers here." They sold maybe two hundred. Barracks got filled up again, the same bullshit.

I was in from November '42 to March '45. I got sick in England. I was in the army hospital for about eleven months, got discharged. Came back to the States, I contracted dermatitis. I didn't wanna get out. I was still wavin' the flag. Bein' discharged with a disability. I was tyin' my hands to the bed not to scratch myself. The other guys were puttin' GI soap under the arms to break out an' get discharged. They saw what I was doin'. See, I wanted to stay in 'cause everybody else was sacrificin' their lives. I didn't wanna get out. I was still wavin' the flag.

How was it in the neighborhood when you came back?

This bunch would give you such a terrific rag and everything else. Especially if you were a cook or a pill roller—a dog robber, takin' care of the officer's quarters. That's beautiful, isn't it? I'm gonna go back an' tell everybody I was a dog robber, right? I was disappointed in a way, because I did not achieve what I wanted to be. I didn't find out what I wanted to find out. I wanted to be in combat. I wanted to be with a gun, 'cause I figured this is my way of defendin'. This is what I believe you go in the military for. Same thing as bein' a police officer. You be a police officer, you're supposed to be fightin' crime, not write tickets. I mean, that's the way I look at it.

World War Two is naturally different. I don't know much about Vietnam except what I read. Vietnam was treacherous fightin'. Lotta times even their Vietnamese turned against them. A lotta times they hadda be careful even of these little kids. They were carryin' bombs and everything else. You hadda frisk 'em an' everything. They were hittin' all over. It was a different type o' war. I saw this movie—what the heck was it?—*Green Berets. First Blood,* saw part o' that, too.

Another thing, World War Two, everybody was behind it. Five

hundred percent. Vietnam, they resisted an' everything else. They were real, real strict in World War Two. If you went AWOL, they'd come after ya. To put the fear o' God into ya.

Da trut' is, I didn't do too much in World War Two. I gambled. We shot dice, played cards. I wasn't farin' too well. I wanted to do my patriotic duty. I run into the orderly room: "I wanna volunteer for the paratroopers." Captain says, "You stay here." I says, "I wanna serve." He says, "Just get out." I think they respected me, but I got more respect from this gamblin' part.

Over there they used to play table stakes, no limits. Every payday. First payday, I go broke. Second payday, I go broke. So I was a little scared. I figured I gotta get over this scaredness. Anyway, I made the mistake of not buyin' cigarettes an' askin' a guy for a cigarette an' he says buy your own an' I tell 'im stick 'em up your ass. I'm pickin' up cigarette butts here an' there an' everywhere else.

Now I get to the point. I sit down an' play cards again. Think I had maybe $40 left. I got busted again. Now I'm chasin' one of these guys around that lends money 6 and 5. Gotta give him 25 for 20 on payday. Back in the game. I'm mad at everybody. I win a few pots here, a few pots there. Comes this one particular hand. This guy bets $54, which is a big bet. He's bettin' into me. He's bettin' for a one-card draw. I says now it's all up to me, 'cause this guy's got a big hand or he's got shit. I says I gotta call 'im. I says if I'm gonna bust the table, this is the spot I gotta get over. Anyway, I called him and he didn't have shit. I got about $300. Then I started gettin' confidence. I'm bluffin' 'em an' everything else. The game went on until six o'clock in the mornin'. The first sergeant went broke. One particular guy hadda break three times an' borrowed. I broke the whole table. I won $1,400.

Next day the news goes around. The first sergeant wanted to cash a personal check for a $100. I said, "Sure, sergeant, I'll cash it." But I'm sayin' to myself it better be good 'cause now I ain't takin' no shit from nobody. The next day he comes around, hands me $100 cash. I give 'im back his check. Everybody's lookin' at me. The word got around.

Gettin' back to this guy with the 20 for 25, right? He says, "I heard you had a little good luck." I says, "That's right, I owe you $25." He says, "That's right." I says, "Our agreement was payday. You got thirty days to wait for your $25. You want 23 now or you wanna wait for your $25 for thirty days?" He's lookin' at me. I says,

"Make up your mind." So he says, "Gimme the 23." See? I got the respect of him.

Now payday after payday I'm winnin'. I didn't wanna bust everybody. I picked up two or three hundred and everything else. I didn't relent to these other drivers. They used to put me on KP once a week. So I give a guy fifteen dollars, even twenty, he'd take my place and I'm off for the rest of the day. I can go to town an' I had money when everybody else was broke.

With anybody in the military, it was pride on top o' pride. Everyone in the neighborhood, they had their sons or somethin' like that, they all bragged about it. It was respect everywhere. Everyone went out four hundred percent.

I'm getting up in age. I'm sixty. Today, looks like there's more o' that shit of dog-eat-dog now. One person tryin' to outcon the other.

That's why I didn't wanna be a dog robber in the war. I wanted combat and never got it, so I'll never know, right?

REFLECTIONS ON
MACHISMO

JOHN H. ABBOTT

Though his is the long gray beard and glittering eye of the Ancient
Mariner, his face appears unlined. Incongruously youthful. Imagine a
genial John Brown.
A small house in Canoga Park, California.

We were ready for a war. We'd had a long depression. People needed
a change, and a war promised to make things different. Get off those
bread lines. Build another bomber for peace. They just changed the
slogans. (Laughs.) That was the most popular war we ever have had.
People sang, danced, drank—whoopee, the war.

I was born in 1918, so I was eligible for the draft. I'd been thinking
for a long time about how I would act toward people when the war
came along. Or if I was drafted.

It started a long time ago, when I took my brother's .22 out in the
woods and shot a bird out of a tree, and was so sick about that I
couldn't sleep. That was in Scarborough, New York.

I went to my friend's father's library—his father was a doctor—
and got some medical books out. Each page showed a step-by-step
progression: from a hamburger to a human being. It was a person who
fought in World War One, a casualty. How the thing was put back
together. I thought, What did this man do to himself? For what? Why
should I get involved with that? I was in grade school then. I never
heard of a pacifist or a Quaker. I didn't even know what a C.O. was.
(Laughs.)

When war broke out, I was in my second year at Pratt Institute
in Brooklyn. Everybody in class was eligible. We got our questionnaires just like we were being handed a test. I was shocked. The
second questionnaire was for conscientious objectors. Do you believe
in a Supreme Being? Do you believe in God? If you didn't believe,

you're in bad trouble. (Laughs.) You weren't gonna get your C.O. classification.

I didn't decide to be a C.O. The draft board did. All I put down on my questionnaire was that I wasn't gonna comply with the war effort. I wasn't going to have anything to do with it. Although I had only attended a Presbyterian Sunday school for a year, I felt qualified. My religion was like anybody else's, except that I worshipped in the woods. I didn't go to any church. What the hell business was it of theirs anyway what I believed?

My draft board knew very well what kind of person I was, knew how I felt before I got there. They weren't gonna mess around with me. (Laughs.) They gave me a 4-E: conscientious-objector classification.

They had orders to send me to camp. I hadn't finished my schooling. It was in violation of the law. I told 'em I wasn't gonna comply with their orders. I went to the district attorney and told him. He asked me to go see the Quakers in Philadelphia and let them show me what the camps were like. I did. In World War Two, the Brethren, Mennonites, and the Quakers agreed with government people that they'd have this camp system.

He also asked me if I'd go see a psychiatrist. I did. He was a Selective Service psychiatrist. He invited me to go to his house over the weekend. When I realized what he was asking me to do, I got highly indignant. (Laughs.) I had never been proposed to before. (Laughs.) He was trying to get me a 4-F, as a homosexual. If they'd go visit him for a weekend, he'd promise to give them a 4-F.

They ordered me to go to camp. I went to two camps. One in Campton, New Hampshire, and another at Chilaya in California. I was transferred involuntarily. (Laughs.) The work was brushing pine needles off the road in the campsite areas so the people who had gasoline, even though it was rationed, could visit and have pleasure. We'd repair the latrines, do maintenance work, trail work. Also volunteer to fight fires.

I got kicked off the work crew in very short order because I was so disruptive. I was talkin' to everybody, tryin' to get 'em to quit work, quit camp. I felt that being in those camps was aiding the war effort. To me, anything you did for the Selective Service System, which is the provider of bodies for the war, was aiding the war effort.

The work we did in camps was called of national importance. We called it work of national impotence. These gasoline stickers for rationing that you had on your windshield had a little note on it: Is this trip really necessary? We'd scratch out "trip" and write "war": Is this war really necessary?

When I got transferred from east to west, the trip across the country was absolutely fascinating. The good ladies were out at the railroad stations with candy and food and magazines. They were standing there as the troop trains went by. They would offer gifts to the men that were going off to serve their country. The train that we were on, there were two cars of marine recruits, without uniform, going to San Diego. And one car full of conscientious objectors with no uniforms. We'd spill out of the cars onto the railroad tracks, the ladies didn't know who the hell was which. So we ended up with a lot of these goodies.

When word got around that there were some yellowbellies on this train, the ladies would actually go around and yank us by the arm and say, "Are you one of those damn yellowbellies? I want my cookies back." Give me back my apple. Give me back my *Life*, you yellowbelly. (Laughs.) They were really irate.

What's the matter with you, you yellow bastard? "Yellow" was the word. Oh, I'd go hitchhiking when I had leave. I'd get in a car, pretty soon the man would say, "How come you're not in uniform?" I'd say, "I'm a conscientious objector." He says, "You're what, you yellow bastard you?" Down would go the brakes. Open the door. "Get the hell out of here."

You'd go in a bar to have a beer. All these guys in uniform. Pretty soon: "Hey, what's the matter with you? Where's your uniform?" I never figured there was any reason I shouldn't say what I was. When I told 'em I was a conscientious objector, they were either gonna fight me there or they were gonna take me outside.

Were you ever physically attacked?

Oh yeah, lots of times.

I never claimed I was a conscientious objector. They gave me this classification, 4-E. (Laughs.) I never felt I was anything. I never thought I was even a pacifist. But when you were asked, it was easy enough to explain by using those words.

We had old friends who were like part of our family. They visited our house on Thanksgiving and Christmas and birthdays. Friends around for years, you grew up with their sons and daughters. When it got known that I was a conscientious objector, these friends would tell me, "Don't call us. Don't come over. Don't bother my daughter or my son. We don't want to see you ever." They didn't want to be tainted. It was like I had some terrible disease and knowing me was like being connected with it. Like being a Jew in Germany. Or Japanese on the West Coast of the United States. (Laughs.)

My mother didn't understand what I was doing or why. When I came home from my draft board and told her I wasn't gonna comply with their wishes, she asked me, "Who told you to say that?" Because I had been anti formalized religion all my life, refused to continue at Sunday school, hated Bible-thumpers, I replied, "God told me to say that." It made her so sick that she was in bed for three days after that.

My father was different. Remember, he was in charge of helping the U.S. government send material over to Europe to supply that war. He was a dollar-a-year man in Washington. He was sympathetic to me as a person, but not to what I was doin'. He said, "John, you're knocking your head against a stone wall. It won't do you any good. I won't try to dissuade you. I want you to know if there's anything I can do to help you, I will do it." That was the best thing I heard from anybody. He did what he could. He was in contact with the prison system, wardens, anybody.

When I got out of camp and went to prison and came home on parole, I walked with my father after supper as we'd done often in our lives. I said, "Dad, I understand how much it must have hurt you to reveal to your friends that your son is a conscientious objector sitting in prison. I feel that must be a real blight on our family name. I'm sorry." He turned to me and said, "You don't have to be apologetic. If you knew what your forebears had done, you'd be surprised." For the first time in my life, I found out that my great-great-grandfather had done things like treating a Negro as an equal in the South.

My older brother tried mightily to get into the military. He tried every way he could. They wouldn't accept him because he was too short and too underweight. He was very gung ho. While I was sitting in solitary at the reformatory, my brother wrote me from Los Alamos. He was working on a device which would shorten the war and save lives. Later on, I heard there was an explosion at Nagasaki and Hiroshima. That's what my brother was working on to shorten the war and save lives. (Laughs.)

My sister married a military man who was also a tennis player, nationally ranked. He spent his entire time in the service playing tennis all over the Pacific. My sister didn't appreciate my stand. She thought I was crazy.

My friend's mother, who lived down the road, was sympathetic. She wanted her four sons to be conscientious objectors. But they didn't. (Laughs.) I had another friend, an artist. He didn't like the word "objector." I didn't either. He showed me that standing up for your rights means doing something positive. So I tried to get everybody out of the Selective Service System.

The Quakers were sympathetic, but they had to hew to certain lines. People of religious denominations have their requirements you have to meet, too. I was making trouble from the day I got there.

I walked out of camp and went to the Huntington Memorial Hospital in Pasadena. I applied for work. During the war, the hospitals didn't have any help. The men were all off fighting and killing. The women were making the most money they ever made as Rosie the Riveter. So I went to the hospital because I knew that was a place where they were trying to help people. They needed a gardener.

I told the lady that I left a camp for conscientious objectors and would ultimately be arrested for it. She said, "Who gives you the authority?" I said, "I do." "Who can reassure me that it's okay to hire you?" I said, "Call the FBI if you want to." She did, and the FBI told her they didn't have jurisdiction over me until the report had come through from Washington. It might be a matter of months. It was okay by them if she wanted to hire me. So she got her okay from her God. (Laughs.)

I went down and told the FBI where I was gonna be. I was having room and board at the hospital. (Laughs.) Anytime they wanted me, I'd be glad to come and turn myself in. They said, "Don't bother about that." I later realized that they get paid extra for coming and picking a guy up.

When I was eating lunch one day at the hospital—I had this metal knife for gardening in my pocket—they came up behind me, one on either side (laughs): "We want you to come along with us." I stood up and the knife was sticking out of my pocket. "Put that knife on the table." (Laughs.) They said, "This is deadly serious." I said, "It's whimsical." So they took me to the county jail in L.A. Booked me, classified me, took all my stuff. I was handcuffed, chains on my feet, when they transferred me from the county jail to the courthouse. It was very humiliating. I felt like I was some sort of criminal. All I was doing is saying I refuse to murder people. Hey, everybody else wants to murder, but I refuse to.

First I pled not guilty. Then I pled nolo contendere. I wasn't gonna comply with whatever it was. The judge sentenced me to two years in the federal prison. Tucson, Arizona.

On the train, I talked to the others. There were some conscientious objectors, but most had robbed a car, broke into a house, stole some money. Two of the C.O.'s wanted to know how come I walked out of camp. I told 'em I didn't want to comply with Selective Service in any way. I told 'em if we complied with the prison system, which was the enforcement arm, we'd still be complyin'. The judge had only sentenced me to spend time. He hadn't told me I had to comply with anybody. He didn't tell me I had to do any work. So we decided on the train that we were going to not work.

We got together with most of the other prisoners. There were some American Indians who refused to fight the white man's war. We called a work strike. We spent our time using typewriters, office equipment, paper, writing position papers. Mailing them out to friends and district attorneys and attorney generals, the heads of the prisons. (Laughs.)

What did the authorities do about it?

Nothing. Not for a couple of days. Finally, about two o'clock in the morning, they got three of us, handcuffed us, put us in the back of a sedan, and drove us all the way to La Tuna, Texas. Just above El Paso. We were met by a Texas warden. We were stood up in front of him. He had his big goon guards hovering all over us. With his cowboy boots and his big cigar sticking out of his mouth, he told us that his son was out there fighting the Japs and if any hair of his son's ever got hurt by those yellowbelly Japs, he was gonna see that we paid for it. He wanted to know right then and there: Were we gonna comply and go along or was he gonna have to call his boys to work us over? Each of us, one right after the other, said we're not gonna comply to anything you request. So we started out to make changes in that prison.

We were segregated. We were not in the compound with the other inmates. We went to chow in a different section of the dining hall. When we had yard privilege, there were no other prisoners out there.

When we'd have a chance at the library, nobody else was there.

They realized this poison we were spreading. The word was getting around, so they broke us up. They sent me to El Reno, a reformatory in Oklahoma. I smuggled a letter out and left it on a seat in the railroad station when I was sitting there handcuffed, waiting for the train.

I told the warden at El Reno as soon as I got there, "If you're interested in reforming me or rehabilitating or changing me, you must explain to me why you got these guys in here who have been convicted of murder and why you've got me in here, too, because I refused to murder people."

What'd he say?

Nothing.

I was in solitary most of the time. They'd say, "What do you want to do in prison?" I'd say, "I'd like to write a book about prison life." "We don't have jobs like that. You can work in the laundry or the kitchen or out in the field." I wouldn't work at any job.

While I was in solitary, a prison employee in charge of the Selective Service files had been drafted. They needed somebody to fill that job. The warden said to me, "You're the only one I can trust." Because if you know the truth of the inmates—and it's in those files —you're the most powerful person in that prison. I said, "No, I'd be working for you as well as Selective Service." He said, "I don't want you to do anything. Just sit there." I said, "Okay." So I just sat there. That was the only time I ever complied with the prison system.

I really got to know how it was to face four walls every day: a bed, a toilet, a washbasin, a little table, a forty-watt light on all the time. Windows painted over. I would touch them to feel what the weather was like. I could stand up on the bed and talk through the air duct in the ceiling to prisoners in the other cells. I danced. I sang. I did yoga exercises.

I hid under the bed when the guards would come around and look through the peephole. When they couldn't find me, they'd come in, look around—he's escaped! (Laughs.) It would really frighten 'em. When they'd open the door, I'd walk out. I'd start walking around and visit with some of the inmates I hadn't seen before. The guard would blow his whistle and two or three other guards would come in and carry me back to my cell. They didn't try that very often.

I'd been in three different federal prisons and I made trouble in every place. When they took me down to the railroad station, they said, "Don't come back. We don't ever want to see you again."

I was paroled to a job in a New York hospital. My parole officer wanted me to report to him all the time. I didn't for a couple of months. Finally I said, "I'll come see you just this once." He said, "Here's a list of rules. Have you violated any of them?" I said, "Yes, I have. I've violated any one that I didn't want to comply with." He said, "We're gonna have to send you back to prison." I said, "You better write and ask them before you threaten me. I don't think they want me." So I told him I wasn't ever gonna come back and see him.

What happened?

Nothing.

When the war was over, I realized that I'd lost my civil rights because I was convicted of this felony. I wanted to vote. I wanted the right to serve on juries. I went to the ACLU and was plaintiff in two cases. They both went to the Supreme Court and were landmark decisions. We won the rights for all ex-felons to vote. Once in a while a young law student comes up and says, "It's wonderful to talk to somebody we read about in our textbooks."

The military and the prison deal with numbers, not names. They used to call out my number in prison and I wouldn't respond. I said, "I've got a name. When you call me by my name, I'll respond." I spent most of my time in solitary. (Laughs.) I wasn't gettin' called very much.

All prisons are the same. All wars are the same. In war, both sides are trying to kill each other over a "principle." And the principle Thou shalt not kill got lost in the shuffle.

What about Hitler?

What about Hitler? He was one person. They were all doing what Hitler said. What do all prisoners do? They do what the warden says. The only power Hitler had was the power the people gave him. I felt the whole world had gone absolutely mad, crazy. They were in love with war.

After the Vietnam War, people are a lot more sympathetic to noncompliance. They've mellowed. They really saw what war was like in Vietnam, went along for ten years and were just absolutely sick of it. It didn't make any sense. To me, neither did World War One or World War Two or any other war.

ROGER TUTTRUP

He's seated on the steps outside the apartment house in which he lives. It is a neighborhood of old people, Asiatics, Hispanics, blacks, a compote of ethnics, and many, many small children. He appears to know most of his neighbors.

He shakes my hand. Ouch! an ironlike grip. "I'm still being a marine. I have my hair cut short. I work out, stay strong. I weigh less now than I did in the middle stage in the Marine Corps. I'm at 150."

We continue the conversation upstairs. He helps an elderly neighbor unlock her door. We have a drink or two.

I wanted to be in it. I was fifteen. I felt I wasn't doin' anything constructive. I was spottin' pins in the bowling alley, besides goin' to high school. I figured I should be doin' somethin' else. I guess it was a year later, I went to work in a war plant. Some of my friends started goin' into service. I figured: Why the hell don't I? I'm no dog, right?

I lied about my age and tried to get in in '43. I was sixteen now. My mother wouldn't sign. She wanted to get rid of me, but not that way. (Laughs.) Then I passed the air corps test at Oak Park High. I passed real good, like I do in everything. Then I figured, what the hell, you're gonna be two years training, the war'll be over. Go in the Marine Corps.

I wanted to be a hero, let's face it. I was havin' trouble in school. I was havin' trouble with my mother. They didn't know what to do. The war'd been goin' on for two years. I didn't wanna miss it, for Chrissake. I was an American. I was seventeen.

I don't think it was more than four or five days I was in there, we hadda get up at four-thirty in the morning, shave, and clean up. Then go out for inspection. This big drill instructor, Sergeant Lynn, he had a hand on him like—so I'm standin' on inspection. He said, "Did you shave this morning?" I said, "Yes, sir." You always hadda say "sir" in those days, right? So he said, "I see a little patch on your skin.

I don't think you shaved. So I'm gonna ask you again: Did you shave this morning?" I said, "Yes, sir." Then he puts his hand on my throat. I mean his hand is bigger than my throat and he practically lifts me off the ground. He said, "I told you you didn't shave. You got a patch there." Honest to God, nobody without a microscope coulda seen it. So he puts me back down. He said, "I'm gonna ask ya one more time. Are you callin' me a liar? Did you shave this morning?" And you know what I said? "No, sir." Know what I hadda do? Me and a guy named Harrison, we walked into the DI's office. With our razors, no water, no lather, no nothin', we stood there half an hour, scraped our faces.

I didn't cry about it. It didn't really hurt me that much. It made me feel like a nothin'. But on the other hand, they did so many things that made me feel like I was a person, that I could tolerate that.

These people, they really put you in your place. That's a polite way of sayin' it. They humiliate ya, they make ya do things that you don't think are physically possible. At the same time, they're makin' you feel you're something. That you're part of something. When you're there and you need somebody, you got somebody. It was the high point of my life.

I'm looking at a photograph. Platoon 280, U.S. Marine Corps, San Diego, 1944. Below: Semper Fidelis. Third row, second from left, is young Roger Tuttrup, clean-cut, earnest. Seated first row center is, unmistakably, Sergeant Lynn, the size of a pro football tackle.

I was somebody. I was in an organization sometimes I'd get mad at, sometimes I didn't. 'Cause I was kind of a rebellious guy. Somethin' like you. Anyway, I was with people I trusted, that I had confidence in. Most of the time, I woulda gone to the moon with these guys. Jeez, I don't wanna get tearful.

I've always been a great IQ guy. So I got high grades, so they put me into radio school. So I got there and school's filled. So I do mess duty. Until there's an opening. You're up at four o'clock in the morning. You serve two shifts. This is June 1944. He said, "You wanna go out to the maritime unit?" So some of the guys say, "We can't tolerate this shit any more, mess duty. So let's try the maritime—" We didn't know what the maritime unit was. It was a little place tucked away at the north end of Camp Pendleton. Right near Richard Nixon's San Clemente. It's this underwater demolition outfit, the OSS. They got these scary kind of people. We were just maintenance people, really. We cleaned up and we cooked the food and we got liberty every night.

Then one day I got an interview. One of these heavy-type psychiatrists. Hey, man, we're havin' a good life there. I mean, it's not bad. But we're gettin' bitter because that isn't what we came into the Marine Corps for, this nonsense. This guy starts workin' me over. You know how to speak French? Such and such a background, why don't you join us? He implied I'd be with these swimmers, goin' behind the lines. They tried to recruit me. OSS. It eventually became CIA.

The best guy in our outfit was Sergeant West. He fought with the Raiders down in the Solomons. He looked me right in the eye and he said, "What'd you join the Marine Corps for?" I said, "'Cause I thought I'd see some action." He said, "Stay in the Marine Corps, don't go with those freaks." So I applied for a transfer back to the Marine Corps infantry.

This was January 1945, right? I spent Christmas Eve in Pearl Harbor. We couldn't get off the ship. The officers could. So we just sat there and sang a few carols. Right next was the battleship *Missouri,* which was beautiful. The sailors were just gorgeous in their uniforms. Sure, they all got liberty, but we didn't. C'est la vie.

C'est la guerre.

C'est la guerre, too. Then we go overseas. We were attached to the Second Marine Division. Where did I land? Saipan. Bullshit people say I never saw any combat. Well, I got records to prove I did. Not as much—I want you to know I'm no fuckin' hero, but I'm no nobody. I'm in what they call a replacement unit. It's a part of the invasion force of Okinawa, which was to be the last battle of the war. All we did was load and unload ships.

Everybody embellishes the truth a little bit. I don't lie, but I don't always tell it a hundred percent. So I says I was in on the invasion of Okinawa. That's true. The outfit I was in made a diversionary trip to the southern end of Okinawa. Then we went back to Saipan. We saw Kamikazes and everything else. You never saw anything in your life that makes you sick to your stomach, it's these guys divin' these planes in. Whack 'em into an LST or somethin'. They know they're gonna die. I couldn't understand. I was willin' to give my life, that's why I enlisted. But not foolishly. These people . . .

So we took some shitty little island over there. I got shot at a few times, but I was no fuckin' hero. I was just a guy, period.

All of a sudden, we get this word: It's over. Hiroshima. And everybody sits down. I just can't understand the second one: Nagasaki. They were beat on the first one. Why do you have to do that twice? 'Cause they were beat. The people had already given up on Okinawa. The generals had committed suicide. Hiroshima? I figure it probably saved my life, okay? Can't say much more than that.

When the war ended, I was sent into the First Marine Division in the mortar platoon. And soon we went off to China, occupation duty. We go to Peking. Except in those days it was called Peiping.

A yellowed souvenir book is brought forth: North China Pictorial, U.S. Marine Corps. There are photos of American generals. One of Chiang Kai-shek. It reads: Welcome, glorious allies.

(Points a finger at Chiang's photo) Bang, bang, bang. To repatriate the Japanese was the alleged purpose. The real purpose, as we found out later, was to keep Chiang Kai-shek in power and keep the commies off. We saw what Chiang Kai-shek's people were doin' and we saw what the other people were doin' and we knew whose side who was on. We once made a parade for Henry Luce. The *Time* guy. He was right up there with Chiang Kai-shek. When I got out of the service, I switched to *Newsweek*.

We hated Chiang Kai-shek. 'Cause it was all rich people. I met people there that were classier than anybody I've ever met in the United States. With paintings, tapestries, real wealth. Tell ya one thing I hate, though, is Chinese music. I went to the Peking Opera once . . .

We got transferred down to Taku, a port city. They made us an MP company. The people were so poor, it just broke our heart. People would throw babies away. Somebody had thrown away a baby and there were some wild dogs. These dogs were eatin' up the baby. They called for some MPs and we got in a jeep and we go out—boom, boom, boom—shoot the dogs. That's what we didn't like.

We were up there protectin' a very corrupt government. We had cheap girls, we had cheap liquor. Life wasn't too dangerous. But we were doin' it for a lousy son of a bitch that was bein' protected by the American government and we couldn't understand it. Marines are supposed to be tough people, huh? But when you look at the kinda crap, and our damn government was backin' this guy. I mean, this was disgraceful.

(He is opening one of the huge batch of letters to his mother) You're holdin' the last one she saved. See? Lutai, China, April 4, 1946.

"Dear Mother: As you can see by this letter, my departure for home was delayed . . . The way things look now, I probably won't be leaving until sometime after the twenty-first . . . Right now I'm on guard duty and I'm teaching some Chink—"

(He interrupts) That's the way I wrote it then. I was just a punk kid, I wouldn't say that now. Keep reading.

"—soldiers some English. They have progressed as far as lighter and cigarette. They're getting me to write their names on their belts for them. I pronounce them and then I write them. Doesn't help my Parker 51 very much either. We're out in the country and it's a lot healthier. It isn't so dirty and it doesn't smell at all like Taku. That's about all for now, so I'll close."

When I think of the war, first image that came to my mind is when that Sergeant Lynn grabbed me by the neck. I knew I was gonna be livin' a different life. I went into the Marine Corps and they made me a different person than I might have been. The last image that comes to my mind is what we were taught about the Japanese. The Marine Corps taught us that, too. That the Japs are lousy, sneaky, treacherous—watch out for them. Well, my God, I mean, who was doin' all this stuff? Who's brainwashin' you on all this? I've been married for twenty-four years to Satsuko—Sats (he indicates his wife, who has just entered the room)—Miss America here, that's a super person. She's the best thing ever happened to me.

TED ALLENBY

He is a columnist for Gay Life, *a weekly newspaper in Chicago.*
"I was at home in Dubuque, Iowa, listening to the New York Philhar-

monic, John Barbirolli conducting Brahms's First Symphony. The announcer interrupted and said Pearl Harbor was attacked. I was seventeen.

"Dubuque is a very religious town. Hetero or homo, we were all very repressed people. It was an atmosphere of ignorance. For a long time, I didn't know I was a homosexual. I knew I was different.

"It was a very patriotic town. So was I. I wanted to sign up immediately, but I was too young. I enlisted in December of '42. I turned eighteen by that time."

I enlisted in the Marine Corps. This had a good deal to do with my being homosexual. In my middle teens, I made a discovery. My dad was a pharmacist. In his drugstore they had a lot of bottles, some of which had a skull and crossbones. That's how I perceived the label "homosexual." I'll wear a skull and crossbones, and I'm not gonna let anybody see this. It's bad, it's a disease, it's a poison. This is my dirty little secret.

How do you deal with it? You deal with it by trying to prove how rugged you are. After all, homosexuals are sissies and pansies. You're not a man. You're not a male, you're not female, you're nothing. I chose the marines for that reason. It's the toughest outfit. This business about the Marine Corps builds men became a slogan. It was something we believed. This is the elite. You really gotta be tough.

I was sworn in at Des Moines and sent to a marine detachment of a navy V-12 unit at Denison University in Ohio. I didn't want to go to school. I wanted to fight.

I was feeling very aggressive for a number of reasons. Like every other young American, I was superpatriotic. And, being a homosexual, I had that constant compelling need to prove how virile I was. I was very restive in this V-12 unit and managed to get myself kicked out. I was a little overaggressive. I had a mean streak in me and was getting into too many fights. To deflect suspicion that I was a homosexual, I'd go out on the weekend, get drunk, get into a fight and come back bloodied or bloody somebody else up. I had a lot of hostility and fear. They got sick of that. That's not officer-candidate material.

I went gaily west to San Diego and boot camp. I wound up as a Marine Corps bandsman. I wanted to play trumpet, but the band director needed flute players. That made it all the worse. The flute is a girl's instrument. (Laughs.) But I got pretty good at it. Every once in a while, the guys would kid me about it and there'd be another fight. I did enjoy music and became a member of the marine base band at San Diego. I was sent overseas and on February 13, '45, I landed on Iwo Jima. They took my flute away and gave me a machine gun.

You have good buddies. It is something subconscious. I had one in San Diego. We were lovers, but never had a sexual encounter. There was the intimacy, the closeness, deep, deep feelings, little subtle things that you reserve just for that special person. He was a deeply religious kid, Baptist. We were both homosexuals, but neither of us would dare use the word to each other. He didn't go to Iwo Jima with me. War brings people together very quickly and separates them just as quickly. It was a traumatic experience when I said goodbye to him.

As I look back, there were other marines at boot camp who were probably homosexual, but they were as frightened and furtive and as much in the closet as I was. Military officialdom didn't seem to care one way or the other. The only time homosexuality was ever discussed was in barracks banter and filthy locker-room jokes. Let's go out and roll some queers tonight. Or, you goddamn cocksucker.

Did you take part in the banter?

Of course. You have to, otherwise somebody'd suspect you. You develop quite a repertory of tricks to prevent detection. Be even more vociferous than everybody else.

I think the Marine Corps is a kind of sadomasochistic outfit. A great deal of sexual feeling is expressed. In those days, we marines wore leather belts. They got rid of them because marines were using them as weapons in fights with swabbies or with each other. You'd take that leather belt and wrap it around your fist and it became something like brass knuckles. I remember when we'd slap each other with 'em, back and forth. It was a game of skill, to see how quickly you could dodge and duck and how hard you could hit the other guy. We'd have these welts on our back.

There's an old axiom: If you can't love, you gotta hate. If you can't show affection, show aggression. A great deal of homosexuality was expressed in the barracks. Part of it was the anticipation of combat, wonder when, wanting to, yet fearing it. It was never done with real meanness. Instead of a pillow fight, we'd fight with these leather belts. But we were macho. You can't find a more macho outfit than the Marine Corps.

I joined the Fourth Marine Division on Maui in Hawaii. We all lived in tents. We staged there for Iwo Jima. Tokyo Rose told us we were going there before our officers did. We picked her up on the radio all the time. When we were near Saipan, where our task force was gonna rendezvous, she said, "When the Fourth Marine Division gets to Iwo Jima, there won't be enough of it left to put in a telephone booth." Iwo Jima? Where the hell's that? Never heard of it before. We were told that it would be fairly easy. A small island, only eight square miles. It shouldn't be any problem. (Laughs.) We found out otherwise.

The men who landed on D-Day, February 19, 1945—well, there aren't many of them left. The casualty rate was enormous. It was ghastly. Iwo was a volcanic island with very little concealment. Cover is something you hide behind—a tree, a bush, a rock. Few trees. No grass. It was almost like a piece of the moon that had dropped down to earth. I don't think there's been any place with more dismemberment, more bodies cut to pieces. You get to the point where fear is numbing and you begin to run on just reflexes and nervous energy. I was there about a month.

I had another one of those close friendships. We were in the same regiment. We saw each other constantly. His tent was just a couple of rows from mine. We were drinkin' buddies before we embarked for Iwo Jima. We were on the same ship going there.

I had a new poncho, an all-purpose tent, raincoat. I printed my name on it in black ink: a big T. ALLENBY. The damn thing got stolen. One day, my buddy was running along and he found a dead marine. His body by this time was decomposed and maggoty. He saw that poncho with my name on it. The guy who was killed was probably the one who stole my poncho.

He and I were assigned to the same ship after the battle was over. He was standing on the deck, looking over the mess that was Iwo Jima. I swung up on the cargo net to the main deck. He saw me. He blanched. A ghost. He'd run across the body on Good Friday, and now it was Easter Sunday and I was alive. The resurrection of the dead. (Laughs.)

I don't suppose I was ever greeted by anybody in my life as I was then. He grabbed hold of me, hugged me, and couldn't let go. He was crying uncontrollably. He was a human being rehumanized.

My rehumanizing occurred on the island, when I was sitting on some ammunition crates, dirty, filthy, smelly, but safe. Big trucks came up with dead marine bodies. Bulldozers cut a huge trough and guys, assigned to this ghoulish detail, just tossed all the bodies off the trucks like cordwood and lined them up in the trough. That would be the cemetery. My crying was uncontrollable, too. One way or another, that's how most of us rehumanized ourselves. We lived like animals. We lived in holes called foxholes, appropriately named after an animal. I sat there weeping when I saw all those bodies of what once had been beautiful young men and now were being thrown into a trough.

That's how Barrett rehumanized himself. Good Friday became Easter and his friend had been resurrected from the dead. It was a joyful moment for him. It has to do with the very deep emotions that men can have for each other, gay or not. Unfortunately, in our society, men aren't supposed to show that kind of affection except under such stress as this. If Barrett and I were to have done the same thing in the street in San Diego—Oh, a couple of queers.

We settled back into the routine for the long trip back to Hawaii. It was five times longer than it needed to be, because of the zigzagging you did to avoid sub detection. Had our usual nightmares. Weird being on board ship at night, listenin' to guys screaming and hollering. My recurring nightmare was a ghastly one. (Laughs.) There was this dead Jap, maggoty, decomposed, with a rusty rifle in his hand, and he gets up and chases me. You're running, but your feet won't go fast enough and he's gaining on you. Then I would wake up in a cold sweat.

Do you know if you killed anybody at Iwo Jima?

Yes, of course. I was a machine gunner.

Back on Maui, they took away my machine gun and gave me another flute to play. I was with the Twenty-third Regimental Band of the Fourth Marine Division. We were then planning for the landing on the Japanese mainland. Right after Hiroshima, our intelligence people told us we would have landed at Chigasaki. Ten years later I was in Japan as a navy chaplain. One day, I got off the train at Chigasaki and walked down to the beach where we would have landed. I got a chill. It was Iwo Jima magnified a hundred times. The mountains, looking down, would have been bristling with artillery, all pre-zeroed on that beach. They would have wiped us out.

Right now, I'm totally against war in any form. I say yes, that bomb was a ghastly thing. I was in Hiroshima and I stood at ground zero. I saw deformities that I'd never seen before. I know there are genetic effects that may affect generations of survivors and their children. I'm aware of all this. But I also know that had we landed in Japan, we would have faced greater carnage than Normandy. It would probably have been the most bloody invasion in history. Every Japanese man, woman, and child was ready to defend that land. The only way we took Iwo Jima was because we outnumbered them three to one. Still, they held us at bay as long as they did. We'd had to starve them out, month after month after month. As it was, they were really down to eating grass and bark off trees. So I feel split about Hiroshima. The damn thing probably saved my life.

On Maui, I had another love affair. We felt a terrible guilt about it. It was the abominable sin. You could go to hell. This was before the Uniform Code of Military Justice. Each branch of the service had its own body of laws. In the navy, it was called rocks and shoals. I don't remember if there was a clause making homosexuality a crime. So I remained in the closet, feeling very, very ashamed of even having these desires.

But there was no witch-hunting. I'd even hear reports of guys found secretively having sex with each other, and nobody turned them in. Officialdom made no big thing about it. There was a war on. Who in the hell is going to worry about this shit?

After his discharge in February 1946—"I came out of the war somewhat disenchanted"—there was attendance at a religious college; a further-ance of guilt; a turn at journalism and at social work; and a return to the service as a chaplain.

I joined the navy and was sent back to the marines. I was assigned to Camp Fiji in Japan, the sacred ash heap. I was navy chaplain circuit-riding nine ships. The Marine Corps doesn't have its own chaplains, so I was assigned to them. I was regarded as a very good counselor. I was always out on maneuvers with the troops. Identified with 'em.

Finally, I got shore duty back in the United States and was assigned to the naval training center in San Diego. That's where I really had to deal with the subject of homosexuality. I was in navy boot camp with young kids, seventeen, eighteen years old. I had to sit and listen to the tales of woe of an awful lot of young gay kids. There was only one person they could go to and that was the chaplain. They had joined the marines for the same reason I did: It'll make a man of me. I'll show 'em how tough I am. When they got there, they were frightened, not knowing what to do. My advice to them was: Get out. I advised them to do what I did not do.

By this time, trapping homosexuals had become quite a hobby, especially of military intelligence. Unlike World War Two, the military had considerable preoccupation with homosexuality. We had a ghastly thing that we had to read to recruits. They wouldn't trust us chaplains to ad-lib it or give our own talk. We were ordered: You will not interpolate. You will give it exactly as it is. It was a gross thing: Homosexuality is a mortal sin. It is a crime. If you get caught, dreadful things will happen to you. Most homosexuals are also dope addicts, so you will probably wind up on narcotics.

This was the aftermath of the McCarthy era. It was definitely believed that homosexuals were potential security risks. That was the main justification for kicking them out.

Of course, the kids were terrified. Scared they might get caught. When they came to me I simply said, I can't turn you in without your permission. What you tell me is privileged. But if you give me permission, I'll pave the way for you to get out as soon as possible. Because if you slip and get caught, they'll just chew you to pieces.

Meanwhile, I was still living a circumspect life, sublimating by playing football at the age of thirty-four. I was known as the jockstrap chaplain. I was a damn good athlete. After two years, I got out and went to graduate study at the Pacific School of Religion at Berkeley. I was still in the reserves. I was broke again. So I accepted orders in October of '61 to First Marine Division, Camp Pendleton. That's where I got in trouble.

My assistant was gay, too. A year and a half, we carried on like a couple of lovers. It was clandestine. I rented an apartment off the base, or sometimes we'd go to a motel room. Matter of fact, I always felt, after we got caught, they shouldn't have kicked us out. They should have put us in charge of planning an operation. (Laughs.) Just the logistics of carrying on an affair like that right under their noses.

One day I was placed under arrest. The division chaplain's office called: "You're wanted immediately." I drove down there, and two big men in dark civilian suits flashed their badge and said, "You're under arrest." They took me down to San Diego at naval intelligence headquarters and put me through interrogation. The charge was violating Article 125, Uniform Code of Military Justice. That's sodomy. The UCMJ came in in the early fifties.

The interrogators went into every clinical detail of my sex life, the kind of stuff you wouldn't even tell your shrink. Questions dealing with the most intimate matters, in front of all these hostile people. With a great big fat lady taking it all down at 120 words a minute. There were about five or six in the room. They wanted every detail. It was all part of a scene to torture you. Nothing physical, all psychological and emotional.

I was discharged under conditions other than honorable and ceremoniously kicked out of the navy. I lost all my veteran's benefits. Everything I earned by being in the Marine Corps in World War Two was all wiped out. That was in '63.

Partly because of Vietnam, the military was liberalized. After a period in civilian life, a person with such a discharge can request that it be reviewed. A lawyer took up my case—this is seventeen years after my discharge. The review board voted unanimously to award me an honorable discharge and restored my benefits. So now I have an honorable discharge.

Now I'm out of the closet and I don't care who knows I'm a homosexual. I'm not hiding any more.

As I look back, it was a war that had to be fought. It's probably the last one. I don't think there ever will be another war that has to be fought. All war is evil. What is unthinkable is fighting a war that is unnecessary.

BOOK TWO

HIGH RANK

ADMIRAL GENE LAROCQUE

A rear admiral, U.S. Navy, retired, he is director of the Center for Defense Information. "We keep an eye on Pentagon spending. We're a group of retired military officers, trying to hold down the growing influence of the military and industry so that citizens can have a bigger say."

He had worked in the Pentagon for seven years and lectured for seven years in the war colleges. "At one time, I was assistant director for strategic plans, the best damn job you can get. I could have done anything from then on: three stars, four stars. I'm surprised they made me an admiral. I didn't want to be one."

I grew up in a little town in Illinois, along the Kankakee River. I was an Eagle Scout. Although I was just a pint-size, I won three medals. I liked ROTC. In 1936, the middle of the Depression, I worked my way through. One summer, while building a road, I saw an advertisement: Join the Navy. Go to Panama and Cuba on a one-month cruise. All expenses paid.

They put us on an old battleship, the *Arkansas,* three hundred of us college kids. They put these sailor uniforms on us, with a blue band around our hat. We got ashore. We thought we'd do much better with the girls than enlisted men, but we were dismal failures. The regular crew members had told all the girls in Panama that the blue band meant we had gonorrhea.

He was commissioned after attending midshipman school at Northwestern. He won a sword as the outstanding student among twelve hundred. He stayed in the navy as an ensign.

In the summer of '41 I asked to be sent to Pearl Harbor. The Pacific fleet was there and it sounded romantic. I was attached to the U.S.S. *MacDonough* when the Japanese attacked. We got under way about ten o'clock looking for the Japanese fleet. It's lucky we didn't find them; they would probably have sunk us. I spent the whole war in the Pacific, four years.

At first I thought the U.S. Army Air Corps was accidentally bombing us. We were so proud, so vain, and so ignorant of Japanese capability. It never entered our consciousness that they'd have the temerity to attack us. We knew the Japanese didn't see well, especially at night—we knew this as a matter of fact. We knew they couldn't build good weapons, they made junky equipment, they just imitated us. All we had to do was get out there and sink 'em. It turns out they could see better than we could and their torpedoes, unlike ours, worked.

We'd thought they were little brown men and we were the great big white men. They were of a lesser species. The Germans were well known as tremendous fighters and builders, whereas the Japanese would be a pushover. We used nuclear weapons on these little brown men. We talked about using them in Vietnam. We talked about using our military force to get our oil in the Middle East from a sort of dark-skinned people. I never hear about us using the military to get our oil from Canada. We still think we're a great super-race.

It took a long time to realize how good these fellows were. We couldn't believe it. One time I was down in a South Pacific atoll that we'd captured. There were still a few Japanese ships in the harbor. We ran into two Japanese who hanged themselves right in front of us rather than be captured. We hated them during the war. They were Japs. They were subhuman.

I hated the boredom of four years in the Pacific, even though I had been in thirteen battle engagements, had sunk a submarine, and was the first man ashore in the landing at Roi. In that four years, I thought, What a hell of a waste of a man's life. I lost a lot of friends. I had the task of telling my roommate's parents about our last days together. You lose limbs, sight, part of your life—for what? Old men send young men to war. Flags, banners, and patriotic sayings.

I stayed in the navy because I believed the United States could really make the world safe for democracy. I went around to high schools in uniform, telling the kids that I thought war was stupid, to ignore all this baloney that shows up in poetry and novels and movies about gallantry and heroism and beauty. I told them it's just a miserable, ugly business.

After the war, we were the most powerful nation in the world. Our breadbasket was full. We enjoyed being the big shots. We were running the world. We were the only major country that wasn't devastated. France, Britain, Italy, Germany had all felt it. The Soviet Union, our big ally, was on its knees. Twenty million dead.

We are unique in the world, a nation of thirty million war veterans. We're the only country in the world that's been fighting a war since 1940. Count the wars—Korea, Vietnam—count the years. We have built up in our body politic a group of old men who look upon military service as a noble adventure. It was the big excitement of their lives and they'd like to see young people come along and share that excitement. We are unique.

We've always gone somewhere else to fight our wars, so we've not really learned about its horror. Seventy percent of our military budget is to fight somewhere else.

We've institutionalized militarism. This came out of World War Two. In 1947, we passed the National Security Act. You can't find that term—national security—in any literature before that year. It created the Department of Defense. Up till that time, when you appropriated money for the War Department, you knew it was for war and you could see it clearly. Now it's for the Department of Defense. Everybody's for defense. Otherwise you're considered unpatriotic. So there's absolutely no limit to the money you must give to it. So they've captured all the Christians: the right of self-defense. Even the "just war" thing can be wrapped into it.

We never had a Joint Chiefs of Staff before. In World War Two, there was a loose coalition, but there was no institution. It gave us the National Security Council. It gave us the CIA, that is able to spy on you and me this very moment. For the first time in the history of man, a country has divided up the world into military districts. No nation in the world has done that before or has done it since. They have a military solution for everything that happens in their area. They write up contingency plans—a euphemism for war plans. General Bernie Rogers has intelligence, has logistics, has airplanes, has people, has an international staff. There is not one U.S. ambassador in Europe who makes any significant move without checking with Bernie Rogers. He's the most important man in Europe and he has tenure. You can't fire him.

Our military runs our foreign policy. The State Department simply goes around and tidies up the messes the military makes. The State Department has become the lackey of the Pentagon. Before World

War Two, this never happened. You had a War Department, you had a Navy Department. Only if there was a war did they step up front. The ultimate control was civilian. World War Two changed all this.

I don't think I've changed. I was a good ship captain. I was tough. I worked like the devil to see that my ship and my men were the best. I loved the' sea and still do. I think the United States has changed. It got away from the idea of trying to settle differences by peaceful means. Since World War Two, we began to use military force to get what we wanted in the world. That's what military is all about. Not long ago, the Pentagon proudly announced that the U.S. had used military force 215 times to achieve its international goals since World War Two. The Pentagon likes that: military force to carry out national will. Of course, there are nuclear weapons now.

Nuclear weapons have become the conventional weapons. We seriously considered using them in Vietnam. I was in the Pentagon myself trying to decide what targets we could use. We explored every way we could to win that war, believe me. We just couldn't find a good enough target. We were not concerned about the opprobrium attached to the use of nuclear weapons.

I was in Vietnam. I saw the senseless waste of human beings. I saw this bunch of marines come off this air-conditioned ship. Nothing was too good for our sailors, soldiers, and marines. We send 'em ashore as gung ho young nineteen-year-old husky nice-looking kids and bring 'em back in black rubber body bags. There are a few little pieces left over, some entrails and limbs that don't fit in the bags. Then you take a fire hose and you hose down the deck and push that stuff over the side.

I myself volunteered to go to Vietnam and fight. I didn't question whether it was in the nation's interest. I was a professional naval officer and there was a war. I hope as we get older, we get smarter.

You could argue World War Two had to be fought. Hitler had to be stopped. Unfortunately, we translate it unchanged to the situation today. I met some Russians during World War Two, officers from ships. They looked to me like human beings. I had been burned before, having been taught to hate the Japanese with such fervor. I saw no good reason, at that point, to hate the Russians, who I knew had fought valiantly in World War Two.

I think they want to be accepted as a world power and perhaps spread their hegemony around the world. I think we have to compete with communism wherever it appears. Our mistake is trying to stem it with guns. It alienates the very people we're trying to win over. The Russians really have influence only in the buffer areas around their country. They've been a flop in other countries. Yet the Russian bear determines just about everything we do. I wonder how much of my whole life and my generation has been influenced to hate the Russians. Even when I didn't even know where it was. I remember a Tom Swift book when I was thirteen: beware the Russian bear.

World War Two has warped our view of how we look at things today. We see things in terms of that war, which in a sense was a good war. But the twisted memory of it encourages the men of my generation to be willing, almost eager, to use military force anywhere in the world.

For about twenty years after the war, I couldn't look at any film on World War Two. It brought back memories that I didn't want to keep around. I hated to see how they glorified war. In all those films, people get blown up with their clothes and fall gracefully to the ground. You don't see anybody being blown apart. You don't see arms and legs and mutilated bodies. You see only an antiseptic, clean, neat way to die gloriously. I hate it when they say, "He gave his life for his country." Nobody gives their life for anything. We steal the lives of these kids. We take it away from them. They don't die for the honor and glory of their country. We kill them.

I went to a church in Champaign, Illinois, about three weeks ago. There's a plaque in front near the altar: In honor of the men who died, were wounded, and served in World War Two. The left-hand side says, For God. The right-hand side says, For Country. We've made war a religious act. Somewhere in the Bible it says, Render unto Caesar the things that are Caesar's and to God those that are God's. What happened to that?

GENERAL WILLIAM BUSTER
_____

Lexington, Kentucky. He was from Harrodsburg, too young to join the town's National Guard unit that became Company D, 192nd Tank Battalion. Fifty-six of its members were in Bataan and Corregidor and spent three and a half years in Japanese prison camps.

"I was assigned to the Second Armored Division and made the invasions of North Africa, Sicily, and Normandy on D-3."

Almost immediately after I reported to Fort Knox, the expansion of the army began. When I graduated from West Point in 1939, the standing army of the United States was 186,000 officers and men. The people stationed in Washington weren't even allowed to wear their uniforms. There was no military presence at all in Washington at the time. The military was on the back burner, de-emphasized. It was not until the German invasion of Poland that things started to happen.

The first realization of a change in the air was the speech at our graduation. The officer was telling us we were coming out as second lieutenants, but if war was declared we'd be majors within a year. (Laughs.) We laughed, of course. But it actually happened. I was a lieutenant colonel when the war ended.

When we went into North Africa on November 8, 1942, we had absolutely untrained troops. They were green and we had to train them from scratch. These young boys came into the reception center at Fort Benning, some of them without shoes. All they had was the shirt on their back and a pair of trousers. They had no toilet articles, no baggage, nothing. They were from Alabama, Kentucky, the Carolinas. We had a lot from Louisiana. They were away from home for the first time. I mean, absolutely green. The expansion of the army was so quick, there was no preparation.

The ships were combat-loaded in Norfolk for the African invasion. Everything was put on backwards, to be taken off and go onto the beach in proper order. For example, the vehicles were put on last, so they could come off first.

The invasion was in three groups. The Western Task Force, the one I was in, attacked Morocco. The Central landed at Oran. The third, at Algiers. Actually we were opposing the Vichy French at the time. It's absolutely remarkable that in two years an American army could organize such an invasion force. The boys on the ship had no idea where they were going. It was a strongly kept secret; none of us really knew. I didn't know until we were at sea.

The ship was loaded with all these crates of weapons that nobody had ever seen before. (Laughs.) Bazookas. We didn't know what bazookas were. We had no training with them at sea. There were a lot of things we didn't know about them. You'd fire it, and unburned powder grains would hit you in the face as the projectile went out. The first guy that pulled that trigger had red spots all over his face.

(Laughs.) We found out that you had to wear goggles and keep your face covered.

The French capitulated very quickly after some desultory fighting. We went into intensive training, not knowing why they didn't send us up into Tunisia. Here, early on, the American forces got the heck kicked out of them at Kasserine Pass. Here we were, the best armored division in the world, we thought, sitting back three hundred miles from the action, not being used. We found out afterwards we were keeping French Morocco from getting involved in the war. We were also a strategic threat to Spanish Morocco and keeping the Nazis or the Italians from using it as a base.

In the winter, we moved up to Oran and prepared for the invasion of Sicily. There was a lot of controversy between Patton and Montgomery. Patton was the task force commander of the American forces. Tanks don't operate very well in the mountainous country of central Sicily, so we made an end-around run and captured Palermo in a few days. We occupied Palermo and stayed there until we were shipped to England to prepare for the invasion of France.

We went in on D-3. The beachhead had been fairly well secured. Almost immediately, the Germans attempted a breakthrough on the hinge between Utah and Omaha beaches. It was the most lightly held element of our line. We had over a month of defensive warfare. We had the same boys all the way through. They now had lots of experience. It was in Berlin they began discharging the high-point soldiers.

Unfortunately, we bypassed Paris. (Laughs.) We were upset that they sent the French Armored Second through the American Armored Second for the purpose of capturing Paris. Had we entered Paris, our country boys might have sung: What ya gonna do back down on the farm after you've seen Paree? (Laughs.) We stopped just short, went on across northern France into Belgium, and across Belgium into Germany.

My division was scheduled to occupy Berlin just after V-E Day. This is when we became aware of the treachery of the Russians. When we were driving across France, there was nothing in front of us. We had reached the Elbe, we had troops across, and we were ordered back. Then the Russians came in.

There was a bridge we had to cross to get there, to occupy our portion of Berlin. It was in the Russian zone. On the appointed hour, on the appointed day, we pulled up, and the bridge had been all of a sudden torn up. They said it needed repairs. They worked on it all day and we're set the next morning, and it was torn up again. This went on for several days. Finally, we said forget it and bypassed the bridge and went in.

On the way to Berlin we met some Russians and found them very pleasant, but we were amazed that, in addition to American equipment, they still had horse-drawn artillery and some very primitive weapons. That may be one of the reasons they wouldn't let us go into Berlin. They wanted to get their ragtag troops out and their elite troops in to show us something.

I left the division in August of '45 and came back to an assignment in the Pentagon. I immediately found out that our division was slated for the invasion of Japan. I made a facetious statement that we still had business in Europe. We'd begun to run into trouble with the Yugoslavians. Remember, they shot down one of our C-47s. Actually, the Eighty-second Airborne in Berlin had been alerted and we had troops in this country ready to move into Italy, because of the situation there. The Russians, by this time, had begun to abrogate all their agreements. We had a very anti-Russian attitude because of their lack of cooperation.

The immigration quotas were relaxed considerably. The big job concerned the displaced persons. I became an expert. (Laughs.) One of the problems was the infiltration of Jews into Germany and into Austria. It was a very knotty problem. The German economy was in terrible shape and there was no place for these people to stay except to house them on the German people. It was an expensive thing. We figured that it cost about $811 to delouse, clean up, refit each of these people and all that sort of thing.

I had to grow up in a hurry in the army. When I walked out of West Point, I really didn't know which end of an aiming circle to look in. At twenty-five, I was commanding a battalion in combat. (Laughs.) Responsibility was forced on you very quickly.

The dedication and patriotism of the American people that was evident in World War Two just wasn't there in the others. If people know there's a good reason for what they're doing, they're enthusiastic about it. But when they have doubts, it's difficult.

Just a short time ago, I read Bernard Fall's book on Vietnam, *Street Without Joy.* Anyone that read that would have serious doubts about getting involved. I think it was necessary. It's just too bad we didn't go all out and do what we had to do. But it really would have been a tragic thing if we'd done all we had to do to win.

I think the pendulum has begun to swing. I'm certainly not war-like. I always think, Blessed be the peacemakers. But somebody's gotta take care of the peacemakers while they're makin' peace.

THE BOMBERS AND THE BOMBED

JOHN CIARDI

An American poet.

I had no attraction to the military, yet we had to go out and do something. I was terribly innocent at twenty-six. I was the tanglefoot civilian who did not know what he was doing. I did not want to go in the navy. I would not under any circumstances get into a submarine. I didn't see any point in being a footslogger, sleeping in the mud.

I had dreams of being a pilot, so I signed up as an aviation cadet. The army decided I was not pilot material. The army was right. They sent me to navigation school. I would have come out as a navigator and been sent to the Eighth Air Force. As a graduate student, I had signed some petitions in favor of the Spanish Loyalists. When I came up for graduation from the navigation school, I was classified as a PAF—a premature anti-fascist. The Dies Committee had wired in. I did not get a commission. A year later, I heard that all forty-four men of my graduating class were either KIA or MIA, dead or missing in action.

When we got to Saipan, I was a gunner on a B-29. It seemed certain to me we were not going to survive. We had to fly thirty-five missions. The average life of a crew was something between six and eight missions. So you simply took the extra pay, took the badges, took relief from dirty details. Now pay up.

There was a way out. Any man who was tired of flying could report to the squadron CO and ground himself. He would be put on permanent garbage detail. Permanent garbage detail is better than burning to death. Yet in all the time we were there, most of a year, only two men in the whole squadron put themselves on permanent garbage detail. Not a one received any wisecracks from anybody. Everybody knew that if he dared, he'd be on that garbage truck with 'em.

I don't think it was patriotism. I think it was a certain amount of pride. The unit was the crew. You belonged to eleven men. You're trained together, you're bound together. I was once ordered to fly in the place of a gunner who had received a shrapnel wound. I dreaded that mission. I wanted to fly with my own crew. I didn't know those other people. I didn't want to run the risk of dying with strangers.

I was saved by two more flukes. The first was the Dies Committee.

We got to Saipan in November of '44, in time to fly the first raids over Tokyo. Those were long missions. We were in the air normally about fourteen hours. Most of it was over the open Pacific. We had to get over the coast, make our bombing run, and then make it back to Saipan. We took some rather heavy losses. Sixty-five percent of them, as I recall, were due to engine failures. The B-29 tended to catch fire. They finally flew the bugs out of this new plane.

At one time, one of the blisters on our plane was damaged—the plexiglass bubble out of which the gunner tracked. There were no spares on the island. We sat it out almost all the month of February of '45, waiting for a replacement. During that time, we lost a lot of crews. We were out surfing, playing in the ocean, spear fishing. I would give myself at least a forty percent chance of having been killed in February, except for this blister thing. Instead, it turned into a vacation.

The third time was a pure fluke. I was halfway through the tour of missions. I know it was over fourteen. You got an air medal for surviving five missions. If you survived eight more, you got another air medal. The next one was a DFC. I got two air medals, so I must have had fourteen or fifteen missions. I received orders to report to headquarters. The colonel in charge of awards and decorations said, "We've run into real trouble with our program. We need somebody with combat-crew experience who can write. You've taught college English, you've published a book. You're now working for me. You're going to take charge of the awards and decorations."

This program was raided by the brass, so that decorations were pointless after a while. Anybody up to the grade of a captain, you may assume earned it. Anybody from the grade of major up who has a high decoration *may* have earned it, but you don't have to believe it.

"Go to your squadron," the colonel said, "pick up your gear. We'll keep you on flying pay. You'll have to fly back and forth to Guam

to report to the board. While you're at it, sew on an extra stripe."
I was then a staff sergeant. I couldn't make tech for having been shot
at, but I did it for grinding out words.

A few missions later, the crew I had been on took a direct hit over
Tokyo Bay from an unexploded flake shell. It went right through the
wing gas tank and the plane just blew up, disintegrated in midair. Just
one of those flukes.

That's three times I should have been absolutely dead, except for
flukes.

I feel sorry for the kids in Vietnam. They couldn't have figured out
what it was they were fighting for. I knew why I was there. That
doesn't mean I wasn't scared. I don't know what I would have done
in Vietnam. I mean, I'm a botch as a killer, as a soldier. But as an
American, I felt very strongly I did not want to be alive to see the
Japanese impose surrender terms.

On the night before a mission, you reviewed the facts. You tried
to get some sleep. The army is very good at keeping you awake
forever before you have a long mission. Sleep wouldn't come to
you. You get to thinking by this time tomorrow you may have
burned to death. I used to have little routines for kidding myself:
Forget it, you died last week. You'd get some Dutch courage out
of that.

We were in the terrible business of burning out Japanese towns.
That meant women and old people, children. One part of me—a
surviving savage voice—says, I'm sorry we left any of them living.
I wish we'd finished killing them all. Of course, as soon as rationality
overcomes the first impulse, you say, Now, come on, this is the human
race, let's try to be civilized.

I had to condition myself to be a killer. This was remote control.
All we did was push buttons. I didn't see anybody we killed. I saw
the fires we set. The first four and a half months was wasted effort.
We lost all those crews for nothing. We had been trained to do
precision high-altitude bombing from thirty-two thousand feet. It was
all beautifully planned, except we discovered the Siberian jet stream.
The winds went off all computed bomb tables. We began to get winds
at two hundred knots, and the bombs simply scattered all over Japan.
We were hitting nothing and losing planes.

Curtis LeMay came in and changed the whole operation. He had
been head of the Eighth Air Force and was sent over to take on the
Twentieth. That's the one I was in. He changed tactics. He said, Go

in at night from five thousand feet, without gunners, just a couple of rear-end observers. We'll save weight on the turrets and on ammunition. The Japanese have no fighter resistance at night. They have no radar. We'll drop fire sticks.

I have some of my strike photos at home. Tokyo looked like one leveled bed of ash. The only things standing were some stone buildings. If you looked at the photos carefully, you'd see that they were gutted. Some of the people jumped into rivers to get away from these fire storms. They were packed in so tight to get away from the fire, they suffocated. They were so close to one another, they couldn't fall over. It must have been horrible.

I have one image of an early raid in which a Japanese fighter plane bored in. I saw his goggled face as he went over the top of our plane. I got a burst into him and he was gone. I got a probable for it. After the first raid, nothing came at us from behind. The Japanese lined up across the sky and came in to ram. They would all swarm on the B-29 and finish it off. That happened from time to time.

We were playing a lottery. A certain number of planes had to be lost. You were just hoping that by blind chance yours would not be. When news of that atom bomb came—we didn't know what it was —we won the lottery. Hey, we're gonna get out of here! We may survive this after all.

I never had any ambition to be a warrior. I had to condition myself, to sell myself against my own death. One measure of that is hatred. I did want every Japanese dead. Part of it was our own propaganda machine, but part of it was what we heard accurately. This was the enemy. We were there to eliminate them. That's the soldier's short-term bloody view.

I was never really a soldier. I was caught up in the army, a civilian putting in my service. When it was over, I had a longer view. It's anyone's universe. Anyone has as good a right to it as I have. Who am I to want to go out killing people?

I think the Germans of that era were guilty. On the other hand, I think any people subjected to a propaganda barrage, with their patriotic feelings worked on, could become savage.

When you're on a mission and you saw a Japanese plane go down, you cheered. This was a football game. When one of your guys went down, you sighed. It was miserable. One of the saddest things I ever saw, when we were flying wing on a plane that got hit, was the barber's-chair gunner in the big bubble at the very top. He was right there beside us in plain sight, beginning to go down. He just waved his hand goodbye. There was nothing you could do. You couldn't reach out to touch him. Of course, that got you.

You were under a compulsion to say nice things about the guy. You saw a plane break up. You saw it catch fire. You saw two chutes, one of them burning. Whatever it was, the truth is—the dark truth—you were secretly glad. It could have been you. It was a superstitious ritual we were playing. There were a certain number of blackballs to be passed out. Every time another plane went down, it was taken out of play. Somebody had to catch it, and somebody else caught it for you. It didn't make any sense, but that's the way we felt. That's a dirty, dark thing to say. When we go to funerals of old friends these days, in one corner of our minds we're saying, Well, I outlived that old bastard.

When the news came that so-and-so's crew had been hit and gone down over Tokyo, you made sounds: Oh, my God. But somewhere, very deep down in your psyche, is, It could have been me.

My first poems of any consequence, I feel, were war poems. I'm not a war poet, but just about that time they were beginning to come together. I found myself writing a lot of elegies for friends of mine who did not make it. Then it occurred to me that the way things were going, I might not make it. So I decided to write my own: "Elegy Just in Case . . ."

He recites:

> *Here lie Ciardi's pearly bones*
> *In their ripe organic mess.*
> *Jungle blown, his chromosomes*
> *Breed to a new address.*
>
> *Here lies the sgt.'s mortal wreck*
> *Lily spiked and termite kissed,*
> *Spiders pendant from his neck*
> *And a beetle on his wrist.*
>
> *Bring the tick and southern flies*
> *Where the land crabs run unmourning*
> *Through a night of jungle skies*
> *To a climeless morning.*

And bring the chalked eraser here
Fresh from rubbing out his name.
Burn the crew-board for a bier.
(Also Colonel what's-his-name.)

Let no dice be stored and still.
Let no poker deck be torn.
But pour the smuggled rye until
The barracks threshhold is outworn.

File the papers, pack the clothes,
Send the coded word through air—
"We regret and no one knows
Where the sgt. goes from here."

AKIRA MIURI

He is a professor of Japanese language and literature at the University of Wisconsin, Madison.

The day the war broke out, December 8, Tokyo time, I heard the Pearl Harbor news on the radio. Though we had been reading in the paper that this sort of thing might occur, it still came as a shock. I was fourteen, in middle school. My father was an English teacher. Both my parents, two brothers, and four sisters were all living together. We were at first elated by the news of this victory. It overshadowed worries about the war. We weren't thinking about how it would turn out.

My father's feelings were ambivalent. He had studied at Oxford for a couple of years and came back to Japan to teach. I suspect he was pro-West secretly, but suppressed these feelings and became quite patriotic.

In '43, students who had enjoyed deferment were beginning to be drafted, especially students who had been in the humanities. The sciences were not touched as much.

My older brother, who was two years older, was drafted. They made him a reconnaissance officer. One day his plane crashed. He and the pilot were killed. In '45, just four months before the end of the war. Two of my sisters married just before the war. Both their husbands were drafted. One was killed in Okinawa. There were a lot of casualties among our relatives and friends.

In Japan, we were not drafted until we were twenty. Toward the end of the war, draft age was lowered to nineteen. I was a few months younger than nineteen when it was over, so fortunately I was never drafted.

Even before the war, Japan had been under military rule, so our education didn't change that much. We did spend more time with patriotic material in history classes and were being taught how to march and how to shoot. We took it in stride without much questioning.

In the beginning, the war was still distant to us. We sent off our relatives and friends with cheery smiles and military songs. We didn't see any bombing yet, so we were not really aware of what war was like.

Doolittle's raids began in '42 and '43. When I saw a couple of American planes in the sky, I realized it was coming closer. After Doolittle's first attacks on Tokyo, nothing happened for a time. America started invading all those Pacific islands. When they took Saipan and built a huge airfield there, it really began. We saw these bombers high above Tokyo. They came in droves early in '44.

In '44, all the high schools were closed so the students could work in the factories. Everybody was mobilized for the war effort. My classmates and I were sent to a metal factory, where they were building airplane parts. I was seventeen then.

The younger kids were all evacuated from Tokyo and sent to the countryside. The air raids were now getting worse and quite heavy. I was awakened by air-raid sirens and could see the western sky lighted up by fire bombs. It looked like a big display of fireworks. Fortunately, the residential area where I lived was not hit. We were very lucky, because in Tokyo it was hard to distinguish factory areas from dwelling places.

Downtown Tokyo was completely destroyed. The Ginza area was pretty well wiped out. I saw people fleeing, their faces covered with soot, their clothing torn off. It was happening almost every night. We had some shelters, but they were so primitive they couldn't do any good.*

I studied at the Tokyo University Law School for one month, and then in May '45 I was sent to a navy factory outside the city. It was just three months before the end. There wasn't enough material to work on, so we ended up as farmers, growing potatoes and pumpkins. Before the pumpkins grew big enough to eat, the war ended. (Laughs.)

We knew we were losing the war. First we lost Guadalcanal and then we lost Saipan. The government was saying we weren't losing the islands, we were just retreating strategically. We didn't believe them. They were hiding the bad news. We didn't know that the Imperial Japanese Fleet had by this time been ninety percent destroyed. We thought it was still intact, hiding somewhere. There were some diehards, hoping, lying to themselves, but most of us were having doubts.

At first it was hush-hush. Nobody dared express his doubts. We knew that life was getting more and more miserable. We didn't have enough to eat. We didn't even have rice. Without rice, life means nothing. (Laughs.) We were eating all sorts of junk, like seaweed, the kind we would never touch. We were eating awful fish we had never heard of. (Laughs.) Everybody was getting thin and losing much weight. The American planes were dropping leaflets from the sky: The war will be over soon. If you don't surrender now, we may have to drop more bombs on Tokyo.

We didn't know what to expect from the Americans. The hard-core militarists were warning us that all our men would be made into slaves, would be sent to China to do hard labor, and all our women would be made prostitutes. It was a great relief when the Americans came and no such things happened. (Laughs.)

The day after Hiroshima was bombed, there was a headline telling

---

*"Le May decided to launch massive night incendiary raids on Japanese cities. On March 9, 1945, over 300 of his B-29s destroyed 16 square miles of Tokyo. It was the most destructive air raid of the war. As the superheated air generated fierce windstorms and consumed the oxygen, tens of thousands of Japanese collapsed 'like so many fish left gasping in the bottom of a lake that has been drained,' as one survivor put it. The death toll probably exceeded that at Hamburg, or Dresden, or even Hiroshima and Nagasaki. LeMay's bombers· moved on to other Japanese cities through the spring and summer, omitting only a few to serve as 'virgin' targets for the atomic bomb." (From "The Slide to Total Air War," by Michael Sherry, *New Republic*, December 16, 1981.)

us about a special bomb. They didn't say "atomic bomb" because they didn't know what it was. They said it was extremely powerful and a tremendous number of people were killed. We were all discussing it: What is this thing? It was a scary feeling.

I remember August 15, 1945. I got the day off from my farm work to go to Tokyo for some dental treatment. A friend and I listened to the radio broadcast by the Emperor, announcing the end of the war. He was using all kinds of highfalutin' expressions to make things sound vague, but we realized that Japan had surrendered. We were very sad, but at the same time we both had a tremendous sense of relief. We felt we had suffered enough and things had to change. There was a naval base right near the factory where we worked. Some fanatical officers wanted to fight on. To lose honorably: to die fighting. They were exhorting everybody and getting nowhere.

I got back to Tokyo ten days after the war. When winter came, we were really miserable. We had neither food nor clothing. There wasn't anything to eat in Tokyo, so they closed the university for two months. They declared a winter vacation. (Laughs.) We were told to go to the countryside and find food wherever we could. There was nothing in Tokyo.

The liberal professors, who had been fired during the war by the military powers, came back. There was a feeling of freedom we hadn't enjoyed before. Strange as it may sound, the Emperor's speech had a tremendous influence on everybody. He said we had to fight this war, of course. But now that it was over, we had to usher in a new era of peace and rebuild our country. People had to believe the war was not in vain in order to live on.

We still didn't have enough food or clothing. Very few of the university students could afford the black school uniforms. Many had returned from the war and were still wearing soldiers' uniforms to class.

The Occupation forces began distributing American food to the Japanese people. Everything was rationed, and we stood in line. We sometimes received American potatoes and we couldn't believe how huge they were. (Laughs.) Japanese potatoes are much, much smaller. These were two, three times as large. The canned goods may not have been great by American standards, but to us everything tasted great.

One day I saw a group of American soldiers marching along the street. It was about two weeks after the war. It was the first time I had ever seen American soldiers. I remember clearly how scared stiff they were, too. They didn't know what to expect either. They thought there might still be some fanatics around. We were scared stiff because we thought maybe these soldiers would do something wild. They were such young boys. These scary moments were over quickly when we learned they were okay and they learned that the Japanese were quite peaceful now. Of course. We were so tired of fighting, we had no energy left. (Laughs.)

After the war, when a lot of Americans came to Japan, they all looked so well-fed and well-dressed, so healthy. In contrast to us, who were all emaciated. That was the first thing that hit us so hard. We said to ourselves, Why did we fight these people? We couldn't have won. (Laughs.) They brought all kinds of food and equipment and were building all over Japan. They even erected some American villages, naming them Washington Heights, Grant Heights, Jackson Heights. (Laughs.) These places were so different from where we lived in Tokyo. We didn't have enough electricity or gas. They were living in absolute luxury. Two or three hours a night, we had electricity. The rest of time we used candles. They were using electricity like water. There was some resentment, of course.

One nice thing came out of the war. I met my wife. Her father was a U.S. Army chaplain who came to Japan in 1948. His wife and my aunt had attended Mount Holyoke College way back. Our family was a very academic one. Most of us turned pro-American, a feeling that had been suppressed during the war.

JOHN KENNETH GALBRAITH

Economist, memoirist, former ambassador to India.

The great principle of American war strategy is: We have airplanes, therefore they must be effective.

Sometime in 1944, Roosevelt came to the conclusion that there was a large element of exaggeration and pure guesswork in what the air force was accomplishing. He responded to several suggestions that there should be an independent civilian commission established, to go with the troops as they moved into France and Germany to find out what really happened.

In the spring of 1945, I was brought into this by George Ball and

Paul Nitze. The three of us formed the core of the operation under Henry Alexander, who came in from J. P. Morgan and Company. It had the advantage that you operated well out of the range of guns. Quite a few people find this advantageous in war, including some generals.

The results were not in doubt. The bombing of Germany both by the British and ourselves had far less effect than was thought at the time. The German arms industry continued to expand its output until the autumn of 1944, in spite of the heaviest air attacks. Some of the best-publicized attacks, including those on German ball-bearing plants, practically grounded the Eighth Air Force for months. Its losses were that heavy. At the end of the war, the Germans had ball bearings for export again. Our attacks on their air-frame plants were a total failure. In the months after the great spring raids of 1944, their production increased by big amounts.

The reasons were threefold. First, the machine tools were relatively invulnerable. They'd be buried under rubble but could be dug out in a day or two. Second, it was possible to decentralize production: to move the machinery into schools and churches. It was reorganized in much less time than was imagined. The Germans discovered that it wasn't necessary for production to be in a single factory. They also discovered a large range of substitutes. It was possible to redesign a lot of equipment to reduce the use of ball bearings. Third, it was possible to reorganize what had been sporadic and less than diligent managements.

The most disappointing of the attacks was on the airplane plants. Production was taken away from Hermann Goering, who was expansively incompetent, and put in the Speer ministry, which was much better. This more than offset the damage done by the bombers.

A similar case was in the bombing of Hamburg. It destroyed the center of the city and made available a large number of people—restaurant workers, cabaret performers, bankers, teachers, salesmen. They all became available as a working force in the war plants at the edge of the city.

There had been two broad strategies. The British bombed at night and went for the central cities, because that was all they could find. Naturally, working-class areas were the most damaged. The middle classes lived on the outskirts and were hardly touched. This was true of most cities, ours and theirs. In general, poor people lived in the center and the affluent lived on the edges. It was the East End of

London that was hardest hit by the Luftwaffe. Or a working-class city like Coventry. The same thing went for German cities.

American strategy involved daylight raids. We aimed for the plants themselves. The problem was targeting. In a large number of cases, we couldn't hit them. There was a saying in 1945: We made a major onslaught on German agriculture.

I don't want to exaggerate. Some of the big plants were hit. One in central Germany, which produced synthetic fuels, was hit repeatedly. The attacks on the German oil supply had a considerable effect on the mobility of their ground forces. They were only successful because it was an enormous plant covering acres and acres. And we hit it repeatedly. The Germans had some hundreds of thousands of people at work repairing that plant all the time.

The war for other people ended in the summer of 1945. For us, it continued on through that autumn in a major row with the air force. Naturally, they were far from enchanted with our figures as they became available. The instinct of the air force was first to deny the figures and then to suppress them.

The over-all conclusion was that wars were won by the slogging progress of the troops across France and into Germany, with a good deal of help from tactical air power: support for the actual movement of troops on the ground. It was an extended form of artillery. Strategic bombing was designed to destroy the industrial base of the enemy and the morale of its people. It did neither.

Need I say that this conclusion was less than popular at the time?

What about the fire bombings of Tokyo?

We concluded that, on the whole, the Japanese industry did not have the same recovery capacity as the German. When the Japanese war plants were hit, they were more likely to stay out of production. You have to remember that from 1941 to 1945, Japan was a very small country with an equally small industrial base. It was stretched very tight and had little of the resilience of the German economy.

Yet the fire bombing of Japanese cities was not a decisive factor in the war. The war in Asia was won by the hard, slow progress up from the south and across the Pacific.

All of war is cruel and unnecessary, but the bombings made this one especially so. The destruction of Dresden was unforgivable. It was done very late in the war, as part of a military dynamic which was out of control and had no relationship to any military needs.

Didn't the dropping of the A-bomb on Hiroshima and Nagasaki shorten the Pacific war?

The bomb did not end the Japanese war. This was something that was carefully studied by our bombing survey. Paul Nitze headed it in Japan, so there was hardly any bias in this matter. It's ironic that he has since become fascinated with the whole culture of destruction. The conclusion of the monograph called *Japan's Struggle to End the War* was that it was a difference, at most, of two or three weeks. The decision had already been taken to get out of the war, to seek a peace negotiation.

The Japanese government, at that time, was heavily bureaucratic. The decision took some time to translate into action. There was also a fear that some of the army units might go in for a kind of Kamikaze resistance. The decision was not known in Washington. While the bomb did not bring an end to the war, one cannot say Washington ordered the attacks in the knowledge that the war was coming to an end.

Would not millions have been lost. American and Japanese, in the projected attack on the mainland, had it not been for the bomb?

That is not true. There would have been negotiations for surrender within days or a few weeks under any circumstances. Before the A-bombs were dropped, Japan was a defeated nation. This was realized.

This experience, as a member of the commission, had an enormous effect on my attitudes. You had to see these German cities, city after city, in 1945 and then go on to the utter horror of Japanese cities to see how frightful modern air warfare is. There is nothing nice about ground warfare: twenty thousand men were killed on the first day in the Battle of the Somme in World War One. But this didn't have the high visibility of Berlin, Frankfurt, Cologne, Mainz. And to see Tokyo leveled to the ground. I was left with an image which has stayed with me all of my life.

POSTSCRIPT: *"I was somewhat more vulnerable than others. I grew up in Canada. My father was a major influence in the community, where there were doubts about the justification of World War One. It was a feeling that this was something not the business of Scottish clans and Canadian farmers. The notion of resistance never crossed anybody's mind. On the other hand, my father had himself made a member of the draft board in order to exempt anybody who didn't want to go.*

"My greatest memory is of a brilliant spring day in 1918. My father, a farmer, had a broken kneecap and was disabled. On this day, teams of horses with seeding and cultivating equipment appeared from all around. They were in the hands of people my father had exempted from service. All of our crops were planted in the space of forty-eight hours. It was all done as a surprise to us.

"Out of this background, I approached the whole subject of war with considerably less enthusiasm than some of my generation. I accepted the necessity of it in World War Two. I was, on the whole, glad when we got in. I had been in Germany in 1937 and 1938, and there was no doubt as to the nature of the Hitler regime. Japan left no doubt after Pearl Harbor. But the visual impact of the air attacks and the horror of it is something I've lived with to this day."

EDDIE COSTELLO AND URSULA BENDER

Most of his work life, he had been a journalist. He is semiretired. Ever since her arrival from Germany, she has worked for a publishing house.

They have known one another for several years, but this is the first time they have talked of a city they both remember: Frankfurt, which he bombed; Frankfurt, where she lived.

EDDIE: World War Two for me is a sore asshole. World War Two for me is four years of nervous diarrhea. World War Two for me is a chance to look back on it, even now, and tell sea stories: to take what happened and enlarge it, embroider it, and come out maybe not smelling like a rose, but smelling a little better than I do.

I began as a seventeen-year-old adolescent patriot. Anything my President said was okay for me. Just before I went in the navy, I worked in an arms plant. I lied about my age when I was fourteen. I made it sixteen. I had a job straightening machine-gun barrels. '38, '39, '41. Everything is very vague now. I make it that way. When the war fever began, the manufacturer had sweepers going around with a can of yellow paint and a stencil making signs on the concrete floor of the plant: GIVE 'EM A JOLT WITH SMITH & WESSON or SLAP THAT JAP. That was the truth.

I was second pilot on a Catalina. It was a flying boat. My first pilot was a Mustang with twenty years in. He was a great father figure. I revered him in an unhealthy way. We landed in the water and I went out on the wing to fix a pontoon that jammed. My first pilot forgot that I was out on the wing. In order to maneuver, he gunned the engine when I was directly behind it. Flew me fifty feet in the air, blew me in the water. Later, I said to him, "Aw, sure, that's okay. You forgot I was on the wing." I would have forgiven that man anything, because he was my father *in extremis.*

He taught me so well that I ended up a better navigator than he was. I could shoot, compute, and do a three-star fix in under ten minutes. But I did a lot of drinking. I learned about women and I learned how to fuck off. (A long pause.) At one point, I developed a terrible fear of the single-engine aircraft—one I was on had lost power and I went over the side at nine hundred feet. Luckily, my parachute worked. I decided to spend the rest of the war in multi-engine aircraft. I ended my days flying sector searches in the Gulf of Mexico for downed aircraft. My war was a quiet war.

The only exciting part came when my girlfriend left me and I needed a charge. I had a ten-day leave. And I got a ride over to England, where I met a guy there in a bar I'd gone to college with. He said, "Come joyriding with me tomorrow. We're gonna have a little flight." I had no idea where it was. Because I was spending all my time drunk. We had a carousing night. The next day, we were briefed and I was smuggled onto his plane. I learned that he was going to Frankfurt on an ordinary run. I had never bombed anything before. But his second pilot was hung over, so I flew in the right-hand seat. I was second pilot on a bomber.

I had never flown a bomber before. We bombed the hell out of Frankfurt.

Years later I made a business trip to Frankfurt. One evening, I was walking around the Opernplatz. It was a misty night and there was a little wind. Suddenly, I found myself downwind of this bombed-out opera house. I could still smell the burning. It was eerie, an uneasy sensation. I got back from my trip and told Ursula (he nods toward Ursula) about this weird feeling. She said she was there that very night. I was bombing somebody who was later gonna be a friend of mine. What Ursula doesn't know to this day is that I was drunk. Bombed out of my mind.

Haven't you ever smelled that smell in a neighborhood after the fire department has put a fire out? That smell. It was faint, but it was detectable.

URSULA: I will never forget that. This incredible memory is the beginning for me of the war. It lingers on till this day. I was five. I was on the toilet seat, on the middle landing. Rüsselsheim, just outside Frankfurt. It's a factory town. They were building airplanes at the time, so it was strategic bombing. The sirens went off. My mother and I were alone in the house. My sister was evacuated in the country.

I went off the pot with my pants hanging down, running into the basement. The next thing I knew, I fell asleep. I woke up and I was alone. My mother had disappeared. I wandered out into the completely burning neighborhood. The smell of burning is one of the stronger images for me of the war. It's that smell of mortar, of brick, of cement that has been hot and cooled down. Since we lived in this town that made airplane parts, we were bombed constantly.

I found her in a chain of women passing buckets from one to the other. There were no men. There were only women and old people. The whole neighborhood had really been bombed out.

I'm now six, this is '44. We were standing outside in the gardens looking at these planes flying over. I remember waving at the American pilots. They came very low and escaped the flak. Flew so low that they practically touched the roofs of the villages. I can't tell you why we weren't scared. I saw my first theater in a bunker. That was a way of life. You had your little place in the bunker, you had your dolls. You could get there very quickly. It was not as scary as it was for the grownups. A six-year-old child has a very different perception. There was excitement, a certain adventure. Your life took place with your neighbors, with your friends. You had places where you played.

We stayed in the Rhineland for a year. Then we went to what is now East Germany, until late '45. We were with the Russians when the war ended. I remember sitting on the lap of this Russian general who gave me beer. We were in an area where the Germans had retreated, set everything on fire, and said, Take what you can carry. The population was allowed to loot as much as they could. The smart women did.

My mother took seven sacks of sugar and two little wheels from an airplane. She turned into a Mother Courage. She wheeled all her little collectings back to Frankfurt, which is about a thousand miles away. Parachute silk. For years we had blouses made of parachute silk. She bartered with that later on. She brought all this back to Frankfurt and became a merchant. Our house was never destroyed, so for years we lived on these goods.

My mother was an incredible woman. She always saw a good situation. The Russians would steal from us, we would steal from them. They would come and steal our little things that we collected. She would steal food from them. They would come and show family pictures. They would come around at night and talk about their families in very broken language. A lot of Russians didn't know what to do about the toilet and washed their heads in them. A lot of the generals with the higher ranks were very polite, but the others were raping. Every night we would sit under the roof, hiding, because they were going through the town raping anything in sight.

The Americans had been there for five days. The next day the Russians are there and that's it. I remember these two Americans knocking on the house across the street, saying, "Open the door, Richard, and let me in." Isn't that a song? I remember my sister and I giggling later on. Being afraid of these guys who were saying, "Open the door, Richard." (Laughs.)

There was a much larger fear of the Russians, because there had been rumors of Russian hordes. That was in our mind, whether it was fair or not.

There was a very eerie scene in that village. I'm going to have nightmares tonight. During the German occupation, there were prisoners behind chicken wire. They made little straw boxes. They'd sell them to the villagers. My sister still has one. When the Russians came in, they were freed. They were the worst. They were illiterate and were really for the first time in their lives let loose on the population. The Russians themselves had a hard time controlling them. They were from the Ukraine, people the German army had taken prisoners. Once they were free they came and took revenge on the population. I don't know whether in fact they did. There must have been an enormous guilt among the Germans. The panic—"The Russians are coming"—was transferred to the children.

EDDIE: I had only one experience with POWs during the war. I was in preflight school at Chapel Hill, North Carolina. Our every move was controlled from sunrise to sunset. We marched in formation to a gigantic dining hall and we were served our meals by German POWs. We were forbidden to speak to them in terms other than orders. More sauerbraten, please. No fraternization was allowed. I was—what?—seventeen, eighteen. My view of these people was that they were simply harmless captured drudges who were there to serve the *Ubermenschen*. Us. I imagine if there were German women POWs I might have gone to a government brothel for sex.

When I was eighteen, I was gung ho, completely a creature of my country's propaganda machine. There was right and there was wrong and I wore the white hat. (To Ursula) Your folks and the Japanese wore the black hats. Some of my best friends are Germans, but I still feel uneasy about the Germans as a people. I feel uneasy about rednecks, too. I really distrust Bavarians. They are the Texans of the Teutons. They have a great sense of style and they're very crude. What a silly thing. I don't know many Bavarians, maybe half a dozen. These are the guys who wear regional costumes in exactly the same way that a guy from Dallas will wear a cowboy hat and boots. They're the guys with nicknames who take you around and bullshit you and bribe you and are despicable. If they were Americans, they would chew tobacco and hang blacks.

My son is keeping company with a girl, Aki Yoshimura. When I first met her father, Mr. Jap—my son will have my head when he hears me call a Japanese person a Jap—I felt very uneasy, because he flew in the Pacific in World War Two. Before I met him, I felt like I feel about the fucking Bavarians. Very uneasy. (Laughs.) But friendship, intimacy, changes everything.

I can think back to World War Two and I can idealize the whole thing, because I don't have a guy over the back fence reminding me of the crappy way I behaved then. My leaders told me to do this because it was good. And I took their word for it, because I didn't know any better. I followed orders, it's as simple as that.

There's no such thing as a just war. Everything is perverted. Recently I heard a government official jokingly say, "Because of the financial doldrums we're in now, what we need is a good war. That's what took us out of the Depression."

URSULA: These things you live with. The word "Jew" wasn't ever mentioned. The first time I heard about concentration camps was when I found a book called *Yellow Star.* I was twenty-one, alone in this room.

I'll never forget. I'm part of that generation that grew up with silence. Don't forget, Germany did not start to talk about these things in schools till into the sixties. I remember going to England and staying with educated people. They couldn't believe how ignorant I was.

There was no attempt by my parents to explain. My mother died when I was twelve. My stepmother didn't know the family history. My father suffered too much and didn't want to talk about it. My sister didn't know about it. So when I opened *Yellow Star*, which was pictures taken in a concentration camp by the Americans, I just sat there. My God, what is this? I was writing letters to my father—they lived in Cologne, I was still in Frankfurt—demanding an answer.

EDDIE: I'd rather forget about the war, except when I'm at a cocktail party and somebody gives me an opening: "Tell me about the time . . ." And I come out with these terribly well-worn stories. They bore everyone around me except the people who haven't heard them before. Sometimes I look at it as the time I had the least responsibility. And then the fun was over.

URSULA: You said the fun was over. I remember the day before the end of the war. Everything was burning. Somebody was instructing the withdrawing German troops in how to use a hand grenade. I'll never forget that. He dropped the grenade. That's the first time I'd come in touch with death really. I'd seen houses disappear, but I'd never seen dead people. This time, you see these kids under your window. Most of them killed, others crippled for life. We're talking about sixteen-, seventeen-year-old kids. About ten of them. The moaning, the screams, the blood. My mother was throwing out the gauze, rolls and rolls of gauze that she had collected. She got rid of her loot. She went down and helped. To me, that was the end of the war. I got one glimpse and my mother pulled me away: Don't you dare go to that window again.

The war was mainly the territory of the grownups. Children were excluded. In all this horror, my mother tried to shelter me—from something. I was never told what really happened when my father, although he was partly Jewish, was finally allowed to go into the army in 1943. There was always this cloud. I was always kept from something.

I'll never forget in 1962 when I came home. My father and step-mother were high up, mountaineering. He was by now in his late fifties. I said I was seeing somebody and we were very friendly. I told them his name. My stepmother said, "That's a Jewish name." My father looked around and said, "Sshhh!" This is ten thousand feet up in the mountains. There is nobody near or far except this poor old schleppy couple in the ravine below us. I've never forgotten that. Ssshhhh. 1962. I felt shame for his cowardice, sad for him.

I guess we're talking about innocence, aren't we? Seeing that grenade dismember so many people, although I was allowed only a glimpse—life wasn't the same any more. No more waving. Within a week, I was sitting on the lap of these Russians and drinking beer. We still have it at home, the little aluminum can that I drank my first beer out of. I remember them as kind, good people. They wanted to be friendly with us and treated us well. This all happened within a week.

JEAN WOOD

She is a matronly-looking Londoner visiting New York, where her daughter has a job.

I was a dancer on the stage and just beginning to make my way. I was married and had one baby. My mother took care of her, so I was free and the world was my oyster. I was twenty-five. That war cut out my life till I was thirty-five.

Although the war ended after six years, we still had rationing and tightening our belts and, at one stage or another, no roof over our heads. My husband was in the Royal Artillery. He was wounded. He was never the same man again. He died from his war wounds, some years afterwards. I get a minute widow's pension.

I was due to have another baby when the blitz was at its height. That was 1940. We had a lull between 1939 and the summer of 1940. When the war broke out, I was dancing at a seaside resort. Ballet. I remember gazing out over the English Channel: how could people go to war on such a lovely day and kill each other? It was so unreal.

What was real was that everybody around me downed their tools and clambered to get to the recruiting office. Stores were left unattended, banks closed down. I'd left my little girl with my mother. I said to my husband, "For God's sake, let's get our little girl out of

London." So we got her out. The government said, If you're out of London with a child, please stay put. You're more of a nuisance coming back to London.

I went back to seaside. They said there'd be a lull. They paid you to be evacuated. We were billeted in different people's homes. I had a terrible billet. The woman wouldn't even let me boil a kettle of hot water. She wouldn't let me iron my baby's clothes. She wouldn't let me keep the baby carriage in the house. She said, "Outside. It stays in the rain." I had to put the baby in a damp carriage.

The first day war was declared, the air-raid siren went off. People dived under the most ridiculous places, thinking the Luftwaffe was coming over. (Laughs.) They did feel silly when it was a false alarm. My God, is that what we're going to do? Fling ourselves down into the gutter and all that?

My husband said, "I'll go to the nearest big town and try to put the money down on a house. So at least you'll have your own roof and be safe." On the way, he volunteered to go into the army. He didn't have to go. He was thirty-four, and they weren't calling up that age yet. He said, "I may as well go in now and get it over with." I had to stay with this dreadful woman for a while. He went off and left me.

The war didn't start until the blitz. In October it started. First they bombed two schools in daylight. The kids were all laid out. We couldn't believe it. That was in Croydon.

The seaside was worse than London. When I'd been there, we'd had 109 dogfights overhead. I'd seen our Battle of Britain boys spiraling down. I'd also seen them do a victory roll when they shot a German airplane down. These boys went up day and night, in these Spitfires, almost stuck together with chewing gum. The mother of two of them lived quite near me. She lived in fear and trembling. We lived near the Spitfire airfield and we got terrible bombings. Here is where we were supposed to be safe.

One day I took my little girl shopping in the main little street. A German plane came down and started to machine-gun us. I ran into a store and put her and myself under the shop counter. I had my behind sticking out. (Laughs.) The machine gun was going bang! bang! bang! all up the road.

They had public underground shelters. They held maybe a couple of hundred. You could dodge in any time there was an air raid. There was no warning in these dogfights. You just looked up and saw planes coming down, machine-gunning. It was mostly bombers; our Spitfire boys were fighting back.

We also had our own air-raid shelter that the government issued. In the country, it was a steel table. You had it in your bedroom or living room. You all crawled underneath it. It was not very high, and if you were pretty big, it was awful to get under. (Laughs.) You'd stay under it for hours.

If you were in a big town, like London or Manchester, there was one in the garden. I don't know which was worse. The garden one was concrete or old tin and it was terribly damp. It used to be up to here with water. Such was the fortitude of the ordinary working class that they made little cozy living rooms in it. (Laughs.) They took their bird down there or their cat. The cat was always the last one: "Where's the cat?"

I had an aunt killed through coming up to make a cup of tea. The siren had just gone all clear. (Demonstrates pitch.) She came up the steps, said to her husband, "I'll make a nice hot cup of tea." They'd been there all night, listening to the crashing and bombing. She put the kettle on and with that, the bomb threw a direct hit on the house.

It was nothing to have the people who lived opposite's furniture blow through your window. We acquired all kinds of furniture we never owned. We ended up with a medley of furniture. Most people did. I had an old aunt of eighty who ended up like a film star's dressing table. How it shot into her garden, all that lovely furniture. (Laughs.)

You had air-raid wardens who were very good. These were men who weren't fit for service or worked in key jobs, and after they finished work, they'd be air-raid wardens. They would help you. They would drag the dead out. My husband once was coming home on leave through London. He was days late because he kept stopping at buildings, pulling out the dead. It was awful.

I had four daughters, all except one born during the war. When I went to have one of them, we didn't have ambulances. I had to go out into the blitz with all the fires raging, to try to get to a phone you could still use, call my doctor. He sent two men with a little truck, with a plank across it. I lay on it. There was no light and no signs, in case the Germans came. These two men were so hopeless, I almost gave birth in the truck. We fell down a big bomb crater and I almost tipped over. But you took it all in your stride. It looked as if you were going to live this way the rest of your life.

When I had my third baby, I stood in the room and said, "Please, God, if you're going to kill us with these bombs, let's all die together now, at night." One didn't know how many children to take under you, like a bird, put them under your wing. I thought if I had two here, and that one was over there, she might get killed and leave me with these two. You had to sort of lay on top of them, so that you'd all be killed together. Never thought I had it in me.

I never thought I could sit and read to children, say, about Cinderella, while you could hear the German planes coming. Sometimes a thousand a night came over, in waves. We had a saying, (says it staccato) I'm gonna getcha, I'm gonna getcha. That's how the planes sounded. You'd hear the bomb drop so many hundred yards that way. And you'd think, Oh, that missed us. You'd think, My God, the next one's going to be a direct hit. But you'd continue to read: "And the ugly sister said"—and you'd say, "Don't fidget, dear." And you'd think, My God, I can't stand it. But you bore up. And I wasn't the bravest of people, believe me.

You had hunches. About half past three you'd say, "I won't sleep over there tonight. I'll put them all over here 'cause I have a hunch that that part of the wall will come down." Or what few neighbors were left would say, "Why don't you bring all the kids over to me tonight and let's all sing and play cards. We won't bother with Jerry tonight." Now would it be safer that side of the road or this side? We'll go over there.

I did fire-watch. And that's frightening. You got up on the roof with a steel helmet on. You're supposed to have a protective jacket. The fire bombs were round balls. They'd come onto roofs and start fires. So the government gave you a bucket of sand and a shovel. Charming. (Laughs.) You stood there till the bomb fell. And you'd shovel it up quick and throw it into the bucket of sand. I didn't do that for long, because I fell pregnant again.

Most of the bombs were in working-class areas. I know there was a big thing about Buckingham Palace had a bomb, but they were all under a beautiful shelter. The working class caught it the worst because of the dock areas. And gasometers and electrical power stations. They aimed for those things. They thought if they demoralized the working class, they weren't going on with the war. For some reason, that never happened.

I had an aunt who was bombed out three times. My grandmother, who was eighty-odd, was bombed out and left clinging to the stairs, with her hair alight. The air-raid wardens got her out. She said, "I must go back for my hat." They took her in a truck with a lot of other elderly people to a safety zone.

I had to stay with my mother-in-law once. Sometimes the raids came before the siren went off, so you weren't down in the shelter. Land mines came down by parachute and laid whole streets low. It was like a bombed-out piece of land. This airplane was very low dropping the fire bombs, dropping them everywhere she was going. She did this terrific zigzag all across this field, hopping and leaping, hopping and leaping. Afterwards, people ran to get the parachute, 'cause with this parachute, we could make ourselves clothes. Clothes rationing was terribly strict. My husband got me a piece, and I made the children little dresses out of this nylon.

A lot of flowers grew on these bombed spaces, especially one in particular. It was a stalk with a lot of little red spots. It was like a weed, really. It was called London pride.

There was the blitz, when all London caught fire, except Saint Paul's Cathedral, thank God. That's why every time I go to Saint Paul's, I say, Oh, you're still there, thank God. Everything was in flames that night. It was like daylight, the flames.

I saw schoolchildren killed one Saturday morning. No warning. That's when the V-2s came. They were like big telegraph poles that shot through the air. No pilot, no nothing. They went into a building and laid low a whole street. On this morning, kids were shopping at Woolworth's. You couldn't buy much. You couldn't buy candy without your coupons. My mother's house was two blocks over and we heard this terrible crash. We all ran out to see. It was this Woolworth's and all these kiddies' bodies were brought out. They said they buried them. They don't know what arms and legs belong to people's arms and legs. They had cardboard coffins. We made so many, but we never made enough.

Then we had the V-1s. They were the planes that came over belching fire. It was amazing when the first one came down—in a working-class area, as usual. The fire went *chuchuchu, chuchuchu*. When the fire stopped, they circled and circled. You could almost pinpoint where it's going to land. We all ran to see it. When's the pilot going to get out? We were going to take him prisoner. But there was no pilot.

After that, there was another lull while they thought up the next monstrosity: the V-2s. You had no warning of those. At least with the

V-1s you could hear a *bububu, bububu* with the fire. You could see the fire. If the war had gone on ten days longer, they might have had the atom bomb. All these things were getting up to that. The blitz began in 1940 when the French let us down at Dunkirk, and lasted until the Normandy landing.

We had bouncing bombs, too. They dropped a bomb here and it didn't stay there. It bounced over a building.

There was a great camaraderie, too. People were down there with their sleeping blankets and their bags of goodies or rations. I don't know of one case where anybody took advantage of you. Even going to the bathroom, they might try to hang a little curtain or something. It was "After you, luv." "That's all right, duck, you go." People developed terrifically high morals.

Being a dancer and a singer, I took over an empty house with my bunch of evacuees. These were very poor people. They hadn't even the little things in life. They didn't know which way to turn. Their husbands were in the war. God knows if they were dying or what. So I said, "Come on, girls, let's all get together to scrub the place out." We managed to get a rickety old piano through these rich ladies. I used to play songs and keep 'em all singin' in the afternoon while another two ladies made cups of tea and served little cookies. That cheered 'em up. We'd say, "Come on, let's have a singsong." And we turned the top floor into a playpen with Girl Scouts taking care of the babies to give these poor mothers a break. They, who had babies by day and night, with landladies who were horrible to 'em.

One time when I was evacuated, I was given a house that people had just fled. It was a lovely place. I could never have had one like it in my normal life. These very upper-class people said, "You look a nice type. We know you'll take care of it, so we'll give it to you as long as we're gone." It had a swing in the garden and everything. It was all done through an evacuee council. They commandeered any empty house. In wartime they can make laws overnight, so people who left their property had it confiscated for the duration.

It was getting near D-Day. Normandy, 1944.

They let me stay in their house an extra five years after the war, because I didn't have anyplace to come back to in London. They were a vicar and his wife, who'd lost a son in a Nazi prison camp. The old vicar had died, and this lady was going to New Zealand and live with her daughter. I paid a very minimum rent. It just paid her taxes.

At that time, you were lucky if you had a corner in somebody else's room. There were no houses for people to come back to. It was surviving as best you could. I know Americans have never had the experience of being bombed out. I don't ever wish it on them, either. But I do wish they wouldn't be so keen to get into wars, because one day it will come back on your territory and God help you. I was sorry for the Germans, too. They must have suffered. You have such silly ideas when you're young: Oh, if I could see Adolf Hitler, I'd shoot him myself tomorrow. Oh, Hitler's dead, isn't that marvelous? But that's not the end of your troubles.

When the war ended, we thought it was going to be a better world. I remember feeling so elated, I really do. I don't think I've ever had such good feelings since. I could see everybody being kind to each other 'cause we'd been through such dreadful things.

The housing was terrible. When the men came back from service and found their wives sleeping in these subway shelters and weeks went on, they took over the Savoy Hotel and became squatters. It was the best hotel in London at the time. The working people rallied around them. They went to these big hotels and the servicemen would let down buckets on ropes and we all put what bits of food we had in them. They occupied those hotels for ages. The authorities were petrified. They thought it was going to be Bolshevism or something. The squatting went on spasmodically for about six months. Then they put up prefabricated houses. They built them in one day. Every available construction worker was busy putting up these houses.

At that time, our family had no home. So my husband said he'd be a sandwich man. You know? Wear a placard in front and back with a sign and parade up and down: You have houses for the tourists, but none for your servicemen. I called a newspaper and told them this is what he planned to do. Within two days, we were offered a nice place to live.

The war took a disastrous chunk out of my life. I gave up thinking about my profession. I had a war-wounded husband and four children. I became a different personality. Before the war, I saw everything through rose-colored glasses and lived for music and my dancing. After the war, I began to study things. I had to help educate my children. I had to adjust to never ever having any money, 'cause we existed on my husband's war pension. I put behind me looking into store windows, 'cause you knew you never were going to be able to buy anything in the way of pretty clothes. Never coveting anything off anybody, because that would only make you old and hateful-looking.

It's taken a lot of maybes and pleasures from me, but I began to see people and events in a certain light. I'm always looking for the economic reason why people do this or why a government does this. It's not always nice to know. (Laughs.)

Maybe I'm pessimistic. Maybe we'll see a lovely new era come. I'm so worried now for my grandchildren. I feel so sorry for them. But then, maybe somebody should have felt sorry for me, growing up in World War Two. (Laughs.) Yet with all its horrors, it made people behave better toward each other than they thought they could.

Housewives during the war were far better cooks than they've been ever since. Can you believe that? We had so little to manage with, we became inventive. If one managed to get a little bit of rice and you had a piece of chop meat, you would mix the two together and make it spread further. If you managed any sultanas or raisins, you scotched all the bits of bread you had together with water and made a gorgeous pudding. If you managed to get some syrup and some brown sugar, if you were lucky, you could make toffee for the kids. So we did fantastic swaps.

I had a very nice lady and her husband, neighbors. She was having her son on leave and she didn't have any meat for him. But that particular day, the butcher let me have some rabbit. In wartime, we et horsemeat and whale steaks, so rabbit was a taste treat. I didn't want the rabbit, 'cause I'd rather give my small children an egg, if I could get eggs. So I took the rabbit round to her. She was so thrilled. On that particular day, her son was killed. We could have flung the rabbit anywhere, for all we cared. He was such a nice boy, a young officer, nineteen years old.

GROWING UP:
HERE AND THERE

JOHN BAKER

Editor, Publishers Weekly.

When World War Two broke out, I was in Ipswich, about forty miles from London. I was seven. We kids were fascinated by aircraft recognition. They gave out these charts of what German planes looked like. The charts were called Know Your Enemy. We instantly memorized them all. My parents were scared, but to me it was all exciting and sort of a game.

There was a terrific flurry of building shelters in early 1940. There were two kinds. One, you built in the garden. This was called an Anderson shelter. A local builder dug a deep hole and shored up the walls with boards. Then he'd put a piece of corrugated iron over the top and fill it in with earth. It was comfortable for four, just enough for a family. There was no room for neighbors.

Being in the shelter was like having a little den. You'd go down there and have secret meetings and take candy and chocolates. You'd pretend you were hiding from something. It was fun.

If there wasn't time to run outside when the air raid sounded, there was a shelter built inside the house. This was called a Morrison shelter. It was built with beams and struts in the middle of the living room. You could get under this thing and if the house fell down around you, it would bear all the weight. It was like getting under a very, very strong table.

There were two kinds of sirens. The alert itself was an up-and-down howling sound. (He imitates it.) It went on for about three minutes. At this, you were supposed to take cover. The all-clear was a long single note, without any wails. (He does an all-clear.) It was like living in a boy's adventure story. We really wished something would happen. When the siren went off and nothing happened, we were disappointed. When the all-clear was heard, we were doubly disappointed.

They issued gas masks. They were convinced the Germans would try gas attacks. Never happened. At school we all lined up in the playground with these rubber masks, like something you go snorkeling with. I don't think they would ever have worked. We'd make faces with 'em. When you breathed into 'em, they made funny noises, like a fart. (Laughs.) We'd do that a lot, being small, laughing boys.

One afternoon I did have an experience. German planes returning from an air raid machine-gunned our street. It was just a bit of terrorism. They were so close we didn't have time to practice our aircraft recognition. They were no more than a hundred feet above us. We really couldn't believe they were machine-gunning us. But being kids and curious, we searched around the bushes and found a lot of these spent bullets.

Shortly after this, the children of the big cities, London, Manchester, were evacuated. It was during the Battle of Britain in late '40. They were kids mostly from poorer areas. They'd be loaded into trains and boarded out with people they didn't know. My sister and I were sent out to an aunt in the country. We stayed there three years.

The people of our country town disapproved of these new city kids, who came in en masse. They regarded them as dirty and their language as bad. They felt their way of life was being trampled upon. I had a little friend from London, a tough little kid. I took a fancy to her, and my mother wasn't keen on this at all. She said Gillian was dirty. Don't play with her. I did anyway.

One night, it was terribly noisy. We could hear explosions and gunfire from a long way off, it seemed. In the morning, we realized it was Coventry. One of the great blitzkrieg attacks of the war. It was no more than thirty miles away. That wasn't considered close in those days. You could bomb one part of town and nothing would be felt on the other end. It would take several bombs to knock down a large building. More damage was done by the fire bombs than by explosives. The scale of terror has changed since then.

She is a faculty wife. Her husband is a professor of political science at the University of Wisconsin in Madison.

"I grew up in Kanazawa, an old feudal city on the west coast of Japan. It means 'golden pond.' It was a college town, much like Madison. I thought I'd run away from it, but I didn't." (Laughs.)

Her father was an ophthalmologist who taught at the university. "We didn't talk politics very much. His teaching, his practice, was all that interested him."

I was born in 1936. I was immediately aware of how rigid school was. It was military, even for first-graders. I remember my first day at school so clearly. All the students had to assemble in the assembly hall. The principal gave a speech about the Emperor and the need to support him.

There was a tiny door on the stage, behind the principal. He opened this door of beautiful burnished wood. There was another door behind it. He didn't open that one. Behind that second door was supposed to be the Emperor's picture. We never got to see it. It was too holy, too divine, to be looked at.

I got in trouble on that first day in school. We were told to look down the minute the principal touched the first door. We were not to raise our head to look at what was there. But I was too curious. I looked up. (Laughs.) The teachers were all standing along the wall and picked out every student who looked up. We had to stand in the back of the assembly hall. Then we had to go onto the stage, say our name, and apologize. I have never forgotten that.

I really hated this military discipline. I could not understand why you couldn't look up. It was an ordinary neighborhood school, but all the regulations were very strict. I strongly resented these rules.

We had one class called *shushi,* mastering your mind. It was a sort of moral education, but it was more patriotic than religious. How divine Japanese history was, how we were a special people. Though the war had begun, we were unaware of it. There was no talk. One time my father said that all this fighting was stupid. That was the only comment I remember him making. The soldiers passing through town were very young boys. They were put up in people's homes, five or six of them together.

Shortly after Pearl Harbor, we were trained to wear certain head-gear. All the mothers made them for their children. It was quilted and covered you all the way down to the shoulders. It was our protection in case of an air raid. (Laughs.)

There were neighborhood shelters, dug behind a low hill. Like a fox's house. It was just carved out of mud. Could hold two or three families. We played war games in them, with sticks, running around chasing enemies.

Now we were not allowed to go to school alone. We formed neighborhood groups. I was the leader of one such group. I always had six, seven children walking behind me in two lines. It was my responsibility to get them to school and back home safely. I was about seven or eight.

I wasn't scared. There was a feeling that whatever came, we were resigned to it. Anyway, our city had no target and we were never bombed. My grandmother used to credit it to our holy Buddhist cloud that covered our city. We were known as a religious town.

By 1944, some of my father's friends started to go to war. They were physicians. I remember them, home on leave, telling stories. The whole atmosphere was one of resignation or treating the whole thing as stupid. There was no enthusiasm at all.

By this time, Tokyo and all the major cities were being bombed. The capital of the next prefecture, Toyama, was bombed completely flat. Our family was in this shelter in the mountain. We looked out and saw the whole sky over Toyama was bright red, burning, burning bright. American planes were flying all over. We heard all kinds of stories about American planes flying very low, shooting down people, and you could see the pilots smiling.

Funny. That's precisely what we heard about Japanese pilots.

Food was getting very scarce. By the time mothers and children were moved to the countryside, it was terrible there, too. My younger brother began to look like one of those starving Indian children: skinny, toothpick legs, and large, distended stomach. When the war ended, there was a feeling of great relief.

On August 15, 1945, at noon, the Emperor announced it on the radio. There was a lot of static, the radio was old. We had a hard time understanding what he said. He sounded almost incoherent. Most people felt it was a very unclear speech. I, a small girl, felt personally very relieved. I didn't like the rigid schools. I didn't like being hungry. I didn't like running at the sound of a siren. I found nothing good about the war. (Laughs.)

When we came back to Kanazawa, things were even worse. Japanese money became worthless. There was inflation and confusion. The only people who had food were farmers. Nothing was available in the stores of Kanazawa. Food meant potatoes and rice, nothing else. The farmers would not accept money because it was regarded as worthless. So my mother started exchanging her beautiful silk kimonos for third-grade rice and a few potatoes.

In the fall of 1945, American soldiers showed up. They drove in jeeps. I remember Japanese girls on the jeeps with Americans. During the war, we had strict clothing and hairdo regulations. We had to have straight hair, no permanent waves. We had to wear no kimonos while out on the street: they were considered luxurious and decadent. We wore trousers, bulky in the middle and narrow and tight at the ankle. Like today's fashionable pants. (Laughs.) Silk was forbidden. So was makeup. We were wearing cotton. These girls on the jeeps had permanent-waved hair and bright lipstick. We considered this in very bad taste. They were called *pan-pan* girls. It had a bad meaning.

The other thing that shocked us was seeing adult men chewing gum. Americans. Eating on the street was considered very bad manners in Japan. Not even candy. It was unthinkable for a well-brought-up person to do so. Grown men chewing while on the street! (Laughs.) Yet the Japanese people liked the American soldiers. Instantly. They were young boys, healthy, smiling all the time, very friendly.

American officers were occupying the better houses. The people had to evacuate. There must have been resentment, but I personally never encountered it. In fact, if your house was chosen, it was proof of status: you had a good house. When I told this to a German, he was astonished. He said when Americans came into Germany, all his friends who had good homes messed them up so they would not qualify for the officers. In Japan, it meant you had a home preferable to your neighbors'.

It took some time for the food to arrive. Until then, we were always hungry. When the white rice came, it was bartered like gold. When the Americans gave us dark bread, we couldn't swallow it; most of us had only known white bread. We had no sugar, no sweets, for a long time. One day Cuban sugar arrived—that's what we called the brown crystals. We made puffed caramels. Oh, it was like heaven.

School changed overnight. Almost all the old rules disappeared. They went overboard, 180-degree change. We could talk back to teachers. We could discuss things. The first English phrase we learned was "panel discussion." (Laughs.) We elected a student council. This was still in elementary school. In 1947, we held citywide student council meetings. I was part of them. (Laughs.) We really liked this new freedom.

The teachers said everything they taught before 1945 was wrong. The war was the fault of the Japanese military. They had led the nation the wrong way. We were now to run a democracy and learn new ways of doing things. Everyone was equal. They made no distinction between boys and girls. Girls could run for speaker. Girls could be class president.

Because there was a paper shortage, we hardly had textbooks. Almost no notebooks. We used newspapers for the toilet, and even the newspapers were scarce. We assembled the textbooks ourselves, with thread and string, hand-printed five-page things.

The clothing situation was very bad for several years after the war. We wore shoes of wood and straw. I didn't get my first pair of leather shoes until 1948. My mother made me a winter coat out of an old blanket. (Laughs.) My friend used to go to school in his sister's dresses. We still have pictures of him in a girl's dress. It's funny now but it wasn't funny then.

While in high school, I contracted tuberculosis. That was a very common disease in Kanazawa. The weather was terrible, but the lack of nutrition worsened things considerably.

By the time I graduated high school in 1955, it was back to normal life, to the old ways. The school system was getting more rigid, the pressures tighter. Ten years after the war, Tokyo was rebuilt. Cars everywhere. Now . . .

As late as 1955, you'd see unemployed, one-legged soldiers at the Tokyo subway stations, begging. This was before the government revised their war-compensation rules. People resented these beggars very much. They were a bad memory, standing there with little tin cans, playing accordions, one-legged, one-armed, begging. People passed by them, so cold, hostile. Why must they remind them?

If you were to ask me what was the biggest influence of the war on me, I'd say it's the way I look at authority. I hated it as a small girl and I still feel the same way. My father, who never said very much, saw the war as a meaningless loss and the military world as an empty one.

POSTSCRIPT: *"For several years, America was paradise in Japanese eyes. The Occupation was considered wonderful. Americans were fair, kind, generous, and rich. More than anything, rich. Students who came to the United States didn't want to go back. Coming here was a dream for many of us.*

"Now it's completely changed around. America is no longer considered paradise. To common Japanese people, it is a place of crime, violence, and unemployment. In 1980, when I was in a Tokyo taxicab, I told the driver I lived in America. He was shocked. He said, 'My brother went to Los Angeles last spring and he had to drive half an hour to find a Japanese restaurant.' (Laughs.) I was reminded of Americans in Tokyo in 1955, frantically looking for a steak house." (Laughs.)

WERNER BURCKHARDT

He is a German jazz and folk-music critic.

The conversation took place in 1963 at his apartment in Hamburg. After midnight.

During the war I started high school in Hamburg. We were lucky. We had a teacher in Latin and Greek who was a pathological democrat. He took dangerous risks in his lectures, this Dr. Drude. When we translated sentences from Latin into German, he wrote on the blackboard: Dr. Gobelius. It was quite obvious to everybody in the class that he was referring to Dr. Goebbels. We had two shaped sentences in Latin: Somebody is lying. Dr. Gobelius is always lying. He was playing with his life.

When there was this strong axis of Rome and Berlin, Dr. Drude came into class one morning with an axle in his hand. He would ride a motorcycle to school. He was a hippie before his time. He pulled this axle from his motorcycle and held it up before the class: "You see, boys? Even an axis can break." We all knew what he meant, of course. Don't you think it was rather daring at the time?

There were twenty-seven of us in class. Fourteen, fifteen years old. It was a miracle that nothing happened. I'm sure the students told their parents. I know quite well that at least three of the fathers of my friends were Nazis. One was the director of a big insurance firm owned by the Nazis. Nobody betrayed him. I think it was the respect for this man. Maybe they guessed that the end was not too far away for the Hitler regime. That Dr. Drude gave us something that would help us endure. Some kind of humanity.

My father had a dry-cleaning shop in the center of Hamburg's Jewish community. On one side lived the lawyers and doctors. They were assimilated Germans. You did not think of them as Jews. On the other side lived the purer Jews. And the poorer. They owned little shops and lived in small, not so well-looking houses. They were all customers of my father.

When Crystal Night came, I was a small boy. This was 1935. I was seven. This was the night Nazi anti-Semitism broke out in a big way. My father took me by the hand, Sunday morning, and he showed me the broken windows of the Jewish department stores. All the valuable clothes, silk and all these things, were lying in the dirt of the street or thrown into the water of the Alster River.

My father never talked politics. He was not a sophisticated man. He didn't talk highbrow or intellectual things. He showed me all this debris and he said this is crazy. You must remember, also, my father was a merchant and he didn't like to see all this destruction of goods. (Laughs.)

My father and I didn't talk too much together. There was a silent agreement. We knew these things were wrong. They wanted him to join the Nazi Party. Recruiters very often came into the shop. He said no, he didn't want to. He said he just doesn't have time for these things. He has so much work to do in the shop. He is not interested in politics. He was just evading. No, he didn't defy them. My father hasn't been a hero. He just didn't want to have anything to do with these people for whom he had such contempt. He very clearly saw it as opportunism and that they didn't believe it themselves. He knew some of them personally. These weren't the idealistic type of Nazis. So they felt it was just a waste of time talking to him, and left.

I felt funny when all the Jews were leaving. The richer Jews left for the Netherlands and France. These very big cars stopped before the shop to pick up their wardrobes, cleaned and pressed. The poor Jews picked up whatever they had. They all left and nobody talked about it.

It was just too dangerous to be too frank. Dr. Drude's survival is a miracle. I know that the owner of the café around the corner vanished for a long time. He would talk a lot. Maybe he had been a bit too frank. He came back, but he was now a silent man. It was understood.

Hamburg, you must remember, had a strong democratic tradition. Social democratic, even communist. Because of the port, working people from all over the world came through here. Hitler hated Hamburg. He was only here two times. I even think he was afraid of Hamburg.

When I was at the *Gymnasium*, I had to attend Hitler *Jugend* classes, also. We all had to wear a uniform, and every Wednesday we got the life of the Führer told to us and had to repeat it word by word. Not omitting anything, not adding anything. Just as it was. Every Saturday we had to go to the suburbs and play war games. Sort of child play, like hide-and-seek. But there was always this background of war behind it.

When the bombings began in Hamburg, they took all the young boys and girls away to the southern part of Germany and even to Czechoslovakia, to a *Kinderland*. When I came back in '43, I had to go to the Luftwaffe. I was in the flak brigade, to shoot at Allied planes. I was fifteen.

We observe a photograph of a young boy, almost a child, in uniform. It is Werner Burckhardt.

I don't think I look too happy.

We had to get out of bed every night at eleven o'clock and stay up till two o'clock in the morning. We still had our school lectures. Every morning a teacher would come out in the snow and ice to our camp and give us Latin and Greek. One day that, another day German and history. A third day, mathematics and chemistry. All this and the flak brigade.

In '44 I was now sixteen. They wanted to send me to the eastern front. I was caught by the British and became a prisoner of war. I was in this camp till June of '45. They took our watches and we got a little bit beaten, too. (Laughs.) They were angry and far away from home.

With the war over, I went back to school. It was in the fall of '45. We had to get the stones out of the ruins and rebuild. I went to the university, Hamburg, and the rest is now.

The old are trying to deny. But in the people who were very young in the Hitler regime and caught a glimpse of the horrors, and in the young today, maybe there is reason for a little bit of hope.

OLEG TSAKUMOV

It is a beautiful Sunday morning of June 22, 1941. The sky is clear, the day quiet. All Leningrad is in a holiday mood. It always is at this time of the year. The summer solstice has begun, when the sun does not set in Leningrad. Girls in their pretty dresses and young men in their white ice-cream pants have been walking all night long on these streets, their arms entwined, singing songs.

Suddenly, a voice on the streets' loudspeakers is saying, Vinomania! Vinomania! Attention! Attention! Hitler has attacked and his armies have crossed the Russian border around four o'clock that morning.

The siege of Leningrad was to begin on the seventh of September and go on unrelenting for nine hundred days. Nobody knows how many people in Leningrad died. It was surely a million. It may have been a million five. Almost half the people of the city died. Imagine New York or Chicago with half its people dead.

They were months of horror. The bones and remains of people at the end of the siege were stacked higher than buildings.

In the winter, there is no light. No heat. It is 20 below zero. A slice of bread a day—bread made of sawdust and glue. There's no water, no transportation. How did people survive under those conditions? I don't know.

When the radio was on, the metronome tick-ticked. It was like the city's heartbeat. Without it, there was no outward sign that this city was alive.

—Harrison Salisbury, reflections on a summer day in 1982. It was shortly after we visited the mass grave at Leningrad.

A poet, living in Leningrad.

I was six when the war began. That Sunday morning, my family took me to the Pushkin Museum. After that, everything was wiped out.

What I most remember is the snow, winter, cold, fog. It eats people. The houses were like dead houses. The smoke was alive, the people were dead. The smoke came from the damaged houses, the fire bombs. One hundred thousand were dropped on Leningrad.

When I was seven, I spoke on the radio. I read a poem, "To the Victory Day." It was long before the victory. It was important for the soldiers at the front to hear this childish voice on the radio, to know that the children of Leningrad were alive. This was no less important than the projectiles. Later, much later, I read my own poem about a very young, small, skinny, very hungry boy who was so small he could walk under the table. Myself, of course.

The most difficult days were when my mother could not get up from bed to go to work. She was too weak from hunger. I went to the kindergarten by myself. With my steps as a man, it is not a far distance. To a man, they are snow heaps. To me, this little boy, they were snow mountains.

In this silent city, there came these sudden bursts of sound. The explosions. I was very frightened, and it was such a long distance to school.

We ate what you give to horses. Oats. In the summer, we picked up grass, boiled it, and ate it. It was food on our minds all the time. Morning was the best time of the day, when you get up. You think something might turn up, you might get something to eat. All the days became one long day and night. Imagine nine hundred such days. It seemed forever.

Victory day? On the ninth of May, 1945, we went to a small opera theater. It was *Iolanthe.* Suddenly the performance stopped and the director came out and said that the Germans surrendered. Everybody in the theater went to the square. I saw hundreds of thousands of people dancing, embracing each other. Tossing the soldiers in the air. They were crying and kissing each other. I was nine years old.

SHERIL CUNNING

La Jolla. We're seated in the lobby of an elegant old hotel. We're facing the Pacific Ocean. She doesn't live here. It is merely our rendezvous.

We lived three blocks away from the ocean, in Long Beach. I was only seven when war was declared. Fear didn't come right away. In no time, the whole beach where we used to walk was completely covered in camouflage netting. Underneath it were all kinds of huge artillery. Hundreds of anti-aircraft guns. Cannons, great things with long huge barrels.

What was so funny is that it was supposed to camouflage the coast. Traffic was still allowed to drive along that street, which was right next to the ocean. Anybody walking down the street could see it. Yet everywhere you went, there were signs that said: Sshhh. A picture of Uncle Sam with a finger on his mouth. It said: There's other people listening. If spies were walkin' around town, they knew the guns were under there. (Laughs.)

The guns were inanimate. We never saw them shoot. I saw much of World War Two as a big game. It was unusual and exciting and it was only three blocks from home. To this day, just any kind of siren makes my hair stand on end. And the searchlights going off. I guess they call 'em spotlights now. Every time they have a new shopping center opening, the big thing in Escondido is to get a spotlight that goes across the sky all night long. It still sets up panic and anxiety in me.

We did hear shooting. We never knew whether we really had an attack or whether it was a false alarm. I don't think they want people to know how close anything came. It's just now being revealed that paper balloons from Japan that carried bombs may have lit on the Oregon coast. Nobody ever said we were really under attack that night. But the shrapnel was coming down like rain. From American guns. We collected it and saved it as remnants of World War Two. My grandmother had a whole dish of it that stayed on the dining-room table all my growing-up years.

Lotta kids, their fathers were actively in the war. Carol's father was in the Coast Guard. We would always look at letters from her father. It was a house with a woman and child growing up all those years alone and living on letters. I think Nora's father was killed. Shirley Somebody's father was away. We talked about it at school all the time. Absent fathers.

Our Japanese friends ran the produce section in an open-air market. They were there one day and the next day they weren't. I don't remember too much about these people, except they were always kind to us. I remember my mother complaining that we couldn't get any decent produce after they were taken away.

When my children were eleven, twelve, they had very close friends. The mother was a Japanese woman. She went through the bombing of Japan and was now living here with her Japanese-American children. Those children would watch the World War Two era movies, especially the Japanese things where John Wayne is in the big airplane zeroing in: I got that dirty Jap. Tojo, here's one for you. These children had no part of that war. Nobody had ever told them about this war, until they saw this movie.

Their mother had all kinds of cultural things from Japan on the walls. They now felt guilty about being Japanese and they were very, very confused: Well, I'm an American, too, and I should feel proud when John Wayne shoots down those dirty Japs—but I'm Japanese. They wanted to know who was right and who was wrong. They didn't know who they were after seeing those movies. The day they questioned me was one of the saddest days of my life.

There wasn't too much talk about the Jews being persecuted or hauled off to Auschwitz or anything. Yet Long Beach had a large Jewish population. Any time we got stuck in a restaurant with a bunch of Jewish people, my grandfather would say, "Oh, the kikes are taking over." We were taught in Catholic school to love everyone and war was terrible. Yet Catholics were saying the Jews killed Jesus. We're supposed to be against Hitler, yet we were talking anti-Jew all the time. I always felt set apart from my family. I didn't believe what they were saying.

After the war, when the blacks moved in all around my grandmother's house, the same kind of talk went on about them.

We were always playing war games. My sister and I had a plan. If the Japanese ever came through the front door, we had a back bedroom with a closet. My mother had huge garment bags, rubber, cold and sort of slimy-feeling. We figured we could run in this closet and nobody would find us behind the big gray rubber garment bags. But just in case they did, we would sprinkle ketchup on ourselves and play dead and then they wouldn't bother us. (Laughs.)

There was so much that went around about torture. The Germans tortured and the Japanese tortured. I remember somebody telling us that the Japanese would put bamboo splints under your fingernails and light them on fire. Torture seemed to be in our childhood conversation all the time.

We'd open up *Life* magazine and there were all those pictures of bombed-out Europe. One image after another of children in rags, huddled. I was just beginning to read. We thought any minute we could be like that, too. They could get us to eat our dinner, make us behave, do anything we didn't want to do—it was just: "Think of those kids in *Life* magazine, think how lucky you are."

My mother and all the neighbors would get together around the dining-room table, and they'd be changing a sugar coupon for a bread or a meat coupon. It was like a giant Monopoly game. It was quite exciting to have all the neighbors over and have this trading and bargaining. It was like the New York Stock Exchange. (Laughs.) This was our social life.

There was a spirit of camaraderie. There was a large vacant lot and everybody got together and had a gigantic communal Victory garden. My sister and I thought it was a wonderful place to go, because it was like Alice in Wonderland to get out there on a Saturday morning and all the neighbors were watering their squash and their green beans. They'd give things away to everybody. Nobody said, This is mine. Everything was upbeat.

Long Beach was a military town. There were several parades a year. We'd have miles and miles of tanks driving down Pine Avenue and everybody standing and cheering and clapping and waving flags. It was a constant reminder of this mighty strength and everything was going to be all right.

Some people were looking back at World War Two and saying that a lot of it was Hollywood and Madison Avenue. It took maybe twenty years to look back and say, Hey, what was all this? All these Hollywood musicals, keeping everybody's spirits up. I hear a Kate Smith record today and I just get all mush inside. That was the essence of America, Kate Smith singing "God Bless America." The patriotism was so thick you could cut it with a knife.

One Christmas, one of these soldiers sent us a huge box of Milky Ways. So much chocolate where there was no chocolate at all. I sat and cried. It took up the better part of the refrigerator, just like a turkey. We didn't even want to eat it. Because we knew that when it was gone, there wasn't gonna be any more. (Laughs.) It was a big treat just to open the refrigerator and see this chocolate.

Yes, and another thing, after the war. My cousin Jimmy who was killed had a sister, Fay. She married a GI who lost a leg in the war.

Fay brought him home for dinner. He came on crutches, his pant leg turned up. Everybody at the table was nice as pie. After they left, all the old clucks started in: He's not a real man. She's gonna have a life of woe, and wouldn't you think she'd know better than to marry a cripple?

Immediately after the war was this rush: We're never gonna suffer again, we're gonna have everything bigger and better, and we're gonna build, build, build. Long Beach had been a very small town at the beginning of World War Two. You could get in a car and drive only three miles and you were out in the orange groves. Long Beach grew enormously after the war. And they built those teensy little tract houses all over everything and they didn't fall down.

I never let my kids play with guns as they were growing up. Now they're twenty-one and twenty-three and they go out and they buy guns. One of them is only too anxious to get drafted. I don't think I raised them through broken legs and all kinds of accidents to shuffle them off. I don't think another war would be a good war. No war.

For one thing, we invented the bomb. There will never be a good war after that. My kids think we could win it. When we dropped the bomb, they said there was gonna be peace. There was marching in the streets and everybody's rushing out of their businesses and shouting and waving and celebrating. We ignored the whole consequences of the bomb.

The communal spirit was breaking down. Everybody was tired of sacrifices and beginning to nag and gripe. Although *Life* magazine showed those pictures plain as day of all those people that suffered the effects of the atomic bomb, my father was saying how beautiful the mushroom cloud was, how majestic. We were just turned off. It was like a curtain rang down.

My boys feel like their days are numbered. That the bomb is going to get them eventually, so why be careful of this. They drink and they drive. They've lost numerous friends in accidents, it doesn't cure them. That gun accident my boys had when they were ten and twelve did not cure them. When I lecture on drinking and driving and guns, they say things: Oh, it doesn't matter, what the heck, what will be, will be, it's a crazy world, who cares? They don't come right out and say the bomb's gonna get us all one of these days soon, or we can't really look to a future. They say, What does it matter? They don't value life as much as my generation does. It's frightening.

She is a designer living in Chicago.

"I was born in 1939 in Bochum, Germany. Near Düsseldorf and Essen, it is known as the Pittsburgh of Germany." When she was one year old, she was sent to her aunt in a village near Paderborn.

When you're a child and you grow up with war, it is a way of life. Lots of refugees from the eastern zone filled up the house. They came from bombed-out towns and actually smelled of fire. They came from Prussia, from a different planet. In 1944, when I was five, I remember soldiers sitting in the living room, telling my grandmother her son was just killed. She lost three sons. All on the eastern front, I think.

Paderborn was leveled and burned out. I remember we all went up in the attic to see the fire, maybe twenty-five miles away. The whole sky was lit. It was like a sensation: Look, Paderborn is burning! When a bomb fell on the field, everybody ran to see the crater. (Laughs.) Look, see the crater!

We hadn't seen many men around. I grew up in a society of women. Except for uncles, who were old, and the country doctors. There were mothers and aunts and grandmas and neighbors—all women. All of a sudden, in 1945, these soldiers came in, Americans. There were black soldiers and others. We didn't see the difference as a child. We'd get chewing gum and chocolate.

As a child you have no feeling for segregation at all. American soldiers, some were blond, some were dark. It didn't make any difference. They all smelled the same. They had jeeps in those days with leather seats that smelled strong. And a cigarette smell. And the smell of chewing gum and chocolates. Like the smell of fire on the refugees.

Our house was first occupied by the British. They ruined our house, made a whorehouse out of it. They had orgies in the bedrooms with some of the older German girls. They just went wild. They had no respect for the Germans at all. The British ransacked the house. Cut mattresses, broken bottles. They played darts with the knives on the furniture.

The Americans came, had a different attitude. They came out of a different setting. They didn't come out of a bombed-out London.

They were more neutral. They didn't have that revenge.

My mother would send me to the American soldiers to get some egg powder, in exchange for cognac. She had a basement full of wine. My father liked to live high and he had these things. He was a doctor, an officer in the army. In the thirties, he was in France and brought some things back. He was also on the eastern front.

This was my first contact with men of that age, twenty-two, twenty-three. Americans. This whole generation of Germans was gone. I remember competition with my little sister. I felt jealous if she got more attention. She was two years younger. She was three in 1945.

Our house was occupied by American majors. We had to evacuate it. When the majors were asleep in the afternoon, my mother would go in and get things out of the drawers.

When the German soldiers came back, suddenly our whole world was filled with men. They hadn't been with women for a long time, in English prisons, so they and the American occupiers were interested in my older sisters. One was fifteen, the other seventeen. The soldiers used me to make contact with my sisters. I was now about eight. So sexual awareness had already started.

When my father came to visit, still during the war on his leaves, I was always eager for his attention. He was missing early in my life a lot, so whoever came along I would use as a substitute. (Laughs.) My own sexual experiences began early because of the war.

Oh, the war had a lot to do with my outlook. I'm a survivor. I grew up in a very basic way. We didn't have electricity. We didn't have hot water. We had a pump outside. And a kerosene lamp. In real, real cold winters, we had hot bricks in the bed. But it wasn't deprivation for me. I always say I grew up in the Middle Ages. (Laughs.)

I had a very rich childhood. The women around me had this healthy survival instinct. It was a farm community. I would go in to neighbors and get hot milk and honey and pancakes. It was Catholic, and on holidays there were processions and I was dressed up in white clothes and a wreath, as a little angel.

I didn't get back to the city until '48. Everything was bombed. Rubble and ruins. All the kids from the neighborhood would put on their old-fashioned roller skates and we'd cross town to the rubble and play there. It was exciting. There were no cars, so we had the whole city to ourselves.

What I had trouble with was school. I hated it. I was in first grade and I was afraid of the teachers, gray monsters. Later, when some pupils had the guts to ask about the war, they were ignored. Some of these teachers had been soldiers. In our history books, there were ten lines about the Hitler regime. It went from Bismarck to Kaiser Wilhelm, this little paragraph about Hitler, and right to Adenauer.

My mother was in the black market. She did whatever she could. She rode a bicycle to different farms and made exchanges. She was like a hamster, the little animal who gets all this stuff and digs in. She used to say, "My whole past is in this suitcase." Because she was a businesswoman, my mother didn't have much time for us, not during the war and just after. I was independent very early. For me, the war was no interruption because I was born into it. That's the way I grew up. I wouldn't have wanted to grow up in some other time.

JEAN BARTLETT

She is blond, slim, and attractive enough to appear in one of those television you'd-never-guess-my-age commercials. She is in her mid-fifties. I study a photograph of a pretty girl in a white bathing suit, pre-bikini. "I was fourteen, trying to be Rita Hayworth. Everyone said I looked like Joan Bennett.

"This was in Berkeley. They really didn't have a middle class in those days. You were either rich or poor. We didn't have the status we do now. My father was a milkman. My mother was a housewife. She wasn't called a homemaker, just a plain housewife."

We were on our way to the movies on Sunday afternoon. I was twelve at the time. My dad loved Abbott and Costello. We were going to a matinee. We saw them all on the way to the theater, the car radio was on. "Oh, my God!" my father said, "Pearl Harbor!" I said, "What's a Pearl Harbor?"

"We can't go to the movies," he said. He turned around right away. There was an outcry from the back seat: "We wanna see Abbott and Costello!" My two sisters were eight and six.

We had a complete shutdown, 'cause they had no idea what was going to happen. My father became a block warden. They issued gas masks and helmets. It had a circle with a CD for Civil Defense. My bedroom had blackout paper, like tar paper. It was called the black room. They'd call in and say we're going to have an air raid. So we'd go in this room and all get in the same bed. My mother would tell us stories. She was a wonderful storyteller. We sang and ate popcorn. It was fun. She was like a child herself, she never grew up. The war changed her life, too, because she was never exposed to anything.

My family was hard-working. They were not readers. There was no television. *Amos and Andy* and *I Love a Mystery*, those were our life. I had a sort of sheltered life. My father wanted to join the navy, but he had three children and he was thirty-three. I remember how frustrated he was. So he joined the state guard. It gave him a feeling he was doing something. I wanted to do something, but I was too young.

He went to work in the Oakland shipyards. That's where the money started getting good. It made a big difference in our life-style. We had a little more than we used to have. We didn't have to worry about which child will get shoes that month. We could pay the bills. I didn't hear my mother complaining, We can't pay the rent. We didn't know about savings or T-bills. There wasn't any money in the banks. My mother had a history of physical problems and there was no Medicare. When you went to the doctor's, it may have been ten dollars, but that was maybe a third of my father's salary as a milk-man.

His hours changed drastically when he went to the shipyards. He went on the swing shift, four to twelve, and then graveyard, twelve to seven. My father was not a strict disciplinarian. I was never spanked, which I should have been a few times. He'd yell a lot. I used to hate to hear him yell, so I'd kinda behave.

I belonged to a little church. The minister would go out on Sundays and bring in young sailors, marines, that were roaming around with nothing to do. The ladies of the church would give them supper. I would go with my girlfriends to this little church every Sunday. We became the best churchgoers. We couldn't wait till Sunday to see what new crops would come in. (Laughs.)

The boys were very lonely. They were on their way overseas. We had Treasure Island debarkation. Also the Oakland naval base and Alameda. Here I was—what?—fourteen? We'd pick out a few we liked and invite 'em home. My dad wasn't home through all this because he was working. My mother enjoyed it, too. She was only thirty-two years old, and probably lonely, too, with my dad gone. We'd bring 'em home and she'd play a honky-tonk, rinky-tink piano, very well really. I sang. I really had a nice voice.

A lot of them would keep coming back. I would say, "I'll write to you." I ended up with a file box with all their names. I was writing ten and twelve letters a week. My grades went completely downhill, 'cause I was so busy entertaining the troops. I'd get sometimes four, five letters a day back. The sad thing about it, being that age and not understanding, each one of these boys thought I was going to be home waiting for them. They all thought I was older than I was.

My little sisters were a nuisance, especially the youngest. I'd bring some fellow home who thought I was sixteen. She'd come dancing in the room and say (sing-songs), "Barbara's only fourteen, Barbara's only fourteen." I'd have to chase her out. (Laughs.) A couple of guys would get up and leave. They got scared. They still talked about jailbait in those days.

I had a couple come back at the same time off the same ship. They both called the same day, and I had to juggle them around. One fellow even brought back an engagement ring. My mother had to say, "Why, she's only sixteen." This was two years later. He said, "I thought she was sixteen when I was here two years ago." He was angry: "That's the only thing that kept me going. Her letters."

I remember young girls in threes, arm in arm, shuffling along the pavement in their saddle shoes. They were called Victory girls.

I was one of them. I knew very little about sex. Neither did these boys. They were kids out of high school who didn't know any more than I did. Most of them were from small towns. I had one little marine from Alabama. As soon as he got in the house, he took his shoes off. He said, "My feet are killing me. I never wore shoes until I got in the service." A lot of these boys had just grits and greens and never had a cheese sandwich. It was just a lot of fun meeting these different boys.

Every day was excitement. With my father gone and every day a different boy, sometimes two or three. Sometimes fighting over me. My ego was just absolutely unbelievable. I thought I was the most gorgeous thing on earth and there was nothing I couldn't do. I know there were times when I was cruel. I didn't mean to be, but I was just so sure of myself. (Sighs.)

When you go through fifty or a hundred people that you're writing to, I couldn't keep track of what they looked like. They were just coming through this revolving door of my life. I'd get out my card and I'd write. It wasn't "I love you dearly" or "I'll wait for you." I tried to tell them what was happening at home and send cookies. I must've made tons of cookies whenever I could get sugar—remember, we had rationing. And took lots of pictures. I felt that was my contribution to the war. It was my duty.

Even after the war, I continued. All through high school. I was never without four or five boyfriends. I never heard of Friday, Saturday, or Sunday without a date.

I had one that I had given a little ring. The ship went down and he was rescued in a lifeboat. He still had that ring on, all corroded and broken. He was the one that was serious about me. When he got back, I said, "I just gave you that to keep you going." He said, "You're the one that kept me surviving."

I don't think my mother told my father too much. She was having a good time along with me. Some of the men that came there were older. She was getting some attention she was lacking. She wasn't too attractive but had a wonderful personality. She was very bubbly, friendly. A Mother Earth type. As I got older, I think there was a little jealousy.

When my father decided to go on days, there was a crying uproar from his daughter and wife. I guess he felt maybe it's time. But it wasn't much fun because he'd sit there and look the boys over. It was a little more difficult. (Laughs.)

We had a *National Geographic* map in my bedroom. That's the one way I kept track of where everybody was.

The only time the war directly affected me was when my cousin was sent to Bougainville in the army. The war was just a game to me. I didn't know what it was. I had a number of letters come back, they were marked Deceased. I didn't know what that meant. One said Expired. I had to look it up. I thought it meant my stamp wasn't any good. I wasn't even sure which boy it was, because they all became one uniform.

They were worried about spies. Loose Lips Sink Ships. But it was very easy to find out where the troops were going. I always knew when the boys were sailing. I used to wave to the ships on the long pier at Treasure Island. I had a fake pass I had made up. I hope after forty-two years they don't arrest me. (Laughs.) They'd call and say, "I called to say goodbye. We're leaving tomorrow morning." I'd take the train over. All of us could get on and off the base any time we wanted.

I must have been engaged fourteen times. I thought, This one's gonna work. It didn't work. So I thought, I'll join the marines. My father wouldn't sign for me because I wasn't twenty-one. So I joined the reserves. I was uniform-crazy. I'm still that way. I should have been a boy. I was born the wrong time and the wrong shape. (Laughs.)

The mothers didn't want their little girls to play with me. They thought I was fast, 'cause I had all those sailors at the house, from the time I was thirteen. A lot of the girls followed me around because they wanted to meet who I was meeting. But the mothers wouldn't allow it.

When my dad was gone, I would sneak out the back window. The streets were not like they are now. I'd meet some of the guys that were off duty and we'd walk around. There wasn't anything bad. A lot of them just wanted to be with somebody. We'd go to the park and swing on the swings, little-kid stuff. At the Rose Garden in Berkeley, they had seesaws and sandpiles. We'd make sand castles till twelve o'clock. I'd sneak back home before my dad got there.

There were one or two fellows that drank, but they were older. Whiskey and Coca-Cola. Uch. You couldn't get anything good. The only time I really drank was the day the war was over. Everybody got bombed. I was sixteen. They thought I was eighteen by then. I was always two years ahead of myself. (Laughs.)

Some of the boys smoked cigarettes, but not many. I never smoked. And we'd roller-skate. Go to a lot of movies, 'cause we'd get in for a dime, some of 'em for a nickel. They had a special serviceman's pass. Dennis Morgan was my favorite.

At this time, I was almost sixteen and said I was gonna marry this one boy. I can't remember which one it was. I was getting rebellious and told my father I was gonna do it whether he liked it or not. The only time he hit me was that day. He slapped my face and said, "You've been out of hand too long."

I think that's why he joined the state forestry as a game warden. We moved to a remote area in northern California. Oroville. A hunting lodge up in the mountains. I had to go thirty-five miles to school on a bus with these hick kids. I had a terrible time. All the boys thought I was fast 'cause I looked older.

I had a date with the most popular boy, football. I'll never forget this. He started driving out into the field. I said, "Where are you going?" He says, "Well, I hear you're fast and I want you to come across." In the back seat, he had three of his buddies hiding. So I got out and walked home.

I feel the war had a lot to do with the way I developed, because of the attention I received as a young pre-teen. I was exposed to a lot of young men, seventeen, eighteen years old. If there hadn't been a war, I would have stuck to my twelve- and thirteen-year-old schoolmates.

The war absolutely ruined me. The more men I had, the more my ego was fed. I had no attachments at all. In later years— I've been married three times. With my first husband, I couldn't stay faithful. There was no chance for me, because I saw something that looked good. What was holding me back? I was married the second time seventeen years and had struggled the whole time to keep away from men. Till finally I couldn't keep back any more. I had an affair and lost my marriage. The older I got, it got harder and harder to have everything I wanted, because there wasn't all these men attracted to me. All of a sudden, I'm forty. What's gonna happen to me? After three years of therapy, I'm able now to handle one relationship.

What I feel most about the war, it disrupted my family. That really chokes me up, makes me feel very sad that I lost that. On December 6, 1941, I was playing with paper dolls: Deanna Durbin, Sonja Henie. I had a Shirley Temple doll that I cherished. After Pearl Harbor, I never played with dolls again.

MARCEL OPHULS

A film director. He is best known for The Sorrow and the Pity, *a reflection on a French industrial city and the behavior of its citizens during its occupation by the Germans. His father, Max, had been a highly gifted, celebrated director in pre-Hitler Germany and in France. The conversation took place in Paris.*

Before we escaped from France, we were in Aix-en-Provence. My father was in hiding. We had no money and the three of us lived in a very small hotel room. Across the street, they were playing the Nazi film *Jew Süss.* They had a billboard, primitively painted: the Jewish caricature profile, the hateful one. People were queuing up to see it.

I was about twelve. My mother, who had been a German actress, was a goy. Very, very German, built like a Gothic cathedral. (Laughs.) We had left Berlin in 1933, the day after the Reichstag fire. My father had just had his first really great success, *Liebelei* of Arthur Schnitzler. It was just after Hitler had come to power in February 1933. I didn't know anything about Nazis. Once in a while, people would be marching. Across from the villa, I'd see them drilling on the roof of a building.

My father was a big splurger, a sort of Bohemian. He was thirty at the time and quite frivolous. With his first movie hit, he had bought a villa. We even hired a cook. My first political memory: he came into the kitchen of this great big house and said, "Pack a bag, we're taking a night train to Paris." We took the Pullman, of course.

My father was a light-hearted fellow. He liked women more than he liked politics, but he was very clearheaded, too. Most of his family, who were rich German Jews with department stores all over, all wound up in Auschwitz.

"He considered himself very left-wing. One time, in 1937, we went to Russia because he had an affair with the Russian ambassador's daughter in Paris. It was like a scene out of Ninotchka. *It was the beginning of the big show, purge trials. They knocked off their best generals. We got out by* le peau des fesses, *by the skin of our ass. (Laughs.)*

"It wasn't politics that brought him there. The ambassador's daughter had promised my father that he wouldn't have to do a movie about tractors. The Russians really wanted comedy. When he got to Moscow, he got a script that was full of tractors. (Laughs.) He had expected a good hotel. The commisars who came to the station with their fur hats to greet us were very proud of themselves, because they'd found a three-room apartment. It was sort of a cellar. (Laughs.) I think it shook his faith in Marxism considerably. This apartment wasn't really up to Champs-Elysées standards." (Laughs.)

In France, my father had contributed to their defeat, because he was in the army, a private. (Laughs.) We had become naturalized Frenchmen in '38. Since he was a Jew, a real goddamn foreigner, the French military were not too pleased. They put him into a regiment with Arabs and blacks, people of inferior races, cannon fodder. He was thirty-nine at the time.

He had also done anti-Nazi broadcasts in German for the French government during the phony war. It was between the time the war started and the time of the blitzkrieg, when France was defeated in three weeks. The war was declared in '39 and the invasion was in May 1940. They came walking in through Holland and Belgium, just walked around the Maginot Line.

He was on the list for immediate arrest and deportation because of these broadcasts. A very nice captain sent him on a phony mission to the Spanish border to do a movie about the Foreign Legion. So he picked us up in Paris and we stayed a few miles ahead of the Germans all the time. After hiding in Aix-en-Provence, we transited to Switzerland, to Spain, to Portugal, and boarded one of the last commercial transports to leave Lisbon. We came to America a few months before Pearl Harbor.

"On the trip across, my father met a German. A red-haired fat fellow, with very short-cut hair, almost a caricature of a German. He loved this guy because he hadn't seen a German for a long time. They spent evenings at the bar and going to pieces with sentiment.

"At Bermuda, the British came aboard, in their shorts, and arrested my father's friend. They took him off the boat and shot him. He was a German spy. (Laughs.)

"A longing nostalgia for Germany is a German-Jewish syndrome. The German Jews were almost more German than the Germans. The greatness of the culture is an antidote against generalizing too much about German guilt."

We got to New York and the Statue of Liberty. I remember the morning, coming out of the fog into clear sunshine. Here was New York, the Manhattan skyline. It brought tears to our eyes. There were always the three of us. It was a problem, being an only child, moving country to country.

With the little money he had, my father bought a beautiful white Chevrolet with red leather seats, a convertible, of course. We headed out for California on Route 66. The Mississippi disappointed me, after reading *Huck Finn* and *Tom Sawyer*. I remember the first cowboy we saw. He was sitting on a bar stool with real spurs on and a big Stetson hat. He turned out to be Jewish. It was a terrible disappointment. (Laughs.)

After driving what seemed to be days through the desert in an open car, very hot, we came to a lot of sleazy-looking bungalows and dusty palm trees and gas stations. My father asked an attendant (assumes

German accent), "Vere iss Hollyvood?" The guy said, "You're there!" (Laughs.)

My father's years in Hollywood were very difficult. He was out of a job for four years and living more or less on United Jewish War Relief. He did some work for the OWI. The four Hollywood films he made were after the war.

Hollywood was a very clannish place. There was a German-Jewish colony, a French colony, a British colony. Bertolt Brecht was a great friend of my father's. My father would tell me, "He's a great German poet, you must get to know him." I was a Hollywood high school kid of fifteen. What the hell was a German poet nobody ever heard of? I thought he dressed rather funny, because he was always trying to look proletarian. His shirts were always frayed.

Our best friend in Hollywood was Fritz Kortner, the great German actor. He came on weekends with grocery bags. He knew we didn't have anything. He had good jobs, he was always playing Hungarian waiters in anti-Nazi films. The German-Jewish colony always played in anti-Nazi films. When Alan Ladd was being parachuted somewhere, here was Fritz Kortner or Otto Preminger coming in, looking sinister.

Helmut Dantine was the handsome Nazi. There were all the ugly Nazis like Otto Preminger and Alexander Granach. They were all Jewish. Some of them played Resistance people, too. It always seemed like the same restaurant they were walking into. Alan Ladd would be sitting there in a sort of black thing, and you'd hear boots outside. It was always a small restaurant in Hungary or Norway or France, Italy. Always the same restaurant, always the same actor. (Laughs.) Only the tablecloths were changed. You'd hear the boots, so you'd know the Nazis were coming. Otto Preminger would be standing at the door: "Achtung! Nobody leaves the premises." I still have that in my ears.

Kortner and my father were constantly getting into fights with other Hollywood Jews. Both had non-Jewish wives. Both believed that Goethe and Schiller shouldn't be held responsible for Hitler. In our homes, we always spoke German. Other Jewish refugees would say, Ve never speak German, ve speak English now. They got into arguments because they didn't approve of the bombing of Dresden and Hamburg. I remember my mother crying through the night. Her family was still in Germany and, of course, she couldn't express her feelings. You'd get those exultant headlines: Nazis are bombarded into oblivion. In a way, Kortner and my father were schizophrenic.

I remember one evening at Brecht's house, they were quietly discussing the fate of German children. My mother hadn't been saying anything, just sitting there looking sad. Suddenly Brecht, who was non-Jewish, got into one of his fits of vile Bavarian temper: "Hilda, get out of my house! You look like a goddamn Nazi to me." A couple of hours later, he called to apologize.

My father dreamed of going back one day, I believe. But he was a pragmatic man. He wanted to get a job in Hollywood and once he did, he fell very much in love with it. He didn't share the views of the European intellectuals who were snooty about Hollywood. He was a show-business guy and loved it. He would have stayed in Hollywood. It was quite accidental that he came back to Europe after the war.

We had come late to Hollywood. By that time, various waves of refugees, talented directors like Murnau and René Clair, had been there for some time. They had contracts. From one week to another, my father would wait for the phone call: Pasternak called, M-G-M called, you must call right back.

There was a great deal of solidarity in the colony. They tried to help each other. Paul Henreid was marvelous. He tried to get jobs for others, get them to meet studio executives, Harry Cohn, Jack Warner. Henreid would always invite my father to his parties. My father never went to movies, so he couldn't really tell Clark Gable from Cary Grant. When one of the big tan fellows would walk up to him, he wouldn't know what to say. My God, this is one of them, but which one? (Laughs.)

At Hollywood High, I was learning English and having a frustrating time. I couldn't make out with the girls because they were going out with football players. It was a sleazy place. This is where the pioneers in drugs and dropouts went. The offspring of studio executives went to Beverly Hills High School.

Before the war, I had been a normal kid who liked sports, who liked companionship, who liked to get into a fight once in a while. But the change in culture, in scenery, and my loneliness put me on the defensive. I became a terrible snob, very much against American sports and against football cheerleaders, because I couldn't make out. So I became very French. I became sort of anti-American, always thinking of the chestnut trees in Paris. I was waiting for the war to end so I could go back to that dreamland, the Paris of my childhood.

My father was different. He was an international film maker. When he made films, he was happy. When he wasn't making films, he was unhappy.

I knew more about the horrors of the Second World War than most kids at school. What amazes me is how insensitive I really was. When I was twelve, I knew what we were fleeing from. I knew about my uncles being in the camps. I knew what it meant being a Jew in Occupied Europe. One would assume, then, I'd be more sensitive to the racial attitudes here, toward Mexican Americans, toward blacks, toward the Japanese being interned. When the war ended, I was seventeen, nonpolitical, and shared the prevalent attitudes. I wasn't particularly aware at all of racism in Hollywood films.

I got drafted in the American army at eighteen. This was in '46. So I was a GI during the Occupation. I spoke perfect French and German and knew Continental Europe, so they sent me to Japan. (Laughs.) I'm grateful. Otherwise I'd have never been to Japan. I enjoyed the army very much, and that's where I became Americanized. I became more and more aware of how much an American I had become. I have passports, one American and one French. But I really don't have roots any more. The grass is always greener on the other side. It's a tendency, I suppose, that will stay with me till I die.

I wanted to make it back to Hollywood as a film maker. My goal in life was to have my name on the credits behind Leo the Lion. This has to do with my childhood. That was, to me, the symbol of success, M-G-M. That's what I thought then. Now I'm fifty-four and I'm never going to be a great Hollywood director.

When I made movies—like *The Sorrow and the Pity*—about the behavior of ordinary people in crisis situations, one of the things that kept me from being too self-righteous is my memory of the Japanese kids who were in my class one day and gone the next. I have absolutely no recollection of protesting or questioning. I wasn't a six-year-old child. I was fourteen, fifteen at the time. Why didn't I react with more sensitivity? So, in my films, I can't be a prosecutor or a hanging judge.

POSTSCRIPT: *"Did you see* Mephisto? *It was based on the career of Gustav Gründgens. He had been the great German actor-director during the Nazi period. He had not been a Nazi himself, but he was certainly one of the favored people. Though he helped an awful lot of people get out of Germany, he was an opportunist. He was a culture hero.*

"After the war, he invited my father to come back to Hamburg to direct Beaumarchais's Marriage of Figaro. It's a very revolutionary, funny play. My father, who had been a stage director in the Weimar Republic, was anxious to go back to Germany. The play was a fantastic success and there were fifty curtain calls on opening night.

"My father became ill at dress rehearsal. He never got out of the hospital. As he lay dying, he kept screaming—this pro-German Jew—'I want to go back to France. I don't want to die in Germany.' His ashes were shipped back to Paris and there was another ceremony there. Even in death, we were a rootless family.

"My mother had arranged for Gründgens to give the speech at the German graveside. She didn't want to hurt anyone's feelings. He was director of the theater at the time. I was shocked, furious: "Why didn't you call Fritz Kortner to come up?" Kortner was back in Germany. Remember, he was a great Othello, Macbeth. Why should he stay in Hollywood doing Hungarian waiters? I told my mother, 'It's one thing to accept an invitation to direct a play for six weeks with the former director under the Third Reich, but it's quite another thing to have this man give a speech over my father's grave.' I didn't want to hurt her feelings or get into an argument with her at this time. So it happened: Mephisto made a speech at my father's grave. Horrible, when you think of it."

D·DAY AND ALL THAT

ELLIOTT JOHNSON

His way is gentle, though deliberate. He wastes no words, though details are terribly important to him. He has for many years been the general manager of a company in Stockton, California; cool young executives of a different era, of a different set of values, are moving in.

Four of us were in an upstairs Chinese restaurant in Portland, Oregon, when the little Chinaman came bursting through the double doors of the kitchen. He was carrying a portable radio and turning up the volume. We learned then that Pearl Harbor had been attacked. We were furious. No one's gonna come in our country. We immediately went to the marine recruiting headquarters.

There was a line over two blocks long. A marine was at a card table set up right at the front door. When it came to me, he said, "Step out of line, you're getting a Dear John letter from the President." The next day, Monday, I got a letter from the President of the United States. Greetings. On January 12, I was inducted into the army.

What about your three buddies?

One had poor vision. He tried to enlist in every branch of the service. He would not give up. He was going to do something for his country. That was the spirit that prevailed in those days. He ended up with the merchant marines. Another joined the Marine Corps, was at Guadalcanal. The third was too short, but he stayed in bed four days to put on an extra half-inch in height. His mother drove him and he laid out on the back seat all the way down there. He got on the scale and he hit the height. He was in. The air corps.

We arrived about one o'clock in the morning. It was snowing, and they showed us one of those perfectly horrid films on social disease. They fed us coffee, which I swear was laced with saltpeter. The man that issued my pants measured my waist and then to hell with it. I swear the man they made those pants for wore stilts. They dragged out eighteen inches in the back. There was a young GI who recognized this opportunity and he brought a sewing kit with him. He was right there when you tried the pants on—(claps hands)—just like that. He said, "For fifty cents I'll alter them." He fixed 'em beautifully and they fit like a top.

Some of the boys there were from the hills. They couldn't read or write. You may call them ignorant, but when it came to those guns, they could make us look stupid. They'd take the parts, put 'em in a bag, dump 'em on the floor, and put 'em back together again, blindfolded. Made up their own songs. The verses rhymed and they had a message. It was a real education for me.

At OCS I had another learning experience. We lived in half-tents in Fort Sill, Oklahoma. There were eight of us in each tent. I was stationed with seven other Johnsons. I was the only white. I kept that thing cleaned up. There wasn't any question what would happen if I didn't. I was in the minority and they had had the short stick for all their lives.

Was this your first acquaintance with black people?

There was one black boy in high school in Portland.

I reported for duty as a lieutenant at Camp Gordon, Georgia, where the captain made me stand at attention for so long. I could see him, in my peripheral vision, swinging back and forth in his swivel chair, staring at me. It was so hot. The perspiration came down my forehead, down my nose. He didn't return my salute. I was getting dizzy. Finally this voice said, "You a northerner?" I said, "I'm a westerner, sir." I heard him say, "Relax, fella." He got up and shook hands with me.

Now I'm in the artillery of the Fourth Infantry Division. We're a self-propelled unit, so we travel with the infantry. We trained intensively for a couple of years before we actually went into the invasion of Normandy. There were people who had been in the army for years. I had to learn to work those guns as good as any one of them.

We started for Normandy on June 3, I believe, or June 4. We lined up in long rows, vehicles under shade trees. Beautiful roads in the English countryside, with trees coming all the way across, making arches as you drive through. The English, I'm sure, knew why we were there and yet no word was said at all. The channel was very rough, so we turned around and came back.

On the morning of June 6, we took off. I can remember that morning. Who could sleep? A lot of the boys played poker all night. I wanted to take a bath. Don't ask me why, 'cause I can't explain it. It was against the rules, but I took a shower anyway.

I was on an LST, a landing ship tank. It was three hundred feet long. It had a great mouth in front of which was the ramp that let down the smaller craft. I remember going up to the highest part of that ship and watching the panorama around me unfold. In my mind's eye, I see one of our ships take a direct hit and go up in a huge ball of flames. There were big geysers coming up where the shells were landing and there were bodies floating, face down, face up.

The LST, as we vacated it, was to become a hospital ship. The boys who had gone first and been wounded were now being brought out. This continued my education: recognizing our body as finite. I remember one young boy who was so badly hurt he was gray, like a piece of flannel. I thought he was dead. They gave him a transfusion and I could see his color coming back. The relief I felt that this boy was gonna make it—I can't remember whether he was German or ours. It didn't matter. Isn't that interesting?

It came our turn to go into the little craft, and we went in. We had a young navy officer who wasn't gonna take us up that beach. I knew dang good and well that if we took our 155 off in that water, that would be all she wrote. We could swim ashore, but we'd never make it, we were loaded with so much paraphernalia. So I ended up taking my gun out on him. Shoved it in his mouth. Can you believe that? He wanted to get the hell out of there. He was the guy in *The Caine Mutiny,* the one rattling the steel balls in his hand. He wanted to dump us. Yeah, that's close enough, go on. He finally got us to where we were in about three feet of water and he said, "I just can't go any more." Fine, let down the ramp.

This self-propelled 155 is nothing but half a tank. Instead of a turret on top, it has a 155 howitzer. You don't have a steering wheel. You just pull on this and you go to the right. The other way, you pull to the left. Pull 'em both, you stop. For some reason, we got our signals crossed. Corporal Rackley was driving and watching me. I threw up my hand. He thought I meant stop. So I assaulted the beach of Normandy in the inglorious fashion of somersaulting through the air and landing on my back. All I could see was this tank out of which

I had pitched. It couldn't stop in that soft sand. The guys for a long time teased me that they had never seen me move so fast. (Laughs.) I just got out of the way. It would have gone right over me. I've always contended that when the Germans saw that kind of clown-acting, it scared the hell out of them. (Laughs.)

I looked around and saw this causeway filling with water very fast. It would have locked us on the beach. I told Rackley to hit it. We made it to one area that was only under one foot of water. That became our road and we got across, off the beach.

Part of my job was standing near the driver because we had a .50-caliber machine gun mounted up there that I would operate if necessary. We looked back and there were the Germans. Beyond them were the Americans, still on the beach side. So I was able to shoot at the backs of the Germans.

We weren't the only ones that got across the water. There was an anti-aircraft crew. This was the dangedest thing. You can't imagine all this noise and all these shells exploding and fellows being hurt and killed, and here's this crew sitting smoking cigarettes and reading a comic book. I couldn't believe it. We stopped a hundred feet from them. I could see them out of the corner of my eye.

All of a sudden—wham!—they were galvanized into action. I looked up and nobody had to say anything. All of us dove out of that thing and crawled under, 'cause here came these three German aircraft. These guys didn't do any hiding. We did. It's a good thing we did. The Germans hit that thing with those .50-caliber machine guns. And these guys hit every one of those three German airplanes and knocked them down. Every one of them. Only two parachutes opened and we were yelling and jumping up and down: Where's the other parachute? Obviously, the boy was killed. We were rooting for him. Yeah, the German guy. Funny, eh?

I had a colonel who was a great instructor. He helped a lot of us. But he couldn't take combat. Long before we ever landed, he was just stoned out of his mind. He came walking by, hanging on to his command car because he was so drunk. He waved me down the road: "Git outa here, git outa here."

Now way down the road I saw, on my right, these dead German boys. On my left, going across the field, is a French peasant leading a cow, crading its head in his arms, protecting it with his body as much as possible. He had come back to get his cow, leading it away from all the noise and death.

I looked up. There was a two-story house across the road to the woods. I could see this German boy silhouetted in the window. I finished laying the guns and with a couple of others went around to the right flank. We had incendiary grenades and set the house on fire. Pretty soon the boy came out. He was my first prisoner. I told him, "Take your shoes off." He didn't understand, so I got down and pulled them off. He had thrown his gun away. All you do is point him back down the road. What happens to him, you could care less. He's out of the war. Everybody that sees him knows he's been captured, as long as he's in uniform and barefoot.

On the way to the house, I had come across a paratrooper sergeant helplessly entangled in a tree. He had a broken leg, compound break, blood coming out of his pants. As soon as we sent the German boy down the road, we cut this boy down. He was so humiliated because he had been up there since before daybreak. It had been a shock to his system, so his bodily eliminations had functioned. He was so mortified he didn't want us to get near him. We just cut off his pants and gently washed him all over, so he wouldn't be humiliated at his next stop.

I was very calm in laying my battery. We got our first order to fire. There's 6,400 degrees in an aiming circle. We were 90 degrees off. We'll never know where those shells came down. I just hope and pray I didn't hurt anybody who was out of the war. I hope it went into the ocean.

This was the first day, all the first day. A lifetime in one day.

I wasn't scared until the third day. When we landed on the beach, our mission was to turn west and go all the way to Cherbourg and clean it out. We could then proceed across France. So I'm going to this huge old chateau. We heard there was a lot of good wine in the cellar.

I had to cross a road and I was learning already about the German 88. You could tell from the sound when it was pointed at you. I heard this *chok!* and I knew it was mine. I was right in the middle of this road. I gave a dive over this hedgerow and went straight down into a moat, all covered with green slime. That killed any desire I had for wine. I was through. All I wanted to do was get back. I raced across the road and got behind another hedgerow. Not before he took another shot at me. He was up in that church steeple and he had a telephone going straight down to that guy. When he'd say fire, the guy'd pull that lanyard. I was the target.

They were so fast and, oh, so accurate. They came close. I had one more road to cross. One more. He had been following me all the way across. This guy was a terrific shot. I began to realize I didn't have a chance. I got a running start from a crouch. He barely missed by being too low. I got a fragment right up here. (Indicates thigh.) It's the only wound I had in the war. I was so embarrassed I never told anybody. 'Cause I'm going after some booze and I get hurt. (Laughs.) The fear hit me a few days later. Fitzpatrick, a wonderful young man, was walking across one of those entrances and an 88 hit him direct and there was nothing left of him. Just exploded his whole body. Eighty-eight millimeters, a little howitzer and very versatile.

The fifth night we were there, we were in dug-in foxholes, in a very checkered position. There were Germans ahead of us and Germans in the back of us. Americans over there ahead of these Germans. The infantry and the artillery were side by side. There was no infantry out in front. When the infantry moved, we moved. There was no straight front line. It was a mess.

We were surrounded by hedgerow fences. One corner would be cut down so cattle could go and drink. In one such corner, there was a sniper. He was shooting at us. Every time, I'd stick my head out of the foxhole, I'd get shot at. I called two very dear friends on the telephone. We fanned out, each of us with a grenade. At a given point, we pitched our grenades and accomplished what we had to do.

I avoid using words like "kill a man" because I like to divorce myself from that. We recognized that we were in a war, but we recognized that they came from families like we came from families and that they had loved ones and they were good guys and they were bad guys. We were called on by our government, that our country was in jeopardy. Therefore we had to fight for it. Personally, I had no malice at any time toward the Germans.

There were only one or two times we ever had face-to-face confrontations with storm troopers. The SS. They were the elite. They were so brainwashed they were impossible to reason with. Those people made me angry.

The ordinary Germans, the boys we took prisoner, were so glad to be out of it. We'd take their shoes and they'd walk down the road. The last thing they'd do is come back and either shake hands with us or embrace us.

We were so mixed up, Americans and Germans. People were shooting at my dear friend Ed Bostick, our forward observer. This was on the second day or third. He jumped into a ditch on the side of the road. The only thing that saved him was a dead Germany boy who he pulled on top of him. He lay there for hours until he felt safe to move. When he came back, he fell in my arms. Imagine what he'd been through, using a dead boy as a shield.

I went back to my foxhole and I was suddenly drained. It was about one-thirty in the morning. I had to stay on duty until two. Ed was to come and relieve me. I couldn't stay awake. I was just plain exhausted. We never turned the crank or rang the bell on the telephone. When you are an officer—and this included the top noncoms —you went to sleep with your headset at your head. Instead of ringing the bell or speaking, we'd just go (whistles softly), and that would waken you from a sound sleep. This voice came on and said, "Yes, El?" I said, "Can you relieve me? I'm just bushed." He said, "I'll be right over." He came walking over to where I was and for some reason he began to whistle. I'll never know why. A young artillery man, one of ours, I'm sure had dozed off. The whistle wakened him. He saw a figure and fired.

I was out and running, and I caught Ed as he fell. He was dead in my arms. Call it foolish, call it irrational, I loaded Ed in a jeep. I had to take him in for proper care. Now! I went to our battalion headquarters, and I was directed to this drunken colonel. He came out and said, "Get that goddamn hunk of rotten meat out of here." You have no idea of my feeling toward him. It's remained with me for a long time, hard to get rid of. That was a very, very hard experience for me, even to think about now.

That was my fifth day.

At one point, I had been reassigned to be forward observer for the entire battalion. To live and work with the infantry, which I did for the major part of my combat career. One morning in December, it was very cold and snowing, about 2:00 A.M., we were on our way to crossing the Aare River. It was ice, water, and more ice. There was a steep slope on the other side with nothing but snow. We knew Germans were over there and it would be trouble. We had to get across the river. We had inflatable rubber boats to row very silently across. That was fine except for human nature. One of the boys had gotten his hands on some Calvados. He came down the river singing "Row, Row, Row Your Boat" at the top of his lungs. The sky absolutely exploded and the mortars came in on us. It was terrible. It seemed like half a day. Actually it was a few minutes. We made our way across. Oh yes, we had heavy casualties.

It was just beginning to be daybreak. There was a row of houses on each side of this little winding country road. We had to go through each house looking for German boys. We came to the last house. You get inside and you have the gut feeling there is someone in here. We had met some and they were perfectly willing to surrender, no trouble at all. But this one—I had a terrible feeling in my stomach. I searched the house. I knew I had to go into the basement. It was dark down there. No flashlight, no nothing. If he sees my silhouette first, he'll blow me away.

I went down into the cellar. It had windows. Daylight was just coming through. I could see two forms huddled over in the corner. It was a French peasant and his wife. He was holding a rooster to his breast. She was holding a hen. I said, "It's all right." They kind of understood me. The last I remember, they were walking down the road together holding on to their precious treasure.

As a forward observer, if I wanted to bring in an entire division, I called a singsong on a code word. If I wanted a huge amount of fire power, I'd call for a serenade.

I was looking down this steep bank into a very narrow valley, just wide enough for a road leading into a rectangle of heavy forest. All day long, I watched German tanks and vehicles move in. Enormous numbers. I asked for a serenade, the whole thing. I asked for one-half white phosphorus, which I hated and still hate today. And I called for one-half posit fuses. These would get so far from the earth and detonate. A rain of steel would come down. Just terribly destructive. If white phosphorus hit your flesh and started to burn, you couldn't stop it. I asked for I don't know how many rounds. The devastation on that little piece of land, the accuracy of those boys in firing, was incredible. It's one of my bad memories, the suffering.

A day or two later, I was in my foxhole. I was separated from the rest of the company. The snow had melted so I was in two, three inches of water. Night came and it started to freeze. My feet were ice, so I had to get up and walk around. Not ten feet away was a German lieutenant looking around to see what he could see. His back was to me. I just went down into my foxhole. (Laughs.) I just couldn't shoot him in the back. I had a Thompson submachine gun. He didn't have a chance. The next day, I thought I should have done it. And then I thought, how stupid to alert the world, here I am.

You'd have five days up and five days back. They never stayed with it. You'd go five days up, you'd come back, take a bath, change clothes, and the next morning you'd be back. That's because of the casualties. On the way back, I saw the little French peasant and his wife walking back to their house. They had survived with their chickens.

Altogether I was in combat from June of '44 to May of '45. France, Luxembourg, and Germany. We landed on June 6. On July 4, I was able to take my shoes and socks off and change clothes.

There were some cement bunkers I had to go through. There was a German boy. Reflex. Again, an unpleasant memory. It was my first experience with face-to-face combat. It was during the battle of Hürtgen Forest. Our worst, I believe. Our division had four hundred percent casualties.

One time I was sent back to get a truckload of replacements, young boys. They hadn't the benefit of the long training we had in the States. I told them, "If I hear anything coming in and if I tell you to jump, do exactly what I do." We had to be alert for interdiction fire, artillery shells lobbed at an intersection. We came near this intersection and I heard one in the distance going *chok!* I told the guys, Get out of here! I dove over the rail of the truck into the gutter beside the road. Out of the twenty or twenty-five boys I picked up that day, ten were dead.

I was a forward observer at Hürtgen Forest. I had a crew of three. All of us carried radio equipment. I was sent to a forester's tower. At the base of the tower, some trees had been knocked down by shells. We arranged two logs parallel and the others perpendicular to form a roof. We crawled under that and it was our house. When the shells came in and hit the trees and fragments of metal came down, we were protected by these logs.

The second day I was there, I saw another forester's tower. There was a German lieutenant looking right at me. We waved at each other. I marked him on the map. I got my guns zeroed in on him, and I know in my heart he did the same thing to me. He was also an artillery observer. Along my ridge was a road. German tanks rolled along there. My target. He would watch my shooting. He was interested in my effectiveness.

I was bringing the artillery in. One day there came several German vehicles in line. Three ambulances were in the middle. That was hands off. I was just watching them go by. Suddenly somebody started shooting artillery at them. I looked over at the lieutenant right away. I shook my head as hard as I could. He thought I called the fire on those ambulances. I saw him pick up his telephone and I hit the ladder. I barely got in my house and he laid it on us. Almost knocked the tower down. Just his precision shooting. After he lifted his fire, I went tearing up the ladder again. I had my hands up and I was waving and shaking my head: not me. He looked at me. Then he took off his helmet. That was his apology to me.

One day I went down the tower to the edge of the woods to urinate. A German boy was standing not five feet away, behind a tree. I'm holding my organ in my hand as I turned toward him. My friends never let me forget it: I pointed my gun at him. I sat him down, took his shoes off, and he handed me his gun.

I knew another forward observer. He went out with his crew. White phosphorus was thrown at them. Two of the men burned before his eyes. He came running to where I was in another part of Hürtgen Forest. I went down the road to meet him. He was sobbing and falling into my arms. He kept saying, "No more killing, no more killing, no more killing."

There were so many signs that the German surrender was near. I was sent on a route to do something with a jeep and a driver. I came into a meadow and there was an entire German division. No sense in being afraid now. I drove up to a German soldier and I said, "Where is your commandant?" He showed me the tent. This very fine general came walking out. I stood at attention and saluted him and he saluted me. He handed me his sidearm. He surrendered. I had no idea I'd run into this.

I radioed in and told them what happened. They said, "Take him to Bamberg." I led the caravan. He and I rode together. He spoke some English. We got along fine until we got to the prison camp. Everyone who entered those gates had to be deloused. He was furious that he was included.

There really was no celebration on V-E Day. A caravan came winding down a hill with their headlights on. I knew then it was over. Until that moment, it wasn't real.

I was raised in a house that believed in God. All right? But it took something like this to hammer it home to me: I am totally averse to killing and warfare. I saw it with my own eyes and it didn't do a dadratted thing. And the wonderful boys we lost over there. It took four years out of my life.

When the Vietnam War first started, I felt that if the President said we should be there, we should be there. When my son went, I was very proud of him. I still am. But as to the necessity of his being there, I'll always question that. It was an immoral war. My son was a marine in Vietnam. He has no elbow now. His hand is shrinking away. The number of times we went into the Michelin rubber plantation and left our blood there . . . stupid and such a waste.

There's something in some men that will seek power and the rest of us will follow. There are a few dissenters, too few. If there is another war, there will be no winner. It is madness.

CHARLES A. GATES

He is wiry, agile; he moves about the hotel room with the grace of an athlete. Not surprisingly, he had in his younger days been a swimming and tennis champion in Kansas City.

He is visiting New York, attending the thirty-fourth annual reunion of the 761st Tank Battalion. "Every year we have to sadly report that someone has passed. We had tried at the close of World War Two to get someone interested in reading our record and hadn't been successful. In '66, it was introduced in the House and it died as usual; '67, it was introduced and died. After President Carter'd got into office, he said, 'Write the White House if you have a problem.' I wrote him a letter. On January 24, 1978, he signed our award for a Presidential Unit Citation."

We were the first black tanker group to be used in combat.

I was twenty-nine when I joined the service on April 10, 1941. I was sent to Fort Riley, Kansas. You had the Ninth and Tenth cavalries there, who established a heck of a record. I might attribute my success to the training I received from old soldiers who had no more than a fifth-grade education. Regular army men. I had noticed that every new white officer who came there was told to observe the old black sergeants.

They asked if I'd be interested in goin' to OCS. I said no, I wanted to do my twelve months and get out. The regimental commander said, "Do you know any question about the Field Manual, FM 105-dash-one?" I said yes. He said, "What are you supposed to do when a commanding officer requests you to do something?" I said, "Request in that particular case is considered as an order." He said, "Well, I'm requesting that you just sign these papers." So that's how I got stuck and ended up goin' to Officer's Training School. I did that in July of '42. Fort Knox, Kentucky.

I had been strictly an outdoors man. To be inside a building and listen to a monotone all day long, I couldn't take. I did nothing but sleep those first days. The instructor said, "You sleep in my classes, you'll not get anything but a bunch of demerits." I said I didn't want to come here anyway. After six weeks, we had our first examinations. Fifty percent of every OCS class lost in the first examination. I ended up with an average of ninety-six-point-something. So the last six weeks, they just said, Let him sleep. (Laughs.) It came as a result of the training I had gotten at Fort Riley.

I was a lieutenant at Camp Claiborne, Louisiana, until December of '42. The company commander had three platoon leaders ask me questions, to test me. I answered, they were satisfied. I then said that I have questions for them and I'll let them have a month to find the answers. They had searched every field manual and couldn't find them. So I politely told them the answers are in the field manual which they've been waiting to receive. Their manual is obsolete. I said, "This is a lesson for you. Let us work together and we'll accomplish a hell of a lot more than we will by trying to trick one another."

It was cold and damp during the winter. Immediately we'd get in the field and the fellas would jump out of the tanks and start building fires. I called all my platoon in and told them, "Now, gentlemen, you know these tanks cost $60,000 apiece. So the first thing for you to do is concentrate on learning how best to use these things. My first order of the day is put out those damn fires and get in those tanks and I'm gonna ride the hell out of you, because you're gonna have to do what I say. Now I like to play as well as anyone, but when you see me working, that means you work." We worked on that principle and got the job done.

The nearest town was Alexandria. Our placement in camp was down in the sewage area. All black. When you went to town, you were faced with nothing but white MPs. We had to change that. They required the Negro officer not to carry a sidearm. Yet the others carried sidearms. So I went in town with a sidearm. They questioned me: "You don't need any sidearm." I said, "Is everybody gonna be without sidearms?" "Oh, no, no, but you don't need 'em." I said,

"I'm performin' the same type of duty you're performin'. I'm gonna be equally as well prepared as you." They knew I was right. I was very foolish, maybe.

They threatened me with charges. I told 'em my parents would be just as proud of me as a dishonorably discharged private as they would if I were a general. It don't matter to them and it won't matter to me. But since I'm in this thing, I intend to do my best according to rules and regulations. And I do study rules and regulations. After that, we carried sidearms.

I had experienced so much prejudice in Louisiana that when I got to Europe, it was a joke. (Laughs.)

We went to Fort Hood, Texas, early '44. We trained against the tank destroyer outfits and consistently made monkeys out of them. They had both white and black. We established quite a reputation.

In '44, General Patton requested the best separate battalion they had left in the United States. He wanted 'em for the Third Army. We weren't in a division. Patton had made a statement that Negroes were incapable of being tankers. The equipment was too technical. And who should General Patton see when he went into the armored field? Us. Here we come, the best they had left in the United States. (Laughs.)

He viewed us for quite some time. Finally he said, "You're the first Negro tankers ever to be used in the American army in combat. I want you to establish a record for yourselves and a record for your race. I want you to make a liar out of me. When you get in combat —and you will be in combat—when you see those kraut s.o.b.'s, don't spare the ammunition." Of course, the Negroes whooped because here was a white man tellin' the Negroes to shoot white people. Well, that really tore us up. (Laughs.)

The average life of a separate tank battalion was from ten to twelve days. Then they'd just redline it out and the few men who were left were attached to somebody else. So when there was a bad spot, they'd send the separate tank battalion in the area and the division would just bypass it. You were just gun fodder really. We went 183 days without relief and damn few replacements.

We had all but ten people in the outfit were black. There were ten whites, officers. Two of 'em were company commanders. One of 'em lasted two days. The other lasted about two weeks. Then there was nothin' but Negro officers and enlisted men on the front from that day on. This was in France, Belgium, Holland, the cracking of the Siegfried Line, West Germany. We finally ended up in Steyr, Austria. Always in combat. No other unit has any record to compare.

In that particular time, we received 250 men from quartermaster units, engineers—types who had never been in combat, had never been in a tank. I had to train these men while we were fighting every day. Those who came through, we kept. The rest, we sent away.

I was captain by then. When the company commander of C Company, Charlie, had been injured—they had lost about eight men killed, thirty-six in the hospital—I took over until the finish of hostilities.

We started out with 750 men. All through the 183 days, we had 35 men killed in action. We had 293 who received Purple Hearts. We had 60 who received Bronze Stars. We had 11 who received Silver Stars. Remember, these awards were granted through the divisions with whom we'd been attached. A division naturally is gonna take care of its own first. So for us to have received that many awards meant to me that any man who received a Bronze Star should have received a Silver Star and any man who received a Silver Star should have received a Congressional Medal of Honor. Because we got only the crumbs. So we must have done a very creditable job. They were very well trained and disciplined. We had a job to do and they did their best.

The German army couldn't see how we could be in so many darned places. We were split into three platoons and the platoon was split into two. We were scattered all over the darn place. To hear the story of the 761st Tank Battalion, it seemed impossible.

On one combat mission, we were having difficulty getting the Germans out of the woods. We kept firing low. Finally I told 'em, "Gentlemen, raise your fire so it will explode up in the trees." That'll send more shrapnel around, also some trees down, and get those people out of those woods. They came out waving white flags and calling, "Kameraden." I told the men to remain in their tanks with the hatches buttoned up, and when the enemy got abreast of 'em, just direct 'em back to the infantry. Well, some guy opened up his hatch a little bit early. The Germans looked and they said, "Schwarzen Soldaten!" Black soldiers! That word just went through the bunch and they started runnin' back to the damn woods. We figured, We'll be damned if you're gonna get back to those woods. Finally, they figured they'd better go along with these black soldiers. (Laughs.)

They couldn't understand how we could be just a separate tank battalion. We were in too many places. They had us plotted on their maps. They were very curious. Their major was questioning us: How many divisions of Negro tankers are there? Of course we didn't tell 'em anything.

It was seldom any of this news got to the States. Most people didn't know that we had a Negro tank outfit. The campaign for a Presidential Unit Citation started back in '45. It took us thirty-three years.

Though you have records, the division is not gonna tell you the story. We had discovered that at least twelve other units to which we had been attached had received Presidential Unit Citations. About eighteen had received the French Croix de Guerre. How easy it has been all through the years to conceal the history of the Negro soldier.

At the close of hostilities—that's when strange things started happening. They started checking the areas where Negro troops were located, and they tried to poison the minds of the people.

Who's they?

Our intelligence. Army intelligence. I'm tellin' you exactly who it was. Saying the Negro soldier was an unworthy person, undependable. While we were in England, they'd gone so far as to tell the English that Negroes had tails like monkeys and things like that. We just ignored that. We were on the front all the time. They've asked me time and again, Did you experience much prejudice? I said, Yes, the first two or three days. But after that there was no prejudice, because you don't have time for prejudice in a foxhole.

They actually made surveys in every area the Negro soldiers were in. I recall one case. I was ordered to have my men stand in formation. The officer, a full colonel, said, "We have a lady who says one of your men raped her." I just told him point-blank, I said, "I don't have my men fall out for anything like that." Just at that particular time, a little German lady, I guess she weighed about 102 pounds, passed by the window, pulling a loaded hay wagon. They didn't have any horses. I said, "Sir, can you step here a minute? See that lady? See what she's doin'? Do you think you can rape that woman?" He just turned a little red and left.

I became very bitter in a battle at Hunskirch. We had been ordered to make an attack. We were able to spot all the major defenses of the Germans. I told this colonel that our approach was very poorly organized and would be pretty tough. I delayed the attack about four hours. Finally he gave me a direct order to move my tanks straight down a road. It was in defiance of good tactics. Within five minutes, we lost five tanks. Now this colonel had been given command of an infantry regiment. All the combat experience he had was as a finance officer in the United States. He didn't know a thing about combat.

I became bitter because I lost one man. I got shot out of my tank, and two of my men from the same tank had to go to the hospital. I made up my mind that day: since I'm going to be on the front, I give less than a damn what their rank is. *I* will tell my men whether they can perform the operation. And that's the way I worded it.

That was one of the major reasons I got out of the service. I didn't bawl anybody out who was my rank. Generally, it was full colonels and brigadier generals. I said to myself, They're gonna think back and say—now, there's a man I'm gonna get. I would have gotten close to home, but I would have been in Leavenworth, not Kansas City. (Laughs.)

My mother was ill and I wanted to get back home. I went to Tuskegee, studying veterinary medicine, but because her health was bad, I just stayed in the postal service.

They wanted to start a Missouri National Guard unit. I was asked for a list of available Negro soldiers in the area. Would I be commander of the unit? I said I can for one year. That was 1949. I retired from the guard in 1964. (Laughs.) The reason I accepted was because a Missouri congressman said that Negroes were incapable of running a military headquarters. I was determined to prove he didn't know what the hell he was talking about. We ended up with one of the most outstanding National Guard units in the Fifth Army area.

They named three streets at Camp Clark for outstanding national guardsmen. The names they chose were President Truman, a general from Camp Girardeau, and, surprisingly, me. (Laughs.) So there at Camp Clark, at least one of the streets is named Gates.

Did General Patton recognize you?

Yes, he did. He was a person who came to the front frequently. When he'd come around to us, he'd talk just as you and I are talking now. He'd start relieving people of the units to which we were attached— starting at the top. At Hunskirch, he wanted to know why we lost five tanks in such a short period. Within two weeks, this colonel of whom

I had spoken had been shipped back to the United States. I have respect for him. He might not have liked the Negro any more than anybody else. I know his headquarters didn't, because they never accepted our record.

Our particular motto is Come Out Fighting. After the close of hostilities, we just kept on fighting. It's just that simple.

ROSEMARY HANLEY

It is the wall of family photographs that first catches your attention: children, grandchildren, themselves in younger days; another. We have cake and coffee; this is not a special occasion; it's there for any guest.

Joe Hanley heads toward the back porch with a beer. It's better, he says, for her to be alone as she remembers. He'll say his piece afterwards.

It's one of those changing neighborhoods on Chicago's North Side: white working-class, Hispanic, some blacks, lower-middle-class hold-overs, and the old. It is the last who most reflect the neighborhood: been around, stubborn and fading.

I was twenty-two when we were married, Kevin and me. My first husband. Luckily, he was in the States for a while. I became pregnant with my first child in '43. She's now forty. Of course, he went overseas, and he was killed in '44 in the Battle of the Bulge.

My present husband was his very best buddy. They were together when Kevin was killed. Jim ran one way when the bombing started and Kevin ran the other way. And Kevin, he got it. Joe says he don't know why it happened that way, because he knew Kevin was married, with a child, and he wasn't. It took a lot out of him when Kevin was killed. He did write me some letters telling me what had happened, how it happened, sayin' how he felt. When he came back in '46, he came to see my daughter. With that, we developed an acquaintance-ship. We were married in '49.

There's a sadness in my life, losing my first husband. But then, meeting Joe and marrying him—we had three other children—it seemed like it was a continuance of my life. It was like he came back instead of Kevin. I know it's not right to feel that way, yet I think maybe there was a purpose to it. Kevin meeting him, becoming good friends, and then he came back and my life continued.

When Kevin was away at camp, I did get a chance to go down after Diane was born. I took her, and his mother came with me. They didn't want me traveling alone. We went to Texas. He worked in the office, doing typing. He was a very good typist. When things got where they really needed fighting men, they put him in the infantry. He went overseas in October of '44. He was killed in December.

At the time, you're living your own life and you're taking care of your child and you're going to work. Finally, we were made to know about the horrible things that went on during that time. Then I think, was his death justified or not? Was it all in vain? That has often gone through my mind.

I had a brother in the war. He was in Africa, fighting. I had friends at work that were all gone also. Every one of them came back. They would come and see me. In my own little world, he was the only one, see? I thought, why? That I had to learn to live with. I shouldn't have felt bad that they all came back. You know? And yet I felt, why to me, the only one? That's what hurt. It took a long time to make me accept that fact.

I became very withdrawn. My in-laws, they were just wonderful people. They would come over and visit me and the baby. I was living with my mom. They'd say, "Rosemary, you just can't be sitting here, you're too young for all this. You've got to start doing your stuff and going out a little bit." They had a daughter, she was my age. She said, "We're gonna go to the Green Mill Ballroom." His brother, my brother-in-law, was in the orchestra. We're gonna go dancin'. I said, "Oh, no, the baby." My mother-in-law said, "I'll be glad to take the baby." It was rather strange, but I did do it. I did get out of myself. And then I did go to work.

When he came back, after we were married, Joe found it hard, too, getting himself together. He loved horses and did get this job being a bookie. Then he went into insurance. Then he was a policeman for the Chicago Police Department.

There were days when I used to say to myself, Did I do the right thing by marrying him? Because he never forgot Kevin. Especially when December comes. The fifteenth of December, he goes into this little shell of his. I don't even want to express it to him, but I know what he's feeling. It always comes back to him. There were times, especially when we were younger, I used to think maybe I didn't do the right thing by marrying him. Maybe I bring the war to him. It never leaves him, it's always between us.

He was even more so when he was younger. Now that he's older, some of it has left him. But it's always there. He must relive that episode. He would always explain to me what happened. In fact, he carried Kevin himself, 'cause they were in the like terrain. He himself brought him to a field area where there were medics. But he said it was too late.

They met at Camp Claiborne in Louisiana. They were Chicagoans, that's what made them so close. We still correspond with some of their buddies that came from Chicago. With Christmas cards. There's a closeness that these boys feel with their buddies, because they didn't know from one minute to the next whether they were gonna be, you know . . . There's a bond there that I think never is broken.

My children, knowing their dad, can tell when he's very depressed. We named our youngest after Kevin. It's hard for me to say what goes on inside of him. He'll say, Oh, c'est la guerre. He always has that. To him, he feels he lived over and beyond, he should have gone during the war. This is his attitude.

It never leaves you. It's always little thoughts, any little thing, a song. "Bésame Mucho" had just come out. Kevin and I were driving in the car, listening to the radio, and he said, "That song's really gonna make it." Now when I hear it played forty years later, I say to myself, Well, it made it. (Laughs.) It's little things like that.

His parents, you know the feelings they had with losing their son. When they'd see me and Diane, I used to think, did it bring it back to them? Did this bring Kevin back to them more? I was happy I had a little child because they felt this was part of their son and this they were happy about, too.

Yeah, I felt bitter. When you think of the young lives that were taken in their prime, there's bitterness. Even now, I think, Why can't things be settled without the turmoil in different parts of the world? Seems like things are not getting any better.

When the war was over, it was a time for rejoicing. But I was sad because I knew he would never come back. (Cries.) I heard the celebrations on the radio. There was no celebrating in our family.

Maybe if Joe had been with someone else, it might have left him. But here he's got Diane and myself right in front of him. (Laughs.) How is he ever gonna escape it? We're all part of it. But we've got three other children, they're just wonderful, and we love them and Diane. So life continues.

While Rosemary Hanley is in the kitchen brewing coffee, preparing the cake, he and I are observing the photographs on the wall.

Of course, those pictures wouldn't be there if I hadn't made it. Maybe the wall would be there, maybe the pictures would be there, but they'd be different. That's my wife's pride and joy. Always in the hopes that there'll be another picture added from year to year. (Laughs.) You live for the grandchildren.

I was always a rebel. I always march to a different drum. From the time I first entered grammar school, I thought to myself, who are these people that are imposing their superiority over me? I never liked it.

I was twenty years old. Of course, I thought I knew it all. But little did I know that I knew nothing. I was just a happy-go-lucky kid. And I went into the infantry. The 103rd Division, 411th Infantry Regiment, Company G. I was with them throughout the war. (Sighs deeply.) There's many nostalgic memories, but it wasn't nostalgia then. It was just the daily grind of it all. It was a changing point in my entire life. Little did I realize that one day I'd be a killer. (Laughs.) But there I was and tried to be the best soldier I could possibly be.

Combatwise, there weren't too many months involved. You're an old-timer if you survive twenty-four hours. (Laughs.) I never had hand-to-hand combat with any of the enemy, but I know I was responsible for many deaths. It's so easy when you're swinging a BAR, a Browning automatic, firing away. It's a machine gun. I liked the weapon and every time I got the opportunity, I used it. I had qualified with every weapon. I was a so-called expert. Still am. I scare myself with my qualifications. (Laughs.)

Actually, for all intents and purposes, the war was won. We were there simply to mop up, get out the ones that refuse to surrender. Of course, it was a little more than that. We had the Battle of the Bulge coming up. We were on the right flank. We were not the people that were surrounded by the enemy. We had orders not to withdraw under any circumstances. We stay in our foxhole, do or die. And that's what we did.

All I remember was we had advanced many, many miles and suddenly the order came to retreat. It was just madness. We had to get out in a hurry, and nobody knew what the heck we were running from. It seemed like such a waste of time after crawling on our bellies for all these months. Suddenly we have to turn around and run like rabbits. (Laughs.) But run we did.

I lost many, many buddies over there. Some I don't even remember their names. I can still remember their faces, I remember how they died. A few last words and then there was no more.

One buddy, of course, was the husband of the woman I married eventually. He literally died in my arms. He was hit by shrapnel. That was December 15 of '44. We were engaged in a battle that's probably unknown to most people. They called it the Climb to Climbach.

The enemy had high hills. We had the low hills. We were climbing up. They had the advantage artillerywise of pickin' us off like flies. And they did just about that. It rained 88s. This particular buddy, Kevin, we were together at the moment. He went in one direction and I went in another, hit the ground, and the next thing I know I heard him call out to me. I went over to him and found he was wounded. I made a joke of it, so to speak: "Well, you got a miracle wound. Now you're goin' home and you'll be with your wife and baby pretty quick."

It continued to rain 88s. I moved over several yards and the next thing I know, I looked up and he looked at me. There was something in his eyes, like he was trying to tell me something. I couldn't hear because of the noise, of all the bombs. When I finally did get over to him, he had passed away.

When the war ended, I had the opportunity of writing his wife and telling her the facts as I knew them. I said I'd call on her, with her permission, and maybe straighten out a few things. Families like to know little things that do occur. In '49, we became husband and wife. We have three children. But thoughts of Kevin come back many times over. His picture's on the wall. We wouldn't be without him.

December 15. That date comes back many times over. You don't want it to really come back, because you feel so helpless over it. It was so ridiculous for him to die and me to live. I feel like I walked in his combat boots when I came home. I didn't know what I was going to do. Certainly I didn't think I was going to marry his wife. Yet it was like the power was there.

I always feel guilty. I don't know why. It's like maybe I should have done something. Maybe we should have went in different directions or some darn thing. Yet I know I was powerless. You think to yourself, How can I go through all that and not get a scratch? Oh, I've got a few pieces of light shrapnel in me that I never reported. Didn't even know I had 'em until I come home and said, What the heck! You start scratching and you get a little piece of metal out of here, out of there. I lost my helmet one time, and little did I realize that I'd actually been hit in the head. Very minor. I still got a little discoloration of the scalp. I didn't know it until I started losin' my hair. (Laughs.)

Why do you think it should have been you instead of him?

I had no responsibilities. I had no wife and kids or nothin'. If I'da died on the battlefield, so what? It wouldn't have made any difference to anybody. Maybe my mother. My dad had died in '44.

If you had died, those pictures on the wall wouldn't be there.

That is true, yeah. That's the madness of it all, ya know? And the wonderment of it all. I'm so happy that, yes, it's on the wall. It's all like it was in the deck. The cards were shuffled and this is it. That's what it's all about for me.

I had a different personality before the war. I was more conscientious about a job. I was more introverted. My girlfriends were few and far between. I could sit down at a table and draw pictures for hours at a time. I had some kind of dream that maybe one day I'll be another cartoonist. When I came back, the only time I could sit down was if I sat at a bar.

I never drank before I went into the service. But after walking from Marseilles to the Rhine River, most of it on my belly, I got to the point that my canteen never contained water. Always cognac, the best I could find. I lived on cognac. To this day, I don't drink water. I drank pretty heavy when I first came back. And for many years.

One of my first jobs was bartender in a local tavern. And also the neighborhood bookie. (Laughs.) I liked the action. I just wanna have fun and a few bucks in my pocket. No more drawing, no more cartoonist dream. I didn't really care any more where I was going. I felt life is a joke. Why worry about anything if within a moment or two you might die? Why get serious about it? What the heck, what's it all about? We don't know. (Laughs.)

In my solitude, if I'm feeling particularly blue, it sometimes scares me. If I had a pistol handy, I might blow my brains out. I haven't done it all these years. But I always think, Am I cuckoo or suicidal? Because death doesn't scare me, you know? I don't like the idea of it, but I know you're gonna go someday. (Laughs.)

As time went by, I kind of took on suicide-type jobs. Hadda have action. There was never enough action. Gambling didn't do it. I figured I'll get something where there'll be some danger. So I became a police officer. There wasn't really enough action there, either. Not as I knew action. Oh, I had a few gun battles as a policeman, but, heck, this is kid's play. This is not the real thing. (Laughs.)

The war's in my daily thought, always. Something will come up that will remind me of an incident. It seems like it was predestined. As a kid in grammar school, it seemed like everybody knew there was going to be a big war and I was going to be part of the cannon fodder. The sacrificial lamb. Nobody really cared about you whatsoever. It was a big surprise to everybody when you came home. What are you doing here? You know? (Laughs.)

I was a late homecomer, '46. I had on the army overcoat, my duffle bag, and the little ruptured duck. When I got off the streetcar, I seen a bar there: "I'll have a shot and a beer." He pulled out a big glass of whiskey and gave me the beer. He didn't take any money. He said, "Welcome back, kid." I stayed there for three or four more drinks. (Laughs.) He was the only one.

I never used the GI Bill. I applied once when I was considering purchasing a home, but I never followed through. I never joined a veterans' organization. They rub me the wrong way. These guys want to perpetuate something that should have been finished.

No wars can be just. During combat, I would say to myself, This whole damn thing isn't worth one ounce of American blood or anybody's blood. You're wondering, What am I doing this for? How did I get into this mess? (Laughs.)

POSTSCRIPT: *After victory in Europe, he was given another assignment. "The Germans, in their retreat, left behind a number of their prisoners. They were Russian slave laborers, working in the factories around Mannheim. It was my job to administer to their needs. They liked to sing and dance and get drunk as often as possible. For some reason, they were hastened out of Germany as quickly as possible. We thought we'd have difficulty putting them on the train and heading them back to Russia.*

But strange thing, they couldn't get on the trucks fast enough to get back home. They were happy to go.

"Then we got German prisoners of war. They were continuously telling us, Within ten years, you'll be fighting the Russians. You should have continued through and licked them. Of course, everybody thought that was a lot of bunk then. (Laughs.) The Germans brought it up. We never thought of it."

TIMUEL BLACK

A Chicago schoolteacher.

We had met on the train to Washington heading for the 1963 Civil Rights March. "This reminds me of one other experience: the liberation of Paris. The exhilaration, the exuberance of the French people. We marched down to Paris, after giving the FFI—the French Forces of the Interior—the symbolic right to free the city. As bedraggled as we were, with dirty and dusty uniforms, all these people were paying tribute. Not to us, the American soldiers, but to the idea of freedom. The firin' was still going on in the streets. The FFI was chasin' the last of the German snipers. The Champs-Elysées, on that day, was an experience I'll never forget."

In 1939, I was sitting in a friend's living room listenin' to some jazz music. We were kids, workin' in a grocery store. I was about seventeen. News came over the radio that Poland had been invaded. I said to my friends, "It won't be long before we're in that war." They weren't quite as serious. My awareness had come much earlier. I was fortunate in having some excellent teachers in high school. DuSable. It was all black.

I began to realize that things were going on in Europe not to my liking. I'd worked for a Polish-Jewish family. They'd gone back to Poland and when they returned, they were tellin' me about the ghettos and the camps.

December 7 was my birthday. I was twenty-one in 1941 and we were celebrating. My good friend, George, was very patriotic. He says, "Let's have a drink: Here's to Christmas in Berlin and Easter in Tokyo." He joined up right away.

I was drafted in 1943, right after the Chicago and Detroit riots. We had this influx of war workers, both white and black, from the South, especially in Detroit. The tensions continued to mount until they exploded. We weren't talking about integration. Should the blacks or whites have the Brewster Homes? That was the new housing project in Detroit. There was no place for black young men, who'd been ignored, left to the side. Suddenly, they were soldiers. In a very segregated army, of course.

My father said, "What the hell are you goin' to fight in Europe for. The fight is here. You should be goin' up to Detroit." He was a militant kind of guy. He would've gone with me. We couldn't get to Detroit, though we had relatives there. The buses and trains were carefully screened. The roads were blocked. Right after that, they began to sweep the streets clean of all eligible young black people by the draft. They had just begun to let blacks in the navy in menial positions.

I went to Camp Custer, Michigan, for induction and then to Camp Lee in Virginia. All officers were white. We had done well enough on the AGCT, the Army General Classification Test. We believed we should have been officers. If you scored over a certain level, you could apply to OCS. I took one of those tests and I know I did well. We knew all our scores. Very often, our noncoms had access to those records and we'd find out. We could look at the records and see that we'd scored well on our first attempt. All black soldiers got was one attempt. Some of our superior officers had taken the exam two or three times. Can you imagine the kind of tensions set up between the white guy who is giving you orders and the black guy who has to take those orders, when both of them know the black guy has superior qualifications?

Most black GIs were put in the Quartermaster Corps. I was. We handled supplies: food, clothing, equipage. In Europe, we handled ammunition, too. We were really stevedores. Many of those young blacks wanted to be in combat units. I went into Normandy with combat troops. We serviced them.

Generally they made illiterate blacks from the South the noncommissioned officers to be over us, who had more education. Most of us were from the North. Here you have a somewhat resentful southern black guy, glad to have a chance to kick this arrogant northern city slicker around. (Laughs.) Deep underneath, those of us who came from New York, Chicago, and Detroit did consider ourselves a little better than our southern less-well-educated brothers. We did carry that attitude of haughtiness.

We were shipped overseas. On board, blacks had their quarters and the whites had theirs. We didn't associate with one another. Different mess halls, different everything. We zigzagged our way all across the Atlantic, because of the German subs. We stayed in Wales, getting ready for the invasion.

Black soldiers and white soldiers could not go to the same town. The ordinary British were absolutely amazed, looking at these two armies. I guess they hadn't thought about their two armies, too: the colonial and the regular. But they were chagrined by this racial situation, which they'd never seen. White soldiers would say, Don't have anything to do with those niggers. They have tails, they howl at night, all kinds of funny stories. Very often if we got into fights, the British guys and gals would be on our side. (Laughs.)

Blacks were given the least desirable towns to go to. Often, some of our more aggressive young men would say, I'm goin' to the nice town. I'm not gonna go to that crummy town. They'd have a conflict. We were fightin' a war before we went to the real war.

If a young black fellow, eighteen years old, would get together with a British girl, sixteen, that girl would be encouraged to say she was raped. We had a number of young black soldiers who were hanged. We had one in our outfit who was hanged.

We're getting ready now for the main battle. We're taken down now close to Southampton in great secrecy. Our outfit was originally assigned to go in D-Day, but they took another QM group. Our guys were disappointed, except me. I didn't want to do that. (Laughs.) Two days later, we went in. We went into Utah Beach. Omaha was the hot one, but Utah was hot enough for me.

It was a weird experience. Young men cryin' for their mothers, wetting and defecating themselves. Others tellin' jokes. Most of us were just solemn. I was thinking, Boy, if I get through this, it'll never happen to me again. What happens when you finally get off this LST? All you know is you wade into that beach. You hear the big guns.

The Germans aimed at our supplies. We were direct targets. I'd been on six-by-six trucks many nights when the Luftwaffe was strafing us. We had good air cover. But it didn't feel good when they were droppin' those small bombs and firin' those machine guns at us. We lost a few fellas.

We were responsible for keeping the German saboteurs from blowing up our ammunition dump. If they had gotten us, we would have been pushed right back into the beach. The Germans had dropped young fellas who lived in places like New York and Chicago and spoke perfect English. They could talk about the Brooklyn Dodgers and the White Sox. You couldn't distinguish them from Americans. You didn't know whether the white person was an American soldier or a German saboteur. They were really crack troops.

They had to take all the white American soldiers off the streets at night and use the black soldiers to do patrol duty. If there was a white person on the street at night, we had orders to pick him up or shoot him. We were doing double duty. Keep the supplies movin' and patrol at night. My whole outfit was decorated with the Croix de Guerre.

We stayed in Normandy until Patton came through. We went from Normandy to Brittany and moved toward Paris. And we came there on this beautiful day. How can I describe it? Know how I know they'd retained hope and dreams? They'd buried their jazz records of people like Louis Armstrong and Duke Ellington and Coleman Hawkins. (Laughs.) They said, (tries a French accent) "M'sieur, ze music, le jazz." They hugged and embraced us. It was the feeling of acceptance. I seriously considered not returning to the United States. They respected something from my own culture so openly, jazz music. I said, God, what kind of craziness am I involved in? It was an eye-opening experience.

We were in Belgium during the Battle of the Bulge. We were at one time feeding three million soldiers: the First, the Third, the Ninth, and the British Seventh. We used German prisoners to do our loading. Some weren't bad, but there were a lot who were arrogant, who considered us inferior.

Often white officers accepted their interpretation. It was frustrating. One time I had a bale of fatigues that had to be carried from one place to another. This German chap refused. I knew he was friendly with our lieutenant. He said, "You can't tell me what to do, you're a black man." I insisted. He resisted. I put the bale on his back, as he was at the top of the stairs, and I put my foot to his behind. He tumbled all the way down, and the bale followed him very quickly. I was reprimanded by the officers for mistreating a prisoner. But they never considered his mistreatment of me as his superior in this situation.

Guys like me were constantly on the spot. On one end, some of my black brothers felt I was endangering them. They were getting away with things by sneaking around, and I wanted to do things because I was an American soldier and wanted fair treatment. On the other end, the officers resented what I did. It was very lonely.

In one last shot, the Germans began to use the experimental buzz bombs. They were inaccurate. That's what made them so terrifying. You didn't know where they were going to wind up. (Laughs.) There was Axis Sally tellin' us all sorts of interesting stories on the radio. At the Bulge, we were under siege from Thanksgiving until Christmas of '44.

The mail had been sidetracked. We had no idea what was happenin' in the world outside. We had no outside. Psychologically, it did somethin' to me. I wrote a letter home: "You've forsaken me. You don't write and I'm gonna die." Finally, my mother was able to get the Red Cross through to me.

We're now up to '45. The Germans were getting ready to surrender en masse. Just thousands and thousands. Kamerad, kamerad. And that's when we came to Buchenwald. I *think* it was Buchenwald.

You begin to approach and the first thing you get is the stench. Everybody knows that's human stench. You begin to realize something terrible had happened. There's quietness. You get closer and you begin to see what's happened to these creatures. And you get— I got more passionately angry than I guess I'd ever been. I said, "Let's kill all the son-of-a-bitches. Kill all the goddamn Germans. Anyone who would do this to people, they're not worth livin'." On reflection, I know not all Germans did this. But my feelings were, how could they let others do it?

This was the clincher for me. If this could happen here, it could happen anywhere. It could happen to me. It could happen to black folk in America. I guess more than any single event, it was this sight that crystallized my determination to do as much as I could to bring about some sanity in a very insane world.

During the time I was in, I'd heard all sorts of anti-Semitic remarks from white gentiles. They'd come up to me and say, "Hitler was right about the Jews." I'd say, "Get away from me." I'm a quartermaster. Hell, I can cut off his goddamn food. (Laughs.) Some of the Germans I met said, "Well, it won't be long before the United States and the Soviet Union will be at each other." What kind of insanity is this?

V-E Day had now occurred. I was in Marseilles. We were being processed for the invasion of Japan. I got word through *Stars & Stripes* that an instrument had been dropped on Japan such as boggled my mind. A city had been devastated with one instrument the size of a golf ball. Most of the soldiers were elated. I was saddened. I wish we had gone and taken our chances. I sensed a new world I had never dreamed of. I went back to my bunk and lay there. What does this mean?

V-J Day was declared and we're on the journey back home. I still had a heavy heart. I had considered seriously staying for a while in Europe, but my affection for my family was tugging at me. My father, my mother, and I were very close.

We're coming up the Hudson River. You could see the shore. The white soldiers upon deck said, "There she is!" They're talking about the Statue of Liberty. There's a great outburst. I'm down below and I'm sayin', Hell, I'm not goin' up there. Damn that. All of a sudden, I found myself with tears, cryin' and saying the same thing they were saying. Glad to be home, proud of my country, as irregular as it is. Determined that it could be better. Just happy that I had survived and buoyed up by the enthusiasm of the moment. I could no longer push my loyalty back, even with all the bitterness that I had.

DR. ALEX SHULMAN

He is a surgeon, practicing in southern California.

He refers, on occasion, to a small, slightly tattered black book: the diary of his war years. As a young army surgeon, he apparently kept meticulous records.

"Our record is so much better than what happened in World War One. Antibiotics played a big role. And new techniques. We had blood, we had plasma, which we didn't have in World War One. We had better anesthetics. And were more skilled. The finest talent in the country was giving us a crash course in the neurosurgery of injury. And transportation: getting people into operating suites faster. The Korean War and Vietnam changed medicine completely, but I believe the big jump took place in World War Two."

I was in Belgium at the time of the Bulge. Winter, '44. I was doing neurosurgery, head surgery. This German youngster was brought in. He was fourteen, fifteen. Looked like a lost little boy. Hitler was takin' the kids and the old men. This kid was cut off from his outfit several weeks before, and he hid in a barn. He was a sad, dirty-looking kid, with a terrible gash in his head. It was actually a hole through his scalp and his skull.

When I first saw him, he was covered with old straw and manure and blood, and it was all caked together. I didn't know what to do with him. What is his injury? We always pictured Germans as having short-cropped hair. It was the GIs who had short-cropped hair. The German boys had long hair, long before our boys did. So did this kid, and his hair was matted together.

As I took him to the operating room, he started to cry. A little kid. I said, "Stop crying." I could speak a little bit of German, and a little bit of Yiddish helped. All I did was get a basin of hot water and some soap and washed his hair. Here was a captain in the United States Army washing the hair of a little German boy. I finally cleaned him up and looked at the wound. It wasn't bad. Nature had done quite a job healing it.

Then he really started to cry. I said, "What are you crying about?" He said, "They told me I'd be killed. And here you are, an American officer, washing my hands and face and my hair." I reminded him that I was a Jewish doctor, so he would get the full impact of it.

"Paris had been liberated just a few weeks before in '44. The boys in our outfit were given permission to go to the first Rosh Hashanah services in Paris. We went to Rothschild's synagogue, a great big place. The service was just about finished when a well-dressed guy came over to us. In broken English, with a bit of French: 'Would you like to be our guest for lunch?'

"He and his family told us stories of how they were always barely one jump ahead of the Germans during the four years of occupation. They brought out their little yellow Stars of David. They said, 'We're Sephardics. We would like you to go to our temple.'

"It was a little temple with a Moroccan configuration. We were the only Americans there. I was introduced to a man who had been a Paris surgeon. He was just released from a concentration camp. At this point, we didn't know about concentration camps. This was my first knowledge of it.

"This white-haired man gets up on the podium and starts to talk. They say his hair turned white shortly after he got there. He tells the audience, who are his friends and neighbors, what he saw in the camps: 'I saw your

sister being taken off somewhere and tortured. I saw your mother being dragged naked onto a truck . . .' He told personal stories to these people, who were all weeping uncontrollably.

"The rabbi gave his benediction. Through the Hebrew and French, you could catch the names Charles de Gaulle and Franklin Roosevelt and Winston Churchill and even Joseph Stalin. A Boy Scout and Girl Scout choir broke into the 'Marseillaise,' and the entire congregation got on its feet, tears streaming down their faces.

"I said to my friend, 'Let's get out out of here, I can't take it.' We started to walk down the aisle and they wouldn't let us out. Kissing our hands, hugging us. Merci, merci. We became representatives of the United States."

I was impatient while in England, waiting to cross the channel. D-Day came and went and other days went and you start thinking, oh, my God, the war's over. Anyway, on D-11, I landed in Normandy. In those days, you thought, oh, you missed the whole show. I was twenty-six when I got in, and at twenty-six, you're immortal.

Among the first we talked to were captured German officers. They were patients of ours. They kept saying, It's all over for you. When our panzers let loose, we're just gonna knock you out of France. We were really quite concerned about it. Hitler really thought this was a fake landing. He always expected us to land in Calais.

We saw a lot of slave labor around, working the farms. As soon as we started capturing a little territory, they appeared at our hospitals. To get a free meal, a cigarette, a place to sleep, pick up discarded American uniforms. There were a bunch of Poles, in these discarded uniforms, who wrote "Poland" on their helmet liners. They became part of us. Our ingenious GIs, who were litter bearers, said, Why do we have to carry litters? We got all these guys. Next thing I know, twenty or thirty of these fellas are our litter bearers. Our guys became supervisors, of course.

I was working in the shock ward. Our job was to get people out of shock by giving them blood or whatever they needed. Then they'd be taken to the operating room. Our rule was, Americans were always treated first. The Germans got the same treatment, but after our boys.

One day I got some Germans in pretty good shape and I sent 'em off to the operating room. A phone call comes from the operating room: "What the hell's goin' on? These guys are in shock. They got no blood pressure, they got no pulse. I don't understand it." We found out that the Poles who were carting these guys on their litters would dump them off and shake them up as much as they could. They were getting back at the Germans. This was the only way they could. (Laughs.)

By the time I got to Normandy, several villages had already been captured. We'd just set up a tent hospital. It was unbelievable. I was the admitting officer. We were on the highway to Cherbourg, which had just been captured. There were supposed to be several evac hospitals to pick up the wounded. But something went screwy that day. I had a tent full of wounded that had just been brought in by ambulance. A sergeant came in and said, "Captain, you better come out and take a look at this."

I went out, and as far as the eye could see, for miles up the highway, there were ambulances waiting to get in. We had a four-hundred-bed hospital and we were already filled. Then he said, "I want you to look out there, too." I looked around and there lying in the field are several hundred wounded. I said, "My God, what do we do? This is incredible." Somebody screwed up somewhere.

So I said, "Sergeant, get me about twenty syringes and twenty shots of morphine and we're goin' out for a walk." It was a bright, beautiful summer day. The two of us wandered from group to group. I had a vision in my mind of the Civil War, with all the wounded in the fields. In little groups. Those Mathew Brady photographs. Relived on this field.

Whenever I went to a group I said, "Are you fellas okay?" They'd usually say, "We're okay, but take care of him." They always pointed to some other guy. Even though they were wounded, they were pretty well off compared to the other guy. I'd give this other guy a shot of morphine and say, "We'll get to you as soon as we can." I did this for several hours around the field.

At the front we were twelve hours on and twelve off. As a designated neurosurgeon, I had certain responsibilities, head wounds. My idea of neurosurgery, before I got into combat, was there'd be an occasional head wound, maybe one every three, four days. In the meantime, I'd be doing the things I knew best, abdominal surgery and that sort of stuff. Well, out here from day one there was one head wound after another. We finished one case, three or four were waiting. Nobody else would ever touch a head, because in this territory if you didn't know your stuff, stay away. So I had no help. There was a period of three, four weeks in Normandy where I was working day and night. (He flips a page in his diary.) I see that I fell asleep one day, standing in the operating room. I'd been going about thirty-six hours continuously. What was a day like? It was a thirty-six-hour day. (Laughs.)

(He reads from his diary again) July 14. Bastille Day, huh? Our statistics show that at our hospital we had seen 5,000. We operated on 2,328. There were 57 deaths. That was from June 19. A little over three weeks. Let's see: July 15. To date I have done 28 major brain cases. I have here: one died. He was in deep coma, stopped breathing before we started. Postoperative mortality is therefore 4 percent. In World War One, it was 60 percent. At least.

After the Battle of the Bulge was the crossing of the Rhine. The hospitals would leapfrog each other. As we moved forward, a new hospital would come up and the first would rest. Later, they'd leap-frog to the front again. A half a dozen of these hospitals kept leapfrog-ging. They were all tent hospitals. In Germany they took a hospital that had been sitting in the rear for the entire war and put them way up front. It was like a football match, where you have a kid who hasn't played all season, so we let him play for a few minutes so he'll get his letter. They did this with hospitals, so you could get credit for something.

Here the war was almost over, a few weeks to go. I'm in this new hospital where they've barely broken their stuff out of their packages and they don't know anything. By now I'm a veteran with five battle stars. I've been going at it eight or nine months. I remember working in the operating room and saying, "My patient needs a bottle of blood." Somebody came in with a piece of paper and said, "The major in charge of the laboratory says you can't have it unless you fill out this form." (Laughs.) I said, "You tell that major to go screw himself. I want that blood." They had to learn that in war, you did things differently. (Laughs.)

The more you went east, the more refugees you saw. The Russians pushing this way, the Americans coming this way. Most of those wanted to get away from the Russians into the American zone. They started crowding into these towns. It looked like Saturday afternoon: thousands of people in village squares. They didn't care where they were going, to get away from whatever fighting there was, and certainly away from the Russians. At the end of the war, we got all kinds of prisoners. People from Dunkirk, from Tobruk. Allied soldiers, released from German prison camps.

I got to Buchenwald, too. Did you know that Buchenwald was a zoo? On the gate, engraved: Buchenwald Zoological Gardens. The ultimate humiliation. They didn't let us in, but we could look in. The smell and the bodies all were still there. So nobody can tell me it didn't happen. (Laughs.)

Americans have never known what war really is. No matter how much they saw it on television or pictures or magazines. Because there is one feature they never appreciated: the smell. When you go through a village and you suddenly get this horrible smell. Everybody's walking around with masks on their faces, 'cause it's just intolerable. You look out and see those bloated bodies. You no longer see humans, because they've been pretty well cleaned up by now. You see bloated horses and cows and the smell of death. It's not discriminating, they all smell the same. Maybe if Americans had known even that, they'd be more concerned about peace.

I had to get in that war. I had a compulsion. Maybe it's because I'm Jewish. I knew how horrible it was. There was nothing more horrible than to see youngsters with heads partly blown off. The tragedy was bigger than even that. The refugees—the war seemed made up of refugees. Every war, I guess, is.

I'm glad I participated. I felt that whatever little I did was something. My job was to save lives. I was asked, How could you take care of those Germans? Doesn't that bother you? Oh, I started looking at them at first as Germans and Nazis. Then I started looking at them as victims. Especially at the end, when I saw the kids and the old men. Could I blame that kid for what his parents or the Nazi leaders did? It was a terrible, mixed feeling. Why shouldn't I take care of a sixteen-year-old kid that's been shot to pieces?

FRIEDA WOLFF
_____

She is a retired schoolteacher. For a brief time she had been a concert singer.

"I had a Spanish father, who was a magnificent teacher. My uncle,

*an engineer, died on the beaches of France, a refugee from Franco Spain.
Until that time, I had been politically naive."*

To me, there doesn't seem to be a beginning to World War Two. I
suppose it began in Spain, because of what had happened to some
of my family.

In 1939, I was teaching in Sacramento Valley. Sons and daughters
of migrant workers were in the same school as sons and daughters
of the Associated Farmers. I had a marvelous class. I had considerable freedom. It was at the time of the invasion of Poland. As background, I was interesting them in the history of countries, in Latin
America as well as in Europe. They got so excited that some who
couldn't read, within two weeks were reading, because of the subject
matter.

In 1941, I was teaching in Petaluma, the Bay Area. I was having
a difficult time because youngsters were coming into class saying they
hoped the Russians would get whipped, quoting the principal and
others. I felt, at that point, I had to do something else. When the
principal walked into the classroom and said, "What will you need
next year in the way of books?" I said, "I won't be here next year."
I didn't know I was going to say that. I just heard myself saying it.

I went to work for navy public relations. I was interviewing Pacific
survivors: burn victims, basket cases, the real horrors of war. I used
to feel it would be terrible to expose the public to the sight of these
people. Then I felt it would be criminal not to expose them. The
public has to know what war is.

I joined the Red Cross because I wanted to go overseas. In England
before D-Day we did a great deal of moving around from camp to
camp, hospital to hospital, doing the best we could to keep the GIs
from becoming too depressed. I was sneaked onto a plane and flown
across to watch the action two days after D-Day. I saw absolute
horror. Kids being blown up. I finally went across with a Red Cross
unit, driving a truck.

When we left England—at night, of course—we rode our trucks
onto an LST. As I wandered around in the dark on this vessel, I heard
a lot of Spanish spoken. It was the last thing I expected. They were
transporting across the channel a Free French armored outfit. A
number of Spaniards who had been exiled to hard labor in North
Africa had managed to escape. They had joined the Free French, had
come to England, and were now going over.

I saw one lone figure standing by the railing. I tentatively addressed him in Spanish. Sure enough, he was Spanish. He was an eighteen-year-old boy who at age thirteen had been exiled to hard labor in Spanish Morocco. His family had been wiped out. His brother and two sisters had escaped to the beaches of France, where all three died because of the horrible conditions there. He was the only survivor. The only smile he had was when I called him Danny. His name was Daniel.

I said to him, "But, Danny, what are you doing here? This isn't your war." He looked at me for the longest time. There was a dead silence. Then this dead-serious young man said, "Señorita, it's strange to tell a Spaniard he has no need to fight fascism." That brought me up. I grew up a lot that moment.

Three days later, when we were in a makeshift hospital near Cherbourg, they brought in bags and bits and pieces of people. Danny had been in a tank and the tank had been blown up. I knew those bits and pieces in that one bag were Danny's bits and pieces. In that bag was the Red Cross pin I had given him for good luck. So I have always felt that Danny knew more than I did at that time. He taught me a lot. My dead-serious Spanish boy was really a dead, serious Spanish boy.

For a time I worked with an outfit called Cinemobile. We had trucks equipped with motion pictures and with a stage. I had the freedom to drive wherever I wanted. Sometimes we were right up at the front. Sometimes I sang. Those are terribly important moments when they have time to think about home and what's ahead of them. And time to be afraid. Don't think they weren't afraid. When they were in staging areas, just before they went across to France, belts and ties were removed from some of these young men. They were very, very young. In their fearful anticipation, they might do themselves damage.

I remember at one point hearing General Patton addressing these thousands upon thousands of young Americans. Some of them had never seen anything outside of their high school. The hardest drink they ever had was a milkshake. He said to these young boys, "With your blood and my guts—" I'll never get over that till the day I die. Your blood and my guts.

Later on, I asked to be transferred to hospital work. I served in evacuation and general hospitals.

We came over on the *Queen Elizabeth*. There were thirty thousand troops on the ship. Because of the crowding, they were divided into the reds, the whites, and the blues. They took eight-hour turns for sleeping on the decks. The officers had marvelous food. The GIs had fish heads.

The weather was rotten. I was so damn seasick, I barely made it to one of the GI decks. A couple of GIs helped me at the railing. I started singing with them. I found out there were a number of them so talented that you couldn't believe it. They had been musicians with big name bands.

Every once in a while, the loudspeaker would come over: "Will all Red Cross personnel get off the GI deck and come up to the promenade deck." I never did. They hid me. I realized this was a wonderful way to cross the ocean. I went to the Special Services officer and told him I could get together a great show. He said, "Do it for the officers." I said, "No way." I said, "We'll do one for reds, one for whites, and one for blues. If we're still on the ocean, we'll do one for the officers." We put on absolutely fantastic shows.

The Red Cross told us to buy an evening dress, just in case of anything. I never wore the evening dress once we got overseas. I had bought a fantastic red dress. I don't know how the GIs knew I was going to wear that red dress for our show. When I came on, the band just started playing "The Lady in Red." And the GIs were singing it. It was beautiful.

When we unloaded at Scotland, we all had on our Red Cross uniforms. There were numbers on our helmets. Mine was 22. I'm sitting in this tender and GIs are still on the ship. Like one big voice, came this shout: "Hey, Twenty-two, sing us a song." Later on, in one of the hospitals, was a GI I didn't recognize. He had both of his legs amputated. As I came through, he said, "Hey, Twenty-two, sing me a song."

I kept running into these young guys in England, in France. In one evacuation hospital, I was meeting all the wounded who came in. I stayed up for four days without going to bed. Thank God, I have terrific kidneys. (Laughs.) I went to the bathroom exactly twice during those four days and four nights. (Laughs.) I had to meet every litter that came in from the field, because I knew they'd try to get them out right away. Some of them, to a general hospital. Some of them, home to die.

It was my habit to talk to them as soon as they came in and offer to write a letter or send word or something they'd want. I was in an evacuation hospital that Patton would visit. It was his habit to ask the army doctors to segregate the so-called SIWs. Self-inflicted wounds.

Just because they were listed as self-inflicted wounds does not mean they were self-inflicted. Many of them had faulty weapons and accidentally discharged and shot a foot or leg. There were many. They were all called SIWs, if there was even a suspicion that they had been responsible for their own wounds. They would sometimes wait for as much as six months before they were court-martialed. And you know what the maximum penalty was for an SIW. Imagine the state of mind of those GIs labeled SIWs, waiting all those months before they came to trial.

Patton always asked for the SIWs to be pointed out to him. On this one day, there was an SIW, so called, lying in this bed. There was a young man lying beside him. He was told that the second young man had been wounded by enemy fire. Here was the so-called SIW lying next to him. Patton went to the first boy's table and ripped him up one side and down the other. He said that hanging and drawing and quartering were too good for him. That his fingernails should be ripped out. I mean, I heard him say this. This SIW, this traitor, this thing that should not be called an American. Next to him lies an American hero, who he personally was going to recommend for the Silver Star.

After he left, I went to this American hero, who wouldn't talk to me. I kept saying, "I'm not going to insist, but if you have a mother or sister or somebody you want to know that you're okay, I'll be glad to write the letter. Just let me know." Finally, after several trips to him, he said, "You don't wanna talk to me. If you knew the story, you wouldn't wanna talk to me."

He says, "General Patton was right here and said I was an American hero. He's gonna recommend me for the Silver Star. I didn't even have the guts of the guy next to me, if he did shoot himself. I wanted to. I was so scared, I stood up there. I didn't know what else to do. I stood up and exposed myself and that's how I got wounded. I didn't have the courage to shoot my toe."

I saw young men who had crossed the river a number of times. One had made three parachute jumps. He was brought to this rest area for twenty-four hours before he went out again. He was sweating. He kept wiping his lip, wiping it, wiping it. I asked him why. This was a young hero in combat three times. He was absolutely terrified. He said, "I just don't know what to do, I'm so scared. What's the matter with me? Am I a coward?"

So many were afraid of being called cowards, some of them in trenches for thirteen days and nights. Hadn't been able to take their boots off. They had trench foot, everything. Yet afraid of being called cowards.

I was at a general hospital in Verdun. Some of the damage from World War One hadn't been repaired. It had about two thousand patients, a third of them so-called SIWs. There was a boy with a terribly damaged right leg. He was awaiting court-martial. They didn't know whether to amputate or give it another chance. I set up a therapy program for him, something to keep him occupied. He had been married and had a child. His wife had gone off with somebody else and he was fighting for his parents to get custody. So all three things are waiting for him: court-martial, possible amputation, and a court fight. I saw him for four months without missing a day.

We finally managed everything. We got custody for his parents. The leg was saved. And he was exonerated at court-martial. It was proven that he had a faulty weapon. The last time I saw him was at a dance I organized. He came on a crutch, limping badly, and said, "Hey, Red Cross, do you wanna dance?" We got on the floor and he did what he could about dancing.

I always violated rules. I never ate in officers' mess. I always ate with GIs. Nobody could court-martial me. I was not an officer in the army.

When I'd visit the ward, I would never tell them I was coming. But they always had an eye out for me. Sometimes they'd pretend they were asleep. Somebody would start to giggle and here would come the spitballs. It was then you'd realize how really, really young they were. Like little children.

I was stationed at Bastogne in Belgium. I'd been asked to set up one of the first rest centers. I saw to it that each had a cot with partitions between. It was so long since they had any privacy. This was just before the Battle of the Bulge. There were so many miscalculations and crossed signals, I really don't believe the Battle of the Bulge was necessary at all.

They did have information. They had captured some Germans who had given away the plans. I was there a few days before the breakthrough, before Bastogne itself was invaded. The news was available to everybody. Two days before the breakthrough—was it the fourteenth or the twelfth?—the Belgians who had previously had signs all over: Welcome Yanks, took down all their banners. The day before the breakthrough, there wasn't a Belgian on the street. The place was absolutely deserted. The Belgians had known about this before the breakthrough. We hadn't taken appropriate action. I know there was a lot of criticism about how long the front was. The Eighth Corps was defending a tremendously long front and it enabled the Germans to come in and, of course, do a pincer.

I was there the day of the actual breakthrough and then evacuated. We joined a convoy of retreating Americans. We were on that road in that convoy for hours and hours and hours. It was sleet and it was rain.

I was still working at that general hospital in Verdun when V-E Day came. I came home and traveled around the country for the Red Cross. The cold war started. For me, the war was not yet over. Franco was still in power in my father's country. I worked for the refugees. And now, I'm simply antiwar, that's it.

Frieda Wolff died on March 22, 1984.

BOOGIE WOOGIE
BUGLE BOY

Don't sit under the apple tree with anyone else but me,
Anyone else but me, anyone else but me, no, no, no,
Don't sit under the apple tree with anyone else but me
Till I come marching home.
Don't go walkin' down lover's lane with anyone else but me,
Anyone else but me, anyone else but me, no, no, no,
Don't go walkin' down lover's lane with anyone else but me
Till I come marching home.

MAXINE ANDREWS

Along with Patty and Laverne, she was one of the Andrews Sisters.

I remember we sang it up in Seattle when a whole shipload of troops went out. We stood there on the deck and all those young men up there waving and yelling and screaming. As we sang "Don't Sit Under the Apple Tree," all the mothers and sisters and sweethearts sang with us as the ship went off. It was wonderful. The songs were romantic. It was a feeling of—not futility. It was like everybody in the United States held on to each other's hands.

I felt we were invincible. Right is right and we were right and we're gonna win. But the news was not encouraging. Remember Boak Carter, the commentator? My father would listen to him every night. We were in California, doing a picture with Abbott and Costello: *Buck Privates.* I would look on the set and see all those wonderful young men. It would go through my mind: am I ever gonna see them again? This was '39, '40. We were not yet in. But I had this great fear.

My sisters and I were so involved in our work, we didn't have much time to think of anything else. But oh, I remember the day war was declared. We were in Cincinnati. It looked like we were gonna break the house record in the theater. It didn't matter how cold it was or how high the snow, people were lined up for blocks. Every morning I'd walk over to the theater, seeing the lines already formed. This Sunday morning, I walked over and there were no lines. I thought, Now, this is funny. I walked onto the stage, which was very dark. The doorman and the stagehands were sitting around the radio. They had just one light on. They were talking about Pearl Harbor being bombed. I asked the doorman, "Where is Pearl Harbor?" Of course, the rest of the week there was no business.

But after that, as the war continued, attendance was tremendous. There was a sort of frenzy and a wonderful kind of gaiety. There was more money around than there had ever been. Our records became big sellers. Remember, during the Depression it was terrible. We closed every RKO theater in the country from north to south to east to west. We were doing three shows a day. With the war years, we did five, six shows a day. We toured almost fifty weeks a year in theaters.

No matter how many shows a day we did, we always went to the camps. We always made the hospitals when they started bringing the boys back. We were the only girls allowed in Oak Knoll Hospital when they were brought back from the Solomon Islands. They were known as basket cases.

We were working at the Golden Gate Theatre in San Francisco when a Red Cross nurse asked us if we'd come out and do a show. She kept us outside for a while. She said it would be something different from whatever we've seen. The most important thing was that we must not break down. The last thing the boys needed were tears.

We walked into the first ward and it was very quiet. When we were announced, there wasn't any applause at all. It was a very long ward. We were ushered into the middle. There were beds in front of us, beds behind us. We finally looked. The sight was terrible. We saw boys with no arms or legs, with half-faces. The three of us held on to each other, because we were afraid we were going to faint. The terrible thing is to hold back the tears.

We sang for about forty-five minutes. I think some of the fellas realized how we were feeling. One of the boys, all clothed in bandages, started to cry. He was crying throughout the numbers. Finally, one of the fellas yelled, "Don't pay any attention to him, he's just dreaming about his girlfriend." We stayed there for about three hours, going from ward to ward.

As we were leaving, a male nurse came over to us: "I have a young patient who would love to hear you sing." He asked us to sing something soft. Nice and easy and relaxed. We went down a long, long hallway and stopped in front of a door that two male nurses were guarding. We were ushered in. We were in a padded cell. The two guards closed the door behind us. We were alone.

In the corner, we saw a figure facing the wall. We started to sing "Apple Blossom Time." About halfway through, we began to hear this hum. It was discordant and got louder and louder. When we came to the end of the song, we didn't stop. We just kept singing. We repeated it and repeated it. The figure turned around. He couldn't have been more than nineteen years old. His eyes were looking at us, but he wasn't seeing us. He was lost in another world. He was just humming and humming. He was so handsome and so young.

A few months later, at the Golden Gate Theatre, the doorman came to us: "You have a visitor." We were just about to do our last show. In walked a serviceman. On his back was another serviceman, with no arms and no legs. One we had seen in the ward. He had his artificial arms on. He said, "I never asked you for your autograph, because I said that one day I was going to give you mine." He leaned over on the dressing table and he signed his name: it was Ted.

We went overseas for the USO. Our last date was in Naples. We were billeted in Caserta, eighteen miles away. We did all our shows at repo depots, where all the guys were being shipped out. We had one more show to do. It was loaded with about eight thousand of the most unhappy-looking audience you'd ever seen. They were hanging from the rafters. All these fellas were being shipped out to the South Pacific. They hadn't been home for four years, and it was just their bad luck. We were trying to get them into good spirits.

We were pretty well through with the show when I heard someone offstage calling me: "Pssst. Pssst." Patty was doing a little scene with Arthur Treacher. The soldier said to me, "I have a very important message for Patty to tell the audience." I started to laugh, because they were always playing tricks on us. He said, "I'm not kidding. It's from the CO." I said, "I can't do it in the middle of the show." He said, "You're gonna get me in trouble." So I took the piece of paper. I didn't read it. I walked out on the stage, saying to myself I'm gonna get in trouble with Patty, with Arthur, with the CO. I waited until the skit was over. Patty said, "Stop your kidding. We can't read that here. We've got to finish the show." I shoved the note at her. She finally said, "All right, I'll go along with the gag."

So she said to the fellas, "Look, it's a big joke up here. I have a note supposedly from the CO." Without reading it first, she read it out loud. It announced the end of the war with Japan. There wasn't a sound in the whole auditorium. She looked at it again. She looked at me. It was serious. So she said, "No, fellas, this is from the CO. This is an announcement that the war is over, so you don't have to go." With that, she started to cry. Laverne and I were crying. Still there was no reaction from the guys. So she said it again: "This is the end, this is the end."

All of a sudden, all hell broke loose. They yelled and screamed. We saw a pair of pants and a shirt come down from above. Following it was a body. He came down and fell on the guys sitting downstairs. Patty said, "You want to go out and get drunk? Or you want to see the show?" "No, no, no, we want to see the rest of the show." We made it very short.

We got into the jeep, and all of a sudden it hit us. Oh heavens, if this is a joke, they're gonna tar and feather us. We'll have to swim all the way back to the States. We suffered until we got to Caserta. They reassured us that the announcement was true.

A few years ago, Patty was working someplace in Cleveland. She checked into the hotel and was in the elevator. This elevator man said, "Don't you remember me?" He was a short, baldheaded guy. She said, "Should I?" He said, "Yeah, remember Naples? Remember the guy that fell off the rafter? That was me."

He was a famous trumpet man from out Chicago way,
He had a boogie sound that no one else could play,
He was top man at his craft.
But then his number came up and he was called in the draft.
He's in the army now ablowin' reveille.
He's the boogie woogie bugle boy of Company B.

BOOK THREE

SUDDEN MONEY

RAY WAX

He is a stockbroker, living in a middle-class suburb just outside New York City. It is a recent endeavor. Previously he had been a builder and a real estate broker. In his younger days, he hawked long-stemmed roses at subway stations.

His words pour out torrentially. He is restless; a fever possesses him, though in these later years it is lowering. A touch of resignation is setting in.

I'm lucky to be alive. Though I thought that war was important, I really didn't want to go. I was drafted in 1940 and looked upon the regular army as Cossacks. It was made up of people many of whom joined to avoid a small conviction. The judge would say, Do you want six months or a tour of the army?

I was on the beach at Santa Monica when someone said Pearl Harbor had been attacked. We all got up in our swimming trunks and headed back to camp. A day or two later, they shipped us all out to protect the coast. What we really did was terrorize the Japanese up around San Francisco.

America became paranoid after Pearl Harbor and decided that the Japanese were gonna attack the West Coast. We put a curfew on the Japanese villages that ran above and below San Francisco. I remember two bandoleers around me with a hundred rounds of ammunition and an M-1 rifle, riding in the back of a truck making Japanese farmers observe a six o'clock curfew. So help me God, we were told to shoot anything that moved.

If there's anything more goddamn bloody boring than the infantry, I don't know what it is. How many times can you break down a machine gun and reassemble it? I fought continually to get out of it. One of the main things lacking in the whole goddamn army was any kind of recreation. I had a chance to go out and do a show for the guys. My captain said, "If you go on that show, I'll never get off your ass. Goddamn it, you're in the infantry." When that thing broke up and I got back, the son of a bitch had me cleaning aluminum stoves for six weeks, every day. I found out later, in regulations, no man can do KP more than once every thirty days. It didn't make any difference in the regular army.

I was in the first group they used to call your thirteen-week wonders. I was training to be an anti-aircraft officer. I bullshitted 'em that I knew mathematics. I was goin' up against these college kids. That's how I got in OCS.

All the officers alongside me thought we had it made. We could stretch out the rest of the war training troops in the South. I decided I wanted to do something about the war. I was still trying to read things that interest me. I read a guy who was amazingly accurate: he said the Russians would stop the Nazis at Stalingrad. I used to lecture that in front of my troops. My first lieutenant used to grab me: "Goddamn it, Wax, where do you get that shit?" I'd say, "From the infantry journal, lieutenant." He'd say, "Goddamn it, I don't see it in the infantry journal." I'd say, "It's there."

I conned my major to release me from his training group and I went overseas. I landed in the south of Wales, Swansea, in December of 1943. We were shipped to a place outside Birmingham. We lived in some houses alongside civilians. The factory girls were hungry. They used to walk in front of our apartments. All you hadda do from your window was nod and the women popped in and there you were in bed. I'll always remember a guy, Murphy. He said, "I'm knockin' off three a day." (Laughs.) It wasn't my game, though I did pop one or two. But I didn't want to just sit there and look through the window.

They didn't have computers then. They had punch cards with holes and everybody had a form 20. They picked out categories, where you belonged. Somehow they found out I had managerial experience, and they assigned me to a PX. Instead of invading Europe, I was to run a PX in England. I got drunk.

I took a look at the TO—table of organization—and I suddenly realized I had an empire. I had 4 officers and 144 men under me. I took over and had a ball.

I went to the south of England and set up the first PX for the men that were coming over, the replacement army. The ships were coming faster then. I was in Yeovil, a charming little town. I set up five exchanges, some in tent camps on the hills. Brought beer from

Bristol, beer from London. I had barber shops and watch-repair shops. I had control of all the Zippo lighters in the south of England. I was quite a power.

I handled a lotta money. I did $40,000 a month in beer. I did over $125,000 a month in PX supplies, and that just with cigarettes and candy. I had a terrible choice to make in the first hour: I had to say to myself, Ray, you gonna steal or not? I just decided I couldn't steal. How many people in your lifetime hand you a cigar box with $40,000 in it that wasn't counted? I had that workin' for me for seven months before invasion. All I got out of it is a bike, which I left when I moved on.

I had two sergeants I really liked. They used to run one or two of the other camps. I thought I had an unbeatable system to make sure nobody stole. But those two guys, when it was all over, were in Chicago running one of the biggest auto-supply houses I'd ever seen. They had made a score. You see, they went on to work for somebody else when I walked away from the PX.

There were guys who trafficked in gasoline, cigarettes. Two guys used to send Patek Philippe watches home every week. They had to be worth five hundred dollars in America. You can't buy a Patek Philippe watch today for less than one thousand dollars. The lieutenant who took over from me used to send a weapons carrier to Paris, loaded with cigarettes. By the end of the war, he was a rich man. I didn't begrudge him. Anytime I wanted a carton for anyone, I always got my carton.

I was determined to go to the European theater. I went to my colonel and said, "I don't want to run a PX any more." He put me in intelligence and information.

I landed D-21 in Normandy. By that time, it was a breeze. They had cleaned out the hedgerows and you could move down. Anybody who was lucky enough to come in behind the guys who made the first hits was alive. I was with the Third Army, Patton's. It was called the Lucky Rear.

I noticed they sent back to us from the front lines a lotta guys who were whacked out. In the First World War, they called it shell-shocked. We called it battle fatigue. There was nobody to treat them. I went to my colonel and said I can set up movies, and I can run 'em by day. He said, "How the hell you gonna do that?" I said, "I'm gonna go back to the beaches, pick up crates, and I'm gonna build myself a shadow box." That's what I did. There were gigantic crates floatin' around. I took two-and-a-half-ton trucks, loaded them up with these sides of wood slabbing, and got the men who were sittin' on their ass to build me a shadow box. I used charcoal and had the guys black down the interior, and I was able to show films during the day. I could seat three hundred men in front of that box. That was the first real recreation in the replacement depot in France.

The ingenious Germans had these prefabricated houses. I hit these places and found prefab sections of flooring. I put together six sections and I had a portable stage. I went to my drunken colonel, who was marvelous, and asked him for a two-and-a-half-ton truck. The army always said, Never volunteer. Fuck 'em, I always volunteered. He gave me the truck and I carried these six sections of prefabricated flooring. Everywhere I went, I could drop down and I had a stage. I put that stage all across France. I put on Dinah Shore. I put on Bing Crosby. These were the live shows comin' in behind the men.

I had a sergeant to protect me, 'cause everybody would kinda wanna talk to me. Everybody had an idea. Again, I was doin' the power-and-glory shit. Someone came to me and said he wants to organize a band. I said, "Who've you got?" He said, "I play sax and I think we got a piano player." I talked to this piano player: "What's your name?" "Dave Brubeck." I said, "Who do you play like? Stan Kenton?" He said yeah. I said okay.

I pulled his form 20: Brubeck was a rifleman, an infantryman. When I pulled his form, he couldn't move forward. It's like he disappeared. That's what I did with eighteen people in the band: I held their form 20s. They stayed alive and I had a band. I had the power of life and death. I really thought I was doing something valuable. I bumped majors and I got my fine drunken colonel to back me. I was able to do any goddamn thing I wanted.

I made something happen for those men. When a man goes to a replacement depot, he doesn't belong to a unit. He comes up and you can look in his face, and sometimes you know he's gonna live and sometimes you know he's gonna die. Because that man is lost. He's being channeled like a piece of cannon fodder into some unit that lost a dozen men. And he's goin' right into battle. You could tell the guys who were scared shitless and wouldn't make it. Anything you did to take a little pressure off the guy that made it possible for him to get through the next few days, that was great.

Everything was in flux. We were moving. We heard that Paris had fallen. Fontainebleau is not that far from Paris. I said to my next in command, "Witty, let's take a goddamn half-ton truck and go to Paris." As we came down the road and headed into Paris, women, men, French peasants, townspeople, ran to the truck and threw flowers at us.

We'd gotten into the back of Leclerc's Second Armored Division. The American armies had passed Paris. It was a tremendous gesture by Eisenhower. He was determined to have the French take Paris. I was in Paris the day it was liberated. But I blew it.

At a moment in history somebody says, "I was there." I wasn't. They were marching down to the Arc de Triomphe and I didn't know it. All I knew is I wanted some perfume and scarves. I went to the Galerie Lafayette, a great department store. Nobody was on the street. We walked through the store, wearing boots, with the .45s on the hip and wearin' a helmet. Great. Out from behind the counters came all those little French girls. They followed us: "Ohhh! Marvelous Américain." We bought scarves and all of a sudden someone said, in broken English, they are firing on the Place de la Concorde. The diehards were in the eaves of the building sniping at the parade. They had to rout 'em out. But I wasn't there. I didn't see the parade. I wasn't on the Place de la Concorde at this marvelous moment in history. I was in the goddamn Galerie Lafayette buying perfume and scarves. Shit.

Later, as we drove out in the street, we tried to get in a restaurant. They said, "You can't get in." The Free French, the maquis, had taken all the restaurants. So we sat in the middle of Montparnasse. The windows opened and the wives sent their husbands down with bread and wine. We sat in this open half-ton truck eating and drinking. A couple comes along and says, "We'll take you to a black-market restaurant." It became one of those great, marvelous Hemingway kind of nights. We went on to a bar. I still remember, it was called Chez Mama. One o'clock in the morning, I was on a fuckin' piano singin' "Hurray for the Flag of the Free." Just out of a bloody storybook. Somewhere around three o'clock, someone took me by the hand across the street to a hotel called, of all things, L'Ecole. The School. Took me upstairs and put me in the sack and I had a marvelous night. In the morning, we crawled back to Fontainebleau.

We holed up for the winter in the little town Neufchâteau. I'm running the Hotel Moderne and the officers' mess. We had a major from Kansas City who claimed to be a drinking, poker-playing buddy of Truman. He was a vicious anti-Semite. We were drinking in the officers' mess, he was smashed. He came at me: "Why is it, Wax, there are so few Stars of David in the cemetery?" I ran for him and grabbed him and I said, "Goddamn it, we oughta open a hole in the lines for you and let you through Lublin." They'd just discovered the death camp there. They parted us. I couldn't sleep that night.

The following day, I went to the adjutant and said, "I want to volunteer for a direct-combat assignment, and I also want to bring charges against this bastard." The windup is they got me to withdraw my request and drop charges against the guy. He agreed he'd never drink again while he was in that command, and made a personal apology to me. He never again opened his mouth about Jews. Know what they did? They made him a lieutenant colonel and me a captain. Ain't that a fuck?

Now I'm racin' for glory. I'm handlin' everybody comin' through Europe. I'm doin' bit pitches on the character of the war. I'm turnin' out a paper called *Hitler's Bromides, or The Daily Belch.* 'Cause we were hearing all the propaganda they were aiming at the GIs. I'm workin' with big maps, describing where the Russian forces are and the Americans are. The main thrust of all this shit was to convince the GIs they weren't fighting alone. There were some three hundred Russian divisions moving toward the western front and we had, all told, maybe a hundred divisions. Three to one. Yet you couldn't convince a GI anybody was out there fightin' the fuckin' war but him.

I worked with three, four thousand men at a time, with mikes. I used to say, "You guys think I'm fulla shit, but I'm gonna do one thing for ya that you'd never expect. I'm gonna show you a big map." I'd get a big howl. Then I'd go with a pointer and do the whole piece of shit.

As the war began to wind down, we raced across into Germany. I made a run for the only thing that really mattered to me—the Nuremberg Opera House. I wanted to see the opera house. It had Hitler's box in it. I was in Nuremberg about a half a dozen days after the Third Army smashed it and went into Munich. They were swinging south.

They wouldn't let me in: "We have direct orders not to let anybody in." I went to the guy in charge: "What the hell's goin' on?" He said, "We're guarding sixteen ballerinas." I said, "I don't want the fuckin' ballerinas. I just want to run shows in it." We hassled for a while and he gave me half the opera house. It had a big hole in the roof, one hit. It had Hitler's box. It had Goebbels's box. It was a great opera house. I did the Lunts in that house, Alfred and Lynn Whatshername. They were marvelous.

We were ready to come back home and I didn't have a goddamn bean in my pocket. I knew I had to go back, pick up the rope, become a civilian, and I just didn't have a fuckin' idea in my head. Didn't know where I was goin' or what I was gonna do. In the next few months they were gonna put you on a train, ship you to Le Havre, and put you on a goddamn boat to America. I felt there was nothing there for me. I just knew I had to pick up and start all over again.

The last thing I did in the war was take a troop train from Bamberg to Le Havre. That train brought in the 101st Airborne out of Berlin. They'd fought alongside the Russians and didn't want to tangle with 'em. I listened to hotshot American officers saying, "We ought to finish 'em off now." They weren't talkin' about the Nazis, they were talking about the Russians. They hated their guts. They thought they were animals. Maybe they were animals. Coming all the way from Stalingrad to Berlin, they'd been turned into animals. They were the best killers in the world. I couldn't find one paratrooper who watched 'em with their burp guns ever wanna fight 'em. I think the greatest goddamn lesson for every American woulda been to be stationed in Berlin alongside those Russians.

I'm sure when they met at the Elbe they met with a great deal of joy. I'm sure they threw their arms around each other and the Russians bought Mickey Mouse watches and the Americans wound up with Russian vodka. But that didn't last long. We had to exchange a lot of ground in Czechoslovakia and in Bavaria, and everywhere the Russians were hard-nosed. I'm sure the same thing happened when they got into Berlin. I heard anti-Russian talk almost immediately after the meeting with the Russians. I guess that's been our position all along.

When I took that train, I heard there was a crap game in which a lot of money changed hands. We set up camp, waiting for the boats to move out. Word came down that there was a limit on the money you could take out. Every officer could take out $1,500 and every GI could take out $500. Here these two guys had won $68,000. Here's how the juices work for a guy when he's on the balls of his ass.

I'm layin' there with about three, four guns, big French .44 and a Luger and somethin' else. I'm trying hard to figure out how I can put together a couple of bucks when I hit the States. All of a sudden the lights go on. I ask a GI where I can find the guys who made the score. I went into their tent. I said, "Look, you're gonna have trouble gettin' the money out. I'll give you sixty cents on the dollar and I'll get it out for ya." They were tickled. They turned over about $30,000 to me. Didn't give 'em a receipt. I went to every officer who was busted and I said, "Carry $1,500 and I'll give you twenty points." I kept twenty. They got $300 and I got $300 and I handed $900 back to the guys for each $1,500.

When I crossed the parade ground to find 'em, they were a little bit teed off. Apparently, the Red Cross was willing to do it for twenty points instead of forty. They had laid off the rest of the money. But that's how I made the $5,000 dollars I landed in America with. The new immigrant. (Laughs.)

I musta picked up another $400 for the guns. I didn't want to see another gun again. That was my grubstake when I hit America. I joined the 52-20 club. It was all over, and I guess you just hadda pick up and go on from there.

It's a terrible thing to say, but it was the most exciting span of time that I ever spent. The most romantic. If you're lucky enough not to get killed or maimed, and you go through it, it's much like a hospital experience. You never remember the pain, you remember the ass of the nurse who came in and bent over you. I forgot all about the boredom of being an infantryman and spending hours doing mindless tasks. But I do remember all the chances I had as a personality to do something that affected the lives of other people.

There was a time of good feeling. The country felt it had done something worthwhile. The guys came back feeling they had accomplished something. Then they moved into a highly competitive society and immediately they had to go back to living routine lives.

When I came back, I felt there wasn't anything I couldn't do. The sky was the limit. The only thing is the brass ring, is the big buck. That calls for dedication, a singleness of purpose: making money regardless of cost or who you damage. It's the food they eat, the dreams they dream. It finally came down to how many people you can get to swing their ass for you. I couldn't do that. That's why I'm not a rich man. I have no regrets.

I work in an office with thirty people. I swear I really know only one or two. When it comes to feeling or real ideas, you hesitate to expose yourself, to say what you really feel or believe. I sometimes let out a howl of anger where I work, because of so many terrible things happening. I frame it as though it were a joke. As that Dow-Jones ticker goes by, nobody lifts a head to complain as you hear one kind of atrocity and another. I don't have as much trust in my fellow man as I once did. I have no trust in my peers. They're burnt-out cases. In the war, I was living alongside people I cared about. I was trying to do something useful with my life . . .

A QUIET LITTLE BOOM TOWN

Seneca, Illinois is seventy miles southwest of Chicago. The Illinois River, a tributary of the Mississippi, flows through. It is a sleepy little town, a Currier and Ives print come to life. It is Corn Belt country.
Between June 1942 and June 1945, 157 LSTs were built here.

ELSIE ROSSIO

Hers is a little gingerbread house. "My curio shop," she calls it. She is Spring Byington in appearance and manner. She has prepared a splendid country lunch.
A widow, she has lived in these parts all her life. "I remember the narrow wooden walks and the hitching posts. Everyone knew everyone."

Around late 1940, we began hearing rumors that the government was going to build a shipyard here. The men who did not have work were excited. We were still feeling the Depression. The trucks began rolling in with great loads of material. In my lifetime, we never had this traffic. Then came the new people, cars and cars and cars.

You'd hear the *rat-a-tat-tat* of hammering all night long. The traffic seemed to be going on all night, too. Even the dogs knew enough to hide. You didn't see them running across the street any more. People didn't stand on the street and visit like they used to.

At the time we were only about a thousand people. One restaurant, an old hotel, that was all. All of a sudden Seneca and the surrounding area had about 27,000. You would wake up in the morning and someone would be rolled up in a blanket on your front porch. Everybody took in boarders. Then the government built barracks and new housing for the workers.

The merchants did very well. It was so crowded that we had to stand in line the longest time with our ration books and food stamps. We weren't used to this. On the whole, the feeling toward the new people was good, although there was some resentment here and there. Many came from the South and we heard all sorts of strange accents. I found it interesting.

The merchants were slightly conservative. They made a good deal of money, but they didn't brag or show off. They didn't begin to drive Lincolns and that sort of thing. They continued their old life-style. They made money, but they didn't show it.

The taverns were the ones who did really well. On Friday and Saturday nights it was exciting. Strange as it seems, there weren't too many fights. These were older men. The younger were in the service.

Oh yes, the war changed my life. I went to work in a doctor's office. Otherwise, I would have lived my life out keeping house and washing clothes. I enjoyed the work.

When the war ended, the shipyards people went back home and we went back to our old ways.

GEORGIA GLEASON

Marseilles, Illinois is five miles away.
A print of Buffalo Bill is on the wall, and a large Holy Bible is on the coffee table.

I believe Mr. Toopes was responsible for bringing in the government work. He managed the Chicago Bridge and Iron that built river barges before the war. When all the people came in, he opened up the grill and I got the job as cook. Before that, they'd go to the grocery, get cold meats and milk, and sit on the curbstones to eat. It was that crowded.

I'd start out at four-thirty in the morning and work till one. Then I'd come back at night and bake fifty to eighty pies. That was every night. We served between 900 and 1,200 people a day. We were using sixty dozen eggs for breakfast, besides the ham, the bacon, and the pancakes. Oh, it was hard work, but I was young in those days.

People were apprehensive, frightened of the strangers. They weren't used to all this commotion. It boomed just overnight. And the money came in so suddenly. It was a poor little community, and all of a sudden there's everything. They got over the fright because of the money.

When the war ended, Seneca settled back to being Seneca again. Just a little country town. The people who lived here were conservative and hung on to what they had made. Whereas the people who came from Oklahoma and Kansas and Alabama didn't take anything back with them. They spent it as fast as they got it.

What bothered most people about the war was the rationing. They couldn't have everything they wanted. But they all survived it. It was fun, being young, with all that excitement.

AT THE BAR

It is a quiet afternoon. An overweight farmer is the only other patron.

On Friday nights, it was three deep at the bar. You couldn't get near it. That was payday. The slot machines were always busy. We never had slot machines till the war. Now we know all about one-armed bandits. (Laughs.) I don't remember any hookers comin' to town. They didn't need 'em, because there were a couple of cathouses in the town ten miles away.

I just turned eighteen and got a job at the shipyards. What I remember is the merchants forgot their old customers, with all that money comin' in. Like cigarettes. They gave us all those bad brands and kept the good brands for the outsiders. They were spendin' more money than we were, that's why. Can't blame 'em too much. When the shipyards closed down, they had to go back to the old customers. We just went back to the old ways. The war didn't change us at all.

POSTSCRIPT: *Elsie Rossio tried her hand at poetry to commemorate the coming of the shipyards to Seneca. The first appeared in the local paper in 1940:*

> *For overnight my hometown has become a teeming tide*
> *Of trailers, trucks, and lumber, and folks from far and wide.*

Yes, Seneca's a boom town, working for defense,
For Uncle Sam and Freedom, and the project is immense.

Everyone is making money, renting rooms and trailer space;
And it really is our duty to find these folks a place.
So I don't mean to be disloyal, but just between you and me,
I know I'll miss the easy ways of the town that used to be.

Everyone has made some money; some have saved and some have lost;
But the LSTs have given recompense for every cost.
So I revise my past opinion, and just between you and me,
It will be sort of hard to get used to the town that used to be!

GEORGE C. PAGE

Millions of visitors have been impressed by the George C. Page Museum of La Brea Discoveries. The house of paleontological findings is a monument to the donor's enterprise and philanthropy.

His home, an estate, past the gates and winding roads of greenery, offers an all-encompassing view of the city. Greeting you at the door is not Citizen Kane; rather, he is a slight, small-boned man, built along the lines of Frank Craven, the celebrated narrator of Our Town.

A Horatio Alger hero, he had come out of the Nebraska plains to Los Angeles, a sixteen-year-old farm boy with $2.30 in his jeans. "I was a born entrepreneur." As a busboy and soda jerk, "I moonlighted from seven in the morning until midnight and saved $1,000."

In southern California's tropical fruits, exotic to the rest of the country, he envisioned an enterprise: the holiday tradition of sending fruit packages in fancily wrapped gift boxes and baskets. Mission Pak, beginning with one rented store, grew, in twenty-eight years, to more than a hundred. A thousand people were employed.

Just before the war, I got into industrial development. It was discouraging in the beginning. They called it "Page's Folly." The prevailing wisdom was "He made it in fruit but he'll lose it in these buildings." I had acquired a thirty-eight-acre parcel of property in the south part of Los Angeles. I had no success at all in selling these sites. No takers.

So I built models of 10,000-, 20,000-, and 30,000-foot industrial plants of brick. This was toward the beginning of the war, and the government was handing out defense contracts. Immediately, I had people wanting to rent. They were short-term leases, for a year or two. There was no telling how long things would last.

I went ahead and built more and larger buildings. The tenants were now asking for 50,000- and 100,000-foot plants. I soon had Northrop Corporation, Hughes Aircraft, National Cash Register, and a number of other blue-chip tenants, all on short leases. The banks shook their heads: I was taking a big gamble, they said. It worked out. When their leases were up, they had spent so much on electronic equipment and improvements that they couldn't afford to move. I was able to increase the rent each time the leases were renewed. It became an extremely lucrative business.

In the meantime, I had bought lots along the Malibu oceanfront. It was during the war, when people were afraid the Japanese might invade. Everything was dark along the beach. I bought them for $30 a running foot. Later on, I sold them for $300 a foot. A tenfold profit, but I sold them too soon. Today, those same lots are worth $6,000 a running foot. I had reasoned that more lots could be made inland, unlimited, as they terraced the foothills. But the number of beach lots was absolutely restricted. There were just so many. They couldn't do other than go up. My only mistake was I didn't keep them long enough.

When the war came along, I was of an age when I could have been drafted. I thought I should contribute more than just operate a luxury nonessential business. I went to the proper authorities and asked what I could do. They said, You have a packing house. We desperately need frozen and dehydrated food. We'll gladly send you to Berkeley to learn how to make one or the other. I made the unfortunate choice of deciding on dehydration. I reasoned that dehydrated products were so concentrated that there would be a good demand after the war as well.

It turned out that after the war, people were not interested. One of the reasons was that in Guadalcanal and other such places, they didn't realize that a five-gallon can could feed five hundred men, it was so concentrated. A dozen or twenty men would take a cupful of river water with no seasoning—they developed a hatred for dehydrated products. When they came back, I hardly dared mention dehydrated foods. However, during the war, it worked out very well. I made millions of pounds. We shipped a lot to Russia and other countries.

When the fighting ended, the government weaseled out of the contracts with me. Noncancelable, I thought. They sent inspectors out. They'd take a handful of carrots and say I had too many imperfect tubes and reject the lot. Here I was stuck with a mountain of these large five-gallon tins of carrots. Fortunately, I had a restaurant friend, the one I had worked for years ago as a busboy. He took some of the tins off my hands and came up with the idea of the carrot cake. It became so popular that other bakers used it. Every pound of those carrots was taken off my hands. I got out of everything.

I still continued Mission Pak in half the building. We had restrictions on metal at the time. So I went to Fresno and bought little pieces of equipment from packing companies and improvised. It was all successful.

Sugar was rationed during the war. I learned to use honey as a substitute. It wasn't rationed and I was able to keep all the bees of California busy. (Laughs.) The price of honey was frozen, so they could charge only five cents a pound for it. In that way, I was able to keep going in my candied-fruit business.

I have never had an investment where I have lost much, if anything. If I had been more greedy and willing to gamble, I could have had industrial plants all across the United States. I could have been the richest man in the cemetery very easily. But I have an underdeveloped want gland. I can sleep in only one bed and eat three meals a day. There's a limit. I like to keep my life simple.

I've thrown the lion's share of my estate into a foundation. The tax gobblers can't touch it. After having the fun of making money, I now have the fun of giving it away.

LEE OREMONT

He had been a certified public accountant, living in Los Angeles. "I drifted into the supermarket business. I had a client who had a small chain of markets. I joined him in 1938 as comptroller and became a partner in 1942."

The Depression ended with the war in Europe. The market business at once ceased to be competitive. The problem of making money disappeared. It became automatic. The immediate concern was how to avoid taxes. All of a sudden, there was an excess-profits tax. It was avoided by increasing officers' salaries, inflating expense accounts, and handing out large bonuses. I remember salesmen coming in to sell you gadgets or systems. Their first selling point was: "It doesn't matter. Uncle Sam pays most of it anyway." You could spend money very freely. It was the government's money.*

When we started out, our net worth was $65,000. I told my partner, with all the problems coming up—rationing, shortages, labor scarcity—if we could hold on to this at the end of the war, we'd have done a good job. Instead, business jumped crazily. You could sell anything you got, it just walked off the shelves.

It was hard to get certain merchandise. Bags, for instance, were in short supply. You did without. Customers brought their own shopping bags. Every shortage became an added profit. If you were short of help, you did with less. You couldn't get new equipment, you used old stuff. The net result was substantial profits. During our first year, we made $100,000 out of a net worth of $65,000.

People had defense jobs, money. If they had problems with cars and gas, they splurged on food. We had price controls, so liquor was scarce. We once managed to get five hundred cases of Ancient Age pints, as a favor from the distillers. We had probably bought some worthless Argentine rum from them. We limited it one pint to a customer, and we had a line waiting outside two blocks long. The same thing with cigarettes, stockings. You sold all you could get.

We bought five hundred cases of canned pears from some outfit in Philly. At the time, they weren't rationed, they had no points. They were terrible. The labels all but warned they were unfit for human consumption. By the time they were delivered, the government had announced they'd be rationed the following week. We were cleaned out of these awful pears in one day. The stuff just jumped off the shelves.

We had a buyer who had meat connections. He had made arrange-

*As a radio disk jockey in 1944–45, I was encouraged by my sponsor, a mob-controlled beer company, to buy as many recordings as I wanted, no matter how expensive, and never mind the cost. I spent $500 one memorable afternoon at my favorite music store. I reported to my sponsor, somewhat self-consciously. He laughed: "You're cheap, kid. You only set us back seventy-five clams. The Uncle takes care of the rest."

ments with some independent packer to get several carloads. He probably paid the man a couple of cents a pound under the table. We leased a store for only one week. It had been shut down since the Depression. We opened the meat department only. It was sold out in two days.

Meat had become extremely scarce with rationing. It was available, but it took black-market money. I had problems with that. With my upbringing, it was against my grain. In the second place, we were doing well enough. We didn't need to go out on a limb and risk jail in order to make a good thing a little better. In the third place, I was an accountant. I couldn't figure out how you could get the money to pay under the table—big money—without reporting sales. So we had very little meat most of the time. But we got by very well.

The meat business was in small hands locally. Your major packers —Swift, Armour, Cudahy—weren't black-marketing, as far as I know. They had no need to. But many of the independents were doing business out of their pockets. They were buying and selling with cash under the table. Between conscience and fear, we managed to do fine without black-marketing. We started with two stores and wound up with twelve by '45.

Before the war, competition was hard. You often ran an ad offering an item below cost to attract customers. You'd give things away. Now they were crowding in and taking whatever you had to offer. It was the difference between a thin-margin business and a highly profitable one.

It didn't take a genius to make money during the war. I know a number of people who still think it was their brilliance that made them so successful. They get pontifical and tell you how efficient they were, how hard-working and smart. Bullshit. They happened to be in the right place at the right time. All you had to do was to open a store and not get dead drunk. You had customers ready and willing and able to buy all you could get. It didn't take any brains or hard work. If it was true of smaller firms, imagine how it worked for the big ones.

We were offered a chance to invest in a housing development. Our stores were in the heart of the aircraft industry. We put in $15,000. In six months, we got double. We were just small investors. The builders were getting financing from the government. They built tracts in ninety days. They started out selling the houses for $4,000. By the time they were ready, they were getting $6,000. That extra money was just clear profit. Right now, those houses are easily $60,000.

I'm really pissed off by people who have such horror of price controls. Price controls really saved us from a devastating inflation. I don't think they went up more than five percent. In spite of being violated in a chickenshit way by black marketeers. Overall, prices didn't go up. Interest rates were down.

They had a drive to sell war bonds. We bought a $100,000 bond. The Bank of America lent us $95,000 at two percent. The bond paid two-and-half percent. We made one-half percent for underwriting the government. And we got our picture in the papers for doing a great patriotic service.

The regulation that is today called oppressive turned out to be beneficial for the very ones rapping it. If you complied. I remember a supermarket convention. Everybody was tossing darts at the government man about all the red tape. He came back: "We'd have no trouble making a simple one-paragraph regulation if you fellows only tried to live by it. But the minute we make a regulation, you guys hire a lawyer or an accountant to try to figure out how to get around it. So we have to think about defeating your machinations, and a simple regulation becomes a three-page document."

Most of the money made during the war was done legitimately: playing pretty much according to the rules and bitching all the way to the bank.

All of a sudden, I myself became a businessman. I never believed the money was going to stay with me. I came out of the Depression. I thought it was just play money and would disappear.

I think the war was an unreal period for us here at home. Those of us who lost nobody at the front had a pretty good time. The war was not really in our consciousness as a war. In spite of the fact that I think I'm politically aware, I never had the personal worry of somebody in real danger. We suddenly found ourselves relatively prosperous. We really didn't suffer.

THE BIG PANJANDRUM

THOMAS G. (TOMMY THE CORK) CORCORAN

During FDR's first two terms, he and Ben Cohen were special advisers to the President, "troubleshooters." They were known as the wonder boys. "Ben thinks of himself as a high priest, a Cohen who believes in the perfectibility of man. I'm just an old-fashioned Roman Catholic who believes in original sin." (Laughs.)

At the time of this conversation in his Washington, D.C. office, he had been a successful corporation lawyer for many years. He was ebullient, uninhibited; his words flowed freely.

He died December 6, 1981.

I worked like hell for FDR when he ran for the third term. He called me in one day and said, "Tommy, cut out this New Deal stuff. It's tough to win a war." He'd heard complaints from the people who could produce the tanks and other war stuff. As a payoff, they required an end to what they called New Deal nonsense. I helped run the campaign against Willkie in '40 and then I quit. Ben and I felt since the New Deal was through, we'd better get out of the way.

My first client was Henry Kaiser.* Henry and I got the magnesium plant going. With government assistance. What do you know? The goddamn plant blew up. (Laughs.)

By great luck, along comes Chennault.† Eight months before Pearl Harbor, I was put into the China war. (Laughs.) And putting Ameri-

---

*"Kaiser [a shipbuilder] revealed a flair for borrowing necessary capital against still unrealized income, for acquiring raw materials according to a precise timetable, for organizing groups of workers in transitory communities to which he provided better services than usual and from which he evoked strong loyalties and steady performance. He also proved his skill in negotiations with government officials. . . . He managed, too, to enlist, as one Washington agent, that incomparable lobbyist, the former New Deal wonder boy, Thomas G. Corcoran." (John Morton Blum, *V Was for Victory* [New York: Harcourt Brace Jovanovich, 1977], p. 112).

†General Claire Chennault, an admirer of Chiang Kai-shek "and a romantic about the potentialities of air power in the war in China" (ibid., p. 269).

---

can fliers in planes. I was put in China Defense Supplies. The front man was Frederick Delano, the President's uncle. I was always sent out as the fellow who put difficult people together and got them to play ball.

Long before Pearl Harbor, everybody was concerned with the Japanese invasion of Manchuria. The British had always seen the Japanese as their counter against the Russians. They wanted somebody else to fight the Japanese and then move in. (Laughs.) Eventually, the British began to see that as the Japanese moved down, the British market in the Far East was periled. And Hong Kong was periled. So they came around.

Chennault and I were in this China racket. We sent the Flying Tigers over eight months before Pearl Harbor. Chennault went back to China, and I helped him form an American-managed airline, Air America. That's how I got involved in the whole Pacific business. Detaching Southeast Asia from the communist philosophy is the most important thing we've got. I have a hunch that we're the repository of the civilized forces that are left in the world. I was in a completely new world over there, with the Chinese and Singapore and Malaya and the rest of it. It was the great adventure of my life.

Look at the maps. (He indicates maps on the wall.) I still believe maps tell you more than all the books in the world. See where the green stuff is? See in China? That's the only place where there's fertile land. See Manchuria up there? Where the coal mines are. See little Formosa? Formosa is a fixed airplane carrier. As long as it's in our pocket—not in our pocket, I don't use that word—as long as it's with us—goddamn it, I'm so fascinated by the Far East, I can't tell you.

I always represented clients who were somehow connected with what I thought was a development possibility. I was in the business of getting gas out of Canada, gas out of Mexico. I was in the business of working out the problems of the first nuclear ships. All my clients have been the most interesting people. You see, I was an idealist, but I believed in arithmetic.

Oh, I was very active. I set to do this South American job. They were worried about how you take the Argentines. (Once again, he indicates the map.) See that? This resource business starts with agriculture and then becomes mining along the coast here. The Germans went in early into the colonization of Latin America. The English were there first. But there was this famous German company called Bayer, which discovered the coke-tar derivative Novocain. All the rest of these things, particularly Atabrine, were German inventions. Bayer controlled the whole chemical business of Latin America. Roosevelt knew that the funds which supported German propaganda in Latin America were all derived from their monopoly of the pharmaceutical business.

Atabrine was the only antimalarial there was. So I was asked to go down and do that job. I fished my brother out, who'd been in Asia for eight years as the representative of American automobile interests in Japan. General Motors. I put him in charge of it. He did one hell of a job. We pushed Bayer out and started the penetration of the American pharmaceutical industry around the world.

We created a new company and went in and beat 'em. Bayer had been a high-priced outfit, but didn't know anything about radio advertising. So we introduced it into Latin America. We gave a little nightclub performer, Evita, her first radio contract. (Laughs.) Way before she ever got mixed up with Perón. We'd take a sound truck with a radio program and we'd run it all through the back country. We took the goddamn place over.

I wasn't too excited about the Atlantic war. The Europeans are gonna fight among themselves. They'll never get together. There was a period when Churchill wanted very much to have the Irish in the war and give him submarine bases on the southern coast. The row about the Irish was very deep in New York. Roosevelt didn't invite Jim Farley to the reception for the King and Queen of Britain up at Hyde Park. That's when their split began.

Joe Kennedy, we know, was against the war.

I knew a great deal about Joe. Joe said, "You know perfectly well that the British can't hold Hitler." Of course, that's why we took the Russians in. No matter how bravely they handled it, there wasn't enough power left in Britain to handle Hitler, unless he were diverted by the Russians.

Joe used to say, at that time, that the British should have made a deal to preserve their empire. Let Hitler get rid of the Russians. Let him take over Europe if he was gonna. Somehow, he said, we could have dealt with German totalitarianism in some way. We could have assassinated Hitler, but we can never do business with Russian totalitarianism. I was always a little bit afraid of Joe.

I was always suspicious of the Russian link. Harry Hopkins said to me, "Tommy, the trouble with you is you're too Irish to trust the British and you're too goddamn Catholic to trust the Russians." (Laughs.) I had no doubt that we'd eventually win the war, but I always wondered what the Russians were gonna do. I know it didn't come out the way we thought it would.

I was always on the edges of things (laughs), never completely responsible, but always the fellow who tried to fix little things that happened.

POSTSCRIPT: *Tim Corcoran, Tommy's son, is also a member of Corcoran, Youngman and Rowe. "I was born in April 1942. The story they all told me was that Marshal Timoshenko, at the time, was defending Moscow from the Germans. Although my Christian name is Thomas, they nicknamed me Tim, because I was such a red baby. (Laughs.) All my baby clothes, I'm told, had 'Timoshenko' on them."*

JAMES ROWE

Tommy Corcoran's partner at Corcoran, Youngman and Rowe. "I worked for Corcoran in a variety of New Deal agencies. I eventually came to the White House and worked for Roosevelt, from 1938 till '51. Moved over to the Justice Department for two years, went into the navy, and was never in government again." (Laughs.)

When I joined the navy in early '43, Washington was changing. To use Roosevelt's phrase, it was Dr. Win the War instead of Dr. New Deal. It upset the New Dealers. We had a big PWA building program. Roosevelt took a big chunk of that money and gave it to the navy to build ships. I was shocked. All the New Dealers were shocked.

A large number of businessmen came down as dollar-a-year men. Men who knew how to run industry. Roosevelt was taking help anyplace he could get it. Before we were actually in the war, he was building a large staff. Jimmy Byrnes, Fred Vinson, and all that crowd came to the White House to work purely on war problems. There was a quick change into a war economy.

When Bill Knudsen of General Motors was running the show down here, we used to check on the businessmen. Find out if they were

Democrats or Republicans. They were always Republicans. (Laughs.) One time Roosevelt had to sign the list of appointees, he gave up and let Knudsen do it. He said, "Bill, you fellows slipped. I found a Democrat." Knudsen said, "Don't worry, Mr. President, he's a Willkie Democrat." (Laughs.)

The New Dealers were still trying to carry out many of the reforms. The businessmen were trying to get on as they always did. The conflict was sharpest in the antitrust laws. Exemptions were given to business to, in effect, violate the laws, with the promise they wouldn't be prosecuted. Thurman Arnold has been the great trust-buster. Because of this, he retired and became a federal judge. He claims he was bumped.

As a young New Dealer, I believed business had been a bad influence on the country. In a sense, they were pretty incompetent before Roosevelt came in. When I was in Justice, we were always on their tails, prosecuting them. I used to see quite a few of them. Now I work for them. (Laughs.)

Over the years, I've changed. We get a little more conservative as we get older. I remember Tommy said, "I really don't have too much faith in you." I said, "Why?" He said, "You're really a government lawyer. It'll take years to change you around." I think he was right about that. I got to switch around. Eventually, the government clips one of your clients, you think unfairly, and you say, "Why, those bastards." By the time you get to my stage, you're against the government—as are a great number of lawyers here, all of whom came from the government.

You get rather fond of the people who pay you.

I think the war itself made a difference. Roosevelt was struggling pretty hard and he couldn't move the country very far. He told me once, just before Pearl Harbor, that he was quite discouraged because he was told the Japanese ships were moving south into Indonesia and he couldn't send the navy after them. The country wouldn't stand for it. Along came Pearl Harbor and it unified us. I have a son who did not go to Vietnam, went to college instead. He always said, "If it were your war, I'd fight it."

There came this great burst after the war, a very prosperous time. The working man got his own house, his car, his refrigerator, and became middle-class. These damn Republicans win elections these days because the New Deal picked up the working man and gave him a chance. He's now conservative.

In the spring of 1941, I was put in charge of organizing price control. There had been a huge increase in prices—a doubling—that left us with a fear of inflation. In retrospect, it was exaggerated. I was there until the middle of 1943. It was a watershed in my life. I went in as a young, unknown economist and came out of it with a nationwide reputation, for good or evil.

Among us, there was a sense of collegial loyalty to Roosevelt that had existed before the war. We were for strong measures of conversion to war production. The foot-dragging was associated with those whose loyalty to FDR was not so great. Our proudest mark was that we were Roosevelt men.

There is with World War Two no memory of inflation. Unlike World War One and Vietnam. It was partly due to our coming out of the Depression. There was an enormous opportunity for expanding output as distinct from raising prices. In the war years, consumption of consumer goods doubled. Never in the history of human conflict has there been so much talk of sacrifice and so little sacrifice. Another thing was the mood of the country. The war, unlike Vietnam, had almost unanimous support from the people. There was a strong objection to people who tried to circumvent controls. There was a black market, but it was small. There were troublesome moments in the case of meat, but there was a great deal of obloquy attached to illegal behavior.

We greatly feared we'd hold the prices and see a decline in quality. It didn't materialize. Manufacturers, protecting their trademarks, were unwilling to risk reducing quality. There was a certain flow of shoddy goods, but it was unimportant.

We had a problem with women's hosiery. We attempted to set standards on rayon hose, a substitute then for unavailable silk and nylon. That produced a storm. The Wholesale Dry Goods Institute had powerful spokesmen on the Hill. They were always looking for us.

The canners set up a major row when we tried to couple price control with the grading of canned goods. That produced a political storm, too. We feared it would reduce the number of peas in the can. It didn't happen.

What we discovered in 1942 was that we couldn't fix prices one at a time. I was given the job on the basis of a paper I had written. It was wrong in nearly all its details. It concluded that consistency was the last resort of a small mind. It didn't take long for my attitude to change. We had started limiting controls to things in particularly short supply, which might be rationed: things especially vulnerable to war demand. We found that was administratively impossible and inequitable. People who had their prices fixed looked at those who didn't and wondered why.

In the spring of 1942, we put into effect the General Maximum Price Regulation, which fixed them all. Exceptions were some farm prices, protected by law. In special hardship cases, we eased back and adjusted as circumstances required. Chester Bowles, who had succeeded Prentiss Brown as over-all price administrator—Leon Henderson was the first—conducted some of the first polling ever done by the United States government. It always showed huge public support.

Those who had their prices fixed, especially farmers, continued to complain. They were quite bitter as well as politically powerful. It took very few cattlemen in Washington to keep you from feeling lonesome. The farmers had suffered two decades of very bad prices. With the war came a chance to retrieve. The barrier was price control. There was a good deal of opposition from them.

We also had trouble with the smaller, more dispersed industries where the market was competitive and the producers numerous. The larger companies were much easier to handle; they already had control of their prices. And there weren't very many of them to deal with. I once laid down a law: There is no great problem in fixing prices that are already fixed. Anyway, they were reaping gains in that their costs were controlled and in the enormous expansion of output.

Price control was in effect until 1946. If it hadn't been for price control, we would have had doubling and tripling of prices, no question about it. There has been little appreciation of how great inflationary pressures would have been in the absence of controls, including restraints on wages. The pressures were great on all of us in the matter of rationing, as well.

In 1942, we put into effect coffee rationing. It was extremely unpopular, especially in the Scandinavian and German communities. In retrospect, we perhaps shouldn't have done it. We should have left coffee to the market. There would have been less antagonism to shortages than to regulated supply.

Leon Henderson was one of the unsung heroes of World War Two. He had been the administrator of prices and civilian supply as well as a powerful figure on the War Production Board. There has been an enormous literature on Albert Speer and the way he was presumed to have organized German production. Henderson, with a few younger colleagues, of whom I was privileged to be one, organized the United States far more effectively than Germany had ever been. The man whose organization failed is celebrated, while the man who had in mind the successful national venture is lost to history. Day after day, he came back wearily from meetings, having fought the battle for some necessary action against recalcitrant trade associations, business executive types.

The businessmen who came to Washington were generally industrial bureaucrats, public relations types, who could best be spared at home. There were many times when we nearly forgot there was a war going on. Our conflict with them was not ideological. It was over the fact that they never wanted to move. We have a public picture of the businessman as a dynamic figure, always ready for action. His wartime image was somebody who could never bring himself to action as the situation required. He would come to the conference and say, "Let us wait awhile. I think this is something we can accomplish on a voluntary basis. I'm sure business will see its responsibilities. This is not a time for radical action." We really had to fight them all the way.

JOE MARCUS

"Though the public had not accepted it yet, Washington was convinced we had to be ready for war. Roosevelt had set up a National Defense Advisory Committee. There had already been a big increase in England's demand for military goods."

A New Deal economist, he was appointed in 1940 head of the Civilian Requirements Division. "If, say, we buy ten billion dollars worth of military goods, what would the civilian requirements be?"

Most of my time was spent fighting with representatives of industry. Did we have the capacity to make enough steel, enough copper, for military as well as civilian needs? Our reports showed we didn't. The top industrial boys resisted this very strongly. They had gone through the Depression and, from their standpoint, there was an excess of capacity. They weren't going to fiddle around, increasing the capacity just because some screwball kids tell them they don't have enough.

What happens in a severe depression is that your consumption goes down, say, twenty percent. With a decrease in construction and in the demand for machinery by about eighty percent, it's devastating. From '32 to '39, there is recovery. But there are still ten or eleven million unemployed. The production of consumer goods is still low. All they're doing is replacing worn-out equipment. Why add more machinery? Why build more factories? Let's say they have the capacity to produce 80 million tons of steel and the demand is for only 70 million. Why should they listen to some screwballs in Washington who say, If there's a war, you're going to need 150 million tons?

We were young New Dealers who found the military in their planning stodgy and backward. They thought we didn't have the industrial capacity to produce more than, say, 5 billion dollars worth of military goods. So a group of us wrote a memorandum showing that there were so many unemployed, so much machine-tool capacity, that it was possible to produce 75 billion dollars worth. It flew in the face of the military statements.

Roosevelt had that memo on his desk on the day of Pearl Harbor. When he reorganized the War Production Board, with Donald Nelson as head, he insisted that the boys who wrote the memo watch the program. He set up two committees on the board. One was planning. The other was program progress control. I was yanked out of my previous job and made program progress control officer. (Laughs.)

When we got into the war, everything was a mess. Suddenly you've got to produce an enormous number of planes, tanks, build an eleven-million-man army, supply the British and, soon afterwards, the Russians. And the Free French. We needed an enormous jump in production. There was a bottleneck: machine tools.

Nelson got on the radio and said the machine-tool producers were not doing their job. They were not working around the clock, not working three shifts. The Machinery and Allied Products Institute, the trade association, says to Nelson, We can't run three shifts. Nelson tells them not to bother him, to talk to the guy who wrote the speech. So they came to see me.

Now my studies were based on statistics. I don't know how to build a machine tool. I barely knew one machine tool from another.

(Laughs.) They insisted I make a tour of the machine-building industries. I accepted the invitation. I came back with my report: the Machinery and Allied Products Institute was wrong. I had visited factories across the street from each other, one working three shifts, one working one shift. Now they wanted me to take over planning and controls for the tool industry. (Laughs.)

I hesitated. It was a challenge: I was a critic, now I had to do something. It was a question of the war, too. I felt it was important. I was young. I was Jewish. I had never met a payroll. So I accepted the challenge.

Here I was, an outsider, reorganizing the whole goddamn thing. It was insane the way they were operating. You take government people: they don't know where the hell the factories are, don't know the possibilities. You take the industry people: they're concerned about their business after the war, doing things the way they have traditionally done it. They had no sense of the war needs and planning.

The heads of these divisions were dollar-a-year men. They kept their company salaries. They were the leaders of industry. Now, down below, you had heads of companies who actually knew their business. You also had guys the industry wanted to get rid of, executives they didn't know what to do with. Washington wants someone in charge of ball bearings? Send this clown there.

The first job I tackled was machine tools. Say an auto factory, an airplane factory, had all the lathes it needed but didn't have milling machines. Another factory, making tanks, was all ready to go with milling machines but didn't have lathes. I looked into it: how did they distribute these machines? I discovered it was done on the basis of conflicts within the military forces themselves. The army wanted machine tools for army products, the navy wanted theirs, the air force theirs. Ten percent went to one, five to another, three to a third. It made no sense. It had no connection to what the actual needs were. Someone had to take over, to allocate machine tools on a priority system. So I did. I couldn't have done it without support from some of the top people who really understood. It was a way of thinking different from what they'd been accustomed to. Others, well . . .

They all were patriotic, but in different ways. Many worried about how their regular customers would react. If I said, Send this abrasive to such and such a firm which was not their standard customer and wouldn't be after the war, don't send it to one which had been their customer, they were bothered—and how! Many fights took place.

In the early days, some of these industrialists wouldn't sign major military contracts until they had the right kind. The right kind? When the war ends, who's stuck with the supplies? What payment do we get when you terminate? Who's gonna pay when we move it out? They wanted to make sure of every cent of profit.

The concessions in these contracts was the biggest thing of all. The war had to be won. Dr. New Deal—with all of FDR's talk about economic royalists—goodbye. Dr. Win The War, hello. The government gives in. The military, of course, is much more sympathetic to business. They feel more comfortable with them. They're the same kind of boys. (Laughs.)

The railroad industry didn't like what I was doing. They brought in their own people with Dun & Bradstreet reports. Everything, they said, was fine. My report remained downstairs. One day, Bernard Baruch shows up. He starts to yell at the top guys of the War Production Board: "You guys aren't doing anything. You're not prepared. There's not enough steel, not enough copper, not enough aluminum." So they rushed down and got me to come up with my report. To show him they were thinking about it. (Laughs.) That's the only time they ever paid any attention to my reports.

One of my early reports showed that there won't be enough railroad cars to move the wheat, the iron ore, the coal because an awful lot of cars were in disuse, needed repairs. We must build more cars. Otherwise, when push comes to shove, there'll be no way to move things around unless we have government controls. Well, do you know that my report, an internal report, was used by the Association of American Railroads in full-page ads in the *Washington Post,* all over? Scare headlines: Socialism proposed by the government.

Pearl Harbor comes along. We're at war. A system of controls of raw material is set up. According to priorities. At that point, guys from the Association of American Railroads come to see me. They want to wine and dine me. They say, "You understand our problem. Will you help us get our allocation of steel? Otherwise, we can't repair the cars." I did help them. But do you know they were so stupid, they never really did it right, as far as I'm concerned. There's resistance in industry to the idea of planning. Comes the big crisis, they'll learn.

We were a group of young people, idealistic, who came in with the New Deal. We were not career-minded. When it came to the New

Deal, we carried out its basic principles. When it came to the war, it was to win it. That meant getting production out. It was as simple as that. Though we worked with big industrialists, we were not subservient to them. We understood their problems, but we had the nerve to fight 'em on policy matters.

Roosevelt dies. Truman is President. The seeds of the cold war had already been planted. I saw an awful lot of things. Cables came over my desk. Part of the Lend-Lease was supposed to go to the Russians. This was one of the major areas of—I won't call it sabotage—of things going wrong in the War Production Board. Machines would get broken. Orders would get lost. Allocations weren't made properly.

There were two important secret projects. They had code names. One was the Manhattan Project. We all know what that is now. The other was the Arctic Circle Project. I didn't know what the hell it was. Certain kinds of industrial chains were needed by the Russians for pulleys on ships or something like that. I was supposed to worry about these things. Seems like a simple thing. It had White House priority. Top. The decision was made to build a factory to make that chain. I don't recall it ever being built.

Five percent of machine tools were to go to the Russians under Lend-Lease. This was violated again and again. There were always problems. Shortly after the end of the war, the question of a loan to Russia came up. Generals and ambassadors were all sending cablegrams: Don't do it without making demands. Along with the wartime alliance was an underlying antagonism, that these guys were bastards, that we're gonna have to tangle with 'em. Oh, I felt that cold war coming in my bones.

The first casualty of the cold war was debate on foreign policy. It was eliminated. It was simply assumed that the Soviet Union is the enemy. Let's go from there, why debate it? We knew all the answers. We knew how Third World countries could develop best. We were the papa. We were in charge. It's seeped all through our society. The war devastated the rest of the world. We came through stronger than ever. So if the world's to be reconstructed, we'll do it.

The most single important legacy of the war is what Eisenhower warned us about in his farewell speech: the military-industrial complex. In the past, there were business representatives in Washington, but now they *are* Washington. And with the military buildup beyond all our imaginations, we have a new fusion of power. It has become a permanent feature of American life.

He had been President Roosevelt's emissary to Great Britain and to the Soviet Union in 1941. Later, he served as ambassador to the Soviet Union (1943–1946) and to Great Britain (1946).

He was preparing to celebrate his ninetieth birthday at the time of this conversation.

My job as Roosevelt's representative to Churchill was a simple one. He wanted me to recommend any aid that would, in his words, help Britain stay afloat. The big change came when we went from just giving aid to intervention.

Roosevelt was the one who had the vision to change our policy from isolationism to world leadership. That was a terrific revolution. Our country's never been the same since. The war changed everybody's attitude. We became international almost overnight.

I found that Churchill felt it was very important to help Stalin. I certainly agreed. There was that meeting at sea between Roosevelt and Churchill. I attended it. Churchill decided to send Beaverbrook* and Roosevelt decided to send me. We both went to Moscow in October 1941. We both agreed that Stalin was determined to hold out against the Germans. He told us he'd never let them get to Moscow. But if he was wrong, they'd go back to the Urals and fight. They'd never surrender. We became convinced that, regardless of Stalin's awful brutality and his reign of terror, he was a great war leader. Without Stalin, they never would have held.

Much of the aid we first gave to Russia we took away from what we promised Britain. So in a sense, Britain participated in a very real way in the recovery of Russia. After that, the Russians got mean. Poland, of course, was the key country. I remember Stalin telling me that the plains of Poland were the invasion route of Europe to Russia and always had been, and therefore he had to control Poland.

It was fear. He didn't want to see a united Germany. Stalin made it clear to me—I spoke with him many times—that they couldn't afford to let Germany build up again. They'd been invaded twice, and he wasn't willing to have it happen again.

There was a great hope with the United Nations. I was at the 1945

---

*Lord Beaverbrook, a powerful British newspaper publisher at the time.

meeting in San Francisco. I didn't expect quite as much as most people. I thought it would be of assistance, but I didn't expect it to solve the world's problems. I remember a meeting with a number of columnists of the day. I predicted we'd have trouble with the Soviet Union. Our ideas and their ideas were irreconcilable. I said we'd have to adjust our differences or else. I had dealt with the Soviet Union since 1926. I was under no illusions. Two men left the room and said, I won't listen to this warmonger any more. One was Raymond Gram Swing. He apologized to me inside of a year. The other was Walter Lippmann. He never apologized to anybody. (Laughs.) They couldn't believe that when the war was over the Russians wouldn't be friends of ours.

I haven't changed one iota from the position I took in 1945. We had to recognize that their objectives and ours were different. But we had to adjust our differences. We have to understand them. We can't assume that they're something they're not. It's my opinion that the Russian government today wants to come to an agreement on the most important subject: arms control.

The weaponry that came out of World War Two, nuclear weapons, is what has changed the world. We can no longer shake fists the way we used to.

There's a myth that Roosevelt gave Stalin Eastern Europe. I was with Roosevelt every day at Yalta. Roosevelt was determined to stop Stalin from taking over Eastern Europe. He thought they finally had an agreement on Poland. Before Roosevelt died, he realized that Stalin had broken his agreement. I didn't see FDR again after Yalta.

I think Stalin was afraid of Roosevelt. Whenever Roosevelt spoke, he sort of watched him with a certain awe. He was afraid of Roosevelt's influence in the world. If FDR had lived, the cold war wouldn't have developed the way it did, because Stalin would have tried to get along with Roosevelt.

FDR had a faculty of keeping negotiations open. Between Roosevelt and Stalin, I think negotiations would have gone on many months further. The cold war wouldn't have started so soon.

HAMILTON FISH

He was Republican congressman from New York from 1920 to 1945. He was chairman of the first congressional committee to investigate communism in the United States: 1930. It bore his name. His immediate successor was Congressman Martin Dies of Texas. The committee subsequently became known as HUAC (House Un-American Activities Committee).

"Dies wrote me a nice letter. He said, 'You're responsible for it. I want this known by everybody—you were the one started this whole investigation.' It was a beautiful letter."

He's about six feet six. His posture is soldierly, erect. Though there are but two others in the room, his grandson and I, his voice booms out orotundly; evocations of DeWolf Hopper offering "Casey at the Bat." He is addressing multitudes.

My family always backed any war we were in—once war was declared. I was outspoken against the Vietnam War because there was no declaration by the Congress of the United States. This is what the Communists wanted us to do, to get us down into the swamps and jungles and keep us there. If we declared war, we'd have won it in one year, because we'd have had the *right* to bomb 'em; that's war. We went in there with our hands tied and stayed for ten years. It was the most terrible, stupid thing we ever did. I backed 'em once we got in, 'cause I always back 'em.

Franklin Roosevelt took us into a war without telling the people anything about it. He served an ultimatum which we knew nothing about. We were forced into the war. It was the biggest cover-up ever perpetrated in the United States of America. But in 1941, December 8, the day after the Japanese . . . I made the first speech ever made in the halls of Congress over the radio. I'd been speaking every week to keep us out of war. The day after the attack, as ranking member of the rules committee, it was my duty to speak first. I damned the Japs and upheld Roosevelt's day of infamy. I called on all noninterventionists to go into the army until we defeated the Japs. For fifteen minutes I talked to twenty-five million people. People told me they cried after. I made the only speech because I took up the whole time allotted.

I'd led the fight for three years against Roosevelt getting us into war. I was on the radio every ten days, BIG radio. I stopped him until he issued this ultimatum. That is the greatest thing I did do in my life. He would have gotten us into the war six months or a year before Pearl Harbor. We would have been fighting those Germans, plus probably the Russians, 'cause they made a deal with them. EVERY

American family owes an obligation to me because we would have lost a million or two million KILLED. That's the biggest thing I ever did, and nobody can take it away from me.

Russia is our enemy and always will be because of jealousy of power. They wouldn't think one minute about pressing the button to kill one hundred million Americans.

Aren't you fearful that somebody here might also press the button?

NEVER! We're a God-fearing country. We have no enemies. We don't want any territory. They want to communize the world.

I'm not afraid of death. I know I have to think about the hereafter, so it doesn't bother me at all. I believe in God. It's been handed down to me in my family Bible. I think most Americans believe in some kind of God, in the heavens or somewhere inside you. It doesn't matter. My life has been a very happy one.

VIRGINIA DURR

A native Alabaman, she was among the first white southern advocates of civil rights. Her work and reputation extended beyond her state, often at a considerable personal expense.

During the war years, she lived in Washington where her husband, Clifford, had been counsel for the RFC and later for the FCC.

Until the Holocaust, I was really an innocent. I really believed that men were fundamentally good. Evil was something you had to fight, but it was not pervasive. I'd seen suffering in the South, but I still thought the world was a good place. The Holocaust changed my entire view of the world.

My father was a Presbyterian preacher who had gone to Germany to study the new theology. He was taught that the Bible was written by men and was not literally the word of God. He studied at the University of Heidelberg and at the University of Berlin. When he returned, he was expelled from the church because he would not swear that the whale swallowed Jonah and three days later spewed him up alive. So I came up with the feeling that the Germans and my father stood for the truth. I thought of the Germans as a civilized, kindly people—my father's word was *gemütlich*. When Hitler and the Holocaust came, I lost my innocence.

I was still fighting the poll tax in 1939 and '40. I still had cheap servants. That's one of the ironies of my life. My freedom was bought at the expense of black women, whom I paid the regular wage. Very little. I worked every day at the anti–poll tax office. We did get a bill through to relieve soldiers of the poll tax.

Mrs. Roosevelt was our supporter and friend. She told me, just as the war was getting under way, that Mr. Roosevelt could not do anything further on the race issue. He needed the support of southern senators in the war effort. All during the war, we kept the poll-tax fight going, though everybody was completely absorbed elsewhere.

A young English couple had come to Washington. Esmond and Decca Romilly.* His uncle was Winston Churchill. Esmond went up to Canada to join the Canadian Air Force. Could Decca stay with us until the baby was born? Word came that his plane was shot down. She refused to believe he was killed. She refused to go back home. Her sister Diana had married Oswald Mosley, the British fascist. Her other sister, Unity, had been a great friend of Hitler. Except for her sister Nancy, and the youngest, her family was fascist. When Churchill came over, the first thing he did was invite Decca to stay at the White House with her baby. He finally convinced her that Esmond was dead.

So we had an English refugee, an amazing person (laughs), and her baby. My mother had come to live with us. I had four children and another one on the way. And Mr. Yamasaki. He was Lowell Mellett's Japanese butler. Lowell was a member of the President's staff, with a hot line to the White House. The authorities didn't want a Japanese butler answerin' the phone. We found a job for him with a general, who wasn't scared of him a bit. He brought with him a wife and baby. (Laughs.)

We had a household of thirteen, fourteen people. There was a problem of food and ration books. The black women who had been my lifesavers working for $15 a week got jobs at the torpedo factory at $100 a month.

At this point, the FBI began to call on us almost every week. I had a Japanese national in the house. The British embassy was watching Decca because of her relatives. She was under suspicion, too. We

*Jessica Mitford.

were constantly monitored by the FBI. Usually two young men would ring the bell. They took away Mr. Yamasaki's radio and his camera. They came in one day and insisted on looking through his trunk. He was very embarrassed and pleaded with them not to do it. They found a false bottom. They were sure he was a Japanese spy. They ripped out the bottom of the trunk. What he had was a whole layer of Petty pictures. Girls with no clothes on. He and his wife were so humiliated.

We were under eternal vigilance. By that time, I took it casually. The children would cry out, "Mother, milkman's here!" "Mother, laundryman's here!" "Mother, the FBI's here!" (Laughs.) That was the beginning of our surveillance. Two years ago, they were still watchin' me.

We were great friends of Lyndon and Bird. I became very devoted to her. He was a big ole country boy in cowboy boots, who always voted against the poll-tax bill. I used to fuss at him, and he'd always put that long arm around you: "Honey, we ain't got the votes. I promise you the minute we get 'em, I'll pass that bill." In 1965, he did pass that bill. It took thirty years.

I was protected in many ways. My brother-in-law, Hugo Black, was on the Supreme Court. My husband was in a position of power on the RFC and the FCC. He was giving these people money to build defense plants. He was giving licenses, which meant fortunes. When you think of the money he doled out and how little we had . . . (Laughs.) He was a perfectly honest man. When we got back to Montgomery as poor as church mice, his brother asked him, "Why didn't you invest? You knew McDonnell Aircraft was going to receive billions. Why didn't you buy stock in it?" He said, "You can't take advantage of inside knowledge." His brother could never understand that. (Laughs.)

When we dropped the bombs on Hiroshima and Nagasaki, Mr. Yamasaki and his wife, Sayiko, came to us. She was one of the sweetest, gentlest people I've ever known in my life. They came into the living room and sat down. They said, "We hate to tell you this. You've given us a home and have been very nice to us, but we cannot stay here." I asked why. She said, "Twelve members of my family were evaporated in Nagasaki." He said, fifteen of his family. Made into atomic ash. They said, "We know that you are good people and you wouldn't have dropped the bomb, but we just can't stay with white Americans any more. We have to be with Japanese people." They left. I never felt so terrible in my life.

My brother-in-law, Justice Black, became quite irritated with me, having all these people in the house. He felt they'd try to get at him through me. That's exactly what happened. When Eastland was running for the Senate in Mississippi, he accused the Supreme Court of being influenced by communists, because it was going to integrate the schools. His slogan was, It's only one step from the schoolroom to the bedroom. He was actually aiming at Hugo, accusing us as his pawns. Eastland, who hated everything I stood for, was head of the Senate Internal Security Committee. He accused me of trying to overthrow the government.

When the war was over, we felt the United States was the most benevolent, the best, the most generous country in the world. I still had this feeling of triumph. It wasn't a year before everything had just turned upside down. McCarthyism started.

I sensed the cold war and its effect almost immediately. In every respect. We tried to revive the fight against the poll tax. We had offices in the Railway Building for free, because Senator Wheeler's daughter worked with us. He was a great friend of the railways. But they came to us and said, "You have too many blacks coming into your office. I'm afraid you have to leave."

We were working with all sorts of groups: women's, church, CIO, AF of L, ACLU, NAACP. A man from the Anti-Defamation League called up one day. They were prepared to help out. He said, "I have the attorney general's list. I want to make sure none of the people on it are allowed to attend meetings." At that point, I'd been tried enough. I got so mad. (Laughs.) I said, "You are the kind of Jew that made Hitler."

This was the breakup of the whole Roosevelt coalition. This was the beginning of the red-hunt and the hysteria. Cliff resigned in '48 and started a practice of his own. He immediately defended these people who were caught on the loyalty oath. His practice and eventually his health got completely broken up by red-baiting.

At this point his mother called from Alabama: "Come home, I've got a big house." Here she was, ninety years old and wasn't but four feet tall. She was a traditional southerner who didn't agree with anything we believed in, but she was devoted to her son. We went home and that's where we've been ever since.

Cliff would wake up every morning and say, "Thank God I'm in Alabama. Back here, I'm home. I know who the sons of bitches are and where the attacks are comin' from." As soon as he was able to open his law office, we got right in the middle of the whole civil rights fight. Martin Luther King. E. D. Nixon. We got Mrs. Parks out of jail. It was thrilling and exciting.

JOSEPH L. RAUH, JR.

Washington, D.C. "I'm a public-interest lawyer. Our little firm represents unions when we think they're right; union dissidents when we think they're wrong; poor districts that don't get enough money for education; black students and parents who want integrated schools. We represent those who can't buy representation."

He represented the Freedom Democratic Party in the 1964 Democratic Convention. "That was the end of segregation in the Democratic Convention."

There may be no such thing as a good war, but at least World War Two had a purpose. Washington in '39, '40 was like the rest of the country, confused, mixed up, didn't know what it wanted. We had a neutrality act that was ridiculous. It made sense only if you thought the whole world was the same. You couldn't make any distinction between England and France on one hand and Germany on the other.

In '40, I was in the Federal Communications Commission, just dyin' to get into the war. I did what we called Hatch Act work. Under the Hatch Act, no federal employee could work in politics. All I can say, brother, is that's all I did in 1940, 'cause I was for stoppin' Hitler, getting in. We used to joke about it: "What were you doin' last night?" "I was engaged in Hatch Act work."

In '41, I went to work for the Lend-Lease Administration. I had no reservations about being a hawk there. Most of the young New Dealers felt as I did.

In June of that year, I got a call from my boss, Wayne Coy: "Get your ass over here, we got a problem." I must've run ten blocks. I come in all out of breath and Coy says, "Some guy named Randolph is going to march on Washington unless we put out a fair employment practices order. Do you know how to write an executive order?" I said, "Sure, any idiot can write an executive order, but what do you want me to say?" He said, "All I know is the President says you gotta stop Randolph from marching." "What's it all about?" He says, "We got defense factories goin' up all over this goddamn country, but no blacks are bein' hired. Go down to the Budget Bureau and work something out."

By the next morning, we had a draft executive order saying that if you were a government contractor you had to nondiscriminate. We wrote this goddamn thing in about eighteen hours. I'm half dead, and Coy calls up: "It's not strong enough. Mrs. Roosevelt and LaGuardia are negotiating with A. Philip Randolph, and he says it's not strong enough. Come over here." We try again, strengthen it a bit. Same thing: Randolph says it isn't strong enough. I thought, Who is this bastard? Later, I became his lawyer. He had scared the government half to death. Finally, he did agree. It was issued as Order 8802. This was the first real executive blow for civil rights. It was the war that caused it.

Roosevelt wasn't a radical. He was really doing patchwork on the economy. When he badly beats Willkie in '40, you feel that shift from the Depression as a cloud to the war as a cloud. The big boys came down for the purpose of protecting their companies. We were trying to get less cars made and more tanks. We had automobile bastards come down here to fight that. There were some vicious bastards, but there were some good guys among them. The spirit of the time was national unity. So was the Cabinet.

In the spring of '42, I went into the army. I was on General MacArthur's staff. Australia, New Guinea, Hollandia, Manila. My last job, I was in charge of civil affairs. I was sort of the mayor of Manila. It was ironic that I was on the Oriental side when my heart was in Europe. But it was the only way I could get in the war. I was thirty, a wife, two kids, lousy eyes. I took what I could get.

As we were planning to invade the Philippines, I didn't know from nothin' about how to administer civil affairs. MacArthur refused to accept any plans from Washington. A friend of mine says, "I've got it." He hands me John Hersey's book *A Bell for Adano*. He says, "It's better than any goddamn War Department documents." I read that book. I know it by heart. I can tell you about the carts and the carabao —it was the greatest thing. MacArthur's battle plan for civil affairs was all in *A Bell for Adano*. (Laughs.)

You have no idea the problems you face. One night we get an order: From now on, everybody will drive on the right side. The Philippines is one of those places where it's on the left. Try that sometime, brother, to figure out in three days how you're gonna move people from the left side to the right. Tell that Filipino guy with his carabao to go on the other side of the road. (Laughs.)

I came back at the end of '45 and have been practicing law here since. A lot of my friends from the New Deal days disappoint me. Their practice is totally on the other side. Among the saddest things in my life are how few New Dealers remained New Dealers. I worked for Ben Cohen and Tommy Corcoran. One of my great heroes was Tommy Corcoran. He's represented every stinkin' interest against public interest in this country. Makes me sad. I like him.

Right after the war we had this drive for civilian goods. I was working as a deputy housing expediter. There were shortages. There weren't nails to build houses. We had priorities. You couldn't get a goddamn piece of plywood unless I said okay. You had such a bureaucracy, it couldn't work. In the thirties there were more goods than you could consume. After the war, there was a shortage. And more purchasing power. It was the kind of thing that works during a war, but now it was too much. We had a real mess.

There was a strong antigovernment feeling. The election of '46 was a landslide against regulations. Truman went along, fired Paul Porter, ended price controls, and fired my boss, Wilson Wyatt, and me. Regulations were being killed.

About this time, Churchill makes his Iron Curtain speech in Fulton, Missouri. The cold war begins. In '47, you get the Truman loyalty order. That affected my life as much as anything. I handled a lot of the loyalty cases.

It's all related to the war, the hot one and the cold one. And the Depression, too. There were still ten million unemployed. Whether we would have pulled out of the Depression without the war, God only knows.

EARL B. DICKERSON

He is ninety-two. He appears every workday morning at his Chicago office. He is president emeritus of the Supreme Life Insurance Company of America. He had served in the city council as an alderman in the late thirties.

He had been appointed by President Roosevelt to the first Fair Employment Practices Committee and served from 1941 to 1943.

Around 1940, '41, the war industries were set in motion: Lockheed, Boeing, all the rest. If this was a war to see that democracy prevails, preparations should involve all our people equally. Since blacks had been to a large extent excluded, A. Philip Randolph and Walter White* planned a march on Washington. I knew both men intimately. To prevent this from happening, Mr. Roosevelt put forth Executive Order 8802. This set up the Fair Employment Practices Committee. I was one of the first named.

Because I was the only lawyer in this group, I was always sent out in advance of any hearing. With some investigators, I prepared the cases for the committee when it met.

One of the first hearings was here in Chicago at City Hall. It was a wonderful three days, examining these people from industry. I remember some fellow from LaGrange. It was one of these General Motors subsidiaries. We had him on the stand: "How many Negroes do you employ?" He replied, "One."

I distinctly remember the hearings in Los Angeles. I had gone out a week before the hearings with a couple of investigators. Lockheed had employed some twenty thousand people in the war effort. No Negroes. Not until the morning of the hearings did they employ any. I asked the head of personnel, "Are you familiar with the contents of Executive Order 8802?" He said yes. I said, "Do you have any Negroes in your employ?" He said yes. "How many do you have?" He said nine. I said, "In what department?" He said, "In the custodial department." That meant they were sweeping floors. (Wryly) Well, that was a beginning.

Another company, there were no black bricklayers. The reason given: one or two couldn't work alongside whites. They'd have to get enough to work one side of the building. Since they couldn't find that many, they'd employ none.

I distinctly remember the hearings in Birmingham. One of my colleagues on the committee, a southern newspaper publisher, called me on the phone a few days before the scheduled hearings: "Earl, perhaps you shouldn't go down there. There have been all sorts of threats." I said, "I want you to read Executive Order 8802 again. It says, 'the jurisdiction of this committee shall be in all states and territories of the United States.'" I had it before me. "The question I ask you now is, 'Is Birmingham within the jurisdiction of the United

*Executive director of the NAACP at the time.

States?' " He said yes. I said, "That being the case, I'll be there."

When I got off the plane at Birmingham to walk to the terminal, a man about six feet four, a tall Caucasian, came to me and said, "Are you Mr. Earl B. Dickerson?" I said yes. He said, "I'm the United States marshal in this district and I have been requested by the Justice Department to protect you during your trip here." In those days, blacks couldn't stay in hotels in Birmingham. So he would come and pick me up each of those three days. And in the federal court, where the hearings were held, he stood beside me the whole three days.

There was another black fellow on the committee. He was very black and I'm sort of brown. The newspapers came out and described us as the black and brown babies from Chicago. That was around 1942.

You must remember Roosevelt had to be pushed. I had no personal relationship with President Roosevelt until he issued Executive Order 8802. It was June 25, 1941.

We had hearings in Washington, D.C., from time to time. The streetcar system did not employ blacks as motormen or conductors. This was during the war, and every day there were ads in the papers advertising for people to apply for jobs as motormen and conductors. The civil rights people there told blacks to apply for these jobs. They had no luck. We set a date for the hearings on this. I was the acting chairman at the time and prepared the case. It was in all the newspapers.

Just the day before the hearing, I got a call from a fellow named McIntyre. He was Roosevelt's secretary. He said, "We understand you are having hearings tomorrow. President Roosevelt has asked me to request that you postpone the hearings until some later date." I said that all the newspapers not only here but throughout the United States know about these hearings tomorrow. We have prepared the case, a noted lawyer from New York has come in, and it will be at Dumbarton Oaks. I said, "I can't go out to the public and postpone this case unless Mr. Roosevelt himself would tell me."

This was about one o'clock in the afternoon. He called me right back. "At two-thirty this afternoon, the President will meet with you in the White House." When I walked in the White House, Mrs. Mary McLeod Bethune was sitting just outside his office. She was the most influential black around, very close to Mrs. Roosevelt. I think Mrs. Roosevelt was one of the sparkplugs behind Executive Order 8802.

After she hugged me, Mrs. Bethune said, "The President asked that I be in on this conversation."

Well, the President simply told me he wanted permission to defer the hearings. I said, "I'm just wondering why it is, Mr. President—" He said, "I want it delayed until I return." I said, "Very well, Mr. President." Of course, the next morning we read about Mr. Roosevelt having flown to Yalta to meet with Churchill and Stalin.

Soon after this, Attorney General Francis Biddle came up with a proposal to reorganize the commission. All the members were reappointed except me. It was one of my major disappointments in life. I knew it was because I had been so aggressive. I had been the leader of all the agitation that went on in the committee.

What did they give as the reason?

They didn't have to, did they? Oh, they had hearings, but not the kind of aggressive ones I'd been pushing. Nobody ever criticized me. I was in all the newspapers throughout the country.

Roosevelt wanted to go slow. I was taking 'em too fast. When you talk about him, he was not unlike any other Caucasian in that position. The blacks had never challenged authority like that before, except for individuals. Here was a collective attack on the practices of the American people.

Do you know that my work on that committee has affected my life? Years later, when Governor Kerner appointed me as one of the first members of the Illinois Fair Employment Practices Committee, I had to be confirmed by the state senate. This fellow Broyles was chairman of the Illinois Un-American Activities Committee. On the day of the hearings, on the wall of that room, they had my files posted. My membership in the Soviet-American Friendship Committee, my membership in the National Lawyers' Guild—*and* all my activities on the Fair Employment Practices Committee. The fifteen Republicans voted no, the thirteen Democrats voted yes. I was not confirmed.

It was in World War Two—because it was so clear, it was against Hitler—that the blacks began to measure the rights they had as against the rights that the whites were given. Now I tell you, this measuring will never end. Not until they have the rights the others have.

FLYING HIGH

LOWELL STEWARD

Black airmen in World War Two destroyed or damaged 409 enemy aircraft, including the last four victories of the Army Air Corps in the Mediterranean Theater of Operations. They flew 15,553 sorties, and 1,578 missions. 200 of these missions were as heavy bomber escorts deep into the Rhineland, during which time not one of the heavies was lost to enemy fighter opposition. 450 Negro pilots of the 332nd Fighter Group distinguished themselves, culminating in a Presidential Unit Citation of March 24, 1945.

—*Robert C. Rose (Tuskegee Airmen, Inc.),*
The Lonely Eagles

It is a pleasant, tree-lined community in Los Angeles. The lawns are evenly mowed; the private homes reflect an air of easy comfort. It is archetypal middle-class. It is predominantly black.

He's a vigorous sixty-four, though he says, "I count 'em by the day now." A photograph of him during World War Two in the flying gear of the 332nd indicates a sense of whimsy. Perhaps.

His longtime friend and war comrade-in-flight, Colonel Edward Gleed, is visiting. "He was our flight leader," says the host. During the conversation, there is an occasional comment by Colonel Gleed.

World War Two was not a pleasant experience. It's anti everything I stand for. It was a frustrating and revealing time of my life.

I was born and raised in Los Angeles. I'd never been south. I had not too much experience with discrimination. I went to integrated schools. And the first time I reached manhood, things were frustrating. When I left school to sign up for the air force, I found out I could not go into the service with my friends. I was the only black on the basketball team. We had decided among ourselves that we would all go into the air force. The others did. When I went down to sign up, they didn't know what to do with me. Just told me they couldn't send me to the air force. Ten months later I was finally called. That's when they decided what they could do with me. I was sent to Tuskegee, an all-segregated base, deep in the heart of Alabama.

COLONEL GLEED: "There's a story about Ace Lawson. He tried to enlist along with some of his white contemporaries. This major at the recruiting place told him, 'What are you doin' here, boy? The air force doesn't need any night fighters.'"

The summer of '42 is when I went through the training phase, graduated. I had various brushes with Alabama bigotry, such as my wife trying to buy a hat. They'd tell her, "If you put it on, you have bought it." You couldn't try on anything. You had to eat in separate quarters, of course. And live in separate places.

Ran into it again when I went overseas. I could understand the white American soldiers' antagonism to black soldiers who dated white girls. Then one day I was assigned temporary duty in North Africa. The white soldiers there were antagonistic to black soldiers dating black girls. This got kinda fuzzy. This I couldn't understand.

During the war, we took short terms of rest and rehabilitation from the rigors of flyin' combat missions. Maybe for a week. The Isle of Capri, the rest camp for the area, was off-limits to black pilots. We had a few confrontations at the local USO. Now this was in the theater of war. Somebody got us a private, completely equipped segregated rest camp in Naples. The 332nd Fighter Group with that combat record. These things all mount up, one on top of another. This is why World War Two doesn't read popular things in my mind. They were fighting fascism and letting racism run rampant.

I think the reason the 332nd was trained at Tuskegee was it was down South. As one of the officers in charge put it, if it doesn't work out, it'll be down South and nobody'll see 'em fail anyway. The whole idea was that blacks could not fly an airplane. We'll give 'em a chance. If they succeed, I guess it won't hurt anything. If they fail, we'll hush it and nobody will know about it.

It was a tremendous success, beyond their wildest dreams. So they established quotas. They were gettin' so many volunteers for the air force, qualified young men, that they had to limit the size of the classes. They had so many pilots graduating, in spite of Washington washing pilots out of flying school for ridiculous reasons, such as not wearing your hat on straight or not saying "Yes, sir" to one of the instructors. You got washed out because of attitude, not flying ability. One fellow that washed out in advanced training as a pilot was hired two weeks later as a flying instructor. (Laughs.)

Mayor Coleman Young of Detroit, who was one of the Tuskegee Airmen, recalls: "I was washed out as a fighter pilot. I'm told it was because of FBI intervention. I had already graduated from officers' school in October of '42, at Fort Benning. They literally pulled guys off the stage, 'cause FBI, Birmingham, was accusin' them of subversion, which may have been attendin' a YMCA meeting in protest against discrimination."*

There was a lot of pressure to get blacks into the front lines of the war. There was pressure to get blacks in the air corps from the NAACP, the *Pittsburgh Courier*, the *Chicago Defender*, most of the black press.

COLONEL GLEED: *"There was a study made by the War Department back in 1925. It governed the thinking of the people between World War One and World War Two. It definitely established the idea that the black was inferior. He had a smaller brain than the white. He couldn't socialize with whites. Certainly blacks were not capable of learning to fly or maintain airplanes. This brought you up to '39 and '40 when the clamor was heard: Hey, why can't we fly? If I'm gonna go to war, I don't wanna walk to war. I want to fly." (Laughs.)*

Flying airplanes was my type of fightin' the war. I had no flying experience. I was brainwashed as a child that I would not be able to fly. This is what I wanted to do when I was a little kid.

At Tuskegee, they assembled black men from all over the United States to go into this flying school. They recruited All-American athletes. They had mathematical geniuses. They had ministers, doctors, lawyers, farm boys, all down there trying to learn to fly. All the fellows we were with were of topnotch caliber.

According to Mayor Coleman Young, "They set up this Jim Crow Air Forces OCS School in Tuskegee. They made the standards so damn high,

---

**American Dreams: Lost and Found* (New York: Pantheon Books, 1980), p. 360.

we actually became an elite group. We were screened and super-screened. We were unquestionably the brightest and most physically fit young blacks in the country. We were super-better because of the irrational laws of Jim Crow. You can't bring that many intelligent young people to-gether and train 'em as fighting men and expect them to supinely roll over when you try to fuck over 'em, right? (Laughs.)" *

We got the nickname Lonely Eagles because we flew alone. The 332nd was not readily accepted when they were sent overseas and attached to white groups. A group is usually composed of three squadrons. So they attached this one black squadron to the three white squadrons, which made it the fourth. (Author's note: Origi-nally, the black pilots were of separate squadrons: the 99th, 100th, 301st, and 302nd. They were later combined into the 332nd Fighter Group.) They still kept us segregated. They put them on the other side of the field. They had to take off, in many instances, in the wrong direction in order to join up with the flying group. It was after several missions before they were really accepted as equal flying partners.

In Naples, we were transferred to the Fifteenth Air Force, which was long-range bomber escort. We flew from that base to support bombers flying into southern Germany and all the Balkan countries. Front-line combat. We were flying to Ploesti, Munich, Berlin, Vienna, Graz, Bucharest. We protected the bombers from enemy attack until the end of the war.

Once our reputation got out as to our fighting ability, we started getting special requests for our group to escort their group, the bombers. They all wanted us because we were the only fighter group in the entire air force that did not lose a bomber to enemy action. Oh, we were much in demand.

We didn't have much social life. We shot pool, we played bridge, we played Ping-Pong.

COLONEL GLEED: *"The units were all separated by several miles. So you didn't really get a chance to fraternize, except amongst your own people.*

The War Department would not allow mixing. We still had our own private rest camp. There was a wonderful camaraderie among the black pilots. We'd talk about flyin' escapades. All our pilots were

*Ibid., pp. 359–60.

really good, for the simple reason that we had extensive training. In the beginning, they didn't know what to do with us, so they just kept on training and training and training us. When we went overseas, most of our fliers had three times the flying training that white pilots had. So we were consequently three times as good. Let's say we were twice as good. (Laughs.)

COLONEL GLEED: *"Let's stick with that for just a second. It goes conversely, too. You would get some white commanders that said we weren't any good, because it took longer to train us than it does the normal white person. No matter what we did, we couldn't win." (Laughs.)*

It was as bad up North at Selfridge Field, in Michigan, as it was in the South. It was separate but not equal. They had always one magnificently furnished officers' club for whites. Then they would take one end of the barracks and put a couple of chairs in it as an officers' club for black officers. It was the same at all the fields, so the guys were getting pretty well ticked off.

Mayor Coleman Young describes his experiences: "We're now, forty-five of us, at Godman Field, attached to Fort Knox. We're boxed in, Jim Crow. The white officers could go to the officers' club as guests of Fort Knox officers. Nobody invited us. . . . We began hearing rumors that they were going to make the Godman Officers' Club all white and the black officers would go to the noncom club. To add insult to injury, we had a few thousand bucks in the officers' club. We swore we weren't going to take this. Well, they shipped us out, one squadron at a time, to Freeman Field, near Seymour, Indiana.

"They were prepared for our arrival, expectin' trouble. MPs were there to keep us out of the club the night we arrived. We decided to go in groups of eight and nine. We were gonna scatter, play pool, get a drink, buy cigarettes. I'm in the first wave. This white captain says: 'You can't come in here.' We just brushed past him and scattered. The commandin' officer was livid and placed us under arrest, at quarters.

"It was my job to convince the other guys that they should go in and get arrested. (Laughs.) After the first nine, it was tough gettin' the next nine. But we broke the ice, and two more groups went in and were placed under arrest. . . . They wanted to put us in a position of disobeying post command.

"The commanding officer read the damn thing and ordered each of

us to come up and sign it. If you did that and disobeyed, they could prosecute you. The post commander says: 'Do you recognize that under the sixtieth article of war, in time of war, disobedience to a direct order can be punished by death? Okay, give him an order. I hereby command you to sign this.' He knocked off a bunch of guys. I'm lucky. They called us alphabetically, right? (Laughs.) I got a little breathing spell. I remembered an article of war that roughly is the equivalent of the Fifth Amendment. We devised a strategy. We'd go through all the formalities, salute properly and say, 'Yes, sir.' Where he gives you the direct order, you say: 'I'm sorry, sir, but under the sixty-sixth article of war, I'm afraid this might incriminate me. I refuse to sign.' There were a hundred and one guys who stood up under that one, one by one. We were all placed under arrest."*

Mayor Young recounts the chaos that followed, word reaching Washington, pressures. "They sent in investigators and they were never able to get one out of a hundred and one guys to identify a leader. That, I think, is really something. . . .

"As a result of that incident, they published a war department memorandum, 450-50, which was the beginning of integration in the army."†

Colonel Gleed became a career man. He stayed in the service and got out in 1970 after thirty years. I returned home from the war and taught flying at Tuskegee for about a year. I couldn't get promoted, saw no future, so I came home, back to civilian life. I had a college degree in hand, a teaching credential, went back to get the job promised me when I left for the service, passed a new exam. They wouldn't let me have the job.

I got sick of the runaround and decided to become an airline pilot. At the Long Beach Municipal Airport, where they had an army reserve unit flying B-51s, which I was proficient in, they told me they didn't have no niggers at this base. I was pretty bitter by then. But bein' a good boy, I had saved money, was married, and had a little child.

I went to buy a house in Beverly Hills, advertised for sale for veterans. I had the qualifications and the financing. They told me I couldn't buy it. So I started studying real estate. I've been at it thirty years. My main reason for going into real estate was to find a good

*Ibid., pp. 360–61.
†Ibid., p. 362.

home for myself. A lot of work I've done much of that time was finding neighborhoods and homes that blacks could buy. That's the way I've made a living for thirty years.

World War Two has had a tremendous impact on black people as a whole. There have always been strides for black people after every war, especially that one. But after the war is over, they revert back to bigotry. That war has definitely changed me. Colonel Gleed and I are just two of the 996 black pilots of World War Two. He's changed as a career man and I, as a civilian minute man. We helped win the war for our country and now I'm back home.

UP FRONT WITH PEN,
CAMERA, AND MIKE

JOHN HOUSEMAN

Actor-producer. During World War Two, he had worked for the Office of War Information (OWI). It was the overseas branch, known as The Voice of America.

"I was hired because I had worked with the Mercury Theatre of the Air, had radio experience, and was trilingual: French, German, and English.

"The domestic OWI, by far the bigger organization, was under the leadership of Archibald MacLeish. Robert Sherwood and Bill Donovan were joint heads of the overseas branch."

Up till that time, the United States had no machinery for propaganda. They were perfectly happy to live by advertising, by huckstering. That changed in the summer of 1941, about six months before Pearl Harbor. William Donovan and Robert Sherwood exerted pressure on the President to set up some kind of machinery for expressing the views of the United States to the rest of the world.

Robert Sherwood made a speech to his fellow writers, telling them they could not live in an ivory tower, that it was important for them to participate in the affairs of the world. He had a theory that the Voice of America should be an extension of the voice of FDR.

I had been with OWI about three months when a split occurred. A strong difference of opinion. Donovan was interested in the use of the Voice of America as a weapon of war: covert operations, known as black radio. He was for putting secret stations inside Germany, a spying approach. The British were very strong with black radio. They had stations all over Norway and Sweden and inside Germany.

Sherwood didn't deny the usefulness of this, but he emphasized the straight news. This was important at the time because we had nothing but bad news. It was Sherwood's theory, on the assumption of our ultimate victory, that if we were honest in telling the facts, disagreeable though they might be, if we every day announced our defeats, our credibility would be much greater.

We didn't fill our broadcasts entirely with bad news. The thing we plugged day after day after day was that America was strong, and it's just a matter of time. We would repeat over and over and over again: this year, 50,000 planes, 40,000 tanks; next year, 100,000 planes. This was believed to be the most eloquent thing we could possibly say to the Germans. Japanese propaganda was conducted entirely from the West Coast. By none other than Owen Lattimore.

We were jealously a civilian operation. This led to problems. Neither the army nor the State Department was happy with our independence. They kept treating us as amateurs. Around Sherwood and Joseph Barnes of the New York office, there gathered a most extraordinary collection. Half the great newspapermen of the country joined our branch. We had about twenty-six language desks. The biggest, of course, were the French, German, and Italian. But we had all kinds: Serbo-Croat, Hungarian, Czech . . .

I was in charge of the broadcasts, not the news. Newsmen would prepare the newscasts, from all kinds of sources. The editorial comment was checked very carefully by the State Department so that it conformed with American policy at the time. How strongly should we support De Gaulle? The State Department was very anxious not to break our ties with Vichy at the time. This created all sorts of problems. We had a control desk that pretty much held us down: giving us complete freedom with news, but not with comment. We had to conform to what the State Department and the Chiefs of Staff told us.

By the summer we had about 750 broadcasts a week. We worked essentially by short-wave. A good many of our broadcasts would be picked up in London and rebroadcast on medium-wave into Europe. The only thing wrong with this was the Germans could tap our wires. Short-wave, of course, was forbidden in Germany. It was a question of how much was getting in. Our first broadcast in German was on the sixteenth of February, 1942.

The underground, or any citizens who were not slavishly nazified, did form little groups. One man would have a short-wave set and he'd rediffuse among his friends. In France, we were more widely listened to than in Germany. By the summer of '42, Swiss newspapers were actually publishing a schedule of America's short-wave broadcasts.

There was one record we made of Franklin Delano Roosevelt's voice speaking in French. He spoke a strange, tourist French, which the French would have regarded as slightly comic. There was a process that through a throat mike, we could actually get the resonance of FDR's voice, yet the articulation was somebody else's. So he wound up speaking in pretty good French. In selling this, we had a record of Caruso singing "The Star-Spangled Banner" in perfect English.

The North African landing was a secret that was not very well kept. We went through the motions of its being very hush-hush. I remember a naval officer sitting in my office for six hours, waiting for the word before we could put this on the air. I remember him saying— as clearly as if it were yesterday—"This is a beginning. This is only a skirmish. You know where the real war is, don't you? It's against the Russians." This was in 1942. These were our allies who were being killed by the millions. Already there were elements thinking about the next war, the war against the Russians.

We were all civil service, so everyone was investigated. Sometimes it took up to six months. One of our best writers was fired because he'd been with the Abraham Lincoln Brigade in Spain. Among the investigators were many who had worked for Henry Ford as union busters. They invented the term "premature anti-fascists," PAF. It was used in adverse reports that we received on people.

There were all kinds of crosscurrents. It was very tricky. The French were unhappy all the time we were playing footsie with Vichy. This became a very serious problem when we went into North Africa. We were there as the result of a deal that Ambassador Murphy made with the Vichy people. Some of our OWIs went on the air and criticized what they regarded as collaboration with the wrong French elements. A real feud developed between the State Department and the army and the OWI. Eisenhower once said he was more afraid of the OWI than he was of the Germans. (Laughs.)

Little by little, as we began to win victories, just before the invasion of France, the Voice of America became, quite rightly, the voice of the military. The invasion was a very delicate operation, and the army wanted certain things said to the civilian population.

When the war was over, the OWI went back to independence of the army. But it was taken over by the State Department. Today, it is the department's branch. Of course, the war still rages. The administration had made a big move to make Voice of America much more overtly anti-Soviet. This had been resisted by some in OWI. They weren't Russian lovers. They had a tradition of pride in their objectivity.

With the cold war, people like Joe Barnes and Owen Lattimore were crucified. Joe had been head of all foreign news for the *Herald-Tribune* and got in the doghouse for being too friendly with Joseph Davies, who wrote *Mission to Moscow.* Barnes invented the term *One World,* which he wrote for Wendell Willkie. It was described as globaloney, as they took out after him.

There's an irony in my case. I was born in Rumania and had encountered great delays in becoming an American citizen. For a long time, the Rumanian quota was filled. Finally, I was a legal resident of this country. But when the war broke out, I was still technically an enemy alien. Enemy aliens were not permitted near short-wave radios. Here I was, technically an enemy alien, running the radio-programming operation for the Voice of America.

For me, it was a madly exciting time. I was in contact with these brilliant newspapermen, writers, philosophers, poets from all over the world. I had the feeling I was right in the center of things, of the world, of history.

HENRY HATFIELD

He was a professor of German at Williams College beginning in 1938. With the war under way, he taught, in addition, aerial navigation, "which I first had to learn myself. Everything had to be retooled, so they retooled some of us. We taught this twenty-four hours a week on top of any other teaching we were doing. I didn't suppose I knew much more than the kids I was teaching. I've never understood how we won the war, but apparently we did."

I was approached by the OWI. Would I broadcast to Germany? They preferred me with my middle-western accent to somebody who spoke one hundred percent good German. They figured if the German audience heard somebody who was perfect in German, they would say, Aha, a traitor! However, if you're talking some kind of American German, it's a different matter.

There were two kinds of war radio: black radio and white radio.

The black radio was underground, playing tricks all the time. They didn't give a damn whether something was true or not, as long as it was good propaganda. We needed this to counteract Goebbels's stuff. The British did this a lot.

I was in white propaganda. It was much more respectable. We didn't broadcast anything we didn't believe was true. Sometimes we omitted things we didn't want to broadcast, but we weren't lying. (Laughs.) As radio propaganda goes, we were rather virtuous. I did it in London from April of '44 to the middle of June, '45.

I also did something a little less white. I went out and got recordings of German prisoners of war. They could either send nonpolitical messages, using their own names, or anonymous messages of anti-Nazi propaganda. There were thousands of these PWs all over England.

It sounded so nice. Here, you poor sap prisoners, send your message home for free. We would use these little nuggets of messages as bait. We would give five minutes of news and three minutes of PW messages. At Christmastime, we broadcast nothing except these messages for three days. It was bait to make people tune in the radio and then get our other message. It was not a hundred percent ethical, but compared to what the Germans were doing, we were angels.

Every day we had messages by German prisoners: how to surrender without getting killed, wait till the tanks go by and then surrender to the infantry. They'd say how they got the same food as the American soldiers. True. There were always references to penicillin. If you're wounded, you'll get cured much faster in one of our camps. That kind of thing.

Most of this happened after D-Day. That's when the great wave of prisoners came. Most of them were quite willing to cooperate with us. The officers were a little more reluctant. But as it became clearer and clearer that we were going to win, they saw it was to their advantage to be nice to the Americans. (Laughs.)

My first feeling wasn't one of hatred. If they had still been in Nazi uniform, it might have been. I felt a certain amount of pity that they could be so stupid. Also a good bit of suspicion. Are they really anti-Nazi or are they putting us on? We uncovered a half-dozen of their agents who were playing a double game.

The British had a camp of anti-Nazis, supposedly. On the whole, they were fairly good guys. But there was one we had suspicions about. My colleague asked him, "Where are you from?" "Brooklyn." My friend starts to talk to him in Brooklynese. The poor damn German didn't understand him. (Laughs.) He didn't know who the Brooklyn Dodgers were. It was an open-and-shut case.

We found one person in an American camp who was running a real racket. He was a member of the Nazi Party, as it turned out. This was late in '44, and badly wounded soldiers could be exchanged. We had an old Social Democrat spying on this spy. (Laughs.) He was sending back, under the bandages of his pals, lists of Germans who were cooperating with the Americans. The idea being that their families would be terribly punished. We stopped that.

The head of my shop in OWI asked if I'd like to fly over Germany in a bomber and make a broadcast of what I saw. I said, "If it's an order, I'll do it, but I've seen enough ruins around here." I saw what the V-1s and V-2s did to London. I don't see that destroyed German cities had any propaganda value. The war was, in effect, over. I don't think the American people liked to gloat over it.

London was a mess. Though the Germans asked for it, the destruction of their cities was vastly greater. Dresden is the one thing I'm really ashamed of. I mean hellishly sorry. We were behaving like the Nazis. The war was as good as over. It was an open city, full of refugees coming back from the eastern front. Who can say that wrecking this beautiful, nonmilitary city shortened the war? It was like that second bomb on Nagasaki.

Paradoxically enough, though it was a great victory and as wars go, a just war, it led to the reluctance of young Americans to be in a war. A lot had to do with the atom bomb. And there is the ironic fact that our one-time enemies, Germany and Japan, are doing much better than we are. (Laughs.) I think we've become more sophisticated and more skeptical.

MILTON CANIFF

He is a cartoonist. Terry and the Pirates *and* Steve Canyon *are his most celebrated comic strips.*

I had a call from the chemical warfare department saying that if we're hit by anything, it will be by air, a fire bomb probably. A la the blitz in London. We know so little about it. Could we get together a poster on what to do in case of an air raid?

I hotfooted down to Washington on the first plane I could get. The next day you couldn't get a plane. I'd left on December 7, 1941. Lotta people in Washington had expected something.

We just sat there at the Fairfax Hotel and finished this thing. They printed it in one night and got it out to the West Coast. We were doing it, step by step, in a cartoon style, easily understood. A big one-sheet poster: If you're hit by a fire bomb, this is what to do.

It was distributed up and down the West Coast. They didn't expect anything east of the Sierra Nevadas. I think they expected it in San Francisco rather than southern California. If you remember, there was an actual attempt, a pitiful one, of a bomb raid on the West Coast.

Terry had been running since 1934. We laid the story line in China because that was the last place anything could happen. The first strips were the usual adventure stuff. But when the war began to loom— you could see it coming—I started using Japanese uniforms. I used them exactly as they looked. We had plenty of pictures of Japanese uniforms and the meatball flag. The *New York Daily News* and the *Chicago Tribune* felt they shouldn't get involved in this thing, so I just called them the invaders. I never called them the Japanese, but everything was absolutely authentic.

This was about 1937. It'd been going on for a couple of years, Manchuria, the whole thing. By the time Pearl Harbor hit, I was all armed and ready. The Pentagon thought so too, or they wouldn't have called me down.

Terry was carried by about four hundred papers. It reached its peak during the war. I quit it right at the end of the war. I'd been doing a strip called *Dickie Dare*. Joe Patterson of the *Daily News* called me in and said how about something adventurous. A kid like Dickie Dare and a big guy to do the muscle work and a place like China, the last outpost of adventure in 1934. He suggested two books: *Pirates of the China Coast* and, would you believe, *Wuthering Heights*. Pat Ryan, the muscle man, was Heathcliff, in love, unrequited, with a girl named Normandie who married a bad guy. Terry Lee was just a kid.

The most memorable character was the Dragon Lady. She was the chief pirate. Started out as an ordinary villain. I thought it would be a thousand times more interesting if the bad guy is a bad girl. She was Eurasian, a beautiful dame. An Anna Chennault type. I made drawings of her as the Dragon Lady. She loved it.

The Dragon Lady was a pirate queen until Pearl Harbor. Suddenly she became a good guy. She was a guerrilla. The only opposition the Japanese had when they moved into the mainland of China were the pirates, the armed brigands, and the war lords. Until we got into the thing with the Flying Tigers, they were the entire opposition. Except the reds, who were hangin' out in the hills. They stayed out of the fighting. They moved in when the other guys beat their heads together.

Shortly before Pearl Harbor, Patterson called me in and said these invaders are obviously Japanese. We'll probably not lose any Japanese circulation—a ha-ha-ha joke—but maybe we should soft-pedal this political stuff. I said, "Sir, I disagree with you." I could see the others in the office sinking through the floor. He didn't take his feet off the desk. He just looked at me and said, "Son, by an accident of birth, we're gonna do it my way." (Laughs.) I said, "Yes, sir." And then Pearl Harbor. He never mentioned it again.

As for *Terry,* it was a rule of thumb: if anybody in the military told me anything, I didn't use it. But if I figured out something on my own, I did it. The FBI was on my tail three or four times. Three or four times, I was on the button. (Laughs.) I got to something before it happened. It was simply a matter of playing general. I'd say, What if I were Eisenhower or MacArthur, would I do thus and so? So I just went ahead and did it. The FBI wanted to know: Where'd you learn that? (Laughs.)

I'd read an item in *Stars & Stripes** about some GIs in Calcutta who'd been arrested for wearing black shoes. The issue was brown. It turned out they were navy men. I started thinking about this. Why are these guys there? It wasn't just an accident. This was toward the end of the war, and MacArthur was about to invade the mainland of Japan. The bomb hadn't been dropped yet.

I was thinking about those guys with black shoes. If they wanted to establish a beachhead, they'd need a radio checkpoint up in the hills of the coast and they'd have their triangulation there. So who mans this radio station up in the hills? These guys in the black shoes. They wouldn't be army, they'd be navy types, 'cause you were gonna be in touch with the navy, the marines, the landing force. Had to be navy.

*A GI newspaper widely read in theaters of war.

I gave it a code name, as you always do with those things: Happy Valley. About a month after the strip appeared all over the world, the door opened in my studio. He pulls out a badge: FBI. So I said, "Fine, let's see your other badge." I'd read all that stuff, I was a smart-ass. (Laughs.) So he pulls out the miniature thing, the proof. This is stuff I boned up on, the way I did everything else.

He said, "How did you happen to know about Happy Valley? That's the radio station up in the hills to triangulate ships." I said, "Holy smoke!" How coincidental can you get? This guy's lookin' at me. How did I do this? Then I remembered. I got in his car and drove him down the road to a boys' camp about half a mile from my studio. It was named Happy Valley. The navy one was named after the race track in Hong Kong. The reason they chose the name is because it was so incongruous.

After a while during the war, the cartoon got to be a little bit closer to reality. Parents would send clippings out to their kids at the front. The Flying Tigers were the first and then the Fourteenth Air Force. The guys began feeding me stuff back. I was getting it from the horse's mouth. The *Stars & Stripes* carried *Terry* every day.

My characters never moved out of the Pacific, except once. When the Germans overran Norway, they let the newspapers publish American comic strips. This was their big gesture. One Sunday, I had a page. The scene was China, but I showed an obvious Nazi and an obvious Italian Black Shirt in conference with an obvious Japanese. A firecracker explodes and these three guys go out the window, with their dignity. And the Chinese are laughing at these goose-steppers. The Germans moved in and blew up the newspaper plant which carried this comic strip. That was the end of being nice.

The Pentagon was delighted with *Terry*. Naturally, I wasn't going to be critical in wartime. Bill Mauldin could say nasty things about officers because he was an enlisted man. Being a civilian, I couldn't bring myself to do it. If I were in uniform, yes. I was a 4-F.

After I got through with that poster, I volunteered to do a strip for camp newspapers. *Male Call* was for GI eyes only, not for civilians. The subtitle was: The First Complete Collection of Uninhibited Adventures of Every GI's Dream Girl. Miss Lace was a running character. I did one of these a week. It took almost a week to do it, 'cause it had to be absolutely authentic. Every button, every insignia, had to be exactly right.

It was nearly two years into the war before I ever saw a jeep. I had to use photographs.

As the war progressed, I knew they're gonna have to do something in China. They got to come in through the back door. How are they gonna do that? There's no place to land an airplane in the Burma jungle. I'd been reading about these gliders. Leonardo da Vinci and the Wright Brothers. (Laughs.) Why shouldn't we go in there with towed gliders, thought I. That's exactly what they were doing. Nobody tipped me off. I was just sitting there, looking at Leonardo's drawings. (Laughs.)

Gliders were expendable. You'd just land and walk away from 'em. I thought that would be great. I went ahead with my idea. I didn't think it was such a big deal. I was two days ahead of the actual operation. The British thought there were spies, leaks. The London *Express* carried my strip two days before the actual operation. Our GIs weren't bothered at all, 'cause they were familiar with this kind of stuff. It didn't bother the Pentagon at all. The British raised hell about it. So the FBI came around again. How did I know that? I didn't know. (Laughs.)

With the end of the war, the Dragon Lady became a villain again. She went back to robbing junks off the China coast. Now the communists were moving in at this point, so for a long time the reds were a handy villain when you needed a villain. Almost immediately after the war.

I was reading everything I could get my hands on: newspapers, current and pertinent, and listening to broadcasts. I still do. My routine's exactly the same as it was forty years ago.

I was trying to be in on the transition, 'cause the air corps became the Air Force, autonomous. I knew I'd be coming up with *Steve Canyon*. *Terry* was still going on. He was out of the service. He and Hotshot Charlie ran a private airline, Air Cathay. I had the intelligence people come to him and say, Here you are on the scene. You're in the reserves. How about being a spy, so to speak? So he was an undercover man right up to the time I left him on December 31, 1946.

When *Steve Canyon* came along on the thirteenth of January, 1947, the Pentagon cooperated right down the line. They gave Steve a serial number and a combat record. I have it all printed out, very, very kosher. I wanted Steve to do something in the Far East and there's a certain type of flying clothes he needed, 'cause it's so hot.

The Pentagon sent a guy, dressed in this outfit. They knew the publicity was as valuable to them as it was during the war.

Oh, World War Two was a peak for me. I still get big mail. From World War Two people, naturally. But now I'm getting kids who never heard a shot fired by anybody.

I've never been called a tool, so to speak, of the Pentagon. I've avoided it. They know they can ask me to do something and I can say no. In these strips, it's me talking.

BILL MAULDIN

For millions of American newspaper readers during World War Two, his one-panel cartoon, Up Front, *offered the indelible portrait of the infantryman: craggy-faced, unshaven, disheveled, sardonic. His two protagonists, Willie and Joe, became eponyms for the American dogface. He was an eighteen-year-old GI when he first drew them.*

Today, at sixty-one, bearded, he has the appearance of a fin de siècle *Parisian artist. He works out of his home in Santa Fe.*

Eighteen? Gad, that was forty-three years ago. Yeah.

I was in Chicago, going to art school, in 1939 when the war started in Europe. I was living in the Lawson YMCA. There were quite a few young Germans there: quote, students, unquote. When the war started, suddenly there were a lot of vacancies around the Lawson Y. (Laughs.) That was a time when Bertie McCormick* was very anti-Allies and anti-British. The atmosphere in Chicago was not all that unsympathetic to these young Germans. There was a very strong isolationist, antiwar sentiment then. My friend threw a party for these departing Germans. I refused to attend.

I joined the National Guard. It was a truck company. My friends convinced me it was a good way to stay out of the infantry. (Laughs.) It was such a miserable outfit, I transferred to the infantry. That was almost eighteen months before Pearl Harbor. We weren't in it yet.

Willie and Joe were really drawn on guys I knew in this infantry company. It was a rifle company from McAlester, Oklahoma. There

*Robert McCormick, publisher of the *Chicago Tribune*.

were Indians in it and a lot of laconic good ol' boys. These two guys were based on these Oklahomans I knew. People like that really make ideal infantry soldiers. Laconic, they don't take anything too seriously. They're not happy doing what they're doing, but they're not totally fish out of water, either. They know how to walk in the mud and how to shoot. It's a southwestern sort of trait, really. Don't take any crap off anybody.

I never once heard an infantry soldier who'd been in combat refer to Germans as Nazis. Or North Vietnamese or North Koreans as reds, or commie rats, or any of that stuff. There were a lot of ethnic slurs: slopes, gooks, and things like that. I heard about krauts, square-heads. People who fight these wars could care less about ideology. Me, too.

I'm not sure they were exclusively American. I think that kind of attitude goes with infantrymen of any army in any war. There was a general consensus that they should put Montgomery and Patton and Rommel in the same ring and take off the gloves and let 'em go at it. Patton made it clear he loved war. So did Montgomery. The only nice guy of that trio was Rommel. (Laughs.)

I think Willie and Joe would have voted for Roosevelt cynically, sardonically, with a lot of reservations. He really wasn't their cup of tea. They would have considered Roosevelt too much of a bleeding heart. They couldn't bring themselves to be Republicans. Someone like Harry Truman would be more their cup of tea. (Laughs.) I'm really expressing my own feelings. I dug Truman. I still do. It really shows you what my limitations are. (Laughs.)

Willie and Joe are my creatures. Or am I their creature? They are not social reformers. They're much more reactive. They're not social scientists and I'm not a social scientist. We're moral people who do not belong to the moral majority. (Laughs.) One of my principles is, Thou shalt not bully. The only answer is to muscle the bully. I'm very combative that way.

Willie and Joe. Now I think one of them is a member of the Machinists' Union, a lathe worker or something. I think the other is a barkeep or a small storeowner. I really don't see them living in Detroit so much as in smalltown America. That's where my roots are. I'm not a city person.

They were members of the 52-20 club: twenty bucks a week for fifty-two weeks. It was an emergency thing. They came back to unemployment. There was a terrible period of unemployment and relocation. Millions of soldiers applied for it or they would have starved to death.

They would be living in a house. They paid $15,000 for it. It's now worth $86,500. (Laughs.) I think by now one of them would have lost his home. He would have overdone his Visa card, he would have lost his car, his job would probably have folded. The chances are pretty good that at least one of them would be on the bum by now. The dole. I call welfare the dole. There's nothing wrong with that. The 52-20 club was welfare. I've got nothing against welfare.

The last time I did Willie and Joe, I had them under a culvert, where somehow they sort of belong. Guys that are totally out of luck, out of money. I had one of them stirring a little can of something over a fire. They're obviously on the bum. They're not long-time bums. They've got beards but they're not totally unkempt. On September 1, I had one of 'em saying to the other, "And a happy fiscal New Year to you." I have a feeling we'll be seeing a replay of 1932.

I was twenty-two when I got home to two hundred papers printing my stuff. The *Stars & Stripes* released my stuff for syndication. I'd done a book during the last year of the war and the Book-of-the-Month Club picked it up. *Up Front* was number one on the bestseller list for about eighteen months. I came home, and here all my friends were on 52-20. My book sold something like three million in hardcover. Eisenhower and I made the same amount of money on our books. Congress rammed through a special law letting him claim captal gains on it. He kept what I paid, I paid what he kept. (Laughs.) He paid capital gains, I paid through the nose. My income tax was in the hundreds of thousands. I remember signing one check for $600,000. Here I was twenty-three, twenty-four years old, fresh out of the war. I felt like a war profiteer, and here were all my friends on 52-20. I might have gone in as an average citizen but I came out as something else.

I didn't kid myself. I was a student of World War One by that time. The war to save the world for democracy. Our war didn't save the world for anything or from anything. I didn't feel we had accomplished anything positive. We had destroyed something negative: Hitler. I think the war had to be fought, unlike World War One, which didn't have to be fought.

If there's a nuclear war, the civilized world as we know it will have ended. I accept the possibility that the world may be inhabitable, but I don't really believe it. There are worse things than war: losing one without fighting. It's the old business of I'd rather die on my feet than live on my knees.

I smell violence in the air. There's a savagery afoot in the world, and the Russians are exploiting it.

They lost twenty million because Hitler attacked them. They had more reason to stop Hitler than we did. If anybody fought an idealistic war, it was the United States. We involved ourselves, I think rightly. I joined the army the same year the Russians were trafficking with Hitler.

Did you have these feelings in '45 when the war ended?

Oh no, my God. Drew Pearson took a vacation one time and asked me to fill in for him—remember his radio broadcasts for the hat company? I still have a recording of that. It was an open letter from Willie and Joe to Ivan. I think it was in '46 when the Russians were first making it clear they were not going to be easy to deal with. They were not letting their troops consort with American troops. They were beginning to blockade Berlin.

It was a plea. I thought maybe they just didn't understand how we feel. This was really an innocent thing. I was full of good will to them. I was very much against people who were hawks toward them. If you've been an ally with somebody in war, you feel very strongly toward them. The Russians had this immense reservoir of good will in this country. But they weren't interested in being a friend. They just wanted to kick the crap out of us any way they could.

By the time the blockade of Berlin was on, I had awakened and smelled the coffee.

Ideology has nothing to do with it. They could be anything. It's the muscle, the goose-stepping troops coming down my street, that I want to avoid. If the people in my town are so badly off that they want to embrace communism, we should blame something besides the Russians for that. Some of my best friends have been communists. I don't mind them. I just think they're dumb. (Laughs.) I've never had any sympathy for communism because it bored the hell out of me.

I've gotten a little harder-headed with the years, but my basic thoughts haven't changed. If you'll go back and look at the drawings . . .

I went through the war more as an observer than a participant. But

I saw enough of it that it shaped something in me. You have the distinct feeling that you're living on borrowed time, getting a gravy-train ride. You get shot at and missed. Nothing really bothers you that much. (Laughs.) I could be buried at Anzio. It makes you more unflappable. It's the only war I can think of that I would have volunteered for. I never regretted volunteering for that one.

HERMAN KOGAN

Chicago journalist and historian.

In 1943, I wound up in the Marine Corps. It was the last place I ever thought I'd be. When I was twelve years old, all the kids in my neighborhood had joined the Boy Scouts. My parents refused to let me. They said once you're in khaki, you'll never get out.

I had tried to join the service in 1942. Because I was a newspaper-man, I was considered essential for the war effort and exempt. I showed up at the draft board one night. Here were all these people sitting around, trying to get deferred. I said to this stern old Legion-naire, "I'd like to have my status changed." He said, 'You're 3-A, you're exempt." I said, "I want to be 1-A." The old guy said, "Why?" I said, "I want to join the marines." Within weeks, I was on my way to boot camp. Parris Island, the asshole of the world.

Why? I was definitely a non-macho character. It was right after Guadalcanal and marines were getting slaughtered all over the place. I wasn't caught up in the patriotic fervor, though I did want to fight Hitler. As a reporter for the *Tribune*, I had covered some of the German-American Bund meetings. I think the marines were a chal-lenge to me and a carryover from my parents' rejection of the Boy Scouts.

I was almost thirty years old. I wore glasses. Everybody else was seventeen, eighteen. Half of them were kids from the South. Though I knew I'd eventually be a marine combat correspondent, I went through the ten weeks, long marches, drills, the whole thing.

My drill instructor, a guy with a big gut, was in the traditional mold. Profane, vile, insulting, a bully. One night, he called me in. A beer can in his hand, he said, "I wanna talk to you, man to man." He held a sheaf of papers in his other hand. "I see by dese here yer s'posed tuh go to Wash'ton to be a—combat correspondent. What da fuck is dat?" I said, "As I understand it, sir, you write about the men in your outfit." He stared at me. He flung the papers on his bed and they flew in all directions. "Waddaya gonna do? Fight da fuckin' war wit' a fuckin' pencil?" "No, sir," I said. "You shoot first, then you take notes." He kept staring. "You ain't gonna fight da war wit' no fuckin' pencil. I'm gonna countermand dese orders." I knew that a brigadier general had signed the orders. This guy was a corporal.

Then there was a hint of a smile: "I'll tell ya why I'm gonna do dat. You look like a nice guy, but I'll bet deep down, yer an awful prick." He beamed. He had just given me my Phi Beta Kappa key. What could I do? I said, "Thank you, sir." He said, "I wan' ya tuh stay here an' be a drill instructor. Ya'd make a good drill instructor. Becuz ya look like a nice little guy, but I t'ink deep down yer a prick." That fat face, with those beady little eyes, was just beaming.

I did have two days training as a drill instructor. You're taught how to stand in front of a group of boots, with your hands on your hips, and shout your commands. It was a fantastic experience.

I went to Washington for training as a combat correspondent. It was weird, crazy, and dumb. We had to listen to a young major from journalism school explain to us that in order to take notes we needed a good pencil and a notebook.

I was assigned to the Twenty-second Regiment of the Sixth Marine Division at Guadalcanal. This was after the Guam campaign, long after the fight. I was with a rifle company. Our next campaign was Okinawa. We landed there on April Fool's Day, 1945. I carried a little portable typewriter and a carbine. We were told there would be a tremendous number of casualties. There was nothing. The Japanese had gone into caves. I remember my first story of how we were greeted by the little Okinawan people.

Later on at Sugarloaf Hill a lot of people were slaughtered. I talked to the guys after an assault and they'd tell me about some kid who had been killed. There were the Joe Blow stories. That's what they were called. Marine private so-and-so, somewhere in the Pacific. You always said that, until the Washington office was allowed to say where. They were mostly the little human-interest stories. They'd appear in hometown papers. A lot of people in my outfit were killed. And when I'd come back to the command post to type it out, the first sergeant would say, "Shit, you still alive?"

We were right outside the city of Naha. It was called the Chicago of Okinawa. When we finally took the island, a sort of city council was set up in Naha. Naturally, I compared it to the Chicago City Council. (Laughs.)

I was scared stiff very often. I remember being under attack and spending the night in a foxhole with a young lieutenant from Oklahoma City. The following night I was elsewhere, to follow up on a story. Otherwise I'd have been with him again. While I was away, he had his legs blown off.

The assaults on Sugarloaf Hill were almost suicidal. I figured, what the hell, I ought to get a better view of what was going on. I went up there and was so intent on getting a story that I forgot to be afraid.

There was a sense of pride of having been in the Marine Corps, perhaps it was nuttiness. In a perverse, masochistic way, I even enjoyed boot camp. The one thing I carried away with me was the selflessness of some of these kids, with no great philosophical ideas about war or comradeship.

I've often wondered what would have happened to me if I'd never gone into the service. Would I have been a newspaper executive? (Laughs.) Had I not been in, had I not met some of these kids, I might have become a University of Chicago intellectual snob. It was not much different from the first newspaper jobs I had as a police reporter. You met a different class of people. But, I could have done without this experience. No matter how just a war it was, it was war. It never was a solution to anything. Fuck war.

ALFRED DUCKETT

During the early years of the war, he had been a free-lance journalist. His pieces were featured in black newspapers: the Baltimore Afro-American, *the* Pittsburgh Courier, *the* Chicago Defender. *He is now in public relations work.*

The 369th Engineer Regiment was all black. Most of them lived in Brooklyn, where I was born, so I knew a number of them. They did not want blacks in combat in World War Two. They wanted them in work gangs, with dressed-up names like engineer, quartermaster, what have you. After Pearl Harbor, the 369th was transferred to Camp Stewart in Savannah, Georgia.

The government's gonna decide what to do with 'em. Whether they're gonna go overseas, where they're gonna go. They're on alert, so they can't get any leave or passes.

They write home about problems: white officers, who are racist; service clubs, number one for white, number two for blacks; limited to certain places in Savannah. This is par for the course. The big complaint is the treatment of their wife or mother or girlfriend, who is visiting. The black woman is subjected to a demand, on the streets, of a walking pass. Like in South Africa? The town's justification was it wanted to make sure they were not prostitutes. It didn't apply to white women. A lot of guys got into hassles about this. There were a number of incidents.

These guys in the 369th started writing to their friends, to people in Congress, asking for an investigation by the United States Army. Their cries were ignored, oh, for several months. Knowing some of the fellows, I asked Carl Murphy, publisher of the *Afro-American*, to send me to Camp Stewart.

At that time, there was a lot of agitation from black leaders and some white liberals: We've got a war on our hands. Can't we practice at home what we're fighting for abroad? Blacks should have the right to serve in combat, not only as servants. A. Philip Randolph was crying out for equitable treatment.*

Franklin Roosevelt had a meeting with representatives of the black papers. He was disturbed by many of the stories run on the front pages of these papers. He used the old phrase: I don't want to impose censorship, but this is war and we must be patriotic. I would appreciate it, if you print any stories that are liable to create a lot of feeling, let us see them. The black publishers were, of course, disturbed by this kind of request. There was, as I understand, a long pause. Carl Murphy said, "We understand, Mr. President." He was severely criticized. When I asked him to send me to Camp Stewart, he had to clear the request through the War Department. They took their time.

They decided to send General Benjamin O. Davis, Sr., to Camp

*President of the Brotherhood of Sleeping Car Porters, a moving force behind the Negro March on Washington Committee in 1941. Its slogan: We Loyal American Citizens Demand the Right to Work and Fight for Our Country. Executive Order 8802, approved by Roosevelt, persuaded the black leaders to cancel the march. It made national policy: No discrimination in defense plant employment. The Fair Employment Practices Committee came into being. The armed services were still segregated.

Stewart to investigate. He was the first black general. Know how he was appointed? Franklin Roosevelt, on the eve of an election, came to New York. In his party was Steve Early, his press secretary. The security was rigid. Early, without notifying anybody, at Grand Central Station, decided to get a newspaper. On his way back to the presidential train, a black policeman accosts him, because this is his duty. Early, instead of identifying himself, gets into an argument and kicks the policeman in the groin. The story made headlines in the black papers. Mr. Roosevelt, a genius at public relations, immediately appointed the first black general in the history of the United States.

General Davis is assigned on inspector-general duty. If you're a private on this assignment, you can outrank officers. Everybody is supposed to jump when the inspector general comes in. Ole Harrington, a fantastic cartoonist for *The People's Voice*, Adam Clayton Powell's paper, ran a picture of General Davis in a race car goin' through Camp Stewart at nine hundred miles an hour. It was big news among the blacks.

After he visited the post, they gave me clearance to go down there. I was immediately met by a very polite white lieutenant who was to be my guide and host. "First I'll take you to the service club where you'll stay and then I'm gonna take you to the commanding officer, Colonel Ochs, who wants to make you welcome." Colonel Ochs belonged to the *New York Times* family.

We got to service club number two, which was Jim Crow, of course. I checked in, got in a jeep to meet the colonel. When I entered his headquarters, the first thing he said was (in a southern accent): "Mr. Duckett, we are very happy to welcome you to Camp Stewart, and I just hope you're not one of those rabble-rousin' neegras that like to create trouble in the newspapers." I realized right then and there that if Al Duckett was going to get any kind of story, it was time to tap-dance. I assured the colonel that there were no problems. I would do my job as a newsman.

I was taken back to service club number two and discovered that my bags had been searched. And not carefully. I didn't resent the bags bein' searched as much as the way in which it was done, messily and carelessly. It almost seemed to give me a message.

I was down there three or four days. Each day the lieutenant would pick me up after he'd had his breakfast wherever he breakfasted and after I had breakfast in the Jim Crow club, and we'd visit the black troops. Every noontime, he'd bring me back for lunch. Then he'd bring me back for dinner. Then I'd go out and meet with the gentle-men of the 369th.

We had secret meetings, for which I admired their courage. They could have gotten general court-martial for giving me information. Officers and men were together in telling me of the conditions under which they were serving. They also told me about General Davis's trip.

According to them, General Davis reported to Colonel Ochs and apologized for having had to come down on this kind of disagreeable task. Remember, he's the inspector general. Then he orders that the men who made the complaints be assembled in a company street, in front of the officers who they charged were oppressing them. General Davis said to these troops, "I just want to tell you three things. One: I am your color but not your kind. Two: If you are complaining about discrimination and segregation in the United States armed forces, forget about it. Three: The problem you have mentioned in your correspondence about what happens to your ladies who come down here has nothing to do with the United States Army. That's your private business. The army didn't tell you to get married." He went back to Washington and gave the outfit a clean bill of health.

I stayed down there and I corroborated all the complaints they had made. I came back to New York and I wrote my stories. Sent them to Baltimore, to the *Afro-American*. Carl Murphy sent copies to the War Department. They were on the phone within a few hours. High people in the War Department, in the administration, were saying, You cannot print this story. Murphy said, "You don't understand. We had a meeting with the President and he said he would like to *see* anything we were going to print. It's on the press." He knew what he was doing. He agreed to the language. (Laughs.)

Do you know the Lena Horne story? She had been sent to a camp in the South to entertain the troops. She was scheduled to do a performance for the white troops and a separate performance for the black troops and the German prisoners of war. When I was in the service in Fort Dix, the German prisoners would be in the mess line with black troops and you'd have a separate line for white troops. Lena entertained the blacks and the German prisoners and then she left.

There was a tendency to place blacks who were examined for the draft in 4-F. They wanted the number limited only to work battalions. They told me I had a heart murmur. I had no great desire to get involved in fighting the war, but I wanted to write. I checked it out with my private physician and couldn't find any heart murmur. A week after the *Afro-American* published my article, they discovered I didn't have a heart murmur and they placed me in 1-A. I was sent to Camp Claiborne, Louisiana.

The first night we arrived, a white officer told us what the rules were. He ended this way: "We want you to know we're not takin' any foolishness down here, because we don't shoot 'em down here, we hang 'em." Well, I fled into the orderly room (laughs), 'cause it was a safe, strategic place. The colonel found out I was a writer and he wanted me to put out a little regimental newspaper. Too many guys were goin' over the hill. Would I do an editorial in the first issue? Don't go over the hill. I did an editorial: Don't go over the hill. (Laughs.)

We transferred to a camp in upstate New York, preparatory to going overseas. We knew we weren't getting any passes, so I joined the majority who went over the hill one night to see our families in New York. As far as most guys are concerned, this is not a very serious thing. The colonel of my regiment told my company commander that as long as Al Duckett is in the service, he is to remain a private and a member of the 1310th Regiment.

Since I was going over, I'd like to have a job as a war correspondent and go to the front. From England, I wrote to the publishers of the *Pittsburgh Courier* and the *Afro-American* and asked if they'd give me a job, providing the government would oblige with a discharge. Both offered me jobs. I had recommendations from Walter White, Lester Granger,* A. Philip Randolph, you name it. They all wrote saying I could do the war effort infinitely more good as a correspondent at the front.

The request had to go to Eisenhower's headquarters, come over to the Pentagon, and come on down. It went over, got okayed, and came back down. The colonel of my regiment got it and kept it in a drawer. I didn't find out for a month that it had been okayed. He kept me from getting this job.

In France, we were at Camp Lucky Strike. It was huge, a town. Its function was to hold German prisoners who had been captured at the front. They were brought to us to be guarded and worked.

There was an almost psychotic terror on the part of white com-

*Heads of the NAACP and National Urban League, respectively.

manders that there would be a great deal of association with the white women. We had a chaplain who made it his business to visit in advance every place we were going to. He'd warn the people in those communities that in America white people did not associate with us and—I'm not kidding—that we had tails. That we quite often, without provocation, cut people up. A man of God. There was an edict issued by the commanding officer of the camp that no black troops were to associate with French civilians. They meant women, of course.

One night in a Red Cross tent, a member of our regiment, Allen Leftridge, was talking to a French woman who was serving doughnuts and coffee. When a white MP ordered him not to stand there talking to this woman, Allen turned his back on him. He was shot in the back and killed. Another black, Frank Glenn, was also killed during this incident.

Word spread like wildfire among all the black regiments at Camp Lucky Strike. Since we were not combat troops, they used to lock our arms up every day. We would only get arms when we'd drill. When the killings happened, the fellows in my outfit broke into the supply room and got their guns. They started to march. They were determined to avenge the deaths even if they got wiped out. Luckily there were a couple of white officers who everybody respected: "You can't win. The odds are against you." The next day, our outfit was moved out.

I was sending stories back to the black papers, as letters. They were getting through. I sent the one about how Leftridge and Glenn were killed. Allen had about two weeks to go before going home on rotation and for the first time would see his little daughter.

After the war, I ran into one of the fellas from the outfit: "You remember Allen Leftridge?" How could I forget him? He said, "Remember how when he died, he called out his wife's name? Well, I ran into her. Would you believe the army refused to give her a pension because they said he was killed due to his misconduct? She has been trying to find out what caused his death, and they give her a lot of doubletalk. She read the article you wrote and she'd like to meet you, 'cause maybe she could get more information." It wasn't written under my name, but a lot of people knew it was me.

I went to see her, and she had this adorable little girl running around, bein' bad. We talked real late. I noticed that when they started playin' "The Star-Spangled Banner" on the radio she got up and turned it off. She was very bitter about what had been done to her husband, to herself, to her little girl. (A pause, a slight smile.) We got married and the little girl became my daughter. We're divorced, but still very close.

I got in touch with guys from the outfit who were scattered all over the country. We formed the Veterans' Justice Committee. We got Mrs. Roosevelt interested. We demanded that the War Department open the records. The army felt that if they gave us victory, it would encourage thousands of others with complaints. So they refused to review it.

We were on our way to the Philippines, after time in England and France. We were on the water when the radio message came over that the war had ended in Europe. There were fifteen vessels. Seven of them turned back and went home. I was on the eighth. (Laughs.)

In the Philippines, the white officers had done a job in this country, too, where the women were not white. The prostitutes had been told all kinds of horrible stories. You really had to wonder who the enemy was. Some of the guys who wanted to negotiate with the prostitutes were turned down. Did you know there was a Jim Crow whorehouse in Manila, made out of grass? (Laughs.) One night, the guys burned it down.

The war brought some changes for the good: blacks in defense industries, training they might not otherwise have received. Social gains. We've come a long way. But racism is just as alive today, maybe even more virulent. It was the war to end fascism, okay? Do you realize that most blacks don't believe the atom bomb would have been dropped on Hiroshima had it been a white city?

GARSON KANIN

Director, playwright, memoirist.
"After my first month in the army, I got my first pay, $21. I sent a check for $2.10 to William Morris, my agent."

While I was at an air base in Fort Worth, I was secretly, magically picked up, put in a fighter plane, and flown to Washington, D.C. I was ushered into the office of General William Donovan, Wild Bill, head of the OSS.*

There had been a request from the British for someone to work on their team in making a filmed record of the upcoming invasion, known as Operation Overlord. It would involve a great deal of time, a staff of perhaps a thousand, and would be shown publicly in the United States and Great Britain.

This was early in 1943. D-Day was June 6, 1944. They knew then it was going to happen. When I got to London, I began to put together this project with the British director Carol Reed. We were codirectors. It took us nearly two years. It was called *The True Glory*.

I had six weeks in London before I could actually go to work. They were still clearing me. It involved all kinds of security, background, FBI checks. I had an assignment as mail censor. For six weeks, I sat and read mail that our GIs were sending home. They did not want any shred of information about where we were going or when, or what they heard. There was going to be an invasion. Perhaps a new kind of gun had been issued yesterday. Not one letter went through unless someone read it. We had little razor blades to cut out any line or word that might make any reference to a possible invasion.

It was one of the most important literary experiences of my life. They were writing to their parents, their wives, their sweethearts, their friends. I read some of the greatest prose in the English language, written by eighteen-year-old kids who couldn't spell. It didn't matter. It was the feeling.

One day a French officer said, "Why do you go to all the trouble of censoring mail? Why don't you use our system? We never censor. We don't do anything. We take all the mail and put it in big bags, which we put in a warehouse for thirty days. Then we forward it." Any piece of information during the war that is thirty days old is worthless. It's like a thirty-day-old newspaper.

When I was finally cleared, I entered the realm of high, high army intelligence, British, American, OSS, every kind of spy, secret-weapon operation. Remember, the OSS had not only derring-do types. It had scientists, sociologists, chemists, and bacteriologists, who thought up all sorts of crazy, unorthodox things.

In *The True Glory* we trained men who were not cameramen, who

*Office of Strategic Services, precursor of the CIA.

were not professionals. We had to plant at least one man in every battalion. We said, Photograph anything that is there. Carol Reed made only one rule: not one inch of this film was to be staged. We wanted a true documentary. Eventually, there was something like ten million feet of film.

The curious thing we discovered was that men involved in the actual battle itself knew less about it than the people at headquarters who were seeing the film shots. Eisenhower was acting as producer. In one operation, an entire regiment was saved by the air cover, which suffered heavy casualties. A guy we interviewed was saying, "We didn't have one fuckin' piece of cover in the whole battle." He didn't see it in the spot he was. We saw it on film.

We finally put the picture together. It covered the whole invasion from the beginning to V-E Day. From the viewpoint of the common soldier.

No matter what you did, there were complaints. The British would say it didn't include enough of what the British did. The marines complained they weren't given enough footage. The navy said, How come there are not enough ships? Every man wants to feel he won the war, his company, his regiment.

The preparation for D-Day was almost as exciting as D-Day itself. You're talking about hundreds of thousands of men. Food, water, fuel, hygienic supplies, sleeping equipment. Things had been planned down to the last button. We had one whole department of sixty men working on nothing but toilet paper.

Once in the British sector, Carol Reed and I had to go relieve ourselves. The facility was a slit trench about fourteen inches wide. Sitting at one end of it was a lance corporal, at a table. He had little stacks of toilet paper in front of him. As you came up to him, he'd wet the tip of his finger and count off the little squares, one, two, three. Reed, tall, elegant, asked, "May I have another, please?" The corporal said, "I beg your pardon, sir?" Reed said, "I'm making this film for General Eisenhower. May I have an extra sheet of toilet paper?" "Oh no, sir, I can't do that. I have orders." Reed said, "But I do need another piece." The corporal: "No, sir. You'll find the three easily sufficient, sir. It's one up, one down, and one polish." (Laughs.)

Another part of the job was to acquire German and Italian film on the black market. We had to send OSS agents into Lisbon either to steal it or buy it or pick it up. Later, our own men filmed the concentration-camp scenes. We were part of the liberation forces in Buchenwald and Auschwitz.

Back in the late forties and early fifties, during a showing of *The True Glory*, a guy came up to me and said, "You know that shot where the guy falls down, gets up, falls down again, gets up and makes it back—I shot that one." It was his personal moment of glory. And mine, too. It's as important as anything I've ever touched. There was so much about the war that I loathed, though I knew it was necessary. Yet I, and just about everybody concerned with this movie, feel we were part of something big.

RICHARD LEACOCK

A documentary film maker.

"I grew up on my father's banana plantation in the Canary Islands. I went to Harvard after coming to America. When the war came along, I was getting hapless Harvard students to give their blood for the armed forces. I felt like Dracula.

"I had to be drafted because I wasn't a citizen. You couldn't volunteer unless you were a citizen. I threatened to leave the country unless they drafted me. When they drafted me in my senior year, I was delighted.

"I went before a judge and I forswore allegiance to any prince or potentate. I've never known a potentate. I expected not to like America. Most upper-class English people don't like America. I fell in love with it. For the first time, I felt useful. I can't say that going to Harvard is a democratic process. Going into the army certainly was."

It was '42. Nobody gave a hang who I was or where I'd come from. It was beautiful. But then something dreadful happened. The army decided I should be a typist. Company clerk in the signal corps. What did you do in the war, Daddy? I was a typist. Reminds me when I was in the White House years later, they had a marine band playing and a harpist in full uniform. (Laughs.) What did you do in the marine corps, Daddy? I played the harp.

I can't spell. I can't type. After seven weeks, I got up to seven words a minute. They gave up. Some guy interviewed me and I found myself a combat cameraman. I really loved being a private. This is what I wanted.

I was first sent to the Yukon, then to India, and then to Burma. We were a team. We were, of all things, assigned to the British Thirty-sixth Division. Like Ping-Pong, I was back where I started. There was a big difference: I was an American and they called me Yank.

We walked from north Burma to Mandalay. It took over a year of very old-fashioned warfare. The Japanese supply lines were already broken..They had very little food, very little ammunition, few people. We were there in tremendous strength. It was totally unequal combat.

It was jungle warfare. A war of nerves, of sniping and booby traps. It was man-to-man. We were parachute-supplied and had tremendous air power. For the first time, we used napalm. All they did was withdraw and let the forest burn. It really didn't do much.

For a while, I was attached to the OSS. It later became CIA. I thought of it as a sort of boy scout group. We trained these Kachin mountain tribesmen in combat. Vicious little guys, all of them dope addicts. They got their daily ration of opium just as we got our gin and rum. We would do hit-and-run raids, behind the lines. Going into villages, interrogating people, often kicking their teeth in. Executions were summary and brutal. Machine-gunning and things.

Who were they?

They were Burmese. Whenever you'd go into a village, there's some guy that's unpopular and everybody'd tell stories. Maybe he's a collaborator, maybe he's somebody they didn't like. They'd accuse him of raping women or whatever. You had American officers and a few noncoms, and these fighting Kachins; we'd burn villages. I don't think what we did was terribly useful to anybody. We would just set fire to them, if they were—quote—unfriendly, whatever that meant.

It's sort of, to me, the beginning of Vietnam. I was quite shocked by a lot of that, but I was a private and my opinions were neither sought nor of interest to anybody. So I figured the only thing I could do was to film what I could, send it in, and hope to God somebody looked at it. Especially interrogation by kicking people's teeth in. It went somewhere in Washington. I have no idea where.

I wasn't particularly angry at the Japanese and I wasn't terribly enthusiastic about recapturing Burma for the British. At the same time, I learned there *are* such people as heroes. There are people that are unbelievably good at combat. It's very hard for me to understand why they do these crazy things, but they do. They seem to get a big kick out of it.

There are also brilliant military tacticians, usually around the level of colonel. Generals sit around and draw maps and make big decisions. But battalion commanders: it makes a hell of a difference if you've got a good colonel or a bum one.

The one I vividly remember, Colonel Gwyder Jones, was very theatrical. He knew how to deal with every situation. His men knew it and would do anything for him. He was one of those strange British very upper-class characters with a sort of affected accent. Referred to his men as "my dear." What are you doing there, my dear? Always carried a shepherd's crook. I was around him when a shot—*pshoong!* —would come by. He'd go, "Piss-poor shot." (Laughs.)

I had friends who were killed, sometimes in my arms. Having direct contact with death was very interesting. I became much less fearful of it. It was much more comprehensible when a buddy, not a great friend, dies in your arms. You dig a grave and bury him respectfully.

I started having very bad anxiety attacks. Nobody ever talked to me about that. It's like having nightmares. You think you're going to do something terrible, like kill somebody or shit on the floor. I went back for a rest to headquarters at Ceylon. The anxiety attacks went on pretty much the rest of the war.

I got bored eventually, and as we got to Mandalay I spent the whole day filming a group of dancing girls. I got a kickback: What in the name of God do you think you're doing? (Laughs.) We also got complaints when we were filming combat. They thought we were enacting the stuff.

I myself never fired a shot. I was tempted to, in self-defense. You have to choose between your gun and your camera. I always chose the camera. You don't see much. Mostly you hear it, especially in the jungles. It's the sound that's incredible. Oh God, your ears ring for hours after. If a .50-caliber machine gun opens up on you at fairly close range, the noise is unbelievable. If you're anywhere near a 155 old-fashioned howitzer, it's staggering. You have tremendous silence. So when something goes bang! it knocks you out of your seat.

We were sent to the invasion of Rangoon, which, fortunately, the Japanese abandoned before the invasion. Otherwise, I wouldn't be here. It would have been a disaster. The whole thing was postulated on its not raining. It rained.

I look at the age of these kids and I think to myself . . . When we took over Rangoon, I had a couple of hand grenades, a Thompson submachine gun, a .38 police special, and my cameras. It's an interesting feeling. You want a car, you take it, 'cause you've got a submachine gun. We were friendly, liberating troops, mind you. You want a house? Which house shall we live in? Let's take that one. The family moves out or they move into servants' quarters and they become your servants. They're very friendly, and you begin to like having a Thompson submachine gun. And a couple of hand grenades.

Why do we fight? Why do people do it? You find yourself involved in a battle and you find yourself doing crazy things. I don't know why we do it. You certainly are terrified of being regarded as chicken. Especially boys who are brought up to be terrified of being chicken. So you do it.

The young GIs. Why on earth do they keep slogging and slogging? I remember those Hollywood films where people sat in their trenches and had ideological discussions about the beauties of democracy at home. Oh, bullshit! I remember those movies. They were stupid. You don't talk during combat. There's a strange closeness of the men. You've had no sleep for several days. There's pouring rain and constant fire. It's over and everybody just goes to sleep in big piles. It's a weird sight. Guys in each other's arms. You never see that except in the army.

I could very easily have become an officer. But I very much did not want to become an officer. Part of this was because I met different kinds of people that I really enjoyed. The other part of it was I didn't want to tell somebody else how to get killed. I'd much rather be on the receiving end than the giving end. I didn't want to be the guy telling other guys what to do. It's a kind of power I never wanted.

Because I didn't want power, I admired it often. I saw some dreadful uses of it. I saw colonels who, if they didn't get shot in the back, should have been. They had the power and didn't have the brains. That can be very dangerous.

I loved the whole caper. I haven't got a bad memory of it. Except for the sex film, the VD film, they showed. Oh, God. I think that ruined everybody's sex life.

He had been a photographer for the AAA (Agricultural Adjustment Administration) of the Department of Agriculture. It was a New Deal agency.

The war started for me on D-Day morning, June 6, 1944. I was a combat photographer on a boat crossing the English Channel. The Germans were very well dug in. Their pillboxes were really sunk into the side of the hills. Their guns faced the beach.

When I get real nervous and I want to relax, I fall asleep. So I took a nap just before we got into the landing craft. I woke myself up just in time. We were among the first troops to hit the beach. I was attached to an engineer battalion. Our job was to remove the pylons in the water that blocked our boats. As we got off, shells were falling all around. It was the first time I saw a dead person. Around me were dead Americans floating in the water.

One of my first pictures was a young lieutenant swimming in all that mess, bringing back a couple of survivors. I was shooting film all through this, with a 4 × 5 Speed Graphic. I'm not a brave fellow. I really avoid fights. I walk around arguments. But when something like this happens, I'm very relaxed and cool. I seem to lose my nervousness at this point. I photographed what I saw. I had a job to do.

The lieutenant in charge of our unit jumped into a foxhole and we didn't see him for three days. He got scared and hid. The rest of us carried on. I was with a movie photographer named Val Pope. He was great. It was scary, because that afternoon the Germans came over and bombed the hell out of the beaches.

Photographers were very privileged. We had a pass signed by General Eisenhower, which said we could go anywhere we wanted and do anything we felt like. If an MP said you can't go into a restricted area, we'd just flash this pass.

We broke through on the way to Cherbourg and captured Saint-Lô, where the Germans had holed up. A lot of the Germans we took prisoner were just kids in army uniforms. The bulk of the German army were probably done in at Stalingrad and these, many of 'em, were just children. They'd been manning these pillboxes that were so hard to get in. They seemed terribly bewildered, lost and frightened. They were fourteen, fifteen, sixteen. They looked terrible. They stood there crouched over, cold and miserable and unhappy and not knowing what was going to happen to them. We got 'em, turned 'em in, and went about our business. Of course, I took photographs of them.

There were two kinds of Germans we captured: these kids and the SS troops. The SS were impossible. They thought they had won the war, even after we captured them. They were beyond belief. But the average German soldier was just a young man who was drafted.

At Saint-Lô we came across underground bunkers that we didn't harm at all. They were so deep. They were equipped like a luxury Hilton Hotel. The wine cellars were unbelievable. I commandeered a quarter-ton truck and flashed my card to the MP at the gate. I filled the truck to the top with champagne and wine and brandy. And we put a tarp over it. We headed for Cherbourg. We had a great party. (Laughs.)

At Cherbourg, the first personal tragedy occurred, close to me. Val Pope and I were photographing. It's a very fluid situation. You don't really know where you are. There's an army here, there's a soldier there. You go around some building. You really don't know what's going on. Val and I are walking alongside a house. We heard there's a Red Cross unit we want to photograph. There's a sniper in a tree. A row of bullets from a machine gun come at us. They hit Val. A bullet went through his helmet like it was paper. I ran behind a building. I didn't know he was hit at that time. You hear this thing, you run or duck. I peeked around and there he was. I ran, found some GIs to give us covering firepower. Another GI and I pulled him back. He was still alive. We got him to the first-aid station and he died. A very beautiful young man. I took over as the movie photographer.

In the preinvasion bombardment, we killed a lot of French people. When our big planes went over and dropped these bombs, we wiped out half of Colleville-sur-Mer, a little village near the coast. I made photographs of funerals and mass graves. The French people didn't say, What did you do? You killed us. They felt we were the liberators, they understood what was happening. It's one of the sad parts about the war.

After the beach had been settled down, I was called back to the Normandy beachhead. It was Eisenhower's first visit with Bradley at the beach. All the generals came. I was the photographer to cover the event. It was very impressive. But it was funny, too. They were talking like a bunch of kids: Yeah, he's gonna deserve another star for this. What about so-and-so? No, I don't think so. They were handing out decorations as though it was a party they were having. You were told which was their good side and which was their bad side, and you only photographed them from their good side.

We took off one late afternoon in the general direction of Paris. It was getting dark. All the road signs had been taken off, so you really didn't know where you were. Along the way, we ran into a young Belgian kid about sixteen trying to hitch a ride. He was in bad shape, bloody. He'd been a slave laborer and wanted to get back to Belgium. We took him along.

A sight I'll never forget was the Eiffel Tower way off in the distance. That's a thrill on a dark moonlit night. Especially if you've never seen Paris before. We drove through, into the city, with the tower as our guide. We were among the earliest ones to come to Paris.

We were attached to Patton's Third Army, but we didn't live with the army. I'd go to a house and knock on the door and say, "I need a place to stay." The advantage for the farm family was that I had access to army rations. I'd drive the jeep to an army depot, load it up with food, and bring it back to the family. That made me very welcome, because food was so short. We always stayed with civilians. Gave me a chance to practice my high school French.

We came to Munich with Patton. There was a firefight between Americans and SS troops in a square. It looked as though it were a Wild West movie scenario. Only it was real. I was, somehow, with the Forty-second Division. The Americans were taking a tremendous beating. But they were battle-hardened, had lost a lot of guys, and were not to be trifled with. The SS troops surrendered.

It was in the back of a courtyard. I sat down on a long bench against the wall. It was like a stage set. They put the Germans against the wall. I was sitting with a single-lens Eimo up near my eye. There were about three or four Americans with tommy submachine guns. They killed all the Germans. Shot 'em all. I filmed the whole sequence. I still wasn't that battle-hardened, and I thought they did the wrong thing. The Germans were quite brave. They sensed what was happening and they just stood there.

I said, Now what do I do with this film? Do I throw it away? It upset me somehow. It may not have upset me later on after I'd seen what happened. I sent it back to the army and got back my regular critique: This film could not be screened due to laboratory difficulties. (Laughs.)

When you're killing and being killed, something happens. You lose your perspective about life and death. These are guys who've been shooting at you and your best friends may have been killed. And these SS troops were so brazen. They acted as though nothing could hurt them. And they sneered at you. They acted the superrace. I've had a couple of experiences where I came very close to shooting somebody.

The first thing I saw as I went down this road to Dachau were about forty boxcars on a railroad siding. I knew something was here at this place, but I didn't know what. The Germans wouldn't tell you about it. They always denied its existence. I looked into these boxcars and they were full of emaciated bodies, loaded all the way to the top. Forty boxcars full of dead people. I came from a very gentle family . . .

Just before that, we went into a building to check it out. I tagged right behind the troops. I heard a shot inside. They weren't shooting at us. I ran down into the basement. Somebody had just shot himself, a German.

We came to the camp and broke the gates down. A few more German guards were shot in the process. We went into the encampments, we went into the bunkers. It was turmoil. It was quite a scene with the Americans coming in, with these camp prisoners running around crying, going crazy. This was the liberation of Dachau. I shot as much footage as I could. I realized this somehow should be used right away. I didn't want to hang around. I wanted to get the film back to the front *now.* You had to get the film back to the 163rd Photo Company. I had to do it myself. I didn't want to give it to a messenger.

I found a Piper Cub somewhere nearby. The guy said he'd fly me back. We went up in that little plane and it began to storm and get black. We didn't know where the hell we were. This poor little pilot had no idea. Before the storm broke, we flew over Munich and I saw a sight that staggered me. When you fly over a building, you see there is nothing inside them. They're all collapsed. It's surreal. We landed safely and I dropped the film off, but it was scary, with the winds and the rains and this dinky plane.

I rejoined my outfit. That's when I saw the crematoriums. And the cadavers. The survivors grabbed at you, at your uniform. There wasn't terribly much we could do for them right at that time. We had a little food, some C rations.

This may sound strange, but there were little things that happened to me that have led me to be an optimist. The still photographer stayed overnight in a little town. He said, "Let's get out." I said, "No, it's safe." I didn't realize the American army had pulled out and I was alone. Then it hit me. My God, the Germans might be coming back, because everything was so fluid. This guy raced all the way back on a jeep, hunted me out, and hauled me into the car. We weren't great friends or anything. It was just that kind act of personal heroism that I find quite extraordinary.

As we were reconnoitering a little further down the road, I saw a German civilian come out of the ravine and approach our little group. He said he was an anti-fascist and wanted me to come with him through the back way. He said we could get the German troops to surrender, 'cause we could outflank 'em. So I and a couple of others followed him down the road to see if he was telling the truth.

In Germany, there were anti-fascist groups functioning. The crime of it all is that we would take a little town, arrest the mayor and the other big shots, and put the anti-fascist in charge of the town. We'd double back to that town three days later, the Americans had freed all the officials and put 'em back in power. And they threw this other guy aside. Invariably it happened. You see, after you came in, the military government took over.

So we're following this guy—who knows? we might get killed—spearheading down the road. Another German comes out of the woods. He says, "A few of us here want to give up. Will you come?" I tell the other guys, "You wait here. I'll go in and see." It might be a trap. I'm very gullible. I believe people. I go in and, sure enough, there were a couple of hundred Germans standing around. We debated, we argued. Many of them didn't want to give up. Some wanted to give up. "Your cause is hopeless, come on, let's go." I was the only American there. I knew a smattering of German, some Yiddish. I'm surrounded by two hundred Germans and we're having this philosophical debate.

Just as we're talking, two planes come over and strafe us. Everybody runs into the woods. I never knew whether they were German or American planes. They came over very low and so fast. They really had enough by then. They all came back. We continued the discussion (laughs) and they decided to give up.

Being a showman type, I took their guns and strapped them all around my hip. I musta had twenty Lugers. I took all the binoculars and put 'em on my chest. I sat on top of the jeep and I had two hundred Germans walking behind me. I drove up the road to our battalion and gave them to the colonel. (Laughs.) It was very funny. Pure showmanship. We freed a couple of other concentration camps along the way.

At the end of the war, I was in Salzburg. We were among the first troops there. I commandeered a hotel for myself, the driver, and the still photographer. We had this little hotel all to ourselves. With lots of chambermaids we used to chase from room to room. The man in charge of the butcher shop owned the hotel. To curry favor with Americans, he fed us very well.

So the war ended. I was demobilized with five battle stars and I had enough points. My last job was to photograph dignitaries coming into Berchtesgaden. That was my last stop as a GI, up in the mountains at Berchtesgaden.

Back home, you have a feeling of euphoria. Pleased that you had accomplished what you set out to do. The photographer always has a front-row seat. You might get hurt in the process, but you're privileged. You're a participant and an eyewitness. To see fascism defeated, nothing better could have happened to a human being. You felt you were doing something worthwhile. You felt you were an actor in a tremendous drama that was unfolding. It was the most important moment in my life. I always felt very lucky to have been part of it.

POSTSCRIPT: *"Three months later, I was back in Europe again. With a Leica that I had liberated. The American Unitarian Association offered me a job to photograph Spanish refugees in southern France. I toured the camps for three years.*

"When they fled across the Pyrenees to escape Franco, the Vichy French had put them into concentration camps. When the Germans came into France, the French handed them the keys. The Germans put these refugees into forced-labor camps and in mines. They were still in these camps when I photographed them. During the war, many of them would sneak out and commit sabotage. They were among the leaders of the French Forces of the Interior—FFI. Capturing the faces of these heroic people was one of the most rewarding experiences of my life."

BOOK FOUR

CRIME AND PUNISHMENT

ALVIN (TOMMY) BRIDGES

Bay City, Michigan, is one of the Tri-Cities, the other two being Saginaw and Midland. It is an industrial area, hard-hit by the recession.

He had been a Bay City policeman for thirty-one years; during his last four years on the force, he was police chief. He retired in 1968.

It was a useless war, as every war is.

I got into more trouble when I was in the army in saying so. They give us this I-E, information and education. Every time they'd get one of these shavetails up there, just come outa college, sellin' us the idea that this war was essential. There was a whole company o' men there, officers too. I blew up and said, "Is any war essential?" I'm not an antiwar guy, I'd go tomorrow if there were a war. But this world's not gonna last long unless we stop it, this nuclear business.

I joined the army on February 20, 1942. To get somethin' to eat. (Laughs.) I don't know how the war was ever won, because they had no rhyme or reason why they selected a guy for an MP. When I was at Fort Custer, they was three guys ahead of me went in the air force like that, two of 'em in the infantry, and they come to me and said, "You're MP." The training they give us was just like a new sheriff goin' in and gettin' a new bunch of deputies, trial and error. It had nothin' to do with police business.

When we got our first assignment in London, I don't know how we ever made it. (Laughs.) The officers, they were dumber than we were. When I went to Paris, the first guy they sent out was me. They figured I knew all about Paris. I didn't know a hill o' beans about it. (Laughs.)

London, we got there New Year's morning of '43. Stayed till just six weeks after the invasion. When we got to Paris, there's still occupying troops. We were just like a new police department for the GIs.

We had a great amount of trouble with supplies being sold. People were starving to death over there and they would sell truckloads, big trucks, they'd be loaded with anything, didn't matter what it was. They'd sell it. The Frenchmen had all that money right there and they'd buy truck and all. He'd pay the guys and take off. The GI then come runnin' to the first MP station and he'd say, "Somebody stole my truck en route." We'd finally find it someplace after the Frenchman unloaded. And there wasn't a thing left in it. We don't know if it was stole or whether he sold it. He was with his outfit in Belgium by the time we found it. There was no follow-up at all, because there was so many people over and so much going on.

A lot of the GIs had respect for the MP and a lot of 'em hated our guts. Just like policemen. Worse, because we were the only ones who bothered 'em. The policemen in Paris didn't bother the GIs at all. If they were tearin' the place apart, they'd call us. We'd arrest 'em for anything from murder of another GI or civilian to sellin' one of those trucks.

In London, we got thirteen colored soldiers assigned to our outfit. That was the first time they had MPs mixed, colored and white. The only reason we got it was the colored congregated out in the Limehouse district and we couldn't do a thing with 'em. We lost a man in one of those places. It was Lichfield, headquarters of the Ninth Air Force. That's where the colored were support troops. They build the bridges, they build the airfield, they take this metal stripping and lay it across a bog. Not combat. They were second-class citizens from the word go, whether in the army or not. They had about two or three combat units. One of 'em was air force, made out of the college in Alabama, Tuskegee. They were in Italy and they had one of the best records, a terrific record.

A lotta these colored MPs were very nice. This Morton was originally from Alabama. Him and this big white master sergeant from Alabama, they'd call each other all kinda names, just two of 'em, back and forth. This sergeant'd say, "You people haven't been out of the jungle long enough to have your rights," or somethin' like that. And Morton'd say, "How do you know your ancestors weren't in a jungle?"

Our outfit was made up of Indiana, Ohio, and Michigan. And Tennessee, Georgia, and Alabama. There was a hellabaloo about who was gonna work with them colored guys. They didn't know what to do about it. So they said to me, "You're in charge of us tonight. Who you gonna put these guys with?" We had six of these colored guys go on duty that night. And I got hillbillies. First time they'd ever been away from home. Them Georgia boys said, "Sure, I'll work with a nigger." They didn't say colored or Negro. They'd tell me, "If they selected the guys, they must be pretty good guys." And they got along from then on, them Georgia guys and them colored guys. There wasn't a one of 'em refused me. I had two of these guys from Kalamazoo, Michigan, and I said, "Will you work with one of them colored guys?" "Jesus Christ, no." Y'see, them Georgia guys played with 'em as kids. They knew more about 'em than guys from the North.

In Paris, we'd go to these hotels to check on GIs AWOL. They's women galore up these four, five stories and stairs in the middle all the way. Rooms. All you'd do is take your flashlight and look under. If you'd see GI shoes, you'd know there's a GI in the room. (Laughs.) You open the door and nine times outa ten, the French gal would get under the covers and try to hide herself. (Laughs.) A lot of AWOLs from the colored quartermaster outfit.

There were more coloreds in Paris than white. The French women thought as much of a colored guy as they did of a white guy. Naturally they would go AWOL and they would get a French woman, a white woman, and probably that was forbidden where the colored guy come from.

Toward the end of that war, they wasn't a guy in any of those outfits, black or white, that wouldn't go AWOL. They had a damn hard job keepin' those guys up in front as they did winnin' a war. And boy, they'd kill ya, too, they'd kill an MP that interfered with 'em. They was outfits that towards the end of the war, they had to put 'em in straitjackets (laughs) in order to keep 'em in line. I went to North Africa to pick up prisoners there and come back across. When my outfit come to Fort Shanks, it's up in the hills north of New York City, up the Hudson, I looked up to see they had guys with rifles or machine guns walkin' beats on both sides of the thing. I said, "What in the hell are those guys doin' up there?" And they said, "To keep them infantry outfits that were goin' overseas." They'd go into them woods and away they'd go.

It burnt me up. I said to the lieutenant, "What in the hell are we doin', MPs and half of us guys have been overseas and back again, why are they guardin' us?" He said, "They guard everybody that comes into that thing," because they had so many AWOL. It was '42.

When we picked these guys up in Paris, we would go over to headquarters in England. They'd court-martial the guys there. Them guys were goin' AWOL in every direction. Mostly colored guys were tried. There was always a colonel, a major, and a captain—about five or seven at a court-martial. You could tell these guys were top kicks in the regular army. The first time I went to testify, this colonel was in charge. I said this guy wasn't guilty of selling anything. He was just picked up because he happened to be there. The colonel said, "Was he a nigger?" He didn't say Negro, he said nigger. I said, "He was colored." And he said, "Well, if he's a nigger, he's guilty, too." I don't know what they give them guys, because we never waited for the verdict. This could go on and on. Stealin' government property, they could have 'em sent to the firing squad.

Do you know any guys who were shot for something like that?

Oh yes. They shot some of those guys up there that were—if you'd go to a municipal court, they'd dismiss the case. Depending a lot upon the commanding officer. The men that were shot and hung in Shepton Mallet—that was the place Henry the Fifth cut all the gals' heads off. It was close to evening when we'd get there, because of train connections from London.

Those colored guys we got from Lichfield, they had a truck loaded with GI stuff. They'd stolen some of that. Anyway, the things they would shoot you for were incidental compared to a civilian law. Jesus, the Articles of War book looks like a Bible. They can shoot you in wartime for nothin'. Murder and rape, I think they hung. They'd execute 'em the next morning at six o'clock. They might be five or six of 'em shot. Sometimes they'd get five years. I don't know what they done to most of the guys I brought in. I don't know where the hell they sent 'em.

I first started takin' em out of Goode Street. It's somethin' like a holding tank for criminals. When we'd get 'em, we'd leave London with 'em. Normally, they would send two of us MPs when we went to Shepton Mallet. This particular time I was alone. Sergeant says to me, "This guy's gonna be shot." He would handcuff me to that guy, left hand. You had your gun on your right side. He was a kind of half-past-eight guy anyway. I don't know what the hell he was in there for, but he was supposed to be shot. I think he killed another GI. He was out of this world. Maybe he was doin' it deliberately, I don't know.

The conductor told me when he let us off, "You're only a short distance away from Shepton Mallet". I look and it's down in the boondocks. The prisoner was more worried than I was. I got a man handcuffed to me that's under death sentence, gonna be shot the next day. I didn't know whether to shoot him right forthwith or wait till he started somethin'. (Laughs.) You don't know how them scuffles gonna come out. Oh, I was tempted a couple times to shoot him. But I sat down alongside him because it was a matter of life and death. That guy might have a knife. I didn't search him, the sergeant did. I certainly was scared, yes.

Why they sent me alone, I don't know. That burnt me up as the war was goin' on. They probably sent fifty MPs layin' around the barracks, not doin' a damn thing, and here I was out in the boondocks with this guy handcuffed to me.

I said, I might just as well get these cigarettes out. My wife run a grocery store at the time, she sent me a fifty-tin of Lucky Strikes. I give this guy a pack of cigarettes when I turned him over to the sergeant, who come by with a carryall to pick us up. The sergeant asked me if I want to come in tomorrow morning at six o'clock and this guy would be shot. This guy was standin' right there. I told him no, I didn't want to see anybody shot. He said, "Well, some guys that bring 'em down like to stay and watch 'em shot."

The thought popped into my mind that when you're supposed to shoot a guy, they have five or six guys and only one guy's loaded with live ammunition. It gives a guy the feeling that he didn't shoot nobody. He said, "Don't let anybody shit you. Every one of them rifles is loaded. When you fire, there ain't no blanks there."

I never liked to see anybody executed or anybody shot. I was a policeman for thirty-one years. I saw a lotta suicides and a lotta murders. How foolish it is to take a life. One boom and that's it. You can't say, Wait, come back here, bullet, after it's been fired one time. I wouldn't give you a nickel to see a shooting or a hanging.

I saw the hangman in Paris, France. He looked so odd. He had on a wide-brimmed hat, they called 'em campaign hats, and a full-dress uniform. He was a master sergeant. An American. They had to have their own hangman. He was a professional, stationed in Texas. He'd bring his own rope. He wouldn't talk. In other words, he was a ghost, as far as I was concerned. He wouldn't talk to nobody. They brought him into Paris there and I guess he hung two guys. I don't know if this Slovik* is one I arrested or not. The kid they shot for desertion. Eisenhower says that's the only guy that was ever executed for it. That's what burns me up, when a gross of them that I know of were executed for probably more minor things than what Slovik was. They said he was the only one. We had to make a show of it. The son-of-a-bitches.

How goddamn foolish it is, the war. They's no war in the world that's worth fightin' for, I don't care where it is. They can't tell me any different. Money, money is the thing that causes it all. I wouldn't be a bit surprised that the people that start wars and promote 'em are the men that make the money, make the ammunition, make the clothing and so forth. Just think of the poor kids that are starvin' to death in Asia and so forth that could be fed with how much you make one big shell out of.

This European war was cruel, no question about it. But the airplane has come in its own, nuclear weapons . . . We don't be in this world for long.

JOSEPH SMALL

On the night of July 17, 1944, two transport vessels loading ammunition at the Port Chicago (California) naval base on the Sacramento River were suddenly engulfed in a gigantic explosion. The incredible blast wrecked the naval base and heavily damaged the small town of Port Chicago, located 1½ miles away. Some 320 American sailors were killed instantly. The two ships and the large loading pier were totally annihilated. Windows were shattered in towns 20 miles away and the glare of the explosion could be seen in San Francisco, some 35 miles away. It was the worst home-front disaster of World War Two. . . . Of the navy personnel who died in the blast, most—some 200 ammunition loaders—were black.

—The Black Scholar, *spring 1982*

*Eddie Slovik, the most celebrated World War Two case of an American soldier being executed.

Somerset, New Jersey. "We have a very quiet community here. The neighbor on my right is white. The neighbor on my left is black. We watch each other's property." The small homes, mostly frame, indicate a working-class neighborhood.

"I do repairs on homes. I'm a carpenter, electrician, a plumber, a painter, a paperhanger. Whatever. I like working with my hands. I picked 'em up along the way, trial and error."

He is a devout Christian. On the wall, enframed: "All Things Work Together for Good to Them That Love God." In the front yard is an old church bus, which he drives. Bible Way Church Worldwide, Trenton, New Jersey. "I'm also an auto mechanic. I rebuilt the engine." He wasn't always religious. "I was a man of the world until 1968. In 1968, I heard the gospel preached in its fullness, and I heeded the word of God and was baptized in Jesus' name. Since 1968, I've been saved."

I went into the navy in 1943. I left Great Lakes, Illinois, as an apprentice seaman and was shipped to Port Chicago, California. It was a naval ammunition depot. Everybody above petty officer was white. All of the munition handlers was black. We off-loaded ammunition from boxcars and loaded it on ships. We handled every type of ammunition that was being shipped overseas, from .30-caliber ammunition shells to five-hundred-pound bombs. We worked around the clock, twenty-four hours, three shifts.

I was an ammunition handler until they discovered that I had the ability to operate a winch. I had no training, but from close observation of the winch operator, I learned how to do it. If I watch somebody do it, I'll do it.

There was constant discussion by the men about the dangers. We got into arguments frequently. I personally had several altercations with my superior. I always received an answer: If it explodes, you won't know anything about it.

The explosives came on boxcars. When we first got there, we loaded only on one side. The ship was moored on one side. It later expanded to a ship on either side of the dock. We were pitted one against the other divisions. If my division put on three thousand tons of ammunition during our shift, the next division had to beat that tonnage. We were pushed by our officers. They bet between them as to what division would put on the most tonnage at any given time.

We complained that it would add danger to the already dangerous job. But we were assured that since there were no detonators in any of the shells or bombs, it was impossible for them to go off. None of us believed that.

We worked under these conditions because we had no alternative. If you complained, you got KP or you got restricted to the base or you got extra duty. We were sailors, under government jurisdiction. So we worked.

Now, there was an attempt by the union to take over the stevedore work. We didn't know anything about it. All this came out after the explosion. The union did offer to send in professionally trained men to handle that ammunition. We were untrained. We had no knowledge of ammunition handling. It calls for special operators to handle special machines. I took over by accident when the winch operator got sick.

We all knew the danger was always present. When a boxcar came in with ammunition, it was loaded to within two feet to the top of the door. Men had to crawl up there, build a ramp, and then roll the ammunition down the ramp, which was about eight feet above the dock. It would hit the side of the ship and then somebody would throw a two-by-four in front of it, and then they'd roll it into the net. Now these bombs weighed as much as five hundred pounds.

There were continuous complaints. We discussed it among ourselves. Some of the fellas wrote letters, to no avail. We had many of the fellas went AWOL. Many tried various means of obtaining a discharge. We had one fella tried to get out on a section 8: mentally unsound. Every morning, just about daylight, we'd hear horseshoes clinking. I went to the window; there was this young man, he had his shoes tied around his neck, had on his skivvies, and was pitching horseshoes. They gave him all kind of psychiatric examinations. He stayed around the barracks all day and slept and did nothing. At least that way he escaped work, and that's what he was after. He survived the explosion because he wasn't on the docks at the time.

On July 17, 1944, my division had left the dock at three o'clock and we had come back to the barracks. Most of us had sacked out. At 10:19 that night, that was the first explosion. It was five or ten seconds after, we heard a second. I have understood since then that there was really one explosion.*

*John H. Grove, a chemist working at a laboratory in the Berkeley Hills "some twenty airline miles away," recalls: "I felt a rumble. It was like an earthquake. I distinctly heard

---

▼

I was laying on the top bunk on my stomach when I heard it. Then the barracks just started to disintegrate. All the windows blew out. I was picked up off the bunk and flipped over and landed on my back. But I had gripped the edge of the mattress, so it was on top of me. That prevented me from getting cut by the glass and the dunnage and the lumber and everything that fell into the barracks.

Many of the fellas lost arms and legs, some were blinded, but I was one of the blessed. I didn't receive a scratch. It took about an hour and a half to get the medical men there. They loaded all the badly injured on buses and cattle cars. I didn't have a chance to go down to the docks. I was very busy tending to some of the fellas there that was cut. I got a minor cut after I gave a boy my shoes and then I walked on glass.

A mop-up crew was down at the docks to clean up. They came back and told us that the docks were leveled, were gone. Both ships were gone. You could see the prow of one ship sticking up out of the water. The black ammunition handlers, two hundred, were all killed. Quite a few white sailors were lost. One ship had a full company, ready to sail. The other ship just had a maintenance crew.

I heard rumors of one ammunitions handler who escaped. He was asleep, hid away in a gear locker. It blowed the gear locker away, but he survived because of the gear. There could be a moral. Shirkin' pays off at the right time. (Laughs.)

Early the next morning, before daylight, we were shipped out to Vallejo, another ammunition depot. We were placed in a barracks to await further movement by the navy. We had no idea what was happening. But we're sailors and we're obligated to obey orders.

I was sort of an unofficial leader of the men. We had black petty officers, but all the men considered them air-bangers. Brownnoses. They weren't very effective as leaders of the black men. So I was accepted by them as their leader. I always marched outside the ranks. I called cadence. When it was time to get up in the morning, muster time, I would come to the bunks and shake the men gently: "All right, fellas, let's go." The petty officer would stand in the front door and

---

two explosions. Then we heard that two ammunition ships blew up. Just leveled the civilian area of Port Chicago, which had another name, Bay Point. There were rumors that the naval officers were in competition to see who could get the ships loaded fastest. The longshoremen raised hell about it. They said that a lot of people were killed. I didn't know they were black. I heard there was some sort of mutiny and a trial. I don't remember if it was in the papers. There was wartime censorship. They tried to hush the whole thing up."

curse: "All right, you so-and-so's." He lost the respect of the men. They would follow my orders more readily than they would those that were appointed to give them orders.

We settled down to life after the explosion. We had no duties, no assignments. This went on for about ten days. Then they posted a notice on the barracks wall that all divisions will muster that next morning in front of the barracks at 0700 hours. We were there. The petty officers gave the order: right face, forward march. About 240 men marched off toward the parade ground.

A lieutenant was standing at the entrance, on the platform. As we approached him, we got the command: Halt. We halted. He said a few words about our obligations to the navy as sailors and to the country as Americans. Now, he said, "We're going back to work." He gave the order: Forward march. We had about a hundred feet to march before we had to either turn left or right.

He gave the command: Column left. We knew the layout. Column right meant the parade ground, column left meant the docks. Everybody stopped dead in their tracks. Everybody stopped as one. He said, "Will you go back to work?" Nobody answered. Then he called me: "Joseph Small, front and center." I marched up the side, across the front, came to a halt, made a left turn, and stood right in front of him. He asked me, "Small, will you return to duty?" I said, "No." As I said that, someone back in the ranks said, "If Small don't go, we won't go either." So that put me in the front of it. They marched us back to the barracks. Next thing we heard, we were going to be tried by general court-martial for mutiny.

Prior to that, the men said, "Small, get up a petition." I canvassed the men and everybody gave their opinion, how they felt about going back to work. This is why they charged me as being the leader of this mutinous assembly. I didn't instigate anything. I didn't persuade the men to vote one way or another. Most of them was against going back to handling ammunition. For one reason: we were afraid. We were afraid of it before the explosion. After the explosion, we were definitely afraid.

We were put on a barge. We were marched under marine guard, fifty or sixty at a time, to the mess hall, served food, and returned to the barge. We were packed in like sardines. Continuous fights. I was the one that kept down the disturbance. One night, I called a meeting. I told 'em: "We're gonna have to play it cool or we'll all be in trouble."

One of the men had fashioned a knife, and he cut a marine. That set the marines against us. See what I mean? For any reason whatsoever they would jump on you. I let the men know we were in a ticklish situation and we had to walk very carefully. In order not to be considered dangerous and sentenced to death by shooting. I said, "Fellas, if we don't start anything, they can't do anything to us." I used an expression: "Fellas, we got 'em by the balls." That was the primary condemning thing in the trial. They had a spy in that meeting. He recorded everything that was said and took it back to the officials. This came out in the trial that I said, We got 'em by the so-and-so. That meant I was starting a mutinous gatherin'.

There came out a list of 50 men that were considered the most dangerous of the whole group of some 240. The 50 men was held over for general court-martial. The other 190 men were sent back to duty, were given summary court-martials. Some of 'em did go back to loading ships.

I was the head leader of the fifty men. (Laughs.) An admiral called me to his office. He said, "Small, you are the leader of this bunch. If you don't return to work, I'm gonna have you shot." Just like that. Then I did something stupid: I blew my top. I said, "You baldheaded so-and-so, go ahead and shoot." That branded me as a mutineer. (Laughs.)

The fifty of us were transferred to Yerba Buena Island and held for general court-martial. We had navy-appointed lawyers. There was one civilian lawyer in the audience in our behalf: Thurgood Marshall, for the NAACP.

Each one of us was put on the stand. We were asked about what went on, who said this, who did what. They had rebuttal witnesses for the prosecution. We knew in the beginning how it was coming out. Everything was rigged. I've said this quite often: You can't beat Uncle Sam. You can fight him, but you can't beat him. That's why I have no hard feelings against the navy. If I had cowarded down, if they had broke me down and I had done something I didn't want to do, then maybe I would have hard feelings. But I didn't lose any respect and I got what Uncle Sam thought I deserved. As far as I'm concerned, the navy is the best branch of service in the world.

I have two sons and both of them went through the navy. They know about it. They also know why it happened. They know I was a victim of circumstances rather than a victim of my own actions. A father chastises a child sometimes because he deserves it. And other times, because he can. Uncle Sam chastised me because he could do it, not that I was guilty of anything. How many fathers do you know would allow their child to slap them without doing anything about it? We felt that we had a right to do what we did. Uncle Sam, being Uncle Sam, had the power to do what he did. We were found guilty. We were sentenced to fifteen years of hard labor with a dishonorable discharge.

Hard labor was anything they wanted you to do. We didn't have any really hard labor. We built nets for the ships. We learned how to weave rope and how to splice. We picked up driftwood, cleared the beaches. Sometimes we were assigned to breakin' rocks. This was mostly as punishment. We'd be given sixteen-pound sledges and make little ones outa big ones. Most of the marine guards were human. But once in a while, you'd find one, he had a .45 on his side and a club and he made the best of it. I had one put a .45 at my temple and say, "You black so-and-so, I'll blow your brains out." What could I say?

I've always been on the religious side. I've always believed in the Bible. While we were at Yerba Buena, I had a dream. I dreamed I was in a snake pit and I was bitten by this deadly snake. But the snake died and the wound healed up. I told this dream to the men the next morning. You'll be surprised the effect it had on everybody. I said, "We're gonna be found guilty, we're gonna go to prison, but it won't last." That relieved those men. They believed me. It happened just that way. We stayed in prison sixteen months and we were let out.

We were celebrities in prison. (Laughs.) "The fifty Port Chicago boys are here." We had clear sailing. Nobody bothered us. The picture they had painted of us was that we were murderers, we were deadly, we were cobras ready to strike. If you say anything to one of us, you're liable to get your head chopped off, see what I mean? They were afraid of us. The white sailors, the guards, handled us with kid gloves. Not that we were that bad, but the word had gotten around before we got there. Wherever we went (whispers): There go the Port Chicago boys. The black sailors respected us.

After sixteen months, all of a sudden, without any forewarning, they told us to pack our bags. You're shippin' out. They didn't say where. About five-thirty one night, they loaded us all on a truck, took us out, and put us on ships. There were five or six of us on each ship. We went aboard, it was daylight. When we woke up the next morning, there was no land to be seen. I asked one of the sailors, "How far is land?" He said, "About two miles—straight down." I'd never been to sea before. We rode the ship to all over the South Pacific. We had no assignment. Ship's company had work to do. We were five passengers.

There was no resentment. There's five guys sittin' here, doing nothin'. When they found out we were the Port Chicago guys, everybody sympathized with our position. The white guys. There was plenty curiosity. They used to come down and talk with us. We were asked questions. When they heard what we'd been through, they said they'd have done the same thing.

I don't remember how long we were there. Oh Lord, we traveled. We left San Pedro and we went to Okinawa. Left Okinawa and we hit some other port. We spent three months in Leyte in the Philippines. We left there, we went someplace else. We never went ashore.

The Man Without a Country.

That's what we were. I read that.

We were finally returned to Seattle. That was the old Kaiser shipyards. We policed the grounds, picked up paper, garbage, stuff around. I was assigned on board a ship for three months. I was the only black seaman that had ever been on the ship. There were two other blacks, but they were stewards. We had a skipper, referred to as a ninety-day wonder. He assigned me to duty on the fantail, relaying his orders. He was on the bridge. I had earphones. Now the crew was white. They were doing hard pulls and I was standing giving them orders. They resented it tremendously. I think the skipper was trying to prove to me he was not discriminatory. He was from Massachusetts, see?

The chief bosun's mate was an Alabamarite. He was about six foot three, musta weighed 260 pounds. The first time I went to crew's quarters to eat, he sat down opposite me. He said, "By God, this is the first time I ever ate with a nigger." I hit him with the mug. I threw the coffee on him first. Before he could get straight, I was across the table on him. At that time, I weighed about 145 pounds.

We fight. I mean we tore up that dining room. I was so fast he couldn't hit me. He was so hard I couldn't hurt him. We both got dog-tired. The skipper came and broke it up. He said, "You wanna fight, put on boxing gloves and go out on the fantail." We put on the gloves. He would swing at me and he would swing where I was. I would hit him, but I couldn't hurt him. We got dog-tired again. So the skipper said, "All right, knock it off. Shake hands."

We became the best of friends. We would go on liberty in San Francisco. Wherever I went, he was there. We would go in a bar and he would say, "Gimme two beers." They would set one up on the counter. He'd bounce over the counter and pour one for himself and give me the other. He told me, "Randy"—that was my middle name, Randolph—"I found out something. A man is a man." Up to that time, he had been taught that black men were inferior. When he found one that was half his size, but still wasn't afraid of him, it made him realize somethin'. He never knew I was one of the Port Chicago guys. All they knew is that I was another seaman.

I used to run a poker game in Seattle. I used to make four hundred, five hundred dollars a night. Go to Seattle and Portland to operate it. I had accumulated a whole five-gallon full of coins when we got new orders.

Finally, they loaded us all on a train and we were shipped to Lido Beach, New York. We received a discharge under honorable conditions. It's not a dishonorable discharge and it's not an honorable discharge. It doesn't entitle us to any veterans' benefits. I couldn't go to a veterans' hospital if I got sick. I lost my GI insurance. If I was to die under conditions that warranted a military funeral, I couldn't have it.

The black community had raised such a stink about the case—Thurgood Marshall, Walter White of the NAACP, the black papers. They brought so much adverse publicity against the navy until they rescinded the fifteen-year sentence with a dishonorable discharge.

Know what happened as a result of that explosion, that trial? The whole base was integrated. They put up a tremendous recreation facility there, bowling alleys, tennis courts, swimming pool, everything. Before the explosion, the streets were ankle-deep in mud. When you stepped off the sidewalk, you stepped into mud. What does that tell you?

I ran into a couple of the fellas recently. I really don't know how they feel, because we didn't discuss what we went through. We just shook hands: How you doin'? Whatcha doin'? And so-and-so and so-and-so. But we never discussed the past.

It didn't have any concrete effects on me. I was drafted. I did my time. Some of it was under adverse conditions, but God spared me. I returned home sane and whole. For that, I'm thankful. I don't hold any grudge against the navy or anybody in there. In fact, I consider what I went through an experience worth having gone through. I hold no animosity against anybody.

I think that God had his hand on me all through my life. This was just another incident where I went through and the protecting hand of God kept me for the work I'm doing now.

What—if on that parade ground—you'd have said yes instead of no—?

If I hadda consented to go back to duty, I would not only be betraying myself, I would have been betraying them. But I wasn't speaking for them, I was speaking for me.

HANS GÖBELER AND JAMES SANDERS

I bought a sailboat last December from a doctor in Key Largo, Florida. He was German. He told me he was a prisoner of war and had been interned. "How come you were a prisoner?" I asked. He was on a submarine. It was depth-charged and sunk. I said, "Do you remember who sank you?" The Guadalcanal, *he said. I said, "Oh, my God, that's my old ship."*

I'm buying a sailboat from him thirty-eight years later. We have met the enemy and bought his boat. (Laughs.)

—Dr. Johanson, an American physician

At the Museum of Science and Industry in Chicago, a German U-boat reposes. It is the U-505. It was sunk by the carrier U.S.S. Guadalcanal *two hundred miles off the coast of West Africa, June 4, 1944. It was salvaged and brought here.*

On this September day in 1982, there is a reunion of most of the surviving members of the crews of both vessels.

Hans Göbeler was a mate on the German submarine. James Sanders was junior flight officer on the American carrier, U.S.S. Guadalcanal.

GÖBELER: Every man, especially the youth, can be manipulated. The more you say to him, that's the way of life, the American way of life, the German way of life, they believe it. Without being more bad than the other is. That was why a lot of German people were running behind Hitler. There's a great danger all the time. If you get that much of people without work, if someone would come and say, "I will give you work so that your family doesn't have to suffer," they will run behind him.

I guess if the same would happen in the United States, a lot of people would run behind Adolf Hitler, too. They don't care about what that man will do after they got work. That's the great danger in the future, too. If people don't think more than they do now, someday perhaps there will be one or two other Adolf Hitlers in another name.

SANDERS: It could happen. People could be fooled. Memory is short. I have two friends who married German girls. One girl, her family were dissenters. They couldn't open their mouth. The other girl's father was a storm trooper. I saw pictures of him in his uniform. She tells how she, as a young girl, strutted with her Nazi emblems in front of American occupying troops. They both came from educated middle-class backgrounds.

GÖBELER: In 1928, my father was without work. I was a boy of six. Most of the time when we awoke, we didn't get enough bread to eat. My father was without work four years. Then came Hitler. (Imitates Hitler) "You German people, you will get work." In 1933, most of the German common people voted for Hitler because they got enough to eat. There were some strong people standing behind him. They were tryin' to make big business. Krupp and whatever they were called. They brought up Hitler, not the common people. If they would have voted some other fella, the industrialists wouldn't have given them their okay.

After 1933, my father got work. I watched as a German boy. I've been in the Hitler Youth. Every German who comes here, my age, and says, "I haven't been in the Hitler Youth"—he lies. Every one.

We could make journeys, we didn't pay anything. You could go without money from Hamburg to Munich. When the war started, I was fifteen years old. I tried to join the navy. I didn't care about that it was the fault of Hitler. It was the navy I was looking at. When I was seventeen, I joined the navy.

I was proud to be a submarine man. I recognized what danger it was to be on a submarine. When I heard U-124 didn't come back, and a few days later, U-542 didn't come back, I knew what happened. Perhaps it was luck that I could join the U-505. Perhaps if I were in the land infantry, I could be killed. We knew that ninety-seven percent of our submarines did not survive. That's why I am thankful the Americans caught us. I never looked at them as personal enemies. I helped my children think the same way. I'm wantin' to help keep the peace.

At first, on the submarine, we had forty-nine men. At last we had to take fifty-nine. Because every ride, we lost some. The submarine was built for forty-nine, not for fifty-nine. We had less food. Life was getting harder and harder when the Americans started their machinery against us. Every day and every week.

We only knew what we were told: our duty. We got the feeling that someday we would die together from the Americans and the Russians. But we had given our oath. That's a bad soldier, who forgets he put up his three fingers. Everywhere in the world, in every force, soldiers have to think the same way.

We saw that each time when we came back, there was a big hole in more boats. We couldn't count them. We knew we lost the battle in the Atlantic.

SANDERS: I wanted to get in the war and get it over with. As far as Germany went, I felt we had to put 'em out of commission, so we'd change their system. We never could end the hostility until Hitler was removed. At the time of the event in '44, I was twenty-five.

GÖBELER: I was twenty-one. Our second skipper, he was twenty-five. He had done duty on that boat ten times by the age twenty-four. I can't imagine what made him kill himself. During a depth charge. It was too much for a man, twenty-five, to lead a ship through the Atlantic Ocean, through the Caribbean Sea, through the Gulf of Mexico, through the Panama Canal, and down to South Africa. He had responsibility for that thing, full of power, full of danger. Once he was knocked down, he didn't know what to do further on.

The war was getting harder, day after day. The submarines had to pay the highest price. From thirty-nine thousand submarine men, thirty-two thousand were killed at sea. Most of them very young men.

June 4, 1944, when our skipper put up his periscope and looked around and he was seeing one, two, three, four, five, and another big ship in a wide circle, he knew it was over. I was standing beside him in the conning tower. He said, "Take the locks off in case we get bombed." And we will get up to the surface and one or two can escape. We got too much air pressure. We couldn't even breathe normal. He said, "Open the valves, we have to go up." They open fire at the same moment we come up to the surface. Only one man was killed out of fifty-nine. The radio man, I can't understand it, he went crazy or something. They didn't shoot too long at us. Most of us had jumped into the water. We were with five guys to make the big lifeboat. A large wave took me away. They threw me a rubber raft.

Perhaps some other American commander would have given us hell. Here, they ceased fire as soon as possible. You have to shoot as long as you get your order to shoot. Someone must have said right away: Cease fire.

SANDERS: They gave a cease-fire, but I didn't hear it. It did stop suddenly. We could see there was nobody on your deck. The *Guadalcanal* turned away, because we didn't know how many submarines there were. We didn't want to get torpedoed. In the Pacific, a number of ships were torpedoed because they lingered on the scene.

When we heard that fifty-eight out of fifty-nine were saved, most of us were very pleased. We didn't care whether you were Germans or Africans or what. We had other German prisoners before. We got a young boy one time from a submarine who was the only survivor. Everybody wanted to talk with him. The guards were always talkin' to him. I remember this young American corpsman, guardin' him. He was sittin' with his gun across his lap and these two kids are sittin' there, talkin' through a weak wire screen. Within a week after the guy was captured, they were just talkin' like a couple of kids that grew up in the same neighborhood.

GÖBELER: Our captain was unconscious. They didn't let us wait too long in the water. They started their salvation. There came some whale boats and picked us up. That's what I will never forget. Because I know some other crews, they were killed in the water. That's the truth, I can put up my three fingers. Perhaps the man who was shooting lost his brother two or three days before. He doesn't give any pardon to the enemy who killed his brother. That's the big danger at that moment.

When we came aboard, the first time in my life I have seen dark people, black people. I thought—oh . . . (Laughs.)

SANDERS: The officers' mess stewards.

GÖBELER: I put my face over the side of the boat, there was a black one, he took me and threw me aboard the destroyer. He has got some chewing tobacco, he said, "Come on, have some." I was scared. They didn't look like soldiers at that moment. I thought, Oh, God, perhaps it would have been better to be killed.

SANDERS: If you'd have asked these Americans, if a fella was witty, he might have said, "That's our special night-fighting force." (Laughs.)

GÖBELER: The black took me inside. I think it was a mess for enlisted men. He gave me some cake. At once, there came a petty officer and he was shouting against the soldier that he had taken me in that room: "Get him out of here."

SANDERS: The colored fella may have taken you into the officers' wardroom. He probably wasn't angry, probably spoke in excitement.

It was the *Pillsbury* that picked 'em up. In the afternoon, they were transferred to the *Guadalcanal.* We all lined the rail to look at them. I didn't think any of these boys looked awful worried. Some of 'em were smiling. They didn't look as if they were having bad luck. I thought the general appearance of your group was one of relief. You seemed to know nobody was gonna really hurt ya.

GÖBELER: No one of us was willing to give his life for Hitler. We knew that death would not be a thing to smile at. We have seen too much at sea killing. I have seen some poor survivors from merchant ship burning off in oil. We only knew we had to do our duty as well as the American sailors did. Perhaps I'm wrong, but I think sailors all over the world, whatever they are, when they see one sailor in the water, he doesn't care what nationality or color of his skin, he is supposed to help him.

SANDERS: That was the attitude of the American navy as I knew it. Some fella I went to flight school with, I heard him braggin' about shooting up a canoe full of gooks out in the Pacific. I remember thinking what a miserable crumb he was.

Captain Gallery gave strict orders not to fraternize. His fear was there might be amongst the Germans some fanatical men, who might possibly try to seize guns. He wasn't afraid they'd take the ship. But our officers had side arms and he was worried that somebody'd grab a gun and kill a few people. The sailors disregarded the order, as much as they could.

GÖBELER: (Laughs.) I know. The man who was guarding me told me his address. He told me after the terrible war's over, we will get connected, we will write each other. After four years, when I came home out of captivity, I wrote a letter to his address. A few months later, I got a letter from his parents. They told me he was killed one year later in Pacific.

SANDERS: The guards were chattin' with you fellas all the time. I never saw an officer light into them. I never talked with you fellas, because I didn't want the sailors see me breakin' orders. (Laughs.) If I coulda gotten in the corner where no sailors were lookin' on, I would've talked with ya.

GÖBELER: It was a terrible feeling for us because the enemy has got our boat. We thought if we have won the war, they will put us in jail in Germany. We will have to be responsible that the enemy has got our ship. Two or three times, it was going down, we were thinking it was sinking and we started singin', happy. So nobody would be responsible.

I came home in December of '47. I been one year and eleven months in the United States and the rest of the time in England for two more years. That's one thing I can't understand. The war was over.

SANDERS: I suspect they were holding submariners to see if they were gonna be subject to charges of war crimes, such as strafing lifeboats. Those war trials were being held after the war. One of the fellows tried was Admiral Doenitz, right?

GÖBELER: It was hard at first in America. But we knew how to talk to people. At one farm in Texas, that farmer wrote me letters. I was in Louisiana first. We picked cotton and cut woods. If we didn't cut our weight three times, we were put in jail. You only got one dollar a day.

In my free time, I was drawing pictures and making small models of submarines. So we could get Coca-Cola and cigarettes. In Louisiana, at first, they were fearin' us. But after one, two weeks, they saw that we were the same people as they were. All this time, they kept us in a secure place. Nobody's supposed to know about us. We were apart from the other German prisoners and from the Italians.

SANDERS: I think the news was being kept from the enemy that the Americans got this sub.

GÖBELER: It was supposed to be a secret that the American navy used the U-505 to find out secrets from the German navy. After a quarter of a year, the German submarine command gave news to our parents that we must be dead. My mother was very sick and I was the only son. But she had a certain feeling inside her. She always said to my father, "He must be alive." Nearly four years later, I telephoned from the railway station. If I would have appeared at the door, something could happen to my mother.

Now I sit here and I only think Jim is my friend, and I believe he is thinkin' the same.

SANDERS: I never had any personal hostility toward the German people. Nor really the Japanese people. There's a maturing with thirty-eight years.

CHARLIE MILLER

We're facing the Pacific Ocean on a salubrious Sunday afternoon. A small house in La Jolla, California.

He is national commander of American Ex-Prisoners of War, a voluntary organization seeking recognition and rights for ex-POWs. His effu-

I was young and goin' about my daily life and all of a sudden the sky
opens and there we are: World War Two. It was chaos.

I was twenty-one years old, lived in Bridgeton, New Jersey. I was
a high school dropout. Doing jobs, working on farms, pickin' fruits
and vegetables. Just menial labor.

I was drafted in August 1942 and went into the air force. My wife
came from our hometown. We had grown up five blocks apart. We
were married April the first, '43. I left for overseas as an armored
gunner, April 9, '43.

I flew decoy missions on a B-17 over the English Channel to draw
flak and so forth. I made two bombing missions into Germany on the
thirteenth and fourteenth of May. The fifteenth of May was my third
mission. We were shot down over the North Sea. As we were hitting
the water, I was thrown through the radio door, and jammed my
elbow and couldn't get out. The plane was filling with water. All the
other people got out. One man did come back and freed me. My arm,
my back, my shoulder, fouled up pretty good. When the plane
ditched, we released a life raft. We lashed two of 'em together with
a nylon cord. There were six sergeants and four officers. Ten guys,
five on each raft.

The first thing we did, we reached for medication. Some kind soul
from England somewhere along the line took all the medication. Our
radio operator had been hit in the face with a shell. So we had
nothing, no water, no food, nothing. I would say the morale was great,
we were laughing and trying to sing, tell jokes, pass the time of day
saying: I think I hear a plane, I think I hear a ship. Which of course
we were always imagining.

So it was eleven o'clock in the morning. As evening came, the
North Sea becomes very, very cold. And rough. The waves were so
high, you could not see the other raft.

Approximately twenty-four hours later, a German seaplane came
over. He flew around us for probably a half an hour. He had a cannon
pointed at our raft. We figured that was it. When the German spotted
the British fighter plane, he headed back to the mainland. When the
British plane wiggled its wings, we were jubilant. We figured this is
it. He chased back the flying boat. We waited and waited. Nothing.

The next thing we saw was a German patrol boat pull up to us, took us out of the rafts, and put us on board. The first thing you see are the swastikas. At that point, it dawns on a person that this is really it. The enemy now has you. I do have a record from our archives that there was no search attempted at all. Maybe it was just chaos.

The captain of that German patrol boat was a very understanding person. He understood it was war. He had his sailors actually come down to the raft and lift me aboard the patrol boat. They put us in their mess hall. Like a picnic table in the middle. It had a red-and-white-checkered tablecloth like you see in our Italian restaurants.

Two of the Germans undressed me. They dried me off with a towel, picked me up, and put me in one of the bunks.

We had been told to expect, once you're captured, the beatings, starvation, things like that. I was taken sick again and passed out. When I woke up, there was a German sitting on the edge of my bed with my head in his lap. He also was wipin' my face. I found out that he was educated in Cleveland and spoke English fluently. They put us on a mailboat goin' to the mainland. Then they put us on a train and we went to Frankfurt. That was the interrogation center. You have a light hangin' from the ceiling, in a very little cell. Absolutely solitary confinement. They would come in at any time. They come in and talk to you for three, four minutes and leave. Come right back and interrogate you again. Our crew stayed there seven or eight days.

After Frankfurt, our officers went to Stalag 3. There were a few British people there, some French. There were a lot of political refugees there, if I remember correctly. They were thrown in with the Russians. There were many, many Russians there. We didn't intermix much with the Russians. There was probably thirty, forty feet separating our compound from the Russians. There was a common street that went right through this camp, a little dirt road. We'd go in the Indian compound. They'd receive some British Red Cross packages. They did not eat meat, they did not smoke. So we would trade them cookies or whatever for meat and cigarettes. See, we'd go to the French compound and trade them our Nescafé for biscuits. In turn, we'd trade our biscuits to the Indians, which by the way are a very fine people. We used to bribe the German guards with cigarettes. They used to bring us blood sausage. I never liked it.

We had Red Cross packages occasionally delivered. So we would take our bread or big chunks of sausage, whatever we had, and we would throw it to the Russian compound. The Russians would come out of their barracks and they would fight among themselves for a little piece of bread. These poor people, they had nothing from their country.

I think there's a natural hatred with the Russians and the Germans. They fed the Russians just enough to keep them alive. See, the Russians would go out and work. When we'd throw them cigarettes and things, they'd break ranks and have a regular brawl tryin' to get somethin' to eat. The Germans would take their bicycles on the back wheel and beat the Russians with the front wheels as the Russians were rollin' on the ground. They beat 'em with rifles and they also had dogs.

The Germans used to have a great sport. At night, they'd leave their dogs run through our barracks, and everyone'd climb the upper bunks. One night, they let 'em go into the Russian barracks, and there was a lot of confusion. When the Germans finally went in, lit the lights, the only thing they retrieved were three halters. The Russians had in fact killed and ate the dogs. (Laughs.) It's very humorous, but to them it was survival. We loved these Russians. We thought they were outstanding soldiers. 'Cause I was liberated by the Russians.

We got along great with the British, except they wouldn't gamble. (Laughs.) We'd play dice, poker, blackjack. For bars of soap, whatever. This is '43. We were there exactly two years to the day.

I went to seven different camps. I escaped seven times. That's not sayin' too much for my intelligence, 'cause I was captured every time. (Laughs.)

In 7-A, two other men and myself, we went through nine barbed-wire fences, actually cut through and escaped. This other fella and I, Steve—he incidentally was shot by the Germans for tryin' to escape one other time—he and I walked through the city of Vienna until nightfall. We mingled with civilians. As long as you don't get trapped in conversation, you're all right. We window-shopped. (Laughs.) Steve and I pooled our knowledge. He was a city boy, worldwise. I was a farm boy. I could get around railroads pretty good.

We almost made a fatal mistake in Vienna. It was getting dark and we spotted a girl. There was no one around. I said, We'll go to this girl and hopefully she won't turn us in. We followed her and made the mistake of pinning her against the building. We were trying to tell her we were American, American. She panicked, and you can't blame her. We sort of panicked and we started hollerin'. She screamed. She bellowed. (Laughs.) We took off, and she ran in the opposite direction.

I had on an old brown pair of pants and an old jacket. We broke into a shack along the railroad, where they kept hoes and rakes. We were lookin' for food, and we didn't find one person we could ask for help. You could easily identify the Russians. They were POWs. Most of 'em had no shoes, they would have burlap bags wrapped around their feet. They were forced labor, cleanin' up in villages, farms. Communicatin' with the Russians was very simple. You say, "American, American." And they would laugh, 'cause we were all buddy-buddies. They had bread or whatever, they'd share it with us. But we couldn't find a one this time.

We walked through Vienna until dark. People walked by and smiled: "Morgen," you know, "Morgen." But we never got trapped into a conversation. At nightfall, we walked five, six miles out of town and got on a train. We thought we were headed for Trieste. We'd been told by the British that there was a great underground in Trieste and they could get us on an American sub or Allied sub and get us back. Instead, we went right on into Hungary. These boxcars had little rooms in the back where the brakeman could stand. We rode in these. Daylight, we'd jump off and hide all day long. Early in the morning, you could see the Russians. They weren't guarded that closely, 'cause they had no place to go.

One evening, these Russians just told us to come with 'em. They took us to a little shack just outside this village. They showed us a big wooden fence, about twelve feet high. They made us understand at dark we're to go over the fence. This is where they were living. We spent the whole night with the Russian forced labor. We had eggs, potatoes, and everything. They were gettin' it from the Austrian farmers. It wasn't through the goodness of the Germans.

We stayed there all day. The following night, they put some food packaged for us, like the CARE packages. (Laughs.) And told us to leave. They gave us a map. They told us what train to catch. Imagine, we couldn't speak Russian and they couldn't speak English. They took us right past the Germans who were walkin' around, down to the railroad. They were tryin' to tell us: a certain train, when it pulls out, will be goin' slow, get on this and it'll take you to Trieste. Instead of that, we wound up in Rumania. We goofed up. We stayed on it too long. We could've gotten off and made Trieste. We kept contacting workers. Rumanians. And had very good treatment. Just say "Amerikanski."

This one night a German brakeman spotted us. Put his flashlight on us and started to scream. We ran. I got on a coupling between the two boxcars. Steve went up to another boxcar and got under it by the wheels. Other workers were there with their lights, runnin' towards the guy who was hollerin'. When he put his light on me, I grabbed him. I panicked. My hand grabbed one of these metal plates where they put the ties together and I whacked him on the head. Steve came out, we split and ran to the woods. And kept goin'. We had another worry, 'cause this guy is dead, I think. Not only were we in civilian clothes, but you're doin' somethin' else, right? After we were captured, they never mentioned anything about it.

Now we find some Frenchmen, forced laborers. This is just a few miles from downtown Trieste. (Laughs.) We stayed with them. You could see these workers all over Germany and East Prussia. "Stay all day," they said. "We'll let you know." The following evening, they told us it was time to go. Great. "You'll see a water trough and someone will approach you." They sure as hell did. (Laughs.) Two men came out and talked with us, a little pidgin English with a French accent. Great. We told them who we were. They were gonna take us under their wing and we'd be on a ship, possibly submarine, leave Trieste, before long we'd be home. Fine. Next thing, out comes the damn guns. They were Gestapo. So they took us to the city jail. (Laughs.)

So now the German military got into it. They accused us of sabotage and espionage. We were put on trial, back towards Vienna. We had a civilian trial and a military trial. A German Luftwaffe officer came in, told us he's our attorney. Christ, this is great. We're gonna have a German attorney defend us, right? (Laughs.) I forget where the hell he was educated, somewhere in this country.

Before they turned us over to the military, the Gestapo first interrogated us. We're young, what the hell! So what should we do? Okay, let's tell 'em we're British officers. We kept on sayin' that. They kept sayin', You're American. See, we inadvertently created chaos with these people, because what are British air force officers doin' here at this time of the war? Are they droppin' paratroopers or what?

We actually went through two trials. We were waiting for the hammer to drop on this guy got whacked on the head. So he probably survived 'cause they didn't bring that up. So the military people said that was it, we were gonna be shot. So the attorney got us off. We left there and went to a civilian jail, where they clobbered us up pretty good. Civilian police. Remember, their families are now bein' killed by bombs.

Another trial, the same thing: guilty, you're gonna be shot. This same Luftwaffe officer shows up here, our attorney. He was neat. When you rationalize this thing, it doesn't really make sense. Maybe he was using psychology. He kept harping: "I know you're not British. I know you're American. I lived there so many years. If I tell 'em you're American, they'll just send you wherever you came from." We still insisted we were British.

Why did you still insist you were British?

Originally, just for the hell of it. So we just stuck with it, I don't know why. One day, after they told us again we're gonna be shot, he came in and said, "You guys are goin' back to camp 17-B." They traced us through our damn fingerprints. He said, "I told ya." When we got in camp, they put us in solitary. They allowed us to go back to our barracks on Christmas Eve so we could be with our friends, and locked us up on Christmas evening. The German mind.

When we got out of solitary, we were in barracks 40-A. It was about thirty feet away from the wire fence. They're dual fences about twelve feet high. Rolls of barbed wire in between. So a gang of us decided to dig a damn tunnel—ten, twelve of us. In the washroom. It was concrete. Material was easy to get. You'd get a hammer from a German for a cigarette. But how do you break through this concrete without makin' all the noise? Well, good old Americans, they had bands. The YMCA would send instruments over. Some of the guys were professionals. They started playin', and a gang of us broke through this concrete. It had to be the finest idea of any escape in Germany.

You've seen television where the prisoners fill their pockets with sand and they walk out? Most of those were officer camps, right? Maybe the sergeants knew a little more. (Laughs.) We had some guys living in mining countries. One guy got the brilliant idea to take a sock, hang it over the faucet, pour the dirt in the bucket that's slashed full of holes. It wouldn't make any noise at all, and the dirt went down and never plugged the drain. Great, but we were discovered. We never figured on the vibrations when our iron stake hit the ground.

There's a little warning fence. If you went past that little one wire, you were open season. They could shoot you if you stepped over that little wire towards the big fence. We used to line up along this fence. There were these German girls with the army, learning to operate flak batteries. They used to walk by in the evening. Quite a few of 'em spoke English. You know what they'd do? They'd put their leg way up on the fence: "Wanna come home with us tonight?" and all this. (Laughs.) The German guard in the tower would be laughin'. Twenty feet of barbed wire and a machine gun lookin' at ya.

Eighteen of us were shipped out, to Czechoslovakia, straight north to Pomerania. Oh yeah, I got moved around.

There was one guy from New York, a character. He was the type of guy, you'd say, "Hey, Brinken, do this," and he'd do it. So we told him to get some chewing gum. I'm gonna keep this guard who had a machine gun busy. This guard put the gun down, and Brinken (laughing throughout the anecdote) took the damn chewin' gum and rolled it and rolled it and rolled it and stuffed it down the barrel of his gun. Great. Now if this guy does shoot at someone, this gun's gonna blow up.

We always figured Brinken would do anything. He comes up to me and he says, "Why don't you burn the straw?" So we can escape in the excitement. German trucks are there to pick us up from the boxcar. So I take a cigarette, wrap some matches around it, and I flipped it. Some of the guys were already on the ground. Christ, the flame went up. But the damn thing went off before most of us even got out of the boxcar. This German who had the machine gun was trying to fire his weapon, and he went on his ass. He's screaming. It's a madhouse. The Germans were hollerin'. They mighta killed us, but this Captain von Mueller, in perfect English, says, "Get off this boxcar and behave yourself." (Laughs.) He saved our lives.

They moved us sergeants by train to another place, which was about seven miles from the Lithuanian border. We stayed there till the Russians were making pretty good advances. We had a crystal set, and some of the Germans would tell ya, too. By now, every day the Russians are gaining miles. So the Germans decided to evacuate us. They put twelve hundred of us into the hold of this coal barge. We're going down the Baltic to Stettin.

On the way to Stettin, we get caught in an American air raid, 'cause there were all kind of German battleships there. At Barth, where we got off for a time, the railroad station was absolutely wiped out. We had these Red Cross things, we'd started to open 'em. A redheaded German sergeant said, "Put that stuff away." Because the German civilians around us were screaming. Not just for the food, because their town had been practically demolished. The redhead had these German guards affix their bayonets, they formed a half-circle around us, an' he was tellin' the crowd, "Stay away, these guys are prisoners of war." That guy saved eighteen of us.

We get to Stettin, they handcuffed us, two guys together. We hadda run, it was about four damn miles to that camp. We were told if you drop out, you're gonna be shot. If I go down, you either carry me or do somethin'. I'm with this guy from Philadelphia. He was funnier'n hell. Like Art Carney, looks like 'im, acts like 'im, talks like 'im. I said, "Rook, I'm gonna go down." I saw him at the end of last September, this year, and he still remembers this. He looked at me, he says, "Aw, Jesus Christ, Charlie, do somethin'. Keep goin'." (Laughs.)

A lotta people say how was the camps? The only answer I can give 'em is, the commandant is like your boss. You've worked for neat guys and you've worked for guys you hated their guts. The best ones were the older guys. They were soldiers. The SS, the Gestapos, are different. They really beat up the guys. We were beat, Jesus, it was a mess. One guy had sixty-seven cuts.

At this one camp, a cheer came up. What the hell is this noise? Everybody went to the fence. It was one guy—this big strappin' young guy. He had his barracks bag over his shoulder and that son of a bitch was running, not dogtrotting. And there was a German right beside him on a bicycle. He made a complete circle of that compound. Carryin' all that stuff. He was runnin' for the hell of it. To say, Damn it, I'm not beat. What was so funny, the German on the bicycle, his guard hadda laugh. (Laughs, snaps fingers.) That was a shot of medicine for the rest of us.

It was a few months to go before the war ended. The Russians were makin' another drive. Now, the German mind again. They marched our guys southwest. Some of the same guys wound up in 7-A. They're marchin' all the way from the Baltic. A couple of hundred of us were sent by train back to Barth. That's where we were liberated by the Russians, May the fifteenth, '45. It was actually two years to the day that I was shot down. You could hear the gunfire and everything. Every once in a while, someone would holler, "Come on, Uncle Joe." He'd say, "Kick 'em in the ass, Joe." Because by now, the Germans are tellin' us the Russians are not gonna get far.

One night the British broadcast came in. They actually had it on the loudspeaker. It was about where the Russians were and everything. When we woke up the next morning, the Germans were gone. We stayed on two, three days.

Even though you are a prisoner of war, your officer is still your officer. Our colonel told everyone to sit tight, don't leave the camp. You're not gonna tell a bunch of Americans not to leave the camp. So while he was trying to control this, the Russians came in. The first Russian I saw was riding with a German man in an old flat-bodied truck. It had no cab on it. It was just open. He was followed by a mob. It was supposed to be the Russian army, but it wasn't really organized as an army. They were people with civilian clothes, some of 'em on bicycles, some on old trucks, some were horseback. There was a Russian corporal who seemed to be in charge. The story goes that his family was butchered by the Germans. He had his troops tear part of the fence down, rope over and pull 'em down with horses, everything else. In the meantime, our superior is sayin', "Stay put." Is he kiddin'? We went in the village.

They were a mob scene. All kinda weapons. They brought in a big truck and they let the sides down. And they had a musical. What the hell, the war's only a few miles from 'em to the west, and they had guys playin' musical instruments and women dancin'. This Russian major I palled up with, he told me that it's really not their army. Those people are sent into areas like Barth to break the civilian resistance down. They send this mob scene in to terrorize 'em. By the time the army really comes in, there's no resistance. I had the privilege to see a big wheel from the Russian army who was a good friend of Eisenhower's—Zhukov. He came and talked to the Russian prisoners. We had a lot of 'em in camp. Now, the Russians went into the village and they looted everything. Broken bicycles, anything. They brought all these parts back and rebuilt bicycles. They left, headed back to Russia. I understand that most of these people who went back to Russia immediately were put right back in camp as prisoners. I've never verified it.

I am not convinced that the people I knew, the Russian people, the soldiers, and our people, Americans, the prisoners of war, hate one another. Dislike, if you please. I don't think people can change like this. The way some of the press may lead it. What I'm sayin' is, it's public officials. I think it could be worked out. What I do understand, the Russian people do not have as much say in the government as we do. Once our people are elected, we really do not have much anyhow. Governments are strange.

JACQUES RABOUD

He had been a parish priest in France and in the United States from 1951 to 1964. He quit the priesthood because "I did not like the changes in the liturgy. I am a conservative in religion and a liberal in politics." Within a month, he will be returning to the Church.

In '40, we know we are losing the battle. The Germans are arriving in Paris very fast. My mother is preparing luggage because we are going to leave for Brest. Her family has a café there. My father was in the French army. I was sixteen.

We arrived in Brest three days after we left Paris. During the trip, we had German planes machine-gunning the train, diving down. We had to go under the train. Three days after the armistice,* the Italians were machine-gunning all the civilians on the road. Many people were hit. Some women were on top of the children, for the children not to be killed.

My father stayed in Paris because there was no room on the train. It was stupid for me to go to Brest. The German arrived at the same time. I came back to Paris. It was now Pétain time. My father was back, too. He was a German prisoner, but he was already in his mid-forties with chest trouble so, by Red Cross, he was sent back. My mother was a model for Jean Lanvin.

My father was buying food on the black market, because he's worked for Peugeot and made a little money. The people in the neighborhood, it's like everywhere else. Fifty percent would fight to be liberated. Maybe thirty-five percent would say, They're here, so we have to make the best of it. You had the others, who were really collaborating with the Nazis.

My father sees other people and talks about resistance. They invite

*It was shortly after the German army had broken through the Maginot Line, during the time known as "the phony war." The armistice was signed at Compiègne, where the Germans had surrendered in World War One.

each other home, talk around the table: what can we do to push the German out? Oh yes, we knew the collaborators in the neighborhood. (Laughs.) We knew who to trust. I said I can be of use. I'm going to be seventeen. I talked to several friends in school. So we joined our fathers.

A member of the Resistance had a farm twenty kilometers from Paris. An Englishman knock at the farm door. He was trapped behind the lines. We were looking for these people. We were hiding them, giving them civilian clothes. And sending them to Spain, Portugal, to England, and back to work with Free French.

I had a bicycle and (he whispers) the documents were in the pump. It was dangerous. We had some Jewish friends across the street. The father had been arrested. The daughter and her husband could not get out of Paris. We put a beret on them and passed them to Toulouse, the Spanish border, and to Free French. We passed thirty-five families from '41 to '43.

The late John Howard Griffin recalls: "I was twenty, a research assistant at the Asylum of Tours. When the war came . . . I was immediately ordered back to the U.S. I refused to go because France had formed me. How can I flee at this time of need?

". . . I got involved with the French underground, smuggling Jews out of Germany, across France, into England. We would use asylum ambulances, put our refugees in straitjackets, and move them that way. They didn't have to speak. Many of them didn't speak French. They didn't have safe-conduct papers, of course. We didn't know how to steal, we didn't know how to forge. We were infants in this, but we did the best we could.

*"The Nazis were moving in. I will be haunted to my death by these scenes. We brought the people inside these rooms and kept them hidden. We had to tell parents who had children under fifteen that we weren't going to make it. Suddenly, I experienced a double reality. The first: a parent said: 'It's all over for us. Take our children.' We would move anybody under fifteen without papers. You sat there and realized these parents were giving their children away to strangers. The second: I could go downstairs into the streets and find perfectly decent men who went right on rationalizing racism. I feel, unless we can view these things from inside such rooms, we are lost."** *

*American Dreams: Lost and Found (New York: Pantheon Books, 1980), pp. 282–83.

One of my friends was arrested. Very stupid. He had an argument with a German boy. He hit him. He was arrested and they found papers on him. They took him to the Gestapo and tortured him. He told names. One day, while my father was away, the ringing of the bell. It was at night. There were three guys. They had this leather coat. I knew what they were, just to look at them.

They ask for my father. I tell them he is away. They said, "Do you know Henry Duvall?" I said yes, he is a friend. "Do you know where he is?" "No." Then they began to tell me all the names of my friends. They said, "Come with us." They pushed me. I said, "Let me take a jacket." They said, "Come the way you are." Another takes everything out of the drawers. My mother was screaming. They did not find anything, because my father had all the papers with him. He was passing on a Jewish family.

I was in jail four days and four nights. I had interrogation after interrogation. I was beaten black and blue with a rubber hose, on the muscles. In the cell were six people. One guy said, (whispers) "Do not talk. The guy in the corner is from Alsace, he is an informer."

They put me on a train and sent me to Germany. It was a forced-labor camp in Delmenhorst. It was now '43. I didn't see my mother until I was liberated in '45. There was rubble and cadavers from the Allied bombing. We had to clean this up.

We were in a trench, trying to put back the pipes. The SS is going back and forth with their bayonets. A middle-aged German man was looking in the window of a camera shop, very near. He had a big package in his hand. Without turning, he talked to us in French. He said, "Boys, I am sorry for the way you are treated. I was once a prisoner of war in France during the First World War. I was treated by the people on the farm very good. They fed me and I will always remember. I will be here every day and I will feed you." After the SS turned their back, he threw the package in the trench. He came for three days and he fed us. We were very, very hungry. I will remember always this man.

They transported people wherever they were needed. I was sent to Schlesien near the Polish border. Salt mines. It was continuous work, five-thirty in the morning until seven at night. We have fifteen minutes to eat. Sawed bread, like wood. I was very sick. I have seen many people die around me. After I was liberated, the doctor said it was a good thing I was well fed before that because I would be dead, too.

In June of '44, we had to evacuate because the Russian army was invading. They sent us to the Ruhr. The bombing from the Allies broke all the pipes in the camp. In the middle of the winter, we had to go to the pump. We were even able to see the pilots from the Spitfires when they were machine-gunning.

We were beaten all the time. We were twelve in a cell. There was this canister with the smell. When you have soup only, you have to relieve yourself very often. In the morning at five o'clock, the SS would open the door and say, (shouts) "Schnell, schnell, schnell! Raus!" They gave us three minutes to relieve ourselves. We had to take the canister with us to empty. It was very heavy. We had to rush, rush, rush, rush. The last man in line was always beaten in the back by the SS with a rubber hose. We took turns to be last, every twelve days.

It happened it was my turn. My God, how can I not be beaten so much? I have an idea. I put the canister behind me, instead of front. Instead of hitting me with the hose, he hit the canister. It was so heavy, it fell on him and he was all covered. (Laughs.)

I could not work for four days, I was so beaten. It was the worst time in my life. They forced me to work. How I did not die, I don't know. We are coming home from work, almost falling down, and they want us to play, naked. It was snowing, very cold. One of the SS had a whistle. Each time he was whistling, we had to make a somersault in the snow.

One of my friends was asthmatic. After maybe twelve or thirteen tours around the camp, he could not breathe any more. He had to stop. The SS come by him: "Go, go." He couldn't. He sat in the snow and they beat him, beat him. When they decided it was too cold for them, they left, and he was in the snow to die. We heard him all night. That is always in my mind. (His voice breaks.) I have the impression I hear him still. If we had been able to, we could have killed all the SS. We know he is dying and we cannot do anything. (Sobs.)

The only thing we had in mind was food. The Germans were clever. They were doing everything they could to make us suffer. But not enough to let us die from malnutrition. Just enough to survive. I was so weak, when I was dropping something on the floor, it took me five minutes to pick it up.

In the cell, we had nothing else to do but talk. It was food, food, food, food, food. Oh, when I come back to France, I'm going to tell my mother to cook some pork chops. We had almost the sensation of smelling the pork.

The people who were desperate, who said, It's the end—they all died. They let themselves go. The people who said, I'm going to come back—they came back.

There were Italian soldiers in camp doing forced labor. It was against Red Cross. They were very religious and have all kinds medals and rosaries. When the Allied bombs were coming, they were praying. The bombing was terrible. The dirt was trembling and was coming up on us and penetrating our skin. (Reveals scars.) When I came back, they had to operate to take out the gravel.

The bombs were always coming by seven. In the trench, I was on top of this Italian. (Laughs.) He had on a very heavy coat. Each time the bomb was coming, I put my teeth in his coat. It was all chewed up, the coat. You become so powerful when you are afraid.

All the people were there. We had the Belgian, from the Netherlands, Norway, Denmark. The only nationalities we were afraid of—or what can I say? doubtful—were the Polish or the Estonian or from Lithuania. The Germans used them as overseers. When the Russians invaded Poland, the Germans gave them uniforms and some of them signed in the SS.

By this time, most of Germany had surrendered. We were in this pocket of resistance. It was the American army on one side and the Russian army on the other. We were liberated on the fifth of May, 1945. Three days before V-E Day.

I was down to eighty pounds. During the bombing, a cow was killed. The snow fell during the winter. Around March, when the snow began to melt, the cow appeared. We ate the cow. I got dysentery.

On the fifth of May, Americans surrounded the camp and the guards were not able to escape. I was inside the camp. I was not able to walk, but I was feeling happy inside. If only I had some strength to welcome the Americans.

There was a captain. He saw all this. I could see his face. (Cries.) He said, "How can it happen? What did they do to you?" People looked as starved as people in concentration camps. You could have counted my bones. He was so horrified.

All the SS were prisoners. They had their hands behind their heads. The captain said to us, "I am going to withdraw for a while. I give you two hours. You can do anything you want with them. I will not see anything."

I am very peaceful. I would not hurt anybody. But that day, I did.

All the hate came back. The three years of forced labor came back. I said to this one particular SS man, "You make me suffer, you are going to suffer. I have only two hours, but you are going to get it." I have no strength. (Laughs.) I took a stone and I cut his ear. It was hanging. I had enough strength to do that. All the other people did more horrible things.

The camp *Führer,* a lieutenant colonel, they took him and put him in the latrine. He was in the excrements up to his waist. They gave him a water glass and asked him to empty it. Then they took them all and they stoned them. They were a bloody mess. They must have their marks still today, if they are alive.

I was in a stretcher, almost in a coma, at the military hospital in Paris. They fed me intravenously. My mother and aunt came to visit me. They were preparing my burial. My aunt was asking my mother, "What kind of sheet are you going to bury him in?" After three months, it was all right. I said, If I recover, I will do something to thank God for what he did for me. I was liberated. I was alive and I was in Lourdes. I decided to become a priest.

It's really difficult when I think about the war. If we answer hate with hate, it will never end. For my generation, it is difficult to erase.

Very often, you hear some German saying, "We didn't know." But who allowed the Nazi to take over? They were very, very happy when Hitler took France, took Europe. At Delmenhorst, we had these guards. They were married, they had families. Don't tell me when they went back home, they were not talking about what is going on. The people of Delmenhorst for pastime on Sunday were coming around the camp. They were looking at us like we were zoo animals.

Is this uniquely German?

This is human. It happened before. The Spanish, in the Inquisition, under God, destroyed an entire population. What about the Albigenses? It can happen again. We are all good people, but if we are led a little too far, we are going to believe everything we are told. We are ordinary people, who can also be weapons for evil Hitlers.

Southwick, an industrial town, ninety miles outside Boston. A commu-nity of ranch houses and two-flats. "Most are hard-working people," says Olga. "Very nice quiet town. Very nice for bringing up children."

We are seated in the kitchen. On the wall is The Last Supper, *painted on a dish. Beside it, the framed legend: "Boze Blogoslaw Naz Dom" (God Bless Our Home). More than ample portions of kielbasa, dark bread, and cheese are proffered the guests.*

He has been working at the same paper mill for thirty years. It coincided with his and his wife's arrival in the United States.

WALTER: The Germans took me to forced work to Germany. I was in Poland, 1942, close to Russian border. I was seventeen. My family used to have a farm. They took one person from the family. I was the person. SS would come and give orders to the mayor of the town. He came with the list and he tell me so many people must go. Mayor will have a meeting and say one from each family must go.

I was the oldest. My brother was two years younger. And my father and my mother. My father, he wanna go himself. I said, "Pop, no." I was sick, so I was thinking I would not pass, they send me back. So that's why I say I go.

I remember. They took me from my home to the city. Dubno. It was a big camp. We stayed two days there, and they loaded us into the train.

OLGA: I was from the same county. I was born in the town where Walter's family came from. I was sixteen. The first thing for me was 1939, September, when the Russians just come in with the military tanks. They took over. They walked in without any asking, as you please. We were under the Russians eighteen months.

The war started really 1939, when the Germans took over. There was the whole turmoil. The Russians now start deporting people, whoever have any connection with the government. The Russians went back with the political prisoners. The Germans took over. Now everybody was thinking we will be better off.

The Germans took our quarters, because they have the military base. The Jewish people went to the ghetto, we take the Jewish people's place.

The same time as Walter, they took me. Supposedly my father was on the list. My mother was not well, so I decided to go. I was the oldest. Two younger sisters. Same train as Walter. That was a big open car. They transport everything, wood, cement.

When we were leaving home, everybody knew you better have something with you. So they were baking some cakes, they had some hot sausage, smoked meat that don't spoil.

WALTER: We went through my town. It was a tragedy for me because my father and mother and brother, they find out somehow what time the train was going by and—I see them, just like today, they was waving. Last time I saw them. I was ready to jump, but I was scared because they could shoot me.

OLGA: I didn't see my family either. That was the last time. When I said goodbye, for me—just awful. (Cries.) Being young you think you survive everything, and you come back. (Cries throughout.) It's very painful to say goodbye to your mother, your sister, your father. He told me, "Olga, you have bringing-up here, you have your instructions. I trust you never bring shame on your family." He said, "I trust you because I know what kind person you are." These were the last words to me. War is a pain for many things. Sometimes the wound will heal. But the broken heart feels hard to mend. That's life, to say goodbye.

WALTER: The trip was around twelve days. Just standing all the way. No sleep, no sleep. With machine guns and everything around it.

OLGA: It was very tight, crowded, and people were pretty considerate. It was June 9 when we landed in Cologne. The camp used to be an old theater, a beautiful place. In the back, you have the Rhine. In front, you have a big gate and there was a bar. Years back, people were coming with carriages in that courtyard. They separated us by six-feet boards.

WALTER: Girls on one side . . .

OLGA: . . . and boys on the other. The next day, they tell you, "Tomorrow when you hear the whistle, you run to the kitchen, get your hot water."

WALTER: So you walk to work in a column, about four miles.

OLGA: This was a big factory. They did make motors for submarines, heavy trucks, and jeeps. There was forty thousand people working three shifts.

WALTER: The beginning, we work eight hours. Later on, when the bombs started falling down, we worked twelve hours a day. But not only in the factory. We waked up a little bit early and we carried the tape machine, all the office equipment, to the cellar.

OLGA: More and more German men were drafted, no matter what age. So they start having the war prisoners taking their place. The French war prisoners, the Russian war prisoners. They had people from Yugoslavia, the Hungarians. Whoever they could grab, they grab. When the Russians started pushing them back, they took more displaced people.

WALTER: We work there till war ended, 1945.

OLGA: I was in the same place, except my story is a little bit different. A doctor connected with this camp took me as a nanny to his baby, two-months-old daughter. When the bombs started falling, his wife, with the baby, wanted to go into mountains. Being a baroness by birth, she wanted to take me with her. But they don't want them too attached to foreign people. So they tell her, "You can't take this girl. There are thousands wherever you going. Get yourself help. This girl is coming back."

When I work for this woman, when the alarm come, the Luftwaffe start shooting the American, English planes, I take the baby and go in the basement. Don't help a lot because everything started falling apart. People were buried there.

When it started getting tough, the Germans were afraid to lose this machinery. So they shifted us to Aachen for a very short time. So I came back, working in the factory delivering blueprints from one section to another. You run from morning to night, no elevators. Running all day.

WALTER: I met Olga the first time I was staying outside in a line. I like to have coffee. Some grass in a big bag and dump it in hot water.

(Laughs.) She was standing in line and I said to her, "That would be a nice pair, you and me." (Laughs.)

How could you court? How could you have dates?

OLGA: Very easy. You come from work, you are going on lines. It's dark, so people will sneak with each other. Marching to work, at least you hold hands. When you come back, even tired from work, you have this public washroom. The toilets were separated, washrooms not. He's coming in, I'm going out. You're standing in line for the slop they give you. He came behind me. I was going with his friend, no big romance. He was funny, his friend, he played harmonica and we would all have this fun. Then Walter came and he grab me from behind, he lifted me up and he turned me towards him, like face to face. He said, "Don't you think we would match together?" So we were joking from that time and having this little going out and sneaking here and there.

WALTER: I said to Olga, "I like to have permission from your father." She said, "Okay. I will give you the address and you write to my father."

OLGA: He did, in that old-fashioned way. We did have mail coming, very little. Last letter I have is January '44. He said all the fences have been taken down, meaning the ghettos. The trees are down, just look like bare ground. Remember the woods where you were going for mushrooms? The letter penetrates something. I said, "Oh, my goodness, the Jewish people were all killed."

I was telling Walter that during wartime, we shouldn't think too much about anything for the future, just survive. There was no possibility to marry there.

WALTER: I wrote her father, couple of words on a card. I got the answer. The father said, "I think you are old enough and God bless you."

OLGA: You better tell what you promised me. (Laughs.)

WALTER: What I promise, when the war will be finished, when we come back home, you will not have to do anything.

OLGA: He means I don't have to do any farm work. You don't need to milk the cows and whatever. He can bring his wife and just put her on a chair and that's it.

Walter don't wanna wait till we get home, because, he says, when we get home, that's goodbye, Charlie. (Laughs.) An English expression. So I said, "Walter, I like you very much." We were sticking with each other very close during wartime. In a situation like that, you show your feelings and you figure out a person sooner than just regular courtship. I'm not sorry when war ended and Walter tricked me into marriage. (Laughs.)

Because we moved among people like us, there were paid informers. I almost got transferred to a concentration camp by that crazy informer. I was walking to the washroom, was evening. There the Russian war prisoners were standing. They were amazing. When they go mad, you could kill them, they will not budge. I was speaking fluent Russian. They refuse to eat the slop. I asked them why. They said, "Oh, this crazy spinach." One of them tastes it and they start throwin' the thing in the barrels. The German says, "If they don't want to take this food, they get nothing." Oh, the Russians were stubborn, challenging them.

So this person asks me what happened. I tell him what the Russians said. I didn't know he was an SS informer. I'm preparing for bed, the SS come and say, "Come." They tell me to march through the gate. They put me overnight in a city jail. I couldn't figure out what I did.

This SS man, the informer, told the other guys such-and-such a person, me, was telling the Russians: "You stand up to them, they will give you something else." But I wasn't that dumb to put myself in that basket, because I knew what would happen. I wanted to survive, go back.

I got out through Walter. Someone start running in the barracks, saying that the SS men took me.

WALTER: I have no power, but I speak to the supervisor and he help a little bit. I said, "Why they take my girlfriend?" He said, "Who take?" I said such-and-such SS. He said, "They are not supposed to take anybody without me knowing it because I was responsible for this people here." He said to SS, "We need her to work, to be messenger. We need Walter." Okay, finally it ended.

OLGA: Americans liberated us. And taking us with them because they needed all the help digging ditches for the military. When they settled the zones, the English took over. The Americans brought us to Menden.

There is a white flag on city hall and people start yelling. Somebody took the flag down, these fanatics. So the Americans start giving them back: first you want to surrender, now you don't. The Americans were booming all over the place. We were in the basement and the whole walls and floor started shaking. Being young and not to have enough brains, we start running to the shelter.

WALTER: Almost I got hit. After the war was ended, too.

OLGA: In the shelter, you have the Germans and all this nationality. American tanks come straight to the mouth of the shelter. They have interpreters in all kind of languages. They start going through loudspeakers: "Everybody start coming out." Naturally there was cheering right away. They tell us, "For you people, it's all over. You have forty-eight hours freedom. You can do what you please." We didn't like that.

Why not?

You don't have any kind of authority. Nothing is over anybody. Some people start getting revenge. Some people were hungry, some people start running stores, knocking windows, taking things, stealing.

WALTER: I was thinking it is 'bout time we have freedom. But I was not the type breaking windows. Never, never. Whoever was mean to these working people, they took revenge. They didn't kill them, not that I know. Maybe there were instances. If somebody was working on a farm and somebody was mean, they took the clothes that they pleased because they were walking in rags and barefooted. Food was the first item. The Russians were wild.

Didn't you have any feelings of anger about the way you were treated these three years?

I have a bad feeling, but I thank God I survive. Let it be that way.

OLGA: That we go home now.

WALTER: Some the German working people, sometime they was fresh to me. Just like all over, you meet all kinds of people. Sometimes they even give me half a sandwich. A man gave me half can of soup. They share with me in the work.

OLGA: We are liberated. We are in camp in the city of Menden. The American government, after forty-eight hours, arrive, tell all the Nazi families, the whole town to evacuate. Just suitcases and out. Now *they* are refugees. That's how it happen. The English took over. They were a little bit softer. They were explaining that the immigration will start processing. That some people were going to Canada, some to Australia, some to South America.
   We got married in this camp.

WALTER: I will never forget that. That was in May, right? 1945. Finally we decided to marry.

OLGA: *We?* Who decided?

WALTER: I decided. (Laughs.) She had no right dress for the wedding, so she made one herself.

OLGA: I didn't have shoes. The old German man lose his son in the war. This guy was so kind, seeing the girl barefooted in wedding dress, he brought his son's shoes. Men's shoes, much too big, the laces up to here. But it was better than barefooted. How could you go to church in men's shoes?

WALTER: I have pocket watch from home, little short chain. I was going to Russian camp and I exchange. They gave me women shoes.

OLGA: They rob everything after liberation. The people were going there and exchanging for other goods and items. Anything you please. One size was bigger on one foot than the other, but the same style, same color.

WALTER: Oh, the wedding day. I set up the alarm clock for one o'clock you're supposed to go to church. Something happened to the clock. I was late, almost the mass was over.

OLGA: Other couples were married together. About a good thirty people standing before the altar. The priest was waiting. The people wouldn't let us go from the back. They were thinking we are just lookers. The priest saw us and he just make a way, said to Walter, "Where you got ring?" Walter says, "No ring." He took from another couple a ring. We exchange vows, and Walter was thinking he will buy me the ring later. But at that time, you have no money. Where will you get the ring?

People start making moonshine, playing cards, going wild. The English were building a monument for war prisoners and they asked volunteers. They will give them more cigarettes, more meat. So Walter volunteers. I was very glad that he didn't start getting this bad influence, when you get yourself tipsy and wipsy. He isn't the type.

We were thinking of going back where we come from, to Poland. But we can't, because the Russians took over there. We wait the news. Where will we go? People start a rumor. This one wanna go here, this one wanna go there. We didn't have too much choices. In between, I have a first child.

(Indicates an elderly couple, who have been visiting, at the time of this conversation. It is they who had brought the rolls of kielbasa from Detroit.) We met these people in that camp in Münster. They were waiting to go to the United States, because his mother was there already, through some Catholic organization. When they got to America, they arrange through Caritas for us to come. They were the sponsors. They didn't have any kind of job to offer us, but they arranged.

How did you get to Southwick?

WALTER: Because I have 'nother friend and he found out in the paper.

OLGA: They were advertising in the Polish paper, the boats and who's on it. He read that Walter Nowak with his family is arriving on the *General Sturges,* New York Harbor, November 11. He went to his pastor and said, "I know this man and I want him transferred here."

WALTER: I am in the same factory, same building, from the time I come to America.

OLGA: Our life wasn't easy. But we were always cheerful with hope. We have worries, but we did have a goal: to give a better future for our children. Because we go through hell and we come to heaven and we like to leave something behind that will be worth a while. If we didn't think of our children's future and just show you this glitter here, we die, we leave nothing. Because this is just rust and dust.

Walter never went back to Poland because he don't want to go have bad memories. 1969, I went to Poland to see how people live. I had from strangers the best reception. They gave me the red-carpet treatment. I keep contact with these people. They were freely talking to me, knowing that they were safe.

The biggest mistake I made was when I went to Auschwitz. History is my bug—ancient or Middle Ages or Dark Ages. So I will go see. I see the pictures of the people that were exterminated and the women and the men and the skeletons. Then I come to the clothing and the shaved hair behind the glass. And the letters that people were smuggling to their families, and when I read what this man said to his wife and the child, "I will not see you" and give his blessing, I just collapsed there, crying. (She weeps throughout her recounting.) All of a sudden I was in the gas chamber and where they go on to be burned. We come out from that bunker and the man is saying they brought at night Eichmann, on a train, because people would tear him piece by piece. I said, "What justice was that?" So many million people were exterminated and they were afraid that other people would tear him in pieces. I'm no really a person of violent things, but I tell you when I come there and I hear their logic—God, I tell you, I was sick. I couldn't forget. Took me a whole week to come back.

I don't know why I did go. I questioned myself already hundred times and I can't figure it out. That was my destiny, if there is such thing.

Since this country give us home and take us in, the orphans we were, we very grateful. You sweat, you work, your time didn't go for nothing. What else we can say? We are just happy. The other thing is almost behind us. But I tell you we still carry deep scars. We never, never could hear from the family and what happened to them. They don't know what happened to us. You just live to survive. We can't dwell and live backwards.

We face the River Alster in Hamburg. "The other Germany, the Germany of Goethe, Heine, Mann, of the Weimar, always had to struggle against the romantic, arrogant." In pre-Hitler Germany, he had been the "Benjamin," the youngest member of the Hamburg city-state parliament. "I was among the first to read Mein Kampf. *When I read its text to the council, they laughed. Later, they were surprised these terrible things happened. Why? He announced it from the first day."*

The conversation took place in 1967.

Under Hitler, I have been a coward. Cowardice under a dictatorship is legitimate. You cannot be brave every day. I have tried to be courageous, but to be courageous completely isolated from morning till night is very strenuous.

During the Third Reich, I had to quit as a journalist and was sent to work as a foreman in a sewing-machine plant. There were slave laborers and prisoners of war, mostly from Russia and Ukraine. There were German workers too, mostly women. The men were in the army. I tried to remain clean. I tried to protest as far as I could, but I did too little.

I really have been astonished at the human attitude in this plant. The Russians, especially, were fed poorly and dressed very poorly in the wintertime. It was forbidden by the Nazi Party to help them with shoes, with clothes, with food. But some of the German women brought them these things, even soap. It was a human solidarity of a wonderful kind.

When Stalingrad was lost, we didn't know it. The Ukrainian female laborers knew it, I don't know how. They went into their barracks and danced happily. This was found out by a Nazi female spy. She told it to the Gestapo. They came in with steel helmets and carbines and mistreated them so that their faces and bodies were deformed.

The next morning, I met one of these women and she showed me her wounds. I told this to the secretary of the general manager. She became pale. At this moment, an SS man entered the room. We became silent. He said, "Why are you so quiet? What did you tell each other?" She told him. I was surprised. This girl, she was quite young, said, "I feel ashamed being German." What was more surprising, nothing happened. He kept quiet. He didn't betray her.

We were afraid at home, with every chime of the clock. All the time, I was afraid they'd find out my real opinions. One of my brothers was already in a concentration camp. He had been a bookseller. You know, before the millions of Jews were thrown into the camps, there were hundreds of thousands of German democrats, poets, ministers, students, labor people, thrown into camps.

My record followed me wherever I went. I was checked and questioned by the Nazis all the time. On the other hand, I could not live without listening to BBC, London. And the Voice of America, I heard the speeches of Thomas Mann. Many Germans heard him. After the capitulation, I met Mann in Zurich. I told him that his words made it possible for me to survive.

For a time, I left Hamburg and joined the underground.

After the war, I wrote books and articles about the Hitler time. I was attacked by neo-Nazis and old ones. At one of their meetings, I spoke of the double life of all decent Germans during the Third Reich. An old officer of the marines rose up to protest: "I am an old soldier and I didn't do anything else but my duty. I didn't know of any of the crimes." I interrupted him: "If you were a marine, your health had been checked, especially your eyes. So you haven't been blind. Didn't you see the smoke rising over the burning synagogues?" He said, "Yes, everybody knew the synagogues burned." I said, "If your double life did not begin at that moment, you should be ashamed. If you don't feel shame, I feel this shame for you."

I have been a soldier. It was safer than being a suspected civilian. I refused to become an officer. I took a personal oath. I would not shoot against those who fought Hitler. The Allies shot against me, but I could not shoot back. In this respect, I was perhaps a bad German. I did not want to earn a decoration with a swastika on it.

I had a wonderful opportunity when I became an American prisoner in Italy. I was in a camp with 140,000 prisoners, among them Hitler boy soldiers. I edited the PW paper and spoke over the camp radio. The line of the psychological warfare of the time was to re-educate these prisoners. But that is directed from the outside. It creates a resistance. I tried what I call self-education. You see, I belong to a nation which has always been rich in military heroes, but is underdeveloped in civil courage. It is this and the other Germany that I was talking about. The young are beginning to understand.

A poet, documentary film maker, and physician living in Kiev, Ukraine.

I was seven years old when I see my first terrible war poster: Jews of Kiev, you must be on Lvov Circle. Those who will not be there will be killed. It was September 1941. Kiev was a multinational city. We have up to two hundred thousand Jews. The German army invaded Russia June 22, and on September 19 they were in Kiev.

They kill people from the third day of their occupation. It was Yom Kippur, Jewish holidays. They throw them in Babi Yar. It is an abyss, a very, very deep hole in the ground.

Nobody believed this would be done. It is done so easy. I ask those who came from Babi Yar. They say they believe these people are quite normal and they take you somewhere to nice places. Some people believe they will go to Palestine. Nobody believed at first they will be killed.

The Germans said, You must take food for three days travel, clothes, and what you have of jewelry, gold and things. You must close your flat. If you touch anything in it, you will be shot on the spot. In first week, the Germans killed thirty-three thousand Jews and more. We found this document in German papers after occupation. In the first two weeks, they killed practically all the Jews.

Then they start to kill the partisans whom they catch. It was a hole deep enough to place a lot of people. More than a hundred, two hundred thousand, nobody knows. In the end, they start to burn these bodies. We asked the German war prisoners and they tell us that they burn to ashes two hundred thousand, maybe more.

In 1943, nobody can believe it. When we start to open documents. The prisoners from other camps, who burned these bodies, they were killed too after two weeks of their work. Each evening, they were kept in old house standing near to Babi Yar. They dream about escaping. They looked in the pockets of those dead bodies for keys. The people who were killed in Babi Yar, they take keys with themselves. They think they are going back. For me, this is the metaphor! Keys for freedom in the pockets of the dead.

More than three hundred war prisoners run away. Only fifteen escaped. SS men killed all the others. Six of them still live. I know five Jews who survived Babi Yar.

They tell me the story and I filmed it. They speak about such details: two or three trucks with children's shoes, which Germans take from Babi Yar in two weeks. How many children must be killed to fill one truck with shoes? They speak of looking for gold teeth, those who try to smash bones. Fascists do this in very practical way. They are very orderly.

They take people in parties—a hundred, two hundred. They take them to edge of deep ravine and from the other side, machine-gun them. They fall in Babi Yar. A kind of industrial production. When I read the captured documents, they never write about killing, they write: liquidation. It was like a business.

I ask survivors, "Why you go there?" They tell me, "These young men laughed when they were around us. We cannot believe that these young men who laughed would kill us." Young German soldiers. Maybe they feel those people whom they kill are as flies, not as people.

I think it is the terriblest thing in nationalism, when you feel you and your nation is the best and others are nothing. To kill them as I will kill a fly, a snake, I can sleep without any suffering. They know that Jews, Slavs, they are *Untermenschen*, not people. Something which must be killed to free this earth for better people. For them, it was not killing, not a crime. They do something good for everybody who is cleaner and better. They kill those dirty people to free the earth for better people.

Some Jews who were killed didn't believe it, because they knew European culture. They knew Goethe's *Faust*, Heine's lyrics. They did not believe that in one nation it is possible to have Heine, Goethe, and Hitler. Beethoven and Himmler. I know Jews, who lived near us, who tried to speak in Yiddish to the German soldiers. They thought they'd understand, because it is quite near in language. They were having a conversation. They tried to speak with them about what it will be after the war.

After the war, all German documentary film come to Soviet archives. In every German battalion, there will be one movie operator, who'll take miles and miles of these films. Sometimes, they never opened them. When we start to open them, it was terrible for me. It all came back to me. We work more than two years with those movies. I became crazy looking through it and looking. Sometimes it looks like the world after the neutron bomb. Because there are only things, no people. Everybody dead. Like Babi Yar.

These poor people came there with their things, with their warm clothes, everything, and were killed. I don't know why the Germans filmed all these things.

I had visited Babi Yar during my encounter with Korotich. The irony was overwhelming: the loveliness of the greenery; the awareness that the once-deep ravine had become almost shallow; human ashes were, in effect, the compost.

Under that grass are dead bodies. When we were youngsters, even now looking for something from the war, we know where dead bodies are. Grass is highest and darkest in those places. In Babi Yar is the highest and darkest grass in Kiev.

Always children make museums of war. Sometimes children look for documents of those who died. They look for soldiers' capsules,* with addresses and names. They look for unknown graves, for signs. Nobody knows names of those uncounted people who were killed in Babi Yar.

I was with my grandmother in country place. She was very old, very ill. I was seven years old, free and young. My father was in prison camp. I was parentless child. It was nobody who keep me at place. I go look for my mother. From this country place to Kiev was three hundred kilometers. There were a lot of motherless, homeless children, hundreds of thousands, traveling, looking for something. We moved as masses. In thousands, we were knockin' on doors or around marketplaces, where we asked for somethin'. It was possible to live this way, but it was terrible.

Everybody gave me food. Only once I was robbed. One man give me something to eat and took my short trousers. All other times, I always receive. Even once, an old German soldier give me a piece of bread and a harmonica. He wept. I remember this man. He was such a poor soldier in this command, near kitchen. He was standing near a dish stand. He tell me a lot of poor people were practically arrested and thrown into the war, not just killers. He wept a lot.

I find my mother because she looked for my father. He was big

---

*Michael Kuzmenko, my young companion, explains: "Very often, soldiers, deathly wounded or encircled by the enemy, who knew they'll soon die, spilled out powder from their cartridges. Inside, they squeezed messages to their wives or relatives. Very many children now go looking for these and digging in the tall, dark grass. Here, there is a boom. It's like a treasure hunt. When they find these cartridges, with these letters, they are delivered to wives of these soldiers. They were young then. Now they are old women."

microbiologist and was dean in Kiev Institute. Till now, he live, but he cannot be alone in closed room. After Gestapo. He must know he can open the door. He cannot travel in trains because door is closed. He cannot travel in planes. He has this complex from war.

Babi Yar only exist when you have it inside yourself. Each man on the earth must have Babi Yar inside. When we have it, it will be something against repeating of Babi Yar.

JOSEPH LEVINE

Fort Wayne, Indiana. He is director of the city's Jewish Historical Museum. He was one of the first American social workers who went to Germany to work with death-camp survivors, from 1945 to 1946.

His desk spills over with yellowed documents, faded photographs, newspaper clippings, old letters, books with torn cloth, and crumpled papers. Throughout the conversation, he refers to them.

My assignment was to direct relief work in Munich. I got word that about 250 Jews were roaming the streets in the little town of Schwandorf, about forty miles north. I found men and women, who had wandered in. No children. They were living in barns and cellars and attics. They were not yet registered with UNRRA, so could get no food or housing or anything. I got them all registered. I had to fight the American town major to requisition homes of Nazis. Later on, as the Jews wanted a place to worship, I requisitioned an old beer hall that had been closed for years. We turned it into a synagogue and dedicated it on Chanukah.

They were all alone in the world. As I traveled from town to town, I'd fill the car with six or seven people, and listen to their stories. One would tell how forty members of his family were butchered by the Germans. Another would say, That's nothing, and I'd hear a story of sixty people killed. My chauffeur had enough. He began to hum a song, a Yiddish or Polish or Russian folk song everybody knew, and they'd start singing.

Schwandorf was a stinkin' little town where Jews hadn't lived for centuries. If they had once, they were kicked out long ago. I slowly discovered Jews in a lot of these godforsaken towns, living over manure piles and in abandoned houses. There were mass graves outside these towns, in the beautiful hills of Bavaria.

The Germans, at first, didn't provide homes for them. I had the simulated rank of lieutenant colonel with the Fourth Armored headquarters in Regensburg. I would pull out Eisenhower's orders to show that these Jews were entitled to homes. I gave these quickly appointed burgermeisters twenty-four hours. That's how we got the housing.

Not a single German of the hundreds I talked to admitted to guilt of anything. They talked about "those terrible Nazis." It wasn't until my last day, on the train from Frankfurt to Bremen, that the porter was the first and only one who admitted the Germans were at fault.

The numbers of these wanderers increased. Jews appeared from Poland after the Kielce pogrom in '46.

'46?

Poles began to kill Jews who had come back from Germany. They didn't want them back. Slowly, Jews began to come into the American zone from Russia. Slowly, some food was sent in from Holland. This was the time when the Russians were also dumping hundreds of thousands of Germans back into the U.S. zone from Czechoslovakia and elsewhere. They emptied mental hospitals.

One day, I found a message from the general of the Fourth Armored Division. He had decided to put the Jews in one big camp. Mind you, they were living in twenty-one Bavarian towns and were beginning to start life again. He wanted efficiency. I said, "Are you nuts? I'll have nothing to do with it." The insensitivity of it—from a death camp into another camp.

However, there was no housing. The camp they had in mind was in Pocking, where Goering once had a tremendous air base. He said there were hundreds of Hungarians living there and about two thousand Poles. The Poles had been slave labor, but the Hungarians, who had come here with their wives and children, had worked for Hitler. The Hungarian women were walking around with their fur coats. We examined the camp and told the military if they got rid of the Hungarians and Poles, we'd take it. Within six months, there were nine thousand Jews in this camp.

Shortly after it was opened, the general called me and said there was trouble: the Jews were burning their beds. I went down there and heard the complaints. We discovered that when the Poles left, they took all the wood with 'em. When the army requisitioned saws and hatchets, they never got to camp. Somebody sold it on the black market. So the Jews had to burn the beds to keep warm.

I ran into thirty kids sleeping on straw mattresses. A sixteen-year-old girl was their leader. I asked her, "What is it these children need?" She didn't ask for clothing. She didn't ask for candy. She said, "These children have to go to school. Give us paper. Get us pencils."

The first child I saw in three months in Europe was a little girl named Ruthie. Her father was killed and her mother hid her with a Polish family. She was stunted, paper-thin. She'd been hidden in cellars and attics. I asked her what she wanted. Her exact words were, "I am ten years old. I never went to school. Help me go to school."

We found hundreds of youngsters, who'd been hidden by Christian families, living in monasteries and elsewhere. Brought them back into the American zone.

A gentleman was sitting with a kid about ten years old. He'd been a partisan in Poland during the war, living in the forest, killing. I asked the little kid, "What did you do?" The father said he was a *partisanchik*, a little partisan. The kid, in Yiddish, said, "At night, other kids and I sneaked into town to steal food. If we had to shoot, we shot."

About twelve hundred Jews survived Theresienstadt, the Czechoslovakian death camp. They were shipped to the American zone and landed in Deggendorf. One of my jobs was to help them make connections with their families in other parts of the world. A Jew would come to me and tell me he had an uncle named Sam Goldberg who went to America in 1915, or Abe Silverstein who lived in either Cleva-land or Nev York. (Laughs.) Could I find his uncle?

I cabled to America, got telephone books from the large cities. We sat up nights writing letters to the Goldbergs or the Cohens in Chicago, telling them that Sam Goldberg of this town, his parents were so-and-so, was coming to America. Are you, by any chance, his relative? We'd send these letters to Canada and Argentina, as well. Some of our great moments was when I'd get a letter saying, This is my long-lost brother. We'd reunite them.

(He holds out an old newspaper) This is the first Yiddish paper published in Germany after the war. I was there when the first copy came off the press.

Three men had come into my office in Regensburg in the winter of '46. One of them was Nathan Silberberg. Before the war, he'd been editor of the *Moment,* the largest Yiddish paper in Poland. He said, "You're getting us food, clothing, and shelter. Now we need something for the *Geist,* the spirit. A newspaper. There's a company in Frankfurt that I dealt with for twenty-five years. I know where they kept the Yiddish type. I'm sure if I went back there, I'd find it. These two men will go with me up and down Germany to locate Yiddish typesetters. We've found a German in Regensburg who'll let us use his equipment. We located a German who has ink that's hidden from the army. We've located a German warehouse where they have the paper. We need money to finance it and a requisition from the army." The paper was published.

It was read eagerly by the Jews in the area. They described some of their experiences. There was information of people lookin' for relatives. They described what was happening now. Other camps published their own newspapers. (He tugs another paper from under the stack) Here's one from Bergen-Belsen: *Our Word.*

I got a frantic call: they're killing Jews at the railroad station. I hurried there and found six hundred Jews sleeping in freight cars. I learned that the night before, they were in a camp in Linz, Austria. They were given one hour notice, a couple of slices of bread, no water, and put on the train. Just like the Germans did. They were being transferred to a camp near the Czech border on American orders. The locomotive broke down. During the night some GI punks shot their guns in the air, so the people in the freight car thought they were killing Jews.

About midnight, I got a call from Silberberg, the editor in Munich: three Jews escaped from the transport. "They're in my room. They have no identification cards. Come over immediately." I jump in a jeep, get there, and meet the three. One had been a leading novelist in Germany. The second was a rising poet who somehow survived in Germany and in Russia. The third was an essayist. The paper, Silberberg said, is going to press tomorrow. "If you'll give me permission to spend the money, I'll reset the paper and publish an article, a poem, and an essay by each of these men, to let the world know they're alive."

Within a week, I ran into a strange kid in Bamberg. He was holding a copy of the paper in his hand, like a hot potato. He was shaking. He said, "My father was a writer in Lodz. He was in Warsaw meeting his publishers, and I haven't seen him since. I spent the war years in five slave-labor camps. When the war ended, I've been marching up and down Germany and Poland looking for my father. I came home last night and found this paper in the kitchen. There's an article by my father. Where is he?" We reunited father and son.

In Regensburg, I found a man with his two boys praying from the same book. They were of an extremely orthodox sect. He believed he and his two boys were among the fifteen survivors of fifteen thousand in the town of Zalachov, Poland. It was a 150-page book. Look at it, all by hand. (He opens what appears to be a rare book, meticulously hand-printed.) This man had been hiding in a Polish cellar where he didn't have room to stand up. Somehow he got ink and had an inkwell around his neck. He found paper somewhere. He didn't know whether he would be alive. The Germans destroyed everything in the synagogue, every vestige of Jewish life. They tore up the Torahs. "Children have to pray," he said. So he wrote this whole prayer book by hand, in the cellar, in the dark.

There was still something else I had to do. I knew that Dachau was not too far away from Munich. So on a beautiful October morning, I went there. My driver was reluctant. Behind the wall, Germans in uniform were playing soccer. I went into one building and I didn't see anything else. I had walked into the gas chamber. It's a museum today with clean, white-painted walls. When I was there, the walls were still covered with blood. People had banged their heads against it as they were dying.

I walked into the next room and there were two or three ovens. Over it was a big sign: "It is the duty of Germans to be clean. Wash your hands." I went downstairs. They don't take anybody downstairs now. Mind you, this was 1945, no guards, nothing. The two of us wandered along. I found myself in a room lined with shelves on which were earthen jars. There were two barrels of human ashes. I froze. I turned to my right and grabbed at something. I had to get out in the sunlight. The driver said, "What have you got in your hands?" The jar covers were glued to my hands. (He holds up the two pieces.) See the date? October 6, 1945, Dachau, Germany.

I discovered who the Germans playing soccer really were. When Dachau was freed, many of the guards were killed, others were prisoners. These guys were some of them. The army was feeding them 4,000 calories a day. The Jews in Munich, survivors of the death camps, were getting 1,600 calories.

The driver quietly said to me, "Do you know why I was reluctant to come here? I was on the last transport brought to Dachau. When the Americans were approaching, as my train pulled in, they took this whole transport of about a thousand people and began a death march. The Germans killed about half of them. I was one who wandered into Munich. That's where you found me. Who'd have thought that some-day I'd walk through the gas chamber and come out alive?"

That same month, I attended a wedding in Nuremberg. It was on a kibbutz that was once Julius Streicher's farm. The next morning I drove into the stadium. Can you picture one jeep driving into this stadium where Hitler addressed a quarter of a million peo-ple? I passed the Court of Justice. The first of the Nuremberg trials was on.

I had my driver stop. I was still in uniform. I gave my revolver to the driver.

Why'd you carry a revolver?

For safety's sake. I traveled at night much of the time. I could be robbed and killed by anybody, Germans or people who were just hungry. They were roaming the streets. This is postwar Europe, you must remember. (He flashes a pass and reaches once more into the stack.) Here is the seating arrangement, the floor plan. Goering, Hess, Keitel, Ribbentrop, Rosenberg, Frank, Frick, Streicher, the whole lot. I found all these men in front of me. It was a group of well-dressed men, with briefcases, newspapers, magazines in their hand. You would think these were members of the board of directors of IBM prior to a meeting.

As Goering and Hess came in, I noticed that some of the Germans clicked their heels and shook hands with them. A couple of guys turned their backs to them. Goering wrapped a huge blanket around his rear end, sat down, dropped his head, and slept through the hour or two I sat there. Hess, sitting next to him, began to write. Schacht stared at the ceiling all through the damn things. There's Keitel and all these others, sitting there, bored.

On the stand a surviving witness was describing how the Germans filled up the synagogues with Jews, set the buildings on fire, lined the outside with machine guns, and killed the fleeing Jews. I was sitting there in the third row. I looked at these bored characters, I can say with honesty that if I had my revolver with me, I would have begun to shoot and I would be dead.

What bothers me, I'm seventy-five years old, and God knows I'm not a religious man. I do go to services. Everybody has his reasons. I pray for peace. But I realize what's going on all over the world, the suffering. What has man learned? I saw people with the indomitable will to live. But as long as some men want power, we're gonna have wars. And all this praying . . .

A TURNING POINT

JOSEPH POLOWSKY

*April 25. He stands on the Michigan Avenue bridge, Chicago. Some-
times he bears a sign. Sometimes he hands out leaflets. It is as much a
mission as it is a vigil. He has been on this bridge, on this day, for the
past ten years. He is commemorating a moment in his life and, he feels,
in ours. On April 25, 1945, an American patrol of GIs met the Russians
along the Elbe River. He was one of that group.*

*At the end of the war, he organized the American Veterans of the Elbe
River. He has arranged reunions, on occasion, of his buddies and the
Russians. He has written thousands of letters, longhand, to presidents,
congressmen, newspaper editors, commentators. He has issued releases
uncomputable. He is a man possessed.*

At sixty-six, he is a retired cabdriver. He has terminal cancer.

I was a rifleman, private, Company G, 273rd Infantry, Third Platoon,
Sixty-ninth Division, First Army. We had seen plenty of action. We
were in a quiet area along the Mulde River, a tributary of the Elbe.
A town called Trebsen, twenty miles west of the Elbe. This was April
24.

I was called into company headquarters. They were checking on
documents of Germans, suspects and former Nazis and those who
wanted to be officials. I was the only man in the company who had
a good working knowledge of German.

A phone call comes in from battalion headquarters. They want a
patrol to be formed immediately, seven jeeps, twenty-eight men, to
go about five miles in front of the lines to see if they could get some
signs of the Russians. They were supposed to be anywhere from
twenty to thirty miles in front of us.

The best platoon leader in our company, by general consensus, was
Lieutenant Kotzebue. He was quiet, young, about twenty-two years
old. I was twenty-six. He quickly assembled the jeeps and the men.
He took a map of the area. I was in the lead jeep with him, because

I spoke German. We were warned before we left that platoons from other companies had been badly shot up by the Germans in this region.

It was seventy miles from Berlin, directly south. The Battle of Berlin was being waged north of us. Every available German soldier was called up to the defense of Berlin. There were many deserters, however, that we ran into. A continual stream. Some of 'em actually dressed up in women's clothing. The great mass was the German civilian refugees, fleeing the Russians. They were continually blocking the road. Mostly women, children, and old men.

To show you how slowly we proceeded, we had just managed to get about seven miles and we'd started about noon. We holed up in a little town called Kübren. Kotzebue pored over the maps all evening. We interrogated anybody who had any idea where the Russians might be.

Actually, we weren't supposed to meet the Russians. If we met them, we were gonna take the consequences in case anything was fouled up. At Eisenhower's headquarters, they were making detailed plans to meet the Russians. We were just on patrol. We were told that after five miles, we were going at our own risk. If anything went awry, instead of being heroes, we might wind up being court-martialed.

They were afraid if the two armies met at full speed, there would be casualties. Two armies, even friendly armies, going hellbent toward each other, there would be some guys who would be hurt. So Eisenhower and Zhukov decided that the two armies would stop about twenty-five miles short of each other. That's why we stopped at the Mulde and they at the Elbe.

When we holed up for the night, we'd gone only a third of the way. As dawn broke, Kotzebue made a decision: we're going ahead. There was a tremendous cheer. We all hopped in the jeeps and proceeded. We didn't know what faced us. At noon, we also saw long streams of liberated civilians from concentration camps, slave laborers, Allied soldiers who were freed.

Would you believe it? There was a tremendous burst of lilacs as we approached the Elbe River. This exaltation of being alive, after all those days trapped in a trench war. There were even jokes that we were approaching the River Jordan, crossing into Canaan. Of course, we were saddened to learn that President Roosevelt had died about two weeks earlier. We also knew that the United Nations was being born in San Francisco on the very same day, twenty-fifth of

April. Can you imagine? The very day we linked up with the Russians at the Elbe River.

It was a tremendous feeling to see the Elbe. This was about eleven-thirty in the morning. The Elbe is a swift-running river, about 175 yards wide. Kotzebue shot up two green flares. After about ten minutes, with shouts and the wind blowing towards the east, our voices were able to carry across the river. The Russians waved at us and gave the signal to approach their lines. The problem was getting across the river. The Germans in retreat, the Allied forces dropping bombs along the bridges, the Russian artillery blowing up the bridges: between the three, there was no bridge to cross. We were at Strehla, about sixteen miles south of Torgau.

At the far side of the Elbe, the Russian side, there was the remains of a steel bridge which jutted out maybe fifty yards into the river. On our side, there was a heavy chain attached to a barge and two sailboats. With a hand grenade, Kotzebue exploded the chain. About six of us piled into the sailboat. There were makeshift paddles. With tremendous effort, we managed to guide the boat into the girders protruding from the opposite side. As we climbed up, there were three Russian soldiers approaching the bank. Why were there only three? On the road ahead, we saw many Russian soldiers.

What happened was this. That bridge had been blown up at least three days. A tremendous wave of civilians, mostly Germans, a great mass, had approached the bridge, fleeing the Russians to go west. So they were piled like lumber at the bridge, along the whole bank. Fifty yards on each side was literally covered with bodies of women, old men, children. I still remember seeing a little girl clutching a doll in one hand—it was right there. She couldn't have been more than five or six years old. And her mother's hand in the other. They were all piled up like cordwood at the bank.

How had it happened? Who knows? Part of it was German fire, maybe Allied planes bombing the bridgehead. Probably the Russian artillery from a distance of several miles. It was a depressed area, impossible to see. It was an accident. There were so many in the war.

Actually, it was difficult for the Russians to pierce their way into meeting us. Because of the bodies. Here we are, tremendously exhilarated, and there's a sea of dead. Kotzebue, who is a very religious man, was much moved. He couldn't talk Russian. The Russians couldn't talk English. He said, "Joe, let's make a resolution with these Russians here and also the ones on the bank: this would be an important day in the lives of the two countries and the symbolism of all the civilian dead. Talk to them in German." As I was translating to Kotzebue in English, one of the Russians who knew German was translating to the other Russians. It was very informal, but it was a solemn moment. There were tears in the eyes of most of us. Perhaps a sense of foreboding that things might not be as perfect in the future as we anticipated. We embraced. We swore never to forget.

When we got to the top of the embankment, there was Lieutenant Colonel Gardead. He greeted us, and again we took an oath. Kotzebue's main mission was to immediately contact the Americans. Our radios were in the jeeps on the other side of the Elbe. So Gardead said go and come back. We'd been drinking and embracing and toasting. The Russians had brought some vodka and some German wine and beer. We were real drunk, but not because of the liquor. Gardead said, "It's important you tell the others. After you've done that, pile into your jeeps, cross onto a ferry, and we'll continue our celebration here." He sent a couple of Russians to accompany us.

As soon as we got across, Kotzebue gets in touch with headquarters. He gave them readings where we were at Strehla. But there was radio interference. As often happens, radio communications in combat rarely work perfectly. An hour passed. We're getting impatient. He wants to make firm contact with the American forces. To either bring the Russians back to the American lines or Americans to come up.

After we made the communications, we piled into the jeeps with the two Russian guys. We went about three, four miles north into this hand ferry and we all crossed again into the Russian lines. As we crossed the bank, Kotzebue tossed me the map. He said, "You've done a good job, here's a little present for you." I kept it as a souvenir. I was actually offered a very considerable sum of money for it. Of course, I wouldn't dream of givin' it up. It's not for sale.

As we learned later, there were mixed feelings on the part of the American headquarters. We weren't supposed to meet the Russians. They were, of course, secretly glad that we met them without casualties. They really dispatched a helicopter to Strehla, but there were no seven jeeps. Something had been fouled up. Meanwhile, there are tremendous celebrations in the Russian lines.

We drank and there were accordions and balalaikas and music and dancing. They played American songs. Some of the other guys could play the guitar. And there were some from slave-labor camps. Russian girls dancing. It was a strange sight. I was so captivated by the event, that it took possession of me for the rest of my life. It has colored my life, in spite of difficulties I've run into—general indifference. It has become a nonevent.

I always felt that American-Russian relations were plagued by bad luck right from the beginning. If we had gotten publicity with the Oath of the Elbe, there would have been a certain depth in the feelings. Just think of the millions who died on the Russian side and the tremendous effort on the American side, amidst all those dead women and children and that little girl clutching the doll in her hand. Nothing.

He urges a photograph toward me, his guest, of American GIs in a jeep surrounded by Russian soldiers. They are all grinning. Standing up on the jeep, cigarette in hand, is young Joe Polowsky. The weary sixty-six-year-old ex-cabbie observes his guest's face.

There was another patrol of Lieutenant Robertson. He and three others in a jeep made the main contact with the Russians. He arrived at the Soviet lines at four-thirty in the afternoon. That was four hours after we met the Russians. He ran into the same problem of scattered fire across the lines. He went into Torgau, a quiet town of about twenty thousand. He made a makeshift American flag and went up in the tower. He was recognized by the Russians. He crossed in a skiff into the Russian lines.

There was a great celebration. This was the only patrol mentioned in the communiqué of Truman, Churchill, and Stalin. He was able to get four Russians into his jeep and go back to the American lines. He raced back to Trebsen. There were almost four hundred American and Allied correspondents. They were champing at the bit. They knew something was up. They were just waiting to break the news that the whole world had been waiting for since Stalingrad. And since Normandy. It was a moving and wonderful thing (a long pause) but there was this special thing of the Oath of the Elbe. It would have been better.

We were still back in the Russian lines. When we got back, Kotzebue got a Silver Star and we all got Bronze Stars.

They were angry when Robertson got back, too. But they got over it fast. There'd been a news blackout, in effect, because they wanted to wait until Truman, Churchill, and Stalin made the announcement. It was better the way it happened. When ordinary soldiers meet, as we met and Robertson met, it's more informal. That's the way armies should meet.

This time he offers a copy of the Stars & Stripes, *April 28, 1945. "A souvenir edition issue, over a million copies. It was issued on Saturday. We met the Russians on the twenty-fifth. The twenty-seventh was the tripartite announcement. This came out the next day." An emblazoned headline:* YANKS MEET REDS.

The lead piece is by Andy Rooney, Stars & Stripes *staff writer. It is headed:* GOOD SOLDIERS MEET. TRADING DAY ALONG THE ELBE:

"There was a mad scene of jubilation on the east and west banks of the Elbe at Torgau as infantrymen of Lieutenant General Courtney H. Hodges, First U.S. Army, swapped K rations for a vodka with soldiers of Marshal Kornian's Ukrainian Army, congratulating each other, despite the language barrier, on the linkup.

"Men of the 69th Division sat on the banks of the Elbe in warm sunshine today with no enemy in front of them or behind them and drank wine, cognac, and vodka, while they watched their new Russian friends and listened to them as they played accordions and sang Russian songs.

"If today was not an extraordinary day in the lives of most Russians along the Elbe at Torgau, the Russian soldiers are the most carefree bunch of screwballs that ever came together in an army. They would best be described as exactly like Americans, only twice as much. . . . You get the feeling of exuberance, a great new world opening up. . . . This is Andy Rooney talking."

There is a memorial in Torgau. It must be a good two stories high. It shows Americans and Russians shaking hands. It has the American flag on one side and the Russian flag on the other. It's on a beautiful stretch of green, right as the Elbe River flows. I'm getting to be an old man. I will be buried at Torgau.

When I stand on the Michigan Avenue bridge every April 25, I pass out a statement: Halt the spread of nuclear weapons. If a passerby asks who I am, I tell 'im about the meeting at the Elbe. It's a matter of nonrecognition. They're generally polite. But I'm out of sync with the times. I'm pretty much of a nonperson. But I'll be at the bridge next April 25, God willing. (Laughs.) I hope I make it.

Joseph Polowsky died October 18, 1983. He was buried in Torgau on November 25, 1983.

MIKHAIL NIKOLAEVICH ALEXEYEV

He is a Russian author and magazine editor. "All my literary work is related to the war or life on the farm." He and his wife, Galina Alexeyeva, attended a Soviet-American writers' conference in Kiev in 1982. During a break, they reflected on their personal experiences in the Great Patriotic War, as they termed World War Two.

He is sixty-five, though there is as much muscle as flab. A heavy, medium-sized man, he resembles almost any older patron of any tavern in any American ethnic neighborhood.

The interpreter is Michael Kuzmenko, twenty-two.

I was born in a village in Saratov County, in a farmer's family of average income. When I was six, I began working in the fields. I went to a pedagogical high school, but I didn't manage to be a teacher. So I was enrolled in the army. From 1938 until 1955, I served in the army. I began as an enlisted man, and at the end I was a colonel.

I faced this war here on the Ukrainian soil, near the city of Sumy. I was in the artillery when the Germans began approaching these regions. I was in a special detachment under the command of General Chesnov. This formation went to the front. In the territory of Poltava, not far from Kiev, I participated in my first combat. It was early in July 1941. The Germans were very near.

The Germans managed to encircle our troops in this region. I was heavily wounded and sent to a hospital. Later I was in a hospital in Uzbekistan. In December of 1941, I was sent to a newly formed division near Stalinograd. It has nothing to do with Stalin. This is from virgin land. I was ordered to form a company to shoot mortars at flying guns, 82-millimeter. In March 1942, this division was at Tula, a town near Moscow. We were there until July of 1942. The Germans were on the offensive in the south and captured Kharkov. They were approaching the Don River in the direction of Stalingrad.

If you go up the Volga River four hundred kilometers, there is Stalingrad. It is still the low flows.

This was the time when the Germans were very sure of victory. They thought they would easily take Stalingrad on the way. It is the end of July 1942. Our division was taken to the railway station near the Don. Our regiment marched to the Don straightway without waiting for the other regiments. Our task was to defend the river and not let the enemy cross it. It is where the Don River is closest to Stalingrad. After the war, a canal was built which connected the Don and the Volga.

My mortar company was defending in the village of Nizhniy. There are defeats. Of course, there is resistance, but the Soviet army is being pushed back. We are delaying the enemy on the Don, but the forces are not even. Our army is being slowly driven back to Stalingrad. Especially hard combats have been taking place near the railway station in the village of Avgenyerova. The local people told me that for many years, they have been collecting skeletons and have been burying them. They called this the white field, because it was all white with skeletons and skulls. Of Soviet soldiers and German soldiers.

When we went to attack, the Germans were shooting us with machine guns. When they went on the attack, we did the same to them. In the beginning it had been very even ground, but as combat continued, it became steep because it was covered with human bodies.

The left wing of the German army approached Stalingrad on the twenty-third of August after a massive attack by German aircraft. During this day, the twenty-third of August, Stalingrad was practically destroyed, because of the German preponderance of aircraft. Our right wing had to retreat all the way to the suburbs of Stalingrad. There we organized our defense and never left our positions, until the twentieth of November. There were attacks and counterattacks, terrible combat. We did not give an inch.

On the nineteenth of November, the attack of the Soviet troops began. Our division joined this attack a day later. On the twenty-third of November, the Germans were encircled. Approximately 330,000 German soldiers and officers, led by General Paulus, were surrounded. As the combats continued, we were making the circle smaller, tightening the vise. General Manstein was trying to break the circle from the outside. He managed to move ahead, some thirty, forty kilometers through it. But at the Avgenyerova railway station, his tanks were defeated. There was no longer any hope to break the circle and free General Paulus and his troops.

Now the agony of the Germans began. A little before the tenth of January, 1943, Soviet General Rokossovsky was proposing a surrender. Not just to continue shooting people for nothing. The proposal was rather humane. They guaranteed life to all the defeated troops, all the Germans. They offered medical aid. They promised that the officers could leave there with their hand weapons, like knives, and to keep all their military awards.

The German command refused, on orders from Hitler. On the tenth of January, all the troops of the Stalingrad front began the big offensive. Very few of the German aircraft reached the encircled troops. By that time, we had a preponderance in the air and in anti-aircraft artillery. We destroyed enemy aircraft before they could even reach the circle.

Somewhere in the middle of January, I could not find a piece of earth for my motor company just to shoot, so many of the German weapons lay on the ground. As the circle was becoming smaller and smaller, the mounds of German guns grew higher and higher. So many and close to one another.

By this time, the German troops numbered about 100,000. The others, about 230,000, were killed or taken prisoners of war. May I give you a detail of their losses? The night before our decisive attack, I was looking for a place to hide until morning, to get some sleep. There were many German positions safe, but nothing was available. I couldn't use them, because the bodies of the German soldiers took up all the ground. They were everywhere, piled high on the fields and in the dugouts. I could find not one piece of open fields nor any unoccupied dugout. There were also so many maggots, because of the dead bodies. And oh, the lice, the lice.

I saw a dugout in the snow. I had warm clothing so I went in there and bumped against something very stiff. It was very dark, so I couldn't see what it was. I thought they were sacks of something. So I made myself comfortable lying on these sacks. In the light of the morning, I saw that I was sleeping on the bodies of killed German soldiers.

The Germans were very orderly people. When they found they didn't have time to bury these bodies, they laid them next to each other in a very neat and orderly way. I saw straight rows, like pieces of cordwood. Exact.

The most surprising thing is that I was not surprised, not shocked by this discovery, so accustomed had I become to death. Now, when you see a dead body of someone, you feel uneasy. Then, I saw it every day, everywhere and so many. I got accustomed to it.

My company was located some three hundred meters from the center, from the Paulus headquarters. We were moving in. Unfortunately, others reached these headquarters before we did. When Paulus was taken prisoner, all the German forces capitulated: on the second of February, 1943.

For many days, columns and columns of German prisoners were passing by. The length of the columns was many, many kilometers long. They seemed never to end. It was very cold and their clothing was very, very poor. They put everything they had about themselves. Women's rags, shawls, anything. They were very hungry. They had eaten all the horses from the Rumanian cavalry corps. There were no horses left. They had no other supply of food, because there was no local population. Very, very few people. The majority had been wiped out when the Germans were bombarding. Many were evacuated when the Germans were approaching. We found a few children in Stalingrad, hiding.

The Germans had committed one strategic and tactical mistake. All their best forces were concentrated on Stalingrad. In the street fights, they dispersed their forces. Their flanks were exposed, because their Rumanian and Hungarian forces were less well equipped. We concentrated on these flanks and broke through.

When this battle began, the Germans were saying in a few days the Russian forces would surrender. Then it became a few months . . . Many years after Stalingrad, I was told that under the debris of one house, they found sacks with letters of German soldiers. They didn't have time to send these letters. In the first letters, one could feel their assurance that they will capture Stalingrad in just a few days. They were very optimistic. One could feel the joy there.

I want to say the truth. When we were retreating, it was very bitter and sad for us. But we couldn't write about it to our families. Once I sent a letter home and put a piece of grass in it. Grass which smells special, a bitter smell. So my relatives who got my letter understood how bitter it was. Remember, when we encircled the Germans, our losses were also very high.

We had been very excited when the combats were actually taking place. But now as we saw these German prisoners walking by in such a pitiful way, you felt a sort of pity for them. We understood that these were people who had some families, relations who were deceived by Hitler.

When I visited West Germany for the first time in 1965, I'll never forget the welcome given us by these former prisoners of war. It was a visit of the Stalingrad veterans. Our hosts explained simply: "You fed us when you had nothing to eat yourselves. You saved our lives." It was no exaggeration. There was hunger in our people and they fed these prisoners. And they came back home alive. No one has written about this so far. If you meet former prisoners of war in Germany, they will tell you this. The Russian people cannot be angry for a long time.

GALINA ALEXEYEVA

Mikhail Alexeyev's wife.

It is the color of her hair that first catches your attention. It is a startling orange-red, obviously dyed. In contrast to her husband, she is skinny, high-cheekboned. He moves slowly, heavily; hers are quick, nervous ways. She is in her late fifties.

Young Michael Kuzmenko is, again, the interpreter.

When the war began, I was in Stalingrad, in school. I lived with my sister, because I did not have a mother. I was in the eighth grade. My sister told me to go to my father because it was safer. I went there to finish my school.

We were also working at digging antitank dugouts, trenches, so it would be an obstacle to the Germans. All the children did that. It was down the river, the Volga. Afterwards, we returned to our homes.

When we came back, we saw that there were lots of wounded soldiers in our classrooms. We began to nurse them, to take care of them. We were trying to help them with everything. We were only thinking how to keep them alive. We young girls were carrying them to where they were making operations. It was a long way from there. Young girls with very thin legs and very thin fingers. The soldiers were very big and very heavy, with broken bones.

There was no place to go between the beds because they were so very close together. We had to lift the soldiers over our heads and carry them out. Believe me, they were very heavy. There was only one thought we had: not to lose the grip of our hands. If we drop him, he will die, because he is already so badly wounded.

When night came, I knew that many of them were so sorely wounded that they will die. Probably I'll help them by killing the bloody microbes, so to say. I was taking icy water and when they were asleep, I was crawling under beds, washing the floor. So they could still have fresh air with no microbes.

This was in the village of Nikolska, in the area of Stalingrad. My father's house.

People came around who put down the names of volunteers to defend the city of Stalingrad. I heard that they were training volunteers, so I went there. I said, "My brother was already killed near Kiev. Take me to the front, as a soldier." I was in a hospital when I got this subpoena to report to where they gathered. Is that what you call it? A greeting? You see, I was already a nurse. I didn't take any examination. They just announced, "You are a nurse." So when I volunteered, I was about sixteen.

When I got the greeting, my father got some foodstuffs and put it in a sack. My father was a very kind man. He knew that in the place where I was going to stop on my way, there were three girls who didn't have any parent. He told me to share my food with them.

My father began crying and saying, "I won't let you go." I said, "How can you say that? You were a guerrilla during the Civil War." This is my memory of him, standing there crying.

She shows a worn identification book. There is an almost faded photograph of her in uniform; a young girl with long black hair.

At first, they had me at a post where I collected messages and passed out cigarettes. I wanted to do something more active. So, after some training, I began to work in communications.

I was there when we crossed the Dnieper River at the battle of Kursk. Also at Odessa. The Twenty-seventh Tank Brigade needed somebody in communications. It was in Kiev and the only girls they had were speaking Ukrainian. One had to be very precise in communications. So I became the communications officer. This was a special armored battalion that was attacking very deeply German fortified areas.

There were a few women like me, but they wouldn't let us inside the tanks. Once we sent a girl in a tank. It caught on fire and all her hair burned off. So we stopped sending them there.

(I had the strangest thought: Could she have been that girl? Was the orange-red hair a wig?)

I volunteered for the combat forces. There were tough combats in Stalingrad. At first, they said no. I was recruited towards the end of the battle. Our tanks were so damaged. The men who were just lying there, wounded, were writing "Stalingrad" in the dirt.

The children were hiding in basements of buildings. When they were coming up to the open air after the battles, they didn't look like children. They had the faces of small old people—dwarfs, yes. The expression in their eyes was not childish any more. They looked like the eyes of old people. One girl had her legs frozen. She was twelve at the time. They wanted to treat it. They put her legs in warm water and—well, the lower part of her legs, her feet, just fell off.

One could talk about this for a long, long time without any end. There were so many heavily wounded people that I saw who were crying, seeing me, Help, help, help, sister. I once saw a soldier from a gun crew with his chest open. One could see his heart beating. When I looked at him, I understood that one couldn't stand him up vertical or his heart would fall out. He needed an operation right on the spot. He would die from his own blood, he couldn't breathe. Sometimes you saw a man sitting when the bombardment was on. You think he's not afraid. You run up to him and something falls. He is without his head.

I saw prisoners of war in Stalingrad and later along the road. I felt sorry for them. Whose sons are these? What was wrong with your life? Why did you come here? What is there which we don't have on our planet? We have rivers, fields. As a former soldier, who saw thousands of deaths, I don't want any war repeated. Peace and war is not a cowboy movie. Don't play around with it.

He was a correspondent with the Red Army during the war. As five veterans are gathered, with a vodka or two to encourage the flow of words, he recalls the day of the German surrender at Stalingrad.

On the morning of 1943, the second of February, they began to surrender. It was snowing a little, the day was bleak. Suddenly, after two hundred days of constant cannonade and shooting, there was silence. Everyone was asking each other, "What's the matter? What's happening?" It is so quiet in the streets. No one understands anything. Someone says, "The Germans are surrendering." They are putting their weapons on the ground. Just hills of weapons.

Then I see this snake, this giant snake of the wounded and the captured. This long, twisting line. This snake was green and dirty. Also, it looked like many frogs. Their ragged suits were camouflage, green, white, black. The line is moving towards the horizon. You don't see the end and the beginning of it. It is growing darker and darker. Dirty snow is everywhere.

Our lorries are moving along with this column and picking up the wounded and the fatigued German prisoners.

Toward the end of the column, I saw a German field lieutenant who was so fatigued he collapsed on the ground. As his friends shuffled ahead, his cry was like a wolf. A howl: "Paul! Paul! Peter! Peter!" His friends just put their ragged coat collars up, hunched their shoulders, and moved on. They never turned their heads. I remember this soldier, he still had a few medals on him. One of the lorries came by. A soldier got out, helped him up, and put him in the car.

I met former German prisoners of war when I visited a cathedral in Weimar. The guide was an old gentleman who spoke Russian very well. I asked him, "How do you happen to know the language?" He said, "Stalingrad."

GRIGORI BAKLANOV

Hotel Sovietskaya, Moscow. We're seated in a huge dining room, once upon a time celebrated for its elegance and the profligacy of its patrons:

the Yar, where dashing officers of the Czar's army and merchant princes,
we're told, tossed large ruble notes at strolling Gypsy players.

"Evenings would begin at the Slagansky Bazaar," says Frieda Lurie,
our interpreter. Figaro, I call her, our general factotum. "They would
continue and last far into the morning in this room, the Yar." The tale,
though true, seems apocryphal, as apparatchiks and foreign guests go
about their business.

He is a World War Two hero whose novels deal with one subject: the
war.

Eight from my family went to the front. Three came back. We were
a lucky family.

When my children ask, "Tell us about the war," I can't tell them
anything. I don't like this reminiscing. A lot of people, who lived after
the war quite a long life, start to recollect. It was miraculous, wonderful, how brave we were then, how close together we were. It is not
a worthy occupation for a human being.

Of my generation, out of a hundred who went to fight, three came
back. Three percent. One should not ask those of us who remained
alive what war means to them.

I live life as if presented to me. I'm surprised that I have it. A
friend asked me, "What's your attitude towards death?" It is absolutely zero. With much more surprise and excitement, I take the fact
that I'm alive. I look at my children and my grandchildren and I
think: only centimeters decided whether they should be on this earth
or not. Whether the bullet went that way or this way. They don't
understand that they live on this earth quite by accident. It was quite
natural that I wouldn't be alive. But I lived and they happened. They
can't understand that.

I think the world is divided into two parts. Half is alive and the
other half is in the shadow. It doesn't exist but in the mind. In my
short story, I recollect a phrase: "The bullet that killed us today goes
into the death of centuries and generations, killing life which didn't
come to exist yet."

I was the only one from our class of all the boys who went to the
front who remained alive after that war. What else is there to say?

CHILLY WINDS

TELFORD TAYLOR

He was chief American prosecutor at twelve of the thirteen Nuremberg trials. He had succeeded Robert Jackson, who returned to the United States Supreme Court after serving at the first Nuremberg trial. He had been a colonel in the army. On his appointment at Nuremberg, "They gave me a star. But I'm not a professional soldier. I've never used the title since I got out of the army." Among his books are Sword and Swastika *and* Nuremberg and Vietnam. *He practices law in New York and teaches at Columbia University Law School and the Benjamin Cardozo Law School.*

"For most people my age, the war and its aftermath were the most intense experiences of our lives. So many crises that overtook me were directly due to the war. I was in no way a military person when I went into the army. I don't think I'd ever seen an American officer in uniform —except on the Fourth of July—until shortly before the war. After Pearl Harbor, all officers in Washington were required to wear uniforms. It became a common sight. There could have been none more unmilitary than my generation. The military seemed a world apart.

"Through all those years—the normality of Harding, the boom, the bust—the army was less than a hundred thousand. It just wasn't part of a normal person's experience. The Pentagon had not yet come into existence. The military budget was, of course, much smaller. The war ballooned the whole thing and it became a major part of everybody's life. The voice of the military, after World War Two, became very strong.

"I got out of Harvard Law School at the foot of the Depression, at the time the New Deal was coming in. Instead of going to Wall Street, I went to Washington. When the war came, I was general counsel for the Federal Communications Commission.

"I went into the army in 1942. At the end of the war, Jackson gave the War and Navy departments a list of lawyers whom he knew and wanted assigned to him for the trials. My going to Nuremberg was not of my choice."

The tribunal that tried the first Nuremberg trial was set up in the summer of 1945, before the Japanese war ended. An agreement had been reached at San Francisco at the same time that the United Nations Charter was accepted. Nuremberg is actually a twin of the United Nations. They were born at the same time, same place, same purpose. Peacekeeping.

The idea was that the punishment of aggression—making it a crime under international law—would help keep the peace. (Dryly) It hasn't worked out very much that way. The four major powers met in London and signed the London Charter, which provided for the establishment of this tribunal.

The first trial was quadripartite. The judges and prosecutors were from France, England, the Soviet Union, and the United States. The remaining twelve trials were conducted exclusively by American judges, prosecutors, and defense lawyers. The other countries were having trials in their own occupation zones.

This international tribunal was set up to consider not only conventional war crimes, atrocities, but also the new idea of making aggressive warfare a crime. A planning offense. Jackson and Henry Stimson, then Secretary of War, regarded this as its most important feature.

Those to be prosecuted need not have been at the scene of the crime?

Most of them were officials who had either given or originated the orders. Or knew about them and passed them down.

There's a very strong contrast, in that respect, between the Tokyo trial of Tojo and the others and the Nuremberg trial. Most of the war crimes committed by the Japanese were not the result of orders from Tokyo. It was very much a matter of the local commander. He might be a son of a bitch, he might be a gentleman. My first wife came from a missionary family and many of her relatives were confined in Japanese prisoner-of-war camps. The treatment varied a great deal from one camp to another. The conduct of Japanese troops going into a captured city varied a great deal. It was not a matter of orders from above.

The attack on Pearl Harbor was indeed planned from above. It was a national enterprise. But the conduct and treatment of occupied populations was very much a local decision by the commander.

The Tribunal of the Far East, as the Tokyo court was called, was in many ways modeled on Nuremberg. Whereas the Nuremberg records are numerous, you can't find, except in one or two libraries, a copy of the Tokyo trial. Little is publicly known about it.

You may remember that when the two German generals Keitel and Jodl were condemned to death and executed, there was a great howl from military circles. Commentators loudly echoed the military view. Except for those two and one other—a General Dostler, who had killed American prisoners in Italy and was condemned by an American court-martial—no other German general received a capital sentence at American hands at the end of World War Two.

With no public awareness, a great many Japanese generals, admirals, colonels, commanders were tried and executed without a ripple of protest from either the military people or anybody else. Nobody ever said it, but I suppose it was race.

Have you seen the Australian movie *Breaker Morant*? It's about war crimes during the Boer War. The pitch is that rules about war are made by civilians, who just don't understand what men in the field are up against. There may be a germ of truth in it, but the idea that rules of war were made by civilians is simply not so.

Who sentenced General Yamashita to death? A military court of seven career generals, whose verdict was approved in a ringing denunciation by General MacArthur.

Military men have been much more severe than civilians in punishing infractions of these rules, if the defendant was an enemy soldier. And equally resentful of efforts to punish their own. There's always been an admiration of the German military in this country in our military circles. This may explain why MacArthur was denouncing Yamashita and signing the death warrant with a great flourish, while at the same time there's an outcry from generals against the conviction of Keitel and Jodl.

We had sized up Keitel at the trial as not very sensitive nor reflective. In his testimony, he was a very wooden man. But in his last statement to the court, he said, "What I never realized was that simply being a good soldier and following orders was not enough. Das ist meine schuld." That is my guilt.

At the first Nuremberg trial, there were twenty-two defendants. Thirteen, if I recall, were given the death penalty. Goering, of course, committed suicide on the eve of his execution. These were the big shots.

Our first trial, after Jackson left, was of German doctors for performing inhuman experiments on concentration-camp prisoners. We had about twenty defendants, and of those, seven were executed. There was a trial of German judges, three trials of SS officials, two trials of military people, a trial of the diplomats. There were three trials of industrialists, Flick, Farben, and Krupp. But things were changing.

With the first trial successfully concluded, the whole climate of the occupation zone changed. The iron curtain came down, the cooperative administration of Occupied Germany had broken up. Came the Berlin airlift and great hostility between the Eastern and Western powers. The sentiment toward Germany, politically and militarily, began to change a great deal. We wanted Germany on our side. That attitude, I think, affected the sentencing in the remaining trials.

Quite a lot of death sentences were given out, chiefly to SS officials who were directly responsible for the Jewish exterminations. A great many of those sentences were pending when General Clay left as head of Military Government of Occupied Germany. John McCloy, who took his place as High Commissioner, commuted a great many of those death sentences. There were only five who were executed after that.

Why did I stay on? Most of the lawyers at Nuremberg had been in the war, were in uniform, and thought this was going to be a big prominent trial and it would be useful to them to have been part of it. After they had a piece of the action, they went home. They didn't stay to see it through. Others, whose belief in it was more fundamental, stayed on.

Initially, I went there with no preconceptions. I wanted to see what was going to happen. After two or three years, I had a growing belief in this body of doctrine, which had both promise and difficulties. It was an experience you could only get once in a lifetime. It didn't do me much good professionally.

When I came back home in 1949, I was already in my early forties. I'd been away from home seven years and was out of touch with things politically. I thought that Washington was still the way I'd left it in 1942. By 1949, it was a very different place. I had left Washington at a time when it was still Roosevelt, liberalism, social action, all these things. When I came back in the late forties, the Dies Committee . . . the cold war. I was a babe in the woods. I didn't know what hit me.

I went into partnership in a very well-set-up New York law firm.

I sat in my office and nobody came. I didn't get any business. Everybody who knew about me from the papers thought I was a general, not a lawyer. So I started to write a book because I had nothing else to do.

Very soon, I became involved in opposition to some of the congressional committees, including McCarthy's. Some of the people who were called before them retained me as a lawyer. I did finally get some business.

I made a few speeches about it. At Sarah Lawrence College, two West Point cadets in the audience invited me to address their Cadet Forum. It was at the time when McCarthy was investigating Fort Monmouth, the Signal Corps research center. At West Point, I gave them my pretty frank opinion of McCarthy and what he was doing to the army. To my astonishment, it went over great. It was all over the front pages of the *New York Times.*

It was not at a good time personally for that to happen. My clients became increasingly people that were in security trouble. Others didn't want a controversial figure like me handling their cases. The commandant at West Point was inquired of by the War Department: How'd you let this guy come and talk to the cadets? I was denounced in Congress. Instead of having been the avenging angel of justice at Nuremberg, I was denounced as a red.

Many years later, I was in Hanoi during the Christmas bombing of 1972. What I was trying to do was to examine the principles laid down at Nuremberg and see whether we had violated them in Vietnam. Whether we lived up to our own principles. I took the position that a number of things we did in Vietnam were violations of the laws of war. As for the bombing of North Vietnam, I did not believe that under the laws of war that was a crime. Maybe it should have been. But there was no precedent for declaring it as such.

Why did we refrain from bombing the center of Hanoi? I suppose because the public is increasingly aware of some limitations on warfare. Nuremberg has built up a body of laws and precedent that needs to be thought about. Why was there such a hullabaloo about the massacres in the camps in Lebanon? I think because in Nuremberg there was a systematic enforcement of these rules. I never would have gone to Hanoi had I not been involved in Nuremberg.

After all, the Holocaust was unprecedented in its scope. Surreal? I don't know. I'm afraid the human capacity for getting hardened to testimony about this sort of thing is unlimited. After you've heard two, three days of it, more of it is not new. Take a small child. He takes everything for granted. I remember when my own children, my two little girls, aged five and seven, came to Nuremberg, I was showing them the bomb-damaged houses. "The houses are broken," they said. After they'd seen one or two of them, they were no longer very interested.

Would you describe the Nuremberg defendants as ordinary people?

A man like Hjalmar Schacht, the banker, was extraordinary in his ability and intelligence. Not at all likable. If you're talking about concentration-camp guards and a lot of the underlings who carried out these bloody and murderous affairs, why, you're right. They were very ordinary people.

Why did they do these things? Because it had become the thing to do. People most of them were followers. Moral standards are easily obliterated. Take Eichmann: a minor electrician in Vienna. He joins the SS and he becomes an officer and a gentleman. He likes that. He gets promoted. He never got beyond lieutenant colonel, but that was pretty good for a Viennese electrician. They so very easily fall into the pattern that their superiors set up for them, because that's the safe way. They may be loving husbands, nice to their children, fond of music. They have been accustomed to moral standards prescribed from above by an authoritarian regime. The safe way to be comfortable in life is that way: following orders.

After I came back, I was quite often asked to talk about Nuremberg. Early in 1950, I addressed the membership of a Jewish synagogue in Brooklyn. I said, The idea that these Nazis of the Holocaust were all a bunch of abnormal sadists is not so. Most of them are very ordinary people just like you and me. You should have heard the uproar that went up from that audience. The same thing happened to me last spring. I told the rabbi that my views are a bit clinical and might not be the right thing for his congregation. He said it's a very sophisticated group. Exactly the same thing happened.

If our general population were subjected to the same trends and pressures that the Germans were, a great many of us would do the same. Maybe not as many, because we're not quite as authoritarian as the Germans. But a lot of us would. I think we do still have some built-in political safeguards, but they're not ironclad. If the depression gets worse—things are already getting more bitter than they were a few years ago—I can see some of the same things developing. But it would take a lot more than I see going on here now to come to that.

Most of our heroes have been ordinary people. The ordinary man is capable of enormous heroism and enormous bestiality. That's the hard lesson of Nuremberg. It's very easy to blame Nazism on the bestiality of these people. If a thousand people are killed by an earthquake, it's a terrible thing, but it's not tragic. There's no tragedy because there's no human element in it. It doesn't teach you any lesson except to watch out for earthquakes. The hard lesson of the tragedy is that ordinary people can be brought into a condition to do these things. That's much more dangerous.

ARNO MAYER

He is a member of the history department at Princeton.

I was born in the Grand Duchy of Luxembourg. We left there May 10, 1940, the morning of the German invasion of France, the big push. We were Jewish. It took us a half year to get to the United States.

I went into the army in early 1944. At Fort Knox, they were going to try and make a tank commander out of me. They thought they needed light-tank people to do some island-hopping in the Pacific. My entire unit was shipped out. I was the only one kept behind. I was sent to Camp Ritchie, Maryland, to be trained in intelligence.

They put twenty-eight of us onto a bus and drove us to Post Office Box 1142, Alexandria, Virginia. There we were to do our stuff. We were not to go overseas. Twenty-seven of the twenty-eight people in this unit were of European birth. They came from either Vienna or Brno or from Prague or Luxembourg. After dinner, instead of going out with gals, we would sit around and read Plato or Machiavelli.

At Post Office Box 1142, I became the morale officer for German generals who had been captured and flown to Washington. They were from the regular Wehrmacht and from the Waffen SS. They all had one thing in common: they had fought on the eastern front. I was to get as much information as I could with regard to only one thing: the battle order of the Red Army. About Germany, not one blessed thing. Even at that time, a few months after D-Day, the thoughts of the American government were already on the next phase of the confrontation.

I was not to do any interrogation. I was to keep these fellows happy, to put them in a good mood so they would readily talk about whatever they knew of the Red Army. I plied them with all sorts of stuff. With liquor, with newspapers. One day I was misguided enough to bring them *The Nation* and a copy of *PM.* * I thought it was perfectly legitimate fare in a free country. When my officers found out that I was handing them literature of that nature, I was told in no uncertain terms that I could give them *Life* magazine and the *New York Times,* and *Reader's Digest,* but for God's sake, not any of that other stuff.

One day during a casual conversation, they told me that Hitler's only mistake was to go after the Jews. Everything else had been perfectly all right. Of course, they knew only too well that was music to the ears of Washington. I exploded at the two officers who had made that statement. I started screaming at them in German: "You people are totally unreconstructed bastards. You know damn well that's what you say to me. To others, you will say something else. How am I to believe you? If you think that's the only mistake, it's one hell of a mistake."

Since every square inch of that installation was wired, by the time I went back to where I had to report, I was presented with a record: the word-for-word conversation between me and the two officers. I was taken by two captains to the camp commander, who informed me my instructions were to keep these people happy: don't argue with them, just make them feel good. I should just listen, keep my mouth shut. He broke the record right over his knee. If this happened again, I would be in serious trouble. I would be court-martialed for disobeying orders.

I also became the morale officer for Wernher von Braun and three other big scientists that were brought here. Of course, by then we were in a dead-heat competition with the Soviets for the personnel that had worked at Peenemünde, the installation where the German rockets were developed. The Soviets, of course, got their own Ger-

*A liberal newspaper published in New York during the forties.

mans. Everybody had his own Germans, getting ready for the next
big bang.

These four were the first scientists to arrive. Of the other three,
one was a specialist in wind tunnels, one in infra-red light, and the
other had another Mickey Mouse specialty that became terribly important for future military technology. They were brought here with
a promise of citizenship after six months, I believe. It was known as
Operation Paper Clip.

Around November 1945, shortly after victory, they came to me.
Behind my back they referred to me as *der kleine Judenbube,* the little
Jewish boy. How they knew I was Jewish I don't know. We spoke
German, but they had suspicions of these people they were dealing
with. Most of us were émigrés of one sort or another. They said, Look,
Christmas is approaching. Conditions in Germany were tough. It was
difficult to get food and clothing. They'd very much like to send their
families back home some Christmas packages.

I said, "My instructions are to do whatever I can to make life
pleasant for you." But I'd have to check this one out. The company
commander gave me a car and he handed me about a thousand bucks.
He said, "Okay, go shopping." There was a car with a chauffeur and
these four German scientists. Wernher von Braun in his full splen-
dor, blue-eyed, blond hair, and all that. The three others were considerably smaller. Here were these four characters, all wearing long
leather coats that reached down to their ankles and wearing Tyrolese
hats with feathers. I said, "Good God, no one's supposed to know
you're here. This is secret stuff. You can't walk around Washington
that way." But my instructions were: Go shopping. So we did.

I had the fiendish thought that it would be nice to take them to
a Jewish department store. So I took them to Landsberg Brothers. We
started on the main floor and bought the usual stuff: cocoa, sugar,
coffee, all the stuff that was in very short supply in Germany. Where
next? "We'd like to send our families some underwear." They
wanted panties for their wives. I was all of nineteen years old and
had never gone to buy panties. We went to the lingerie department.
Imagine these four odd characters, with long leather coats and green
Tyrolese hats, at the panties counter. Accompanied by *ein kleine
Judenbube.*

The saleswoman said, "What size?" Almost by reflex, out came
their slide rules. Centimeters into inches. She came back and held

467

up a panty made of nylon. My four charges, as if it had been orchestrated, threw up their hands: "Aber nein, Unterhosen aus Wolle und mit langen Beinen." Woollies with long legs, 'cause it's going to be very cold. We didn't get our panties. What next? They would like to get some brassieres. The lady was rather puzzled with the four odd men moving up to her. Again, the slide rules came out. At that moment the military police came and took the five of us to jail. The powers that be finally cleared us and we got back to Post Office Box 1142. All of this was in service to the nation.

The Germans considered me a pretty stupid fellow, which I was supposed to be. I remember their trying to convince me that the only reason they mucked around with these rockets is that they wanted to improve the airmail service between Berlin and London. They wanted to get it down to eight minutes. (Laughs.) At that moment, I cracked up, which I wasn't supposed to do.

They tried to give the impression that they never really approved of the Nazi regime. They worked exclusively as scientists in the interest of advancing the cause of science and research. And one fine day we'd get to the moon. They pleaded complete political ignorance. They knew very well when they scrambled away from Peenemünde they'd be a hell of a lot better off being captured by the Western armies than they would be by the Red Army.

They were totally patronizing. They knew I had no power. I had only power to bring them whiskey, orange juice, and the daily newspapers. At a certain moment, there was a question of plying them with women. I don't think it came to that, but there was talk of it. Freud would say I'm blocking this out.

The whole bunch of us were shipped to an island in Boston Harbor. There were about 120 of these types around by now. I remember going with them to church services on Sunday morning and translating the sermons, both Catholic and Protestant. At that moment I thought they could do worse things than worship. It was perhaps the most honorable thing they were doing.

We were just beginning to find out that plans were being made for work at White Sands, New Mexico. It was one of the testing grounds for military hardware. Including the stuff that eventually landed the first man on the moon. It became one of the central experimental stations for the most advanced military technology of the time. I didn't follow it at all.

There was a Quonset hut at Post Office Box 1142 to which I was never allowed to go. You needed a special permit. But since human beings will talk—they were working exclusively on Soviet stuff. Maps of theaters of war in Eastern Europe. These were German generals they were interrogating. And interrogating those scientists who had worked at Peenemünde to find out whether their unaccounted colleagues had gone over to the Russians. The heat race was really on by this time. This was late '45. The war had hardly been over.

When anybody asks me when the cold war began and talks about Truman and 1947, I tell them I was present at the creation. I use the title of Dean Acheson's memoirs, *Present at the Creation.* I was there. (Laughs.)

Weren't your superiors observing you in a certain way? After all . . .

Sure, I was accustomed to that. For me, it began at Fort Knox, in Louisville. I was the only Jew in the outfit. I experienced a kind of anti-Semitism that I wasn't prepared for. It reached a point where I had a couple of teeth knocked out. I prefer to call it anti-Judaism. It's a rather more traditional Jew-hatred, imbedded in a certain kind of Christianity with which Jews can live. It doesn't necessarily take you to the gas chamber. But at the time, any kind of anti-Semitic expression was likely to sit bad with me.

I was not only a northerner, but they felt I was an egghead. At first with hostility, and then fondly, I was referred to as the "intellectual fuck" of the outfit. Whenever I was called to the company commander's office, over the loudspeaker you'd hear: "Will the intellectual fuck come to the company commander?"

At the barracks, we had an orientation hour when the news of the day was read. It was up to me to read that briefing every day. One day, when I had finished, a guy said, "Here's a poem. Would you read this to us as well?" I read out this poem. I remember the punch line: When we finish with the Germans and the Japs, we'll come back and kill the Jews and the blacks. I said, "Hey, I like that poem so much I'll read it to you again, particularly that last stanza." After I read it again, I said, "Now look at me. I'm the Jew you're gonna kill." A real brawl broke out. Not that they were gonna kill me, but they sure as hell were gonna beat me up. This experience gave me another interpretation of World War Two.

To me, the war meant the exhilaration of being in the American army. When victory was won over Nazi Germany, I had absolutely no hesitation about fighting in the Pacific. I would have gone with the same enthusiasm with which I'd have gone to Europe. There was some suspicion on the part of the officers that someone that was an exile from Europe would not take the Pacific theater seriously. I'd have jumped at it.

I was at Camp Ritchie when word came over the radio of FDR's death. I was absolutely disorientated and overwhelmed by a sense of loss. A lot of the officers were overjoyed. He didn't die soon enough. At long last. I heard it many times over. I simply couldn't understand. I was still fairly innocent about American politics.

One thing that is unsettling about these recollections is that at Post Office Box 1142 I took an oath of secrecy. When does this oath come to an end? It does funny things to you. I feel myself bound to this oath of secrecy and yet, obviously, I don't. I wouldn't be talking this way. The puzzle for me is this has nothing to do with what we're talking about. Still, It does funny things to you.

I'm sure that in Germany people also took an oath of secrecy. We know what that eventually led to. If it works that way with us, the sanctions for breaking the secrecy are nothing compared to the sanctions there could be if we're silent.

All these years, I, a historian, inhibited myself to the point where I never really bothered to piece together where my own experiences fit into Operation Paper Clip. Plus the cranking up of what eventually became Cold War Mark Two.

Cold War Mark Two?

The new model of the same war. Cold War Mark One is what happened after World War One: the intervention in Russia by the Allied powers and the quarantine that was set up. I think the two are umbilically connected.

When does the state of emergency come to an end? I'm sure there must be a date that one can fix. Or have we slipped imperceptibly into a state of permanent hostility? And what it does to all of us.

I had won a Yale fellowship. This was about 1950. The cold war was just hitting academic circles. While in Europe preparing my dissertation, I heard of an East-West trade conference to be held in Moscow. Perhaps it could become the cutting edge for some kind of détente. I made my application. I wrote to my professors at Yale telling them that I was going. I wasn't asking for their permission,

I was merely advising them. I got panicky letters back from my professors. They simply said it was a dangerous thing to do. In all probability there would be a headline in the *New York Times:* Yale Fellowship Holder Attends Commie Meeting in Moscow. They'd wash their hands of me when it came to getting me a job. I didn't get the papers I needed to go to Moscow.

So when anybody asked me what I was doing in the army—since I wasn't able to say anything, not about where I was stationed—my answer was invariable: I was preparing for World War Three.

ERHARD DABRINGHAUS

He retired after twenty-nine years at Wayne State University as professor of Germanic culture.

During World War Two, he was a military intelligence officer. "In 1944, I was sent to England as an interrogator. We didn't have too many guys in the American army who knew what they were doing. I worked with the British to learn ruses how to make a guy talk.

"We knew the Germans were good family men. We'd go through their billfolds. They'd have pictures of mothers, wives, kids. I'd say, 'You could help this war end one day earlier, your wife and kids still alive and healthy when you get home. Otherwise, who knows? They might be bombed.' We were bombing German cities by then.

"We used tricks with ketchup. We had a sergeant dressed as a German. We'd throw ketchup into his face, and he'd run out screaming while we're interrogating the guy who wasn't talking. We could not put a hand on a man.

"Whenever a German was especially stubborn, I'd always call Sergeant Kaminski. The German starts talkin' at once. He knew Kaminski was a Polish name and he knew what they'd done to Warsaw. If I said, 'Sergeant Kaminski, this guy doesn't wanna talk,' the German'd say, 'Don't bring him in. I'll tell you the story.' "

I landed D-Day on Omaha Beach. First Infantry Division. Easy Red was Omaha's code name. It was not a happy day. We lost a lot of men.

This first day, I had two prisoners who didn't know what to say. They were glad to be alive. Later on, I found out that German GIs don't know much about the big picture. You have to be an officer.

The German soldier was kept in total darkness. He doesn't know what the hell he's doing. He's only told, Go forward and I'll tell you what to do later on. Same thing with our own GIs. Just say your name, rank, and serial number.

We'd always like to know the route they took, how they got up front, the kind of weapons they carried. Tactical information. It would greatly help our commanders on how to move. That's why prisoner-of-war interrogation was important.

We went through Paris and Belgium and were the first ones to enter a German city, Aachen. That was a tough fight. The Germans fought like dogs. It was just before the Battle of the Bulge, their last effort to slow us down. They were almost successful. We had terrible losses.

Our German prisoners still felt they were winning. We're gonna knock you Americans out, they said. They spoke of their reprisal weapons, the V-1 and V-2, the buzz bombs. This was late '44, remember. When we finally reduced their garrison at Aachen, some GIs brought me a prisoner. I immediately recognized him as the bishop of Aachen. He had his ecclesiastic uniform on. He was known to have stirred up the Germans to keep fighting to the last minute.

Our division chaplain, a colonel, who happened to be a Catholic, was there at the time. When he saw the bishop of Aachen, he came running, kneeled down, and kissed his ring. A half-hour ago, he was blessing our troops, hoping to beat the Germans. And the bishop had just been stirring up the Germans that with God's help they could beat the Americans. Put that in your pipe and smoke it. (Laughs.)

When the war was over in '45, I was in Czechoslovakia. Sudetenland. Germany immediately went on a cigarette-butt economy. The German mark wasn't worth a damn. In order to stay alive, they used cigarettes, coffee, lard as a means of exchange. The three years was nothing else but black market and cigarette butts. When we would light up, the kids would follow us. When we flipped our butts in the gutter, kids jumped on it. Three butts would make one cigarette and that was enough to buy somethin' to eat.

We never occupied a country before. What the hell did we know about occupying Germany? We made so many mistakes. We sent colonels in who needed another year for retirement, we made them military governors of Bavaria. They'd never been in Europe. We taught 'em for a couple of weeks in South Carolina what kind of trees grow in Bavaria.

At this time, I was civilianized and joined CIC, the Counter Intelligence Corps. I was assigned to the city of Augsburg in Bavaria. My commanding officer told me to find a guy named Klaus Barbie. This is all hush-hush. Go to this house in Memmingen, near Augsburg. Identify yourself and you'll get further orders.

I knock on the door and this guy says, "Are you Dabringhaus? I've been waiting for you." I said, "You're supposed to be working for me from now on." Remember, I wasn't told who this guy is. I knew he'd been an SD officer, top SS, top Gestapo. He says, "Meet two friends of mine." Kurt Merk and his French girlfriend, Andrée Simone Rives. She was the daughter of a Parisian police officer. Merk used her as an informant to penetrate the Paris police. This guy and Barbie worked together during the occupation of France, from '42 to '44.

I put him in a nice house in Augsburg, requisitioned by the American army, furniture, housekeeper, everything. Barbie introduced me to a guy who was supposed to be a professor of anthropology, Zarpf. He tells me he was a member of the German Eastern Institute—Das Ost Institut. Their mission, after the invasion of Russia, was to figure out how to exterminate all of 'em, 189 million of 'em and however many there were of 'em at the time. They sat in Königsberg, East Prussia, on this committee, some thirty topnotch Germans, lawyers, professors, judges, SS officers. Their job: figure out how to get rid of all the Russians after the Germans beat 'em. I said to myself, Who needs this guy, for God's sake? I don't even wanna talk to him.

I was told to use Barbie as an informant. I said to my commanding officer, "I hope you know what the hell you guys are doing." Okay, if he's the guy, I'll work with him. Normally, I would arrest this guy.

I got an office downtown. I hired a secretary for Barbie. I said, "I want you to produce at least two, three pages every day." He claimed he had one hundred informants in the field. At the end of the first month, my boss gave me an envelope of money to give him. I opened it up and counted seventeen hundred good green American dollars. I said, "Jesus Christ, this guy is really gettin' paid for that. For this kind of money, he ought to produce."

One day I saw him copy a news report from a Yugoslavian news agency. I said, "Listen, Barbie, I can read that myself. I want the real stuff." The only one important thing he ever gave us was that the Russians were mining uranium near the Czech border in eastern Germany.

While I'm working with him, I learn from his friend Kurt Merk that this guy turns out to be a real good war criminal. When Merk felt he wasn't getting his cut, he'd call me the next day: "If you ever found out what Barbie did in France, during the Occupation, you'd turn him over. This guy killed, on one occasion I know of, two hundred Frenchmen himself, hung 'em up by the thumbs in the basement of his headquarters." He arrested a famous underground guy, Jean Moulin. Moulin got beaten to death. Barbie's job was to break 'em down and get information. His major job was penetrating the French Resistance. Merk told me the guy has killed at least four thousand Frenchmen during the Occupation. We didn't know at the time that he sent Jews to the concentration camps. We kept him in our protective custody.

I reported to headquarters: "You know you're working with a real war criminal?" The answer comes back: "Yes, we know all about it. But he's still valuable. In due time, we'll turn him over to the French."

How this guy was helped to escape, by the Americans, is beyond my comprehension. Throughout the years of his escape, later to Bolivia, I reported to every French consular officer I met. We'd have cocktail parties at the university with the French consul general. I'd say, "Barbie's living in Bolivia. Shouldn't you pick him up?" He says, "Oh, he's out of reach. We can't do anything about it." This is stupid. They could've extradited him any time. I saw Barbie one night on NBC *Nightly News.* I said to my wife, "This is the guy I worked with for eight months." On the same day I reported it, he was actually extradited to France. I hope they do a good job.

I never knew he was the Butcher of Lyons. I knew he was a high enough SD officer to have been arrested. We used these kind of guys for information. Protected them and paid them.

It was June 1, 1948, a new directive came from higher headquarters. We're no longer interested as we used to be in former German Nazis. We're now interested in what's happening behind the East-West border. Communism becomes our most important interest. We're now looking for communists. We want to know about the newly organized government in France, after the war. How many communists are in it? 'Cause Barbie was well entrenched over there for three years. He was informed on French communists. That's what we were looking for from him.

We became so damn obsessed with lookin' for communists—

There was a work stoppage at the gas plant in Augsburg. I was asked to investigate how many communists are involved in this strike. Barbie and I went to a meeting of a communist cell. I was dressed in a German-made suit. I had my .38 special in a shoulder holster. It was in the back of a beer garden. I put a cigarette out in an ashtray and forgot to put it back in my pocket. Nobody ever left a butt in an ashtray. Barbie kicks me: "Pick up that damn cigarette or you'll blow our cover."

I found out there was no communist infiltration in the strike. Actually, these guys were hungry. They couldn't shovel coal into the furnaces because they didn't have anything to eat. We find out that the lard shipments from Hamburg to Augsburg, to ration out to the German workers, were laying out somewhere on a railroad siding. Had nothing to do with communists.

My boss told me, "Hey, Dabringhaus, that's a bad report. We wanted you to tell us that the communists are doin' this." He said, "There's gotta be communist instigation of the strike." I said, "No, these poor bastards are hungry. They're falling over in front of the furnaces with the heat and not enough to eat." If I said communists started the strike, they would have given me a medal. But I had to tell 'em the truth, what the hell.

In November of '48, I asked for a transfer. I was upset workin' with this guy. They said, "You gotta keep goin'. We still got use for him." The Berlin airlift had started. Anyway, I got out of CIC and I was assigned to the constabulary force in Stuttgart, still with military intelligence. My successor took over and worked with Barbie.

I now worked with a network of SS informants. A colonel named Gunther Bernau was in charge. He says, "I have hundreds of friends in the field and they report to me by telephone. We are great friends, and I need your help in keeping them alive." We said, "Okay, you guys give us information about Russia." He said, "Yeah, we got informants in Moscow." There were a lot of SS in the eastern zone and they became good communists. Lotta SS guys became leaders of the German *Volkspolizei.* Once you're on the extreme, you can go to the other in a hurry. The Russians were usin' 'em too.

The guy I dealt with was a member of the Fifth Panzer SS Division, called Viking. It was exonerated at the Nuremberg trials because they were constantly at the Russian front. They were never used behind the lines to round up partisans, guerrillas. That was the only one of the some thirty SS divisions that was exonerated. All his friends are the guys we're still lookin' for, who committed war crimes. The truth is we weren't interested in them at all. They said we got protection of both sides. They were in good shape. They're probably millionaires now, some of 'em heads of corporations.

We all knew he escaped to Bolivia. It was common knowledge. We gave him all kinds of passports.

Who's we?

American intelligence agencies. After they used him. He knew too much about the American intelligence system to turn him over to the French. Then they'd know how we operate. To me, that makes no sense. We're supposed to be allies, aren't we?

Barbie got exit permits from us, went to Genoa, reported to the Bolivian consul in Italy, got a permit, bought himself a ticket on a steamer to Argentina, with his wife and two kids. From there, he went to Bolivia. He lived there twenty-seven years.

The guy's a millionaire over there. You know how he got thrown into the open? He apparently defrauded the government of ten thousand American dollars. A civilian government replaced the military junta. They put him in jail. His attorney paid back the money the next day. But this new government still thought he was too dangerous, shipped him to France. France had been askin' for him for ten years. Most responsible is the Klarsfeld couple in Paris. They'd been tryin' since '72 to get him out of Bolivia. Klaus Altman, he was called, but everyone knew it was Barbie.

Now the French have a big job. They gotta bring him out clean. But there might be some guys in high positions in France who collaborated with him, and Barbie can spring the door on these guys. If the French don't do a good job, it'll be a political football.

Our archives must be loaded with Barbie's interrogations. Where the hell are they? Why can't we talk about it? It's all hush-hush. The guy who hired him must be thinking, What the hell kind of mistake did I make, to pay him 1,700 in American dollars? The guy would have worked for nothing, because he knows we could have turned him over to the French. These are all mistakes our agencies made.

Maybe that is now policy. I hate to admit that my government would make those kind of policies. I know we were watchin' the Russians. I can see why. We have to find out what they're doin'.

When the war was over, the Germans said, Give us some guns,

we'll go to Moscow. You're gonna have to go anyway, one of these days. Today they come and say, See, I told you so. If you'd've gone with us right then and there, you wouldn't have had any cold war or any worries. Our own General Patton wanted to keep on going.

Our GIs, who cheered when the Russians were moving, knew they saved our ass because they killed so many more Germans. Hell, they lost about twenty-five million themselves. Now you're gonna tell 'em turn around and fight the guys they were allied with? In the *Stars & Stripes*, they read every day about the Russians pushin' the Nazis back. Tomorrow you're gonna tell 'em to shoot 'em? Some of the leaders wanted it.

In Stuttgart, I met a couple of guys from the First Infantry Division, the one I was with during the war. I applied for assignment as assistant G-2. We were on maneuvers in Grafenwöhr, a hellhole in central Germany. Instead of calling the enemy the Red Army or the Blue Army, which we did in Louisiana and Texas, we actually called them the Russian aggressors. That struck me so severely. All of a sudden, four years after the war, we've picked them as our future enemy. Today that's the only one we worry about. At first the GIs were a little bit stunned by it. But if that's what we gotta do, we gotta do it.

I came home in January of '50. The McCarthy era. We were lookin' behind every tree for a red. The same thing happened in the military. Somebody decided that the Russians, who were allies during the war, can't be trusted. So the iron curtain comes down not only on the Russians. We are also bringing it down. We are makin' the SS look like good prophets.

POSTSCRIPT: *As we're heading for the Detroit airport, he remembers something. "The war is over May 8, right? On April 12 of '45, I'm driving through a little town in the center of Germany, Neidersach-werfen. It's near Nordhausen in the Harz Mountains.*

"A guy who looks like a skeleton in a white-striped prisoner's suit is walkin' around on the street. He says, 'Have you seen Camp Dora?' I said, 'I don't know what you're talkin' about.' He says, 'Come on, I'll show ya,' and he jumped on the jeep and drove me to this concentration camp.

"I must've been the first American to enter there. It was a large camp where forced laborers were living, who were buildin' this factory in the mountains. This guy was one of the inmates, a survivor. I found this one

barracks that was nailed shut with big boards. I tore the door open and found bodies, people starved to death. That's the only time I saw cannibalism. I saw a couple of bodies on the floor where one guy had his jaw in the ass-cheek of his neighbor. Apparently, that's how they both died. In the last moment, you try to keep alive any way you know how.

"I called the military, and immediately we surrounded this camp. There was nobody left in it except these bodies. The guards had all taken off. That's the camp Eisenhower came to and he brought Patton and a few big shots. He says, 'You still don't know what we're fighting Hitler for? This will show you the reason.' It was in all the papers at that time.

"It's a tremendous calcium mountain. Soft rock. Inside this mountain, they built a factory. It was one mile wide and three miles long. They had elevators going twelve stories high. They had drug stores, hospitals, cafeterias, and a great big assembly room, where the fusilages of these reprisal weapons that the Germans called V-1s and V-2s were built.

"They had beautifully camouflaged exits. We were never able to bomb it.

"This inmate said they took a hundred thousand laborers that died building this factory. Every so often they would string up somebody on a crane and let him hang there for two, three days, to ward off any attempt at sabotage. He told me one guy once took a leak in the corner and he sprayed a fusilage. This was considered sabotage. They hung him up on a chain and let him dangle there for a few days.

"This is a factory that the Russians unfortunately got, in the agreement later on. That's today in the Soviet sector of Germany. The DDR.

"This skeleton had been in hiding and when he saw the American jeep, he came out. It wasn't a secret. The people in the town knew these people were there. It wasn't only Auschwitz in Poland. These guys were killed right in the heart of Germany. First of all, they had to transport all these laborers into that factory every day. The people worked in the fields, in the farms. You just don't keep your mouth shut. You talk. The camp over there got a new load of workers come in. They came in by the thousands because that factory required that kind of labor force.

"Of course, you can say, I didn't see anything. But that would be a lie. Everybody in that neighborhood knew that Camp Dora was there. It wasn't a Jewish extermination camp. It was a slave-labor camp."

History will declare that the six months intervening between the Fascist victory in Spain and the invasion of Poland were a mere armistice in one war—the Second World War.

—Claude G. Bowers, United States ambassador to Republican Spain, 1936–1939

He had been commander of the Abraham Lincoln Battalion. They were American volunteers who fought for the Loyalists in the Spanish Civil War. With other young men from non-Spanish countries, they made up the International Brigade.

To me, World War Two started on July 18, 1936. That's when the first shot was fired in Madrid. A bunch of us were fighting the war long before. In the thirties, during the Depression, they were tearing down the Sixth Avenue El in New York. They shipped all that scrap iron to Japan, and we said it's gonna come back as bombs. Japan had already invaded Manchukuo. We wouldn't go out with girls that were wearin' silk stockings and silk underwear (laughs), because all the silk came from Japan. There were protests and street-corner meetings and boycotts. We were collecting money for Haile Selassie when the Italians were bombing Ethiopia. I was putting in sixty hours a week at the Garment Center, but I never slept. We were active in the Anti-Fascist League in any damn thing we could do.

When the chance came to go to Spain, we went. To try to stop the war that was coming. Hitler was involved by this time. We all knew what the hell *Mein Kampf* was about. We knew what was in store for the Jews.

When I came out of Spain, I continued in France. A bunch of us did. The Spanish refugees were on the beaches, in concentration camps in France. They were gonna send them back to Franco. A hell of a lot of 'em would have been shot or jailed. We were tryin' to help them in every way we could. LaGuardia put up a law in New York that you couldn't picket foreign consulates. We did. Right across the street from Saint Patrick's, we tied up noon traffic on Fifth Avenue. Seventy-five of us were arrested.

Vincent Sheean was a friend of mine.* He and his wife were close to Wild Bill Donovan, who had a law office on One Wall Street. By this time, the Nazis had invaded Poland and Donovan was Roosevelt's man working with British intelligence. He said, "You want my office to represent you at no charge?" I said, "Jesus Christ, yes" (Laughs.) We never had a One Wall Street lawyer defending us. (Laughs.) We went to jail for fifteen days, and he introduced me to British intelligence.

I went to work for them, rounding up members of the International Brigade that I knew were in this country. We weren't at war yet, but we knew we were gonna be. They wanted guys to drop behind lines in Yugoslavia, Austria, Italy, Czechoslovakia, Poland. I traveled around the country recruiting these guys. We were all in British intelligence and wound up liberating forces in partisan movements in all these countries.

After Pearl Harbor, I went to work for the OSS. The Nazis, through Fascist Spain, had a tremendous intelligence network, especially in the Gulf of Mexico and the Caribbean. Givin' them information on convoys. A hell of a lot of our ships went down. We set up counter-espionage networks through Spanish War and Communist Party contacts. It was very effective.

One of the deals I had with Donovan was to set up a group that would go into Spain and overthrow Franco. To re-establish the Republican government that had been elected by the people. It never happened. Franco was a shrewd bastard. He kept all his options open, and Roosevelt never pushed him very hard.

I left OSS and volunteered for the infantry. I was a machine-gunner in the Spanish War, so I knew my trajectories, my cones of fire, everything like that. I enlisted in June 1942, and I did not fire a shot in anger until the end of 1943. The U.S. Army just did not want me to go to the front. Me and a lot of other Spanish reds.

They screwed us around in Camp Dix for six weeks. Usually you were in and out in a week. My buddy and I got to know the place like the back of our hand. We looked up our files. We were listed as PAF—premature anti-fascists.

Finally, they shipped us out to Camp Wheeler, Georgia. It was a dumping ground for German and Italian nationals, homosexuals,

*A celebrated American foreign correspondent at the time. He covered the Spanish Civil War and much of World War Two.

pimps, gangsters, convicts, and me and my buddy. (Laughs.) It was called Branch Immaterial—BI. We had rifles without firin' pins and locks in 'em. Luckily, we heard that a general there was having a hard time getting guys to volunteer for the infantry. He put in a call for anybody with infantry experience to go on the camp radio and extol its virtues. My buddy and I talked for an hour about wars being won by foot soldiers.

The general said, "You guys couldn't have been in the Spanish-American War." (Laughs.) "No, no, no," we said, "the Spanish Civil War." "What are you doin' in Branch Immaterial? Did you fight on Franco's side?" "No, we fought on the side of the government." He said, "I'm putting you in infantry cadre immediately." We became corporals.

When you come in, you take an IQ test. Anybody who scored over 120, they approach 'em for OCS. We were over 120, so they put the arm on us. I didn't wanna go into OCS. I was already aware of some of our guys, who went through thirteen weeks, bought their uniforms, bars and everything, and had their commissions declared null and void in Washington. I didn't wanna go through that.

The commanding officer said, "It wouldn't happen to you guys. You're too good." So we went over to Fort Benning and became officer candidates. We're at the top of the class because we knew all the stuff. The guy on the next bunk became very friendly with me. Another guy's wife came down with two suitcases of Scotch, and during leave I'd go to their apartment and take my friend with me. On the fourth or fifth week, he comes up to me. He says, "I can't do this. I'm supposed to report on everything you do. I don't know what the hell to report on." So I say, "You want me to write the report for you?" (Laughs.) I wrote up a glowing report on all our activities, and he signed it.

About the sixth week, my captain called me. He pulled an American flag out of his drawer. "Candidate Wolff, is this your flag?" I said, "Yes sir." "Are you prepared to defend this flag?" "Yes sir." He threw the flag back in the drawer and slammed it shut: "I don't know what those sons of bitches in Washington are up to." (Laughs.) He didn't know what the hell was going on. But I knew the bell was about to ring and I was out.

They waited until we went on a field mission. They sent a jeep to bring me in. All the guys were sayin' Wolff's gonna be commissioned in a hurry. He doesn't have to go through all this stuff. I knew better.

When I got there, my bags were all packed and I had orders to report back to Camp Wheeler, chemical warfare. My buddy was sent to the medical hospital bureau to fold linen. This is a guy that later on was a captain, decorated in the invasion of Germany. He's buried in Arlington, but they had him folding linens for a year in Columbus, Georgia.

So I was running the guys, giving 'em a little sniff of mustard gas, a sniff of chlorine, a little phosphorus. Running them through tear-gas chambers, so they could use their gas masks. The lieutenant colonel loved me. He made me staff sergeant. He said, "What do you wanna do?" I said, "I wanna go overseas." He did, too, but he was overage. His wife was Spanish, and he was sympathetic to the Republic. He did everything for me. I said, "Don't do all that. Just send me overseas." He got word that they needed noncoms in England. So he transferred me to an infantry cadre there.

I was sent to Camp Shenango in Pennsylvania. My first sergeant was in OCS with me. He'd flunked out. He was happy to see me. Here's a staff sergeant, me, so he'd assumed I'd flunked out, too. He knew I was in the top ten in the class, so he didn't feel too bad. He showed me the shipment list every time it came through. It had: Staff Sergeant Milton Wolff, Aleutian Islands. I didn't wanna go to the Aleutians. (Laughs.) I wanted to be in the European action. After weeks of the stall, I got fed up. Okay, the hell with it. Send me out there. When I got to Fort Lawton in Seattle, Attu had fallen. They didn't need any replacements in the Aleutians.

I didn't know anything about boats, so they made me second mate on a crash boat (laughs), to pick up downed pilots in the North Pacific. That wasn't my speed, either. I was working like hell to get to the front. It was a real struggle.

Naturally, I had carte blanche up there. The worse punishment you could get was being sent overseas. The first sergeant felt the same way. Anytime they'd threaten to send us overseas, we'd say, "Hey, man, that's where we wanna go." Another first sergeant who knew about Spain and was sympathetic said, "If that's where you wanna go, we're going to England." I had to take a bust to private to get into his outfit.

The day I got transferred, he was sent to Alaska. They brought in a regular army man, who was not sympathetic. (Laughs.) I didn't care, we were going to England. Well, we went to North Africa. I got in touch with Donovan: Take me back. They sent a plane for me in

North Africa, but by the time it got there we were on our way to India.

We were a longshore outfit, two ships. They were tin cans, these boats, just British tea ships. The skins were as thin as possible. The one I was not on was hit by a robot bomb. I think it had come out of some Mediterranean island the Nazis had captured. Over eight hundred went down in oil slicks. All American troops.

I finally got to Calcutta. One day, I saw a GI with blue piping on his infantry cap. I grabbed him: "What the hell are you doing here?" He said, "I'm with Stilwell, on liaison with the Chinese army. We're going into Burma."

Just at this time, the inspector general came to our outfit. The rank-and-file can come in and register their beefs. This is your one opportunity to bypass channels. I'd been writing nasty letters that I know the censors were readin' and my captain was readin'. I was back to sergeant again, 'cause I did my work. My gangs produced. When the IG opened his office, I was the first in line. "I want to join Stilwell." "What are your qualifications?" "I'm a trained infantry-man, infantry officer, know map readings, elevations and arms, cones of fire, and so on." Great. He got me transferred. They flew me to Assam, where I joined Stilwell.

We started the LRP, long-range penetration, into Japan. There was no trench fighting. It was all skirmishes. Sometimes we were in front of them, sometimes in back. (Laugh.) This went on until we got down to Mindanao. Merrill's Marauders were with us. And a British outfit, too. I was assigned to the Chinese Eighty-eighth Battalion as liaison man.

We were stalled at Mindanao. About two thousand Japanese were there. They were not all combat troops, but they were good fighters. They had two old artillery pieces and a couple of Zeroes that came across and strafed. They put up one hell of a fight. We couldn't take 'em. Merrill's Marauders were all sick and out of the picture.

Anyhow, Stilwell brought me back to headquarters and gave me a second lieutenancy. He said I'd have to get a haircut, and gave me his barber. He knew about us, he knew about Spain. He was quite a guy.

They sent me to Calcutta for a uniform and I got malaria. In the hospital, I met a German doctor who'd been to Spain with me, an anti-Nazi. He had no country to go to after the Spanish War ended. Twelve International Brigade doctors—Czechs, Germans, Austrians —went to China and served with different armies there. They married

Chinese women, learned the language, and live there.

I remember once, in the fight for Mindañao, I was bringing a convoy of wounded back. I heard a song that sounded familiar. Here was this little German doctor, teaching these Chinese orderlies to sing "Freiheit" in Chinese. (Laughs.) It was the song we had sung in Spain.

While I was in the hospital with malaria, Donovan caught up with me. They shipped me out to Bari, Italy. I went down to a school in Brindisi training the guys. There was a Frenchman who was an expert on plastic explosions. We had an Italian who was an expert on something else. We had homing pigeons which we sent over to the islands with messages to the Yugoslav partisans. I was in charge of the whole bit. I figured I'd take parachute training. I went to a British school in Italy and made my five jumps and got my wings.

I wanted to go on a mission. I had marched all my life and didn't wanna do any more fuckin' marchin'. I had paratroop training and I figured they'd drop me somewhere. They finally formed a mission and put me on it. It was made up of bankers and trade-union people. There were about thirty-six of us. They put me in there for flavor. We were gonna go into Val d'Isère, where France, Italy, and Switzerland come together. I was p.o.'d. Here I was trained for a drop and we're walking again.

These guys were going in with thousands and thousands and thousands of dollars. They wanted to assure the Fascist collaborators that they would remain in place. They'd be financed and backed by American dollars. The main thing was to put up a wall against communists and socialists and the Garibaldinis, who fought in Spain. That was the mission. This is the winter of '45. Roosevelt died in April. Italy surrendered in May. We knew it all the time, but now it was really happening. My guide wanted to split off from these guys, because he knew what they were about. He knew me from Spain and he wanted to take me straight to Luigi Longo. He was with the Garibaldi Battalion in Spain. A leading Italian red. So we're going our own way.

This was perfectly all right with the commander of this industrial outfit. He didn't know a goddamn thing about war. All they had was money and wristwatches and gold and papers.

It had been snowing heavily. The guy with me says in Spanish, it's impossible. The Germans have spotter planes all over. They'll pick up our tracks. He suggests we go back and arrange a drop-in, instead of walking in. These other characters kept on goin' with their guides and were all captured. The whole mission. The Nazis were enriched considerably with all the loot. (Laughs.) They weren't killed, because by this time Allen Dulles, in Switzerland, was in touch with the Nazi commander, whose name was Wolf. (Laughs.)

Who do I bump into in France but a slew of Spaniards, who had fought with the maquis. They have trucks and rifles and are gonna cross the Pyrenees to undo Franco. I said, "Jesus, that's great. I'm gonna get you some help." Back of my mind is Donovan's promise that we'd go into Spain and get rid of Franco.

I wired headquarters in Florence, I have a battalion of these Spaniards, and I give them a list of things they need: vehicles, machine guns, mortars. We're crossing the Pyrenees into Spain. Up comes an order: Don't let Lieutenant Wolff proceed west of the Rhone River. We're sending a plane to Grenoble to bring him back. The order didn't come from Donovan. He was not there. I came back to Italy and was debriefed. At Naples, the U.S.S. *West Point*, a troop ship fully loaded with GIs, had been waiting two days for me, a lousy second lieutenant.

All these guys on the ship didn't know what the hell they were waiting for. As soon as I came aboard they weighed anchor. Other Spanish vets were on it already. They didn't want any of us in Italy. Who was in Italy at that time? Collaborators on one hand and underground partisans on the other. If the United States Army had not intervened, if the OSS hadn't intervened with large sums of money, Italy would have been a socialist country.

We came back and wanted to go to China. We set up a mission. They said fine, but they never had any intention of sending us there. The cold war was on. I was back at Benning. They suggested I had enough hash marks to get out of the army. I got an honorable discharge and a nice letter from Donovan, sayin' what a great guy I was.

World War Two, besides givin' me the GI Bill of Rights, certainly did not make life easier for me or for the other guys who had fought in Spain. We were still stigmatized as premature anti-fascists. We were harassed by the FBI, Dies Committee, McCarthy Committee. The Subversive Activities Control Board took a year out of my life, defending the Lincoln Battalion before those characters.

I don't ever want to see another bloody war again. There's a certain amount of glamour attached to a guy like me because I was a warrior.

But I've always had more respect for the conscientious objectors. We were in good wars, that's what we should be honored for, but not because we were warriors.

I went to Berlin in 1960. I stood in one of those mausoleums Speer built. It was partially shattered and burnt out. People have defecated and peed in it. I stood in the middle of what was once a magnificent hall. And I felt good. I was glad I was part of this. 'Cause I remember Guernica and I remember Madrid and I remember Barcelona and all that. I felt good standing in that hall, that these sons of bitches got it.

EILEEN BARTH

She was a young social worker during the war. Her husband was in the army.

I had worked for a long time with groups trying to keep us out, trying to prevent World War Two. I was taking part in the boycott of Japanese silk. Not wearing any silk clothing. When I was married in 1939, I wore a white cotton dress. We felt it was important not to deal with Japan. They were destroying China, and we considered them the aggressive country at that time. We were selling steel to Japan and they were selling us silk. For a time, I wore lisle stockings. Not very attractive. (Laughs.)

My first contribution to any cause had to do with the children of Spain, who were suffering terribly. I pledged a dollar a month. (Laughs.) I even remember the amount. That was a commitment that really got me involved. We knew that the Germans were testing their Luftwaffe in Spain. Some of us felt they were practicing for the Second World War. When it came, we were not too surprised.

Now that we were in it, I felt we had to pursue it all the way. A young black man who had worked in my office and was drafted came back on leave. I said, "Of course, everybody knows what this war is about. You know what you're fighting for, don't you?" He laughed. No. Soldiers don't know what they're fighting for. They get drafted, they go in and fight. He was with a black regiment, so I don't know how enthusiastic he was.

When my husband was drafted, it came close to home. It was lonely. But there was a lot to do. Many women went to the camps to spend time with them while they were still in the country. Though I visited my husband once or twice on weekends, I felt it was the wrong thing to do. Even though I missed him, I felt women had important things to do at home: working in a defense plant or anything for the effort. Oh, I was so self-righteous. (Laughs.)

I was puzzled over the lateness with which I received my husband's mail. I thought, well, it's due to wartime. I didn't find out until years later, when my husband received his files through the Freedom of Information Act, that our mail was being opened by army intelligence. It was called G-2, I believe. I was shocked to read excerpts of a letter I had written to him about a film I had seen. At the time, we were helping the Russians. It was a film about them. I think another reason was that my husband had helped raise money for the Spanish Loyalists. The term "premature anti-fascist" came into being later. I think it applied to people like us.

I was longing for the war to be over. At the same time, I was very hopeful. I thought that democracy and progress would be endless. That good times would come and there would be a lasting peace. I really believed this.

I remember an ad in which people were shown as pigs because they seemed to want so much. To me, it was wanting to have things for the first time in their lives. They were able to enjoy life a little more, even get a house in the suburbs. These were people who lived through the Depression, as children, many of them. I guess you'd say a new middle class came into being. Perhaps they concentrated a little too much on the material life. The war did it. The hope was there: the end of all wars. But these hopes were dashed. What can I say?

ANTHONY SCARIANO

A lawyer; a former member of the Illinois Legislature.

I was a young Italian American looking for adventure. Wild Bill Donovan of the OSS was looking for adventurous types. He wanted people who could speak Italian, who were young, energetic, and progressive. I was already overseas, destined to be military governor of Reggio Emilia, just north of the Adriatic. That seemed a little too tame for me.

I became an intelligence officer for the OSS in the Tuscan Archipelago, north of Corsica. We were conducting what was known as dirty tricks. Blowing up tunnels, convoys, barracks, all behind the fascist lines, German and Italian.

It was the fall of '43. We had taken Sicily, had landed at Salerno, and were about to establish a beachhead at Anzio. In the winter of '43, I was sent to Corsica to help with PT operations. We had a small flotilla of Italian and American PT boats. Our object was to create havoc behind the enemy lines.

We landed several parties on Elba to gather intelligence. We were mounting campaigns against the mainland itself. One of our earliest operations was known as the Ginny mission. We landed thirteen men and two officers off the coast of Genoa. Our object was to blow up a tunnel the air force couldn't get to. We put the men on rubber rafts and they rode in to shore. We were to land the men, get them to do their mission, and pick them up. We had walkie-talkies. Just then, we picked up on radar some German F-lighters and E-boats, landing crafts like our PTs. We had to get the heck out of there or we would've been just annihilated. We scattered out.

When we came back, we lost walkie-talkie contact with the landing party. We couldn't pick them up any more. We got a radio message that the boys had been captured but were safe. We discovered later that all thirteen men and two officers were executed by the Nazis. The prisoners' hands were tied behind their backs, their feet were bound, they were blindfolded, lined up, shot, and dumped into a common grave. They had been in American uniforms. This was contrary to the Geneva Convention. If you caught military personnel behind your lines in uniform, you could take them as POWs, but you could do nothing more.

General Dostler of the Wehrmacht, who ordered the execution, was the first war criminal tried by the Allies in the fall of '45. This was well before Nuremberg. He was court-martialed by the American army. His defense was that he was acting under orders from the Führer. He produced telegrams of instructions from Hitler. It was a harbinger of the defenses we'd hear so often during the Nuremberg trials: acting under orders from the Führer. It didn't do Dostler any good. He was found guilty and executed.

We were in touch with the whole partisan movement in northern Italy. They were in control of the region. By September of '43, we were dropping our men by parachute in the Ligurian Alps. Our intelligence was so good that the partisans picked 'em up right at the drop area. They drove 'em twenty miles to their headquarters in the mountains unmolested.

This was right where the Fascists would conduct a *rastrellamento,* a mopping-up operation. Our boys would take to the hills and hide out because there were hordes of these Fascists around. We racked up a pretty good box score: ammo dumps bombed, barracks blown up, convoys attacked.

We would drop material of war and medical supplies by parachute. For food, the partisans lived on the countryside. They lived by barter and exchange. They could get a whole veal for a case of GI soap or cigarettes. We would drop money: Swiss francs, British pounds, American dollars, Italian lire. Usually about a $16,000 fund.

The partisans were superbly organized. We would train them in the use of our weapons. They loved the bazooka. At first, they were largely Socialists and Communists—Garibaldini, they called themselves. They wore red kerchiefs the way Garibaldi did in the war to unify Italy. Later, the Monarchists and the Christian Democrats, and the Liberals joined them. They were really Johnny-come-latelys. They didn't want the Socialists and the Communists to get all the credit in the postwar years. They didn't want it to be said they had no part in the Movimento de la Liberazione.

We were doing things that were not traditional. Army and Navy Intelligence were not too enthusiastic about the way Donovan worked. He recruited anybody who would fight Fascists. He said, "I don't care what the color of his politics is. I just want people who will fight these dirty so-and-sos and save American lives." He recruited guys like Milton Wolff, who fought with the Lincoln Brigade in the Spanish Civil War. They operated behind the lines and risked their lives. Donovan didn't care if they were communists. They were SI, Special Intelligence, and sometimes worked in civilian clothes, mixing with the partisans. We were OGs, Operational Groups, always in uniform.

Toward the end of the war, Colonel McCormick* thought he had a great scoop. It was common knowledge to everyone else who knew

*Publisher of the *Chicago Tribune.*

anything about the OSS. He called it Oh-So-Secret. He emblazoned the front pages of the *Tribune* in 72 type: OSS INFECTED BY COMMUNISTS. The funny thing is that Wolff and the other Lincoln guys in SI did a bang-up job for the OSS.

McCormick tried to make political capital out of this, but he never got to first base. We forget that most Americans didn't think it was a cardinal sin to fight on the side of the Loyalists in Spain. It was, after all, the duly elected government. Boy, Wolff and the others were really calumniated in the *Tribune*.

Our boys, most of us, were somewhat liberal. We were Italian Americans who were recruited from the working-class areas of the big cities: New York, Chicago, Cleveland, Boston, all over. We weren't interned like the Japanese, but we felt, as Italians, we had to prove ourselves. We weren't very political, but we'd sit around the fire in our villa and argue about the war. Would it mean a better America? Would it mean an end to injustice? We were just learning about the Holocaust. We really believed in this war, unlike Vietnam and Korea. The boys really believed that a better world would come.

The camaraderie was absolutely superb. We still keep in touch. We have an association, the OG Veteran's Group. We have a corny name: Donovan's Devils. (Laughs.) We talk about how we won the war all by ourselves. (Laughs.) We ask whether young people know what it was about. We're all a little bit disillusioned, but we do believe, on the whole, it was worth it.

When the war ended, I wrote the company history and citations for the men. Every one of our guys was decorated. Then I went to Georgetown Law School on the GI Bill.

I volunteered in March of '42 and came out in February of '46. Four of the best years of my life, twenty-four to twenty-eight. I still think it was worthwhile. I've gone back to Italy seven times to look up some of the old partisans I worked with. You can't imagine the suffering and torture they endured when they were caught. They were the real heroes.

IRVING GOFF

As a member of the Abraham Lincoln Battalion, he specialized in guerrilla warfare behind enemy lines. He may have been the model for

Robert Jordan, hero of Ernest Hemingway's Spanish Civil War novel, For Whom the Bell Tolls.

"I never saw Ingrid Bergman in all the time I was in the war. If I did, I might still be there. (Laughs.) The way Gary Cooper blew that bridge—like blowing a seam in a coal mine. I've blown bridges. You put a detonator in the thing and then you'd better be twenty miles away. You went after bridges and railroads. Usually it'd last five or six days behind the lines.

"The biggest guerrilla operation was freeing 315 Asturian miners from a Mediterranean prison fort. Thirty-five of us, plus grenades. Another American and I and two Spaniards got cut off. It was almost like a movie scene. We were swimming towards Africa, while the Fascists were pot-shotting at us. The two Spaniards drowned. We saw their swollen bodies later, as we grabbed a rock.

"We're in a little crevice, stark naked. The Fascists are just above us. We hear 'em talkin'. It's four o'clock in the morning. Icy water hits you. We hug ourselves to conserve whatever body heat there was. We wait till nightfall. We swim some more. We spend another twenty-four hours in tiny caves. No food, no water.

"Fascists on one side, the Republican army on the other. Shots going on all the time. We went from rock to rock. We were keepin' our heads below water, just about here, so you could breathe. It took us three days to make it to our lines."

I'm a kid from Brooklyn. I was hardly ever in a mountain. What do I know from guerrilla warfare? I learned everything in Spain. I learned from life itself. One time, I'm carryin' explosives on my back and this Spaniard is tellin' me how they work. In two days, I'm behind the lines, blowin' up a train. It had Italian soldiers goin' to Córdoba. My very first operation. I was never on a plane until I went up for my first jump. I was with OSS then. I was good because I'd been a professional acrobat. You know how to fall and roll and control your body.

Just before Pearl Harbor, Donovan wanted us to work for the British, behind the lines in Egypt. Desert warfare. When Pearl Harbor happened, he said, Hold everything. Our objective was to go to Spain, organize intelligence, paramilitary work, and protect Gibraltar. Franco had forces in Morocco and could almost lock up the Mediterranean. The State Department stopped it.

Remember Kasserine Pass? That was the big battle in North

Africa. A bunch of us Lincoln vets are now with OSS. An anti-Franco Republican fleet was interned there, in a concentration camp at Kasserine Pass. And a lot of International Brigaders were taken out of camps in France to build a trans-Saharan railroad in the desert for the Germans. When we made the landing, they were liberated.

Just at this time, Rommel broke through and there was a massive retreat. We were behind the lines. I'd seen this in Spain. How can you go behind enemy lines without intelligence? You wander into anything. We're under the command of a British major. Courage is not enough. You gotta know what the devil you're doing. We almost walked into an airport, a mile away from Rommel. We would all have been captured. Later on, we were behind enemy lines again, toward Tunis.

Everybody who graduated from the OSS school came out full lieutenants, captains, majors. All us Lincoln guys came out enlisted men. (Laughs.) They considered us all communists. Because of Spain, we knew ten times more than any of the other guys.

When we first went in, we got civilian pay. We were made enlisted men, but we still would've gotten civilian pay. We wrote a letter to the Treasury: We're in the army, we want army pay. We got a letter from the Treasury: Are you guys crazy? He couldn't understand that we're in to fight, not make a buck. We didn't want it said we're mercenary. If you're on civilian pay, you can come out of the war with thirty thousand bucks on ya. (Laughs.) That's not why we were fightin'. This major who'd been in class with me, he wouldn't budge without us. (Laughs.) Any goddamn question came up, he'd ask us.

In North Africa, we're seven miles behind the German lines. Three Lincolns and two other guys. Suddenly, the Germans throw a shell over us at our lines. We have no cover. We were supposed to have. Bang! A shell hits near a Lincoln, Feldsen. I pull out my sulfa pack, just pour it on his wound. I pull him into a ravine and these tanks come out. They yell, Hands up! Tiger tanks, big ones. It is rough, sittin' in front of an 88 tank. I had my nose buried down, I'm close to China practically, I wrapped myself around a sagebrush. Lasowski, another Spanish vet, wrapped himself around a sagebrush. The major, in an Abercrombie & Fitch brown jacket, is visible a mile away. He was silly, but great enough to stand up and divert them to the wounded guy, Feldsen, and himself. They took the two prisoners and rolled back. When I met Feldsen after the war, we talked of eight German tanks in front of us. Here we are, a handful of nobody. (Laughs.)

When we got back, Major Sage and others wrote letters to Donovan: "On our honor as officers and gentlemen, we cannot understand why Sergeant Goff and Sergeant Lasowski and Sergeant Feldsen are not made officers." Donovan comes to the front and he makes us all second lieutenants right at the front. (Laughs.) We had a sort of left-handed reputation. When they began to redbait me, Donovan said, "For the work he did in Africa and Italy, he's on the honor roll of the OSS."

Rommel had only three Panzer divisions, no infantry, and he smashed the American lines. A hub-to-hub retreat. If the Stukas came in, they would have knocked the hell out of us. I'm talking about stupidity. We had tanks and half-tanks. They looked like Tinker Toys. Rommel was toying with 'em. No matter what I think of Nazism, as a military man he was brilliant.

There's a myth that he was beaten by Montgomery smashin' him on one end and we smashin' 'em on the other. Nothing is further from the truth. All the tanks and planes went to Stalingrad. One day, the sky's full of German planes. The next day, you saw nothing. You never saw 'em to the end of the war. All went to Tunis, into Europe. Look at the map. It's not that far to Stalingrad. That's what happened in North Africa. All the rest is nonsense.

We moved from North Africa into Sicily. Donovan's on the boat with us. He's on the beach with us. He's in a foxhole with us. Hell, we hit Anzio on a PT boat together. German plane came down, Donovan's standin' there. He was a great guy, but he had foolish guts. I yelled at 'im, "Get down, general!" He wouldn't get down, and bombs droppin' all around.

The purpose of Anzio was to outflank Cassino. We're really hung up at Monte Cassino. It's twenty miles north of Naples. You have this big mountain range. The Germans were intelligent. They never fought on flat land. When you got to Cassino, they're throwing grenades at you. Tanks couldn't get up there, trucks, artillery, nothing. They bombed the hell out of us for six months, eight thousand casualties.

Lasowski and I are trainin' these young guys how to penetrate the lines and gather intelligence. I'd take 'em with me, come back in a couple of days. We put twenty-two teams across that line. All twenty-two, except me, were successful.

We had no intelligence. Suddenly you're getting all these reports. The Third Division was ecstatic. The one team captured was in a Gestapo jail. Had their nails pulled out, but they didn't talk. We met them in Rome, later on. We didn't lose a man.

Donovan was on the plane with me from Naples to Algiers. He sits down next to me. He's talking about my connection with the Communist Party. Not antagonistic, just curious. "How you makin' out?" He knew all the OSS debriefings here came from me. My prestige with him was pretty high. Jeez, if I asked him for a million dollars, he wouldn't even bat an eye. I told him what the connections were all about and what I had in mind: blowin' up railroads. He says, "We're collaborating with the Communist Party, boy. Isn't that interesting?" He always called me "boy," affectionately. He says, "But in your connection, make sure the Communist Party doesn't come out ahead." I said, "That's valid. They're out to win the war, we're out to win the war. I'll do the best I can to win this war." He said fine, and left.

In Naples, the Communist Party had 150,000 members. All during the Mussolini time, twenty-two years, the railroad workers maintained an illegal, left-led union, underground. The Italian partisans, during the Nazi occupation, were slaughtering the Germans, especially as they were fleeing. Hot water from windows—did you see the movie *Four Days of Naples*? Every sector of the front was commanded by a guy who fought with the Garibaldi in Spain. The guy that captured Mussolini and strung him up by his feet was Muscatalli. He fought in Spain.

North of Rome we're parachuting radio teams to the guerrillas who are known as the Garibaldi Committee of National Liberation. Their leader was a guy who was head of the Garibaldi Brigade in Spain. With 'em was this guy, Italian, who spoke with an Oxford accent. He was spectacular. He and a few of these guerrillas captured a German tank division in the Alban Hills. The British were slow comin' in. So he walks out in a ragged outfit and says in his Oxonian English, "What're you standing there for? I've got 'em all, take 'em." He did it without any tanks, just submachine guns. He turned 'em over and the British made a big to-do about it.

The army took Rome. Now you have Florence, Siena, and the German army in the north. By this time, the guerrillas are a massive force. We had eighteen radio teams, speaking German, French, English, Italian in northern Italy. Every day. Never lost a team. The intelligence we sent was called by Allied headquarters the best from any source. We had house-by-house. Guys would come back with intelligence that high. We had an overlay map of all the German positions. The American army knew where every German was.

General Alexander, the British head at Allied headquarters, put out a bulletin: All Italian partisans go home and wait until final offensive. Then they'll coordinate all the activities. Anybody with an elementary knowledge of guerrilla warfare knows this is impossible. A guerrilla army has to be constantly on the move, searching for intelligence. You send 'em home to sit on their fannies, it's stupid. You can't suddenly assemble a force that's now 300,000 and expect it to function. I told OSS that. I didn't know that Churchill and Roosevelt were meeting in Quebec on a battleship and saying the end of the war is in sight and so on.

I sent out a radio communication that it's necessary to mount stronger and stronger attacks on the German positions. All railroads, all bridges, all ammunition dumps, any kind of factories—we need an enormous amount of intelligence. Eighteen radio teams. (Laughs.) Jesus Christ, I can't believe it myself.

They called me down to Caserta, the top OSS base. They wanted to know what I was up to. I said, It's an all-win-the-war message. How can you fault that? The major agreed. So I went away and forgot the whole thing. Never knew any of the stuff going on with the top officers. There was a guy, Scamperini, one jump ahead of an idiot. He analyzed that everything I was doing was subversive and scheming rather than an all-out-win-the-war effort. Let's face it, they wanted us guys out.

Towards the end of the war, I wrote up a mission to go to China. I got an immediate answer: Accepted. Donovan said he'd put us on the first boat. Don't forget, we still had Japan. Two days later, the final offensive had started. You gotta understand that the partisans captured the German army. Kesselring surrendered to them. The message of surrender came through my radio from two different places. I offered to parachute in with some OSS guys to pick up Kesselring. (Laughs.) They gave it to Allen Dulles, who was head of the Swiss desk, and he sent somebody in. They didn't want us. I didn't expect it. Hell, they held up my captaincy for six months.

Donovan backed us up all the way down the line. He called me to

Washington. The war was over May 8, May 10, I was on the U.S.S. *West Point.* And Milt Wolff was with me. The mission to China never came off.

Donovan tells me there's a twenty-million-dollar appropriation before Congress to wind up OSS work. A few months earlier, we were asked to write reports of what the future of the OSS should be. It turned out to be the CIA. Donovan was supposed to head it up. But now he's under attack for having Communists in his organization. They're putting the heat on him.

He calls me in: "They're holding up the appropriation. We can't finish our work. I'm forced to let you go." Me and the other Spanish vets in the OSS. He gave us a letter attesting to our loyalty in action. I still got it home.

We were shipped to Fort McQuade. It was an AWOL camp. I was supposed to train them for Japan. The commanding officer is reading my record and he couldn't figure out why the heck I was sent here. We did nothing at McQuade except get fat. Didn't do anything. Didn't train anybody. When the bomb dropped, the guy said, "Do you wanna be discharged a little early?" I said sure.

They presented me with the Legion of Merit. And then I was attacked by the FBI, and whoever wanted to get in the act, for being with the Lincoln Brigade, a red. Me and the other guys. Legion of Merit? Oh, it's around the house somewhere.

HANS MASSAQUOI

He is an editor of Ebony *magazine. He lives in Chicago.*
"I was born in 1926. My mother was German. My father was Liberian. My grandfather was Liberian consul general in Hamburg. Before the war broke out, my father, who saw what was happening, decided to leave Germany and urged my mother to leave with me. My mother, on the advice of our family doctor, decided against it. I was very fragile."

I grew up in Germany. German was my language. For a long time, I had no real problems growing up. In my neighborhood, the people were all used to me. I had my friends. I was treated like any other German boy. Whenever I left my neighborhood, I was constantly

---

stared at, I was such a novelty. Little children would tug at their parents' sleeves: Look, there's a *Neger*. That would really get my goat.

Prior to my grandfather's leaving, we lived in relative comfort. Hitler came to power in '33. At first, I wasn't affected. I was too young. I didn't realize that my mother, who was a nurse, was summarily fired from her job because of me. That's when things became rough for us.

In '32, when I started school, I was six years old. In '33, my first teacher was fired for political reasons. I don't know what her involvements were. Gradually, the old teachers were replaced with younger ones, those with Nazi orientations. Then I began to notice a change in attitude. Teachers would make snide remarks about my race. One teacher would point me out as an example of the non-Aryan race. One time, I must have been ten, a teacher took me aside and said, "When we're finished with the Jews, you're next." He still had some inhibitions. He did not make that announcement before the class. (Laughs.) It was a private thing. A touch of sadism.

In 1939 the war broke out. That was my last year in school. I, like many of the other kids, was enthusiastic about the war. Something was going to happen. A change. I had become so identified with the Germans and the Nazi cause that I was just as enthusiastic about them moving in the Saar, into Austria. I was a German. I had not yet gotten the message. It was a long time before I saw what the Nazis were all about.

In 1935, Hitler for the first time visited Hamburg. The school principal had all the kids come to the schoolyard and announced that today would be a very historic day, one that we would never forget. At the time I had no idea how right he was. Today we would see our beloved Führer. A once-in-a-lifetime chance to really lay eyes on him.

School, of course, was suspended for the day. They marched us up to the approach route from the airport, Hamburg Flughafen. We were lined up, just one sea of kids, waiting for Hitler to arrive. I was one of the kids that shouted the loudest when Hitler actually passed by. I saw him with his arms outstretched in his black Mercedes. Can you imagine this little black boy screaming his lungs out? (Laughs.)

There was a drive to enroll young kids into the Hitler Youth movement. I wanted to join, of course. My mother took me aside and said, "Look, Hans, you may not understand, but they don't want you." I couldn't understand. All my friends had these black shorts and brown shirts and a swastika and a little dagger which said Blood and Honor. I wanted it just like everybody else. I wanted to belong. These were my schoolmates.

My mother wasn't at all sophisticated about politics. She even took me to one of those Hitler Youth headquarters. She thought they might make an exception. They laughed us out of the place.

This constant rejection finally made me wonder. The teachers had to explain to the kids about the inferiority of other races. And they had a kid sitting there who was always getting top grades, who in sports excelled, who was better than most of the Aryan students. It made it difficult for the teachers to say, Here is Hans Massaquoi, an inferior being. Some teachers were having such a problem that they began to fudge a little on the grades they gave me. Kids rallied around me, because I was usually the leader.

In 1936, our class had a chance to go to Berlin to watch the Olympics. Not all Germans were sold on this Hitler nonsense. Jesse Owens was the undisputed hero of the German people. He was the darling of the 1936 Olympic games. With the exception of a small Nazi elite, they opened their hearts to this black man who ran his butt off. I was so proud, sitting there.

There again I saw Hitler. He made a point of not being present when Jesse Owens won. He didn't want to witness the victory of a non-Aryan.

In that same year, '36, Max Schmeling went to the United States to do battle with Joe Louis. I was rooting for Schmeling. In '38, when Louis beat him, I was crushed. That's how much I identified with the Germans. It was not a matter of Hans Massaquoi, black. I was a Hamburger and Schmeling was my man.

It's clear to me that had the Nazi leadership known of my existence, I would have ended in a gas oven or at Auschwitz. What saved me was there was no black population in Germany. There was no apparatus set up to catch blacks. The apparatus that was set up to apprehend Jews entailed questionnaires that were mailed to all German households. The question was: Jewish or non-Jewish? I could always, without perjuring myself, write: non-Jewish.

My mother was now reduced to day work. She was so popular in the hospital where she had worked that the doctors were kind enough to employ her as a cleaning lady. That's what she had to do in order to survive.

My scholastic records entitled me to go to the *Gymnasium*, the secondary school. A sympathetic teacher called me aside and said, "You have to be a member of the Hitler Youth movement to qualify. You're not accepted as a Hitler youth. So . . . I'm sorry."

The only thing open to me was an apprenticeship. It is costly to a family, because you don't get any pay. And you're doing three years. My mother wanted me to at least become a skilled tradesman. So I apprenticed as a machinist.

We're building big truck trailers for the military. Every day officers would come to the plant to inspect. By this time, pretty much everybody around me is a Nazi. A lot of my old classmates decided to volunteer. At sixteen, they're ready.

Many of the German youth that followed the call to arms weren't moved by any political considerations to kill Jews or Poles or Russians. It's the old quest for adventure. Hitler made it very attractive. He put the fancy uniforms on his troops. Had I not been constantly rejected, there's no telling how enthusiastic a volunteer I might have been.

Most of the kids that volunteered didn't even know what they were getting themselves into. I saw one friend after another go into the army or navy. One of my closest friends volunteered for the submarines. I was very proud of him. When he came on furlough, we would go out on the town. I still felt rejected, because everyone my age by this time wore a uniform.

A new phenomenon sprang up. There was a group of teen-agers who were rejected and who began to reject the system. They made their opposition to the regime known by the way they wore their hair. Short hair was the order of the day. Nazis would sometimes raid a nightclub and get young people whose hair was too long and march them to the barber shop. This identifiable group also wore their jackets long, like zoot-suiters. They were bitter enemies of Hitler. Of course, you could go only so far.

Their affinity was for English and American records. Jazz especially. If they caught you playing these records, they'd confiscate them or take you to jail and keep you overnight. They'd give you a lecture or a beating. I became part of that group. We were just seventeen, eighteen. We'd meet at certain nightclubs. You could look at us and know we were anti-Nazi.

The Nazis hated our guts. Any chance they had, they would kick us in the pants or make life miserable for us. There was nothing ideological about us. We were nonpolitical, just anti Nazi regimentation. It was just a total turnoff. We didn't want to be bothered by this nonsense.

Many of the young soldiers who were drafted, when they came back on furlough, would grow a little hair. They'd get out of uniform and wear civilian clothes. Sometimes they'd join the swing boys, as we were called. There were still many young people who, for one reason or another, were not drafted. Toward the end, everybody was drafted. Anyway, our group was already hoping for Germany's defeat.

By this time we identified with English and American culture. More American. We would crave listening to jazz. Almost fanatics. Every other night, some band would be arrested because they were egged on by the swing boys to play "Some of These Days" or one of those numbers. A Gestapo man in the audience would arrest the whole band.

One evening, we were standing on an el train by the door, three or four of us. We were singing some of those songs we heard in English. Some people on that train were so furious, we were almost lynched. There were still quite a few gung ho Germans in Hamburg. But there was also a lot of defection. The poorer-class Germans, especially, became more and more disillusioned. As long as Hitler was winning, there was enthusiasm for him. But as the war continued, more people were saying, We can't win this one.

The first bombings of Hamburg started in 1942. The raids increased. In 1943, Hamburg was practically demolished. In three nights, forty-one thousand people were killed. My mother and I were right in the middle of it. On the street where we lived, there was a public air-raid shelter. Every street had to have a shelter, which you could reach in five minutes.

I remember one night, about nine o'clock, the siren started wailing. We grabbed our suitcases and made it down. We'd been in this same shelter many, many, many, many nights before. The shelter was packed. There must have been two hundred, most of them neighbors we knew. There was not a moment when there was no Allied aircraft over Hamburg. It was an around-the-clock affair. The British would attack us at night and the U.S. air force in the daytime.

This night, about midnight, we heard the bombs dropping. It lasted about an hour. When it was over, we tried to get out, but we couldn't. The building over us was hit by an incendiary bomb and was on fire. The outside walls had collapsed and had blocked the exits. People were running around, getting hysterical. Nobody gets out, they were shouting.

About eight the next morning, we heard digging outside. They were removing the walls. We were half suffocated. We couldn't breathe. When we reached the street, that part of Hamburg where I lived was totally burned down. My mother and I made it to an overpass of an el train. All the survivors went there. We were picked up by trucks and taken out of the city. In those days, refugees—and we were all refugees now—could use the trains without paying.

We went to live for a while with my mother's relatives in the Harz Mountains. It was a town near Nordhausen. When I was little, visiting my aunt and uncle on Sundays, we'd climb this mountain. Now the whole area was fenced in and German military police with dogs would patrol the fences.

I asked my aunt what's going on. She said, "Oh, they say it has something to do with the war. They have a lot of prisoners working there." I saw trucks loaded with what we now know were concentration-camp inmates, with those striped suits. Emaciated people. I could actually see the entrance to the tunnel from my aunt's window.

Nobody appeared to pay any attention. There's something going on, but nobody would ask about specifics. If you acted too nosy, you'd run the risk of getting your head chopped off. Well, as it turned out, after the war was over, I found out that Wernher von Braun was manufacturing his V-1 and V-2 rockets with this slave labor. Many years later, I visited my aunt in this area, now East Germany. There is a museum on this mountain. Ovens were there for the people who could no longer work. They'd be dragged over and burned. I did not know about those ovens then.

We returned to Hamburg and it was rubble. We didn't see one intact building. My mother and I were living in emergency quarters in a big school. Thousands of homeless people lived this way. I lived in one classroom with a bunch of old men. They were all staunchly anti-Nazi. My mother lived in the other wing with the women.

Two weeks before the British actually moved into Hamburg, the military blocked the street in front of the school and built a huge tank barricade. They tore all the cobblestones out of the streets and made a huge wall, reinforced with steel beams.

Tomorrow, it was announced, the British would come into the city. Karl Kaufmann, the governor of Hamburg, who had been one of Hitler's staunchest allies at the beginning, rebelled against Hitler's orders. He refused to defend the city. Berlin by this time was completely cut off. So Kaufmann is loved today for his one good deed, although his sins are manifold.

The next day somebody in the classroom woke me: "Hans, your friends are here." I looked out the window and there on the other side of the tank barricade was a long row of tanks and jeeps. And these soldiers in these funny tommy helmets with camouflage nets around their faces: the British troops. You cannot imagine how unthinkable the idea—seeing foreign troops in Germany, that we knew belonged to the Nazis. I said, "My God, I don't believe it."

The Nazis had told the Germans, Your goose is cooked when the Allies come. You'll be executed, your women will be raped. Where my mother was staying, the women were hiding in the toilets and in the closets. (Laughs.) Somebody opened the door and several British soldiers marched in. One had a big walrus mustache. He wants to know if there's anybody speaks English. I said I speak a little. He said, "Okay, you'll have to do. Now go around and tell these people to assemble in the schoolyard."

I walked from classroom to classroom. I had a problem finding half of them. They'd been hiding in various places. (Laughs.) Some were absolutely sure they'd be executed. I quieted them down as best I could. I said, "This officer just wants you all in the schoolyard." In five or ten minutes, about a hundred of us were outside, surrounded by soldiers. It looked ominous. But the officer gave me a cigarette, so I thought there was no immediate danger.

He said, "Tell these people we have to go through this street with our vehicles. In two hours, I want this barricade down. We will supply them with shovels and picks. Everybody has to work, men, women, and children." I led them to a construction firm, where they busted the lock and loaded several trucks with shovels.

I introduced my mother to the officer, and he told her she didn't have to work on the barricade. This created much hostility among my former German friends, because they saw me as a traitor. It was really a mission impossible, removing that barricade. It took weeks to build. He made me the overseer: "Just keep them working." They were furious with me. I said, "Look, fellas, I'm just tellin' you what the man says." (Laughs.)

Large numbers of young soldiers were now streaming back from the front, some wounded, some intact. Everybody was trying to make a living. There was no legitimate business. The black market was the only thriving business. Everybody was hustling. I had a head start. My appearance made it easy for me to make friends with the Allies. They assumed right away, looking at me, that I was not a German. Shortly thereafter, American ships came into the seaport of Hamburg. Invariably they had black crew members. All I had to do was go up to ask for a cigarette. That was my contact. Then I'd say, "I'm stranded here. I want to go to America." I always had an entrée because of my color. I could even pass through military police without any pass and get on these ships.

This is when I started a crash program of learning English. I had to learn it if I was to pass myself off as an American. This was a meal ticket for me.

During the war, I had completely lost contact with my father. I wrote all kinds of letters to Liberia. Some I gave to American soldiers, some to British, some to the Red Cross. In 1947, I get this huge fat letter with big stamps: Liberia. It said, "Dear son, thank God you are alive." He sent me a Liberian passport. I was able to leave Germany because with this passport, for the first time, I was identified as a member of the Allies. I had always identified in my mind with 'em, but now I had the papers.

My biggest disappointment, for those who've really suffered under the Nazis, is the benign treatment of those Nazis by the Allies. We had assumed a housecleaning would follow the occupation. That the British and Americans would come in—as the Russians did—and, first of all, round up the Nazi suspects. And make sure that those who had been in power would not get back in power. Quite to the contrary, within a very short time we saw these same people who terrorized the neighborhoods in charge again. The wardens, the block leaders, all these *Gruppenführer*, all the ex-functionaries, were back in the saddle. A lot of my friends were so disillusioned they left Germany. One particularly brutal Nazi I worked for at a rubber plant during the war was put back in charge of that same plant. This went on everywhere.

Another phenomenon occurred: the disappearance of Nazis. You saw pictures of thousands of them screaming and hollering "Heil Hitler." If you asked anyone, Were you ever a Nazi? Oh no, not me. Just about all these former functionaries appeared in their old positions.

I think Americans were the worst in this respect. They fraternized so readily. The American brass that came over, in an ostensible effort to have things run smoothly, immediately became pals with these old Nazis.

I think it filtered down from Washington. We'd rather deal with the Nazis and have them on our side. Let's not be too serious about this denazification. Go through the motions, but don't step on too many toes. We ultimately will need them.

IS YOU IS OR IS YOU
AIN'T MY BABY?

On a fine November day in 1945, late in the afternoon, I was landed on an airstrip in southern Japan. From there a jeep was to take me over the mountains to join a ship which lay in Nagasaki Harbor. . . . I did not know we had left the open country until unexpectedly I heard the ship's loudspeakers broadcasting dance music. Then suddenly I was aware that we were already at the center of damage in Nagasaki. The shadows behind me were the skeletons of the Mitsubishi factory buildings, pushed backwards and sideways as if by a giant hand. What I had thought to be broken rocks was a concrete power house with its roof punched in. I could make out . . . nothing but cockeyed telegraph poles, and loops of wire in a bare waste of ashes. I had blundered into this desolate landscape as instantly as one might wake among the craters of the moon. The moment of recognition when I realized that I was already in Nagasaki is present to me as I write, as vividly as when I lived it. I see the warm night and the meaningless shapes; I can even remember the tune that was coming from the ship. It was a dance tune which had been popular in 1945, and it was called: "Is You Is or Is You Ain't My Baby?"

These essays . . . were born at that moment. For the moment I have recalled was a universal moment; what I met was, almost as abruptly, the experience of mankind. On an evening like that evening, sometime in 1945, each of us in his own way learned that his imagination had been dwarfed. We looked up and saw the power of which we had been proud loom over us like the ruins of Nagasaki.

The power of science for good and evil has troubled other minds than ours. We are not here fumbling with a new dilemma; our subject and our fears are as old as the tool-making civilizations. . . . Nothing happened in 1945 except that we changed the scale of our indifference to man; and conscience, in revenge, for an instant became immediate to us. Before this immediacy fades in a sequence of televised atomic tests, let us acknowledge our subject for what it is: civilization, face to face with its own implications. The implications are both the industrial slum which Nagasaki was before it was bombed, and the ashy desolation which the bomb made of the slum. And civilization asks of both ruins, "Is You Is or Is You Ain't My Baby?"

—*Jacob Bronowski,*
Science and Human Values

PHILIP MORRISON

The folklore of the day is, the physicists were approached by the army. The army said, We will make you rich and famous. We'll give you the wonderful opportunity to make the world's greatest explosion and all you have to forget is, it's going to make a bomb to kill very many people. A Faustian bargain.

That was not the idea at all. It's a complete misapprehension. *We* went to the army. I mean the scientific profession, Einstein, the pacifist, at its head. We beat on the doors and said, We must be allowed to make this weaponry or we're going to lose the war. Once we did that, we didn't stop. I didn't work a forty-hour week. I worked a seventy-hour week. At night, I sat and I thought. I woke up in the morning and I thought. All my friends did the same thing. What can we do about this war? Physicists invented the bomb.

His office at the Massachusetts Institute of Technology reflects his incredible multi-interests and impulses. There are jagged mountains of books, journals, and dissertations formed higgledy-piggledy on the floor, at the window, on his desk. He will undoubtedly write critiques of some, comment on others; subjects including and beyond theoretical physics, from which he "strayed about twenty years ago," to astronomy, with which he is currently concerned. "I'm really an astronomer today."

During the war, I was a nuclear physicist. Actually, I was an engineer. We made weapons.

Before the war, in Berkeley, California, I was listening to the speeches in Nuremberg, in the middle of the night. Hitler was speaking on the radio. I was a student of Oppenheimer. My friends were in Spain: the Spanish Civil War seemed even more real to me than World War Two. I know more people who were killed in Spain than were killed in World War Two. We felt it was a prelude to the war in Europe. Had the Spanish Civil War been stopped, had the German and Italian aid to Franco been beaten back, the world war might have been aborted. Or so we thought.

The whole thing really began for us in late December, '38, right after Munich. That first paper arrived in German, by Hahn and Strassmann. This queer paper showed that uranium could be changed into barium. Before we could understand it very well, we heard rumors from Sweden that Robert Frisch and Lise Meitner had understood it. Frisch told me this story himself. She was his aunt. They went for a walk in the woods. They sat down on a log. He drew a little something, and she said, "I think of it this way." She drew a little something. They couldn't understand each other's drawings. Then they realized at once, together, that they were exactly the same drawing, seen from two different points of view. The uranium atom was splitting in half. Three days later, they gave it the name: fission. By the middle of January, it was clear to everybody.

We, Oppenheimer's students, drew on the boards all kinds of fantastic designs of atomic bombs. We didn't know much about it. A year later, I wrote an article, but they didn't print it. Nobody seemed interested in physics.

Leo Szilard was ahead of everyone. He had this idea five years before. He was still in Europe, a Hungarian refugee. He understood, somewhat mistakenly, that it was a sign of how to make a chain reaction. For four, five years he toured Europe, trying to buttonhole people. Trying to find a place where he could work on it. He acquired a reputation as this crazy guy, who has the idea of making energy from the atom. He didn't think of the bomb so much then, but of a source of power. He became a figure of folklore.

He came to the United States to look up Enrico Fermi, who had just come here from Italy. He tried to convince him to get to work on it. Then, Szilard and Wigner persuaded Einstein to write that letter to Roosevelt: the Germans are well ahead on the bomb. Let us do something. Their information on Germany was not very good, but it seemed to them plausible. This was the fall of '39. War had already broken out. With the fall of France in '40, we were already on a war footing.

I was looking for a job. Chicago was the place where I went. I was hired by Fermi the day after the first chain reaction, which took place December 2, '42.

For a year, I had been doing war work at the University of Illinois. There was no physicist able to breathe who wasn't doing war work. Physics was totally mobilized. The U.S. was still not at war, there was plenty of war work. After Pearl Harbor, the campus was immediately mobilized. Classes were accelerated. Students were in uniform. They marched to class singing "Sixpence." I was wildly enthusiastic, 'cause I was a long-time anti-Nazi and this was the war I expected and feared. I was caught up spontaneously and naively in this terrible war. It was the great crusade.

I was an air-raid warden at Illinois. I spent the drills on top of the physics building, with my sand bucket to put out incendiary bombs. We even figured out the Germans would send a little aircraft carrier to Hudson's Bay and try to bomb Chicago. But they would miss Chicago, because the lights were off. And they might find Urbana, which was straight past Chicago. (Laughs.) Really bizarre. There was a great sense of camaraderie, of national unity. Everybody was caught up in it.

The day I joined Fermi at Chicago was suffused with excitement. My friend, who'd been working there, said, "You know what we're doing here?" I guessed that they were working on a chain reaction. He said, "We already did that. Now we're going to make an atomic bomb."

This bomb requires fissionable material. A chain reaction does not. It can be made out of ordinary uranium. The idea was to make plutonium, chemically separable from the other elements. After that, it was alchemy: to turn uranium into plutonium.

In Oak Ridge, Tennessee, two factories were built: one for the New York scientists from Columbia University, under Harold Urey; the other, for the Berkeley people, under William Lawrence. The third plant, in Hanford, Washington, was for Fermi's Chicago laboratory.

We had a tight schedule. We had to decide what the plutonium design would be, train the Du Pont engineers, enlarge the work, and develop it: all leading to fissionable material. Then, it would be taken to another place and turned into a bomb.

It was all one single enterprise, highly divided, highly complex: the Manhattan Project, run by General Groves.

We knew the idea was to make the most destructive of all possible bombs. We believed Hitler was well ahead of us. My own personal experience was colored by a notion that came to me about six months after I joined the project. It occurred to me there were other ways of finding out what the Germans were doing, instead of just shaking prisoners and asking them what was going on. Technical means.

I prepared a careful, lengthy letter, which I sent off to General Groves. The same week it appeared on his desk, there was by chance a remarkable similar letter from a chemist in New York. We had never seen each other or even heard of each other before. This coincidence fitted General Groves's own turn of thought. He called us in and said, "Set it up." He gave us a few officers to work with. We set up a scheme for studying German intelligence. This eventually became known as the Alsace Project. I made myself into an intelligence officer. I just sat and read . . .

We initiated a terrible set of operations, the kind you read about in books. In my present view, it was wasteful, but probably justified by the circumstances. We sent airplanes into all kinds of difficult jobs. We sent young men to do all kinds of difficult tasks. Sometimes they were killed for negligible information. We took photographs galore, penetrating far behind German lines, in our fastest aircraft. We'd taken photographs of a Czechoslovakian uranium mine: was it working? We'd measure the number of trucks that came in and out each day.

We studied literature. We got all the magazines from Switzerland that the Germans published. We collected instrument dials from wrecked airplanes and measured their radioactivity. We even got people to fly up and down the rivers of Austria and Germany, at a very low altitude, dragging cotton wicks into the water, to pick up samples. Was the water radioactive?

We assumed the Germans were well ahead of us. They were our teachers. They had been well organized for war. We had a hard time doing that. Intelligence is an impossible task because it is marred by false information. We had heard innumerable stories from Sweden, from Switzerland, from prisoners of war. Yes, the Germans are testing bombs. Yes, they're well ahead. Yes, they have secret weapons. But now, through our other ways, we knew precisely what they did in all detail. We had their notebooks. Of course they were working on it, but they were far behind us.

By December '44, we learned unmistakably, from the Alsace mission, from people who went abroad to do studies of the Germans, by taking Strasbourg—we seized the laboratory of an important German physicist, Fleischmann—that the Germans were not a threat. They could not make the atomic bomb. It was like an open book. They were far behind and arrogant. They said, "We're well ahead of the rest of the world. The Americans can't do it. Even if Germany loses the war, we'll win the peace, because we alone control this powerful weapon." When we read this, we laughed out loud.

The work at Chicago was becoming more and more an engineering job. The plant at Hanford was ready to go by the summer of '44. I was scheduled to head out there with Fermi to work up this enormous power-generating plant. The biggest thing in the world. But General Groves said, "Don't go." The Normandy invasion was under way. We were preparing to go into German territory to shake down any information they had.

A crisis came up in Los Alamos. Here, in the New Mexican desert, they'd be assembling the bomb, making it. They were already working there, under Oppenheimer. It had been formed in the spring of '43. It began to grow enormously, much more than we had expected. They needed help to solve the problem of implosion, when it became clear that plutonium could not be used in the bomb unless a new method of assembly was developed. They'd better get people there in a hurry. The work in Chicago was slacking off. We began to talk about the postwar world and peaceful uses of atomic energy.

I was quite happy to go to Los Alamos, at first, because I felt a great loyalty to Oppenheimer. Los Alamos was a community of great single-mindedness and intensity. We thought of ourselves as being in the front line. We stood in the breach between Hitler and the world. The only way we could lose the war was if we failed our jobs.

Los Alamos was not a city like Chicago. It was an army post with physicists. When I walked down the street, I knew everyone personally. We never had such a sense of fraternity in a little community before. Of course, it was secret. It was surrounded by guards. We could not go out without permission. Our mail was censored, our telephone calls were interrupted. We consented to all this. The payment that Oppenheimer, quite wisely, elicited for our acceptance of control and isolation was that we be allowed to talk freely, one with the other. You knew all that was going on. Within the community, there was a complete openness. Fermi, Bethe, Neumann, Kistiakowsky, Teller were all there. There were no secrets to which we were not privy. We were inventing the secrets. We were writing the book.

"Teller? As Oppenheimer said, 'In wartime, he is an obstructionist. In peacetime, he'll become a promoter.' Teller had an ideé fixe. *He said, 'My work is more important, making a thermonuclear weapon.' It was clear to everyone, you had to make the fission one first. It was clearly in the wrong sequence. It wasn't at that moment a moral question. It just wasn't realistic."*

We spent a lot of time and risked a lot of lives to do so. Of my little group of eight, two were killed. We were using high explosives and radioactive material in large quantities for the first time. There was a series of events that rocked us. We were working hard, day and night, to do something that had never been done before. It might not work at all.

I remember working late one night with my friend Louis Slotin. He was killed by a radiation accident. We shared the job. It could have been I. But it was he, who was there that day. It was a Saturday, We'd get the material and we'd work from nine in the morning to three the next morning. We worked alone in a shielded laboratory, with a couple of guards. The shadowy night outside. A soldier or two, who was technical.

A very important role was played in the Los Alamos project by young men and women who were taken in the army, sifted out of the draft, graduate students in chemistry or physics or metallurgy. They were sent to Oak Ridge, selected, and sent on to Los Alamos. I was the senior physicist. I was twenty-seven. It was exactly the mean age of Los Alamos scientists. We were all young.

What was the right thing for us to do? It was a critical moment. The Japanese war was not yet over. Our work may bring an end to the war, save many lives, start a new world. We were disappointed that the United Nations did not hear about it. Nobody breathed its possibilities to the UN. Acheson didn't mention the weaponry that could transform the world. That puzzled me.

Then came the terrible news of the sudden death of Roosevelt. I think that ended the possibility that anything novel would happen

with the bomb. Yet if Truman had modified the obvious course—
going ahead, using it—he wouldn't have had the power to do so. The
pressure of his advisers was too much.

I don't say I was antagonistic to its use, not at all. But I wondered:
Is this the right thing to do? The idea of dropping it was implicit in
making it. We were not certain just how. Our task was to get the bomb
finished, to find out if it would work. The whole world was depending
on that, we felt.

I was appointed one of the people to make sure of the details of
the test in the desert. The Trinity test. There was talk of the possibility of its use over Japan. There was another suggestion that the
Japanese be invited to see the test. But there was this enormous
uncertainty: would it work? If it didn't work, you'd feel pretty embarrassed. (Laughs.) July 16, it went off in the desert.

The shot was set for Monday morning. I went down the Thursday
before, guarded in a convoy of automobiles, carrying the core, the
little ball of plutonium. I designed the ball. We assembled the bomb
in the high explosive only for the second time. We were all afraid.
Kistiakowsky was afraid for us. When we tried it on the hill, it
worked. We came down in the desert and tried it again. At the base
of the tower, we put the plutonium core into the high explosive. That
was the end of our job. We were done.

We went to the base camp, exactly ten miles away. We stayed there
for a couple of days, hearing gossip, living our lives, getting ready
for the day of the test. It began to rain on Sunday evening. The test
was uncertain. There was much anxiety. In the morning, just before
dawn, the rain subsided.

I had a short-wave set and was responsible for listening to the radio
communications from the people who would actually start it. Fermi,
all the others were there. But those directly engaged with the in-
strumentation were scattered all over the desert, some in shelters,
some far away. I had a microphone and I relayed the countdown. I
announced it: 30 seconds, 20 seconds, 10 seconds, 9, 8, 7, 6 . . .

From ten miles away, we saw the unbelievably brilliant flash. That
was not the most impressive thing. We knew it was going to be
blinding. We wore welder's glasses. The thing that got me was not
the flash but the blinding heat of a bright day on your face in the cold
desert morning. It was like opening a hot oven with the sun coming
out like a sunrise. It was a feeling of awe and wonder and dismay
and fear and triumph, all together. The sound came a minute later.

It went off in a dead silence, a great thunder.

Within a few days, I went from Los Alamos to Wendover Air Force Base at Wendover, Utah. The 509th Composite Group was there. And our transport aircraft. With the core of the bomb, I flew to Tinian. That's where the B-29 bases were. They had been attacking Japan for a year.

I loaded the plane called *Bock's Car*. It had two dice, with sixes showing. It was named after Captain Bock. Somebody else loaded the other bomb on the *Enola Gay*. The takeoff was dangerous, because there was no way of rendering it safe. The airplane just had to take a chance. *Bock's Car*'s bomb fell on Nagasaki three days after *Enola Gay*'s fell on Hiroshima.

We heard the news of Hiroshima from the airplane itself, a coded message. When they returned, we didn't see them. The generals had them. But then the people came back with photographs. I remember looking at them with awe and terror. We knew a terrible thing had been unleashed. The men had a great party that night to celebrate, but we didn't go. Almost no physicists went to it. We obviously killed a hundred thousand people and that was nothing to have a party about. The reality confronts you with things you could never anticipate.

Before I went to Wendover, an English physicist, Bill Penney, held a seminar five days after the test at Los Alamos. He applied his calculations. He predicted that this would reduce a city of three or four hundred thousand people to nothing but a sink for disaster relief, bandages, and hospitals. He made it absolutely clear in numbers. It was reality. We knew it, but we didn't see it. After we saw the event . . .

What was the purpose of the Nagasaki bombing? Didn't Hiroshima do the trick?

That's been much debated. From the viewpoint of the leadership, it was the same event. Two bombs were ordered. Admiral Pernell pointed out to General Groves that if you drop one bomb, after four years of war, the Japanese may think you could make only one bomb in that time. So why don't you drop two in quick succession? Then they don't know how many to expect. That fitted the project's plan: they were both being tested. They were two quite different bombs, with different mechanisms. Each one cost billions of dollars, so you used them both. When they cut the orders, they didn't say drop one. They said drop the first one and, as soon as you can, drop the second.

I was of the opinion that a warning to the Japanese might work. I was disappointed when the military said you don't warn.

Realize this: the air force had bombed sixty-six Japanese cities and towns before the end of the war. Ninety-nine big air raids and sixty-six targets. The place was destroyed. From our point of view, the atomic bomb was not a discontinuity. We were just carrying on more of the same, only it was much cheaper. For that war, it was just one more city destroyed. We had already destroyed sixty-six; what's two more? Fire bombs and high explosives did the job on Dresden and Hamburg and Leipzig.

Would the A-bomb have been dropped on Germany?

Oh, you bet. We would have all struck if it hadn't been. If Roosevelt were still there and Germany had not surrendered, it certainly would have been used. The libido of the physicists was to drop it on Germany. Every physicist felt this.

Through the years, we've heard it said that the A-bomb would never have been used on a Caucasian nation.

I think it underestimates the hatred against the Germans and the bitterness that we felt.

James Franck, a truly wonderful man, produced the Franck Report: Don't drop the bomb on a city. Drop it as a demonstration and offer a warning. This was about a month before Hiroshima. The movement against the bomb was beginning among the physicists, but with little hope. It was strong at Chicago, but it didn't affect Los Alamos. As soon as the bombs were dropped, the scientists, with few exceptions, felt the time had come to end all wars.

Two among sixty-six is nothing, but each of these two big ones was only one airplane. That was the real military meaning of Hiroshima and Nagasaki. It was not that the bombs were so destructive. It was not that the bombs created radioactivity. Terrible, of course. It's that the atomic bomb, now the nuclear bomb, is cheap. That's why we're in this big trouble.

At the height of its mobilization in World War Two, the United States could manage to make six or eight hundred big bombers. They could visit a city and do big damage in one night. If these eight hundred came to a city several nights, they could do the damage of an atomic bomb. So, you could manage to knock off, with all your forces, a city a week. But now, a thousand cities in a night! It's the numbers. It's the cheapness.

In World War One, we saw the first application of twentieth-century science to war. In the Battle of the Somme, the worst, the British and the Germans together could mobilize ten kilotons of high explosives; to shoot ten thousand pounds at a time, cannon shot by cannon shot, into the trenches for fifty miles around. That's ten kilotons a day—ten thousand tons. That's a lot of bombs, a lot of shells, right?

A freight train carries 40 tons a boxcar; 40 times 250 is ten kilotons. That's a train 250 boxcars long. A mile long. Several freight trains of shells were fired off in one day by fifty thousand sweating gunners shooting the shells one by one.

By 1951, the United States could do the whole World War One, which lasted a thousand nights, in one day. By 1952, there was the thermonuclear weapon. By 1958, we could do—not a kiloton as in World War One, not a megaton as in World War Two—a gigaton. A billion tons.

A billion *tons?*

A thousand million tons. That's where we stand now. It is this inordinate scale of change. Destruction has become so available and so cheap. The world still does not understand it.

The physicists have nothing to do with it any more. It's an industry. It's bought and paid for. There are thousands of jobs. The materials are expensive. It's highly technical. The processes are complicated. And high-paid people are doing it.

This is the legacy of World War Two, a direct legacy of Hitler. When we beat the Nazis, we emulated them. I include myself. I became callous to death. I became willing to risk everything on war and peace. I followed my leaders enthusiastically and rather blindly.

The Germans made the rocket. The cruise missile and the ballistic missile are also German inventions; they came out of Peenemünde. They didn't have the atomic bomb, but I believed they would have it. I thought that's why they were making these missiles.

"In my intelligence capacity, I once wrote a letter to somebody in authority: Don't let Churchill and Roosevelt meet in the south of England. It's not safe. Any day the Germans will launch an atomic bomb and destroy any place they please. They'll just kill the leadership at once."

There was the feeling that it was justified. Now, of course, I don't think it was justified. But if I had to do it all over again, I honestly say I would do the same. Nationalism is a terrible force. We're nation states, and people follow their leaders. Sure, there is an international community of scientists, but it's weak compared to the national impulse. You see it every day.

We fought the war to stop fascism. But it transformed the societies that opposed fascism. They took on some of its attributes. All these clichés, all these slogans: Total War. No Appeasement. No More Pearl Harbors.

In cold objective fact, Pearl Harbor was the greatest American victory of World War Two. It mobilized the country. A few battle-ships were sunk, a few thousand sailors were killed. Sure, it's bad. But from the viewpoint of history, no Japanese defeat was as bad for them as their successful attack on Pearl Harbor.

In the same way, I feel all this arming and preparing comes from the same syndrome: we can't afford to be surprised, we can't afford to be weak. That's what the Germans said. And did. They mobilized first. Look what happened to them. The same thing will happen to us if we don't cool it.

As one of Samuel Beckett's tramps asks the other, What's to be done?

End the arms race. It sounds like a slogan, but it happens to be our last best hope. We must wind it down as fast and as far as we can. I'm optimistic. I think there's a great survival instinct. In spite of the cold war, in spite of all the anxiety, the war has remained cold. We've never used the weapons for thirty-eight years. I wouldn't have given it twenty-five years. So we've had, as I see it, thirteen years of grace. Perhaps people will now decide we'd better have a lot more years of grace.

A lot of people went into government, worked at developing these weapons, and came away saying it was the wrong thing to do. The people who made the H-bomb say it was a mistake. I made only the

A-bomb. It took me only one lesson to learn the mistake. I don't know what the future holds. But I do know we're beginning to understand the climate, beginning to understand the oceans, beginning to understand the cell and the nucleus of the cell. We're beginning to understand things we didn't understand before. It is simply not possible to have war and nation states in the old way, with this kind of knowledge and this kind of technology. It cannot work into the next century.

MARNIE SEYMOUR

It was a casual encounter in the lobby of a New York hotel. Fortuitously, a tape recorder was at hand.

She and her husband have four sons, twenty-seven to thirty-four. "Baby boom, you know. The girls I went to school with all wanted large families. We were Depression small families and missed having a lot of brothers and sisters."

Her husband, Harry, had been drafted. He was allowed to finish at engineering school. "We were the only young people left in town. Everybody we knew was in the service." It was Benton, Illinois. "The capital of Little Egypt, coal-mining country." He tried to join the Canadian Royal Air Force, was turned down because of his eyes. Finally, "they drafted people that were half blind."

In '44, my husband was yanked out of the Corps of Engineers and sent to Oak Ridge, Tennessee. Not knowing why. He was sent with a whole bunch of chemical engineers down there. Nobody knew anything about Oak Ridge. He was writing me, but they had an elaborate censorship system. They looked through our hometown papers, fraternity magazines, anything, to see if there were any leaks. It was a well-kept secret.

You had to give three references. We gave the names of our town's most prominent people. Until the sixties, wherever we moved, the FBI would check on us. Wherever we'd move, our neighbors would tell us the FBI had been there to ask about us. It really made a great impression when you moved to a new town to have the FBI checking with your neighbors. Very helpful. (Laughs.) They'd show their FBI badge and say, "We have a few questions to ask about your new neighbors." Our original references would say, "Oh, Marnie, Harry, what are you up to now? We just heard from the FBI again." We'd always tell them we were down in Oak Ridge, saving America. So it was okay.

It was really a hellhole of a place. It was all wooden sidewalks, and the town was swarming with rats. There were more rats than people. It was a walled city. There was this big fence all around. They'd bulldozed this town in the mountains. There was no proper housing for a long time for married GIs. You had to find your own out of town. We lived out in a room at a motel. And we all cooked in this inn.

There were thousands of people, civilians and GIs. There were a few officers. Most of the GIs were engineers. They had three plants. They went by initials: Y-12, K-25, and I don't remember the other one. They were working out three different processes to separate out the U-235—nobody knew which process would work or if any would. They worked around the clock, of course.

I got a job that was crazy. I was running a mass spectrometer in the laboratory. I tested the product out of the stream to be sure impurities weren't getting into it. We had to handle it with asbestos gloves. I never knew how it worked. I don't think very many understood, except the people who designed it. It was a deadly dull job. Nobody could adjust the machine, except some guy in Washington. We could loaf around and read magazines waiting for his arrival. (Laughs.)

I was very proud of Harry, very smug. I thought we were part of the elite, working on a blockbuster. I'm ashamed of that now. I was thankful he wasn't overseas being shot at or shooting at people. My brother was wounded in the Battle of the Bulge. He still has nightmares about it. Gave up hunting. He used to be a big duck, quail hunter. He never talks about it, though.

The GIs worked right alongside the civilians. The only thing is they were getting $50 a month, or whatever it was. The civilians were getting $450 plus overtime. It rankled everybody because they were doing the same job. The best man at our wedding, Pete, worked for Dow Chemical in Midland, Michigan. He'd have been deferred because of his work, but he was a patriotic soul and joined the army. He was pulled out of the infantry and sent down to Oak Ridge. He was doing the very same job for GI pay that he would have done as a civilian if he'd stayed at Dow. (Laughs.) He died of leukemia.

There was a physics book in every office. A whole section about atomic energy. They all seemed to know what they were doing, but what they couldn't figure out was how they were going to defuse this blockbuster bomb. Nobody knew the damage it was going to do. Even Oppenheimer had no idea. I don't think they ever thought about it being used against anybody.

We had a three-day pass to go to St. Louis. It was the nearest city to our hometown. We were sitting in the rathskeller of the Mayflower Hotel, having lunch. All of a sudden, Harry, in his army uniform, jumps up from the table, runs across the room, and grabs this newspaper out of a man's hand. He threw it down and ran upstairs. We thought he'd freaked out. War nerves. We just sat there dumbfounded. What he'd seen in the paper was: A-Bomb Dropped on Hiroshima. He came back with a paper, sputtering and agitated. He said, "Now I can tell you what I've been working on. This." He said, "This is the one day I'd like to be in Oak Ridge." He was delighted to tell people where he'd been all these years, that he was not just loafing around. I don't think he had any conflicts at the time.

His father was head of the draft board and must have wondered all this time why his son wasn't off fighting the Japs in the Pacific. He was very gung ho. Now he could be very proud to say, "My son was down there making the bomb." Good lord, how proud can you be? Our little town was busting its buttons. Those wonderful GIs in Oak Ridge, Tennessee, ended the war singlehandedly by making the bomb. My father was a big Legionnaire and very proud of it all.

I thought after the war they'd close down all the plants at Oak Ridge. I thought it would become a ghost city. I never realized it would go on and on and on. You should go down there these days and see it.

Later that fall, after the war was over, there was an atomic test out in Bikini. Many of our friends went out to watch it. They wanted the excitement of going. People didn't travel as they do now. Hadn't been to the South Seas. Any of the GIs at Oak Ridge could have gone. We hadn't been married very long and I didn't want Harry to go on a two-month jaunt. To the best of our knowledge, most of the fellows who went and watched that test have cancer or are dead of cancer.

I'll bet everybody rushed up to see that glorious explosion. They got exposed to radiation and they died from it eventually. Some of their children are suing the government. Of the eighteen couples out of the motel we lived in, most have never been able to have children.

We are rather fortunate. We have four children. Two have birth defects.

As I got older and became more and more aware, I began to resist any X-rays, even routine ones in the doctor's office. They always wanted to know why. I'd just say, "I was at Oak Ridge and I don't know how much radiation I've been exposed to."

Were we ever warned? Oh, no, of course not. I don't think it was malicious. They just didn't know. I don't think anyone had any idea.

We rode this bus in, most of the wives who worked. Some were nurses, some were secretaries. We stopped all along the road and picked up civilian workers, hillbillies. We called this bus an abortion line, because so many of the girls that did get pregnant miscarried. Young women, healthy young women, don't miscarry right and left. Nobody who rode on that bus carried a baby to term. Maybe one of eighteen did. Everybody thought it was the cobblestone road.

Never are we at airports that Harry doesn't bump into somebody he knew at Oak Ridge. I've often wished that somebody would finance a study of the GIs down there, just to find out how many of them couldn't have children and how many had defective children.

When Harry went back to graduate school, all he had to say was, "I was on the Manhattan Project." The door just opened to any graduate school. He had exposure to all sorts of scientific things that they'd never laid hands on. We were so smug about it.

You know what happened to us? We were living in New Canaan, Connecticut, and Norman Cousins brought over some Hiroshima Maidens. Weekly, we were confronted with these deformed, burned women. I would see them at the supermarket and think, My God, this thing I felt so smug about did this. Sometimes I cry . . .

You must realize we were not a worldly people. We were an isolated big country. We didn't know much about the Japanese and Japanese culture. They were yellow, they had squinty eyes, and they all looked evil. They were always evil in the movies, characters slinking around knifing people. You begin to think of them not as human beings but as little yellow things to be eradicated. They looked different from the Germans. If you were to say to me, You can save only *x* number of prisoners and, say, you've got fifty Japanese and fifty Germans, whom would you let die? I would have fed the Germans. They had been more civilized, at least in my knowledge.

I remember, in the fifties, the air-raid shelters in New Canaan. It is a very swish commute-to-New-York suburb. Our neighbors were going to build a bomb shelter, elaborate, well stocked. They wanted us all to go together. We'd be compatible. Harry talked 'em out of it. He said, "You'd be sizzled to death. There'd be nothing to come out to. You wouldn't want to survive. It would be a slow, hideous death."

Our children are the ones that did that darn duck-under-the-desk. Instead of fire drills, they had atomic drills: when you see the blast, duck under the desk. They did it all the time. It was so preposterous. I'd hear a lot of jokes. I was substitute teaching. The teachers would say, "Oh God, I hope it doesn't come when I'm teaching and I'm stuck at school with all these kids for days before we could send them home." As if we'd be in school, eating in the cafeteria, and when the radiation cleared up, the kids would go home.

This was in the McCarthy days. I thought he was a horrible joke. I didn't know how seriously people took him. I don't remember ever being afraid. I talked to everybody about how awful he was. I've often wondered why the FBI, checking up on us, didn't get me. (Laughs.) I was always outspoken. I can't help it.

The wives at the company Harry works for think I'm misguided. I've read too much, caught up in that intellectual stuff. Once when we attended an orientation meeting—we were going to Saudi Arabia—I asked a few questions. The wives at the picnic said, "Oh, you're the one who asked all those questions." They turned and walked away.

We've lost most of our friends. They've never even written to say, "Now I understand the way you felt." What they really said was, "What you're saying is terrible. You could really go to jail for that."

I think a lot of fellows from World War Two gave their children silent permission to say no to the army. If you asked them, they'd deny it, but they knew it was a different war.

These postwar babies feel that they will not live out their lifetime to expectation. I have one boy who's become a master carpenter. He's not making any provisions, even at thirty-four. He takes off and wanders at leisure. As for getting married or buying a home, he doesn't think there's any future. He's just one of the thousands of young people who grew up ducking under their desks in atomic-bomb drills at school. Why would they think there's a future? All their lives they've heard about the bomb being dropped. That's a sad way to live.

An arbored house in Berkeley, close by the campus. "It's near the radiation lab. It's now called the Lawrence Livermore Laboratory."

During World War Two, we were the pilot plant. We trained people for Los Alamos and Oak Ridge. Our particular job was to purify all the uranium and separate uranium 235 from uranium 238. There were no guidelines. We simply had to improvise and invent as we went along. I was a chemist. We were all part of the Manhattan Project.

They compartmented us for two reasons. One was secrecy: so the left hand wouldn't know what the right hand was doing. The other was for efficiency. We never spoke of the other places. Oak Ridge was X. Los Alamos was Y. Washington was W. There was a big one at Hanford, Washington. That's where they were making plutonium.

When my superior, Dr. Segrè, one of the three great Italian physicists we glommed on to, was sent to Los Alamos, I first knew something important was stirring in the Southwest. At the time, I began to hear of X. There were all these Tennessee Eastman people running around, with badges. I couldn't figure out what they were doing on our project. Nobody would tell me and I wasn't supposed to ask questions. That's how disguised it was.

Eventually, we were ordered to send half our immediate staff to Oak Ridge. We were not told what it was. Just send them. A few of us flipped coins to see who would go. The kids wrote back and said, "We're in Dogpatch." We began to realize it was either in Kentucky or Tennessee.

We called it the Tube Alloy Project. It was a disguise, of course. It gave rise to a lot of jokes. In about two weeks, I realized, My God, this is uranium. Then I began to catch on to what we were trying to do, without ever talking to anyone. We were on the road to atomic power, the atomic bomb. I began to talk to my boss about it, because it was pretty obvious by then. There were little leaks. Some hotshot young physicist, who was new on the project, called me on the university phone. He wanted some highly secret data. I just blew my stack. I said, "Don't you realize that anybody could grab the phone anywhere on this campus and listen in?"

When my partner came back from Oak Ridge, I asked him how big it was. He said, Multiply what we're doing at Berkeley by ten to the fifth. About a hundred thousand times. He said the race tracks there were just unbelievable. So was the red tape. (Laughs.) He sent a teletype asking for a tiny invention of mine. It involved glass blowing. I said, "Why didn't you do it back there?" He said, "We can't even get glass. The warehouses go for miles and miles and you can't even get into them."

Basically, there are no secrets to scientists. There were attempts by various governments to clamp down. Certainly Nazi Germany wasn't releasing any secrets. Neither was the Soviet Union. Didn't the State Department recently crack down at Stanford and forbid any Soviet scientists from coming? But science is universal and it's very difficult to hide these things. Frankly, I don't think there was much espionage going on during the war in that direction.

On August 6, 1945, I was working on missiles at Arroyo Seco, a big canyon just above the Rose Bowl in Pasadena. My girl assistant came in ten minutes late. "I was listening to the radio," she said, "and now I know what you were doing all this time. You were working on the atomic bomb, weren't you?" They had just announced the dropping of the bomb on Hiroshima.

My instantaneous reaction was elation. Then there was a second reaction. (Whispers) Oh, my God! On a city! I went in and talked to my boss. (Whisper builds to a shout) They dropped an A-bomb on a big city, a hundred thousand or so. Why didn't they drop it on Tokyo Harbor or on that great naval base at Truk? Why on a civilian population? My boss was Jewish and he knew about the Holocaust. He said, "What the hell, they're just Japs. Dumb animals." I was stunned. Lost all my respect for him.

The reason for my instant elation: my boss was telling me that if we failed, most of us would go to Leavenworth. We were spending three million dollars on this project—1945 dollars. If we failed, there'd be a tremendous congressional investigation after the war about graft and corruption. We'd serve one to ten in Leavenworth. This was thrown at me, again and again. Particularly whenever I'd try to get a salary raise for my assistants. All of us were just working our tails off. I myself averaged about a hundred dollars a week and, of course, no overtime pay. My assistants, for whom I spoke, were getting a pittance.

There was the feeling that the Germans had a four years' head start on us. If they were as good as we were, that would be the end of the United States as an independent country. We had real worries. It didn't work out that way, but with wartime secrecy, we had no way of knowing.

We had finished on June 30, 1945, two weeks before the Los Alamos explosion. One of our Los Alamos people visited us. He said, "Let your imagination run wild, as far as you can go, and you'll be right." He said it will be successful.

A brother of mine, who had two years flying P-38s in the South Pacific, had volunteered for an invasion of Japan. All his former squadron members said, "You're crazy." He was intensely patriotic. A couple of weeks after V-J Day, he said, "Now I know what you were working on. You saved my life. We figured," he said, "on at least a million casualties." I said, "Yes, but it sticks in my craw, the two cities we bombed." He said, "Yes, it's terrible, but don't you realize what we were doing in Japan? We were all out fire bombing. We were trying to fry the Japanese alive in Tokyo and Yokohama." In his estimation, the atomic bomb was no worse. He said, "We learned that in Dresden. What difference is there?" There was quite a difference. When you think of atomic radiation and the Pandora's box we opened.

Sometimes, I ask myself, Any regrets about working on the atomic bomb? The answer is no. Under the circumstances, I felt that our survival as a nation, as a democracy, was really at stake. I was not so worried about the Japanese as about the Nazi threat. The Hearst papers out here stressed the Japanese menace. Hearst was trying to get us to shift our power to the Pacific, which might have led, hopefully for him, to some sort of understanding with Germany. I felt we had to go all out.

I still regret how it was done. I realize that a threat was not enough. It had to be dropped somewhere. But there were other places they could have dropped it without such a terrible loss of life.

Of course, some people thought of it as a warning to the Soviet Union. We're not going to be allies any longer, so don't get ideas. We're stronger than you.

Today, the development has been headlong. Our military and

political leaders seem to be almost in a trance. They think that if we can get far enough ahead of the Soviet Union, we can somehow settle their hash. I can't see it that way. If a person is threatened, he's gonna fight back. The more we threaten them, the more heavily they'll arm. The more they threaten us, the more heavily we'll arm. Ultimately, this could lead to mutual suicide. We might just blow ourselves off the face of the earth.

BILL BARNEY

We're in an Indiana farm kitchen, some thirty miles outside Fort Wayne. On this delightful autumn morning, we see rich farmland. "It's all now just corn, wheat, and beans.

"Dad had this farm, so I went in with him. I never had much of my own before. It's a different ball game now. There's a lot of farmers ready to go under. I talked to some auctioneer here yesterday. He's got a farm sale every day for September and October. Here we don't have a head of livestock. We have a dog on the place. We can't go out and butcher, live off that. Nowadays there's no way to be independent."

Immediately, there's coffee: a matter of course with any guest, I suspect. There's a shyness, a diffidence; he is not one given to words; his gnarled hands and weathered face—and deep-plowed acreage—tell you something else. He is ideal film-casting as "a man of the soil."

He was a crew member on the flight that dropped the A-bomb on Nagasaki, August 9, 1945.

Golly, I don't know. First thing comes to mind—probably memories of the fellas I was with, the life we had together. Something I know I would never done if it hadn't been for that.

I came out of high school and went into the service, 1943, January. I'd never had to do any thinking for myself at that time. When I first got in, I went into the veterinary corps. (A soft chuckle.) They had to take care of guard dogs, and we was meat inspectors. I didn't care too much for that, so I transferred. This was the air force—air corps, it was. I had a chance to apply for cadets. At the time, they was full, so they put us into gunnery school. Laredo, Texas.

We went to this gunnery school for B-24s. We come out of that, they brought us up to Nebraska. They were just beginning to get crews for these B-29s. So they pulled a bunch of us out and sent us to B-29 gunnery school. Well, I come out of that and they told me I was gonna be a radar operator. At that time, B-29 was the largest combat plane.

We was ready to go overseas in the squadron and all of a sudden one night, there was posted on the bulletin board that our outfit was to pull out. We was told we was going to Wendover, Utah. We didn't know where the hell Wendover, Utah was. Or what it was. We didn't know what we was in.

The training was just more of what we had, only more sophisticated. We was told we was in a highly exclusive secret thing. The first thing they done on our planes was take all the armament off of 'em, except the tail gun. To give 'em speed, so we could pull more altitude.

We experimented with some large bombs. We'd flown a lot of dummy bombs, so we assumed it was gonna have a lot of weight. There was a lot of rumors, but we didn't know what we had until the first one was dropped.

They was having to experiment with how to detonate these bombs. They didn't have any way of doing it. We even experimented with a man on the ground detonating the thing. You'd be up there and somebody down there'd have the switch. There was a few dropped experimentally up the mountains. They decided to give that up and finally decided to arm 'em on the ship.

The biggest thing we had dropped before was these five-hundred-pound incendiary bombs. We didn't know how large these others was gonna be, but when you made it fit up in just one bomb rack, we knew it had to be pretty good size. So we knew they had to be talkin' up in the tons.

We picked up new planes out of Omaha and they put all this new equipment on it. We flew these planes overseas to an island called Tinian in the South Pacific.

We started droppin' 'em on regular missions. We took 'em to Japan. They was nothin' more than seven-ton TNT bombs. We made one run on Tokyo one time. We usually went in on twenty-six, twenty-seven thousand feet and you could see 'em. Just a great explosion, debris. I never did see too much because I was usually tied to the radar set. On occasion, I went to the windows.

When were you first aware of the mission?

We knew that after the first one was dropped. The guys from the plane, *Enola Gay,* relayed it back to us. We really didn't know it was until like you read it in the newspapers. That's the first that we actually knew. I was in barracks over in Tinian. We knew it was called the Manhattan Project, but we didn't know what the Manhattan Project was.

There was fifteen crews, that's all that was ever trained to drop this bomb. We was one squadron: 509th Composite Group is what it was. Nine on each crew.

Did you meet the guys when they came back?

When they got off the plane? No. You couldn't get close to 'em. There was too much turmoil. I talked to 'em later, yes. They was excited like we was excited. But at that time, it didn't mean a lot.

We flew out the ninth. They posted orders about two o'clock in the afternoon for us to take off that night. There was three ships that was goin'. The third one was a camera. I *wasn't* on the one that had the bomb. I was on the second plane. Our ship was strictly to measure velocity of this bomb. That's what I done on that mission.

We went on about twenty-seven, twenty-eight thousand feet—I think the target was Kokura, but I'm not too sure. This one we got wasn't our primary target. We made two passes. We had three targets. Nagasaki was the third one down the line.

Why weren't the other two—?

We couldn't see 'em. We got there, it was covered over. We sent three weather ships up ahead, and they came back and said this Kokura was clear. When we got there, it wasn't. They wanted to do it visually. We could bomb on radar, but they didn't want to do it with this bomb. They didn't want to waste too many lives for nothing.

With radar, it was not as accurate. They knew there was a big possibility that you could get in a residential district. They didn't want to use the radar unless they had to. But you had to get rid of it, because it was armed and we couldn't set down with it. We knew we was gonna run out of fuel. This target we went on was between us and Okinawa. So that's where we headed for, Okinawa. We started to make the run, the last minute, this other plane, he could see it and he took it over and made a direct drop.

Nagasaki.

Right. They weren't gonna let us in Okinawa. See, they'd just taken it and they said you couldn't land one of them things. Chuck Sweeney, which was flyin' the first ship, said, "That's a lot better than that ocean out there." (Laughs.)

We was close. Sweeney was closer than we was. His one inboard died on the taxi strip, he was that close. Of course, he had a bigger load than we did.

Fact is, the third ship never showed up, the camera ship . . . We had enough cameras on board ours to take pictures. That's where the pictures come from, our ship.

When the bomb was dropped on Nagasaki, did you see what happened below?

Oh yes. You could see fires all over, just literally acres of fire. We was probably down to twenty thousand feet.

Do you remember your first reaction?

You could glorify it and say like everybody else did: Oh my God or somethin' like that. But it was—I can't tell you now.

You realize it was big. We done a little chattin' back and forth on the intercom. How much bigger it was than the conventional, how much more destruction it was doing, things like that.

If there'd been a third one dropped, we woulda dropped it, our crew. To my knowledge, only four bombs were completed. One was in the United States. The third was loaded in our ship the day the war was over. Fred Bock was our pilot. That's why it was called *Bock's Car.* The *Enola Gay* was named after Paul Tibbets's mother. That was the Hiroshima plane.

Do you ever run into the guys?

I was with 'em in Chicago a few years ago. They have a reunion about every two or three years. But they always have the damn thing in the middle of the summer when I can't get away here on the farm. This bombardier stopped by the other day. We had pictures and we reminisced.

I know you're asked this every time the subject comes up: Do you or any of the other guys have any conflicts?

There's never been any of 'em to my knowledge. Except one person that had a lot of publicity. He's dead now. I don't know if there was anything to it or not. Eatherly.

Claude Eatherly.

Right. Buck and I were good friends at one time. Whether there was anything drivin' him—He's from Texas. I saw him a few years back. At that time, they said he was nuts, but he talked rational to me.

His book, Burning Conscience.

I read it. (Pause.) He was an erratic person. He was regular, but he'd fly off the handle quick. He was a whale of a pilot. He had a crew of his own. He flew one of the weather missions. I think Buck went on that mission over Hiroshima. He was one of our fifteen crews.

We just got pulled into this. I never did know how our outfit got it. We was there puttin' in time and might as well be doin' that as somethin' else. We didn't have any choice really. I was lucky enough to get in and out of it.

Your first thought is, Hey, I was there. I'm one of the few that knows it firsthand. That thought always enters your mind.

Does it bother you when you read these stories?

Yeah. They don't do it as much as they used to. Right after it happened, there was a lot of discrepancies printed. There was quite a long time when I couldn't sit down and talk about it. I couldn't sit down and talk to you this way, because they hadn't released us still. As to what did happen.

This was just a peanut compared to what we got now. I don't think they'll ever be using it. That's my personal opinion. It's my opinion that it'll just destruct the world if it ever started. Everybody would lose. Say they dropped one on Chicago, it would probably annihilate us here through fumes and maybe clear down into Cincinnati. I assume they got it where they could send it now on warheads where they don't even have to go with a plane.

We never saw them people in Nagasaki. I've thought about that. About the Civil War and things like that. One guy hidin' behind one tree and you shoot a rifle around it and another guy behind another tree. They could actually see them people. All you do now is read about it, just like everybody else.

At that time in Vietnam, I felt we should use it. But you know, I've changed my mind. (Laughs.) I more or less growed up in my thinking.

I came out of school and went into service. You don't do too much thinkin'. When you're in school, you're told to do this, you read this. When you go in the service, you'd be here today, you'd be there tomorrow. You do your job and you're told when. After you get out here on your own, you develop a different personality, a different outlook on life. You mature after you have to do your own thinkin'.

I can understand why the first bomb was dropped. Why the second?

This is my interpretation. They knew what we had. We give 'em a chance to surrender. If they didn't do this, they knew it was gonna take an invasion. We had 'em whipped, but it was gonna take a lot of their lives and a lot of our lives if you had to invade that place, plus a lot of money. This way you just took Japanese lives.

Some people once in a while ask if it bothers me. No, it don't bother me. It's just I think of it more in memories, of what we done, the people I was with, the good times we had.

There's a lot of these do-gooders runnin' around—to kill that many people, you're a murderer. I could see where if I sat down and thought about it all the time, I could drive myself whacky. If you sat around and just dwelled on something.

POSTSCRIPT: *"If that war woulda lasted, it would have been used in Europe, I know. We had a simulated flight, trainer things. You flew two, three thousand miles. Bombardier, myself, navigator. You flew these missions. And they was all in Germany. That's what we based our thinkin' on. Japan was just timing. I think it was a last-minute decision on Truman's part."*

Gray-bearded, slight, nimble, he's a cross between a leprechaun and a bantam prophet. On his T-shirt is the legend: Bethlehem Peace Pilgrim.

Flint, Michigan. A working-class town; the classic depressed area. When he first arrived in 1941 as a parish priest, it was booming. " 'Forty-three, I went into the service and became a chaplain."

Though he is retired, "I am a peace pilgrim." He has walked, with colleagues who have dropped in and out, from Seattle to Washington, D.C. "This year, we start March 17 in Ireland and we hope to get to Bethlehem by Christmas."

His well-used jalopy is decorated with bumper and window stickers. Literature is scattered all over the back seat.

An hour or so before this conversation, he had spoken at the local Masonic lodge. About a hundred members were in attendance, small merchants of Flint. Though the question-and-answer period was spirited, the audience was remarkably friendly. They were listening hard.

At Harvard chaplain school, we were taught how to take care of our charges, how to counsel them, how to conduct religious services. How to make them better soldiers. And what is a soldier? A paid professional killer.

We were taught to keep young men morally fit, help their morale, listen to their troubles—what's wrong with that? At the time it all seemed so good. This was 1943. I was twenty-eight. These kids were my parish, wherever I was. Wright Field at Dayton, Fort Jackson in North Carolina. Overseas. Okay, they've engaged in killing and fighting, but it didn't register. I believed it was perfectly okay.

My father had been a soldier in the Austrian army and I was proud of it. That was a glorious, wonderful thing. A soldier was admired. I looked forward to being a chaplain, wearing the uniform, proud of the flag. You're defending your country, your loved ones. The thought that to do that you have to kill other people who are equally convinced of their cause—who have families, who have sweethearts and wives—didn't seem to enter into it.

I wanted to get into action. I was in the Army Air Corps. Up we go into the wild blue yonder. I was supposed to go with a hospital unit to Germany, but V-E Day came. We were reassigned to the Pacific theater. It was around June 1945 we landed on Tinian Island.

At that time, there was the plan of invading Japan. We island-hopped from Guadalcanal on through the Marshall Islands and on up through Guam. To Saipan and Tinian. Airfields were set up. B-29s were dropping napalm and blanket-bombing the cities. Tokyo was a seventy-five percent burnout.

Another group came over. It was the 509th Composite Group. It was a special group with a special bomb. We knew it was bigger than anything that had ever been dropped. We called it the gimmick bomb.

We didn't have patients yet. I had the time. So I became the Catholic chaplain of the 509th Composite Group. That's how I got to know Paul Tibbets.* Not very well, 'cause he was the commanding officer and he wasn't Catholic. But I got to know Charley Sweeney.†

I remember him and General Farrell, one of the higher-ups, at mass. A very fine group of men. I still admire many of the military people. They, like me at the time, were sincere that war was terrible, but it had to be. Of course, the Japanese had some pretty bad pages. We knew about them.

We knew they had a big bomb, but that's all. They flew dummy bombs every day. Practice, I guess. Runs over possible targets. Even the crew members of the *Enola Gay* did not know they had a live bomb until they were airborne. On August 6, Paul Tibbets announced through the intercom: This is it, we are dropping the first atomic bomb. That's the first time anybody knew there was an atomic bomb, a nuclear weapon. The orders came directly from Washington. It came through no chain of command.

I still have the first *Time* magazine article about it: the entrance of a new world. We don't know what the future's gonna be. It promises either a terrible thing or one of the greatest achievements of man: atomic energy.

It was customary to bless the crew. Not the plane. And not the bomb. I've had this thrown at me many times. But the crew members were part of our parish. They were going on a dangerous mission. These were our boys, our young men, endangered by death. I didn't know they were dropping any kind of bomb until the radio on the island told us. Then, the shock. We suddenly realized that eighty thousand people were killed in that one explosion.

*Pilot of the *Enola Gay*, the plane that dropped the A-bomb on Hiroshima.
†Pilot of *The Great Artiste*, on the flight that dropped the A-bomb on Nagasaki.

We were living on an island where every day hundreds of planes were taking off, dropping blankets of napalm, burning out hundreds of thousands of people. At one time, we had five hundred planes on one mission over Japanese cities. We had read about Dresden and Berlin and Coventry and London. On a walk somewhere in Oregon, I met a pilot of a B-17, who walked with us for several miles. He flew a B-17 over Dresden and described what he saw. Fire bombs. A whole city destroyed. The shock was that here, suddenly *one* plane did what hundreds of planes had not been able to do. One plane, one bomb, destroyed a city.

Instead of a feeling of horror, which I should have felt as a Christian, as a priest, it just went by me. We had heard from other pilots who came back from raids how they saw firestorms in Tokyo, hundreds of thousands burned to death. We should have felt horror then that these were civilians. We had gone through the "just war" theory of Saint Augustine: civilians were not to be harmed. Yet it never occurred to us.

I think the reason it went by us is that no voices were raised by the hierarchy, by any religious leaders. The immorality of indiscriminate bombing. It happened in Dresden, it happened in Japan. Cardinal Spellman came out to Tinian. I remember that, the big mass toward the end of the war. He urged us to continue fighting. We were fighting for freedom, for justice, fighting to do away with the horrors that the Japanese had perpetrated at Pearl Harbor and all that. Just as we had fought to do away with Hitler.

Eighty thousand in Hiroshima. Forty-five to fifty thousand in Nagasaki. Charley Sweeney flew that plane. I don't know why he named it *The Great Artiste*. When that second bombing on August 9 came, none of us on the island knew. I guess many of us were hoping there'd be no more bombing, that Japan would end the war. But it didn't.

What about the other chaplains? Did the subject ever come up?

We never got into the morality of the bombing. I guess we all felt it was terrible, but necessary. Remember, we demanded unconditional surrender. This is also against the principles of Saint Augustine's "just war" theory: you cannot continue fighting when the other party is ready to capitulate. It doesn't mention unconditional. If the term weren't used, there would not have been any need for the bomb.

There were already overtures, made through Geneva and different places. They were on their knees.

And the Soviets were about to enter that sphere . . . ?

That's one of the reasons I think they dropped the second bomb. To hurry it up. To make them surrender before the Russians came.

When the news of Hiroshima hit me, my reaction was a split one. Gosh, it's horrible, but gosh, it's going to end the war. Finally the boys will get home. This was going to save millions of lives. We would have lost a million soldiers invading Japan. But, as a priest, I should have considered: We're killing little kids, old men and old women, burning them to death. I don't recall any feeling of guilt at the time. I must say that there was a little difference in my feelings when I found out that Nagasaki was a Catholic city. The bomb was dropped right on Urakami, a suburb. It was dropped within a few hundred meters of the central church. It was an almost totally Catholic settlement. Saint Francis had come four hundred years before and brought the faith into Japan. That's where the shoguns tried to eradicate the faith and thousands of Christians were martyred.

Here was Charles Sweeney, a good Boston Irish Catholic, piloting the plane, dropping the bomb, killing our fellow Catholics. Brothers and sisters killing brothers and sisters.

I got acquainted with a Japanese priest who was in the prisoners' compound in Tinian. Some Irish Seabees told me about him. We built a chapel for him in the compound. We had a little choir. The Japanese priest said the mass and I said the mass with him. It was still in Latin at the time. All of us went to communion, the GIs and the Japanese prisoners. A Quonset hut, I think it was.

On August 15, the war ended. We had a big mass. It was the Holy Day of Assumption. It's the day we celebrate Mary's assumption into heaven. The war started on December 8—they're a day ahead of us —which was the feast of the Immaculate Conception. We had the mass. We were all happy, but everybody was kinda quiet. There was no great yelling or shouting or anything. Everybody just was walking around. War's ended, we're gonna go home. No more Kamikazes coming over, no more danger.

It was October when our hospital group was assigned to Japan for occupation. The southern island of Kyushu. Shortly after, we disbanded the hospital. The material—jeeps, trucks, medical equipment, everything—had to be taken back. Usually they'd dump it all in the ocean.

Dump it?

Sure. I knew all the valuable drugs we had. So I got some trucks and loaded them up with medicines and all kinds of things and took them over to the orphanage and dispensary run by the Visitation Sisters. There were a lot of hungry and sick people all through there.

You violated military law?

Oh, I violated military law, yeah. I even got cases of cigarettes through the navy and gave it to the bishop there, who sold them, so he and the others could eat. Oh, I felt guilty about that. (Laughs.)

The American GIs in Europe and Japan were tremendously good people. But when we came to Sasebo, going up north to Fukuoka, we'd go through certain villages and the kids would run away. The GIs would hand out candy bars, and pretty soon the kids would come flockin' around. The same way with these medicines. The GIs helped me. This the irony of the whole thing.

In Kyushu, I met some sisters and missionaries who had come from Hiroshima. I had already visited Nagasaki and saw the ruins and talked to some of the survivors. Thousands had what they called the A-bomb sickness. This was the first time, I think, that it really began to come through to me. Here were these little kids, who didn't have anything to do with the war, and they were dying, many of them very quiet, very silent. They were just quiet, just dying. The worm started squirming.

After our hospital unit disbanded, I could have gone home. But they needed chaplains in the northern part of the island, so I signed up. In the course of the occupation, you became acquainted with the Japanese. You start seeing they're not such horrible people.

Again, that worm squirms. Hey, these were God's children. They were hungry. It may have been a carryover from that time I saw the Japanese soldier and the American soldier on the sands, equally dead. They were still clearing out the Japanese on Tinian. There were woods and hills and caves. I came across these two. I recall saying to myself, Hey, this Japanese guy, he probably came from a drug store or a farm raising rice and has a mother and father just like this

American soldier. Had I not been in the Flint parish, had I been in a rich parish, I don't know what would have happened to me.

Remember, strange things can happen if you're a conqueror. Especially if you're an officer. I was a captain then. You were just like God in a conquered country. We'd drive someplace in a jeep. You'd drive up to the railroad station and just say, "Hey, load up my jeep." You could go anyplace. A ferry going across to Sapporo. I came late. This ferry was halfway across. You just stand on deck, wave, and they'd come back. Power is hard to explain, especially for a chaplain. It's seductive. You take it for granted. They were a conquered people. You were kind, but, oh Lord, if they should ever cross you or anything.

I came back after the war and tried to talk about it, but nobody would listen. The war's over, forget it. Along comes Korea. Some of my good friends got killed. I would counsel them. Yeah, we got to defend our country. I tell this to Dick Sheridan. He went over and a week later he was dead. Now the squirming really commences. Something wasn't right here. What are we doing in Korea?

Along comes Vietnam. The mad bombings. I'm recalling Hiroshima and Nagasaki. There's Martin Luther King. I'm now with the blacks, the poor, the militants. That's when the heart attacks came. I made the mistake of taking everything on myself. I don't remember three days at all. Several times they said I was a goner. Anyway, I came through. So I'm walking.

HAJIMI KITO AND HIDEKO TAMURA (TAMMY) FRIEDMAN

They are hibakisha,* *survivors of Hiroshima. He lives in Japan. She, married to an American, lives in a suburb of Chicago. On this occasion, they have met for the first time in a Chicago radio studio.*

They are listening to the words of a young Japanese woman who is also a hibakisha. *It is a tape recording of 1960. She recalls August 6, 1945.*

---

*Hibakisha (crane)—a paper crane—is the Japanese symbol of hope and the name given survivors of the atom bomb. There are four groups of *hibakisha:* (1) people who were directly affected; (2) those who, afterwards, entered the city limits; (3) those, outside the area, who took care of those who were bombed; (4) those who were in their mother's womb.

WOMAN'S VOICE: I was looking up in the sky, trying to spot the airplane. Then I saw a big flash in the sky, so I hid my face on the ground. I remember that I must have been blown away by the impact. When I regained my consciousness, I couldn't find any of my friends. They were either blown to bits or burned. All my clothes were torn away, except my very undergarment. My skin just peeled off and was hanging from my body. I had that over my arms, legs, and face.

The heat was so intense that I jumped into the nearby river, the small river that was running through the city. All my friends were in the river—(She cries. The interpreter stops in mid-sentence and stifles a sob: "I don't think I can say it—")

KITO: (After a long pause) When I hear that young woman's voice, I immediately recall the moment thirty-seven years ago. I was there in the army at the time the bomb was dropped. I was a nineteen-year-old soldier. Young children were running toward me. I remember hearing lots of voices, elementary-school children were coming to us for rescue. What I remember most are the screams for water. There were so many people, you couldn't possibly provide water for a fraction of them. It was just an impossibility. And they did die. We had to carry these bodies and burn, cremate them in some way. Because they were corpses now. I can still hear those voices very clearly.

FRIEDMAN: I was in my home, which happened to be a very protected kind of shelter. My grandfather was an industrialist, and we lived on a huge estate with very thick walls and beams. The house did not collapse to the ground. The thick walls protected me against the effects of radiation. Although I was affected, it was not as intensely as it might have been had I lived in a smaller house.

I was eleven years old. A few days after the bomb fell, I was looking for my mother. I was going through places, amongst the people who were not getting aid. We had very, very little help. It was completely overwhelming to all the communities around. We had depleted resources to begin with.

People were barely having food to eat for themselves, and clothing. All I had were five grains of dried beans in my hand that I clutched all that day. I was well enough to be on my feet, but almost all the others I saw were laying in the spaces, in schoolyards and other public places.

I was going around from place to place, calling for my mother: "If you are here, if you are there, please answer me." I would have been devastated if someone answered, because I wouldn't have known what to do, to help. Yet, a child is desperately looking for her mother. Because I felt so helpless, I devised something in my head. A sort of magic.

I thought I would sing some lullabies that she loved singing, that she used to sing to me. I said in my head, God, I ask you now, would you sort of, like the wind, carry the tune and comfort her as if she could hear it? I remember crying and sobbing as I was singing.

There's a beach near Tokyo, Kamakura. Although we happened to be in Hiroshima at the time, we were from Tokyo. We used to walk along this beach and collect sea shells. She would sing this song. (She sings it. Mr. Kito softly joins her.)

Did you find your mother?

No, she is still listed among the missing, although my father ran into a woman who thought she knew where my mother might have fallen. My mother had to be with a group of people of the block. Neighborhood block groups were organized because there was a mass evacuation. My mother was the one of our family who had to go.

She left about seven-thirty in the morning. Where she went was very close to the center of the explosion. When the bomb exploded, this woman was not too far from her. The woman had small children, and she just bent over to protect her children. My mother, with the flash, put her hands over her ears and ran inside. Then she saw the concrete fall on my mother. This tale was told to my father about a month after the explosion. It's most likely that she died.

My father went to the place where this woman took him. He said there were a number of remains. They were so burned that it was difficult to tell which one might have been my mother. So he collected little bones from each remains and brought them home and we kind of buried that as my mother.

KITO: All my family were in the city of Nagoya, so none of them were injured by the bomb. But my friends in the army with me, there's no trace of what happened to them. I would say, from about the seventh of August, thousands of maggots would infest the wounds of the thousands of injured that I came upon. As the maggots would squirm on the surface of these injuries, it was very painful for these survivors. They would scream to us, plead with us, "Please take these maggots off our bodies." Where there are maggots from head to toe on all these bodies, it was impossible for me, one soldier, to try to help so many people.

We consulted a military doctor nearby. All the medications had been used up, there was no supply left. What should we do?

The doctor said, "This is impossible. We can't do anything." He said, "Sterilize their wounds with salt water." So we boiled water in a large pot and put in a whole jug of salt. Since the entire bodies were infected, we just used a broom. We couldn't possibly do each part of the body with our fingers. We took a broom, dipped it into the salt water, and painted over the bodies.

The children, who were lying down, unable to move, leaped up. In the local dialect, they would say, "I'm gonna run, I must run." I remember this scene very clearly.

A woman in the studio interjects: "The word Mr. Kito used is hashira. *It means 'it hurts.'" The interpreter corrects her: in the local dialect it means "thank you."*

Since I was from Nagoya, I didn't understand that dialect. I thought they were saying they had to run. So I was trying to hold them in place, to keep them still. Shortly after, they died.

Of course there were no family members of these children to take back their dead. What we did was to take the timber from the buildings nearby. We built up a funeral pyre to burn these corpses.

FRIEDMAN: I was going through these very places looking for my mother.

Something devastating happens to your system. It lasts for a prolonged period of time. You are in shock. In order for you to function, you must desensitize yourself. You may be moving automatically, with the simple instinct to survive. You do not feel as if you were in a real situation. You feel as if—I can't believe this is happening to me. As if you are looking at television, something detached, outside your feelings.

KITO: I didn't think of myself as transporting corpses when I was going through the task of cremating them. I was just carrying an object. I was thinking, Okay, today I carried x number of corpses, this is what I did today. This is how objective I felt about it. Any sense of sympathy or pathos about what happened to these human beings was just blown away somewhere. I was just doing the tasks. I needed a very long time in order to return to some sort of normal state.

Did survivors—yourselves, perhaps—ever experience guilt at having survived?

FRIEDMAN: Oh yes. I had a deep feeling of guilt, of depression about that day for a long, long time. I worked it out through hypnosis. I hypnotized myself and relived the time, the event of the Hiroshima explosion. Rather than remembering it as if I'm seeing it on the stage and hearing only loud sounds like exploding ammunition, I began to hear smaller voices and smaller sounds in the background, calling for help. That I hadn't really heard. I saw more things coming back more vividly than my actual recollection of the time. Then I was able to say that this was why I truly felt guilty. That I wasn't able to help them.

KITO: I have come to think that the people who died are calling upon us survivors not to make a meaningless waste out of their deaths. That is how I have been able to change the guilt into activity.*

POSTSCRIPT: *There is considerable discrimination in Japan against* hibakisha. *It is frequently extended toward their children as well: socially as well as economically. "Not only* hibakisha, *but their children, are refused employment," says Mr. Kito. "There are many among them who do not want it known that they are* hibakisha."

VICTOR TOLLEY

A retired postal employee. He wears a button of the Second Marine Division Association.
"I was living the all-American dream when the war broke out in 1941.

---

*Mr. Kito instituted a signature campaign to abolish nuclear weapons. He has gathered, thus far, thirty million signatures.

I had a little house with a white picket fence, a baby girl, a loving wife, and an honorable job. I was twenty-nine, very patriotic and gung ho. I joined the Marine Corps."

I'll never forget August 6, 1945. I'm standing in a chow line on Saipan at approximately eleven-thirty in the morning. On the armed services radio I heard: The President of the United States just announced that a terrible new weapon has been used on the city of Hiroshima, Japan. It'll be a hundred years before anybody will be able to enter that city. The new weapon is called the atomic bomb.

We cheered and we hollered and we grabbed each other and we jumped up and down. Maybe this damn war's gonna end and we won't have to invade Japan. We all felt that way. On August 9, they dropped another bomb on the city of Nagasaki. The armed services radio came out with the same report. It will be a hundred years before you could enter the city.

A few weeks later, we found ourselves aboard a troop transport. We laid out in the harbor for about three days. A young lieutenant said, "We're gonna occupy Nagasaki." I asked him a dumb question: "How can we occupy Nagasaki when they told us it would be a hundred years before anybody could go into that city?" He said, "Marine, you don't have anything to worry about. The scientists have gone in there. It's very safe."

On September 23, 1945, the ships pulled into the harbor of Nagasaki. The first sight I remember is the Mitsubishi factory. It looked like somebody had taken an erector set and stepped on it with both feet.

The next morning, I said to five of my buddies, "Let's get the hell off this ship and go ashore. Let's see what's in Nagasaki and what the bomb did." There's six of us, all alone, no weapons, no nothin', just tourists, walkin' up the main street in Nagasaki. It was just like walking into a tomb. There was total silence. You could smell this death all around ya. There was a terrible odor. You could feel the eyes peering at you from the buildings that were left standing. We were less than a mile from ground zero, where they dropped the bomb.

For the next three months, we lived in Nagasaki. We helped tear down the buildings. We helped clean up the rubble. About twenty thousand troops of the Second Marine Division occupied the town. We were instructed not to touch or go near any Japanese that we saw dropping in the street. We were to inform an aid station. On more than one occasion, I would see a person keel over and lay in the street.

We had no idea what it was all about. I was on the dock one day, doing duty, and here's this beautiful white ship in the harbor. On the side was painted: United States Scientific Expeditionary Force. I turned to my buddy and said, "We've been here about a week and now they send in this scientific force to check this damn city over. We'll probably be sterile." We kidded and laughed about it. We never took it seriously. Hell, we drank the water, we breathed the air, and we lived in the rubble. We did our duty.

Warren Zink was an eighteen-year-old fireman, first class, U.S. Navy. He took part in Operation Crossroads, the atomic bomb test at Bikini, during the summer of 1946. "It wasn't until years later that I realized I had become sterile. My wife and I have been married since 1950. After the first few years of our marriage, it became obvious we were unable to have any children.

"I was developing severe headaches, too. And vomiting. I have a serious respiratory problem. Muscle trouble in both my legs. Often I lose control of them. I used to be a professional blood donor. But I've ceased to give blood because I'm afraid of passing something on to an innocent person.

"Billings Hospital, which examined me, wrote me a letter when I asked for my files. They had a fire and all the records were destroyed. I had a stone the size of a walnut removed from my left kidney. I asked to have it analyzed by a laboratory in Florida, for radiation content. You won't believe this—it was lost in the mail."

At this writing, Warren Zink is seriously ill.

Irene Zink, his wife, picks up the story: "For years, I went to doctors to try to figure out why I couldn't have children. We planned a family of seven kids. We always laughed. His father had five, and we were gonna beat his dad. I went for operations and everything. We never had one. I never, never dreamed they made him sterile.

"My nieces and nephews say, 'It's too bad you never had kids. You'd make wonderful parents.' I know we would. We have an overabundance of love for children. Now it's just too late."

In the back of our minds, every one of us wondered: What is this atomic bomb? You had to be there to realize what it did. I saw young children with sores and burns all over. Miles completely wiped out. There was nothing. Just rubble.

It's a funny thing. We were twenty-four hours in Nagasaki and we made friends with these people. They were not afraid of us. We were not afraid of them. It was as if there never had been a damn war.

One day I got separated from my buddies. Here I am in a strange city. The enemy. I see a group of little Japanese children playing in the street, just like our American kids would play. I yelled at 'em and waved. They saw me, this marine. They all ran. Except one kid. I walked up to him. He couldn't understand English. I couldn't understand Japanese. But we communicated. I tried to tell him I wanted to get back to my base. He saw this bracelet my wife had sent me.

On his arm is the bracelet: Victor E. Tolley, U.S. MCR.

Inside are the pictures of my two little girls and herself. He saw it and pointed. I opened it up and he saw the pictures. His face beamed. He started to jump up and down. He pointed upstairs where he lived. He said, "Sister, sister." He motioned that she was pregnant.

This little kid ran upstairs and brought his father down. A very nice Japanese gentleman. He could speak English. He bowed and said, "We would be honored if you would come upstairs and have some tea with us." I went upstairs in this strange Japanese house. I noticed on the mantel a picture of a young Japanese soldier. I asked him, "Is this your son?" He said, "That is my daughter's husband. We don't know if he's alive. We haven't heard."

The minute he said that, it dawned on me that they suffered the same as we did. They lost sons and daughters and relatives, and they hurt too.

Until that moment . . . ?

I had nothing but contempt for the Japanese. I used to hear all the horror stories. We were trained to kill them. They're our enemy. Look what they did in Pearl Harbor. They asked for it and now we're gonna give it to 'em. That's how I felt until I met this young boy and his family. His sister came out. She bowed. She was very pregnant. I'll never forget that moment.

The kid hung on to my hand when I left. I couldn't give him the bracelet. I gave him the Asiatic Pacific ribbon we were so proud to wear. He was just so happy.

I realized that these people didn't want to fight us. What the military did and what the civilians did were two different things. In December of 1945, I came home and completely wanted to put out of my mind what I saw in Nagasaki.

It's 1979. I'm retired, living in a suburb of San Francisco. I'm thumbing through *Newsweek*, the November issue. I come across this article about a former marine who came down with a rare bone disease known as multiple myeloma cancer. He spent thirty thousand dollars, his life's savings, to fight this disease. The United States government refused any medical aid. This incensed me no end. Here was a man who fought at Bougainville, on Iwo Jima. He was right near the guys who raised the flag on Suribachi. He was one of the advance scouts sent into Nagasaki. He got terribly sick. He always felt it was radiation poisoning. He was a house painter. You gotta paint a hell of a lot of houses to save thirty thousand dollars. He spent it all on his illness, and the government refused him.

He joined a new organization, the Committee for Hiroshima-Nagasaki Veterans. The members exchanged information and discovered that an inordinate number of them were coming down with cancer, leukemia, multiple myeloma, and other rare blood diseases. A larger group, the National Association of Atomic Veterans, was formed. "From that moment on, I became totally dedicated to their cause. I had found my niche in life. If I was put on earth for one thing, I guess that was it."

I may be carrying a touch of radiation myself. If a person picks up one rem it can linger in your cells all your life. It may lay dormant and nothing may happen to me. But when I die and I'm cremated and my ashes are scattered out over some forest, that radiation is still alive. Twenty-seven thousand years from now, somebody might pick up that rem of radiation from those ashes of mine and come down sick.

I believed in my government. Whatever Roosevelt said, by God— and he was God—we believed it. When I was in the Marine Corps, I was totally dedicated. They gave me a rifle and when they said go forward and kill that enemy or be killed, you did it. You didn't question it, 'cause you're doing it for your country. Now I'm sixty-eight years of age and I've had a chance to reflect back on my life.

I've had a chance to sit down and do a lot of reading and a lot of studying. Now, I question. I question my government and I think every American should. I don't think that any individual can say Mom, apple pie, and the President of the United States is it and stop thinking. Whatever the government says is not always right.

Caspar Weinberger and I went to high school together. I sat right next to him for four years. We were friends and we've corresponded. But I can no longer believe in Cap Weinberger and what he stands for. I don't give a damn what Cap or the President or what anybody says, I have to think for myself. And I saw what I saw.

We didn't drop those two on military installations. We dropped them on women and children. The very minute I was jumping up and down and hugging my buddy and was so elated, there was a little baby layin' out in the street charred and burned and didn't have a chance to live. There was seventy-five thousand human beings that lived and breathed and ate and wanted to live that were in an instant charred. I think that is something this country is going to have to live with for eternity.

JOHN SMITHERMAN

In earlier testing years, particularly in the North Pacific region of the Marshall Islands, military participants were required to sign agreements, in which they promised not to discuss their mission. Violators were subjected to a $10,000 fine and/or a ten-year prison sentence. It was not uncommon for armed personnel to be present during the signing. One of the participants recalls being warned that if he violated the agreement, he would never live to see the world outside Leavenworth. Fearing retaliation, men went to their graves without revealing even to their families that they had participated in nuclear arms weapons tests.

—*Thomas H. Saffer and Orville E. Kelly,*
Countdown Zero

Mulberry, Tennessee, eighty-five miles out of Nashville. It is an old two-story house. A dog barks as you enter. Your host calls from within.

You immediately see a large, handsome face. Simultaneously, you see that he is legless. It is his left hand, resting on the arm of his automated wheelchair, that draws your reluctant attention. It is at least five times normal size; roughly ridged, corrugated, grayish; it resembles an elephant's trunk.

He is president of the National Association of Atomic Veterans. "About fifteen thousand strong. They were at various test sights. There was forty-two thousand veterans that participated in Operation Crossroads; twenty-seven thousand of 'em are dead."

In one corner is an old grandfather's clock; the chimes are on the half-hour. On a small end table is a photograph: a husky, muscular young man—an athlete, perhaps? He's a cross between a young Jack Dempsey and Robert Mitchum. It is our host, a number of years ago.

His voice is astonishingly gentle. "This is Jack Daniel's territory. Did you get to see it?

"I was a farmer. I was born and raised on the eastern tip of Tennessee, in the Cumberlands. My father was a coal miner for forty-some years."

Bein' a youngster, seventeen years old, I went into the navy. On my birthday in July of 1945. And spent some of my happy days in the navy. I'm fifty-five, as of yesterday.

I enlisted in Norfolk, Virginia. The last of July, why, I was shipped out on the aircraft carrier U.S.S. *Randall.* We were on our way to England and was hit by a mine. We were transferred onto a destroyer and came through the canal and went to California. We were headed for Japan, when the war was over. We went through two little minor battles in the Philippines, which was nothin' major. We came back to Pearl Harbor and on back to the States. Then we got word that we was goin' back on another test.

The big news at that time was everybody was talkin' about the big bombs that they had dropped on Japan. Nobody knew anything about the big bombs, the two of 'em. For that reason, they told us we'd go back. We would probably be involved in two of 'em. The code name of that was called Operation Crossroads. That was in the Marshall Islands and the Bikini atoll. That was the only word that we received. We had no idea. Not only myself, but the rest of the young men that was on board. It was a destroyer called U.S.S. *Alan M. Sumner.* We were advised there would be nothin' harmful. Just a lot of excitement and have a lot of fun.

Who said it?

The PA system on the ship. Oh yeah, I remember that. I remember also when we got there, before the actual bomb testing, we had to sign what they call a loyalty oath. That oath was not to disclose or talk about any of the explosion of the bomb or any of what we saw on the island. If we had, why, of course, that could mean time spent at Leavenworth or a huge fine. That kind of scared young fellas like myself to death.

After that, why, on July 1, 1946, the first bomb was dropped from an aircraft. We had been in the bay, runnin' around, and early that morning we went to our flagship, the U.S.S. *Mount McKinley.* That's where all the brass were. Also the scientists were on board this ship. We were circlin' around *Mount McKinley* when the bomb exploded.

Mount McKinley was nine miles away. We were just three miles away from *Mount McKinley.* So we coulda been six miles or we coulda been twelve miles from the blast.

We were standin' in shorts. I had a T-shirt on, just like this. I had a little sailor hat on and tennis shoes. The brass on the *Mount McKinley,* they stayed undercover the whole time. They wore heavy clothing all the time. They were protected all the time. They told us it would be a huge bomb, so all us little ol' mountain boys on the ship, we were lookin' for this big monstrous bomb to fall. All of a sudden we saw this huge ball of fire come from the bottom and go up. I don't know how to describe this ball of fire. We felt the heat, we felt the shock wave. We rode out a way from it.

Within ten hours, we were right back at ground zero. And passing by the target ships. The paint had been peeled completely off. Some of the guns were split in the middle and peeled back. Big holes in the bulkheads, and there was a fire on the U.S.S. *Independence.* There were seventy-five target ships.

I was on the topside and they asked for a couple of volunteers to go on the *Independence* to fight the fire. We went on board and we fought fire for one hour on and two hours off. Maybe sixty, seventy guys.

Did they say anything about it being dangerous?

Nah, no. They wanted to make sure the fire was out, because they wanted to check the animals that they had on board. I fought fire for three hours. We went back on the LST while we had came to what they call a checkpoint. A scientist was there with Geiger counters, checkin' us as we come by, if we picked up any radiation.

Did the scientists say anything?

Oh no. We didn't know what they was checkin' us for. Had no idea. They never did tell us. During those few days, we were allowed to walk around, swim. We were drinkin' the water that came through the distilleries aboard the ship. Washing our clothes in it. After we got back on the *Sumner,* we drank water that came from the lagoon there. We swam. We had no restrictions whatsoever. Nothing was ever said to us at all.

I was one of the guys on Bikini that was helping them bring down the cameras from the towers. The tower was steel and it was hot from the sun hittin' it. I didn't know that radiation would hang around steel like that. I had no knowledge. In fact, radiation was never mentioned the whole time we were there.

On July 25, we were told they were gonna detonate another bomb. This was planted ninety feet under the water. We made it out to the *Mount McKinley* and started circlin'. We saw the bomb go off. The code name was Baker. Now that was larger. When this bomb went off, it had a sort of vacuum to it. It looked just like a mushroom starting from the ocean. It just went right up into the air pullin' sand, water, and debris from the ocean. And that formed a huge cloud above us. We were caught in the downwind of that, and the spray from that came aboard our ship. We had to be washed down because of it.

The scientists came aboard with their Geiger counters. We still didn't know what they were doin'. In ten hours, we were right back again on ground zero. There was a lot of confusion going on. There's a bunch of guys got caught goin' swimmin' the second day and they were punished for it. But again, there was no restrictions for us. We had a lot of fun over there, we really did. We didn't think of anything wrong.

Along about the last of August, I discovered some red burns about the size of a silver dollar, five or six of 'em, on both feet and legs. I went to first aid, and they put a white salve on with a tongue depresser, and put a little piece of gauze on every one of 'em, and they give me bed rest. That disappeared. About a week later, both feet and legs begin to swell. They give me bed rest again. And that went away. But it kept comin' back on me, while I was aboard ship. I was still unable to wear my shoes, because of the swelling of feet and legs.

We came back to Pearl Harbor, sometime the last of November. I was admitted to the hospital. They started running further tests on me and said I had kidney problems. They transferred me to California; that was in 1947. I was given a medical discharge.

They told me to go home, and if the swelling continues, just get in bed and elevate my feet and legs until the swelling goes down. But the swelling continued to get a little worse each time. It would come up on my leg a little further. Until they got so severe, why, I was admitted to the VA hospital in '76.

In March of '77, they removed my left leg because it had bursted open so many places that it was so painful. One month later, after being discharged, I was admitted to the hospital with a swelling of the right leg. In August of '77, my right leg had bursted open from the knee down to the anklebone. Then it had to be removed. Immediately before I left the hospital, my left arm began to swell on me.

Within the last two years, they've been tryin' to get me to come up and have my left arm amputated. The last six, seven months, I've been ill all over again. Comin' back from Washington, D.C., in March, I tried to go to the VA hospital to see a doctor. They refused to admit me or refused to allow me to see a doctor. Because I wasn't there on a scheduled appointment.

I entered a private hospital down here. After bein' operated on twice emergency surgery here, within thirty days apart, they found cancer of the colon and liver, and it's terminal. Meantime, I've been fighting with the Veterans Administration to gain service connection out of this whole thing. They have turned me down for the sixth time.

They admit that I was exposed to radiation while over there, but not enough to have created my problem. Their one doctor said it was impossible for me to have been exposed to enough radiation to cause my problem. Three doctors on my behalf said I was exposed to anywhere from a thousand to 1,800 rads. Their doctor from Stanford University said that the swelling I had in the service was not the same swelling I had today.

I'm not angry about it. I forgive 'em. But I don't understand why they didn't find the cancer in me. Cancer doesn't come on ya just overnight. I had really lot of faith there for a while in the veterans' hospital. But they treat you up there like you're one of two: you're either an alcoholic or a drug addict. I don't drink alcohol. I'm what you call a good Christian man. I know I haven't been all my life, but nevertheless, I haven't drank in the last fifteen years. I have been in the VA hospital since 1975, if they would have found cancer on me at that time, I could have probably had a few days more to stay on this ol' earth.

No, I'm not bitter. I'm proud of the way we live. I'm proud of our Constitution, and I'd fight for that any day. If they called me tomorrow, I would go and fight. That's not my point. My point is the Veterans Administration promised all the veterans that they would be taken care of if they became ill or down and out.

The doctors in veterans' hospitals are overworked, underpaid, and they have such a bitter attitude against the government if you talk to them privately. You can't condemn the doctors. I feel they will do what they can. But they're not going to overdo. There you're a number. Or again, you're either a drug addict or an alcoholic.

I fault the Veterans Administration and Congress. Congress hasn't bothered to change the law since 1946. 'Cause I don't know if they're afraid to get into a bucket of worms that would create other problems. All the atomic veterans want is a little treatment for ones that are sick, a little justice.

I draw what they call a nonservice connection disability of five dollars a month.

Five dollars a month?

The reason is 'cause my wife works and she makes over the maximum of $4,800 a year.

The loss of your two legs is not service-connected?

That's a fact. Now they want my left arm removed because it was swollen five times larger than it is now. It was heavy, awful heavy. And it was distorted, so ungodly lookin'. Now I'm watchin' it very close, afraid that gangrene is settin' in, because I'm losin' a lot of weight. I've lost eighty pounds in that last deal. I was a big husky young fella, barrel-chested. Six foot even, 225 pounds. Now I weigh 123 pounds.

When they turned me down from gettin' into Bethesda, the Japanese people heard about this. I received a letter from a doctor in Japan stating that if I could find my way over there, they would treat me the best they could and the best they knew how. The newspapers locally here and the radio station got ahold of that. They started a collection: We're gonna send John Smitherman to Japan. The people of Lincoln and Moore counties did their best in sendin' in donations. They ended up with about $8,200.

On July 28 of '82, I flew to San Francisco and met with a lady doctor from the radiation research center. They had raised enough money on the California side to send her along with me and learn some of their methods of treatments. I stayed over there for thirty-one days and got, oh, a total of twenty-two treatments.

I was called a *hibakisha* while I was there. In Japan, a *hibakisha* is a survivor of the bomb. I met many of the *hibakisha* while I was there. They were laying in various types of beds. Some of 'em similar to my condition, some of 'em with severe burns, some of 'em blind. Some of 'em half the body was gone, but they was still maintainin' life.

The *hibakisha* were so kind to me. The ones that could stand, they stood. The ones that could set up, they did. And the ones that could raise their hands and wave at me, they did. The others just laid there in the bed and looked at me. It was a real choking, breathtaking situation. And made me proud to line up.

I don't believe the President of the United States could have been treated any better than I was while I was there. People would see me comin' down the street, they would run across just to touch me. There were several honors bestowed on me when I was there. But the big honor was that I was the first American veteran to go to Japan and receive treatments. They had a boat called the *Lucky Dragon,* that some of the sailors was caught in the downwind of that and they died. All the fish they had on board were highly exposed. They had me sign the ship's log and makin' me an honorary seaman of that boat. The mayor of Hiroshima allowed me some forty-seven minutes, an interview.

Back home, even the governor of this state of Tennessee hasn't recognized me. It is difficult to understand why we would have to go to the very country that we tried to destroy and receive those type of benefits without havin' any animosity at all thrown against me, none.

I took the same kind of treatment they were takin'. When I came back from Japan, the doctors over there told me it would be shameful if I weren't allowed to continue those treatments over here. Because if I waited six months after that, the treatments I received over there wouldn't do me any good. After comin' back, they tried to get me into several hospitals for this treatment, UCLA, Mayo Clinic. But the government would not allow that, because if I was admitted and treated in this country for radiation exposure, I'd win my case. It would be an admission of liability.

Part of that problem is due to a gentleman whose name is Taft. In his statement before Congress that passed Public Law Bill 9572, which helps Vietnam veterans, there was an amendment tacked on that would help the atomic veterans. He said it would be a detriment to our overseas operations. If they caught wind of it over there, they would have to remove all their nuclear missiles.

I'm not bitter at the government. I volunteered because I wanted to be a proud sailor. But at the same time, I'm angry because they should have advised us of the hazards. I'm proud of our government. I'm proud of the freedom we have. I'm proud of the people. You can go to a church of your choosin'. You have so many rights. I can drive the automobile without gettin' permission. I'm just proud of our society, and I would fight every day to protect that society. I have two girls and I have two grandchildren. I would certainly protect their rights, like my forefathers fought to protect mine. Regardless of what they're doin' to us now.

In the last four, five months, we've found definite proof that was hidden in the vault of a library of one of the Los Angeles branches, of the men that were in Operation Crossroads. The scientists that were there stated there's gonna be a lot of repercussions from the men involved in this testing. We submitted this to a judiciary committee in Washington, and it didn't get any publicity whatsoever.

Those men that did get exposed to radiation, it was just as if the enemy had pointed at you point blank and shot you with a gun. Our injuries didn't show up until thirty, forty years later. It is now hard for me to go back and say, Uncle Sam, hey, you did me wrong as a kid by exposin' me to all that radiation. It's settled in my body and been in my body all this time. See, I had a chromosome test in Japan. The blood cells, they found it. Why don't they run chromosome tests here in the United States on the atomic veterans?

I've written to the President. I've never gotten a reply from him, because he always throws it back to the veterans' office. The veterans' office says: Let's throw it back to the local Veterans Administration.

The Bible teaches you not to be bitter. It also says to turn the other cheek. I thought several times before turnin' that other cheek. Was I wrong, too? I did a lot of soul-searching. I don't believe that I was wrong. I did what I was told to do while I was in the service. My record reflects that. You won't find a blemish on my record, as far as having court-martials or gettin' out of order in any way.

I've been a little country boy from the mountains. When my Uncle Sam told me to do something, I did it. I signed the loyalty oath, yes sir. We never did mention any of this. When I came back, I didn't even tell my wife. I didn't tell my mother about it. But when I started havin' the problems, I said to myself, What could he do to me now that he hasn't already done? So I let it all come out. I feel that Uncle Sam has a duty to protect the veterans.

If my dog that you saw comin' barkin' at you when you came into the house would have bitten you, I would have an obligation to take care of ya. I, for a fact, knew that my dog wouldn't bite you. But if he had, I woulda had an obligation. Now, if Uncle Sam has this monster locked up and he gets out and he harms people, why shouldn't they have the same obligation? I'm not immune to it, but they are.

They knew their dog would bite?

Oh yes. No questions. The very first bomb they tested was in New Mexico in 1945. It was on July 16. That bomb was so wild, they really didn't know what they exploded. Here again just one month later, they detonated two more bombs. Those bombs that destroyed two cities didn't destroy any military installations, but old men, women, and children. Then seven, eight months later, without getting too much data, went right in and detonated two more. They didn't even have the proper equipment to gauge the beta or the alpha radiation that I was exposed to. These tests were certainly not on behalf of any of the men involved. I feel personally we were all used as guinea pigs.

He indicates a painting on the far wall. "You'll notice the picture hangin' above the television there. You see who it's signed by? My wife did that." A proud husband.

A small gold statuette is on the mantelpiece. It is young John Smither-

man, snappy, standing with his legs crossed. Below, the inscription: "My first solo flight, September 9, 1965."

I'm proud to have met my wife and taken her on as a partner. I'm proud to be livin' here in this old 1820 home. I'm proud of the fact that the doors are wide and I can get from room to room in my wheelchair. I'm awfully proud to see her walk in that door. And I'm proud that I can wake up each morning that I have been and smile and get the same smile from her. But when I'm gone, then what will she do? For that reason, with every ounce and up to the very last breath I draw in my body, I will be fightin' to try to overturn what they're doin' to me and the other veterans out there that's in far greater pain than I am. If Uncle Sam don't pick up and give my wife and all the other wives some benefits before I leave this ol' earth, I think that the whole majority will have sinned so much that they will answer some of these days to somebody a little higher.

John Smitherman died on September 11, 1983.

JOSEPH STASIAK

Michigan City, Indiana, is its name; making steel is its game. Row upon row of frame bungalows tell the story: a second- and third-generation working-class community.

He had worked at U.S. Steel. "Oh, I was in pretty good shape. I could handle those wheels, they weigh eight hundred, a thousand pounds. I used to play with those wheels like you'd take a silver dollar and spin 'em. My doctor attributes my stamina, that pulled me through, to the work with these wheels."

His son, Adrian, a large, gentle man built along his father's lines, is singularly solicitous of the sick man's welfare. Joe sits in a specially upholstered easy chair. He appears to be in constant discomfort.

"Right now, I'm just fighting for my life. I had hoped to work until I was sixty-five and get that watch. Every time I go to see my doctor, he wants to put me in the hospital." He describes himself as "a medical oddity": enlarged liver; "something else called hemopneumothorax"; heart and lungs "ballooning. I was like a caricature of Quasimodo. I wished I was dead lotta times."

No one ever thought of radiation. That was one of the best-kept secrets of the war. The doctor says, "Joe, you ever work around radiation?" I says, "No, but I was in Hiroshima right after when the bomb went off and stayed there for quite a time." He says, "That could very well be it."

On V-E Day, May 8, 1945, he was on a ship crossing the Pacific as a member of the Forty-first Infantry Division. On Leyte, "this Japanese had come into my tent, rummaging underneath the cot for food or weapon, I went right on over him. I'm tight as a bowstring. I throttled him. He died. I didn't know I did it till after. I became a light sleeper after that."

On central Mindanao, he used a flamethrower in mopping-up operations on the caves. "I had more than once drilled in my head, 'I don't want you takin' prisoners.' It was told to us that it takes two men to watch one and we ain't got time for that. We gotta win a war."

We landed in Kure, eight, nine miles from Hiroshima, October 6, exactly two months after the bomb. The place is all full of nothin' but vermin. You could see 'em hoppin' all over. We hadda set everything on fire. And this odor—boy, I can still smell it. Not a word about contamination or anything. It was quiet as a mouse. We wouldn't have the foggiest notion that Hiroshima was just next door. The only thing I ever heard was, don't drink the water.

I was there about four days. Here comes this sergeant and he says, "Guard duty." They took me towards Hiroshima. They just let me out, all alone out there: "This is your post." I start walkin' around and all I'm doin' is slippin' and slidin'. These objects under my feet—when daylight come, I could make them out: money. The whole area was deep with copper coins. I was guarding a smelter.

When the Japanese sacked the islands—Sumatra, Borneo—they confiscated all their coinage for the copper content. This place I was at was nothin' but coins. When the bomb went off, this money went naturally all over. The Japanese were melting it for their war effort.

So daylight comes and I'm sitting there and you don't see nothin'. Not a bird, not a sound, nothing. Here I am with all this money and everything. And nothing.

I was there for five days all by myself. Night and day and night again. I was a sitting duck, a patsy. All these rats were gettin' me. I got up on a ledge where some machinery used to be, to get out away from the rats. I was right in the rubble. In that rubble is arms and legs and torsos. The smell of death all over. The place was full of these former people.

I'm up on that ledge. Everything is a haze, I'm out of it. I open my eyes, and standin' in front of me is this man. A walkin' balloon, this Japanese. He's lookin' right at me. I'll never forget. His fingers, it was like giant rubber gloves. Swollen like a balloon. I was gonna shoot him, but he makes these motions like he don't mean any harm to me. He starts to get some words out: "Friend, friend." He spoke a little English. But everything is so swollen, it's hard to make out what he said. I come off that ledge and found out he was a photographer.

He wanted to be by me, 'cause he was like an outcast. He just sat with me for a few hours. You hate 'em and everything, but at the same time you look at humanity like that . . . He kept saying, "You see, you see, you see." I kept lookin' at him. I realized he wanted to show me somethin'. So we make our way through the rubble and we go, we musta gone maybe six or seven blocks. I'm thinkin' to myself, Here I left my post to go with this man. Smoke and drizzle everywhere. Around the corner of this rubble is a crematorium. Bodies and rats. Guys would take 'em and make big pyres out of 'em and burn 'em up. They had these bodies in a cage, and they'd pull a string and it would open up and you'd see 'em all tumblin' down in this big blaze.

All of a sudden, one of these fellas seen us standing there and there comes this screaming in Japanese. I cut loose with a couple of shots over their heads and they fell back. They were comin' toward this man for bringin' me here. They were very, very ashamed. He wanted me to see what the bomb had wrought. But they, I guess, wanted to keep that hidden. This was like a tremendous humiliation.

I took him by the sleeve and we go back to my post and he stayed with me. He never stayed at night. He always went away. I give him a couple of cans that, luckily, I had. He was grateful. He always wanted water. I wouldn't give him mine. I couldn't. I didn't have enough. 'Cause I was there five days by myself. They never did come and get me.

Daylight came and I'm lookin' for this guy. I think his name was Akira or somethin' like that. I was lookin' for him and lookin' for him and he ain't here. I'm gettin' lonesome, too. I'm missin' this Japanese balloon man. Like he's my friend. I go through some rubble and I see some feet stickin' out. It was Akira. I think those fellas came during the night and they killed him. I said, I'm not gonna stay here. So I start walkin'.

I'm walkin' and walkin' and walkin'. I don't even know what I'm doin'. I coulda been walkin' in circles. Hours and hours. I didn't see nobody or nothin'. I had malaria, which I picked up on the islands. Out of nowhere a jeep comes along. They didn't nobody say nothin'. And they take me to some place. I don't even remember.

He remembers being treated and then reassigned to a work detail, supervising Japanese workmen in dumping toxic chemicals into the sea. "That didn't do no good because the current washed it back on the shore."

He was eventually given a kitchen assignment. "They make me the big honcho. Can you imagine me in charge of things? (Laughs.) I gave everything away. I made it so they cooked more and all the leftovers—the Japanese lined up by the fence with their empty tin cans—"(He cries.)

Before I left Japan to come back home, they examined me and hustled me through. I was discharged and that was it. Never a word about radiation when they sent me out there on guard duty. I noticed one thing. It shoulda rung a bell. We even laughed about it. Every Japanese was goin' around with a white face mask. And we didn't. When I got back, my abdomen ballooned from here to there. My left testicle was always as big as this case. My doctor tried to get me in a VA hospital, and they said I have to wait because it's not service-connected.

A Jap I met, when I told him I was in Hiroshima, he said, "The only chance you got is just stay in the water all the time." I've been livin' there. I put in five, six hours a day in that tub. It's the only thing that keeps me going.

Of course, I've got a souvenir of my stay in Japan. A bag of these coins. (He hands me a heavy coin with strange markings.)

POSTSCRIPT: *He shows me a photograph—which the Japanese balloon man may have taken. It is a crematorium. There are bodies and bodies. It is as though it were Auschwitz. Bodies like cordwood.*

REMEMBRANCE OF
THINGS PAST

NANCY ARNOT HARJAN

She is a native San Franciscan; she lives in Menlo Park, thirty miles to the south. She was thirteen when World War Two began and seventeen when it was over, "and very impressionable."

We had in our employ a beautiful Japanese woman named Mae. The edict came that all Japanese in California be sent to relocation camps. We didn't speak about it until one morning Mae brought it up herself. It was spring 1942. I was upstairs, overhearing the conversation. I heard their voices rising, my mother's and Mae's. It frightened me. She said, "Mrs. Arnot, it's really a concentration camp I'm going to." My mother was caught in a bind. She did know that it was wrong. "It's for your own good," she said, "for your own protection" Mae was saying, "Ah ha, I thought you had to be protected from us. Now you're telling me I have to be protected from you." I was so blown away by that as a fourteen-year-old, an idealistic teen-ager.

Mae started to cry. I remember my mother's voice, rising and crying. She seldom did that and it distressed me. So I stayed upstairs. Mae was bitter. She had been saving her money to go to school. She was beginning to think things were getting better for the Japanese.

When she did leave, everybody put on a brave front. We said goodbye and wished her well. I wanted to get away as soon as possible. I ran upstairs to my room. I don't know what happened to her. We never saw her again.

We had another person in our employ, a gardener. He was an Austrian Jew who had escaped from a Nazi concentration camp. He came to this country in 1941. He writes his story, twenty, thirty pages of what happened to him and his family. My mom handed Albert's little portfolio to me. She said, "Nan, read this, because there's a lot of Americans who hear but do not believe what is happening in Nazi

Germany. This is living proof." Losing his whole family. It almost makes you go crazy if you try to comprehend the human cruelty and barbarism. Especially if you are fourteen and have been treated kindly all your life.

We were a very comfortable, privileged family. White Anglo-Saxon Protestant. My father was a successful physician. He was a kind of groovy conservative Republican. Very magnanimous on a one-to-one level, but very naive politically. Did not like Roosevelt and the New Deal. Hated Roosevelt.

I remember the summer of '42. We'd go away to our little cabin in Marin County. My grandmother's cabin. I was becoming conscious of who I was and was asking for the first time, What is the meaning of life? My own answers were, beauty, truth, and goodness. Two days later, I'd be asking, Why suffering? I knew that the Jews were suffering in Germany and I could not reconcile that to my personal happiness.

Some of my schoolmates were anti-Semitic and played down what was happening in Nazi Germany. We were all very patriotic. The girls at this private school and I would knit all kinds of scarves and caps for the boys in the service. We'd go down to the USO and bring sailors home for dinner. (Laughs.) I donated blood at the age of seventeen. I was underage but patriotic. I was delighted to give my blood. It didn't hurt and I was so proud of myself. (Laughs.)

Before the war was over, I went down to the WACs and tried to enlist. They were very nice, but they wouldn't take me. I really wanted to be a woman in uniform and support this terrible war and overcome evil with good. America represented nothing but good to me. Our boys were good. They weren't trained to be malicious killers. We took *Life* and *Look*. Everything seemed so right and good, I even liked Bob Hope.

We saw many war films that showed our boys fighting the Japanese and pictured the Japanese military as utter brutes. I bought all that. But I couldn't hate Mae. We loved her. Yet I felt this detachment. We knew that people of German descent were not being picked up.

I do remember V-E Day. Oh, such a joyous thing! It was in early May. It was my younger brother's birthday and my older brother would most likely be coming home. And San Francisco was chosen for the first session of the UN. I was ecstatic. Stalin, Churchill, and Roosevelt met, and somehow war never again would happen.

Hiroshima hadn't happened yet. They met in June of '45 at the

War Memorial Opera House. They needed ushers, so I signed up to do that. I was still in my little Miss Burke School uniform. Little middy and skirt. I remember ushering as Jan Smuts of South Africa was taking the stand. I couldn't hear that very well. But I was thrilled to be there. I was excited. I was part of it. And so deeply proud.

My dad, my younger brother and I, and my mother went to the Sierras for a two-week vacation. In the middle of it came August 6, the bombing of Hiroshima. The war was over. This wonderful new bomb had ended it all. I remember my father organizing everybody in camp, he was so happy the war was over. He had everybody dancing the Virginia Reel. He was up there clappin' his hands. I was just so proud of him.

Within a week or two, bit by bit, it sank in. Seventy thousand or a hundred thousand or two hundred thousand civilians? It came as a shock after seeing so many war movies with the Japanese portrayed as militaristic brutes. To see women, children, and old innocent civilians brutally burned. And Nagasaki! Two of them?

As the war came to an end, I was totally blown away by how quickly our former enemies became our friends and how quickly our former friends became our enemies. I couldn't understand that. I began to ask, What was it all about?

Since the end of World War Two, I've really had all kinds of questions. I feel let down and disillusioned. I never heard much anti-Soviet talk during the war. My parents may have had some friends who wondered about, ha-ha, these communist allies of ours. But I don't think anyone suggested we were fighting on the wrong side.

I used to argue with my parents. (Laughs.) My father maintained his conservative stance throughout. He would react emotionally. My mother was more reasonable. She would just put her foot on my foot under the dinner table and say, "Bring it to a halt." Then she, my older brother, and I would go talk. It's hard to keep contradicting one's own parents, but during the Vietnam War years my mother certainly came around.

When I was that young girl, I saw on the news films the Parisian people, with tears streaming down their faces, welcoming our GIs. They were doing what I wanted them to do. When the Holocaust survivors came out, I felt we were liberating them. When the GIs and the Russian soldiers met, they were all knights in shining armor, saving humanity. (Laughs.) I believed in that. It's not that simple. It's true, nazism is evil. But nazism is not totally gone. We still have the seeds of all these evils here.

World War Two was just an innocent time in America. I was innocent. My parents were innocent. The country was innocent. Since World War Two, I think I have a more objective view of what this country really is.

PAUL EDWARDS

During the New Deal years, he had been a director of the National Youth Administration in South Dakota. "The Depression was a great shaping force in my life. Then—bang!—World War Two was the other." When I first met him, he was director of information for UNICEF. He has since retired.

I was living in Winner, a little South Dakota cowtown, a rootin', tootin' cowtown (laughs) west of the Missouri River. We'd just spent Saturday night in a pretty rugged fashion, drinking and carousing a bit. So I got up late Sunday. I had a headache. A friend came in and said, "Turn on the radio. The Japanese have bombed Pearl Harbor."

That fall I had been named head of the Junior Red Cross for the county. On December 8, I went down to St. Louis and signed up as a field director for the American Red Cross. I was immediately sent to Fort Riley, Kansas, with the assimilated rank of lieutenant. The Eighth and Ninth Cavalry were stationed there, totally black. The officers were all white. They had been for years a showpiece for parades. They were great horsemen. They were great drill. They were a lot of old-time sergeants with hash marks from here to there, up their arms. They had built a morale of their own. They had pride. Boy, you put those old sergeants out in front of a troop of guys on black horses or bays, you put them on parade grounds, it gave you a thrill. It gave them a thrill.

They had been drafted out of the poorest families of the Midwest. Most of them sent fifteen of their twenty-one dollars a month to their families back home on welfare. They used to pay twenty-one silver dollars. There was this big husky black leanin' up against the wall. He'd drop the silver dollars like a gambler and they'd go clink, clink,

clink. He said, "Man, I'm well off. Hear that money clinkin' in my pocket?" He never had that much money.

Most of the draft boards were composed of men from Main Street across America. They were quite punitive towards the welfare crowd. Volunteerism was not yet in effect. This was before December 7. Most of these kids expected to be let out after a year of the draft. A lot of 'em had plans. All of a sudden they were thrown up against the reality of total war. We had a problem with suicides. Guards were put out at night. They would not issue ammunition. I watched the transition from peace to war.

The role of the Red Cross was peculiar. You were neither man, beast, nor fowl. You were with the army but not of it. You were under military control, but you didn't enjoy the privileges of being an officer among officers. Your assignment often put you up against the army with regard to the individual man. The command didn't like a challenge to their control. You bunked with 'em, you ate with 'em, so this tension made the job difficult.

Things moved fast with the expansion of the army. I wound up at Fort Meade in Sturgis, South Dakota, near home. That's the old Seventh Cavalry headquarters. Custer's. Thousands and thousands of horses were raised at these remount stations, Nebraska, elsewhere. All of a sudden, they weren't needed: the transition to the jeep, the scout cars. The romanticism of the cavalry was still very strong. Officers hated giving it up. I remember old Colonel Hooker at the Nebraska remount station. He pounded the table when the Japanese had sunk two British warships off the coast of Singapore: "I know that country down there. Goddamn it, they'll never take a square foot of it until they get our men down there on horses and donkeys." (Laughs.) There was a lot of resentment as we moved from one era into another, from horse to motor.

All of a sudden, I was sent down to Camp Barkley, Texas. The needs of the soldiers were rooted in the Depression. You jerk a young man out of his family. Next thing you know his father dies. Who'll support the family? He's just been married, his wife dies, he's left with a child. You had the business of AWOL and family circumstances. A black kid at Fort Riley came to me with a telegram. It said, "Daddy died last night. Come home at once. Bring an overcoat." The simple need: bring an overcoat.

It was a segregated army at that time. There were hundreds of labor battalions that were totally black, still under white officers.

They were an abysmal shame to the nation, if the facts were known. They were held to a work schedule, a seven-day week. They were almost imprisoned. It was cold, it was mud, it rained. Here they were pouring concrete bases for the Eighth Air Force. It was hell to pour concrete runways in the downpours. And no leave, no nothing. At that time, there wasn't one black field director of the Red Cross.

Camp Barkley was just outside Abilene. It was a righteous Baptist town, still had prohibition. We had forty thousand troops around this little town of thirty thousand. That made for prejudice against the soldiers. They were patriotic towns, but my God, look at our restaurants, we don't get in. Look at our girls, they're bein' insulted. It was hard to get quarters off the base. Once I rented a converted chicken coop. Yet the town drowned in money.

There was an alliance between the Baptists and the taxi drivers that kept the town dry. The hotel keepers wanted to open it up, but you'd find a lot of Baptist money and cabdrivers boostin' prohibition. 'Cause the drivers were sellin' us booze at five dollars a pint. (Laughs.) The righteous and the unclean. (Laughs.) Of course, they weren't crazy about blacks. I remember a little black singer who came out to entertain the troops. Here were about ten thousand guys, and this little girl worked that show like you wouldn't believe. She ended gettin' them all to clap and sing in a state of ecstasy, almost. She couldn't get a room in a hotel that night. We had to find her quarters.

Out of nowhere, I get a call to Dallas. They need a supervisor in Great Britain immediately. To a country boy from South Dakota, that's reachin' for the moon.

I left for the U.K. on December 7, 1942, the anniversary of Pearl Harbor. We were all rounded up and put on the *Queen Mary*. A whole division. There must've been fifteen thousand people on that ship. This was a time of high secrecy. How the hell you keep the movements of the *Queen Mary* a secret is a good trick. (Laughs.) But you still went around and played spook.

We had a violent crossing. The *Queen Mary* tipped to forty-two degrees and she was supposed only capable of leaning to forty degrees. A big wave hit us and brought us back up. We hotbedded, half down and half up, during the night and day. We had two meals a day, largely of boiled English fish. Everybody was so sick, it didn't make any difference.

We had a remarkable storm one awful night. The portholes were smashed and the sea was coming in on us. There was almost a riot as people rushed for the gangway and the MPs stood there with pistols: "Get back down! Get back down!" The lifeboats had broken loose from their moorings and they came in against the side of the boat. The crash had broken the portholes. We made it to Glasgow.

The Red Cross has a split personality. When the war broke out, the leadership was extremely conservative. It depended on rich donors. The orientation was very upper-class, snobbish. There was a marked difference between these volunteers and the staff. Eventually the pro staff took over because of the dimensions of our chores.

You'll hear those who damn and those who praise the Red Cross. The leadership was loaded with prejudice—to blacks, to Jews. When I first went in, there were hardly any Jews. A gentlemen's agreement. You didn't talk about it. I remember when the first Jewish field directors arrived. Odd, when you think we were fighting Hitler.

Until we were well into the war, they segregated the blood plasma of the blacks from the whites. I must say the Red Cross was the mover and shaker and changer, because not only was there no scientific sense to it, the economics was bad. There was always that double dilemma. There were no black field directors. Many towns were off-limits to black troops. They wouldn't let whites go into others. We had black and white towns. Many racial incidents developed and the Red Cross found itself in the middle. Historically, we came down on the right side.

I'll never forget the first black guy I got as a field director in England. He's an All-American end, about six foot four, a prince of a man. I went down to set him in command. And I just caught Billy-all-hell from the commanding officers. Whaddaya mean sending this nigger down here? I said, "You'll take him or none." They took him. In six weeks, the man was a hero. Even these officers—He just did a job, a heroic one, with the morale of the black soldiers.

We developed these on-site clubs for the Eighth Air Force. I like to think I had a hand in it. When a soldier got a pass in the city, his recreation problem was pretty well solved. But it was while he was on the base, and his buddies were getting shot down, and the mud and the cold, and you're with those guys and the next night they're on a mission—and the next day they're gone. It would tear you up.

I arrived there on the fourteenth of December, 1942, and I stayed until March of '44.

When the first contingent was moved to North Africa, they left behind a lot of pregnant girls, commitments to marry. Remember, the

Americans were dashing and daring and had money in their pockets. The factory girls came from little provincial towns. I tried to arrange marriages by proxy. We did it over the telephone. I tried to get the Church of England—I went down to see the old bishop. Couldn't we get an exemption so we could have these proxy marriages? The old man was about ninety with a secretary about eighty-five. He had one of these old-fashioned trumpets. I yelled into the thing, but he turned me down.

I went to see Churchill's brother, who lived in the south. I told him about this disappointment. He said, "Nonsense, son, don't worry about it. All those soldiers from your country are in good physical condition, aren't they? They're all inspected and examined?" I said yes. He said, "Why, we'll just tell the girls to go ahead and have the babies and we'll adopt them and call them the King's children and raise them. They'll be good for the blood and bone of the country. We lost lots of our best men in this war." Sounded like a stud farm in a way (laughs), but it was quite sensible. He was less bombastic than Churchill, but a real character.

I was called one day to the Command in Grosvenor Square. An officer of General Jake Devers' staff cornered me: "I want you to see this light colonel. He has a problem. We cannot deal with him." The guy in trouble was an oceanographer. He studied the tides and coasts for a landing. A terribly important guy. I went to his apartment, knocked a number of times. Finally, a guy came to the door. He looked haggard, terrible, messy: "I don't want to talk to you." I said, "I was interested in your name, because when I was in high school I played football against a small town in Oregon and there was a guy playin' there—" He started to cry. He was the guy. We played tackle against each other at a football game back in the twenties.

Well, the story is he had an affair with an Englishwoman, who suddenly turns up and tells him she's pregnant. She's threatening to write his wife. He has two nice kids and is scared to death. I said, "Let me talk to the woman." She was demanding a thousand pounds, clear out of his reach. She was a cockney and kind of garrulous. I thought, This doesn't quite ring true. She said, "Make it five hundred and I'll go down to Bournemouth and have the baby." I made an appointment with her, but also with our chief nurse and a police-woman. In the meantime, I had her investigated by Scotland Yard. Turns out she's a well-known hustler. She comes to see me and I have our nurse ready and ask for a physical inspection. And there she was with a padded blanket inside her clothes. So we blew that out of the water.

I go tell the light colonel the facts. He thanks me profusely, he weeps and says, God, he'll never forget me. Two weeks later, I run into him down at the Grosvenor; he looks right at me and looks away and never speaks a word. I never felt too bad about it. The guy had to forget.

In spring of '44, we were staffing for the Normandy invasion. What were our responsibilities? Should we have side arms? Do we go in with the landing? Yeah, we lost four men in the landings. We had very high losses later.

When you were hired by the Red Cross, you were draft-exempt. They took men who were overage or had infirmities. I tried many things to get in the service, but I had this football injury. We had teachers, coaches, this, that, and the other. Most of us were family men. We had a two-thousand-dollar insurance policy, that's all.

Meantime, I'd been sent back to the U.S. to make a cross-country speaking tour. Fund raising, that sort of thing. That's when I heard about the four guys we lost. In Minnesota and Iowa, I ran into the wives of two of these guys. Each had been a teacher. Each left a wife and two kids and a policy of two thousand dollars. I went back to Washington and asked: What about raising the insurance? They go in with the army, why can't we put them under the GI insurance provision, ten thousand dollars?

I got Senator Chan Gurney to introduce the bill. It would have gone through Congress like that. (Snaps fingers.) I thought I'd cut a fat hog. I went back to headquarters and reported to my bosses. And, by golly, they turned it down. It just made me madder than hell. There was no reason for it. We were back to that snob approach. They said, "Well, we were afraid we would lose too much control of our people to the army." That was b.s., because you can't control a dead man, right?

I was so angry—I was still in uniform—I got my cap and said to my wife, "I'm leavin' this." I drove out to South Dakota and went hunting—with Bob Feller, Rollie Hemsley, old baseball players. And I did too much drinking. I got a phone call to come back. I did and ran into the same attitude. So when I got a job with UNRRA, I quit.

My old boss said, "Are you going with that worldwide WPA?" We were back to that contemptuous attitude toward welfare. The word that's been used to beat poor people over the head ever since Roosevelt's time.

UNRRA—the United States Relief and Rehabilitation Administration—was charted in unknown circumstances to help the war-torn areas of the world. To people used to established ways, this kind of venture is a threat to their values. It was chartered in a conference in Atlantic City in 1943 by nations fighting fascism. Its purpose was to rehabilitate nations devastated by war.

I was one of the early employees, about fifty, sixty of us. My first assignment was to go to the Middle East and run the refugee camps. There were thousands of Yugoslavs, fifty thousand, sixty thousand. We brought in something like fifty thousand Greeks, who'd come off the islands through Turkey. I had a Greek camp at Gaza. That was my base. My territory ran clear north to the Turkish border. The Turkish army would take them over, knock out their gold teeth, jerk the gold rings out of their ears, and push 'em over the border into Syria. We had camps along the Suez Canal, camps in Egypt. Palestine was full of refugees.

In Palestine we had Royalist Yugoslavs, and down in the Suez we had thirty-eight thousand Red Star Yugoslavs. Tito's crowd. We had to separate them. They were deadly enemies.

We had areas for tuberculars. We had typhoid, we had typhus, we had scarlatina. They were in terrible condition, starved, dying. Every evening we would have a mass burial in a big ditch.

I had great admiration for the Jugs. They were tough, resilient. One time an airplane crashed nearby. They took the scrap metal and made cooking utensils. They took the tires and made rubber-soled shoes.

I sometimes worked in cooperation with the Joint Distribution Committee, a Jewish agency. When the Germans captured Greece, they shipped a lot of Jews to one of the extermination camps. The JDC and others intervened with Franco, who intervened with Hitler, and they were released on the promise that Americans would take them off his hands. They brought them down in boxcars to Spain. The Americans picked them up and took them to Casablanca. We brought them over by boat to Alexandria, put 'em on a train, and brought them up to my camp, six miles south of Gaza.

We had a ninety-year-old man there. His wife was eighty-eight. Their daughter and son-in-law came in, from up near Tel Aviv, in a little car. They had escaped out through Rumania and Turkey, right?

Would I consider releasing the old couple to their care in their home? As soon as they could get some space. Space was very dear at the time. We got an exemption to bring them to Palestine. The English had barred the advent of any Jews there, right? But I said yes. I never had much regard for stupid regulations. So they left, elated. Would you believe that six miles north of Gaza, there was a sudden storm and a wall of water swept that young couple to the sea? Tell me about fate, friend. How do you break this news to the old couple?

UNRRA soon came under attack in Congress. Because the Soviet Union was part of it. Herbert Lehman was my boss. He had no more personality than a musk ox, but he was always on the side of the angels. It was a fight, always. I sent my last group back home to Greece in the fall of '45.

I was sent to Czechoslavakia as deputy director for UNRRA, under a Russian chief of mission, General Peter Alexander Alexeyev's industrial rehabilitation. We brought the first cotton up the Danube. We got textiles in so their mills could get back to work. We got repairs for the machinery, which was exhausted 'cause the Germans had worked it to death. We helped start the forest industries again. And agriculture.

I was director of Slovakia. It was odd. Slovakia had been collaborationist under Father Tiso. I attended his hanging. God, I hated Hitler and all his flunkies from day one. I started in South Dakota. There was strong sympathy for him in the Lutheran Church. They weren't bad people but the German culture was strong. The president of my college, just come back from Germany, spoke at our assembly: "I've seen a nation that had such poverty and hardship pull off an economic miracle. Everybody has a job. And this at a time when millions in our country don't." Oh boy. As for Russia, the streak of hostility was always just beneath the surface. The Russian alliance was never a thing of the heart. It was a calculated stratagem to defeat Hitler, with the help of American technology. I've had Russian generals tell me what won the war for them was that old Studebaker six-wheel truck. That thing was a genius of transport. It was tough, it was wiry. When the evacuation of Austria came about in '45, '46, I saw a stream of these American trucks coming out of there, older than hell, rusted and spoutin' steam and smoke. But they were still movin'.

In my experience, dealing with the Russians was like when I was a kid ridin' on freight trains. Once in a while you get in a boxcar that had a flat wheel. The wheel goes around in perfect circles, it's fine.

All of a sudden—bump. When I left Czechoslovakia to go to Germany to direct the DP operation, the Czechs gave a big dinner. Alexeyev came up and put his arms around me—(Suddenly cries angrily) Goddamn it, we missed something. This is one of the tragedies of the death of Roosevelt. There was a blind spot. We're on the threshhold of destruction because it didn't work.

I'm not nor never was a communist. Matter of fact, I lost my standing in the international community by helping people escape from the communists after they took over Czechoslovakia. I was there when they took over. Czechoslovakia needed a communist revolution like it needed a hole in the head. Several of my friends were put under house arrest and persecuted. So I took my passports and got seventeen people over the border, including two cabinet members. I had a system: a false stamp which was like a Czech approval for going in and out. We worked the border all the way down to Munich. A car would go in and out. I lost my wife's passport in no man's land between the Czech and German borders. It was picked up by a German farmer and sent to the American embassy. They called me in. They said I abused my American passport. I had to resign, and I left in October '48, I went home in disgrace. I was helping people escape what they supposedly hated. It was one of the ironies of our time. Later on, in the McCarthy era, it came to haunt my professional life. I was marked unreliable.

This is just another small fallout of the cold war. I feel to this day it didn't have to be this way. I've been to Russia a number of times. They're so bloody fearful of us, you can't believe it. To talk about Russian superiority is to be totally unaware of the dysfunctioning of Russian machinery, shortage of skills, inefficiency. Twenty million people killed in World War Two. If you know these things, you get furious.

When I come back to the U.S., here was Walter Winchell, the dean of boobality. He had the American people in a state of total fright. I listened to the stuff, I couldn't believe it. I was living in Czechoslovakia at the time. I remember driving from Prague to Berlin up through the Russian zone. I saw a lieutenant colonel in a buggy behind a horse and a cow. The scarcity of supplies, the thinness—it sickens me to remember the distortions on which this Russophobia is built.

We ran into it in Greece, when we started to repatriate these people. Churchill insisted on putting King George back on the throne, and the Greeks didn't want the son of a bitch. These were just people who resented what was being done to them. The English forced him back there, and they created a communist revolution. The more you fed it, the more it became like a fire.

Fiorello LaGuardia succeeded Lehman as UNRRA boss. One of his men asked me to go to Germany to run the DP operation in the American zone. There were about six million DPs there at the time. I really didn't want to go. You had responsibility without authority. The army ran things. A command decision could just wipe you out. And they did.

This was December '46. We still had about four-and-a-half million in the American zone: Poles, Russians, Ukrainians, Lithuanians, Estonians, Latvians. And some Jews; there only were about 280,000 of them left. While I was still in Czechoslovakia, we moved quite a few Jews out of Russia. They came across Poland and down the border across Slovakia to Vienna and then up into the U.S. zone. I worked with the JDC on that. We diverted food and medicine, what have you, from the Czech mission. It was too pitiable.

I went underground for three weeks before I began to run the office. I'd get in my car and stop in at camps, see who was running them, what spirit prevailed, who was running whom. And I came back to Heidelberg, our headquarters. It was an undestroyed town. We had a staff of fourteen thousand. It involved millions of people and everything from care of infants, to food, to shelter, to clothing, to transport, to death. Some of the social workers tried to work from textbooks. It didn't work. I went to the basics: shelter, food, sickness. That was it, right?

By this time, the warriors had gone home. The whole attitude toward the Germans had changed. The cold war had set in. General Lucius Clay was made head of the U.S. zone. It was his mission— as he told me once—"to get those damn Jews out of here because my job is to rehabilitate the German economy and these people are eatin' up our groceries." The thing was to build up Germany as a counter-force to the Russians, and the DPs were a drag on the economy.

Of course, you had an anti-Russian factor at work among the DPs. A lot of Latvians, Lithuanians, and Estonians had elected to join the Third Reich. And don't think they were coerced. They wanted to go. They killed their own Jews. They didn't need any help. They were a bunch of bastards.

The Estonians and the Latvians, especially, are a beautiful people, and the Germans loved 'em. Blue eyes, blond hair. Almost every officer, if he had a rank of colonel, had one of these women in his bed. They were choice women, right? They were the dancers, the entertainers, what have you. And they had infiltrated our command. We had a G-5 section that had to do with the displaced persons and prisoners of war. It was wildly anti-Russian. It had largely to do with who you're sleeping with. I can't tell you what the influence of the bedroom is on military and political policy, my friend. When I went to Prague, the Pankratz Prison was run by an SS group from Latvia.

They told their horror stories, which were probably true. The Soviets weren't patsies, believe me. They were ruthless, especially when they saw them as German collaborators. I know the Russians were trying to repatriate people. They had persuasion teams. We did no forced returning. The army did, but we didn't. About three million out of the four-and-a-half million went home within a year and a half.

Were the DPs screened by us?

One of the first things I did was put through a *Fragebogen.* It was a questionnaire. Where were you on such and such a date? What work were you doing? I wanted to screen 'em out. The army objected. They raised Billy-all-hell. They called me up to Frankfurt and read the riot act to me. I had a press conference. It hit the old Paris *Herald-Trib* and the *New York Times.* From then on, I was anathema to the army. It was war between us now.

By this time, the combat troops had gone home and the second echelon had moved in. They were all in bed with the Germans and they particularly turned on the Jewish DPs like you wouldn't believe. It fell just short of persecution.

Who's they?

The U.S. Army. You had the sycophants, most of whom had been collaborators, right? The Jew came out of the ovens and he said, Screw you, Jack. He's lost his fear of death, life, hell and fire and damnation, because he's been there, right? All of a sudden the war was over and he thought he was on the winning side. I remember incidents that would kill you.

We were in this camp and a little redheaded guy—a pock-marked, tough little wiry Jew, who's survived the ovens—they were asking him, "Do you think you want to go to Israel?" He said, "I don't think, I'm goin' there." He used good uncouth GI language he'd picked up on the way. They said, "Suppose we don't let you?" He said, "You keep me from goin'? How the hell you gonna keep me from goin'?" He broke down and wept when we came outside.

His story: he'd come out of the ovens weighing somethin' like sixty-five pounds. He'd built himself back, he'd married, had a baby. He and another guy had been walking through the camp, through the streets of the town where Hitler wrote *Mein Kampf.* Two GIs, half loaded, with some German girls, went by, and one of the girls called him *Judensau*—you Jewish pig—'cause they didn't get off the sidewalk. The GIs started pushin' 'em around and these little guys gave it back at 'em and there was a fight and the MPs came and they arrested 'em and they sent this guy to prison for a year. So he was full of this anger when I talked to him.

He joined the Haganah, moved there down through Italy. His wife and son were left in camp. War broke out with the Arabs. I didn't know he'd gone. One morning at Heidelberg, at seven in the morning, a woman came to see me. This guy's wife. She had a letter. Her husband was killed down by Gaza. I put her on the first legal movement, to go to Israel. We moved people illegally by the thousands down through France and Italy.

What more is there to say? After I was canned for my Czecho-slovakian adventure, I ran a ski lodge in Vermont. I was called back as director of information for the islands and possessions of the United States. In those days, Hawaii, Alaska, Puerto Rico, and the Canal Zone, right? One morning I found everything off my desk. The security department called me in and told me, No problem, Mr. Edwards. We just decided we didn't want you. Questions had arisen. It took me four years to find out what the charges were. It was cleared up, and I came back to the United Nations with top clearance. It's a chronicle of a well-used life. And how nutty the cold war makes us.

To many people, the war brought about a realization that there ain't no hidin' place down here. That the world is unified in pain as well as opportunity. We had twenty, twenty-five years of greatness in our country, when we reached out to the rest of the world with help. Some of it was foolish, some of it was misspent, some was in error. Many follies. But we had a great reaching out. We took fifteen, eighteen million men overseas. For the first time they saw pain and poverty in dimensions they had never known before. At heart, Americans had a period of unbelievable generosity toward the rest of the world, of which they knew little. It was an act of such faith.

Now we're being pinched back into the meanness of the soul that had grabbed a new middle class that came out of poverty as did I. We squeezed our soul dry of pity. If it were just pity, that'd be one thing. But reason itself denies this. You can't repeal the speed of sound. You can't repeal the speed of communication. You can't repeal the interlinking of social orders around the world. It's impossible.

While the rest of the world came out bruised and scarred and nearly destroyed, we came out with the most unbelievable machinery, tools, manpower, money. The war was fun for America—if you'll pardon my bitterness. I'm not talking about the poor souls who lost sons and daughters in the war. But for the rest of us, the war was a hell of a good time. Farmers in South Dakota that I administered relief to, and gave 'em bully beef and four dollars a week to feed their families, when I came home were worth a quarter-million dollars, right? What was true there was true all over America. New gratifications they'd never known in their lives. Mass travel, mass vacations, everything else came out of it. And the rest of the world was bleeding and in pain. But it's forgotten now.

World War Two? It's a war I still would go to.

EPILOGUE:
BOOM BABIES AND
OTHER NEW PEOPLE

NORA WATSON

She came from a small mountain town in western Pennsylvania. She remembers miners and hard times. "When I was little, I thought everybody was on strike or laid off." Her father was a fundamentalist preacher. "We lived on what people gave us." She was born in 1943.

We had a radio that worked sometimes. My father made us turn it off when worldly commercials were on—liquor, cigarettes. I was going on three. They talked of POWs and boys coming back. I had the sense of big numbers of people.

We did not go to movies. I did not know about Bob Hope or who Audie Murphy was. I knew nothing of the movie-star war or the principled war.

I first became aware of it when I was twelve or thirteen. It was one of the most important experiences of my life. In the school library, I was looking at photographs of the Holocaust. They were oversized books. I can still see the bindings and the mottled green cloth. It wasn't an assignment. Why was I doing this? It was a new library, new furniture, clean floors. The sun was coming through on the Appalachian hills. In contrast to the photographs, which were grainy, fuzzy. Parents wouldn't want their children to see these photographs.

In those grainy photos, you first think it's cords of wood piled up. You look again, it shows you human beings. You never get the picture out of your eye: the interchangeability of the stack of human bodies and the stack of cords of wood. There is something curious about the fascination with horror that isn't exhausted anywhere. Prior to finding these pictures, there were merely hints of something to a sheltered girl, nothing she could put together.

Something else happens. It tells you that human beings do it to each other. You can go to a school that tells you how a bomb works. You know people can design things that can kill people. You already know that from the histories of wars. But there wasn't any preparation for the manual destruction of human beings on a machine scale. That's what the Holocaust was.

I don't believe the Germans didn't know. It was so labor-intensive. It was not what it would be now if we had a Holocaust. We could program machines to do most of those things. But it took people to cut off hair and use it to make something else. It took people to pull out gold fillings. There had to be railroad switchmen, who had the full schedule of cars going in full and coming out empty. It sets up a distrust. It takes the bottom out of the world, especially in combination with the bomb.

My aunt Sarah was on the porch, it might have been the same year. "How many children do you want to have?" It was the standard visiting-aunt question. I said, "I'm not gonna have any children." "Why not?" "I wouldn't have any children in a world with the bomb." I was a very moral child. Some way I had a picture of the bomb that matched the other pictures of bodies stacked up like cordwood, of faces, pictures of trenches, of men standing over the trenches with rifles. Trees in the background, winter. The bomb was in the sky. They were on the ground. I had the impression of no bottom, no base to the world. The unpredictability. The no-bottom world is unmanageable.

More important, it's not outside of us. It's not in nature, like a flood. It was hands taking clothes off the people's bodies. The walls of the places where the people took showers were scratched and clawed at. Those were hands, too.

It was the industrial scale applied by hands. That's why a certain generation of people, who are not Jewish, who are not European, who don't have any other reason to be so crazy on the subject of the Holocaust, are rendered crazy. I didn't know any Jews. I didn't know any blacks.

If that thing hadn't happened, and the photographs I saw on that sunny day, I'm sure I'd have been thinking differently of human beings. Of myself, too. It reminds me of Rumpelstiltskin. He stamps his feet and the floor opens up. Somebody stamped their feet and the floor opened up. Unlike Rumpelstiltskin, you can't get it closed again. The floor that opened up is knowing the magnitude of what we can do and will, under circumstances we can't foresee, do to one another. I don't mean I know what it was like to be a person caught in the middle. I don't mean I'm exempt from that.

As a twelve-year-old girl, I discovered that the world was not a sheltering place. There was not a place in the world, no matter what its potential, that can be relied upon. We went another step in World War Two, and both sides did it. We did it on a scale that said it could happen anywhere, any time, and you could do it.

My reaction to the Holocaust may be precocious because of an accident I had when I was four. It was a tiny, little-finger-like holocaust. It had to do with fire, which is what the Holocaust is about. Burnt offerings. Holocaust is a religious word that comes out of Jewish scriptures.

It was electricity with me. I don't know how it happened. There was a jump cord, with a plug on both ends. I put it in my mouth. The cord was in the wall. A perfect circuit and a small four-year-old body. I was unconscious. It destroyed a fair amount of flesh in the face. It was eight years until we started plastic surgery. There was an awful lot of talk about God and his purpose, none of which made me very grateful to God.

If I were the only person who felt as I feel, I would think there was some sort of similarity between my experience and what I was seeing in those pictures. But my friend Martha, who is from an altogether different background, saw those same pictures when she was a small girl and went just as crazy. Anyway, mine was an accident, a tiny one, and the other was made by people just like us. Yet even physical accidents can be metaphors. I began to learn that everybody has scars. In most cases, invisible. We don't talk about the Holocaust without talking about ourselves. The scars are inside us. If they're outside, you're lucky, because you have a name for it. This is my mystical doctrine of scars. (Laughs.)

My sister is only four years younger than I am, yet we are a different generation. She was born during the baby boom. It became a different world after the war. She didn't have the sense of peril I did—about going hungry. She felt less vulnerable. She felt she had a right to food. We weren't sure we had that right. When we moved to Canonsburg, we were the first white settlers in a public housing project. That was something new and astonishing. We had hot water in the house.

With my sister's generation, *things* started to be important. Oh, we all liked clothes. We all read *Seventeen* magazine and exchanged patterns, but we weren't hung up on it. When my sister was growing up, shopping centers started. You spent your spare time there. To her, shopping centers were the neatest things on earth. She thinks things are always going to be there. I know they can go away.

What is weird is that both she of the baby-boom generation, who has a sense of material security, and I, who grew up with no sense of material security, both have another kind of insecurity in common. We know we can all die suddenly. It becomes specific for me when I see the picture of the mushroom cloud as not much different from the clouds on the Appalachian hills.

My mother never smoked, never drank, never kept late hours, had no friends who smoked, none of whom were corrupt. She died of massive cancer at age sixty-two. My nephew was born with cancer. My next sister bore a child with a rare tumor. And cancer does not run in our family.

My friend Martha, knowing nothing of my family, showed me a *New York Times* piece on Canonsburg, Pennsylvania. There was a radium-processing plant in town. And they didn't know diddly. They separated radium and put the tailings in Chartres Creek. That's the creek I used to fall into, stepping across the stones to take a shortcut to school. There's a scar for you: radium in our creek. You look at the photographs of the mushroom cloud and you look out toward the Appalachian cloud—and you remember those fuzzy, grainy photographs of the Holocaust. I don't have to be Jewish to be burned up. There isn't any bottom any more. There isn't any foundation any more.

I was alone with my mother when she died. As she got less and less compos mentis, with the medication and the cancer, the only hymn she remembered word for word was "How Firm a Foundation." I sang it to her. (She sings)

> *How firm a foundation,*
> *Ye saints of the Lord,*
> *Is laid for your faith*
> *In His excellent Word.*
>
> *What more can He say*
> *Than to you He hath said,*
> *You who unto Jesus*
> *For refuge have fled.*

1967. We're at a restaurant in Rüsselsheim. It is a resort area near Frankfurt.

In the adjacent room, a German band is playing an old favorite, "Der treue Husar." In the spirit of life mirroring art, I immediately see, in my mind's eye, the last reel of Paths of Glory, *the Stanley Kubrick film adapted from Humphrey Cobb's World War One novel. In a café near the front, a captive German girl is singing this song for a gathering of young French soldiers, who, at first light-hearted and joshing, are caught by its poignance and overcome with loneliness and homesickness.*

Its strains are heard through much of our conversation. I had requested an encore and then another, to the tune of several D-marks.

JOACHIM: I was born at the end of 1944 in a little village in Hesse. My parents first lived in Kassel. It was bombed out. My father had returned from the war. He was wounded at the Russian front. Normally, it was not a very good time to have babies. This time, many children were born. Women who had no children had to work in defense plants very far from home. Therefore, I was wanted.

MARLENE: My father was a marine fighting in Bremen. He had been drafted. I was a vacation child. It was the last leave of absence soldiers had till the end of the war. My parents wanted to have a child, some foundation of family because they didn't know if they were going to live much longer. By this time, they knew the war wasn't going to end good. I was born in January '44, one of the last vacation children.

JOACHIM: My father has talked to me of his experience, but there is always a bit of difficulty. I say to him the war was not a good one. Never. He says at that time he didn't know. It was the government that told him to fight: for the land and for Germany. He had to do it. He was nineteen when the war began in '39. He said he had to obey orders. I said to him, "Even if you are a little soldier and not a general or president, you must think, you must know if the thing you do is correct." I am against all wars, I think all people living in the twentieth century must know this.

I am not an exception. I know other students, not only German, of other nationalities, my age, who will not fight for their land. If the leader of our land said, Now you must go to war, I wouldn't do it. I have many, many friends in other countries. I couldn't shoot at them.

Would you go to jail?

Yes. Thirty years ago, there was not much communication between people. We were told in Germany, all French are bad. We must fight against them. Well, I've been to France and I know they are not bad people. I don't know Russian people, but I am quite sure they are also amicable people. I can't say they are lesser than I. It is not natural that people fight. We have our minds, we can discuss. When people first see a people who are different, it's quite natural to be suspicious.

I have had a very good teacher who told us about Hitler times. It is not enough to say Hitler was bad and forget it and don't do it any more. I think we must find out why Hitler was accepted by the German people. I have had other teachers who said all the Hitler time was bad and now is a good time. They say all people who lived under Hitler were bad because they fought the war with him. That is wrong. We can't say all people were bad. We must find out why they were with him. If you want to make something better, you must know the reasons why it was wrong and what has happened.

My parents didn't know exactly what happened to the Jews. They knew that they disappeared. My mother, when she went to school, knew that four or five Jewish girls weren't there the next morning. All the Germans knew that things weren't right for the Jews after Crystal Night. I think, at that moment, all must have known. I don't understand why they didn't search out what happened to the Jews. I can't imagine that they didn't know about these camps.

When I ask my parents, they say they didn't know. Those who resisted, I know, were few. It's natural there was a fear. And it was easy not to search out. Yes, it was easy not to know.

MARLENE: My parents always talked to me about it. When the war came, my father owned a store in Koblenz. My mother was a photographer. It was hard. We sold cigarettes and a few groceries. Every store was called a German store and everybody had to put up the Hitler flag. No Jews were allowed to buy there.

My father had quite a few Jewish friends who lived in the neighborhood. He kept on selling to them, naturally. They were his neighbors. The word got around: he was the only store around that sold to Jews. That's why he was drafted at the age of forty-two. He had two children already. The subject comes up quite often in our family.

My mother says it was almost impossible to know exactly what was going on. All you heard over the radio was, of course, guided by the government. The German people were told what to believe, how to behave orderly. As she recalls, the SS came to the house of the Jewish family at night, so the citizens didn't realize what was going on. After the Nazi regime took over, they did it openly: break open the door, throw furniture out of the window and dishes and everything. They knew it was going to be bad, but not as bad as it was.

JOACHIM: My father says, "You always accuse us. You always say, Why didn't you do anything?" He says, "Look at now. All the terrible things happening. What are *you* doing?" Often now, he begins the conversation about what happened during the war. I have a feeling he wants to discuss it with me and not be accused. I think he feels that things were wrong.

MARLENE: Yes, there's an urge to talk about it. With a family it arises more. Like something under the table. They would like to know what you think. They don't ask you directly. They talk around it. Naturally, you take your stand and give your opinion. They look at you silent and maybe nod a little.

JOACHIM: I think it's a question in all generations. When I have children that one day, they will have questions in the same way. They will say to me, "What did you do?" I do try now, so later I can say things that I did were not wrong. I don't know if I reach that. Now, we have other weapons.

STEVE McCONNELL
———————————————
———————————————

He is an aide to Congressman Claude Pepper's Select Committee on Aging. "I was born in 1947, a boom baby. We moved from Los Angeles

to the suburbs where my father has had a church for many years."
The conversation took place in Washington in 1981.

I always had a sense that our generation was bigger and better than any that had come before. And probably bigger and better than any that would follow. Every time we turned around, something was happening that we felt we had control over. We had the feeling that somehow we were the chosen, We were gonna make the world right. We were gonna invent the better mousetrap.

Everybody was havin' a good time, hangin' out at the milkshake parlors and the drive-ins. We were all drivin' souped-up cars. We had the run of things. We carried that into college.

I was in the class of '65. With our sense of power, along came uncertainty. Lots of things were changing. We were faced with a war that nobody really understood. We were a generation brought up not to think that war was a good thing. Something was going on that we didn't like.

People began to experiment with drugs. We had the luxury of free time and economic security. It was wide-open territory, like the frontier. You could just go in any direction you wanted. Drugs was just another experience. There was no sense of purpose. A fairly small group of people was working against the war in Vietnam. They had a sense of purpose. But they were few. Some people dabbled in drugs—I did too, a little this, a little that—because they had such high expectations. As they began to realize that they weren't going to be able to meet them, drug use became an alternative, an escape.

We had no sense of the Depression before World War Two. Parents talked about it, but it had no meaning. There was no sense of World War Two, either. It was distant. One reason the Vietnam War came home to us, it hit us directly, fast. I am thirty-four years old, and until this year, I had not been aware that this country had ever suffered economically. I've never had a sense of what people go through when the economy goes to hell.

We went through the bomb-shelter era in the late fifties. I remember it as kind of fun. You could go into a shopping center and at the corner of the parking lot was one of these bomb shelters. Gee, that was neat. Mom, can't we get a bomb shelter in the back yard and store up? Get some great provisions, like campin' out? But there was that sense of nagging that maybe this was more than just fun. Nothing serious was imminent, but . . . there was talk. They'd sell 'em. It was a big marketing thing. They were selling bomb shelters like they were selling lawn mowers. There'd be big displays. Each company would have a little fancier one than the other. It was another consumer item. (Laughs.)

We had drills in school. The alarms would go off and you'd hit the floor and put your back to the windows and cover your head. You were mostly afraid of getting hit by glass. What most of us didn't realize was that that would be the least of our problems. (Laughs.)

Along came Sputnik in '57. That has brought the technology drive to our generation. There was this great push to get people trained in engineering. The thing, next to being an athlete, was to be an astronaut. That was hot stuff, cool.

There was a total fascination with technology. Cars, fixin' em up and soupin' 'em. Technology was the solution to everything. When I was in college, you walked through the humanities building to get to the business school because you didn't want anybody to know you were a business major. That's all turned around, really, in the last ten years.

I played football at USC. I was a defensive lineman during the O.J. years at USC.* We played in the '68 and '69 Rose Bowls. We were national champions one year. I toed the line. I did what was expected.

About 1968, as I was finishing my years playing football, there was a lot of antiwar stuff going on. If you remember, athletes on many college campuses were the enforcers. They were used by the administration to bust heads, to break up demonstrations. We were the jocks who beat up people who burned draft cards. I began to have problems with that. It didn't sit right, sports being used in this way. Anyway, this all started to sink in. About 1969, I organized the phys. ed. department in support of the antiwar effort.

I'll never forget the day that I went to the leaders of the antiwar drive on the campus and delivered the petition that I'd gotten signed by more than a hundred people. The guy was scared to death that I was gonna punch him out. (Laughs.) I handed him this petition and he was beside himself. They made it, they got the phys. ed. department. (Laughs.)

Technology and business. The whole record industry was just another indication. A billion-dollar industry devoted exclusively to youth. We're a generation that can define the tastes of an entire

---

*O. J. Simpson, star running back at the University of Southern California.

---

culture. There was an arrogance that came along with it. Our music was good, your music was not good. Rock-and-roll was our music, our identity. It was almost good that our parents said, "How can you listen to that stuff? Turn it down." It meant you got bigger speakers and a better stereo and you turned it up.

My high school was lower-middle-class, yet the kids had better cars than their parents. The car was the status symbol. You put special markings on it, you lowered the front, loud mufflers. Again, technology. That was your identity. In many cases the car was more important than your girlfriend.

In the fifties, you started getting the fins on cars, bigger and bigger and bigger. Nonfunctional technology. (Laughs.) It was all part of the symbolism of extravagance and wealth. It was driven by the sense that we can kinda do what we want.

Now times are getting hard and what do you find? The Japanese are outdoing American companies in televisions and radios and cars and we're starting to scapegoat them. There are ads that now show the Japanese in very derogatory ways. Especially in California. When I was growing up, you could like everybody. You had the freedom and luxury to be concerned about civil rights. There was more than enough to go around. So you could be very righteous and intolerant of bigotry.

I feel the pressures around me. I feel people seeing the competition and developing hatreds toward other groups. I myself am now a middle-class adult. You have resources. You're interested in protecting. You're concerned about blacks and crime. It becomes a racist thing.

I remember getting into arguments when I was in college: Why do you put so much attention into mowing your lawn, when there's so much suffering? Then I bought a house about four years ago. When I put that money down and became a homeowner, a lot of things changed in my head. My God, I've got a huge debt. That house is worth as much as that community is worth. I don't want that community to fall apart. You get locked into the system.

Our generation didn't have to get plugged into the system. We could stay on the fringe and still do very well. We've bought the values of our parents' generation more than we thought we would. We should have, perhaps. You feel that your generation's cut loose, afloat.

The meaning of World War Two for me was being victorious. That was what the war movies taught us, what John Wayne taught us. We won and we were right. America had proved its strength. We had conquered the world. We were riding it, taking it for everything it was worth. We were the giants. We could do what we wanted to do. That carried over to our personal lives. You could pick your job. You didn't have to worry about failing. If you screwed up one thing, there was plenty more that you could do. (Laughs.) The expectations were astronomical. But it became more and more difficult. Now times are getting hard and what do you find?

As far as wars go, World War Two was a good one. It was a positive kind in our minds. That made it more difficult to deal with the Vietnam War, because there was such a contrast.

We've lost that sense of a generation. We're now scattered all around. The economics have changed and people are grabbing what they can grab before the bottom falls out. We're working individually to survive. People are taking care of themselves first.

It's a bitter pill for our generation to swallow 'cause we had everything. We had such great expectations. Now is the time of diminished expectations. It's probably easier for our parents, having experienced the Depression. We can talk about the need to sacrifice, but it doesn't sit well. It's the first time our generation has had to face the possibility of failure. And we were conceived in victory.

GEORGE SEYMOUR

He's Marnie Seymour's third son. He is twenty-eight. He joined us in the lobby during my conversation with his mother.

Many of my friends, myself, assume that one way or another we won't die natural deaths. It doesn't affect my day-to-day existence, but in long-term planning it does. It's silly to think about what I'll be doing ten years from now. On the other hand, you try not to think about getting blown up or something like that. It's not something we talk about late at night or anything like that, I know it's in the back of my mind. It's just part of our lives.

I can remember talking about it more when I was in high school. It was always there. I can't remember not being aware. The other night, my mother and I were talking about bomb drills in elementary school. I'll always remember going under the desks. I was in second grade. It was never explained to us. We'd go outside for fire drills. We'd go down in the basement for these other kind of drills. I remember having them in kindergarten.

When somebody makes a remark: I don't expect to live real long, I can't worry about that too much. It's always told in joking manner. It's taken seriously, but made light of. It seems so unreal. You can't quite comprehend what it would be like if the bomb were to go off. It almost seems like a dream. It's real, but it's not real.

I don't think my friends feel there's anything we can do about it. We can't take any direct action. I mean, we can't stop the bomb from taking off from a silo. We can't stop anybody from pushing buttons. We can voice our opinions and write letters, but that's it. We have no control of where those letters go or what effect those letters have on the people who make the decisions.

There's a difference between me and my oldest brother. He's thirty-four. He perceives life much differently from me. I remember, during the sixties, my older brother going off to college and getting involved in political action. He felt he could directly affect politics. I don't feel that. I can put my two cents in, but I don't entertain the notion that it will affect anybody.

It didn't work for him, did it? He thought he could change everything, and it changed nothing. I experienced his disillusionment at a younger age. I think of myself as being more pragmatic.

DEBBIE COONEY

She is a student at a vocational high school in Chicago. She is seventeen.

I was around ten when I came aware of the bomb. It didn't have any great impact on me until a year ago, I have a niece who is eighteen months old now. She means a whole lot to me. I mean, she's my first niece and she's learning how to talk and she runs around the house. I want her to have a life. 'Cause she could have a really good life. 'Cause she's really intelligent. I can tell.

I want her to be able to live and go out in the country and just breathe without having to worry or anything. I think a lot of times I do it more for her than for myself because I've at least had seventeen years of life. I've at least had some sort of chance. She's eighteen months old and she's just wonderful. So I just want her to have a chance.

STREET - CORNER KIDS

Chicago, 1965.
There had been trouble in the neighborhood. The young bloods of the project and the pubescent gladiators of the two-flats had several encounters, loud and clear.

This had been, before the war, an old Italian neighborhood, of sons and daughters of Calabrian peasants. Since the war's end, there had been a double migration: from the Deep South and from south of the border. The children of construction workers and the children of sharecroppers and migrant farm workers had been inordinately busy flexing their muscles and their lungs. They were at the moment arm-weary and, due to a surfeit of expletives, suffering from mouth fatigue. These young Italian, black, and Hispanic street soldiers and their precocious camp followers were just plain tired. And, unexpectedly, reflective. Their ages ranged from eleven to fifteen.

JIMMY: Sooner or later, you have to die. You don't have to worry. If you worry too much, you just get gray hair. If there's a H-bomb falls, I die. I do my penance in purgatory and go to heaven. The end of the world's gonna *show.* Not by no bomb. The hemisphere movin' out of its orbits. When that happens, the world shall turn to flames. There'll be a cross up in the sky to show you it's the end of the world. That's when you suffer.

LINDA: It used to bother me to think about what happens if the bomb comes and I die and I'm young. It doesn't bother me now, 'cause I'm happy. I figure as long as I'm happy, whatever happens, it happens.

JOHNNY: The bomb is awfully wicked. If there ever should be a war, that's what they're gonna use. Why go out and fight anything, ya know? The only thing they can do is push a button an' there you go. No more, ya know? Just push a button and you die. (Laughs.) All of a sudden, man. Why go out there and dive on dirt and this an' that? That's a lotta jive, man. Why doin' all that, if you can push a button? But the only trouble is, who's gonna push that button?

FRANKIE: The bomb is your enemy, 'cause that's the one that's gonna put the hurts on you. You're gonna feel it. (Laughs.) For a little while. Everything hurts for a little while. That's all, man, for a little while.

RAYMOND: This might sound crazy, but I'd like to see a world without bombs. I mean, without wars. It would be a lot bigger, the world. Maybe we could enjoy it more. Get a lot out of life, without worrying you be blown up tomorrow.

SAM: I hope I can die of old age, before the world starts the war.

RICHARD: I think the world as it is now is in pretty good condition. By violence, they learn. If the world was peaceful, the people would get kinda dull. They would just sit until they die. They just want some action. Probably they do something bad, but they get enjoyment out of it. Instead of just sitting around and looking at pictures or just doin' nothing. They like to get excitement into their lives instead of just sittin' around.

HENRY: This is like a mad world to me. Everyone's chasing each other. It's just little animals thrown together. If there will be a war, there would be nobody to live. The whole place would be erupted and some people would try to find shelter, but they wouldn't make it. They should be catching up with more better things to do, instead of fighting another war.

MONK: If there's gonna be a war, there ain't gonna be nothin' left at all. Before there used to be spears and hot water or hot tar going to the people's back or something like that. But now it's gettin' worse, where one man could just push a button and the whole world just explode.

FREDERICK: That bomb—when women get pregnant, it do somethin' to their child. The child come out crooked. Some kinda disease that come from that bomb. They shouldn't be makin' stuff like that that'll kill you later on up in the year. You'll worry so and all that. They shouldn't have never discovered that thing, 'cause it's too dangerous. Explode, blow up half the side of the world. Then, later on, up in years, your mother had a child, you don't know what's wrong with her, and it'll be from the atom bomb. They shouldn't be makin' stuff like that.

TONY: God made this world, the plants and everything. Of course he made man and woman. From that, a generation started. He made it a very clean world. My idea of the world would be the same. The people are the image of God. They have two hands, two legs, a face. If I said, I'll make 'em with three legs, three eyes, that's not good. Ain't that what's happenin' with some of them children? From that bomb?

MONK: I cry sometimes when that feeling comes. When I get sore feelin' in my heart. Sometimes a person cry when they're by themselves. I wouldn't like to cry in front of nobody. No older person, I mean. The fear that most kids got, I got that fear, too. They might just tell you they ain't got any future in this world.

Nearby, little girls of eight or nine are skipping rope to the tune of "Miss Sally, Sally." During the breath-catching pause in this complex song-game, the usual simple-minded question is asked: "What do you want to be when you grow up?"

ETHEL: I wanna see if I'm gonna grow up first. I mean, I might not live to be grown up. 'Cause I don't know when my time is up. I don't know when I'm gonna die yet. I never know if I could die overnight from the bomb or somethin'. So the day wasn't promised to me. (Laughs.) I don't know what may happen, uh, my life weren't promised to me.

She and the other children begin to argue back and forth, as they resume skipping rope. It becomes a children's game, the reply to the last comment:

It was . . .

It wasn't . . .

It was . . .

It wasn't . . .

It was . . .

It wasn't . . .

ABOUT THE AUTHOR

Pulitzer Prize-winner Studs Terkel was born in 1912 and grew up in Chicago. He graduated from the University of Chicago in 1932 and from the Chicago Law School in 1934. He has been an actor in radio soap operas, a disk jockey, a sports commentator, a television master of ceremonies, and a radio host. He has traveled all over the world doing on-the-spot interviews. His books include *Division Street*, *Hard Times*, *Working*, *Talking to Myself*, *American Dreams: Lost and Found*, *Race*, and *Coming of Age*.

His radio program on WFMT in Chicago is still broadcast each day, and at present he is beginning to organize the nine thousand interviews that he has accumulated over the years, planning a new series of broadcasts and books based on this incomparable archive.